Canadian Woman Studies
An Introductory Reader

Second Edition

Published by:
Inanna Publications and Education Inc.
212 Founders College, York University
4700 Keele Street
Toronto, Ontario M3J 1P3
Telephone: 416. 736.5356
Fax: 416.736.5765
Email: inanna@yorku.ca
Website: www.yorku.ca/inanna

Printed and Bound in Canada

Cover Design/Interior Design: Luciana Ricciutelli
Cover Art: Alice Williams, "Medicine Wheel Among the Stars,"
Quilt, 61" x 61."

Library and Archives Canada Cataloguing in Publication

Canadian woman studies : an introductory reader / edited by Andrea Medovarski and Brenda Cranney ; introduction by Dorothy E. Smith. – Rev. and updated 2nd. ed.

Includes index.
ISBN 0-9736709-6-7

1. Women – Canada. I. Medovarski, Andrea, 1973- II. Cranney, Brenda, 1949 -

HQ1453.C3557 2006   305.4'0971
C2006-903149-5

Canadian Woman Studies
An Introductory Reader

Second Edition

**Edited by
Andrea Medovarski and
Brenda Cranney**

With an Introduction by
Dorothy E. Smith

INANNA Publications & Education Inc.
Toronto, Canada

Contents

1. Feminist Perspectives

2. Herstories

6. Violence

7. Representations

8. Health

9. Activism

Acknowledgements

As is always the case with feminist organizing, creating this book has not been a solitary pursuit. In determining which articles to include we have relied on the detailed and considered feedback of many instructors who teach Women's Studies in universities across the country. In particular, the editors are grateful to Elizabeth Blaney, Marie Hammond Callaghan, Jane Cawthorne, Cathy Cavanaugh, Nancy Forestell, Theresa Healy, Guida Man, and Kathryn McPherson for all of their generosity. We are grateful for their contributions, which have ranged from a willingness to share course syllabi and other teaching materials with us, to thoughtful suggestions about articles, approaches, or issues to consider as we revised the table of contents. Unfortunately, we were not able to include every article to which they pointed us, and any gaps or omissions in this book are solely our own. We are also profoundly thankful for their stimulating and provocative conversations about their own pedagogical practices, which made the editorial process much more pleasurable. But we are most thankful for their consistent support of CWS/Inanna Publications and all of its endeavours.

The editors would like to extend a separate thank you to Sheila Molloy for all of her work compiling the index to the Reader. This addition will make the book far more useful to readers than it otherwise would have been, and we are grateful to Sheila for her willingness to take on this important task.

Finally, words cannot express the depth of our gratitude to Luciana Ricciutelli, the Editor-in-Chief of *Canadian Woman Studies/les cahiers de la femme* and Inanna Publicationsand Education Inc. Her commitment to feminist publishing is truly unparalleled. She has laboured tirelessly to sustain both the journal and the press in recent years, and we consider it an honour and a privilege to work so closely with this inspirational woman. As with the previous edition of *Canadian Woman Studies: An Introductory Reader*, we dedicate this book to Luciana.

Preface

Andrea Medovarski and Brenda Cranney ⟶

Seven years after the publication of our first edition of *Canadian Woman Studies: An Introductory Reader*, we are pleased to introduce this second, revised and updated edition. As with the previous edition, this book is intended for use in introductory Women's Studies courses, as well as for those who seek an overview of current women's issues in Canada. All selections have been chosen from nearly 30 years of publishing *Canadian Woman Studies/les cahiers de la femme*, with particular emphasis on the sixteen issues that have been produced since the first edition of the *Reader*. We are delighted that this journal can continue to play such a vibrant role in educating young women and men about the various dimensions of both academic and grassroots feminisms, in Canada and around the world.

Much has changed in the last decade since we initially embarked on the first edition of the *Reader*. Our main concern then was specifically to recognize the significance of Canadian feminist scholarship. We produced the first edition in an academic climate in which Women's Studies courses in this country relied almost exclusively on American books published by American presses. Fortunately, there is not the same dearth of Canadian feminist pedagogical material today, and numerous other introductory texts with a specifically Canadian focus have followed in recent years. In this second edition of the *Reader*, we also strive to consider some of the other changes that we have witnessed in Canada and elsewhere. In an increasingly globalized world, this book aims to situate Canada within a broader, transnational context. Our selections consider the regional, urban, rural, linguistic, demo-graphic, and ethnic differences within the nation. But many also examine the ways women located in this country are impacted by various global factors.

To this end, we have made some changes to the section headings. We hope they reflect the emergence of new themes and questions which have been raised in Women's Studies in the last few years, while also considering the issues that have continued to be significant to feminist inquiry in the past three decades. Some sections have been revised or refined since the first edition, some sections have been added, while others have been removed. As with the first edition of the *Reader*, arranging the articles was a challenge and the sections were not easily divided. Questions of gender, sexuality, ethnicity, class, and identity so often intersect, seeping into one another as they shape and inform women's lives. Thus, articles that we have included in one section might easily have been included in several others. Similarly, there are other themes and topics which have not been designated a particular category, but which can be found throughout the Reader. For example, while there is no single section dedicated specifically to ecofeminism and the environment, readers will find various articles throughout the book that focus on this issue.

As with the first edition, the opening section, *Feminist Perspectives*, aims to introduce readers to a range of feminist thought. We have continued to foreground the diversity of perspectives, the multiplicity of voices, and the interdisciplinary approach on which Women's Studies is based. The section begins with the foundation we laid in the first edition of the Reader, with the inclusion of updated version of Dorothy E. Smith's original introduction. The other essays range between a look back to the earliest days of second wave feminism in Canada, an examination of the most recent questions currently being raised by young third wave feminists, and speculations on the futures roles of feminisms both locally and globally.

The second section, *Herstories*, has not been substantially altered from the first edition. Our only changes here have been to add two more articles which take up significant moments in formal and informal feminist organizing. Again, we could not possibly hope to cover all aspects of women's histories in one brief section. Hence, the essays here are meant to provide touchstones for the long and rich history of feminisms in Canada. Some, such as Mary Kinnear and Ruth A. Frager, consider significant moments in organized women's activism over the last century and in various regions. Others, like Sylvia Hamilton, Marlene Brant Castellano, and Franca Iacovetta, focus on familial and community-based modes of resistance to gender oppression.

The essays in the third section, *Difference and Identities*, explore how racialized and gendered identities produce each other in complex and shifting ways. Many of the articles also take up the obverse of this issue. Notisha Massaquoi, Lynn Gehl and Angela Aujla consider how the identities of racialized women are also produced in particular ways by a nation with a long colonial history. Together, the essays in this section aim to think about difference and identity as multifaceted, and official multicultural policies of the last thirty years are juxtaposed with questions about the originary First Nations presence in this nation. And, as Nancy Chater's essay reminds us, whiteness cannot be the unquestioned "norm" against which all other ethnicities are read; it too needs to be understood as a racially constructed identity that sometimes positions white women against their so-called "others" in deeply problematic ways.

Work/Economy continue to be significant avenues of Canadian feminist scholarship, and the articles in this section take up the various dimensions of both paid and unpaid labour in women's lives. These authors provide a nuanced and specific look at a range of working experiences, and the disadvantages—even dangers—women workers face at home and in their places of employment. Articles by Roxana Ng and Ana Isla insist on understanding the impact of an increasingly globalized economy on women's working conditions. Many of the articles look at the ways women workers have organized through formal and informal channels, while others think about the work that still needs to be done both at home and in the workplace to address long-standing gender inequalities.

The next section on *Policy* was also an important element of the first edition, and while we have continued to recognize its significance, in the second edition we have chosen all new articles. We have gone this route so that this section can reflect the most current government debates around women's issues in Canada and elsewhere. These essays, which consider labour laws, migration and border crossings, correctional practices, education, and parental rights, reveal the extent to which states can, and do, discipline nearly every aspect of women's lives in Canada. The articles all speak to the troubling ways that racism, sexism, classism, and homophobia are often upheld, either directly or indirectly, by state laws.

By extension, the articles in the section on *Violence* are a sobering reminder of how these prejudices force some women to live in fear, physically and psychologically. The essays in this section explore the various dimensions of violence against women in Canada and around the world. As Ursula Franklin emphasizes in her powerful address to commemorate the Montreal Massacre in 1989, the most extreme forms of gender-based violence in our society are not aberrations, they are extensions of readily available societal prejudices. Through careful analysis, many of the articles examine the specific loci at which such forms of violence occur, while others aim to unpack the social causes, and effects, of violence against women in Canadian society.

Our next section, *Representations*, explores the social constructions of women's "expected" roles in all aspects of Canadian society. As with the first edition, a number of these essays focus on the role of the media in creating and upholding gendered and racial stereotypes. Some authors instead look at the ways the state, the family, or particular communities, can also reinforce limited and limiting notions of how women are or are not supposed to behave, look, or dress. The commonality among all the articles in this section is their insistence that many complex factors intersect in the social construction of gender, and that these constructions can impact nearly every facet of women's daily lives.

Women's health remains a significant preoccupation in feminist research, and the articles in this section on *Health*, as in the first edition, continue to foreground the importance of interdisciplinary study in reframing academic and policy debates about women's health and well-being. As with the section on public policy, nearly all of the articles here are new inclusions. They take up the most recent questions and concerns facing women as they try to navigate an increasingly troubled health care system. Some consider the struggles women face as they work to provide health care to Canadian society, while others consider the numerous barriers that prevent some women from accessing the health services they need.

Our final section, *Activism*, is a new addition to the second edition of the Reader. The articles included here reflect the ways women from all walks of life, old and young, urban and rural, in academies and communities, work in concerted ways to improve the world in which they live. Some articles focus specifically on feminist organizing, while others explore the roles that women play in broader anti-war or anti-globalization movements. Still others consider the importance of art and cultural production, or of everyday interpersonal interaction, as sites of activism through which to enact change in women's lives.

This desire, to envision and to work toward implementing new possibilities for women, is what has motivated us in the production of this book. We hope that the women and men who will learn from its pages will be better informed about the long history of feminisms in Canada and the current issues which impact women's lives. We also hope that, after considering the questions which are taken up in this book, our readers might also be inspired to work toward positive change, so that their political, artistic, scholarly, and community endeavors might be reflected in future editions of *Canadian Woman Studies: An Introductory Reader*.

Introduction

Dorothy E. Smith ⬦

Some four or five hundred years ago in Western Europe, a new way of organizing society began to emerge, largely coordinated in words, numbers, and images. Its development has mainly been driven by a kind of economy that relies on market processes and stresses the accumulation of capital. A complex set of ruling relations has emerged that connects people's everyday/everynight living and work through the medium of texts, whether on paper, in film or electronically. In these forms of ruling, men, mostly white, predominate as agents, while women and non-white peoples play subordinate parts. Though women are everywhere in the society, established channels of communication—academic discourses and universities, book publishing, the mass media of television, newspapers, even women's magazines—have not been fully accessible to us as a means of being heard, as a medium of representing, advocating for and mobilizing women, of speaking and writing as women for women and as women for men.

The exclusion of women from the making of the text-mediated relations that organize our lives (both women's and men's) is not a function of women's biology. Of course, some of the bases of exclusion are grounded in our relationships, biological and social, to children. But it is important to know of a Western European and North American history of active repression when women ventured to speak authoritatively. In the fifteenth and sixteenth centuries, women who read and became learned in the scriptures and ventured to dispute the interpretations of the exclusively male clergy might be burned as heretics; in seventeenth-century Massachusetts, Anne Hutchison was exiled from the colony because, as a successful preacher and teacher, she usurped male authority; during the Terror following the French Revolution, women leaders of women's organizations were guillotined, again because they were taking on roles of authority that were reserved for men; in the late nineteenth century a woman who took different religious views from her Calvinist minister husband was imprisoned in an insane asylum; in the student movement of the 1960s, women who attempted to represent women's concerns at demonstrations and rallies were harassed and ridiculed. And today women who have tried to raise issues of equity in Canadian universities have also been ridiculed, their representations of inequities trivialized, and their careers in universities distorted if not actually forfeited.

More is involved here than can be met by reasoning. Both social organization and social relations perpetuate the special authority of white men's voices. Take the educational system with which we are all familiar. Look around you, look back into your school days. The educational system still shows marked differences in power and status of women and men throughout. This isn't just an issue of equity employment, important as that may be, but also of what it has to tell us about women's part in the making and transmitting of a common culture and intellectual life. As we go up the hierarchy of status and control of the cultural processes of the society, the subordination of women is more and more marked: In elementary schools, the majority of classroom teachers are women and the majority of principals and administrators are men; at the secondary level, the majority of classroom teachers are men and so again are the administrators. In colleges and universities women may make up as many has half the instructional staff hired on a sessional (temporary) basis, but as we go up the hierarchy to the level of full professors, the proportion of women diminishes radically. And throughout, the vast, vast majority of both sexes are white. Although women's studies has been successfully established in Canadian universities, this does not mean that women's perspectives, concerns, and experience, as they have been developed artistically and academically, are incorporated into regular programs that reach both women and men. Universities in general still function to inhibit the access of both men and women students to the extraordinary renaissance of scholarship, the artistic and literary achievements among women in the last thirty years.

There is a social structuring of authority which is still integral to white male identity and which subordinates and diminishes women and women's authority, as well as the authority of non-white men, to speak and be heard. When we speak of authority, we are speaking of what makes what one person says count. White men are invested with authority as individuals, not because they have special abilities as individuals, but as representatives of the power and authority of the institutionalized structures, the ruling relations, that organize the society. Their authority as individuals in actual situations of action is generated by a social organization. They do not appear as themselves alone. They are those whose words count both for each other and for those who are not members of this category. A circle is thus formed that excludes those whose words do not count, whose speakers have no authority.

These circles can be found at many levels. Only look at the history of philosophy in Western Europe and North America. Not only is it bounded by the centres of imperialism, it is also gender bound. There is something like a conversation over time, mediated by texts, in which men in ancient Greece (a democracy from which women and slaves were excluded) are engaged with philosophers of the Enlightenment who are engaged in their turn with contemporary philosophers critical of the presuppositions of modernity. Women have not been admitted as participants to this conversation. What a woman might say had no authority; it would not be heard; what she had to say would not be allowed to become part of the debate.

Such patterns are to be found at all levels. They are all around us and we, both women and men, participate in them without realizing it. Social scientists who have done studies in this area have provided much that is useful in helping us simply to see what we ourselves are implicated in. One psychologist did a study quite a while ago which involved giving identical collections of short papers on various topics to two university classes. Though the papers were identical, their presentation differed in one respect. Papers in one collection identified with a male author were identified with a female author in the other. Students were asked to comment on qualities such as cogency, style, etc. Where the paper was seen as written by a man it was treated very differently from the same paper seen as written by a woman; the students, both women and men, thought the papers identified with male authors were more serious, more significant, better written, more coherent, and so on. Yet the only difference was the gendered authority, or lack of authority, of the supposed author. A story such as this helps to identify a pattern of which we may not be aware. We may have, without thinking, taken books or papers written by women to be less significant than those written by men. We may think that, as women, what we have to say is not important, and therefore be hesitant to speak out and to say what we think. This is a problem that extends to the writing of papers for publication and even to the writing of doctoral theses. Before the women's movement, I had a serious block about writing papers, particularly when I thought I had something genuinely original to contribute. I suppose I did not see myself as someone who had authority, who had something worth saying as a sociologist to other sociologists. In general women have felt that our own voices and what we have to say is not important, perhaps not worth saying at all. We may have paid more attention to the men who speak up in the classroom, rather than listening to the women and treating ourselves as those who have something to say.

Through such studies, we can get close to our own everyday experiences and begin to recognize the ways in which we, whether women or men, are complicit in them. Social scientists have studied and provided descriptions of patterns that emerge when women and men meet and talk. Characteristically women use styles of talk that throw control to men, as by interjections that reassign responsibility for its meaning to others—they may not finish sentences, or cast them adrift by concluding them with a "you know," or the like. Generally, it's been shown that men control the topics of conversation and women tend to be relegated to supportive roles that they are skilled in sustaining. Male control of conversational topics is achieved by displays of disinterest (giving minimal responses to topics introduced by women), by interruptions that change the topic, and so on. In committees, classrooms, or other occasions of meeting among women and men, ideas or criticisms put forward by women are less likely to be picked up and made part of the topic of discussion. An idea put forward by a woman may simply be ignored, or treated later as if it originated with a male speaker, or, later, be reintroduced by a male speaker as if she had never spoken. It is like a game in which there are more presences than players. Some are engaged in passing a ball between them; the others are assigned to the roles of audience and supporters. They pick up the ball if it is dropped and pass it back to the players. They support, facilitate, and encourage, but they do not become active in the play or in moving the process along. In many situations where women and men meet and work together, we can find this pattern. What women have to say may simply remain unsaid, or if said, unheard, or heard inattentively. It is not integral to the main play of the game which is among the male players.

If we think of a given period of time when people meet and talk—a seminar, for example, or a meeting—as something like a pie to be divided up among different speakers, there are many studies that show that men take up more of that talk space than women do. This is something you can check on yourself in your classroom. Using a stopwatch you can record how much of the talk space is appropriated by men and how much by women. Of course, we know women who do speak up and seem not be functioning very differently from men, yet even here there may be undetected differences. Norms for women's and men's speech differs; the woman who seems to talk so much may be having her talking measured unconsciously against how much women are expected to talk. She may seem to be talking a lot just because she's exceeding women's norm. One study showed that a woman who was seen as very assertive in fact talked less than any of the men including one who was seen as rather silent.

As I've stressed, these are patterns we participate in and often reproduce without realizing, probably largely because we're unaware of the part women play in our own silencing. The specifics may vary, but the over-all grammar of these relationships is understood by both sexes, though largely at a level below consciousness. It is important to realize that they are not simply imposed by men on women and that their reproduction is beyond the normal range of what we can speak about to one another. Hence it is often shocking to both women and men when these patterns are pointed out to them and they discover the extent to which they participate in women's repression.

Though the women's movement has made major advances, perhaps the most important change has been that of changing the ways in which women are able to treat what women write and say as authoritative. Before this movement, it was not only men who did not recognize women as authoritative speakers. Women shared this view. And so it was hard, at first, for women to attend seriously to one another, to listen, and take what was said (or written) as of serious significance. It was hard to develop organization without that essential recognition of how other women's voices mattered. This has indeed changed. A major achievement of the women's movement has been the emergence of a women's media, women's writing, women's poetry and art, women's political thinking, women's scholarship, and so on. These have depended on that first major step: recognizing the authority of women's voices.

The women's movement has its distinctive history and its distinctive struggle against and within the ruling relations because these relations have encysted the gender hierarchy we call "patriarchy." Its critique of patriarchy has often been also a critique of the ruling relations, proposing radically alternative forms of organizing the social relations of knowledge and communication. It revealed, for many women, the taken-for-granted class, gender, and racial subtexts of academic institutions—the hidden boundaries, exclusions, and positionings on which the texts and practices of ruling rely.

A radical critique speaking from the experience of women has been integral to the politics of the women's movement. Insisting on women's right to speak from the actualities of our experience is always potentially disruptive; there is always something new to be heard; there is always rethinking of established positions and representations to be done. The "we" of the women's movement has been open; hence settled positions in it are always subject to challenge. The perspectives and relevances of white, heterosexual, middle-class women built into the definition of women's issues have been disrupted by working class, lesbian, and non-white women opposing that hegemony. Elsewhere women of the "third world" were and are evolving a women's movement or women's movements independent of and in many respects more radical than those of North America and Europe.

New bases of organization have constantly been emerging; rifts and rows have resulted in new activism, realigning and expanding the women's movement's system of communication. We have published newspapers, newsletters, created new publishing houses, established bookstores. And of course we have also tried to convert the established structures for women, most often by creating within them a shell such as a women's caucus or committee, or in universities and colleges, a women's studies course, even a program. We have taken seriously in practice and in theory the universality lent our project by the category "women." Though established exclusions and barriers of race, class, politics, and imperialism were implicit in women's movement practice, they were, and are, always subject to confrontation and disruption. The very claim to speak as women and for women creates its own instability for at any minute another woman will come forward speaking from her experience, saying, "this does not apply to me," "this is not true of my experience," so that the claim to speak for women in general is found not to be speaking for me, for you, for her, for us.

The women's movement is in this respect extraordinary and exemplary. Though positions have been arrived at that have been centred on the experience of white women, the movement in general has been committed to listening to and recognizing the right of all women, of all people, to speak from their experience. Hence any orthodoxy will be challenged by a representation of concerns and perspectives that come from somewhere and someone else. Each new position is subject to challenge, creates new debates, advances new positions, creates new levels of political organization, seeking possibilities for political cooperation or intellectual engagement that transcend or, perhaps better, engage with and build upon the politics of difference. This volume represents exactly such a move. It draws on the richness of women's experience, formulating it for the general lessons we can learn. At the same time it always brings us back to the possibilities that arise when women, when people, can be treated as the authorized speakers of their experience—speaking with authority of what, though theoretically formulated, originates in the actualities of their lives.

 **Feminist Perspectives**

Women's Studies

An Inclusive Concept for an Inclusive Field

Marion M. Lynn ———

Women's studies is about social change; that must be seen as its final goal. Women's studies, in the broadest sense of the term, includes any organized learning experience which enables women to alter the unequal distribution of power between the sexes. Although it is an academic-sounding term, it is not an academic field in the traditional sense. In fact, it represents a new way of integrating material which challenges the barriers constructed by conventional scholastic structures. The content of courses and programs in women's studies refuses to fit neatly into existing disciplines. The teaching method necessarily unites the subjective and the objective, the experiential and the theoretical. It is this inclusiveness which gives women's studies its strength and its power. As we gather information, raise awareness, and gain recognition it becomes obvious that these studies pull together educational processes for women from all backgrounds and of all ages.

Women's sStudies, with its roots in the feminism of the '60s, is developing alongside the women's movement and reflects both the uniqueness and the complexities of the movement itself. The women's movement has developed through a process of social change in which the diverse nature of the issues, the changing leadership, and the unorthodox method of cooperation and communication have allowed a rich variety of talented people to contribute. And the areas of education which fit under women's studies do the same. We must preserve this uniqueness and understand the complexity.

This article defines women's studies as an "umbrella" concept incorporating academic courses, community programming, and affirmative action. These are directed toward women as students, as members of the society, and as workers. They are all new in both form and content, and there is no blueprint for their action or organization. Even within each category, there is no single model. But, although the structures and the politics vary from one program to another, they are mutually supportive in forming a solid basis for change. And they fit under the overall heading of women's studies because within all three areas (academic courses, community programming, and affirmative action), three essential processes occur: consciousness-raising; acquisition of knowledge and formulation of theories; political action and social change.

The following illustrates the relationships that link these three areas of study and these three processes together.

From consciousness-raising to social change

How do these processes come together? They interrelate in the following way. Consciousness-raising occurs when women share their life experiences and conditions and thus become aware of the common ground of their existence. As a woman expresses or describes an event to another, her own understanding of that event becomes clearer. What had been perceived as an isolated incident in the life of one woman becomes one of many such incidents in the lives of all women. The shame, giult, and competitiveness that had previously kept women apart now binds them into a sisterhood.

When women learn to speak out it is a crucial step on the road to liberation. And this is not only because we are at last acquiring a voice, but because facts are surfacing that can be communicated, collated, analyzed, and transformed into banks of resource material. With this information we are formulating new theories which explain the behaviour and situations of women and men. In consciousness-raising groups, women also experience a new form of organization, different from that to which they are accustomed. These groups are more organic and less structured, and are extremely effective. All this knowledge becomes a powerful agent for political action when used to reshape the lives of women and the society in which they live. And changes in our personal and social lives lead to consciousness-raising at an even higher level. The entire process of acquisition of more knowledge and organization for more social and political action occurs again. These processes are interlocking, spiralling, and ongoing.

Two specific experiences described in the literature on women further illustrate this relationship between consciousness-raising and social change. The first refers to a study entitled "Housewives in Women's Liberation: Social Change as Role Making," by Marylee Stephenson. In this study a number of housewives in an early women's liberation movement group in Vancouver, B.C., came together because as individuals they felt that they had failed to live up to the expectations society had of them as housewives. After their meeting each woman realized that her problem was not unique; other women were just as confused and frustrated. From the support of the group, the women were able to re-evaluate their expectations of themselves and of their roles within the family. Many began to cut out blocks of time for themselves, then insisted on sharing of household duties, and in this way their patterns of interaction with their children altered, especially in relation to sex-role behaviour. The significance of individual women making changes within their own families must not be underestimated. It could change the entire structure of family as we know it, and the structure of society. As a result, the women acquired the awareness, the skills, and the confidence to support a new view of their roles as housewives. All these conditions are necessary to bring about social change.

The second example comes from a book entitled *Rape: The First Sourcebook for Women*, by New York radical feminists Noreen Connell and Cassandra Wilson. Women discovered in consciousness-raising sessions that rape, or some form of sexual assault, had been a part of almost every woman's experience. They concluded, therefore, that this type of oppression was not personal, but political—a part of the overall oppression of women. The next step was to hold a public speak-out on rape and then a conference. In order to present papers, members of the organizing committee conducted research on rape. This led to the realization that an understanding of this social—not personal—problem depended upon an analysis of the power structures of such male-dominated institutions as education, law, medicine, psychiatry, films, and the media. What emerged from the conference were proposals for law reform, opening of rape crisis centres, and formation of self-defence courses. This is political action.

The following analysis shows how this same interconnected process leading to social change occurs in each of the areas of women's studies—within academic courses, community programs, and affirmative action.

Academic courses

Both the teaching/learning process and the curriculum content of academic courses in women's studies challenge the authority of traditional bodies of knowledge. In her article entitled "Women and the Power to Change," Florence Howe points out that the academic courses within the field of women's studies provide the strategy for social change because they build on "the social realities of particular lives" in order to develop "consciousness about one's life in contrast or comparison to the norms that prevail." In order to investigate or establish any body of knowledge, e.g., history or psychology, one must have this initial awareness of one's own life and experiences. For instance, in order to understand Freud, we must realize that our experience is the experience of all women, with the result that much of Freudian theory can be debunked.

Barbara Bellow Watson, in her preface entitled "The Proper Study," suggests that one function of women's studies courses is to shed new light on the "distortions and omissions" about women found in the traditional curriculum, and consequently to enable women to know themselves better. Because the study of the individual and of society are inseparable, this knowledge will lead not only to self-realization on the part of individual women, but to a clearer understanding of society. "Every time we correct a misconception about women, we correct a misconception about society. Every time we correct a historical or psychological conclusion, we also correct, implicitly or explicitly, the method that led to that conclusion."

An experience that stays with me occurred when I was teaching a course on "Women in Society." At the end of the term a young woman said, "Taking this course has altered my life." And a woman who knows that her life has been changed by one fifteen-week course cannot keep that change to herself. She will gradually bring about changes in her own family. She will work toward changes in her community, creating more and better daycare, getting more women elected to political office, or improving laws on rape and labour legislation. In fact, continuing contact with students from this course demonstrates that many of them have become involved in some aspect of change for women.

Community programming

One analysis of the effects of community programming can be found in the report, *Learning Opportunities for Women in Canada: Perceptions of Educators*, prepared by Janet Willis. It is based on the results of a cross-Canada questionnaire sent to people involved in community education for women. It clearly demonstrates the overall importance of the various courses, workshops, and seminars offered to women. Whether they come from educational institutions, government, or social agencies, such programs lead to consciousness-raising, accumulation of knowledge, and political action.

According to this research some of the effects of these programs on the participants were: enhanced self-image and more self-confidence; greater sense of competence and power to make decisions; improved physical and mental health, and the conviction that women can begin solving their own problems. As a result of these changes in attitude some of the women entered the workforce or full-time educational programs; some organized daycare centres and library discussion groups, while others went into political offices on local school boards or city councils.

These programs also have an impact on the host agency or institution. A corollary to successful implementation of programming for women is the change in attitudes of staff and faculty, and of administration. People became more supportive towards future programming for women. The report states that in some cases the institutional policies were changed when it was recognized that 30- to 50-year-old women are potential students for daytime programs. The administrators of the institutions involved also realized that these women students need special services and scheduling of classes at appropriate times. And this realization must lead to structural changes to accommodate this new groups of students.

Affirmative action

The third area to be included as part of women's studies is affirmative action. This is a total program of education and change within an institution or organization that has as its goal the elimination of barriers preventing women from reaching their potential in the workforce. The first two steps in any successful affirmative-action program must be commitment on the part of top management, and research to determine where women are in the organization.

The third and crucial step is the establishment of a comprehensive educational program to change the attitudes of women and men in the organization, and to teach women the necessary skills to achieve greater job mobility and control over their careers.

In order to do this it is necessary to provide small group workshops for the women employees. These are at a "grassroots" level and provide opportunity for consciousness-raising and the acquisition of specific skills, as well as general knowledge about women's status and potential. Effective speaking, career planning, power analysis, and assertiveness training all require skills that most women never think about—never mind put into practice. Workshops of this type are educational and point out the need for women to catch up on the skills, and change the attitudes that were acquired while they were "growing up female."

Affirmative-action programs focus on the need for all members of the workforce to reassess their definitions of masculinity and femininity in relation to positions of power and status. For instance, a woman who is competent and knowledgeable in her field should become a top executive, and men who work for her should not feel threatened just because she is a woman. Her expertise should be judged, not her sex.

This view of affirmative action underlines the similarity between women learning to appreciate their experiences through the study of an academic course on "Women in Literature" and women learning in an affirmative-action workshop. The study of women and the law is equally appropriate to academic courses, community programming, and affirmative action. This is why affirmative-action programming should be seen as a basic part of women's studies. As in the areas of academic courses and community programming it provides an opportunity for women to experience consciousness-raising, to acquire knowledge and a new understanding of behaviour, and to act politically for social change.

The philsophy behind this article was in fact thrashed out during the initial editorial board meetings while we were all formulating the How and the Why of this journal [CWS/CF]. The editorial board meetings of the journal all work in one or more of these three areas of women's studies. We want to help to break down the barriers between the education of women in the classroom, in the community, and in the workforce. We believe this will unite women and give them power. By raising consciousness, by sharing knowledge, we will help each other to understand why we have been in a dependent and powerless state. In doing so we will create a structure and a process so conducive to political action and social change that there will be no turning back. This is what we mean by women's studies and this is why this journal is published.

Originally published in Canadian Woman Studies/les cahiers de la femme's (CWS/ cf) inaugural issue, Fall 1978, (Volume 1, Number 1).

References

Connell, Noreen, and Cassandra Wilson, eds. *Rape: The First Sourcebook for Women*. New York: Plume, 1974.

Howe, Florence, ed. *Women and the Power to Change*. New York: McGraw-Hill, 1976.

Stephenson, Marylee, ed. *Women in Canada*. Toronto: New Press, 1973.

Watson, Barbara Bellow, ed. *Women's Studies: The Social Realities*. New York: Harper and Row, 1976.

Willis, Janet. *Learning Opportunities for Women in Canada: Perceptions of Educators*. Toronto: Canadian Committee on Learning Opportunities for Women, 1977.

Towards a Politics of Location
Rethinking Marginality

Joan Borsa ⟶

> *To find someone somehow like us, is to account for our desire, to give it a place from which to imagine and image a writing self: absorbed, drudging, puzzled; at a desk, not before a mirror.* —Nancy Miller (109)

Most of us come to feminism because the social situations we experience necessitate struggle, analysis, and change, but becoming politically and/or theoretically engaged does not magically eradicate the complex relations within our everyday realities. Since I have more consciously identified with that large and always shifting terrain of feminism, I have been plagued by what I will call the politics of location—those places and spaces we inherit and occupy, which frame our lives in very specific and concrete ways, which are as much a part of our psyches as they are a physical or geographical placement. Where we live, how we live, our relation to the social systems and structures that surround us are deeply embedded parts of everything we do and remain integral both to our identity or sense of self and to our position or status within a larger cultural and representational field. While many of us are actively involved in feminism, in cultural production, and in critical social theory, our historical, social, political, and economic realities vary—there is a great deal of structural difference between us. Part of our struggle is to be able to name our location, to politicize our space, and to question where our particular experiences and practice fit within the articulations and representations that surround us.

For example, under the umbrellas of critical theory, postmodernism, and feminism, how have the topics and agendas been established? Who sets the parameters for discourse, representation, and practice and where are we in relation to those agendas? Are our personal and social locations "in" the parameters we take on? And how do we manage that complicated manoeuvre of accounting for our specific circumstances while participating in the larger field that informs, challenges, and affects our individual lives and practice? How do we avoid overemphasizing our circumstances and becoming so self-centred and insular that we fall into a rhetoric of intolerance and indifference—or on the other hand becoming so preoccupied with what is happening elsewhere that we act like tourists or hungry consumers fascinated with the new, the exotic, examining distant locations in a way that comes close to escapism, applying imported methodology and analysis to our specific struggles without an adequate understanding or acknowledgement of the limitations they present? Either way we fall into the old either/or opposition where we accept that the truth lies in wait and that we are about to unearth the solution, the ultimate explanation where we may finally rest. What is missing at either end of these polarities is an acknowledgement of the fruitfulness of struggle, of the benefits of not having the definitive answers, and the productiveness of working through the contradictions and conflicts that surround our particular locations.

Structural difference

The notion of structural difference (the politics of location) seems particularly crucial to those of us involved with feminist struggle and cultural production who live and work in Canada. Except for a handful of Margaret Atwoods, Margaret Laurences, Mary O'Briens, and Emily Carrs, it is safe to say that ours is a marginalized and colonial relationship to the larger field of theory, art, and representation. As we look around us we see a great deal of imported dominant presence(s). The curriculums we study or develop, the representational practices in play, the critical writing styles, the content of gallery exhibition programs all reveal a strong Eurocentric and American bias. And yet this openness to the outside is also a strength, a willingness to explore the boundaries of our own production, to consider other contexts and to "listen" as well as to speak. My concern is that we may be too skilled at listening and too competent at appropriation. More determination is needed in the area of resistance—not as a reactionary defiant stance but as a process of identification, articulation, and representation—a critical positioning which provides a sense of place, a context from which to develop our insights, ideas, and responses, a strategic site that allows sufficient grounding for specific forms of thought, speech, and representation to emerge and gain meaning.

British cultural theorist Stuart Hall emphasizes that cultural identification need not produce "an essence but a positioning," not a fixed point but a point in transition, a place I see as a reference point, and that Hall describes as a site "subject to the continuous 'play' of history, culture, and power" (72, 70). To conceive of cultural identity in this manner brings out the significance of the politics of location—an exploration of the ways we have been grounded and positioned in particular representations of past and present, where frequently history and culture are presented as static, some already formulated space that we merely pass through. To acknowledge that we are engaged in a "process of becoming as well as being"[1] de-emphasizes the notion that cultural identity merely reflects or represents a collective or common experience, a pre-ordained "essence." Emphasizing the "process of becoming" allows for the possibility of a new space, an area of transformation and change where we no longer accept a factual or natural account of history and culture, nor simply seek to retrieve a hidden authentic identity. Although it is crucial to recognize that we have inherited a past that constitutes and positions us in very specific ways and simultaneously to remember that much has been devalued, omitted, or misrepresented, neither position goes far enough. On the one side we seem hopelessly trapped, fixed into inherited systems and structures, and on the other we appear reactive, engaged in revisionary tactics, offering new stories as if in themselves they can set things right.

There is no simple truth that must be retrieved, discovered or brought forward that will easily change our circumstances, but by articulating our specific experiences and representing the structural and political spaces we occupy, we offer concrete accounts of where and how we live, what is significant to our experience of cultural identity, how we have been constructed and how, in turn, we attempt to construct (and reconstruct) ourselves.

Rethinking marginality

For anyone occupying a place that could be described as marginal or colonial it is important to acknowledge that one does not "naturally" occupy a site outside the larger cultural and representational field as if irreconcilably "other," but that whether in the centre or in the margin one always speaks from a position, a context, a place which offers the possibility of exploring identity, articulation, and representation. As American writer bell hooks suggests there is nothing intrinsically positive or negative, inside or outside, about a specific location. Centres and margins—like culture, sexual difference, and identity—have been historically produced. The associations that surround particular "placements" are part of a complex "play of history, culture, and power" (Hall) where a particular privilege (in the form of power relations) is naturalized and other positions (different and less powerful than the first) are neutralized.

Cultural theorist Gayatri Chakravorty Spivak has devoted much attention to the process and practice of "othering," a term she uses to refer to the mechanisms and strategies that construct the orders and relations of power that we come to occupy. In an essay on "The Rani of Sirmur," Spivak addresses the problems in "reading" cultural difference and questions how to get at a particular nineteenth-century third-world woman's historical inheritance, structured as it is within the relationship of India to the British Empire, the Rani's position as woman within an indigenous order of patriarchy, and finally her status as wife of the king of Sirmur. As a colonial, as a woman, and as a wife, the Rani is constituted in power relations and dominant cultural codes that represent her as a supplementary figure—she is brought in and out of historical records during the constitution of India as a British colony to enhance her husband's or son's archives, or to expand the accounts of colonial history, but never is she presented as a subject with her own location, her own stories to tell.

In looking for a missing or silenced archive, Spivak dismantles the layers of dominant inscriptions that have enclosed the Rani. Underneath the mediations, representations, and discourse that have layered themselves upon her, we find not the Rani herself but the space where she resided. Spivak names and politicizes the space the Rani occupied and strips away the naturalness of the power relations that contained her. Spivak believes there is no "real" Rani to be found and that it would be to no one's advantage to invent or substitute a preferred Rani. Instead we must be satisfied with understanding how the Rani was a site of complex power relations and cultural inscriptions, a fragmented historical presence. Spivak's work provides a significant example of the need to explore ways we have been grounded and positioned—the usefulness of examining the conflicts and contradictions that surround our particular inheritances. Spivak suggests ways to begin to unravel the ordering and structuring of dominant cultural codes so that we may better utilize the locations we occupy as sites of resistance—spaces where critical positioning, or a process of identification, articulation, and representation can occur.

Marginality and feminist cultural production

In the visual arts we occupy a rather unique relationship to cultural and representational systems. We have the potential to speak in a form capable of re-ordering and re-symbolizing the power relations and cultural codes already in existence. Through visual practices artists have attempted to destabilize lines of natural authority and have attempted to politicize the different positions and cultural identities they occupy. To this end, I have been fascinated with the Mexican artist, Frida Kahlo (1907–1954) and the ways she articulated a politics of location.

In considering Kahlo's work I take on an artist who, I believe, lived and worked outside the dominant structures functioning at her time. I wish to explore how, within the conditions surrounding Kahlo's production, she managed to construct her own history, how she resisted the spaces designated female and artist as laid out by patriarchal and hegemonic systems, how Kahlo's work articulates the "structural difference" of her placement within gender, art, and discourse hierarchies, and what she did about the marginality that she was presented with. (Obviously this is beyond the scope of an article of this length. I will therefore outline what I consider to be central to my discussion, that is, Kahlo's strategy of resistance.)[2]

Kahlo was a self-trained artist who worked outside the centres and high art traditions of Europe and the United States. As a woman making art she refused the male-dominant language of high art and worked in what has been called a "dialect," which embraced the peripheries of "folk" art practices popular in Mexico at the time. Kahlo's images, numbering approximately 200 paintings and drawings, intimate in scale and personal in nature, are largely self-portraits and references to a private world where woman's body and her own direct experiences come into focus. In Kahlo's work the body and assigned feminine roles are taken on not to celebrate or glorify them but to parody and invert the ways they have been represented.

Frida Kahlo, "Self-Portrait with Thorn Necklace and Hummingbird," 1940.
Oil on canvas, 63.5 x 49.5 cm. Collection Harry Ransom Humanities Research Centre,
the University of Texas at Austin, USA. Reproduction of this image authorized by
El Instituto Nacional de Bellas Artes y Literatura Mexico.

Kahlo continually gives the impression of consciously highlighting the interface of women's art and domestic space, as though in her life (and in her dress) she was drawing attention to the impossibility of separating the two. However, her art also acts as an ironic, bitter comment on women's experience. *The feminine sphere is stripped of reassurance* [my emphasis]. The haven of male fantasy is replaced by the experience of pain, including the pain associated with her physical inability to live out a feminine role in motherhood.... She takes the "interior" offered as the feminine sphere, the male retreat from public life and reveals the other "interior" behind it, that of female suffering, vulnerability, and self-doubt. (Mulvey and Wollen 15)[3]

This passage by Laura Mulvey and Peter Wollen suggests that Kahlo's work plays with the spaces she occupies. She acknowledges and manages both to image the structure that contains her, that codifies her existence and asks her to "perform" in particular ways, and simultaneously to suggest her aware-

Frida Kahlo, "My Nurse and I," 1937. Oil on sheet metal, 12" x 13.75".
Collection Fundacion Dolores Olmedo Patino AC. Reproduction of this image authorized
by El Instituto Nacional de Bellas Artes y Literatura Mexico.

ness and discomfort in carrying this codification. The "interior behind the image" not only suggests an analysis of sexual difference, its formation and impact, but reveals a reworking of the conditions and margins she has inherited. Kahlo's self-portraits, for example, play with the outward appearance of self, the projection and image that is presented for public consumption *versus* the screened, masked, and complex inner workings of the subject behind the representation.

Kahlo's reworking of "otherness" can be seen in her attention to marginality, where cultural contradictions and classifications are always in view. For example Kahlo's painting "My Nurse and I" painted in 1937, like much of her work, is in the style of the popular Mexican ex-voto paintings, religious offerings usually painted on tin or wood to commemorate "miraculous deliveries from death or disaster" (Baddeley and Fraser 122-124). Kahlo presents us with two female figures, one clearly being nurtured by the other, reminiscent of the many religious representations of the Madonna and Child. The large dark madonna figure, the nurse, dominates the space and is presented as if in two parts: a large fertile, nurturing body contrasted with a much darker carved mask-like face. In the nurse's arms a female adult-child is being suckled— clearly the infant is the artist Frida Kahlo. A similar bodily disjuncture occurs with the contrast between the child-like frail body and the adult artist's face and head. As with the nurse, the child's face is expressionless and mask-like, similar to most of Kahlo's self-portraits. In the disjuncture between the bodies and faces several associations or layers of past and present come into play. The nurse's mask-like face, for instance, is reminiscent of an Olmec stone mask. The Olmecs were some of the earliest civilizations of ancient Mexico. Kahlo's detailing of the Indian female body and a pre-Hispanic past suggests a complicated interplay between nature, culture and history, the referencing of Mexico's colonial past, the history of the land, and the continuation of Mexican cultural despite massive interventions, fragmentations and disjunctures.[4]

The usual negative representations of gender and race as oppressed or lacking are transformed in Kahlo's work; the Indian/pre-Hispanic figure represents the power of life and the contingency of history. The traditional gendered image of colonization—the female land as overpowered and plundered—is symbolically reworked, suggesting instead a regenerative and powerful presence. The referencing of Mexico's past and peasantry as Kahlo's own life-line is not isolated to this particular work. Both in her everyday dress (she wore the traditional Tehuana costume of the Tehuantepec women, one of the oldest matriarchal groups in Mexico) and in various cultural codes, Kahlo's identification with Mexican popular culture is obvious. It appears that the language (dialect) and situations that Kahlo understood best, those sites where she staged her struggles and in the end were the closest to home, allowed her to interrogate and speak with the greatest clarity. The structural difference introduced by her particular location as woman, Mexican, and self-taught artist was never a place Kahlo accepted. Her production leaves us with a sense of urgency in its desire to announce and understand difference and above all to remain wary of any practice or process that attempts to speak on one's behalf. In Kahlo's work the concept of margins is not allowed to remain within the boundaries of second-order, peripheral, and deprived status.

Within and across margins

Similarly, American feminist bell hooks emphasizes the political and productive potential of margins. hooks refers to margins as "profound edges" where one can choose to stay—sites with "radical possibilities that allow lived experience to nourish and develop perspective." In a paper she delivered in England in 1988 called "Choosing the Margin as a Space of Radical Openness," hooks describes the complex shifts possible when people use their margins as sites of political resistance. First, they push against the oppressive boundaries that have defined and restricted them and eventually find themselves in a state of transformation where they "move out of their place" (the place of repression that they have struggled against) to find themselves "confronted with the reality of choice and location" (hooks 19-20). At this point they may be tempted or indeed satisfied to leave the struggle behind and "position themselves on the side of the colonizing mentality" (hooks 15). Or they may take full advantage of the ground that has been gained but continue to stand in political resistance with the oppressed, recognizing that frequently even to speak about domination in terms that will be heard requires using a language and representational systems that are potentially repressive. But as Gayatri Spivak and Frida Kahlo clearly demonstrate, one can take on master texts without subscribing to them, without reproducing their meaning. It is this constant search for ways to play with the relations of history, culture, and power, to parody or decon-struct and reconstruct meaning in a way that speaks of structural difference, that much feminist work seems to productively explore.

In a Canadian, feminist, visual arts context and particularly at this point in our history, I see much evidence of struggle around developing a politics of location where margins become positive and productive sites of resistance. Until we individually and collectively can acknowledge the power relations and dominant cultural codes that need to be examined (and that we are inevitably implicated in) we continue to operate in an us/them (Canadian/European, East/West, urban/rural, feminist artist/woman artist) oppositional structure. Ours is a specific fragmented cultural and social landscape which requires assessments and engagements within contexts marked by its own heterogeneous and discontinuous frameworks. We cannot simply adapt theories and practices developed elsewhere without contributing to the development of new and equally problematic master texts. Nor can we reduce our struggles to battles within our own Canadian boundaries—between theoretically informed, politically correct Toronto and spiritual, laid-back Vancouver and grassroots, out-of-step Saskatoon. To begin with, these are all negative, stereotypic, and combative responses to location. We are all sufficiently mobile (culturally and geographically) and sufficiently hybrid to traverse these simplistic codes. Across the regional, theoretical, and political boundaries that separate us are much larger issues of gender, race, and colonial history. We have long since passed the point of needing to ask permission to speak in our own terms but perhaps we need to repeatedly remind ourselves what our specific struggles are—why it is that we came to feminist practice, why we are engaged with a process of analysis and change—what it is that we are attempting to learn more about. That is, what is the critical and collective value of our efforts? Are we not attempting to account for the specific effects of social and historical meaning, while reassessing the terms that have been set in place? And aren't these activities a function of articulating and representing what we know best—issues much closer to home?

Originally published in CWS/cf's Spring 1990 issue, "Feminism and Visual Art" (Volume 11, Number 1).

[1]The phrase "What are we in the process of becoming?" has been used by Juliet Mitchell (294) to suggest that we cannot live as human subjects without accounting for the effects of history. If we deconstruct the histories we have

inherited what do we offer in their place? What are we in the process of becoming?

[2]I have developed these ideas in an article, "Frida Kahlo: Marginalization and the Critical Female Subject," *Body Politics, Third Text* (#12, Autumn) London: Kala Press, 1990. This research was completed in the Social History of Art Programme at the University of Leeds, England.

[3]My reference to Kahlo's "dialect" is also discussed in Mulvey and Wollen.

[4]My interest in Kahlo's work and particularly "My Nurse and I" has benefitted from Baddeley and Fraser's astute discussion of contemporary issues specific to Mexican art and culture.

References

Baddeley, O., and V. Fraser. *Drawing the Line: Art and Cultural Identity in Contemporary Latin America*. London: Verso, 1989.

Hall, Stuart. "Cultural Identity and Cinematic Representation." *Third Scenario: Theory and the Politics of Location, Framework*. London: Sankofa Film and Video, 1989.

hooks, bell. "Choosing the Margin as a Space of Radical Openness." *Third Scenario: Theory and the Politics of Location, Framework*. London: Sankofa Film and Video, 1989.

Miller, Nancy. "Changing the Subject: Authorship, Writing and the Reader." *Feminist Theory, Critical Theory*. Ed. Teresa de Lauretis. Bloomington: Indiana University Press, 1986.

Mitchell, Juliet. *Women: The Longest Revolution*. New York: Pantheon, 1984.

Mulvey, Laura, and Peter Wollen. *Frida Kahlo and Tina Modotti*. Exhibition catalogue. London: Whitechapel Art Gallery, 1982.

Spivak, Gayatri Chakravorty. "The Rani of Sirmur: An Essay in Reading the Archives." *History and Theory* 24 (1985).

Moving Beyond the Feminism Versus Nationalism Dichotomy

An Anti-Colonial Feminist Perspective on Aboriginal Liberation Struggles

Lina Sunseri ——

In writing this paper, I feel that I must clearly identify my position in our "Canadian" society: I am of mixed Aboriginal-Southern White European ancestry. This mixed cultural/ethno-racial identity provides me with distinct experiences which have brought me to a point in my life where I support the anti-colonial self-determination struggles of Aboriginal peoples on this Turtle Island known as Canada. Many times I am asked by friends, intellectuals, feminists, and non-feminists, how I could support any nationalist struggle, especially in light of what has taken place in many parts of the world in the name of ethno-nationalism. Indeed, I often wonder if an Aboriginal "nationalist" struggle can avoid the destructive results that have occurred elsewhere. I also wonder where I would be placed, and place myself, in this struggle given my mixed ancestry. My "hybrid" identity leaves me in what Homi Bhabha would call an "in-between" place, not quite the colonizer or the colonized. Located as I am in this ambivalent place, having the "privilege" of a mixture of cultures, it is not surprising then that I might feel both pulled and pushed towards an Aboriginal anti-colonial movement. This tension is further complicated by my feminist ideology and culture, an ideology that has expressed justifiable skepticism about "nationalisms," especially in light of the latter's relationship with women's rights.

This paper, written in the midst of all these emotions and recent events of "nationalist" movements (such as the Serbian, Croatian, Kurdish and Tamil cases), is an attempt to come to terms with my support for an Aboriginal anti-colonial nationalist movement. Mine is obviously then a situated knowledge, informed by both feminist knowledge and Aboriginal experiences, either of my own or of other Aboriginal peoples. A situated knowledge stresses and validates the importance of lived experiences and it incorporates these experiences within theory (Collins). While recognizing the limitations of past nationalist movements to liberate women, I believe that it is possible to envision a progressive nationalist liberation movement, one which could eliminate oppressive and unequal power relations. Given that Aboriginal women have lived for many centuries in an oppressive racist and sexist colonial society, which has brought them infinite political, economic, social, and cultural destruction, it is not surprising that these women would ally themselves with a movement that wants to restore and reaffirm their inherent right to govern themselves.

I will begin with an introduction to feminism, nationalism, and nation, and then briefly review the debates taking place between feminists and nationalists. I examine the contributions offered by feminist critiques of nationalism, highlighting the argument that there have been limitations to the liberatory aspects of nationalist movements. In most cases, once the post-colonial nation is formed, the position of women has not improved much and, in some cases, it has even regressed. I will argue that nationalism, in itself, is not necessarily evil, just as feminism is not but both have the potential to be exclusionary, and therefore, on their own, cannot resolve all of Aboriginal (and non) women's problems. I will then offer an overview of Aboriginal self-determination struggles. In this section, I will examine some key characteristics and assumptions of these struggles, and then address the specific dilemmas that Aboriginal women face within these struggles both with the Canadian state and with some Aboriginal organizations (e.g. the Assembly of First Nations). In my conclusion, I will attempt to move beyond the feminism versus nationalism dichotomy by arguing that Aboriginal women's participation in the self-determination of First Nations can be seen as both an anti-colonial movement and a feminist one.

Defining feminism, nationalism and the nation

A core part of this paper consists of the debate between feminism and nationalism, and how the two seem incompatible. Some earlier second-wave feminists, believe that women's oppression is unique and tied to a universal patriarchy (Firestone; Friedan; Millett). They sought to unite women through a sense of a shared oppression, and tended to believe that women's interests can be best achieved through a women's movement that places women's rights the first priority in its agenda.

Many Aboriginal women, along with other women of colour and "third world" women, have felt alienated by what they view as "Western" feminist movement that has either marginalized them or not accurately represented their experiences and interests. As Charles and Hintjens point out:

> In the context of the Third World, this rejection of feminism often arises from its association with western, middle-class women and with the negative consequences of modernisation.... However, feminism has also developed a critique of modernism.... Thus western feminism recognizes that women neither automatically share a gender identity nor do they necessarily have political interests in common. Their material circumstances and experiences differ significantly and a unity of interests between women from different cultures (and within the same society) cannot be deduced from their shared gender. (20)

The marginalization of non-White European women within mainstream Western feminism is a reality, and women of colour have challenged the members of the movement to analyse its own racism and its essentialist portrayal of the "Universal" woman. As Charles and Hintjens indicate above, Western feminism has more recently provided its own critique of modernity and taken into account the diversity of women's experience. Although Western feminism has responded to the challenges presented by women of colour and Third World women, and re-evaluated its earlier assumptions, I still believe that more work needs to be done, especially vis-a-vis the further incorporation of issues of colonialism and racism into the theory and praxis of the movement. Until the women's movement completely faces the reality that many of its members are part of the colonial power, and therefore share some of the advantages that their male counterparts enjoy, most Aboriginals and other colonized groups will continue to view it with some skepticism. If we could all come to understand feminism as a theory and movement that wants to fight *all* forms of oppression, including racism and colonialism, then we could see it as a struggle for *unity* among all oppressed women and men. It is this meaning of feminism that I accept, and therefore I can call myself a feminist without reservations.

For the purpose of this paper, nationalism and nation are associated with movements for independence, liberation, and revolution. A classic definition of nation is that of Benedict Anderson, who constructs it as "an imagined community," a collectivity of individuals who feel that they belong to a shared linguistic community. Anthony Smith presents a primordial definition of nation. For him, nation refers to an ethnic collectivity with a shared past. In my analysis, nation means not only a community that may share a common culture and historical experiences, but it is also a collectivity that is "oriented towards the future" (Yuval-Davis 19). Nationalism is that ideology or discourse which promotes and shapes the formation of such communities. There are different kinds of nationalism; some rely on an exclusionary and homogenous vision, but others can be empowering and culturally diverse. Partha Chatterjee argues, in the context of an anti-colonial project,

> the national question here is, of course, historically fused with a colonial question. The assertion of national identity was, therefore, a form of the struggle against colonial exploitation. (18)

It is precisely this anti-colonial, liberation struggle to which I refer when I speak of nationalism in this paper. Within this framework, and within an Aboriginal context, nationalism means a process to revitalize the different institutions and practices of our various Nations (Alfred). An Aboriginal perspective on nation and nationalism differs from a Western one because its basis for nationhood is not rooted in notions of territoriality, boundaries, and nation-state (Alfred). Moreover, other concepts (such as "pure" Indian, status-Indian, national and regional boundaries) are all constructs of a colonial state and are foreign, if not antithetical, to most Aboriginal cultures and ways of governance (Monture-Angus 1995).

Feminist critique of nationalism

Feminist studies on nationalist and other liberation movements have revealed that, after national liberation, women generally have been pushed to domestic roles (Abdo). During nationalist struggles, women are often seen as the producers and reproducers of the national culture, and can aquire prestige and status as the bearers of "pure" culture. However, they can also become increasingly controlled, as their reproductive roles and their portrayal as bearers of culture can also be used to control their sexuality and confine them to domestic roles (Enloe).

Embedded implicitly and explicitly in this discourse of women as the bearers of culture and "tradition," is another discourse not exclusively tied to women: that of ethno/racial identity as immutable and connected to blood. Yet, when identity is viewed as uni-dimensional and biological, it marginalizes those who do not fit the strict categories of belonging to one specific ethnic/racial group, and in the process excludes all those individuals who have "mixed" descent, because their blood cannot be easily and exclusively connected with one group. When ethno-racial nationalist movements connect their concept of belonging to the nation to this notion of purity, we can also see that they need to regulate the sexual relationships of the members of their community. In practice, this regulation is more strictly applied, and with more negative sanctions, against women, because their reproductive roles become extremely important in the discourses of common origin and purity of blood (Yuval-Davis).

While recognizing some of the negative results of some nationalist discourses for women, we cannot ignore that some anti-colonial movements have provided the opportunity to mobilize women in their common struggle against the oppressive colonial or quasi-colonial power[1] as in the case of Algeria, South Africa, Palestine and some Latin American countries. The women involved have increased their political consciousness and, in some cases, made the male nationalists more aware of exploitative and oppressive gender relations. Often enough though, the male nationalists argue that colonialism and/or capitalism has been the cause of women's problems and they have completely ignored or dismissed the patriarchal nature of women's oppression. Moreover, neither a nationalist nor a socialist revolution has yet integrated a feminist discourse (McClintock). Constructing a radical alternative discourse that can smash both the sexist emperor and the sexist "colonized" is not an easy task. This project becomes even more difficult when other forces, both internal and external, such as global capitalism, religious fundamentalism, and reactionary "traditionalism" are at work, limiting the possibility of a full transformation of social relations in the post-colonial world.

Aboriginal self-determination struggles

Aboriginal peoples of North America have in recent decades successfully articulated a discourse of "self-determination," advocating a commitment on the part of non-Aboriginals to recognize Aboriginal inherent rights to govern ourselves. This discourse of self-determination is similar to that of self-government; however, I see it as having a much broader meaning and intent. Some may use the two terms interchangeably and argue that self-government means an inherent right of Aboriginal peoples to "be governed by rules of social, moral, political and cultural behaviour upon which they agree" (McIvor 167). However, I tend to agree more with Monture-Angus and with other Aboriginals who claim that self-government implies a perpetuation of a colonial superior government that still makes the ultimate decisions about the meaning of aboriginal rights and how these are to be implemented (1999). Self-government, then , is viewed by us as a "limited form of governance" (Monture-Angus 1999: 29) that maintains unacceptable and unjust colonial relations. Self-determination, on the other hand, holds a better promise for Aboriginal peoples, because it is premised on the notion that our rights to be independent and to determine our own futures were never extinguished. (Monture-Angus 1999). What we demand is not merely equal opportunity within the mainstream Canadian system, but rather an inherent right of First Nations people to live by our own unique set of values (Schouls). Some of these different sets of values comprise a distinct definition of government, of land, and of land rights. For native peoples, "government" constitutes a decision-making system based on consensus and on individuals maintaining significant responsibilities for their behaviour and decisions (Barnaby). Similarly, Aboriginals have a unique relationship to the land; in fact, this distinctive relationship to creation is reflected in our languages, hence our insistence that our rights to lands be recognized. Ours is a world view that moves far beyond the material utility of natural resources because we view our relationship with animals, plants, water ,and all other living things as a very spiritual one. Land rights are, then, very different than proprietary rights. While the latter translates into individual ownership of land and is usually based on a market economy, the former "needs to be understood in a context of culture and territoriality.... Similarly, tribal sovereignty must be understood in its cultural context, one that reflects self-determination and self-sufficiency traditionally predicated on reciprocity" (Jaimes-Guerrero 102).

Many Canadians feel threatened by the demands of Aboriginal peoples; some fear they might have to relinquish any privilege they have enjoyed at the expense of Aboriginals' oppression, others feel that Aboriginal self-government may weaken an already shaky Canadian national identity. It is important to note that recognition of Aboriginal sovereignty does not automatically become national independence. As Glenn Morris argues,

Given the difficult practical political and economic difficulties facing smaller states in the world today, most indigenous peoples may very well not opt for complete independent state status. Many would probably choose some type of autonomy or federation with existing states, preserving rights to internal self-governance and control as members of larger states. (78-79)

What is crucial here is that it is be the choice of Aboriginal peoples to determine which course to take rather than having one imposed on them, as has been the case with the Canadian state.

As in some other anti-colonial liberation struggles, Aboriginal women have had an important role in the "national" struggle and their roles have not been free of contradictions and obstacles. Colonization of the Americas ultimately transformed all structures, including Aboriginal gender relations. Prior to this, women in most Aboriginal societies enjoyed a large amount of status and power. The *Haudenosaunee* (Iroquois, or a more appropriate translation, People of the Longhouse) women, for example, occupied prominent positions in all aspects of indigenous life. Within the laws of the *Haudenosaunee* people, the *Kaianerekowa*, known as the Great Law of Peace, it is clearly stated that women choose the *Oyaneh* (Clan Mothers), who had a large amount of power in each clan, including the power to remove chiefs, to decide on matters of inter-tribal disputes, and determine distribution of resources (Goodleaf).

The contact with European societies and the eventual colonization of Aboriginal peoples altered the conditions of Aboriginal women of Canada. As Cora Voyageur argues:

> one of the primary reasons for the situation of Indian women today is that Indians, in general, were subjugated by the immigrant European society.... The British North American Act of 1867 gave the power of legislative control over Indians and their lands to the federal government. The Indian Act of 1876 consolidated legislation already in place. The measure depriving an Indian woman of her status when she married a non-Indian was first legislated in the 1869 Indian Act. This Act was also the first legislation that officially discriminated against Indian women by assigning them fewer fundamental rights than Indian men. (100)

Most Aboriginal women point out that, for them, the Canadian law is at the centre of our problems and the patriarchal nature of the Canadian state has different meanings and consequences for Aboriginal women (Monture-Angus 1995). In order to fully understand how patriarchy works in Canada, we *must* look at the oppressive role that the Canadian state has had, and continues to have, in the everyday lives of Aboriginal women. Decolonization, therefore, is a necessary step for the full liberation of Aboriginal women, and it is the one point where Aboriginal men and women can come together as united. By "decolonization" I mean the process by which the longstanding colonial relations between Aboriginals and non-Aboriginals are abolished and new relations formed. These relations will be based on principles of mutual respect, sharing, and recognition of the inherent rights of Aboriginal peoples to follow their traditional ways of governance.

Resorting exclusively to an agenda of decolonization while simultaneously not integrating women's issues into it, as I have warned earlier, can be "dangerous" for women. We cannot be certain that the national liberation will automatically translate into a women's liberation. More often than not, failing to combine a gender analysis with an anti-colonial one can only increase the chances that colonized women's lives will not be improved, as the new male leaders will be reluctant to give up any power they have recently gained. As Aboriginal women, we have an awareness of inequalities and injustices we suffer as women as well as Aboriginal peoples. These inequalities may have been created as a result of the colonization of our peoples, but some may have existed in some communities externally to it, and we need to look closer at this possibility. As Emma Laroque states, it is important to remember that:

> Culture is not immutable, and tradition cannot be expected to be always of value or relevant in our times. As Native women, we are faced with the very difficult and painful choices, but nonetheless, we are challenged to change, create, and embrace "traditions" consistent with contemporary and international human rights standards. (14)

Canadian Indigenous women have, at times, found themselves in opposition to the male-dominated and federally funded Aboriginal associations. The two important historical moments where we witnessed this dissension between male leaders and female leaders occurred during the amendment of the Indian Act which reinstated Indian status to Aboriginal women who had married non-Indian men, and then later during the Charlettown Accord talks, when the Native Women's Association of Canada (NWAC) argued that the collective rights of Aboriginal women related to gender equality were not protected and integrated in the Accord. Throughout these moments, the Assembly of First Nations, the main Aboriginal organization recognized and funded by the Canadian state, did not fully support the positions of Aboriginal women as advanced by the Native Women's Association of Canada (NWAC), often arguing that the women's arguments were based upon an individual rights discourse that undermined the struggle of First Nations for self-determination.

This particular way of looking at the dissension between the male-dominated political associations and the Native Women's Association of Canada ignores a critical issue: "the discursive formation of ethno political identity that emerges as male and female political leaders contest each other's expressed collective aspirations and envisioned future nationhood" (Fiske 71). Many Aboriginal women's groups (which do receive support from many traditional men) use a political discourse that looks at the intersection of ethnicity, class and gender and they want to bring back symbols and images that have been part of most Aboriginal traditional cultures. Some of the symbols include that of "Woman as the heart of the Nation," "the centre of everything" (Fiske). What Aboriginal women envision, then, is a feminized nation, where both men and women equally give birth to it, and following a traditional Aboriginal cultural world view, kin ties are "evoked as symbols of a community and nation: blood and culture, not law, define ethnic identity and citizenship within a nation that nurture and sustains her people" (Fiske 76-77). As I expect the word "blood" to raise many eyebrows, I feel it is important to remark that as my elders and other Aboriginal peoples have told me, many Aboriginal traditional societies were very open to "adopting" members of other "tribes" who acquired their culture. At least, that was the case for the *Hauenosaunee* people. Therefore, it can be clarified that the notion of blood is not as rigid and exclusionary as the one more commonly used by other ethno-nationalist movements. It stands to represent one's affiliation to a clan, and one's membership to it can be obtained either by birth or adoption by the female members of the clan.

For the most part, Aboriginal male-led organizations use a different discourse, one which is masculinist and derived from the same European hegemonic power that they oppose. In this discourse, men are the natural citizens and women instead have to be accepted by the men and the Canadian state (Fiske). This masculinist discourse came into evidence during the proposed amendments to the Indian Act to reinstate women who had lost Indian status into their communities. In a subsequent period, in name of protecting the constitutional "collective" rights of self-government, Aboriginal male leaders were ignoring the gender relations of power that presently exist in Aboriginal communities. Throughout both these debates, Aboriginal women asked for either re-instatement or insurance that gender equality for Aboriginal women be protected in the Constitution, Aboriginal women have always argued that, if we truly want to reaffirm our traditional way of life, women's rights are to be considered collective by nature and to be at the core of Aboriginal notions of "nation."

Moreover, to argue that women's rights (as Aboriginal women) are only individual rights is a colonized way of thinking, because for Aboriginal peoples the individuals are always part of the collective, not outside of or contrary to it. We must also remember that many of the dividing lines (either of status, reserve residency, blood, or membership to bands) now existing in our communities were not originally drawn by Aboriginals themselves, rather by the Canadian state (Monture-Angus 1999: 144-45). During our decolonization process, we Aboriginal women must ask the men and the leaders of Aboriginal communities to respect the powerful roles Aboriginal women held and which are part of many traditional laws (e.g. the *Kaianerekowa*). In doing so, we can then equally walk together towards the same path and have a similar vision, one in which we are, in the words of

Sharon McIvor, " united with our own people, on our own lands, determining our forms of government, deciding rules for membership in our Nations, and deciding who will live on our lands" (180).

Conclusion

In this paper, I have attempted to illustrate the complexities of the ongoing debate between feminists and nationalists. Throughout I argue that there is not a single version of either feminism or nationalism and demonstrate that they can be either progressive or reactionary. For the most part, "Western" feminism has been guilty of excluding, or at least marginalizing, women of colour and Third world women and has only recently begun to integrate issues of race and colonialism in its theories. In the context of Aboriginal women's issues, feminist theories need to look more closely at the issues of land rights, sovereignty, and colonization and the impact this has had on the lives of Aboriginal women. In their critique of nationalism, feminists need to look much deeper at issues of land rights, at the colonial state's erasure of the cultural practices of indigenous peoples, and should not be quick to define Aboriginal women's participation in nationalist struggles as non-feminist and inherently dangerous for women. (Jaimes-Guerrero). However, we Aboriginal women should be also very careful not to prematurely dismiss all of feminist theories. Undoubtedly they have enriched our analyses of power relations, especially of those most directly related to gender. It is also true that many "mainstream" feminists have attempted to reevaluate their earlier assumptions and are beginning to question their own colonization of "others." More importantly, most of the feminist skepticism about nationalisms should be taken seriously.

Historically, women's participation on anti-colonial liberation movements has been vital, but has not translated into enduring gains for women in the new nation. There are many nationalisms, and only one that offers women an emancipatory place in *all* phases of the liberation movement would be the one that I could join. Most importantly, identities which are defined by an ideology of purity of "race" have the potential to be very oppressive and dangerous, especially for women, since they are seen as bearers of the imagined pure nation. We must also acknowledge that "tradition" is not static, but is always transformed by people; therefore, post-colonial Aboriginal nations must accommodate differences of experience and let traditional practices meet the continuously changing needs of their members.

Originally published in CWS/cf's Summer 2000 issue, "National Identity and Gender Politics" (Volume 20, Number 2): 143-148.

[1] I would refer readers to the works of Jayawardena; Charles and Hintjens; Moghadam; and Alexander and Mohanty for an overview of the mobilization of women in anti-colonial movements.

References

Abdo, Nahla. "Nationalism and Feminism: Palestinian Women and the Intifada-No Going Back." *Gender and National Identity*. Ed. Valerie Moghadam. London and New Jersey: Zed Books, 1994.

Alexander, M. Jacqui and Chandra Talpade Mohanty Eds. *Feminist Genealogies, Colonial Legacies, Democratic Futures*. London and New York: Routledge, 1997.

Alfred, Gerald R. *Heeding the Voices of our Ancestors: Kahnawake Mohawk Politics and the Rise of Native Nationalism*. Toronto: Oxford University Press, 1995.

Anderson, Benedict. *Imagined Communities: Reflections on the Origin and Spread of Nationalism*. London: Verso, 1983.

Barnaby, Joanne. "Culture and Sovereignty." *Nation to Nation*. Eds. Diane Engelstad and John Bird. Concord: Anansi, 1992.

Bhabha, Homi K. *The Location of Culture*. London and New York: Routledge, 1994.

Charles, Nickie and Helen Hintjens. Eds. *Gender, Ethnicity and Political Ideologies*. London and New York: Routledge, 1998.

Chatterjee, Partha. *Nationalist Thought and the Colonial World: A Derivative Discourse*. London: Zed Books, 1986.

Collins, Patricia Hill. *Black Feminist Thought: Knowledge, Consciousness, and the Politics of Empowerment*. Second Edition. London and New York: Routledge, 2000.

Enloe, Cynthia. *The Morning After: Sexual Politics at the End of the Cold War*. Berkeley: University of California Press, 1993.

Firestone, Shulamith. *The Dialectic of Sex*. London: The Women's Press, 1979.

Fiske, Jo-Anne. "The Woman is to the Nation as the Heart is to the Body." *Studies in Political Economy* 51 (1996): 65-89.

Friedan, Betty. *The Feminine Mystique*. Harmondsworth: Penguin, 1965.

Goodleaf, Donna. *Entering the War Zone*. Penticton: Theytus Books, 1995.

Jaimes-Guerrero, Marie Anna. "Civil Rights Versus Sovereignty: Native American Women in Life and Land Struggles." *Feminist Genealogies, Colonial Legacies, Democratic Futures*. Eds. M. Jacqui Alexander and Chandra Talpade Mohanty. London and New York: Routledge., 1997.

Jayawardena, Kumari. *Feminism and Nationalism in the Third World*. London: Zed Books, 1986.

Laroque, Emma. "The Colonization of a Native Woman Scholar." *Women of the First Nations*. Eds. Christine Miller and Patricia Chuchryk. Winnipeg: The University of Manitoba Press, 1996.

McClintock, Anne. *Imperial Leather*. London and New York: Routledge, 1995.

McIvor, Sharon D. "Self-Government and Aboriginal Women." *Scratching the Surface: Canadian Anti-Racist Feminist Thought*. Eds. Enakshi Dua and Angela Robertson. Toronto: Women's Press, 1999.

Millett, Kate. *Sexual Politics*. London: Virago, 1977.

Moghadam, Valerie. *Gender and National Identity*. London and New Jersey: Zed Books, 1994.

Monture-Angus, Patricia. *Thunder in My Soul: A Mohawk Woman Speaks.* Halifax: Fernwood Publishing, 1995.

Monture-Angus, Patricia. *Journey Forward: Dreaming First Nations' Independence*. Halifax: Fernwood Publishing, 1999.

Morris, Glenn. "International Law and Politics." *The State of Native America*, Ed. M. Annette Jaimes . Boston: South End Press, 1992.

Schouls, Tim., John Olthuis, and Diane Engelstad. "The Basic Dilemma: Sovereignty of Assimilation." *Nation to Nation: Aboriginal Sovereignty and the Future of Canada*. Eds. Diane Engelstad and John Bird. Concord: Anansi Press, 1992.

Smith, Anthony. *The Ethnic Origins of Nations*. Oxford: Basil Blackwell, 1986.

Voyageur, Cora J. "Contemporary Indian Women." *Visions of the Heart*. Eds. David Alan Long and Olive Patricia Dickason. Toronto: Harcourt Brace and Company, 1996.

Yuval-Davis, Nira. *Gender and Nation*. London: Sage Publications, 1997.

Why I'm a Feminist

Lauren Anderson ~~

> I have put her in my box, I have defined her by my means, and now
> she isn't free because of me."
>
> —Brian McBay, "First Foundations"

It's Wednesday afternoon, and it's snowing outside, and I've got a final exam in less than 48 hours, but am I studying?

Of course not.

Unfortunately, I'm too angry to study. I'm sad to admit it, but my blood is still boiling over something that happened last evening while I was having dinner. I sat down next to my friend Nick, a computer studies major, who ended up spending much of the meal discussing the stupidity and future joblessness of the arts majors at the table. Although I'll admit it annoyed me to some degree, I've gotten somewhat used to ribbing from the science, computer studies, and engineering science students on campus here; you can't go to the University of Waterloo and major in English without expecting to be the butt of some jokes (my current personal favourite is actually quite clever: "What is the limit of a Bachelor of Science in math as your GPA approaches zero?... A Bachelor of Arts!"). Of course, us artsies have to pretend that we're annoyed or the mathies like Nick assume that we really are as stupid as they make us out to be, so I made an been oh-so-witty-and-clever comment (that I don't remember at this point) to which Nick responded in truly stellar form:

"You'd better watch it—I'm not afraid to hit a girl!"

Of course, I responded to this by smiling cutely and saying, "Perhaps you should be afraid of this one. She would very likely hit you back."

And Nick, who must have been pulling a Cyrano de Bergerac with a neanderthal sixth-grade intellect, met my eyes, raised his eyebrows, and said, "Ooooh. A fighter. That's hot."

And so you can see why I'm angry. Or perhaps you can't. I can 100 percent understand if you can't. About this time last year, a friend of mine told me her sister, who was away obtaining a post-secondary education, was majoring in women's studies, and I had a good chuckle. "Why on earth would anyone want to major in women's studies?" I asked my friend, picturing a hairy-legged, bitchy, lesbian.

Since then, I have decided to do my minor in women's studies. Before I continue, though, it is important to note that I don't exactly fit the stereotype of a women's studies student I had imagined. I'd like to think I'm not too bitchy, I am not hairy-legged (well, maybe a little, but it is out of sheer laziness rather than on principle), and I am not a lesbian. I do, however, have a rather shocking confession to make, a little coming out of the closet to do.

I am a feminist.

Okay, so telling you wasn't quite as awful as I expected. I knew you'd understand. Now, you might be curious as to why I am what I said I am. I have never been the victim of rape, of sexual harassment, or abuse. I have never tried to have an illegal abortion, had my genitals mutilated, or been passed over for a job because I am a woman and not a man. I am not a feminist because it is "cool" or because I have been the victim of any form of any crimes against humanity. I am a feminist because of the 173 solved female homicides in 1999, of which more than two thirds were committed by men known to the women (Statistics Canada; Duffy). I am a feminist because in Britain, the United States, and Canada, it is legal for a rapist, defending himself, to keep the woman he raped on the witness stand for hours, and sometimes days, on end, forcing her to relive the rape in order to satisfy his questions. I am a feminist because there are women who die in order to satisfy the contradictory lusts of the man hungry for a 20-inch waist and a 40-inch bust.

I am not a man-hater, and I would never be so hypocritical as to claim that all men are abusive, that all men are selfish, that all men are insensitive barbarians. I love the men in my life and I will never stop being grateful to them for the love and respect they have given to me.

Nonetheless, statistics are statistics.

Statistics Canada reports that an act of sexual violence or harassment occurs every 17 minutes in Canada. Ninety per cent of these acts are against women. It is reported that at least thirty per cent of women with disabilities in Canada are abused, sexually, physically, and often both (Duffy) and by the time a Canadian woman has called the police to report a domestic assault, she has, on average, already been assaulted 30 times (Beatty).

The United Nations reports that approximately 5,000 women world wide are killed each year by their husbands over dowry disputes. It is shocking to note that the most common method men use to kill their wives is to douse them with a flammable substance and light them on fire (Duffy). Statisticians in India fear that as many as 11,000 Indian brides over a three-year period at the beginning of the '90s were killed or forced to commit suicide by their husbands for not providing an adequate dowry. In Sierra Leone, where civil war is still raging, women have been raped by the thousands and many have been forced to become the "wife" or sexual partner of her rapist (Farrugia).

Women in nearly all developed countries have the right to vote, to hold public office, to have equal pay for equal work, to have a career or to own a business, and to choose to be childless, or unmarried, or unmarried with a child. Officially women are equal in the eyes of the law. And yet, women are oppressed, and there is no denying it. Ani DiFranco, in her song titled "Swing," described being a woman as being "weary as water in a faucet left dripping, with an incessant sadness like a sad record skipping," and that, for some unexplainable reason, rang very true with me. There is a constant state of fear and sadness that women live in that can't be explained away. If a woman is not worried about being killed by her partner, she is able to tell you everything that is wrong with her physical appearance without ever looking in the mirror.

Both men and women explain away women's oppression by saying that as North American women, we are free to make choices, to determine how we will act, and how we will dress, and who we will be and why. I agree with that, to some extent. I am fortunate to live in a country where I have the right to make choices about my future. I have chosen the place where I will take my post-secondary education, I have chosen my major, and I'm sure at some point I will be in the position to choose whether or not to be married, where I will have my career, and if and when I will become a mother. But at the same time, I have also chosen to kneel on the floor in the tiny bathroom of my place of employment, with my finger down my throat, trying to force myself to vomit the lunch I had just eaten. I have chosen to wear jeans tight enough that I had trouble leaning over to do up the platform shoes I would later have trouble walking in. I have chosen to call male friends to escort me home from classes, from parties, from work, because I was afraid of walking home on my own.

I made those decisions, and I won't pretend otherwise, but in retrospect it really makes me wonder why on earth people consider women to be free from oppression when we still make choices like that, because if we were honest with ourselves, we would admit that they are not really choices at all. If you consider them choices, be serious for a moment. Who would choose to wear away their oesophagus, the enamel of their teeth, and their dignity by inducing vomiting after eating? Who would choose to wear pants so tight as to inhibit regular movement, eating, even breathing? Who would rather make the choice to inconvenience friends and be a nuisance than walk home, alone, after dark?

A study of high school students in Saskatoon, Saskatchewan showed that 17 per cent of female students control their weight by vomiting, and 12 per cent use diet aids, including diuretics, laxatives, and addictive diet pills (Duffy). The Walk Safe Program on the University of Waterloo campus says that the number of women calling to ask for an escort across campus vastly outnumbers the number of men calling to request the same. The manager of a Smart Set store reports that women will continually force themselves into pants, dresses, and skirts that are too short, too tight, too small, simply because they "can't believe that they are a size nine now. They always used to be a five or a seven, so they buy a five or a seven even if it doesn't fit because they can't bear the thought of buying the next size up."

We all make choices.

A group of men at Queen's University answered an anti-rape "No Means No" campaign by placing posters in the windows of their residence rooms that read "No Means Harder," "No Means Dyke," "No Means More Beer," and "No

Means Tie Me Up" (Duffy). Fifty-one per cent of a random sample of university-aged males reported that there was "some likelihood" that they would rape a woman in a dating situation if they were assured they would not be punished (Duffy). More than half of Canadian high school students surveyed said that they believed that it was alright for a young man to force a young woman to have sexual intercourse with him if she had been a "tease" and had gotten him sexually aroused (Duffy).

I am not a feminist because I am too fat to wear the tight pants, or too ugly to find a man, or too much of a whining, militant activist to be anything but a "feminazi." I am a feminist because no means no, and it doesn't mean "dyke," "more beer," "harder," or "tie me up" and because a few people thought this was even a little bit funny. I am a feminist because "some likelihood" is some likelihood too much. I am a feminist because, like I said, we all make choices.

When I think about the comment that my friend Nick made last night at dinner, I'm not angry at him because he said what he did. Rather, I am angry at what a comment like that represents; namely, that we act the way we do because our gender roles define us, and that because boys will be boys, some girls will continue to live in fear of their husbands and fathers, take laxatives to control their weight, and live lives that are determined by the men they know. If it happens at all, it happens too much.

We all make choices. I chose to get angry over what happened at dinner yesterday evening. I may tolerate being the butt of arts faculty jokes at dinnertime, and even laugh a little because after all, they are pretty funny … but I will not tolerate being the butt of gender jokes. And I will certainly not tolerate violence against women in any form. Why should anyone be expected to?

Originally published in CWS/cf's Winter/Spring 2001 issue, "Young Women Feminists, Activists, Grrrls" (Volume 20/21, Numbers 4/1): 32-34.

References

Beatty, Brenda. "A Montreal Massacre Remembrance" University of Waterloo, December 6 2000.

Difranco, Ani. "Swing" *Swing Set.* Righteous Babe Records. New York, 2001.

Duffy, Ann. "The Feminist Challenge: Knowing and Ending the Violence." *Feminist Issues.* Ed. Nancy Mandell. Toronto: York University, 1998.

Farrugia, Alastair. "Gross Violations of Women's Human Rights" *Imprint.* Imprint Publications, University of Waterloo. 6 December 2001.

McBay, Brian. "First Foundations" (unpublished lyrics).

Statistics Canada, Student Resources. *Homocide Victims and Suspects by Age and Sex*, December 2000.

Feminism and Young Women

Alive and Well and Still Kicking

Candis Steenbergen

Efforts to define "feminism" and attempts to determine the boundaries of the "women's movement" have always been problematic. Characterizing a *feminist* (or worse: *the feminists*) has been even harder. "Feminism," as Geraldine Finn has noted, "does not speak with one voice" (299). Feminists have *always* expressed their desire for social, political, economic and cultural change in a variety of milieus. Feminist activity has *always* assumed a wide range of forms: from militant political activism, to silent volunteerism, to academic research and writing, to the creation of works of art, to so much more. Feminist historians acknowledge that the women's movement in Canada has always had a "diverse, complex, and shifting reality," and agree that feminists have *never* followed a unified political ideology (Adamson, Briskin and Mcphail 9). While all feminisms share certain characteristics, significant differences in political strategy, in vision, in attitudes towards men, in understanding the roots of women's oppression, and in setting priorities also typify the Canadian women's movement ideology (Adamson, Briskin and Mcphail; Hamilton).

Feminism itself has altered and evolved over time as the intricacies of women's positions in society have changed (Wine and Ristock; Adamson *et al.*). In the early moments of the contemporary women's movement, second wave feminists identified, named, analyzed, and resisted women's oppression, particularly as it existed in the private lives of "ordinary" women. The decade that followed has been called "a phase of expansion and consolidation," a period in which the women's movement grew in size and visibility, as well as in organizational and strategic terms (Tremblay).[1] In the 1980s, many of the battles fought by the mainstream women's movement concentrated on institutional policy and political change. The strategies adopted by the women's movement through all three decades were employed in reaction to the political conditions of their struggles. But they were also the result of constant internal checks and balances performed by and among women of strikingly different political persuasions (Hamilton).[2]

Feminism in the last decade has been no different. By the early 1990s, the battlegrounds for feminist struggles had altered again. As early as 1993, Manon Tremblay noted that:

> ... Over the course of the last few years, the feminist movement has
> devoted itself primarily to fighting to maintain what women have
> gained in a climate of political conservatism, of financial austerity,
> and of the affirmation of a neo-conservative right wing. In addition,
> the antifeminist undercurrent which is currently developing in the
> West has led to the belief that the feminist movement has lost its
> *raison d'être* with women now having achieved equality with men.
> (276)

At the beginning of the new century, Tremblay's "undercurrent" is a
commonly heard reproach of feminism and its proponents. The "diversified,
multifaceted, and enriched" nature of feminist activities has been re-inter-
preted (and perpetuated by popular media) as demonstrative of an antiquated,
ineffectual, "splintered and fragmented" women's movement (Hamilton 80).
The evidence supporting those charges has been even more unsettling. The
arrival of a number of North American publications in the very recent past—
written predominantly by young, female iconoclasts—incited reports of the
arrival of the next generation of feminists: self-proclaimed "dissidents" who
herald the coming of feminism's last breath.

In the United States, "feminism's daughters" appeared in the form of Katie
Roiphe's *The Morning After: Sex, Fear and Feminism* (1993), Christina Hoff
Sommers', *Who Stole Feminism? How Women Have Betrayed Women* (1994),
Rene Denfield's, *The New Victorians: A Young Woman's Challenge to the Old
Feminist Order* (1995), and—of course—Danielle Crittenden's *What Our
Mother's Didn't Tell Us: Why Happiness Eludes the Modern Woman* (1999) and
Wendy Shalit's *A Return to Modesty: Discovering the Lost Virtue* (1999), to
name just a few. Almost perfectly paralleling the introduction of *Ally McBeal*
to the television-consuming public, the entrance of these young voices—all
straight, white, and well-educated voices, I should add—announced the
"coming-of-age" of the heirs of the sexual revolution and the new faces of
feminism. *Women have made it*, they say. *Get over it.*

Canada has not been without similar voices. In 1992, Amy Friedman
published *Nothing Sacred: A Conversation With Feminism*. Using Queen's
University as a model, the American-born author asserted that feminism had
mutated and that she was no longer comfortable identifying with what the
movement had become. Over the last 30 years, she argued, feminism has
grown terrified of recognizing differences among women, and has not retained the sacredness of the personal. Individual stories, she asserted, now
served only as "fodder for a statistical mill" (42). Friedman's agitation with
academic feminism was multi-faceted: she "deplored [the] sloppy, inaccurate,
lazy language" used by proponents, was angered by the promotion of "female
knowledge as distinct from male knowledge," and was dismayed by the
apparent feminist belief in "ultimate solutions" for the atrocities of the world
against women (42, 44, 58). She stated: "...The new feminist rhetoric ... was
beginning to sound like other versions of revolutionary fanaticism, and

revolutionary fanaticism, we all know, has sparked some of the most heinous regimes in humankind's history. No matter who the enemy" (60). According to Friedman, feminism lost sight of its original goals and fixated on romanticized images of women as powerless victims, encouraged self-pity, and sought to gain strength in martyrdom.

In 1995, Canadian journalist Kate Fillion published *Lip Service: The Truth about Women's Darker Side in Love, Sex, and Friendship.* Fillion discussed the myth of female moral superiority, and attempted to deconstruct a number of existing stereotypes, including "woman as victim," and "woman as saint." She stated that women today adhere to conflicting paradigms:

> Self-determination is what women want, but the myth of female moral superiority tells us that women cannot be actors in their own right. Apparently, women are too pure to harbor negative feelings and too virtuous to make mistakes. Agency—having some control over one's own life—is confused with happy endings. When things turn out well, women are given full credit, but when something goes wrong, we are absolved of responsibility. (318)

Based on her own observations and a handful of interviews, Fillion denounced feminists for attempting to achieve sexual liberation through the perpetuation of dangerous dichotomies and through the preservation of an age-old sexual script, and argued that, consequently, "the common language used to discuss sexuality in the public arena … [has been] predicated on women's passivity and oppression" (223).

The next year, Donna LaFramboise (also a journalist) published *The Princess at the Window: A New Gender Morality*. LaFramboise attacked "establishment feminism," that group of "people who are recognized by society at large as legitimate feminist spokespersons" (1996: 8). Citing Ann Landers, Ms, Marilyn French, and Catherine MacKinnon, LaFramboise asserted that "the lunatic fringe has taken over main-stream feminism" (1996: 33). Arguing that highly questionable ideas have been elevated to feminist dogma, she claimed that feminism has become extremist, self-obsessed, arrogant, and intolerant. LaFramboise was alarmed by the speed at which such "sloppy thinking" has permeated the rhetoric of popular culture and has influenced public policy, and stated that traditional methods of examining women's issues have become obsolete (1996: 48). LaFramboise argued that feminism has perpetuated the myth of female martyrdom, stated that feminists have deliberately maintained such fictions to ensure its survival, and differentiated between "a feminism that *informs* one's opinions and a feminism that *dictates* how one should think" (1996: 323).

Friedman, Fillion, and LaFramboise presented limited analyses of feminisms past shortcomings and future directions. All three generalized "North American feminism" as a unit based upon their own observations, anecdotes, conversations with friends, content analyses of newspaper columns, and a variety of studies on white, heterosexual, able-bodied, educated, middle-to-upper class women. All of the authors were former students (or graduates) of women's studies departments, and all three targeted the work of feminists in the academy, yet all failed to illustrate an in-depth knowledge of feminist theory or of the history of the women's movement. All of the authors used items from the popular press, provided snippets of contentious quotations from select feminist theorists (mostly American ones), and relied heavily upon personal interviews. All three expressed concern for the current state of feminism, and all provided instances in which mainstream second wave praxis has "failed," but none provided viable alternatives. All three viewed tolerance and flexibility as key elements of future strategies for the women's movement, yet none succeeded in achieving a sound blend of analysis, theory, and practice.

Perhaps most interesting about this supposed "new generation" has been their preoccupation with sex. Those who received the most public attention contend that the women's movement advanced a single, antiquated vision of what constitutes "good" feminism, and "good" feminist sex through the promotion of women's victimization and men's inherent lechery. Their texts present feminism as the mastermind behind stringent sexual and moral codes, as the promoter of a villain-versus-victim mythology, and as archaic protectors of "political correctness." To many, the 1970s granted empowerment and sexual agency to women:

> At the beginning of the sexual revolution, a truce was declared in the gender wars for a few brief years—at least among some segments of the population. Rather than being used as leverage, sex was freely enjoyed. Men and women reveled in each other's beauty, sharing their bodies comfortably and lavishly. (La Framboise 1999: A18)

Instead of just enjoying their newfound freedom, "the feminists," desperate to maintain their stronghold on public conviction, continued promoting their webs of untruth: date rape, marital rape, sexual violence, and so on. To LaFramboise, the point of the sexual revolution was freedom: "freedom from appalling ignorance, senseless guilt, and needless fear" (La Framboise 1999: A18). "The feminists" just weren't getting it.

In these accounts, feminists are portrayed as anti-men, anti-sex, and obsessed with notions of women as hapless victims and therefore *all* feminists hate men, believe in the essential "goodness" of women, lack a sense of humour, and are preoccupied with sexual danger. Fillion and LaFramboise, however, are the antithesis of the second wave stereotype: they are "successful and independent, and less likely to espouse 'dangerous' feminist ideals" (Whelehan 240). As we all know, sex makes for good copy, and mainstream media latched on to the existence of these "new feminists" with vehemence. *Time Magazine*'s 1998 cover story (slyly asking "Is Feminism Dead?" under the face of TV's McBeal) certainly added fuel to that fire (Bellafante). Accepting the insurgence of writings as an indicator of women's successful liberation and the impending demise of feminism, popular discourse perpetuated the idea that Canada, as it approached the millennium, had entered a "postfeminist"[3] era.

Feminist commentators were swift in their criticism of the three Canadian-published books, their authors, and their American counterparts. One reviewer attacked their "highly selective, blinkered vision," and stated that their texts were little more than "in-your-face rant[s]" supported by "extraordinarily inflated ideas" about the prevalence and influence of feminism in Canada (Hurley). Myrna Kostash attacked Fillion for presenting second wave feminism as "a monolithic movement reducible to a single tendency," and suggested that this new generation believes that feminism is anti-male, and that "mainstream feminists hate the very idea of sex with men" (1996: 13). By the year 2000, the presence of a new generation of women, concerned with little more than individual gain, the consumption of material goods, and the exertion of their own enlightened power, was branded into the public mind. The image of the "new modern woman" of the millennium was "bad girl," one who has rejected the "tyranny of contemporary sexual politics" brought about by feminism and who has been aggressively taking matters into her own hands (Dennis 3).

As the last decade's media frenzy suggests, a new generation of women has emerged, aggressively analyzing, rethinking, and challenging the assumptions and strategies of feminism's diverse histories and theories. Unfortunately (but not surprisingly), the popular press pinpointed the wrong group of women. A third wave has appeared within the women's movement; a generation of young women actively addressing the complexities of women's everyday experiences and the personal and structural relations affecting them. Their critiques—as varied as the feminisms that have come before—are intended to further the feminist cause, not to slander the movement or its proponents. Nonetheless, there has been a tendency to deem any comment or criticism of feminism or the women's movement made by women under the age of 35 suspect. The inclination to clump all young women into the media-friendly, postfeminist category has been strong, leading many to assume that the next generation does in fact think the war's been won, that the sole pursuit of pleasure and possessions is paramount, and that feminism, in effect, is passé. Charges by the second wave that younger women are "reinventing the wheel" have been rampant, and have led many to believe that there is "nothing new" about third wave approaches (Greer).

As problematic (and historically inaccurate) as they are, the works of Fillion, LaFramboise and others (and the reviews, critiques, and attacks that followed their publication) have served four auspicious purposes. First, they (albeit unintentionally) publicly announced the "coming of age" of feminism's daughters; those women who grew up with feminism as their birthright and who have come to feminism (or feminist activism) in a markedly different manner than their predecessors. Second, they illustrated that the landscape for feminist activism and theorizing *has* mutated over the last three decades, and that some women are indeed reaping the benefits—sexual and otherwise—of the second wave women's movement's labour. Third, and unwittingly again, they sparked a new and necessary dialogue on generational (and intergenerational) feminisms and on the women's movement's future directions—one that has just begun to take shape. Finally, their fixation on the successes of the sexual revolution and the assumed failure of feminists to recognize them has prompted a much-needed reexamination of feminism's engagement with sexual politics and the body. Ironic, isn't it, that ideological one-upmanship and petty name-calling inadvertently created spaces in which these issues could be discussed.

Despite the mass visibility of postfeminists, young feminist women—raised with feminism as a familiar concept since their birth; the beneficiaries of many of the successes of the women's movement; and those who know that there are still challenges remaining and obstacles to be jumped for women—exist and work and resist in the millennium. And, like the "popular kids" of their age group, many of them are vigorously engaged in exploring the intersections of sexualities, sexual pleasure, and feminism—and challenging some of the feminist strategies of the past as a result. The differences between the two, however, are significant. For one thing, most young women with legitimate concerns and critiques of feminism and the women's movement have not lined bookstore shelves with mass-market bestsellers, done the talk-show circuit, nor made countless headlines. Instead, their voices appear in independently-produced zines, in book reviews hidden in the backs of journals, on walls and across public advertisements, in non-mainstream publications, and in other, less-conspicuous (and *less* financially-rewarding), spaces. Third wave feminists also understand and recognize that there is no feminist monolith, or any feminist "establishment" trying to take all the fun out of sex.[4] As well, young women see the historical specificity of the women's movement's engagement with and inquiries into issues of sexuality and body politics. They might not be thrilled with the way things turned out and want to revisit older strategies and theories (and question and confront those who pursued them), but most have the rationale not to blindly point fingers.

Women's sexual freedom was one of the key feminist goals of the late 1960s and early 1970s, and women's right to sexual pleasure and to control their own bodies symbolized their right to social equality.[5] Women formed woman-centred collectives and organizations and utilized public spaces as forums to speak about, challenge, and try to resolve sexual discrimination and lingering postwar repression.[6] One objective was to denounce and dispel the inaccuracies of "those heterosexual practices predicated on the assumption of the priority of a male sexual urge and a male right to sexual pleasure" (Hamilton 65). Activists sought to expose the double standard that celebrated men for "sowing their wild oats" and divided women as "whores" and "virgins." In public and in the home, feminists challenged socially enforced domesticity, "to wrest control away from the state, the medical establishment, institutionalized religion, pharmaceutical companies, advertisers, pornographers, institutionalized censorship, [and] the violence of men" (Pierson 98).

The struggle for reproductive rights, the revelatory discovery of the clitoris as a site of sexual response, and the publication of woman-centred journals, created "a thrilling sense of new possibilities" for women (Tiefer 115). The "sexual revolution" has been characterized by a surge of public interest in sexuality, an increased focus on the successful pursuit of sexual activity and performance, and the publication of texts concerned with maximizing pleasure.[7] The perceived acceptance of alternative forms of sexual expression, the annihilation of taboos against premarital sex, the subversion of the institutions of monogamy and marriage, and the encouragement of sexual self-expression also led to announcements that a sexual revolution had begun. The generation that came of age in that era contested sexual assumptions and challenged traditional notions of sex, marriage, and family structures. To activists in radical movements, including members of student movements and the New Left, the eradication of sexual inhibitions was pertinent to their cause. In many cases, the liberation of sexuality was "an essential part of the New Left idea of 'living your politics': the sexual revolution … was a democratic utopia to be realized in the present—something one *did*, here and now" (Connell 60-61).

Although the "flower power" years have been depicted (in retrospect) as the "permissive moment" in history, members of the new feminism and gay politics began to ask "permissive for whom?" (Connell 61; see also Parr). The open-minded ideologies of some failed to construct the utopia that it promised for all. As Kostash recalled, the women's movement,

> expose[d] the operations of much of the sexual revolution for what they were: fraudulent. Double standards prevailed in the vocabulary of sexual put-down, [and] responsibility was evaded in the rhetoric of non-possessiveness...." (1996: 113)

Despite the egalitarian overtones, the discourse of the time,

> seemed to be serving a very old conservative agenda: women servicing their men—their activity stripped out of any deeper personal, social or political context which might highlight conflict, confusion or any number of other troubling incongruities of experience. (Segal 99; see also Kostash 1980)

In retrospect, the "sexual revolution" failed to liberate most women from exploitation or from firmly established gender roles. Instead, the fluid perceptions of sexuality,

> only partially modified behavioural prescriptions for women in a sexual relationship and...the use of contraceptives [fell] in line with

conventional gender-role demands, leaving women vulnerable to both old and new kinds of exploitation. (Greenglass 120)

Sexual emancipation proved more complicated than was originally thought as, "endless doubts and heartbreaks about non-monogamy, about faked orgasms, about the political correctness of heterosexuality more or less stifled that first wave of sexual liberation" (Valverde 9).

By the mid-1970s, mainstream feminist praxes had turned its attention away from the personal aspects of sexuality and focused predominantly on legal, political, and social policy-making and change, and in that climate "it was virtually impossible for lesbian, bisexual, or heterosexual feminists to claim the right to sexual pleasure" (Ross 113). Concentrating instead on policy-based issues that they could mobilize around and effectively influence, the now "mainstream" feminist movement became focused on male sexual violence, the legalities of the *Divorce Act*, pornography, and the political and legal battles regarding rape and sexual assault. The sexuality debates had begun to change, and analyses of sexual danger rapidly superseded discussions of women's personal empowerment, pleasure and desire.[8]

The 1980s witnessed a "revival" of interest in the issue of women's sexuality and sexual pleasure, as well as a challenge —by feminists, to feminists—to the perceived fixation on the potential "dangers" of sexuality. Right-wing thinkers and organizations also grew at this time, scrutinizing sex education curricula and contesting the scope of legal rights for lesbians and gay men. As well, anti-feminist writers and groups (such as R.E.A.L. Women) captured the popular media's attention and made mega-headlines. Despite (or perhaps because of) increased attacks by traditionalists and the backlash against feminism, a new vision of an older strand of feminist thought began to emerge. "Pro-sex" feminists wanted to revive dialogue on pleasure and desire and reasserted the need for sexual expression and exploration as a necessary step towards women's liberation.[9] The objective was to "eroticize equality":

> ... it's time to seriously rethink Freud's old question: what do women want? We know what we don't want, and we are beginning to understand how we got into this mess. So the question about our erotic needs keeps coming back to us—the return of the repressed— and we ask the old question with a new emphasis: What do *we* women want? ... Eroticism is about the *what*, the brass tacks of sex. (Valverde 9)

Pro-sex perspectives often called for a reconnection of the complexities of women's personal sexual experiences with theoretical critiques of male violence. While helping to return the issues of pleasure and desire to the sexuality debates, the works of pro-sex feminists were harshly criticized for typecasting second wave feminists as perpetuators of stringent moral standards and anti-sex. In retrospect, it was apparent that the moment for reexamining and perhaps revising feminist theories on and engagement with sexuality had not yet arrived.

When the next generation of women came of age in the late 1980s and 1990s, sexuality was again a hot topic—one that pervaded (and continues to drench) virtually all facets of popular culture, the media, and mass-market advertising. The growth and intellectual development of young women today has been marked by a greater overall awareness of sex, sex identities, and sexualities, and a resurgent interest in the role that sexual identity plays in their everyday lives. The establishment of women's studies in schools, the inclusion (albeit paltry) of feminist and queer theory in other fields of study, and strong and vocal lesbian and gay voices have all contributed to their awareness. Young women also grew up with an expansion of cultural influences: music videos, cable TV, improved satellite communications, the internet, and specialty magazines; all of which have affected and shaped their outlook. Advertising specifically and pop culture generally have become increasingly sexualized and young feminists have acknowledged that "as women become more powerful in real life, their clothes got tighter and shorter in the make-believe-it's-real world of television" (Timson 52). In many ways, postfeminism emerged at an opportune moment in history: feeding off of the backlash of the '80s and utilizing the public fixation with and consumption of sexuality to their advantage.

While not receiving publicity on par with postfeminist literature, the desire to analyze body image, self-esteem, desire, sexuality and sexual pleasure has been strong in third wave writings to date. To many, those pursuits have revolved around continual self-analysis and personal negotiation, an attempt to reconcile the desire to create their own version of "femininity" and the fear of betraying their allegiance to feminism and the struggle for female empowerment. For some, that has translated into a strong defiance of pre-constructed notions of what constitutes a "beautiful" female body and activism against fat-phobia. For others, it has meant indulging in beauty culture: fashion magazines, make-up, hair products, and slinky fashions previously viewed as fodder for the male gaze:

> For me, being a femme means that I take pride in wearing just the right shade of lipstick, drawing the perfect black line above my eye-lashes, keeping my legs smooth, and smelling good. Being a femmenist means knowing I am just as attractive when I don't wear makeup, shave, or put on perfume. (delombard 29-30)

The emphasis has been placed on redrawing the boundaries of beauty, femininity, and sexuality, and the roles they play in every person's quest for self-empowerment.[10] Others have critiqued the mythologies surrounding the "free love" era, asserting that while the sexual revolution,

> was largely about women saying *yes* (to really prove themselves

liberated) a new movement is empowering them to *also* say no, *along with when, where and how.* As a result, women are more closely examining what turns them off—and also what turns them on. (Kamen 1998:140)

Young feminists are conscious of the use of sexuality and sexualized images of women in the media that consistently support and perpetuate traditional sex roles and sexual identities, and actively strive to make sense of manipulative media techniques in their work. A number of young feminist scholars, writers, artists, activists, and critics of the mass media have attempted to link their connection (and attraction) to the hyper-sexualized culture of consumerism and consumption with their identities as women, sexual beings and feminists. The editors of BITCH: *Feminist Response to Pop Culture* explained the rationale:

We are supposedly living in a new age—one that some have dubbed postfeminist. Feminism is over, they say. Just get over it. But television demonstrates that most people still think what a woman is wearing is more important that what she's thinking. Magazines that tell us, both implicitly and explicitly, that female sexual urges are deviant—while reminding us that maintaining our sex appeal is the only way to wring commitment out of a man, without which our lives will be sad and incomplete in spite of dazzling careers and intense friendships. Billboards urge us to fork over our hard-earned cash for the glittery, overpriced wares of companies that depend on our unhappiness and dissatisfaction for their profits.

The negotiation between the attractive, processed, advertised, and consumable version of female sexuality and the difficulties of translating it into a lived reality, has been substantial in third wave analyses to date. In many respects, the approach has been to acknowledge the mixed messages pervading popular culture and account for the "problem desires" that often result. Not surprisingly, the craving for sexual empowerment has paralleled young women's questioning of reality, of the sexual revolution, and—necessarily—of their feminist "brand."

While young feminist perspectives regarding sexuality have just begun to emerge, much of the writing to date begins from a location similar to pro-sex feminists: where the early second wave feminists left off. Early feminist writings that emphasized women's sexual freedom did not ignore the existence of sexual danger in many women's lives. Instead, they argued that women's sexual freedom could not occur without a more thorough sense of women's realities as well as a realization of the need for social, economic, and political rights.[11] It's just that one ended up absorbing the other. The complex sexual context of the current time has made a reconnection of the two necessary and unavoidable, and young women's activism has reflected that. In organizations and campus centres, young feminists have created pamphlets, how-to manuals, and newsletters on everything from surgical operations to enhance, sculpt, or rejuvenate the vagina, to tips on body piercing and tattooing, to info on the morning-after pill, to AIDS awareness.[12] Third wave reactions to body politics coalesce neatly with the intentions of early second wave discussions on the body.

In response to the often contradictory conditions surrounding women's sexual lives in the 1990s, young women have sought to combine radical perspectives on sexual theory with the everyday occurrences of women's lived experiences. That has translated, so far, into a reinterpretation of both personal and collective identities, an interrogation of the women's movement of the past and of the current period, as well the creation of new visions for the future. Mariana Valverde has noted that there have traditionally been two genres used by women to talk about sex: the intellectual application of a number of abstract theoretical frameworks to women's sexual experiences and desires, and "the confessional." The new generation of feminists values both, and has been actively attempting to combine the two strategies in a concerted effort to work through the "lived messiness" of women's lives. The potential that explorations of women's sexuality has is "infinite and incalculable," but the myriad of problems, issues, and concerns facing young women also indicates that their "sexual project is just beginning" (Crosbie xii).

Of course, the issues of sexuality and body politics covered herein are only fragments of the kinds of work that young women are currently engaged in. Like the waves that came before, the third is as difficult to define and as arduous to label and their activism has been as problematic—or more so—to pinpoint. Like their forerunners, their feminisms come in a myriad forms: they all don't adhere to the "feminist" label, they don't follow a single agenda, and they don't necessarily agree, they don't share the same political motivations, priorities, or dreams. Their realities are as diverse, fluid, and complicated as the environment in which they resist. Whether feminism's "third wave" overshadows postfeminist ideology in the public's eye remains to be seen, but a number of things are certain. The new generation of young feminists is emerging, reacting, and acting within a particular moment in history, just as the feminisms of the past have changed in reaction to the ideological, social, cultural and political climates within theirs. The future of feminism in Canada is not postfeminism; it is a strongly supported, vigorously active, dynamic group of young women who are determined to flex and bend their feminisms with where the world takes them, pushing the women's movement into the next century.

Originally published in CWS/cf's Winter/Spring 2001 issue, "Young Women Feminists, Activists, Grrrls" (Volume 20/21, Numbers 4/1): 6-14.

[1]Tremblay notes that the 1970s marked the institutionalization of the women's movement with the establishment of state organizations like the Canadian Advisory Council on the Status of Women.

[2]Hamilton noted that "feminists disagreed not only on the explanations for women's inequality, oppression, and subordination, but also on the means to transform their situation" (54).

[3]"Postfeminism" is used herein to denote young women who have gained notoriety for their pop-criticisms of second wave feminism only. It should be noted that the term "postfeminism" has been used positively in many contexts to describe what I am calling "the third wave."

[4]For a satirical look at one woman's quest for "the feminist establishment" (and for a job therein) see Kamen 1996.

[5]The feminist interest in sexuality and sexual pleasure certainly didn't begin in the 1960s. It has *always* been at the forefront of feminist inquiries. For a thorough look at sexuality in the postwar years, see Adams.

[6]The contemporary gay liberation movement emerged from the New Left as a unified force during this period. See Kinsman.

[7]The Kinsey reports (male sexual response in 1948 and female sexual response in 1953) definitely had an effect on public discourse on sexuality. As well, the 1950s also introduced two major additions to pop culture: rock'n'roll, and *Playboy* magazine.

[8]These discussions continued at the grassroots level. Mainstream feminists, the more visible, public "face" of the women's movement switched their focus to more political, policy-based issues.

[9]In 1985, the Women's Sexuality Conference was held in Toronto, announcing the resurgence of "feminists who wanted to get beyond the lesbian versus heterosexual divide and to welcome women of all sexual preferences, celibate and bisexual women included, to the pursuit of an enhanced understanding of women's sexuality through co-operative discussion and study" (Pierson 108).

[10]The complexities of the body have been addressed through the analysis of "the politics of hair." See Trass.

[11]It should be noted that Valverde (1995), Kinsman, and Ross have all illustrated that pro-sex feminism, gay/lesbian cultural formations, and the pursuit of sexual pleasure through "alternative" means have always existed in Canada, and they did not dissipate when the mainstream women's movement began to target violence and policy issues more actively in the mid-1970s. They just didn't get props.

[12]See AGENDER (Carleton University) and *Challenge the Assumptions!* Both illustrate a concern articulated in the mid-1980s, expressed in McCooey.

References

Adams, Mary Louise. *The Trouble With Normal.* Toronto: University of Toronto Press, 1997.

Adamson, Nancy, Linda Briskin, and Margaret McPhail. *Feminist Organizing For Change.* Toronto: Oxford University Press, 1988.

Bellafante, Ginia. "Feminism: It's All About Me!" *Time Magazine* 151 (25) (29 June 1998): 48-56.

BITCH: *Feminst Response to Pop Culture*. www.bitchmagazine.com/mission.html.

Connell, R.W. "Sexual Revolution." *New Sexual Agendas*. Ed. Lynne Segal. New York: New York University Press, 1997.

Crittenden, Danielle. *What Our Mother's Didn't Tell Us: Why Happiness Eludes the Modern Woman*. New York: Simon & Schuster, 1999.

Crosbie, Lynn. *The Girl Wants To*. Toronto: Macfarlane, Walter and Ross, 1993.

delombard, jeannine. "Femmenism." *To Be Real: telling the Truth and Changing the Face of Feminism*. Ed. Rebecca Walker. New York: Doubleday, 1995. 21-33.

Denfield, Rene., *The New Victorians: A Young Woman's Challenge to the Old Feminist Order*. New York: Warner Books, 1995.

Dennis, Wendy. *Hot and Bothered*. Toronto: The Penguin Group, 1992.

Fillion, Kate. *Lip Service: The Truth about Women's Darker Side in Love, Sex, and Friendship*. Toronto: Harper Collins Publishers, 1995.

Finn, Geraldine. "Conclusion." *Feminism in Canada*. Eds. Angela Miles and Geraldine Finn. Montréal: Black Rose Books, 1982. 299-306.

Friedman, Amy. *Nothing Sacred: A Conversation With Feminism*. Canada: Oberon Press, 1992.

Greenglass, Esther R. *A World of Difference: Gender Roles in Perspective*. Toronto: John Wiley and Sons, 1982.

Greer, Germaine. *The Whole Woman*. London: Bantam-Dell-Doubleday, 1999.

Hamilton, Roberta. *Gendering the Vertical Mosaic*. Toronto, Copp Clark Ltd., 1996.

Hurley, Clarissa. "Feminists Bashing Feminism: The Princess at the Window." *The New Brunswick Reader* 17 August 1996.

Kamen, Paula. "Acquaintance Rape: Revolution and Reaction." *"Bad Girls"/ "Good Girls": Women, Sex & Power in the Nineties*. Eds. Nan Bauer Maglin and Donna Perry. New Brunswick: Rutgers University, 1996. 137-149

Kamen, Paula. "Paradigm For Sale." *Shiny Adidas Track Suits and the Death of Camp the Best of Might Magazine*. Ed. Might Magazine. New York: Boulevard Books, 1998.

Kinsman, Gary. *The Regulation of Desire: Homo and Hetero Sexualities*. Montreal: Black Rose Books, 1996.

Kostash, Myrna. *Long Way From Home*. Toronto: James Lorimer and Co., 1980.

Kostash, Myrna. "Dissing Feminist Sexuality." *Canadian Forum*. (September 1996): 13-17.

LaFramboise, Donna. *The Princess at the Window: A New Gender Morality*. Toronto: Penguin Books, 1996.

LaFramboise, Donna. "Freedom, Baby." *The National Post* 18 March 1999: A18.

McCooey, Sharleen Johnson. "Help Yourself." *Herizons* 4 (1) (Jan/Feb 1986): 39.

Parr, Joy. *A Diversity of Women*. Toronto: University of Toronto Press, 1995.

Pierson, Ruth Roach. "The Politics of the Body." *Canadian Women's Issues: Volume 1: Strong Voices, Twenty-five Years of Women's Activism in English Canada*. Eds. Ruth Roach Pierson, Marjorie Griffin Cohen, Paula Bourne, and Philinda Masters. Toronto: James Lorimer & Company, Publishers, 1993. 98-122.

Roiphe, Katie. *The Morning After: Sex, Fear and Feminism*. Boston: Little Brown & Company, 1993.

Ross, Becki. *The House That Jill Built*. Toronto: University of Toronto Press, 1995.

Segal, Lynne. *Straight Sex: Rethinking the Politics of Pleasure*. Berkley: University of California Press, 1994.

Shalit, Wendy. *A Return to Modesty: Discovering the Lost Virtue*. Toronto: HarperCollins Canada, 1999.

Sommers, Christina Hoff. *Who Stole Feminism? How Women Have Betrayed Women*. New York: Simon & Schuster, 1994.

Tiefer, Leonore. *Sex is Not a Natural Act and Other Essays*. Boulder: Westview Press, 1995.

Timson, Judith. "Bimbo-Watch: Resistant to Feminism, She Just Won't Go Away." *Macleans* 27 November 1995: 52.

Traas, Wendy. "Splitting Hairs: Creative Expression vs. Self-Normalization in Women's Hair Care." Diss. Brock University, April 1999.

Tremblay, Manon. "Gender and Society: Rights and Realities." *Canada and the United States: Differences that Count*. Ed. David Thomas. Peterborough: Broadview Press, 1993.

Valverde, Mariana. "If Freud Were A Woman…" *Broadside* 5 (6) (April 1984): 9.

Whelehan, Imelda. *Modern Feminist Thought*. New York: New York University Press, 1995.

Wine, Jeri Dawn and Janice L. Ristock. *Women and Social Change*. Toronto: James Lorimer and Company, 1991.

The Silencing of Young Women's Voices in Women's Studies

Leah M. Thompson ━━

In speaking with young womin involved in womin's studies in both the United States and Canada, and those young womin involved in more active organizing outside academia, I have come across a shared experience. Young feminists often feel silenced and devalued by feminists of a previous generation who monopolize much of the room and voice in womin's organizing. As I explore in this essay, young feminists, like myself, have experienced silence bind our tongues; we need a forum in which to scream out. Although applicable to all womin's organizations, I am referring specifically to academia and womin's studies in particulars. Within the institution of education and disguised in the cloak of a traditional academic relationship between student and teacher, many young womin involved in womin's studies feel that issues relevant to them, their experiences, and their voices are not being heard or taken seriously. This silencing can only be detrimental as it deepens a divide between womin of different generations. Although this is part of my story in particular, this is a problem shared by many young womin.

The Journey Starts

When I discovered womin's studies during my undergraduate year I was thrilled. I felt like I had energy to change the world and that I finally found a subject I could relate to. I found something that I could fight for ... me. I learned about first wave feminism and second wave feminism, I read about womin who, gathering in their living rooms, explored the neglected and invisible experiences of womin and acted to create change. Those womin seemed so passionate and they had goals, goals that they spoke up for. No, spoke up is much to soft a term, they roared for. One day, I was in a sociology of womin class and I saw a film about feminism in the U.S. The womin who spoke on camera voiced words that were so powerful to me and the womin's force to do something about what they felt passionate about was so enviable, I also wanted to do something. I wanted to be active and make a difference in the lives of womin. Maybe this is what all young university students are like: idealistic and passionate. Either way, I saw myself as a feminist in training.

Shortly after seeing that film I was lucky enough to help some fantastic young womin open a womin's center on our school campus. Imagine that ... a university with a womin's studies program and no womin's center on campus! It was wonderful to participate in the venture and for the first time, rather than simply read words off a page, I was actually doing something. I was convinced I was on to greater things and because I felt like I had so much potential, I applied to graduate school. Maybe I could strive to teach other young womin this wonderful feeling that I had recently learned; this feeling of strength and purpose, this feeling of pride and a sense of belonging, one in solidarity with others who, like me, wanted to speak up about how they felt. Other young womin who had something to say and would not stop until it was heard. Then I went to graduate school ...

Bumps in the Road

And so began boot camp. "Head up, shoulders back, speak when spoken to. Here are the theories, read them, engage with them, criticize them, relate them to other material ... what's that, personal experience you say? Ummm ... well ... as long as you base it in theory and connect it to what is being said here, then it's okay." Suddenly my head was swirling.

"Whoa ... wait a minute. What's going on here?" I asked myself. "I thought what I had to say counted ... I thought it was important. What happened to sharing experiences, feeling heard, respected, and understood? What happened to the ideal of a dialectical relationship? Was I dreaming all of that?" It felt as though my experience was only valid if and when it was grounded in theory.

Theory upon theory upon theory. Talk, talk, talk. I scream, "Can we not *do* something?" There is all this talking and reading and so very little action. I came here to actively create change but there seems to be little room for that. Even my words are deemed weak. In all this speech where is the action? I came to womin's studies with the hopes of "doing" something and being active. But there seems to be little room for this in academia.

And so it continued.... "Listen ... read ... listen ... talk ... read ... listen ... read ... listen.... *Enough!* Please listen to me, I have something to say. Hello out there, is there anybody listening?"

"Yes," I am told, "but first, listen to what the second wave feminists have had to say. This is how they theorize the issue, this is where it all began."

Theory is important, but often times it is abstracted, removed from practice, and students' experiences are seldom reflected within it. A core body of knowledge is continuously reproduced and taught, that, rather than feeling connected to, I have felt removed from and on the outside of. The exclusion of my experiences has led to silence.

Silence is also manifested in classroom discussions. I have sat in classes where, during group discussion after a student's presentation, two or more attending professors have monopolized the discussion, interrupted students and only looked at each other when speaking within the class group. This has not promoted a reciprocal learning process in which those teaching have as much to learn from me as I do from them. It has effectively excluded and silenced the students in the room. Consequently, all too often, discussions that should be fostered in the classroom are privately carried on amongst the students outside the classroom. It is not problematic that such talk should carry on after class, but it is problematic that they are not occurring inside the class.

Furthermore, I have energy to use in active ways beyond the classroom. However, there seems to be little room for this in academia. There has been so much focus on theory that connecting academia to activism in the community is still too little. In previous attempts I have chased the guidance of older feminists, including some professors, to use my energy in the women's community around me. Although at times successful, the chase is a challenge that is far too often fruitless.

Although their perspective is important, so is what I have to say. I have a voice; it may be a voice that does fit the standard academic conception of what my voice should say, but it is still a voice and doesn't that count for something? And if my speech is not formal and does incorporate slang, does this mean that it will not be taken as seriously as someone's with a more developed lexicon? Is (rather ironically) taking on academic language the only way I will be listened to?

I have listened to the past with open ears and a dawning awe, but there is no space for me. I am young; I have experience; I am at times ignorant and I am thirsty. However, by not including young women's experiences in their teaching, thinking, organizing, and events, by asserting authority over young womin based on their own experience and knowledge, and by maintaining a distance between academia and womin's communities outside of it, older generations of feminists are keeping young womin out. Most importantly, they need to actively listen to young womin, open more of their spaces to our ideas and experiences, and help, not direct, young womin in organizing themselves. How often do I hear about how the "way" has been paved for me and other young womin by more experienced feminists? Well it was certainly forged by them but not paved with gold!

The F-word

When I go outside womin's studies or the womin's community I must not forget a single piece of armor in my feminist's iron suit, for there are many moments when I come under attack. Surprisingly, I still encounter many people who cling to an older stereotyped description of what a feminist is and ought to be. This conception often includes the idea that all feminists must be man-haters, lesbians, loud, "ugly" (according to societal standards of beauty), and just plain hard-up. So, when I walk into a social situation that is not related to womin's studies or feminism, and tell people that I am a student in womin's studies, right away many eyebrows begin to raise. "Oh, really … " they say and immediately I can sense an uncomfortable tension. "Does that mean you are a *feminist?*" At this point I have to be honest with you. It is a difficult question to answer because when this person asks if I am a feminist, I presume they have a preconceived notion of what feminists are. Sometimes I answer by explaining that the word feminism does not have one monolithic definition. There are so many varied womin, feminisms, feminists, and also rejections of these. Past definitions have often meant an erasure of class, race, ability, and all sorts of specialties among womin. Consequently, I could explain to the person asking the question what my definition of feminism is but I can not speak for all feminists. However, there are also times that I forgo having to explain myself to the inquisitive person and I poignantly answer by looking them directly in the eye and saying—*Yes ... I am a feminist.*

Then the next question that often comes up is,"What exactly do you study? Um ... what was it? ... womin's studies?" Often I come across the assumption that I study the psychology of womin and why they act the way they do, or because I am a "feminist," I must be studying womin's search for equality. My response usually involves an affirmation of the possibility of the latter, but also, that like any other discipline, I study an array of issues pertaining to womin and because womin's studies is interdisciplinary womin are focused on in many, many disciplines.

Next, my favorite question: "What will you *do* with a womin's studies degree?"! This is the best because when I was pursuing a degree in sociology not many people asked "What will you *do* with a sociology degree?" I mean it did happen from time to time, but it happens so much more with my womin's studies degree. What will I do? When I've posed this problem and question to some of my colleagues they acknowledged that they too have heard this question. And when I asked what their response is I have heard some great answers: "Brain surgery!" says one. "Teach at university," says another, or research, medicine, policy-making, lobbying, international relations, media, technology. Basically our response is we can do anything we want to do.

And the questions do not always end there: How can you accomplish anything in this world while only focusing on half the population? Haven't womin already achieved everything? I mean you are equal now aren't you? What more could you possibly want? You are being to pushy. You are being too demanding. Why do you hate men? Are you a lesbian? In the beginning, when those eyebrows initially raise, it makes my stomach sink because I know I am going do have to defend and explain myself. And most of these problems are centered on the stigma that sill exists for a young feminist and the word feminism ... the "f-word." Nobody wants to hear that word in public!

Afterthoughts

In the last few months my experiences in womin's studies have been like riding a rollercoaster. On the one hand I have gained much valuable knowledge and experience. I would encourage any and all young womin to pursue a womin's studies degree. On the other hand, I was completely unprepared for the academic world that lay ahead of me. I had all these ideals of young womin gathering together to raise our voices and be heard. But I felt silenced, silenced by my lack of academic knowledge, silenced because of my age, silenced because my voice did not count, and most often silenced by womin of a different generation.

There is still much work to be done in academia, but it should also be noted that some positive changes are being made. For example, at Memorial University of Newfoundland the women's studies program has created a new course and graduate programs that focus on activism outside academia. This will potentially foster strong links between academia and the womin's community, and give young womin more opportunity o be active outside the classroom.

Although gains have been made in the past there are still many roads left to travel and young feminists have much to say. I know I am not perfect, that I do not have all the answers but I do not suppose to either. I want to learn from the past but I also want to explore the present. I simply want to be heard without feeling intimidated and that somehow my knowledge and experience is not worthy of academia or the womin's movement. With the barriers voiced here, myself and many other young womin feel on the outside of the traditional womin's movement. Although the Internet and zines are showing to be a way for increased expression, any bit of silencing in womin's organizing and womin's studies can only come at a price of distancing and weakening young womin who have something to say. At the same time, young womin must also value the experience and knowledge of older feminists. The important key being open communication. What is needed by and for all is greater respect, listening, learning, sharing, and giving of resources and experiences so that, as one insightful friend and colleague put it, "The torch may be passed on."

Originally published in CWS/cf's Winter/Spring 2001 issue, "Young Women Feminists, Activists, Grrrls" (Volume 20/21, Numbers 4/1): 136-138.

Local Activisms, Global Feminisms and the Struggle Against Globalization

Angela Miles ⟶

Feminism is necessarily an internationalist politics, for the systems of exploitation and control we resist are global. In North America we understood right from the beginning of this phase of feminist activism that "No woman is free until all women are free."[1] It is now becoming increasingly clear that the liberation of any community of women requires women's liberation in all communities. To win our full freedom, and not merely ameliorate women's conditions, we will have to transform global as well as national and local structures of power.

Women's struggle has a long history in all regions of the world. In the current period feminists everywhere have discovered and reclaimed largely hidden histories of women's resistance. In the West we discovered Christine de Pisan from the fifteenth century, Mary Wollstonecraft from the eighteenth, and Sojourner Truth from the nineteenth. We learned that the suffragists were a mass movement of militant and visionary women, not a tiny group of laughable malcontents as we'd been told; that, in Canada women were recognized as people in law as late as 1920 only after a long struggle. Asian feminists point to Buddha's debate with his followers in the sixth century about whether women could join the order and become nuns and to women's campaigns for emancipation linked with struggles against foreign domination and local despotism in the nineteenth and twentieth century (Bhasin and Khan; Jayawardena). African feminists point to "the key role [of women] in traditional African Society ... which still prevails in many African regions (e.g. in the Akan region, in the South-East of the Ivory coast, in Togo, in Senegal etc ...)" and to "the traditions of struggle" in "Egypt, Sudan, Lebanon, Maghreb" where this was not the case (Baffoun 4).

In the nineteenth and twentieth centuries activist women worked together across boundaries of nation, class, race, and culture in numerous international networks and conferences against slavery and war and for women's rights (Stienstra). Though not as narrow as commonly believed, participation in these organizations and events was predominantly European, Scandinavian, North American, Anzac, and Latin American. Even this geographically limited solidarity supported women's struggles in significant ways in each of their home nations while providing a powerful base for women trying to change the world.

International feminist cooperation today is important for the same reasons. However, it is qualitatively different in scope and potential, grounded in and reflecting for the first time a genuinely global mass movement of women. Participants in these new international networks and conferences come from all regions of the world. Unlike the earlier period, leadership at the international level has tended to come from the economic South where women have been more and longer aware of global systems of power and the importance of global solidarity.

All over the world women are engaged in feminist environmental, economic, health, shelter, food security, social-justice, human rights, peace, anti-debt, anti-globalization, pro-democracy, anti-violence, and anti-fundamentalist struggles of major proportions (Brodribb; Davies 1983, 1986; Morgan; Schuler 1986, 1990, 1992; Wine and Ristock). These activists are cooperating globally to develop analysis and strategy, and to support local and international action through newsletters, conferences, workshops, courses, and joint lobbying efforts at the United Nations (UN), and other international agencies. And they are creating new forms of ongoing dialogue and organization in loose, decentralized networks very different from women's earlier international associations which tended to be based on formal national groups. These new feminist networks are founded whenever a need is felt for global cooperation. So they are more numerous and flexible with generally closer ties to local activism and more opportunity for direct exchange and mutual learning among women in very different situations and struggles.

International issue-defined feminist networks include (to name only a few of many) The Coalition Against Trafficking in Women, Development Alternatives with Women for a New Era (DAWN), the Feminist International Network of Resistance to Reproductive and Genetic Engineering (FINNRAGE), The International Commission for the Abolition of Sexual Mutilation (female genital mutilation), The International Women and Health Network, Women's Environment and Development Organization (WEDO), Women's Global Network for Reproductive Rights, Women Against Fundamentalism, and Women's Rights are Human Rights Network.

Many regional networks and identity-based international networks are also making major contributions to the development of broad and inclusive feminist politics. These more general networks foster dialogue, research, theory building and activism across issue areas and among issue-defined networks. Such Regional networks include the Association of African Women on Research and Development (AAWORD), the Asian and Pacific Women's Action and Research Network (AWRAN), and the Caribbean Association for Feminist Research and Action (CAFRA). Among the myriad of international identity based networks are the well known Network of Women Living under Muslim Laws, Third World Women's Network, Indigenous Women's Network, and the DisAbled Women's Network.

All these varied networks produce important newsletters and organize regular conferences. They are also sustained by and in turn sustain multi-faceted feminist journals and conferences which foster dialogue and organizing among feminist individuals and groups all over the world working on the whole gamut of issues. Examples of such broad international feminist journals are WIN News, WE International, Connexions, and Lola Press (in this latter journal all the articles appear in English, French, and Spanish). Important broad international feminist conferences include the four United Nations Conferences on Women held in 1975, 1980, 1985, and 1995 with growing numbers and diversity of women and ever increasing leadership from the "two thirds world"; the World Women's Congress for a Healthy Planet in 1991; the International Interdisciplinary Congress of Women held every three years in a different city since its inception in 1981 in Haifa, Israel; and the biennial Conferences of the Association for Women in Development (AWID) (United States-based but increasingly international and movement defined). Women's intensive organizing around United Nations Conferences on the Environment and Development (UNCED) in 1992, Human Rights in 1993, Population in 1994, and Social Development in 1995 and their preparatory and follow up meetings has also benefitted significantly from—and helped build—the global capacity of feminism.

Feminist local globalism

Feminists' ability to act together at the global level, as reflected in these international journals, conferences, and networks, is extremely important. However, it is only one facet of global feminist movement which is made up of a multitude of globally aware local feminisms.

The inspiring "World March of Women in the Year 2000,"[2] an entirely new form of international cooperation grounded directly in these local feminisms, testifies powerfully to their vigor and scope and growing global awareness. The March was the idea of Quebec feminists inspired by the success of their ten-day 1995 provincial March "Du pains et des roses" ("Bread and Roses) against poverty and violence against women.

Beginning at the Fourth World Women's Conference in Beijing in 1995, they called on women's groups around the world to participate by organizing local events related to these themes in their own country beginning on March 8, 2000 (International Women's Day) and ending on October 17, 2000 this day to be marked with national marches in all the countries with national coordinating committees and an international March on the United Nations in New York City.

This massive global initiative draws on women's political strengths in 157 countries (August 2000 count) at both the local and global levels and highlights their connection. Participating groups are experiencing themselves and are revealed to each other as unique centres of diverse practice in a multi-centred global movement. The March honours and nourishes global feminism's local roots and women's growing capacity to work together. In doing so it heralds a new level of feminist movement in which any one of its many centres can invoke the power of global solidarity.

Transformative feminisms

In Canada one of our main challenges today must be to foster in our local and global activism the transformative perspectives that are necessary underpinnings of feminist solidarity. Women, as individuals and members of diverse groups, are located very differently, often in antagonistic relation to each other within their local communities and the world system. Our immediate needs, interests, and strategic priorities vary greatly. Only feminisms which challenge the system as a whole can reveal women's common interests in change; provide a basis for solidarity among women of all races, classes, and regions in Canada and globally; and play a role in the vibrant multi-centred global feminist movement.

These transformative feminisms address the whole of society from women's points of view, not just "women's issues." They question not only women's inequality *within* current social structures but the structures themselves; and they resist colonial, race, and capitalist as well as patriarchal power at the local and global level (Bunch; Miles).[3]

Key to these transformative perspectives is an understanding that the unequal, competitive, individualistic, market relations that define this system were established historically through the conquest and control of nature, women, workers, and traditional cultures and communities in both "first and two-thirds world." (Mies).[4] The "globalization" we hear so much about today is a continuation and intensification of these destructive processes.

In the industrial nations of the economic North, we are taught on the contrary, that "modernization," "development," and "globalization" represent unambiguous and benign "progress." Ever since the end of the Second World War when all nations began to keep national income accounts, a country's GDP (Gross Domestic Product—value of market transactions) has been used as a measure of its wealth and well-being (Waring). Growth in GDP and thus the opportunity for profit has become the policy priority of all national governments and development agencies as well as transnational corporations. Yet neo-liberal agendas to maximize the growth of GDP, including privatization, devaluation, cuts to social welfare, downsizing and wage reductions have huge costs for people everywhere and the planet. (Douthwaite; Shiva).

Structural Adjustment Programs (SAPs) enforcing this agenda have long been imposed on countries of the economic south by the G7 countries and multi-lateral agencies like the World Bank (WB) and International Monetary Fund (IMF). Their populations have been resisting for decades. Now, we in the industrialized nations are suffering the same agenda in the "restructuring" imposed by our own governments and are joining the resistance. (Isla, Miles and Molloy; Sen and Grown; Ricciutelli *et. al.*; Sparr).

Anti-globalization movement

Farmers, fishers, peasants, workers, young people, environmentalists, and indigenous peoples, as well as feminists, all over the world are working in their own contexts to end cutbacks, privatization, environmental destruction, corruption, dictatorship, militarism, and violence. And they are working together internationally to counter the draconian undemocratic enforcement of the "growth' agenda by the G7 (the governments of the seven most economically powerful western industrial nations), the WTO (World Trade Organization) and other non-accountable international bodies and agreements (including NAFTA, the North American Free Trade Agreement).

The aims of those involved vary a great deal. Some are merely attempting to moderate the terms of emerging trade and other agreements and reduce the negative impact of globalization. Others, among them transformative feminists, are challenging the core agenda of globalization, the agreements themselves, and the right of the agencies and governments involved to impose them without democratic mandate or accountability.

Many of the key forces opposing globalization at this deep level know well that wholesale destruction of human communities and environment will continue as long as increases in profit and production for the market remain the only aim and measure of value in our world system. However, they have not yet generally acknowledged or addressed the deep patriarchal structuring of the colonial capitalist system they oppose. They do not recognize that achieving a world organized around the sustenance of human and non-human life rather than profit, will require, or rather is the empowerment of women.

Feminists are bringing to this broad field of contestation, the transformative women-centred perspectives they have forged in their varied but connected local struggles and their by now well established global dialogue and organizing. Their demands that women's devalued life-sustaining work and responsibility be recognized, honoured, generalized and supported are core challenges to neo-liberal globalization. Their struggle for the power to make women's concerns for individual and community reproduction, defining social priorities is central to transforming the world system.

Yet this is not generally understood and feminists have not yet gained a defining voice in the fast growing multi-sectoral organizing against globalization. Far from it in fact. Feminist voices are strangely muted and the feminist presence little acknowledged in accounts of the strategic debates around and collective resistance to globalization (Brecher *et.al.*; Hawken; Phillips).

Conclusion

Today, transformative feminists must foster feminist awareness among those opposing global forces at the same time as they foster awareness of global forces in feminist practice. The continued development of a powerful global feminist movement depends on both these things. It may be no exaggeration to suggest that the fate of the world hangs in the balance.

Originally published in CWS/cf's Fall 2000 issue, "Women 2000: Eradicating Poverty and Violence in the 21st Century" (Volume 20, Number 3): 6-10.

[1]"Sisterhood" may be invoked too easily by those who fail to notice and honour important differences among women. However, at its best what has been recently and critically dubbed "sisterhood feminism' is grounded in the radical understanding that the liberation of even the most privileged women requires the liberation of all and that no women in our society, including the most privileged are truly free. "Sisterhood" for these feminists is a political vision of possibilities opened up when we understand and act on the shared interests of women which are revealed only at the deepest level if analysis and transformation.

[2]For up to date information about the "World Women's March in the Year 2000" see the web pages of the International Liaison Committee (www.ffq.qc.ca/marche2000) and the Canadian Women's March Committee (www.canada.marchofwomen.org).

[3]Elsewhere, I have called transformative feminist perspectives, "integrative feminist perspectives" and described them and their significance in more detail (Miles and Finn 1989; Miles); Charlotte Bunch also describes and discusses the significance of transformative feminisms, which she calls global feminisms (Bunch).

[4]For a powerful portrayal of this process in Europe see the video "The Burning Times" about the history of witch burnings. It was directed by Donna Read and produced by Mary Armstrong and Margaret Pettigrew for Studio D of the National Film Board of Canada (Montreal 1990).

References

Baffoun, Alya. "In Search of African Feminism." Special issue on "Feminism in Africa." *ECHOE: Women for Research and Development* II/III (1985): 4-6.

Bhasin Kamla and Nighat Said Khan. *Some Questions about Feminism and Its Relevance in South Asia.* Second edition.. New Delhi, India: Kali for Women Press, 1999. First published in 1986.

Brecher, Jeremy, Tim Costello and Brendan Smith. "The Road from Seattle." *Z Magazine* (Jan. 2000): 40-43.

Brodribb, Somer ed. *Reclaiming the Future: Women's Strategies for the 21st Century.* Charlottetown, Prince Edward Island: Gynergy Books, 1999.

Bunch, Charlotte. *Passionate Politics: Feminist Theory in Action: Essays 1968-1986.* New York: St. Martins's Press, 1987.

Davies, Miranda, ed. *Third World, Second Sex: Women's Struggles and National Liberation.* Vol 1. London: Zed, 1983.

Davies, Miranda, ed. *Third World, Second Sex: Women's Struggles and National*

Liberation. Vol 2. London: Zed Pres, 1986.

Douthwaite, Richard. *The Growth Illusion: How Economic Growth Has Enriched the Few, Impoverished the Many, and Endangered the Planet*. Tulsa: Council Oaks Press, 1993.

Hawken, Paul. "N30 WTO Showdown in Seattle." *Yes! A Journal of Positive Futures* 3 (Spring 2000): 48-53.

Isla, Ana, Angela Miles and Sheila Molloy. "Stabilization/Structural Adjustment/Restructuring Canadian Feminist Issues in a Global Framework." *Canadian Woman Studies/les cahiers de la femme* 16 (3) (1996):116-121.

Jayawardena, Kumari. *Feminism in Sri Landa, 1975-1985*. Reprinted by NY: Women's International Resource Exchange (WIRE) Service, n.d.

Miles, Angela. *Integrative Feminisms: Building Global Visions, 1960s-1990s*. New York: Routledge, 1996.

Miles, Angela and Geraldine Finn, eds. *Feminism: From Pressure to Politics*. Montreal: Black Rose Books,1989.

Morgan, Robin, ed. *Sisterhood is Global: The International Women's Movement Anthology*. Garden City, NY: Anchor Press/Doubleday, 1984.

Phillips, Jim. "What Happens After Seattle?" *Dollars and Sense* (Jan/Feb 2000): 15, 16, 29-32.

Read, Donna (Director). "Burning Times." Studio D, National Film Board of Canada, Montreal 1990.

Ricciutelli, Luciana, June Larkin and Eimear O'Neill, eds. *Confronting the Cuts: A Sourcebook for Women in Ontario*. Toronto: Inanna Publications and Education Inc., 1998.

Sen, Gita and Caren Grown. *Development, Crises and Alternative Visions: Third World Women's Perspectives*. New York: Monthly Review Press, 1987.

Schuler, Margaret, ed. *Empowerment and the Law: Strategies of Third World Women*. Washington D.C.: OEF International, 1986.

Schuler, Margaret, ed. *Women, Law, and Development: Action for Change*. New York: OEF International, 1990.

Schuler, Margaret, ed. *Freedom from Violence: women's Strategies from Around the World*. New York: OEF International, UN International Fund for Women, Women Ink, 1992.

Shiva, Vandana 1989 Full bibliographic details missing

Sparr, Pamela, ed. *Mortgaging Women's Lives: Feminist Critiques of Structural Adjustment*. London: Zed Books, 1994.

Stienstra, Deborah. *Women's Movements and International Organizations*. Basingstoke, UK: Macmillan, 1994.

Waring, Marilyn. *If Women Counted: A New Feminist Economics*. San Francisco: Harper and Row, 1988.

Wine, Jeri and Janice L. Ristock, eds. *Women and Social Change: Feminist Activism in Canada*. Toronto: James Lorimer, 1991.

World Women's Congress for a Healthy Planet. *Official Report, Including Women's Action Agenda 21*. New York: Women's Environment and Development Organization (WEDO) 1992.

 **Histories**

Our Mothers Grand and Great

Black Women of Nova Scotia

Sylvia Hamilton

Very little of what one reads about Nova Scotia would reveal the existence of an Afro-Nova Scotian[1] population that dates back three centuries. Provincial advertising, displays, and brochures reflect people of European ancestry: the Scots, the Celts, the French, and the Irish, among others. There is occasional mention of Nova Scotia's first people, the Micmac. Yet Afro-Nova Scotians live in 43 communities throughout a province which is populated by over 72 different ethnic groups. Tourists and official visitors often express great surprise when they encounter people of African origin who can trace their heritage to the 1700s and 1800s. To understand the lives of Black women in Nova Scotia, one has first to learn something about their people and their environment.

The African presence here began in 1605 when a French colony was established at Port Royal (Annapolis Royal). A Black man, Mathieu da Costa, accompanied Pierre Du Gua, Sieur De Monts, and Samuel de Champlain to the new colony. Da Costa was one of Sieur De Monts's most useful men, as he knew the language of the Micmac and therefore served as interpreter for the French. The existence of Blacks in Nova Scotia remained singular and sporadic until the late 1700s, when 3,000 Black Loyalists arrived at the close of the American War of Independence. Though the Black Loyalists were free people, other Blacks who came at the same time with white Loyalists bore the euphemistic title "servant for life." Both groups joined the small population of Black slaves already present in the province. A second major influx of Blacks would occur following the War of 1812; approximately 2,000 former slaves, the Black Refugees, arrived in Nova Scotia during the postwar period between 1813 and 1816.

African people have a long tradition of oral history; stories about their heroes and heroines have therefore gone unrecorded. When a people begins the process of creating a written record of their champions, an initial tendency is to lionize and revere all. Since they will be paraded for all to see, faults and shortcomings are minimized and criticism is not often tolerated. The making of cultural heroes and heroines is an act of unification and empowerment. This process, just beginning among Afro-Nova Scotians, is integral to the survival of a people.

On Saturday next, at twelve o'clock, will be sold on the Beach, two hogshead of rum, three of sugar, and two well-grown negro girls, aged fourteen and twelve, to the highest bidder.

From her first arrival in Nova Scotia, the Black woman has been immersed in a struggle for survival. She has had to battle slavery, servitude, sexual and racial discrimination, and ridicule. Her tenacious spirit has been her strongest and most constant ally; she is surviving with a strong dignity and an admirable lack of self-pity and bitterness. She is surviving, but not without struggle.

During Nova Scotia's period of slavery, Black female slaves were called upon to do more than simple domestic chores for their masters. Sylvia was a servant of Colonel Creighton of Lunenburg. On July 1, 1782, the town was invaded by soldiers from the strife-ridden American Colonies. Sylvia shuttled cartridges hidden in her apron from Creighton's house to the fort where he was doing battle. When the house came under fire, Sylvia threw herself on top of the Colonel's son to protect him. During the battle she also found time to conceal her master's valuables in a bag which she lowered into the well for safekeeping. Typically, it was not Sylvia who was recognized for her efforts, but her master and a militia private to whom the provincial House of Assembly voted payments of money from the county's land taxes.

Another tidy arrangement involved slave-holding ministers. These men of the cloth adjusted their beliefs and principles accordingly when they purchased slaves. Lunenburg's Presbyterian minister John Seccombe kept a journal in which he noted that "Dinah, my negro woman-servant made a profession and confession publickly [sic] and was baptized, July 17, 1774." Dinah had a son, Solomon, who was brought to the province as a slave and who died in 1855 at age ninety; no record was found of the date of Dinah's death. In 1788 a mother and daughter were enslaved by Truro's Presbyterian pastor, Reverend Daniel Cock. When the mother became "unruly," he sold her but kept the daughter. In the same year, a Black woman named Mary Postill was sold in Shelburne; her price was one hundred bushels of potatoes.

Many slaves could hold no hope of being set free upon the death of their owners. Annapolis merchant Joseph Totten left his wife Suzannah the use of "slaves, horses, cattle, stock etc." and "to each of three daughters a negro girl slave … to her executors, administrators and assigns for ever." Amen. Others who were not given their freedom seized it for themselves. Determined owners placed newspaper ads offering rewards to their return.

While Black women slaves were being sold, left in wills, traded, and otherwise used, Black Loyalist women, ostensibly free, endeavoured to provide a livelihood for themselves and their families while at the same time labouring to establish communities. In 1787 Catherine Abernathy, a Black Loyalist teacher, instructed children in Preston, near Halifax. She taught a class of 20 children in a log schoolhouse built by the people of the community. Abernathy established a tradition of Black women teachers which would be strongly upheld by her sisters in years to come. Similarly, her contemporaries Violet

King and Phillis George, the wives of ministers, carved another distinct path: Black women supporting their men and at the same time providing a stable base for their families. Even though history has documented the lives of Boston King and David George, it has remained silent on the experiences of Violet and Phillis.

What must it have been like for Phillis George in Shelburne in the late 1780s? Her husband travelled extensively, setting up Baptist churches in Nova Scotia and New Brunswick. He preached to and baptized Blacks and whites alike, not a popular undertaking at that time. The Georges had three children; money and food were scarce. On one occasion, a gang of 50 former soldiers armed with a ship's tackle surrounded their household, overturning it and what contents it had. Some weeks later, on a Sunday, a mob arrived at George's church; they whipped and beat him, driving the Baptist minister into the swamps of Shelburne. Under the cover of darkness, David George made his way back to town, collected Phillis and the children, and fled to neighbouring Birchtown.

What of Phillis George and other Black Loyalist women: unnamed women who were weavers, seamstresses, servants, bakers, and hat makers? We can in some measure recreate the society they lived in; we can even speculate on what they looked like. But except for isolated cases, their memories and experiences are their own and will remain with them fixed in time.

One of those rare, isolated instances is that of Rose Fortune. A descendant of the Black Loyalists, Rose lived in Annapolis Royal in the mid-1880s. She distinguished herself by establishing a baggage service for travellers arriving by boat at Annapolis from Saint John and Boston. A modest wheelbarrow and her strong arms were her two biggest assets. Rose's noteworthy activities were not only commercial. She concerned herself with the well-being of the young and old alike. Rose Fortune declared herself policewoman of the town and as such took upon herself the responsibility of making sure young children were safely off the streets at night. Her memory is kept alive by her descendants, the Lewis family of Annapolis Royal. Daurene Lewis is an accomplished weaver whose work is well known in Nova Scotia. She also holds the distinction of being the first Black woman elected to a town council in the province.

Black Loyalists had been promised land sufficient to start new lives in Nova Scotia. However, when the land grants were allocated, the Black Loyalists received much less than their white counterparts. Dissatisfaction with this inequity coupled with an unyielding desire to build a better future for their families provided the impetus for an exodus to Sierra Leone, West Africa, where the Black Loyalists hoped life would be different. In 1792 Phillis and David George, along with 1,200 Black Loyalists, sailed from Nova Scotia to Sierra Leone.

Four years later, 500 Jamaican Maroons were sent in exile to Nova Scotia. A proud people, the Maroons were descendants of runaway slaves who for over 150 years waged war against the British colonists in Jamaica. Upon their arrival, the men were put to work on the reconstruction of Citadel Hill. Of the

Maroon women very little is recorded. We do know they were used for the entertainment of some of the province's esteemed leaders: Governor John Wentworth is believed to have taken a Maroon woman as his mistress, while Alexander Ochterloney, a commissioner placed in charge of the Maroons, "took five or six of the most attractive Maroon girls to his bed, keeping what the surveyor of Maroons, Theophilus Chamberlain, called a 'seraglio for his friends.'" The Maroon interlude ended in 1800 when they too set sail for Sierra Leone.

Between 1813 and 1816 the Black Refugees made their way to the province. It is this group whose memory is strongest in Nova Scotia, for their descendants may be found in communities such as Hammonds Plains, Preston, Beechville, Conway, Cobequid Road, and Three Mile Plains. Some of the earliest sketches and photographs of the Halifax city market show Black women selling baskets overflowing with mayflowers. Basketweaving for them was not an activity used to fill idle time: it was work aimed at bringing in money vital to the survival of the family. This tradition has endured because there are women who learned the craft from their mothers, who in turn learned it from their mothers. Edith Clayton of East Preston has been weaving maple market baskets since she was eight years old; it is a tradition which reaches back to touch six generations of her family. Not only does Edith Clayton continue to make and sell baskets, she also teaches classes in basketweaving throughout Nova Scotia as a means of preserving and passing on a significant and uniquely Afro-Nova Scotian aspect of the culture and heritage of the province.

Many and varied are the roles Black women have played and continue to play within their own and the broader community. It has often been said they are the backbone of the Black community: organizers, fund-raisers, nurturers, care-givers, mourners. When an attempt was made in 1836 by the provincial government to send the people of Preston to Trinidad, it was the women who objected:

> They all appear fearful of embarking on the water—many of them are old and have large families, and if a few of the men should be willing to go, the Women would not. It is objected among them that they have never heard any report of those who were sent away a few years ago to the same place, and think that if they were doing well some report of it would have reached them. They seem to have some attachment to the soil they have cultivated, poor and barren as it is....

Nowhere has their involvement been more pronounced than in the social, educational, and religious life of the Black community. In 1917 the women of the African Baptist churches in the province gathered together to establish a Ladies' Auxiliary which would take responsibility for the "stimulation of the spiritual, moral, social, educational, charitable, and financial work of all the local churches of the African Baptist Association." These women gathered outside around a well in the community of East Preston since the church had no space for them to use; this gathering became known as the "Women at the Well." Some of these same women later organized an auxiliary to provide support for the Nova Scotia Home for Coloured Children. In 1920, for the first time in Canadian history, a convention of coloured women was held in Halifax.

A woman well-respected throughout Nova Scotia's Black communities is ninety-four-year-old Muriel V. States. She was present on that day the women gathered at the well to establish the Ladies' Auxiliary. She was present as well at another historic event: the 1956 creation of the Women's Institute of the Ladies' Auxiliary she had helped to organize 39 years before.

One hundred and five delegates were registered for a meeting whose theme was "Building Better Communities." Among the issues discussed were community health and educational standards and family relations. Muriel States, who was the Auxiliary's official organizer at the time, told her sisters their activities would not go unnoticed:

> Today, we women of the African Baptist Association have taken another step which will go down in history as the first Women's Institute held this day at this church. We feel that we as women have accomplished much and are aiming to do great things in the future. We are already reaping the reward of untiring and united effort in all that tends to the promotion of the church and community welfare.

Since 1956 the meeting of the Women's Institute has been an annual event. In October 1981, the Institute celebrated its twenty-fifth anniversary. Its history tells of the dedicated work of many women: Gertrude Smith, Margaret Upshaw, Pearleen Oliver, Selina David, Catherine Clarke, and many others. Today the Institute undoubtedly records the largest gatherings of Black women in the province; annual conventions draw several hundred Black women.

In 1937 the Nova Scotia teacher's college in Truro had a student population of over 100 students. My mother Marie remembers being one of the college's two Black students; her companion was Ada Symonds. Teaching was my mother's second choice for a career; nursing, her first choice, was not open to Blacks. The bar remained solidly across this door until 1945, when pressure from the Nova Scotia Association for the Advancement of Coloured People and from Reverend William and Pearleen Oliver forced its removal. Two Black women were admitted as trainees in nursing.

Teaching became the selected profession for many Black women. Some chose it because they wanted to teach, others because there were no other options open. These women are remembered in the many communities where they taught. They are especially remembered for their diligent work and commitment in the face of the hardship and adversity of a society which has tried unceasingly to deny their existence. They had to put up with one-room segregated schools, few resources, and little money. They stayed late to devote extra time to those students who had to stay home to help pick blueberries and mayflowers or to help garden. When the school day was over, another day began for them: seeing to their own children, cooking supper, ironing the children's clothes for school, preparing lessons, and attending a meeting at the church.

As they laboured at teaching, nursing, housekeeping, typing, and other jobs, Black women have not led easy lives. Nova Scotian Black women, like their counterparts elsewhere, have always known a double day. Some say the Black woman invented it. Work was and continues to be an integral part of her life. She has not had the luxury of deciding to stay home; with the current state of both our provincial and national economies, it is unlikely she will be afforded that choice in the near future.

Public attention in Canada has been increasingly riveted upon incidents of racially motivated attacks on individuals and groups in some of our major urban centres. The manner in which these cases have been described would leave one to believe such occurrences are relatively new phenomena in this country. Even the most cursory examination of the experiences of Afro-Nova Scotians will clearly demonstrate that, indeed, such is not the case.

In 1946 New Glasgow theatres were segregated; Blacks sat upstairs, whites occupied the downstairs seats. While in New Glasgow, Viola Desmond of Halifax decided to go to the theatre. She bought a ticket (balcony seat) but decided to sit downstairs. Though she was ordered to move, Viola refused, offering instead to pay the difference in price. The theatre manager declined the offer and called the police. Viola Desmond was carried away by the officer and held in jail overnight. The next day she was fined $20 and costs. She was charged with having avoided paying the one-cent entertainment tax. A year later, Selma Burke, a Black woman from the United States, was refused service in Halifax. It is not difficult to see that this environment had the power to dampen spirits, damage identities, and lessen the desire for change. But there were Black women who felt equal to the challenge.

A New Glasgow publishing venture which began as an eight-by-ten broadsheet in 1945 soon blossomed into a full-fledged newspaper. This was *The Clarion*, edited and published by Dr. Carrie Best. Published twice monthly, *The Clarion* called itself the voice of "coloured Nova Scotians." Dr. Best published timely articles on civil-rights issues in Nova Scotia and elsewhere; the paper featured a women's page and carried sports and social news. In 1949 *The Clarion* gave birth to *The Negro Citizen*, which achieved nationwide circulation. But Dr. Best was not moving down a totally untravelled path; one century before, in 1853, Mary Shadd Cary launched *The Provincial Freeman* from Windsor, Ontario. In so doing, she became the first Black woman in North America to found and edit a weekly newspaper. Dr. Best has been awarded the Order of Canada; in 1977 she published her autobiography, *That Lonesome Road*.

Other Black flowers were blossoming as well in the 1940s. When Portia White was 17 she was teaching school and taking singing lessons. Winning the Silver Cup at the Nova Scotia Music Festival paved the way for her to receive a scholarship from the Halifax Ladies Musical Club to study at the Halifax Conservatory of Music. By the time she was 31 Portia White had made her musical debut in Toronto. Four years later, in 1944, she made her debut at New York's famed Town Hall and later toured the United States, South America, and the Caribbean. Of the "young Canadian contralto's" debut, one New York critic wrote:

> as soon as she stepped on to the stage and began to sing it was obvious that here was a young musician of remarkable talents. Miss White has a fine, rich voice which she uses both expressively and intelligently.... The artist has an excellent stage presence ... she was greeted with enthusiastic applause at each entrance. Miss White is a singer to watch, a singer with a bright future.

In 1969, Portia White's estate donated a gift of $1,000 to the Halifax City Regional Library to assist in setting up a music library in the city. The record collection which was subsequently installed is large and varied; few members of the borrowing public, however, know how the collection they so enjoy was originally established.

Recently Black women in Nova Scotia have begun to enter areas where their absence has heretofore been conspicuous: government, law, journalism, business, and medicine. This is not to say the struggle has ended or that we have arrived. While the attitude of the Black woman toward herself has been undergoing changes, the perceptions and attitudes of others both within her own community and beyond it require continual challenges to bring about any significant changes in how she is regarded and treated by others. As Black women begin paying tribute to themselves and their own work, others will pay tribute also. This year the family of Joyce Ross, a daycare director and long-standing community worker in East Preston, held a recognition dinner in her honour. Pearleen Oliver, author, historian, and educator, was one of three women selected to receive the YWCA Recognition of Women Award initiated in 1981. She was the first woman to serve as moderator of the African United Baptist Association and is the author of *Brief History of Colored Baptists of Nova Scotia 1782–1953* (1953) and *A Root and a Name* (1977). When the Recognition of Women Award was announced for 1982, Doris Evans, an educator and community worker, was among the three women honoured. And there are still many others who have experiences that need to be examined and stories that need to be told—women such as Ada Fells of Yarmouth, Edith Cromwell of Bridgetown, Clotilda Douglas of Sydney, Elsie Elms of Guysborough, Ruth Johnson of Cobequid Road. And there are others....

Writer Mary Helen Washington, in the introduction to her book *Midnight Birds*, speaks of the process whereby Black women recover and rename their past. She talks about the monuments and statues erected by White men to celebrate their achievements, "to remake history, and to cast themselves eternally in heroic form." Yet there is no trace of women's lives. "We have," she says, "been erased from history." As research and exploration into the lives of Black women in Nova Scotia continues, a fuller view, one with dimension and perspective, will emerge. We will know then where to erect our monument. Now there are only signposts pointing the way.

Originally published in CWS/cf's Winter 1982 issue, "Multiculturalism" (Volume 4, Number 2).

[1]While the term Black is most commonly used to identify people of African origin, Afro-Nova Scotian has come into contemporary use to identify people of African descent who live in Nova Scotia.

Author's postscript: In the years since this article was first published, language and terminology have evolved as part of a process of self-definition and empowerment. People of African origin in Nova Scotia and elsewhere in Canada, often use African Nova Scotian, or African Canadian, in addition to Black. Aboriginal people in Nova Scotia have used Mi'Kmaq to name themselves. Readers interested in learning more about African descended women are encouraged to consult "Women and the Black Diaspora," *Canadian Woman Studies/les cahiers de la femme (CWS/cf)* 23 (2) (Winter 2004). This volume presents a rich selection of essays, poetry and book reviews by international scholars and writers. My article in this volume, "A Daughter's Journey," is a reflection on my work since the original publication of "Our Mothers Grand and Great," in *CWS/cf* in 1982.

The Ontario Medical College for Women, 1883 to 1906

Lykke de la Cour and Rose Sheinin ➤

Women pursuing a career in medicine in Canada during the late nineteenth century faced numerous obstacles. Foremost was accessing appropriate education. Most existing medical schools refused to admit female students. At the Toronto School of Medicine and the Medical Faculty of Queen's University, where limited enrolment was finally granted to women in the 1870s and early 1880s respectively, the attitudes and experiences encountered were hostile. Obnoxious behaviour and derogatory comments regarding female physicians put unpleasant, as well as unwarranted, stress on female students. Pressure from male students and faculty ultimately resulted in the re-imposition of bans on women at medical schools by 1883 (Hacker 65; Toronto School of Medicine).

Demands for education in medicine for women finally resulted, in the fall of 1883, in the establishment of the Kingston Women's Medical College and the Woman's Medical College, Toronto. These schools were designed to provide female students with "equal but separate" medical education. The former was linked to Queen's University, the latter to the University of Trinity College. In this article, the history of the Woman's Medical College, Toronto, in advancing the cause of women in medicine is examined in the light of an operative strategy of educational separatism. The Toronto college, which in 1894 became the Ontario Medical College for Women, had significant implications for female medical students and women in the profession, as well as women in the community, and must be evaluated accordingly.

On October 1, 1883, the Woman's Medical College, Toronto, opened a small building at 227 Sumach Street. While annual reports issued by the College boasted of lecture rooms, anatomical and physiological museums, a chemical laboratory, and a dissecting room "well supplied with subjects," in reality facilities were quite meagre at first (Woman's Medical College, Toronto, 1886–1887). Faculty repeatedly had to assure guests that the word "college" indeed was not a misprint for "cottage." The chemistry department was "portable." The museum doubled as a janitor's bedroom and heating left much to be desired during the winter months. But as one visitor to the College noted: "All this was nothing in comparison with the fact that here at last girls had an opportunity to study medicine" ("Ontario Medical College for Women").

Initially, responses to the opportunity afforded by a women's medical school were few. Only three women enrolled for the first session of classes; two were reportedly daughters of friends of one of the founding professors (Guest). Enrolment over the next five years averaged four new students per year.[1] In the late 1880s attendance increased substantially, such that 20 women registered for first year studies by the fall of 1888; eleven registered in the following year. By December 1889 plans were underway to erect new premises for the College. A professor at the school was confidently writing to a supporter: "Evidently the College has taken root, and I have very little doubt but its success will be greater year by year" (Duncan). In the fall of 1890 the College moved to a large new building at 291 Sumach Street, where facilities were greatly expanded. The school now housed a lecture hall capable of seating over 50 students, microscopical and chemical laboratories, and reading rooms. The old College building became a dissecting room.

The Woman's Medical College, Toronto, was never empowered to grant degrees, but it qualified female students to sit the medical examinations at Trinity College, Victoria and Toronto Universities. Lectures and demonstrations were given at the College. Clinical instruction was provided through arrangements established with the major Toronto hospitals—Toronto General, the Hospital for Sick Children, and St. Michael's. "Special Hours" in the public wards were designated specifically for female students. Separate postmortem classes were conducted and segregated seating was provided in the operating theatres (Woman's Medical College, Toronto 1891–1892).

Although special attention was given to ensuring that the curriculum provided was identical to that offered in medical schools for men, several features of instruction at the Woman's Medical College were unique to the institution and the medical education of women. Emphasis was placed on courses deemed "of the utmost importance to women practitioners"—gynaecology, obstetrics, and the diseases of children (Ontario Medical College for Women 1898). In an attempt to provide students with added practical experience in obstetrics, a midwifery service was established by the College in 1891. Under the supervision of the Lecturer in Obstetrics and an Assistant Accoucheur, students provided women in the community with pre-and postnatal care and attended home births (Woman's Medical College, Toronto 1891–1892). A Dispensary for Women was created in 1898 by Drs. Ida Lynd, Jennie Gray, and Susanna Boyle, graduates of the Woman's Medical College. As instructors of the College, they offered students essential clinical experience, while providing for the needs of women in the community. In the dispensary women in their primary years of medical studies received instruction in dispensing and pharmacy, while female students in their final years assisted in clinic activities (Ontario Medical College for Women 1898).

Thus, in the process of educating women physicians, the Woman's Medical College initiated health care services novel for the times—medical treatment for women by members of their own sex. Furthermore, as indicated in the College's reports and references in medical journals, the midwifery and dispensary clinics were utilized most by poor and working-class women.

Maternity care was provided by the school for a fee of 50 cents ("The Woman's Medical College, Toronto"), considerably less than the usual rate charged by most male physicians. C. Lesley Biggs notes that, in the 1870s, doctors were billing $5 to attend home births (29). Although poor women in Toronto could use the Burnside Lying-in Hospital in the late nineteenth century, few did so, according to studies on childbirth in Ontario. Social conditions and fear of puerperal fever, associated with hospitals, often kept women away (Oppenheimer 41). It is difficult to ascertain how many expectant mothers actually took advantage of the College's maternity program. Only one Annual Report listed utilization rates: it showed over a one year period, in 1898–1899, 60 women used this service (Ontario Medical College for Women 1899).

The Women's Dispensary, on the other hand, appears to have had a high volume of patients, especially considering the facilities and staffing available. In the first year of operation, 1898–1899, clinics were held three days per week and approximately 1,200 treatments were handled. Increased attendance necessitated the expansion of clinics to six days per week in 1900. By 1903–1904, Annual Reports recorded over 7,500 dispensary treatments (Ontario Medical College for Women 1904). As with the maternity service, special financial accommodations were made for women unable to pay. Medical advice was given free of charge and medicaments dispensed for only a "nominal" fee (Ontario Medical College for Women 1900).

Funding for the Woman's Medical College came primarily from donations and students' fees. Finances, even in the best of times, were a constant source of difficulty. Faculty were not paid for most of the 23 years of the College's existence (Royal Commission on the University of Toronto 146). Apparently, any surplus funds were used to expand and improve facilities.

In 1894 the school experienced a financial crisis. While enrolment had continued to average eleven new students per year, several donations promised for the upcoming session did not materialize (Royal Commission on the University of Toronto 147). In a bid to save the College, a major reorganization was undertaken: the school became a joint stock company, with seventeen faculty members each subscribing $1,000 which they held in stock. The name of the College, now incorporated, was changed to the Ontario Medical College for Women (Limited) (Province of Ontario). These actions coincided with the closing of the Kingston Women's Medical School. Faltering enrolments, as well as financial difficulties, had made it impossible for the Kingston college to continue. With only one women's medical school in Canada and a new financial basis, the Toronto College was optimistic about the future. In its report for 1896, the school announced that:

> ... a new interest has been awakened in the College, and many applications for information have been addressed to the Board giving conclusive evidence that the hopes upon which the Directors based the reorganization were on a solid foundation. (Ontario Medical College for Women 1896)

Unfortunately, optimism at the College was short-lived. Despite the measures taken in 1894, economic problems persisted. The financial report for the year ending 1901 showed the school operating at a loss (Wishart). In addition, enrolment was beginning to decline. After peaking in 1895 with 18 new first-year students, numbers steadily dropped. From 1901 to 1905, first-year enrolment averaged only six new students per year. The reason for the decline was simple—yet ominous for the future of the Women's College. At long last, medical faculties of American and Canadian universities were beginning to admit women to co-educational programs. In 1895 the Johns Hopkins University in Baltimore opened enrolment to female medical students, as did Cornell in 1899. By the early 1900s Canadian universities such as Western, Dalhousie, and the University of Manitoba were graduating women in medicine.

The demise of the Ontario Medical College for Women was, in a sense, inherent in its origins as a facility for equal but separate medical education for women. Although the College was affiliated with the Trinity College University from 1884 to 1906, there is not one single reference to the women's school in a comprehensive history of the Trinity Medical College (Spragge). In theory and practice the future women physicians were nurtured and mentored separately and distinctly from their male colleagues. By the early 1900s students at the Ontario Medical College for Women were increasingly questioning the logic of a university system which would permit women to sit their medical examinations under university auspices, yet ban them from the classrooms ("Medical Training for Women"). Although official regulations still barred women from studying medicine at the university, several had begun to attend medical classes in 1904 and 1905. Academic concerns were also being raised by the female students. Dr. R.B. Nevitt, Dean of the Ontario Medical College for Women, reported in 1905:

> The women feel that as presently situated they have not an equal opportunity with the men of becoming acquainted with the idiosyncrasies of examiners, and that this loss influences their competitive standing. (Royal Commission on the University of Toronto)

In 1905, as a result of the economic and enrolment problems, directors and faculty at the Ontario Medical College for Women proposed the creation of a Faculty of Medicine for Women at the University of Toronto. They suggested that female students use all university facilities, but that their classes should continue to be segregated and taught by a separate faculty. According to the proposal, eleven instructors from the Ontario Medical College for Women (six women and five men) would form the new faculty. Dr. Augusta Stowe-Gullen was recommended for the position of Dean of Women (Ontario Medical College for Women 1905). The University rejected this suggestion completely and instead announced: "the Faculty of Medicine ... is now prepared to register female students" (Royal Commission of the University of Toronto).

In the spring of 1906 the Ontario Medical College for Women closed and female medical students transferred to the University of Toronto. With the closing of the College, Dr. Stowe-Gullen prepared a brief history of the school wherein she concluded:

> … let us feel no sorrow at the order of procedure…. The spirit of the age is monopolistic. Small medical, or preparatory colleges, are not consonant with prevailing thought, and their death knell has been sounded. It is conceded that the interests of the students, the profession, and the public, are best attained by university life, and university training. The greater facilities afforded, concentration of work, combined with a reduction of expenditure in time and energy, constitutes an alluring academic picture; and compensates for the loss of personal interest. (7-8)

But were the interests of female students, women in the profession, and women in the community, best served with the closing of the school? For women students and those in the profession, the closing of the women's medical school had particular and important ramifications. As Veronica Strong-Boag noted, the decline in the number of female physicians in the early twentieth century "was not unrelated to the closing of the Ontario Medical College for Women" (129). Quotas on female enrolment, discrimination in admission criteria, lack of adequate financial support, lack of positive reinforcement in career plans, as well as unpleasant and prejudicial attitudes in university classrooms, resulted not only in decreased numbers of female medical students but also in deteriorated conditions of study.

Dr. Elizabeth Stewart, who graduated from the Faculty of Medicine in 1907, remembered women students as being "cordially hated" at the University of Toronto. Out of ten women with whom she began medical studies, only four reached graduation (Tiel 4). At the Ontario Medical College for Women, six out of every ten students graduated. Women students also lost exposure to female role models when they transferred to the University. Women physicians had instructed students at the College and Dispensary. Although the Women's Dispensary continued to operate after the closing of the school, student involvement declined. Thus, emerging women doctors were faced exclusively with male teachers and mentors—many of whom were actively opposed to women in the medical profession.

For women physicians, the closing of the College represented a loss of opportunities for practical experience. Female doctors formed nearly 30 per cent of the total teaching staff at the Ontario Medical College for Women, whereas there were no female professors of medicine at the University of Toronto. Although staff on the faculty of the Ontario Medical College for Women never received salaries and women were given lesser positions as lecturers, demonstrators, and department assistants (few ever reached the professorial level), the psychological and practical benefits in terms of the teaching and clinical experience provided by the College were nevertheless of significance when no other medical schools would hire female physicians.

Women in the community also experienced losses as a result of the closing of the Ontario Medical College for Women. The midwifery service of the Obstetrics Department was lost when the school closed. Fortunately, the Women's Dispensary continued to operate as an independent institution and was eventually transformed into the Women's College Hospital in 1911.

From 1883 to 1906 the Women's Medical College, Toronto and the Ontario Medical College for Women served the professional and educational needs of women in medicine through the only strategy available to them at the time, that of "equal but separate" medical education. During this period they graduated 111 female physicians. The impact of these women's medical schools on female members of the profession and on women's health was of significance. But what of their effect on medical education and the practice of medicine generally?

The Ontario Medical College for Women appeared at the time to have little impact on the medical profession. Restrictive policies on female enrolment in medical programs at the University were removed through pressure exerted by women students themselves. Women entering medical training after 1906, as students in the Faculty of Medicine of the University of Toronto, were faced once again by male faculty and students who expressed hostile attitudes towards them. Hospitals and medical faculties persistently refused to appoint women to staff positions, despite the growth in the number of female doctors.

Notwithstanding, the Toronto and Kingston women's medical colleges were key events in the evolution of the medical profession in Canada. Together with the Women's Suffrage Movement, the movement for higher education, the earliest women physicians, the graduates of the women's medical schools, and the few men who fought for co-education, the colleges stimulated the development of full and equal education for women in all disciplines including medical science. Moreover, the women's medical colleges helped lay the foundation in a number of important branches of public health and preventive medicine by providing the early medical training of women who would pioneer in these fields. While gender-separatism in medical education did not erode all the obstacles confronting women in medicine, it nevertheless marks the permanent entry and presence of women in the medical professions.

Research for this paper was supported through a stipend from Associated Medical Services Incorporated, Hannah Institute for the History of Medicine. A version of this article was presented to the Canadian Society for the History of Medicine at the Learned Societies Conference, Winnipeg, Manitoba, May 27th, 1986.

Originally published in CWS/cf's Fall 1986 issue, "Canadian Women's History/ L'histoire des femmes canadiennes: 1" (Volume 7, Number 3).

[1]These and subsequent figures for the women's medical college, unless otherwise indicated, are compiled from annual reports for the school located in Series A7, Container 7, Women's College Hospital Archives, Toronto, and Record Groups p78-0121-(02)-029.1/p78-0122-(01)-029.2/p78-0122-(03)-029.2, University of Toronto Archives, Toronto.

References

Biggs, C. Lesley. "The Case of the Missing Midwives: A History of Midwifery in Ontario from 1795–1900." *Ontario History* 75.1 (March 1983): 29.

Duncan, Dr. J.T. Letter to Mrs. McEwan. 16 December 1989. File 5, Series C18, Container 21, Women's College Hospital, Toronto.

Guest, Dr. Edna. "A Message: On the Laying of the Foundation Stone of the Women's College Hospital." 20 October 1934, File 1, Series A9, Container 9, Toronto: Women's College Hospital Archives.

Hacker, Carlotta. *The Indomitable Lady Doctors*. Toronto: James Lorimer, 1984.

"Medical Training for Women," [1906] (Typewritten), Women's College Hospital Archives, Toronto.

Province of Ontario, Letters Patent for the Ontario Medical College for Women (Limited), 29 March 1894, Record Group 55-I-2-B-1, Liber 36, Archives of Ontario, Toronto.

Provincial Secretary, Annual Return for the Ontario Medical College for Women (Limited), 31 December 1895, Record Group 8-I-1-G, File 2025, Archives of Ontario, Toronto.

Ontario Medical College for Women (Limited). "Annual Announcement of the Ontario Medical College for Women (Limited): 1896." Women's College Hospital Archives, Toronto.

Ontario Medical College for Women (Limited). "Annual Announcement of the Ontario Medical College for Women (Limited): 1898." Women's College Hospital Archives, Toronto.

Ontario Medical College for Women (Limited). "Annual Announcement of the Ontario Medical College for Women (Limited): 1899." Record Group p78-0122-(01)-029.2, University of Toronto Archives, Toronto.

Ontario Medical College for Women (Limited). "Annual Calendar for the Ontario Medical College for Women (Limited): 1900. Women's College Hospital Archives, Toronto.

Ontario Medical College for Women (Limited), "Annual Announcement of the Ontario Medical College for Women (Limited): 1904." Record Group p78-0122-(03)-029.2, University of Toronto Archives, Toronto.

Ontario Medical College for Women (Limited) to the Commissioner upon University Matter: November 1905, File 7, Series C18, Container 21, Women's College Hospital Archives, Toronto.

"Ontario Medical College for Women." *Saturday Globe* 17 August 1895: 1.

Oppenheimer, Jo. "Childbirth in Ontario: The Transition from Home to

Hospital in the Early Twentieth Century." *Ontario History* 75 (1) (March 1983): 41.

Royal Commission on the University of Toronto. *Report of the Royal Commission on the University of Toronto*. Toronto: T.K. Cameron, 1906.

Spragge, George W. "Trinity Medical College." *Ontario History* 48 (June 1966).

Stowe-Gullen, Augusta. *A Brief History of the Ontario Medical College for Women*. Toronto: n.p., 1906.

Strong-Boag, Veronica. "Canada's Women Doctors: Feminism Constrained." Ed. Linda Kealey. *A Not Unreasonable Claim: Women and Reform in Canada 1880s-1920s*. Toronto: The Women's Press, 1979.

"The Woman's Medical College, Toronto." *The Canadian Practitioner* 16 (October 1891): 479–480.

Tiel, Jane. "Medicine and Woman's Intuition." *The Globe Magazine* 9 August 1958: 4.

Toronto School of Medicine. Minutes of Faculty Meetings. Meeting, 7 March 1883, Record Group B-73-007.1, University of Toronto Archives, Toronto.

University of Trinity College. Minute Book, 1883–1884. Toronto: Trinity College Archives.

Woman's Medical College, Toronto. "Annual Announcement of the Woman's Medical College, Toronto: Fourth Session 1886–1887." Series A7, Container 7. Toronto: Women's College Hospital Archives.

Woman's Medical College, Toronto. "Annual Announcement of the Woman's Medical College, Toronto: 1891–1892." Women's College Hospital Archives, Toronto.

Wishart, Dr. D.J. Gibb. "Financial Report for the Year Ending October 8th, 1901." 5 December 1901, File 7, Series EZ, Container 26, Women's College Hospital Archives, Toronto.

The Icelandic Connection

Freyja and the Manitoba Woman Suffrage Movement

Mary Kinnear ➤

Freyja, which means "woman," has been described as "the only woman suffrage paper published in Canada" (Kristjanson 373; Cleverdon 49, 53; Bacchi 28). It was produced by Margret Benedictsson and her husband Sigfus in Manitoba between 1898 and 1910. The title page described its purpose as "devoted to woman's political, economical and social rights."

This article is an outline of the interest of Icelandic women in turn-of-the-century feminist issues as reflected in *Freyja*. First, there is a brief examination of the place of the immigrant Icelandic community in Manitoba, with particular reference to the status of women within the settlement. The article then compares the feminist philosophy contained in *Freyja* with the feminism of the anglophone leaders of the Manitoba movement. Finally, an attempt is made to assess the impact of *Freyja* and of Icelandic women in the province on the Manitoba woman suffrage movement.

By 1898, Icelanders had been settled in the province for over 20 years. The community numbered approximately 6,000 people. The 1901 census records 11, 924 Scandinavians in the province composing 4.7 per cent of the total Manitoba population, of which it is estimated that one-half were Icelanders (*Report of the Royal Commission on Bilingualism and Biculturalism*, Book IV, 259). Women were already accustomed to working in the churches' Ladies Aids groups, and additionally in local Women's Societies. These helped new immigrants and the poor of the community but, even in the early days, priority was accorded to education: two girls were given bursaries to study music.The Women's Society also organized traditional festivals, like the Midwinter celebration. A feature of the 1884 Midwinter festival was a speech on equal rights for men and women and a second speech, by a woman, on the cultural position of Icelandic women (*Report of the Royal Commission on Bilingualism and Biculturalism*, Book IV, 259; Salverson; Kristjanson 194).

The women's movement in Iceland was already underway in 1885. The newspaper *Fjallknonan*, Maid of the Mountains, carried the first article on woman suffrage to be written by a woman, Briet Bjarnhedinsdottir. Her ideas were later echoed in many respects by *Freyja*'s Benedictsson. Bjarndehinsdottir stressed the importance of education, and parents' responsibility in seeing that daughters, as well as sons, were adequately prepared for economic independence and for independence of mind. She alluded to the prominent part played by women in the ancient sagas, and encouraged modern women not to be disheartened by contemporary opponents of progress. In 1895 she founded *Kvennabladid*, The Women's Paper, and later in 1907 became first president of the Iceland Society for the Emancipation of Women (*Fjallkonan* 1885). Over the years she corresponded with the editor of *Freyja*.

Margret Benedictsson emigrated from Iceland as a single woman, arriving in 1893 in Winnipeg after spending some time in the North Dakota Icelandic community. She took advantage of a newly-offered course in shorthand, typing and bookkeeping, and soon married. She and her husband Sigfus operated a printing and publishing business, at first in Selkirk and subsequently in Winnipeg. In 1910 she left Sigfus and with her three children went to live in Blane, Washington (*Freyja* 1899, 34–35; *Heimskringla* 1911b). Her importance in Manitoba derives from her editing, printing, and publishing of *Freyja*, 1898–1910. The magazine served a responsive audience.

In general, Canadian Icelanders supported women's emancipation. As with the anglophone women's movement, there was a strong connection with temperance. Helen E. Gregory, in a series of newspaper articles written for the Toronto *Globe* in 1890, noted that "last spring their temperance society held a picnic and debate and the subject chosen for discussion was Equal Rights." The main organizational impetus for Icelandic suffrage organizations came from Benedictsson. After 1905 she encouraged the Icelandic Ladies Aids groups to incorporate woman suffrage into their aims. She was gratified by an editorial statement in 1907 from *Logberg*, one of the two main Icelandic language newspapers in Winnipeg, in sympathy for woman suffrage. Benedictsson announced in 1908 the formation of the "first Icelandic Suffrage Association of America," in Winnipeg, with herself as president. She then joined this organization to the Canada Suffrage Association, and thereby also the International Woman Suffrage Alliance. In November 1908 an Icelandic women's group devoted exclusively to woman suffrage was founded in the small rural community of Argyle; the following year others were founded. These separate organizations each sent petitions to the Manitoba legislature in 1910 and a joint petition was sent in 1912. The bill giving women the vote was introduced into the Legislature in January 1916 by the province's Solicitor-General and acting Premier T.H. Johnson, himself the son of an Icelandic suffragist (*Freyja* 1909, 291; 1907, 294; 1908, 6–7, 181; 1909, 157; *Manitoba: Journals* 1910, 14, 22, 79, 91; *Manitoba: Journals* 1912, 13, 22; Hurwitz 325–345). *Freyja's* own aims were described in the first issue:

> Matters pertaining to the progress and rights of women will always be our first and foremost concern. *Freyja* will support prohibition and anything that leads to the betterment of social conditions. (1898, 4)

For twelve years Benedictsson issued the monthly magazine. About a quarter of its 30 or 40 pages (the issues varied in length) was taken up with advertisements, both in Icelandic and English. Up to half the text was taken up with poetry and a Children's Corner. Articles signed by pennames ("Baldur," "Lucifer") appeared, but most articles were either written by Benedictsson or Sigfus, or were translated by them from the writings of American feminists. Most articles were directly related to "the progress and rights of women."

In this *Freyja* took a distinctively radical line. With regard to women living in poverty, *Freyja* argued that the state should be involved in social welfare. At the same time, attention was drawn to the bind of the married woman who had no choice but to bear children, without the independent economic means of supporting them. Divorce was a topic of particular interest to *Freyja*. "A philosophical divorce" in 1900 described the onset of incompatibility in a marriage: "we have decided to separate without bothering the Court of Justice…. We each go our own way as each member does when a Society is dissolved for some good reason and depart as friends." A couple of years later Sigfus painted a more bitter picture of a couple forced to live together: "… he to undertake to support her forever, no matter how loathsome she became, she to give him all authority over her freedom in both a physical and spiritual meaning." *Freyja* in a subsequent issue disputed Sigfus' view of married women as dependents. Marriage was like a company, with two departments, "the domestic and the provision departments. Both are of equal worth to the company" (*Freyja* 1903, 44–7; 1901, 99–100; 1905, 31–2; 1907, 240).

Freyja recognized that most of the reading audience, Icelandic women, were actively involved in local community work. In an early article Benedictsson offered her view of an ideal Ladies Aid Society, less an institution of a charitable nature and more of an insurance society. Her model was the North American Independent Order of Foresters, Women's Branch, which offered its members life and health insurance (*Freyja* 1898, 20; Strong-Boag, 102).

While never disowning a woman's role as wife and mother, Benedictsson wished to see the woman in the family recognized as an equal partner, as in a business concern. But there was no doubt that she wished to see a woman's role expand out of the family and into public life. She was interested in more than new opportunities for professional and bourgeois women. Benedictsson also emphasized the need to improve conditions for working-class women.

In 1901 *Freyja* printed reports on a society establishing rules regarding work and wages for domestic servants, "working women," in Chicago: "Domestics should be given time off on Mondays…. The householder should have no right to hinder the social life of the domestics. They should be allowed visitors in their time off" (*Freyja* 1901, 176–7).

In support of a more public life for women, *Freyja* articles utilized philosophical arguments based on justice and historical example, contained uplifting biographies of non-traditional women, and reported the activities of women's rights organizations, both locally and in the United States and Europe. At a time of local elections, a thundering editorial used the text "Taxation without Representation is Tyranny" in an effort to inspire women readers to use "a weapon that is sharper than all others"—love—in order to influence men in voting for candidates supporting equal rights for women (*Freyja* 1907, 245–9; 1899, 41–2; 1904, 133–7; 1906, 205–8, 217–8; 1907, 221–4; 1910, 243–5; 1903, 209–10). Benedictsson's view was that justice and freedom applied with equal force for men and women. She was not anxious to maintain or encourage a retreat onto the pedestal. In one revealing piece written in 1904, she identified her personal struggle for independence with that of nineteenth-century countries struggling for freedom. As a young girl she had read about the Iceland patriot Jon Sigurdsson. He campaigned for responsible government and, in 1874, Iceland was granted independence in domestic affairs from Denmark. She was inspired by his yearning for liberty: "Angry and distressed I read the laments of oppressed persons, unhappily married women, and the misfortunes of young girls. And it is this evil that aroused in me ... a yearning to break down all the fetters that tie people to evil and distress" (*Freyja* 1904, 41–3).

Benedictsson's inspiration was different from that of Manitoba "mainliners"; so was her religion, and her ethnic background. As Carol Bacchi has pointed out, most of the leaders of the Canadian women's movement were Methodist or Presbyterian, with few from Anglican or other denominations; they were middle-class; either British immigrants themselves or daughters of Ontario British; housewives, although there were journalists and a few professional women among them; and most subscribed to the prevalent ideology of "maternal feminism" (Bacchi viii, 149; Gorham 30).

Benedictsson shared one passion with the Manitoba suffragists—a belief in temperance. But her views on divorce, pacifism, and the need for women to be in all aspects of public life were generally more outspoken than theirs. They were inclined to appeal to the argument of bringing women's moral superiority out of the kitchen and into the legislature (Strong-Boag 104–6, 134–5, 183). She invoked the ideal of equality rather than superiority. However, they all recognized the desirability of co-operation amongst women committed to social change. Was there joint activity between the groups she had done so much to establish and the English-speaking Manitoba suffragists?

Occasionally there was. In 1902 the Icelandic Women's Christian Temperance Union (WCTU) co-operated with the Winnipeg WCTU in presenting a woman suffrage petition to the Legislature. In 1911 the Winnipeg Women's Labour League met with the First Icelandic Suffrage Association in America in the Winnipeg Trades Hall to discuss whether it was appropriate to present another petition to the Legislature: they decided not to. In 1914 the Icelandic suffrage association accepted the Manitoba Political Equality League's invitation to join in a meeting with Premier Roblin. Again in 1915 the Association joined the League in a delegation to the Premier. Later that year, after the Liberal election victory, Icelandic groups circulated petitions for woman suffrage along with the English-speaking suffragists in order to present evidence of support to the new Premier Norris (*Freyja* 1902, 5–6; *Heimskringla* 1911a, 1914, 1915b). Most of the time, however, little effort was taken by the mainliners to bring about effective communication or co-operation. As early as 1893 one of the Icelandic newspapers related a circumstance which set a rather unhappy scene.

In February 1893 Benedictsson, newly arrived in Winnipeg, lectured on women's rights to Manitoba Icelanders. This coincided with the preparations of the Winnipeg WCTU to stage a Mock Parliament on the subject of equal rights for women. The Icelandic weekly newspaper, *Heimskringla*, reported the efforts of the "English-speaking ladies of Winnipeg" to get a petition and publicity for the cause of woman suffrage:

> These highly esteemed ladies have considered it below their dignity to seek the co-operation of the Icelandic nationality here in this matter.... These English ladies no doubt expect little appreciation of a matter like this from a foreign nationality which has come hither from a remote and poor country.... They do not expect any help from us.

The newspaper went on to describe women's municipal voting rights and educational privileges in Iceland, and pointed out that if the English-speaking women were less stand-offish they could "learn a little lesson from us in some matters" and could get the support of Manitoba Icelanders in the struggle for legal recognition of women's natural rights (*Heimskringla* 1893).

Twenty-two years later, at the time of their 1915 convention, the Manitoba Political Equality League did go so far as to solicit support by placing a notice in the Icelandic newspaper:

> The League particularly desires that Icelandic women attend and address the convention; it would be appropriate because it was an Icelandic woman who first established an association of this nature among her compatriots, although it is no longer in existence. (*Heimskringla* 1915a, 1915c)

Members of the First Icelandic Suffrage Association in America were affronted to learn that their organization was considered dead.

The conclusion must be that the Manitoba Icelandic women, along with their leader Margret Benedictsson and her magazine *Freyja*, had a minimal direct effect on the mainstream Manitoba woman suffrage movement. Examination of *Freyja*, however, serves to remind us both of the vitality of the feminism within Manitoba's Icelandic community and of the ideological diversity in the early Canadian women's movement—a diversity which deserves fuller exploration.

The author would like to acknowledge the assistance of the University of Manitoba Research Board and especially Hrund Skulason and Sigrid Johnson.

Originally published in CWS/cf's Winter 1986 issue, "Canadian Women's History/ l'histoire des femmes canadiennes: 2" (Volume 7, Number 4).

References

Bacchi, Carol Lee. Liberation *Deferred? The Ideas of the English-Canadian Suffragists, 1877–1918.* Toronto: University of Toronto Press, 1983.
Cleverdon, Catherine. *The Woman Suffrage Movement in Canada.* Toronto: University of Toronto Press, 1950, rpt. 1974.
Fjallkonan 5 June 1885.
Freyja I (1898).
Freyja II (1899).
Freyja III (1901).
Freyja IV (1901).
Freyja V (1903).
Freyja VI (1903).
Freyja VII (1904)..
Freyja VIII (1905)
Freyja IX (1907).
Freyja X (1908).
Freyja XI (1909).
Freyja XII (1910).
Gorham, Deborah. "The Canadian Suffragists." *Women in the Canadian Mosaic.* Ed. Gwen Matheson. Toronto: P. Martin Associates, 1976.
Gregory, Helen E. "Icelanders in Toronto." *Globe* (Toronto) 4 October 1890.
Heimskringla 1 February 1893.
Heimskringla 2 August 1911a.
Heimskringla 17 August 1911b.
Heimskringla 4 March 1914.
Heimskringla 11 February 1915a.
Heimskringla 25 February 1915b.
Heimskringla 4 March 1915c.
Hurwitz, Edith F. "The International Sisterhood." *Becoming Visible: Women in European History.* Eds. Renate Bridenthal and Claudia Koonz. Boston: Houghton Mifflin, 1977.
Kristjanson, W. *The Icelandic People in Manitoba.* Winnipeg: Wallingford Press, 1965.
Manitoba: Journals, 1910.
Manitoba: Journals, 1912.
Royal Commission on Bilingualism and Biculturalism. Table A-15, "Ethnic Origin of the Population of Manitoba: 1881–1961." *Report of the Royal Commission on Bilingualism and Biculturalism,* Book IV. Ottawa: 1969.
Ruth, Roy H. *Educational Echoes.* Winnipeg: Columbia Printers, 1964.
Salverson, Laura Goodman. *Confessions of an Immigrant's Daughter.* Toronto: Ryerson Press, 1939.
Strong-Boag, Veronica. *The Parliament of Women.* Ottawa: National Museums of Canada, 1976.

Sewing Solidarity

The Eaton's Strike of 1912

Ruth A. Frager ➤

"Mr. John C. Eaton, 'King of Canada' as he is generally called, is being taught the A. B. C.'s of Industrial Democracy by the striking Cloak Makers of Toronto," proclaimed the International Ladies' Garment Workers' Union (ILGWU 1912b, 1). It was 1912, and the Jewish workers who laboured in the Toronto garment factory of the T. Eaton Company were locked in combat with one of the most powerful employers in the country. The ILGWU charged that:

> ... in this very Kingdom of the Eaton Company, frail children of fourteen years, in busy seasons, work from 8 a.m. to 9 p.m. ...; in slack season, skilled working women, connected with the firm for six, eight or more years, can earn only Five, Four or even less Dollars per week; ... girls are forced at times to take "homework" to do at night, after the long day in the factory; ... foremen and forewomen have power to discriminate most flagrantly in favor of their friends, or vice versa, and may cut wages, ruinously, by intention, or from careless distribution of piece work; and this is not the half of the story of wrongs. (ILGWU 1912b, 1–2)

"Insults to Girls" (i.e. sexual harassment) and "Graft for Foremen" were other complaints against Eaton's (United Garment Workers 1912b, 3).

Eaton's was no worse than many other employers in this period. Nevertheless, this strike is outstanding because it provides a rare example of male solidarity in support of women workers. The strike began in one department of the firm's clothing factory when 65 male sewing machine operators refused to follow new orders to sew in the linings of women's coats on their machines. Although the large Eaton's garment factory was not a union shop, all of these men were members of the ILGWU. They had been making $0.65 per garment without sewing in the linings, and they were now being asked to do the extra work without any increase in pay. Previously, the linings had been sewn in by hand by female workers who were known as finishers. So the new order from management amounted to more than a pay cut for the men—it meant women were going to lose their jobs. Male self-interest and female self-interest now coincided, and the strike became an expression of male solidarity with women workers.[1]

This solidarity was emphasized by the Toronto District Labour Council when it passed a resolution objecting to Eaton's locking out workers for refusing "in the interests of their sister workers, to do work which did not belong to them" (Toronto District Labour Council Minutes 1912a; see also 1912b). Indeed, this solidarity between men and women became the main theme of the strike. "Remember," stated Joe Salsberg, a Jewish immigrant who became a left-wing labour activist, "the Jewish tailors in Toronto went on their first big strike in defense of *undzere shvester*—our sisters." Salsberg explained that:

> The reasoning of the men who worked at Eaton's was a simple one: that these [women workers] will lose their jobs, and [...] maybe they felt they didn't want to do these jobs that the women are now doing, maybe their wages will come down [if the men were to sew in the linings by machine] because the rates fixed for those operations were always traditionally lower because women did [those operations].... I never rule out the element of selfishness and self-interest—which is also human.
>
> But [one of the strike slogans] became the folksy expression of simple, honest working men ..., in Yiddish particularly: "Mir vellen nisht aroycenemen dem bissle fun broyt fun di mayler fun undzere shvester." [In English:] "We will not take the morsel of bread from the mouths of our sisters."

The solidarity displayed by the men was not a simple matter of self-interest. According to the ILGWU's newspaper, union officials believed that "management would have increased the price of operating [on] the garment, but the operators, with admirable solidarity, insist that the finishers shall not be deprived of their share of the work" (ILGWU 1912a, 14).

When the 65 male operators refused to sew in the linings, Eaton's management fired them and physically threw them out onto the street. Almost immediately, over 1,000 of their fellow workers from Eaton's factory went on strike to support them. About a third of these strikers were women, and the ILGWU's head office sent two women organizers to Toronto in order to help lead the women strikers. The sympathy strike spread beyond the ILGWU to include members of the United Garment Workers who worked in the men's clothing departments of the Eaton's factory. And it spread beyond Toronto: workers at the Eaton's clothing factory in Montréal also struck in sympathy with the Toronto workers, and Hamilton's garment workers threatened to join the strike if any of Hamilton's clothing firms attempted to do any work for the T. Eaton Company.[2]

The attack on "Fort Eaton" was reinforced by the call for a nation-wide boycott of the company's goods. The labour press warned its readers not to "go after cheap Eaton bargains" because "bargains at the expense of manhood, womanhood and childhood are expensive in the extreme" (*Hamilton Labour News* qtd. in United Garment Workers 1912d, 2; ILGWU 1912c, 25). The boycott was particularly effective within Toronto's immigrant Jewish community. This was due largely to the support of Jewish women, for they were the ones who were primarily responsible for the family shopping. Here, women's role as consumer was used strategically to support the struggles of male and female producers. In addition, Eaton's mail order business suffered as customers from across the country mailed back their Eaton's catalogues in protest (Kirzner; *Industrial Banner* 1912b,4).

Further appeals for support were made to women's groups outside of the Jewish community. The Toronto District Labour Council asked "Women's Clubs [and] Suffrage Associations ... to defend the rights of the [Eaton's] workers" (ILGWU 1912b, 2–3). The ILGWU's newspaper optimistically reported that "Women's Lodges and Women's Auxiliaries of men's trade unions, and associations of leisure class women" promised to support the strike (ILGWU 1912b, 2–3).

Meaningful solidarity between women appears to have stopped at the class border, however. Alice Chown, a women's rights activist, described the considerable difficulty she had when she tried to persuade non-working-class women's groups to support the Eaton's strikers:

> I tried to interest the various women's clubs, but I was amazed because they had no sympathy with the strikers, unless I had some tale of hardship to tell. The common, everyday longings for better conditions, for a life that would provide more than food, clothes and shelter, were not recognized as justifying a strike. I had to tell over and over the old, old story of the bosses who favoured the girls whom they could take out evenings, girls who had to sell themselves as well as their labour to get sufficient work to earn a living. (Chown 151–152)

Chown also indicated that many women suffragists were unwilling to support women strikers, fearing that strike support work would tarnish the appeal of their main cause:

> During the [Eaton's] strike I had to preside at a meeting of the Woman's Political League. I asked [the woman], who had been sent from New York to conduct the strike, to speak to our association. She made a very wise and illuminating speech. I did not expect an audience who had never considered that justice to working people was a higher virtue than charity, to respond any more cordially than it did. As soon as the discussion started I closed the suffrage meeting, and asked all who were willing to try to awaken interest in the strike to remain. I thought I made it quite clear that with the adjournment of the suffrage meeting a new meeting came into existence, but I aroused a great deal of hard feeling amongst the zealous suffragists,

who were afraid that their pet cause would be hurt through being linked with an unpopular one. (153)

The unpopularity of the strikers' cause in Chown's circle was also because the vast majority of the Eaton's strikers were East European Jewish immigrants—and English Canadians were often intensely ethnocentric and suspicious of foreigners.[3]

The Jewish nature of the strike was a central issue. The ILGWU's newspaper was to the point:

Those affected [by the dispute at Eaton's] are almost entirely Jewish: and the chief slogan by which it was hoped to cut off public sympathy was the report ... that this is "only a strike of Jews." The appeal to race and creed prejudice has succeeded, too, in so far as it has prevented the Gentile Cloak Makers from joining in the sympathetic strike. (1912b, 2)

The failure of Eaton's non-Jewish workers to join the strike was part of a wider pattern of tension between Jews and non-Jews in Toronto's garment industry. Considerable ethnic tension also existed within the labour movement more generally. Garment manufacturers attempted to capitalize on these divisions, by trying to pit non-Jewish workers against Jewish workers, particularly in strike situations. In the Eaton's strike, the non-Jewish strike-breakers protected "Mr. Humpty Dumpty Eaton" from his downfall.[4]

Despite the formidable solidarity between male and female workers and despite the vigorous support of the working-class Jewish community, the "King of Canada" prevailed. After four months, the workers were forced to admit defeat. The effect on Jewish workers was devastating. The ILGWU was seriously weakened, and "for a long time [after this strike]," a union official recalled, "the T. Eaton Company would not hire any Jews" (Kirzner).

Workers' defeats were not uncommon in this period. What is outstanding here is the potential for working-class power that this strike illuminates. Without the unusual solidarity between men and women and without the mobilization of consumers to boycott Eaton's, the strike would never have developed the powerful momentum it did. If the solidarity between the sexes and the solidarity between producers and consumers had been supported by greater solidarity between Jewish and non-Jewish workers, the "King of Canada" would indeed have gotten "the surprise of his life" (ILGWU 1912b, 2).

This strike provides a glimmer of what might have been the basis of a much more powerful labour movement. It highlights the critical need to overcome the deep divisions within the working class. It also highlights the need for women's rights organizations to encompass the interests of working-class women.

Originally published in CWS/cf's Fall 1986 issue, "Canadian Women's History/

l'histoire des femmes canadiennes: 1" (Volume 7, Number 3).

[1]See Labour Gazette; Toronto Daily News; Toronto Star (1912a, 5); Toronto Star (1912b, 2); Industrial Banner (1912a, 1); Kirzner; Shatz; Kraisman; Siegerman. For a more detailed analysis of this strike, see Frager (1992b).
[2]Toronto District Labour Council (1912b); United Garment Workers (1912a, 3); United Garment Workers (1912b, 1); United Garment Workers (1912c, 1); Industrial Banner (1912a, 1); Labour Gazette 856, 897–901; Kirzner; ILGWU (1912a, 14); ILGWU (1912b, 2, 18); Toronto Daily News 13.
[3]On the prevalence of anti-Semitism in Toronto in this period, see Frager (1992a, 12-14).
[4]The reference to "Mr. Humpty Dumpty Eaton" is from ILGWU (1912b, 4). On the tension between Jews and non-Jews in Toronto's garment industry see Frager (1992a, 77-97).

References

Canada, Department of Labour. Labour Gazette (March 1912).
Chown, Alice A. The Stairway. Boston, 1921.
Frager, Ruth A. Sweatshop Strife: Class, Ethnicity, and Gender in the Jewish Labour Movement of Toronto 1930-1939. Toronto: University of Toronto Press, 1992a.
Frager, Ruth A. "Class, Ethnicity and Gender in the Eaton Strikes of 1912 and 1934." Gender Conflicts: New Essays in Women's History. Eds. Franca Iacovetta and Mariana Valverde. Toronto: University of Toronto Press, 1992b.
International Ladies' Garment Workers' Union (ILGWU). The Ladies' Garment Worker (March 1912a).
ILGWU. The Ladies' Garment Worker (April 1912b).
ILGWU. The Ladies' Garment Worker (June 1912c).
Industrial Banner (London, Ontario) (March 1912a).
Industrial Banner (London, Ontario) (April 1912b).
Kirzner, A. [speech, in Yiddish, rpt.; trans. by author] Toronto ILGWU's Cloakmakers' Union. Souvenir Journal, 1911–1936.
Kraisman, S. [speech, rpt.] Toronto ILGWU's Cloakmakers' Union. Souvenir Journal, 1911–1961.
Salsberg, Joe. Interview. Toronto, 1984.
Shatz, C. [speech, in Yiddish, rpt.; trans. by author] Toronto ILGWU's Cloakmakers' Union. Souvenir Journal, 1911–1936.
Siegerman, M. [speech, rpt] Toronto ILGWU's Cloakmakers' Union. Souvenir Journal, 1911–1961.
Toronto Daily News 15 February 1912: 13.
Toronto District Labour Council Minutes, 15 February 1912a, Labour Council of Metropolitan Toronto Collection, Volume 3, Public Archives of Canada, Ottawa.

Toronto District Labour Council Minutes, 7 March 1912b, Labour Council of Metropolitan Toronto Collection, Volume 3, Public Archives of Canada, Ottawa.

Toronto ILGWU's Cloakmakers' Union. *Souvenir Journal, 1911–1936.*

Toronto Star 15 February 1912a: 5.

Toronto Star 16 February 1912b: 2.

United Garment Workers. *The Weekly Bulletin of the Clothing Trades* (New York) 22 March 1912a.

United Garment Workers. *The Weekly Bulletin of the Clothing Trades* (New York) 29 March 1912b.

United Garment Workers. *The Weekly Bulletin of the Clothing Trades* (New York) 12 April 1912c.

United Garment Workers. *The Weekly Bulletin of the Clothing Trades* (New York) 3 May 1912d.

The Convent

An Option for Québécoises, 1930–1950

Barbara J. Cooper ⌁

Within the last fifteen years historians of women in Québec have begun to explore the importance of religious communities of women within French-Canadian society. The emphasis has shifted away from finding heroines and models of piety among the nuns[1] (usually the foundresses or leaders), to an interest in the general membership, its reasons for choosing a convent life, and its various charitable endeavours. Not all agree on the nature of the contribution nuns have made, but more are recognizing the need to examine the religious life as an avenue that was open to women as an alternative to marriage and motherhood.

As recent scholarship has begun to redress the lack of attention paid to nuns over the years, two basic hypotheses about communities of women have emerged. One of these suggests that religious congregations absorbed marginalized women of the society, particularly widows and women *"d'un certain âge"* who were engaging in works of charity on their own (Denault et Lévesque 11). It is Bernard Denault's contention that the clergy actively sought to direct the efforts of these women in accordance with its view of the role of the Roman Catholic Church in society.[2] Although Denault presents a convincing case for the growing hegemony of the Church in the realm of social services, he fails to treat nuns as agents on their own behalf. Denault would seem to suggest that it was the approbation of the clergy that saved these women from a life on the "fringe." At the same time he wants to make the point that it was to the advantage of the clergy to take over and direct the initiative of these women. Nevertheless, it is not at all clear by what magic this group of "marginalized" and "passive" women was transformed into an organization worthy of esteem.

Assessments of religious communities that are more sensitive to the aspirations of women have been put forward by Micheline Dumont and Marta Danylewycz. These historians have argued that the religious life represented an alternative to marriage, motherhood, and spinsterhood. Their approach acknowledges the desire of women to be involved actively in society. Dumont emphasizes the need to analyze the role of communities *"comme pôle d'attraction, pour l'ensemble de la population féminine; c'est d'évaluer leurs fonctions en regard des besoins sociaux de leur époque"* (Dumont-Johnson 82). Both Dumont and

Danylewycz have stressed the fact that religious life was an attractive option for women as long as they were philosophically and economically constrained to attach themselves to a "*foyer.*" Dumont suggests that, in a society in which motherhood was held as the ideal for women, the notion of a "*maternité spirituelle*" (Dumont-Johnson 87) increased both the acceptability and the appeal of the religious life. Furthermore, Dumont argues that, once in the convent, some women used the religious life as a vehicle for occupational advancement and self-expression. According to Danylewycz, the convent offered nuns many opportunities unavailable to their lay peers.

The work of Danylewycz and Dumont also raises some rather difficult questions about the motivations and attitudes of the nuns. While Danylewycz found evidence of what she called "feminist praxis" (1981, 419) among the nuns, Dumont argued more explicitly that "*les religieuses (étaient) peut-être des féministes sans le savoir*" (102). Can one, however, argue that a latent feminism inspired these women to join the convent when, even by Dumont's own admission, many if not most nuns perceived themselves to be responding to a call from God to be of service within the Church? Does evidence of "feminist praxis" mean that religious life was a protest against the role assigned to women within the patriarchal structure of the Church? Or does challenging the authority of bishops and priests with regard to their own communities suggest that the nuns accepted the patriarchal structure, but sought to secure their own place within it? Furthermore, with regard to the "proto-feminism" of some nuns, one might wonder whether this phenomenon actually motivated women to opt for the religious life, or whether it was an out-growth of their experience after they entered.

It would seem that, for the majority of women, choosing the religious life did not constitute a conscious protest against the restricted lives of lay women in Québec. Nuns continue to describe their choice of the convent as a response to a call from God.[3] This is hardly surprising when the very validity of their "vocation" is premised on the fact that their choice of the convent is seen in religious terms. It is quite possible that citing any other reason for wanting to enter may have been unacceptable to those responsible for screening entrants. Since there was, then, a religious rhetoric that was approved, and perhaps expected, it is difficult to assess motives for entrance.

Difficulty does not, however, mean impossibility. Dumont and Danylewycz were right to insist that the lives of the nuns must be examined. One can begin by studying women who entered communities during specific periods of time in order to recreate as closely as possible the nature of the choices available to them. Admittedly it is dangerous to generalize on the basis of one group of entrants. Nevertheless, it seems this is the only place to start to delineate the broader picture. This paper will present some of the findings of a study of a Montréal-based community during the 1930s and 1940s.[4]

The Community under study was chosen for several reasons. This group was involved in virtually every aspect of the social services and numbered both professionals and non-professionals in its membership. One traditional work of the Community even into the 1930s was home-visiting, and the Sisters played an important part in the life of the rural communities in which they lived.[5] Their entrance requirements were not prohibitive, apart from canonical stipulations regarding age and legitimacy.[6] Although good health was seen as an asset, exceptions were made. There were no set levels of education to be attained prior to entrance, nor was a dowry actually demanded (although formally it was a requirement). These factors made this community more easily accessible to women who wanted a life of service to the Church. The young women usually brought with them what they could: a table service, a few articles of underclothing, and whatever their parents might want to give. The Community supplied the rest.

The major source of information for this study was the Community's Register of Membership, which includes the entrants' names and the names of their parents, as well as the occupations of the fathers. It records the location of the entrants' births and the locations from which they entered. The dates at which they progressed through various stages of training are also listed. In some cases a note has been made on their educational training. Necrologies and various commemorative booklets of the Community were also consulted. Although the Community had an English-speaking Novitiate in the United States, this study examines only those women who entered in Montréal.[7] In total we are dealing with 2,007 entrants over a twenty-year period.

The time frame selected for the study, 1930–1950, encompassed both a period of very successful recruitment of new members of the Community (the first half of the 1930s) and a period of ominous decline in new membership (the 1940s). In Québec generally the population of nuns increased by 29 per cent during the Depression and the years 1930–1934 were record years for recruitment of new members. Some have attributed the increase in membership to the economic dislocation caused by the Depression.[8] By contrast, the 1940s was marked by a return to prosperity occasioned by the Second World War, and by the recruitment of women into jobs previously denied them because of their sex. During this time growth of religious communities of women was ten per cent less than in the previous decade. The recruitment to this Community faltered during the 1940s as 40 per cent fewer new members joined. This study examines the extent to which the material conditions of existence may be said to have affected recruitment. The religious/political contexts of both the increase and decrease in membership were also studied.

Some broad patterns and conclusions emerged from the sources.[9] First of all, the ages at which the young women chose the religious life offers an insight into how women perceived their choice: whether they viewed it as their first choice, or their last hope, with optimism and enthusiastic idealism, or panic. The average age of the entrants over the 20 years was 21, and most of the women were between 18 and 24 years of age (the total ages ranged from 16 to 43). The average age of marriage in Canada during these years was 25. Almost half of those who entered the Community in any age category left before it was time to pronounce final vows.

What all of this suggests is that, first of all, women chose to enter the convent at an age younger than that at which they might marry. That so many left implies that there was little stigma attached to leaving before final vows. (By contrast, leaving after final vows was viewed by the Church much as divorce was at the time.) It would seem that many young women entered the convent to test their suitability for the life. Catholic girls at the time were encouraged to consider the possibility of a "vocation," and one could at least try the convent and then get out—unlike marriage. It would appear that most women who decided to enter the convent saw it as a positive first choice, rather than their only alternative when other things failed.

Most of the entrants also came from those areas where the Community had houses, so the young women would have had some familiarity with the nuns. Another factor which may have influenced entrance was that approximately 20 per cent of the entrants had a sibling in the Community. Not only did the presence of a sister in the Community constitute a positive role model, but in an age when contact with family and friends was strictly controlled after entrance, the knowledge that one was not "alone" would have been most reassuring.

To establish the socio-economic background of the entrants, the occupations of their fathers were analyzed. Farmers' daughters were disproportionately represented. Not quite half of those who entered and more than half of those who stayed, came from the farm. Since the nuns did not provide any educational facilities for the elite of the society where upper-class young women would have come to know them, the underrepresentation of professionals' daughters is not surprising. Nor did the poorest elements in society provide many members for this group. In fact, the diversified ministry in which the Community was engaged, and the rural location of many of the convents, put the Community in contact with precisely those kinds of women who entered.

The educational background of the women who entered seems to reflect the characteristics of the general female population. Most had completed the equivalent of Grade 8; many had a year of two of high school. A few had teaching certificates or professional training. Unfortunately, however, the records are not entirely complete with regard to this aspect of the entrants' backgrounds.

To appreciate the choice represented by the convent, one must understand what other options were available to women. In the 1930s, not surprisingly, the economic climate was most unfavourable for Québécoises. Of the women who worked outside their own homes, 50 per cent were engaged in "service." For many, if not most, this meant domestic service, the mainstay of "working" women during the Depression. The professions of teaching and nursing were increasingly taken over by the nuns who, for example, took up teaching positions at a faster rate than the laity. This was understandable when nuns could be hired to teach for a pittance—even less than the already low-paid lay teachers.[10] Finally, the attitudinal climate of the 1930s did not favour women in the workplace. The Francoeur Bill introduced in the Québec legislature in 1935 went so far as to seek to exclude women from the workforce unless they could prove need.[11]

At the same time that there was a great deal of hostile rhetoric aimed at those women who were trying to make a living, the clerico-political elites continued to extol the role of wife and mother within the French-Canadian context. The image of the nurturing female also encompassed those women who would dedicate their lives to the service of others in the Church. So, during the 1930s when most women found the workplace inhospitable, religious communities offered attractive alternatives where women could enjoy legitimate power and respect. Young women were being fed a steady diet of what was acceptable for them and they had the time to try out the religious life—a life that was often linked to a profession.

What changed in the 1940s? As has been shown, the age of entrants and the percentage of those with kin remained fairly constant. Farmers' daughters continued throughout the period to be overrepresented in the Community. What this meant, particularly in the 1940s, was that the Community continued to draw on a diminishing sector of the population. Whereas 27 per cent of Québec males were employed in the agricultural sector at this time, 39 per cent of the recruits came from farms.

Another consideration is the type and scale of work undertaken by the nuns during the 1940s. The eight new foundations of the Community in these years included an orphanage for boys, an elementary school for the children of workers in a munitions factory, a rest home for their own nuns, an educational institute, and three hospitals. The Community was being forced to give its members some occupational/professional training to work in larger institutions, particularly hospitals. Many Sisters were assuming supervisory or administrative roles. Nuns were less frequently to be found making home visitations. In a real sense, the life of the nuns was becoming more professionalized in terms of occupations, and the scale on which they were asked to perform certain works militated against their spending much time with potential new members. Since recruitment depended to a great extent on informal and individual encouragement, this could have been a problem.

Throughout the period under examination, education continued to be a relatively unimportant factor in both entrance and declining enrolment. Catholic women, generally, were not encouraged to receive any other training than that which would prepare them for motherhood. Until education would become a means of occupational advancement for women rather than a preparation for one's "vocation," it seems unlikely that it could be considered a factor in diminishing recruitment.

What did change then? Clearly one must consider the occupational opportunities occasioned by the war. Women in Québec, as elsewhere, took part in war industries and enjoyed the autonomy that resulted from their employment.[12] Unlike other areas in Canada where hesitation about women at work was perhaps a little more muted by patriotic fervour, the Québécoises were exposed to vitriolic attacks by the clergy for their selfishness and wanton disregard for the welfare of their children when they went off to work.[13] In a sense, the clergy laid all its cards on the table in an attempt to keep women at home. One might argue that the experience many women gained in the workplace belied the most outrageous claims of the clergy with regard to their moral jeopardy. This contradiction may have been but one element corroding the credibility and authority of the clergy, especially with regard to their pronouncements about women. It would be hard to argue that the expectations of women did not change over the war years. One might also wonder whether those who worked during the war merely delayed entrance, although there is no evidence to suggest so within this Community. It would seem that those who postponed entrance never, in fact, entered the convent.

Several other factors seem worthy of consideration in trying to account for waning interest in this Community. The occupational explosion for women during the war did not last. Active programs were begun by 1944 to encourage women "to go back home." Most women did, and on the surface, life seemed to return to "normal." Some married women, however, remained in the workforce, and these relatively few women can be seen to have kept the door open for others. These women did not have the best jobs, but their presence in the workforce suggested to others that marriage need not necessarily preclude paid employment.

One occupation that did make a difference for women during and after the war was clerical work. Employment in an office was generally considered an acceptable middle-class occupation, and one that was not already monopolized by nuns. Women were thus able to begin to conceive of work outside the "vocational" range traditionally presented to them.

In another important development in the mid- to late-1930s, rural lay female teachers, and later their urban counterparts, began to challenge the clerical hegemony in their field.[14] These women were actively resisted by the government which seemed accurately to perceive that they were picking away at the underpinnings of a system that relied on the "cheap labour" of the nuns. Similarly, in the mid-1940s, some nurses saw the need to unionize in order to withstand the pressure to turn them into "lay nuns" (see Daigle). While neither of these efforts at organization could be construed as mass movements, they represent an incipient awareness that women who chose not to enter the convent had a right to a profession and to a living wage.

In the realm of provincial politics the struggle to obtain female suffrage continued without success throughout the 1930s. While many see the granting of the vote to women in Québec in 1940 as a political ploy or a class-specific concern, it seems that this event can also be viewed as part of a nascent challenge to clerical control in Québec. The fact that Premier Godbout stood up to Cardinal Villeneuve, threatening to resign and leave his position open for an avowed anti-clerical if female suffrage were not granted, suggests that Godbout knew that he could successfully defy the iron grip of the clergy (Casgrain 92-4).

What all of this suggests is that regardless of how slow or how minimal social change may have seemed at the time, it was probably the most important factor in accounting for declining enrolment in the Community. The emergence of clerical work provided middle-class women with an alternative to more traditional pursuits. The growing militancy of some teachers and nurses was forcing open the doors of these professions for women who wanted a career and an income on which to live independently. The changing attitude which resulted from married women's decisions to stay at, or go back to, work was part of a larger awareness that women had a right to a just wage and reasonable working conditions. Although they faced the hostility of many of their male counterparts, their presence allowed for the possibility of greater choice for women.

Given the religious and socio-economic reality of Québec in the 1930s, then, the religious life can indeed be seen as an attractive option for young women with occupational or religious aspirations. Accordingly, the Community shared in very successful years of recruitment to the religious life throughout Québec. In the 1940s, however, the seeds sown by those women who stood up against the image of women propounded by the clerico-political elites began to bear some fruit in the gradual opening of options for women other than marriage and the convent. In this context the Community experienced a rather dramatic decline in new members as women looked elsewhere for life choices.

In all of this, however, we must not lose sight of the fact that the women who entered the convent spoke of their choice in relation to a specific "call from God." Despite the subjectivity of such an assertion, recruitment patterns reveal much about the nature of their "vocation." As more convent records are made available in the future, the role and importance of these women will be more clearly understood.

The author would like to thank Nora Campbell, Ruth Brouwer, Franca Iacovetta, and Ian Radforth for their comments on an earlier draft.

Originally published in CWS/cf's Winter 1986 issue, "Canadian Women's History/ l'histoire des femmes canadien-nes: 2" (Volume 7, Number 4).

[1]The terms "religious women," "nuns," and "Sisters," will be used without specific reference to any canonical distinctions.

[2]Hereafter the Roman Catholic Church will be referred to simply as "the Church." The clergy mentioned throughout the paper can be assumed to belong to this Church.

[3]A questionnaire was distributed as part of the research for my thesis (Cooper). The responses to the questions, "Who suggested the religious life to you?" were revealing both in content and in emphasis. Almost unanimously the nuns attributed their being in a convent to a call from God. The use of phrases like "God alone" or "Jesus Christ himself" followed by exclamation marks or

periods indicated that there was some sensitivity to the suggestion that they may have had other motives for being there.

[4]The period of the 1930s was the focus of my MA thesis cited above. Subsequently, I profiled entrants to the same community during the 1940s in a paper that was part of the doctoral requirements at York University. The Community requested anonymity in exchange for the use of their material. Consequently it will be referred to as "the Community" throughout.

[5]For example, in the absence of undertakers, the nuns were often called when someone died, and they would take care of the wake.

[6]Canon law required that an individual be at least 21 when she professed final vows. Because the training period in the Community was about five years long, entrants were not usually accepted before the age of 16. Canon law also required than an individual be legitimate or legally adopted. The Superiors seem to have had some discretionary power with regard to this canon because a few entrants were noted as being "illegitimate."

[7]Some who entered in Montréal were from the New England milltowns, but it was assumed that they probably shared in the French-Canadian mentality since they chose to return to Canada and to be trained in French.

[8]The relation between the Depression and recruitment to religious communities is made by Marc Lessard and J. P. Montminy. It is also part of the argument of Bernard Denault.

[9]For a more detailed analysis see Cooper.

[10]One wonders about the extent to which the nuns realized the political implications of their accepting certain jobs. Hamelin certainly suggests that the nuns were resented for taking the jobs from which the laity could have benefitted.

[11]Although the bill was never passed, Madeleine Trottier and Robert Mayer suggest that the bill did not pass not so much for lack of electoral support, but for the administrative difficulties inherent in obtaining the required proof.

[12]The reaction of Québécoises to the wartime experience is recorded by Geneviève Auger and Raymonde Lamothe.

[13]In 1942 the Jesuit-sponsored École Sociale Populaire published the tract, *Le Travail Féminin et la Guerre* in which the authors accused women of being "… *séduites par une propagande intéressée ou aveugle qui faisait consister la dignité de la femme, non pas dans son rôle d'épouse, de mère et de reine du foyer, mais dans l'affirmation de sa personalité,' dans la 'liberté de se faire sa vie,' et dans son 'emancipation'*" (2).

[14]The rise of these unions has been explored by Thivierge.

References

Auger, Geneviève and Raymonde Lamothe. *De la poêle à frire à la ligne du feu.* Montréal: Boréal Express, 1981.

Casgrain, Thérèse. *A Woman in a Man's World.* Toronto: McClelland and Stewart, 1974.

Cooper, Barbara J. "In the Spirit: Entrants to a Religious Community of Women in Québec, 1930–1939." MA thesis. McGill University, 1983.

Daigle, Johanne. "L'éveil syndical des 'religieuses laiques': l'émergence et l'évolution des infirmières de Montréal, 1946–1966." *Travailleuses et féministes*. Eds. Marie Lavigne and Yolande Pinard. Montréal: Boréal Express, 1983. 115–138.

Danylewcyz, Marta. "Changing Relationships: Nuns and Feminists in Montréal, 1880–1925." *Histoire Sociale/Social History* 14 (1981): 413–34.

Danylewcyz, Marta. "Taking the Veil in Montréal, 1850–1920: An Alternative to Migration, Motherhood, and Spinsterhood." Address to the Annual Meeting of the Canadian Historical Association, June 1978.

Denault, Bernard, et Benoît Lévesque. *Eléments pour une sociologie des communautés religieuses au Québec.* Montréal: Les Presses de l'Université de Montréal, 1975.

Dumont-Johnson, Micheline. "Les communautés religieuses et la condition féminine." *Recherches sociographiques* 19.1 (1978): 79–102.

Hamelin, Jean. *Histoire du Catholicisme au Québec: le XXe siècle.* Montréal: Boréal Express, 1984.

Lessard, Marc, and J. P. Montminy. "Les religieuses du Canada: âge, recrutement, et persévérance." *Recherches Sociographiques* 8 (1967): 18ff.

Thivierge, Marîse. "La syndicalisation des institutrices catholiques 1900–1957." *Maîtresses de maison, Maîtresses d'école.* Eds. Nadia Fahmy-Eid and Micheline Dumont. Montréal: Boréal Express, 1983. 171–89.

Trottier, Madeleine, and Robert Mayer. "Images de la femme au Canada français." *Québécoises du 20e siècle.* Ed. Michèle Jean. Montréal: Boréal Express, 1981.

Women in Huron and Ojibwa Societies

Marlene Brant Castellano ◆━━

Native women of the past are a shadowy lot. One remembers their handiwork, quill and bead and buckskin pieces preserved in the museums, but what of their personalities? Very few portraits have been left to us except by the ethnographers, who were more interested in kinship and customs and manner of dress than in portraits of individuals.

What we can piece together is a composite portrait of Native women of a particular tradition or a particular time. Such composite portraits are not inconsistent with the images Native women in the past held of themselves, for they did not seek notoriety beyond the bounds of their community. Their accomplishments were not of the sort to bring them fame. They seemed content to form the backdrop against which the men played starring roles. Yet they commanded a respect and wielded an influence which might be the envy of a modern advocate of women's rights.

The coming of European settlers drastically altered the lifestyle of Native women. New elements of material culture were introduced; the cycle of economic activities was changed; alien laws were imposed. Perhaps the most significant change wrought in the lives of Native women was the introduction of new standards by which they were judged, standards which bore little relation to the measures of excellence by which they had hitherto gained esteem, to which their lifelong education had directed them.

Under the impact of these disorienting experiences, the majority of Native women became, for generations, very private persons, attending to their traditional tasks, largely invisible to the mainstream of Canadian society.

In recent years Native women have emerged from the shadows to voice their concerns, to exercise their talents in a public way, to demonstrate the wit and courage which have always been part of their tradition. This essay selectively illustrates this tradition among one small group of Native women, those of the Kawartha district.

Both the Iroquoian and Ojibwa women who called the Valley of the Trent their home during these early periods belonged to societies which glorified the male roles—those of warrior, hunter, councillor, or shaman. Women took on those domestic, supportive duties which have been defined through history as "feminine." The major differences in occupation and prestige between women in the two culture groups stem directly from the differences between agricultural and migratory hunting and gathering economies.

The Huron people lived in villages organized on the basis of clan membership. Descent was traced through the female line and transmission of titles and rights followed the same course. The Huron dwelling was the longhouse, constructed of bark slabs tied to a wooden frame, 90–100 feet in length and 20–30 feet in width, with doors usually at the ends. The longhouse was divided into four or more pairs of compartments, each pair separated by a central passageway and served by a common fire for heating and cooking. The occupants of a longhouse were the descendants of a senior woman, her unmarried sons, her daughters, their husbands and children. There must have been variations on the rule that a husband took up residence in his wife's longhouse, since a man chosen as councillor served his mother's clan and he would necessarily reside at least in the same village as his constituents. Property belonged to the family and the practice of storing winter supplies in a single compartment at the end of the longhouse rendered the designations of items as individual or nuclear family property largely meaningless.

Mothers continued to wield considerable influence over their daughters after marriage and the intensity of this relationship was increased by the prolonged absences of the men pursuing hunting, warrior and even political activities away from the village. Women who remained at home were responsible for the stability of the food supply. The crops which they cultivated, especially corn, not only provided insurance against the uncertainties of the hunt, they also constituted an important trade item in relations with the Algonkian people further north who had easy access to meat and furs. Pinning family and residential structure to relationships among women served, then, to provide the greatest economic security and the greatest family stability in a culture where men were highly mobile and engaged in hazardous pursuits.

The importance accorded to women in Huron society was reflected in a variety of ways. The Hurons were said to rejoice at the birth of a girl. When injury was done to an individual the criminal was required to compensate the victim's family for the loss. The price levied to compensate for the loss of life was greater for a woman than for a man because, it was argued, a woman was less able to defend herself and was more valuable because of her reproductive capacities.

Young women were accorded the same sexual freedom as men and little emphasis was placed on the distinction between married and unmarried states. Rather, the society recognized a growing commitment between a man and a woman which became stable with the birth of a child. Separation seldom occurred after the birth of a child, although it was recognized that either partner had the right to terminate the marriage. Where a marriage was threatened, the relatives and friends intervened to heal the breach.

If a young girl who had many lovers became pregnant, it was customary that all the men involved claimed the child and the girl had the option of choosing her husband.

In addition to the tasks of food production, preservation, and preparation, and the domestic chores related to child care, hospitality, and clothing making, Huron women participated in many activities practiced primarily by men. They gambled; they belonged to curing societies; they participated in ceremonies, including those confirming political appointments.

The picture of Huron women which emerges is far from the myth of female-dominated matriarchy which has been attached by some to Iroquoian society. Still, it is clear that Huron women of the seventeenth century enjoyed respect and autonomy which was not yet dreamed of by their white female contemporaries.

If the dominance of Iroquoian women has been exaggerated in history and myth, the submissiveness of Ojibwa women has been similarly exaggerated, affected by the image of the warrior's woman walking docilely two steps to the rear.

The Ojibwa people were migratory hunters and gatherers. They followed a seasonal cycle of activities in which the social unit varied from a single nuclear family to a band consisting of up to 15 or 20 families. Bands harvested the resources of a particular area and gathered each year at familiar sites. For six to nine months in the winter, nuclear families lived in isolation from each other. The scarcity of game made dispersion desirable so that hunters would not be in competition for the big game and fur-bearing animals on which they depended. Family hunting territories were demarcated and fear of retaliation through sorcery was an effective restraint on violations of territorial rights. In March and April families came into closer proximity as they gathered maple sap from groves which often were owned by women in particular families. Although families might share a tent during this season they carried on their economic activities independently.

In summer up to 15 or 20 families might gather around a favourite site to fish, gather berries, hunt small game, and engage in ceremonial and social exchanges. In August families went to the wild rice beds to harvest grain. In October individual families left for duck hunting, and by November they dispersed to their traditional family hunting territories.

The economic unit maintained throughout this cycle consisted of a hunter and his dependent relatives. Dwellings were wigwams or tents suited to the needs of a highly mobile nuclear family. Although relationships with more distant relatives persisted in the band or might be established with members of neighbouring bands, the intensity of these contacts was diminished by separation during much of the year.

When a young couple married, they established an independent household and though the marriage might have been arranged on the initiative of parents, the rule was that once the young people established their independence in a separate household they were no longer subject to controls from their families of origin.

In Ojibwa society there was a clear distinction made between male and female roles and public recognition went almost exclusively to the activities of men. The exploits of the hunter, warrior, and shaman were celebrated in stories told in the lodge. The legends recording encounters with the supernatural deal with the affairs of men. The role of women was to send men on their journeys with proper ceremony, to welcome them back with appropriate mourning or rejoicing, to hear and applaud the accounts of their achievements.

Ojibwa women were more, however, than passive complements to the life of their men. They were essential economic partners in the annual cycle of work. They were needed not only to perform the normal domestic chores of cooking, sewing, and child care, but their skills were also essential to weave the fish nets and paddle the canoe during the duck hunt, to construct protective fur robes and roof the birchbark wigwam, to tan the hides and harvest the rice and maple sap.

It was the recognition of their economic contributions which gave rise to the one rigid prescription imposed on Ojibwa women: that they should marry. A bachelor girl was regarded as anti-social. She was the subject of gossip for thinking herself too good for any man. Since men were prevented by their training from practicing women's work, the lack of a female partner worked economic hardship on a bachelor.

The very fact that Ojibwa society's expectations and rewards were focused so predominantly on men meant that women were free to deviate without censure from the normal course mapped out for them. If, once married, they found that state uncongenial, they had the right to terminate the union and seek another mate. They could, alternatively, shun the protection of any man and follow those masculine pursuits which were necessary to survival. Especially if a girl was the only child, a favourite or eldest child, she might be taught masculine skills of hunting or doctoring by her father. Women could acquire supernatural protection or power necessary to the practice of shamanism. If they chose to join a war party, it was assumed that they had had a vision to protect them in this pursuit and they were accepted as warriors, not as abnormal women.

While most traditionally feminine activities were carried on quietly without fanfare, some women were known to have exceptional talents and to follow their vocations with energy and devotion, in the same manner as men called to a particular career. One such renowned woman was known in her region for the quality of her crafts and the beauty and intricacy of the songs and dances she composed. Still, this fame did not alter her lifestyle or her status within her own lodge.

The nineteenth century saw the advance of settlement in Upper Canada, a succession of treaties and land surrenders to which the Mississauga Ojibwa acquiesced, and the virtual disappearance of the migratory tribal lifestyle of the Native people inhabiting the Kawartha district. By 1830 an official reservation policy had been articulated, the objectives of which were to collect Indians in considerable numbers, settle them in villages, introduce them to agricultural practices, and instruct them in religion.

The transition to a sedentary life on reserve land had a shattering impact on all Native groups, but the effects were particularly disruptive for migratory groups like the Ojibwa. Men whose education from infancy was directed to preparing them to assume the roles of hunter, warrior, visionary, saw the opportunities to exercise these skills shrink into virtual non-existence. While the role of men underwent drastic change, Ojibwa women retained many of their traditional roles. They cared for the children, processed the materials available for family use, and added colour and beauty to the daily round of subsistence work through the creation of handicrafts.

Traditional Native standards of behaviour and excellence were progressively eroded with the spread of Christianity and increasing social and commercial contact with European settlers. A succession of laws was passed, designed to promote the "gradual enfranchisement of Indians and the better management of Indian lands." An Indian Affairs administrative structure was established, and reservations became cultural fortresses within which Native languages and Native customs were preserved in isolation from mainstream Canadian society.

In 1868 the first legislation touching Indians was passed by the Canadian Government; in 1968 Native people became involved for the first time in a national dialogue with the Federal Government and the Canadian community. The intervening period has been called a century of neglect. It was a time when Native women were essentially remote and silent, emerging only sporadically to explore the bright lights of the city which promised joys but seldom delivered them.

The drama of women who left the protection of reserves and met a tragic fate in the city, as portrayed in the play *The Ecstasy of Rita Joe*, has tended to create a stereotype of Native women, as those whose souls have been destroyed by white contact. Again the exaggeration of one facet of the Native experience has tended to obscure the reality. The majority of Native women did not disintegrate. They bent their energies to surviving, as they had always done, although the boundaries of their world had diminished. For many Native young people today the associations which have the deepest meaning are the ties they have with these survivors. The grandmothers maintain that unbroken lineage of loving, courageous, resourceful, and creative women who carried the responsibilities of full-fledged human beings in tribal society, who won the respect of the most observant European immigrants, and who, during a long and difficult period, kept alive in their communities a sense of continuity with the past and hope for the future.

Native women of today are breaking their silence to lobby for improved social conditions, to protest the injustice of white man's law, to practise and teach Native arts, and even to run for public office. They are not breaking from traditions, as some have suggested. They are women who share the same concerns as their mothers and grandmothers before them. They are actively engaged in the protection of the quality of family life, in wresting necessities from a harsh environment, and infusing beauty into daily experience. Contemporary Native women have simply accepted the reality that achieving these traditional goals in modern society requires that they put aside their reticence and work out their destiny in public as well as private endeavour.

This article was originally published in Portraits: Peterborough Area Women Past and Present *and was reprinted with the permission of "The Portraits Group" in CWS/cf's Summer/Fall 1989 double-issue, "Native Women" (Volume 10, Numbers 2/3).*

Recipes for Democracy?

Gender, Family, and Making
Female Citizens in Cold War Canada

Franca Iacovetta ⇌

During the past several decades, feminist and left scholars of immigrant and refugee women and women of colour have exposed—both through empirical documentation and careful rethinking of conventional categories of nation, immigrant, and citizen—the material and ideological processes central to the "making" of nation-states and national identities. Many now acknowledge that nation-building is premised on the political and social organization of "difference," and that it creates both citizens (or potential citizens) and non-citizens denied rights. That First World nations in the EU and NAFTA champion globalization and free trade zones while at the same time "police" their borders against "others" (especially Third World migrant workers) speaks volumes on the topic.

Studies of contemporary migration note the growing female presence among migrant workers around the world, while those focused on Canada show how racist, class-based, and heterosexist paradigms continue to define mainstream definitions of Canada and Canadian. This situation prevails despite the long history and enduring impact of immigration to Canada, and its increasingly multi-racial profile especially since the 1970s. Immigrant women of colour from the Caribbean, Asia, Africa, and other "Third World" nations—who are exploited as temporary workers but discouraged from settling permanently and stereotyped as sexually promiscuous single mothers undeserving of citizenship—experience most directly the cruel hypocrisy of liberal capitalist countries that promise opportunity and freedom to all, while simultaneously creating pools of unfree labour and perpetuating damaging race and gender stereotypes. Immigration and citizenship policies are also sexualized and shaped by bourgeois and heterosexual norms regarding reproduction and motherhood. Lesbian women face particular challenges in the face of hetero-normative discourses, and women of colour are eroticized in ways that affect adversely their claims to citizenship.

Specialists of migrant, immigrant, and refugee women workers in Canada have sought to disrupt the dominant liberal construction of Canada as "an immigrant nation" that has always opened its doors to the world's peoples. As their work documents, liberal histories of Canada erroneously depict state-sanctioned racist policies, such as the infamous Chinese Head Taxes and other laws prohibiting the entry of wives and children of Chinese male workers, as blips in an otherwise smooth and linear development towards mature nation-hood. Similarly, nationalist boosters, past and present, see the presence of "successful" white ethnic and "non-white" Canadians as proof of even greater national progress. We must remain aware of the critical distinctions between, on the one hand, an official liberal and highly flawed policy of multiculturalism, and, on the other, Canada's historical and continuing transformation into a multi-racial society and the reality of many Canadians who in daily practice live multi-cultural, multi-racial lives.

As a historian of post-World War II Canada, I wish here to tackle the dominant liberal framework of Canada as a land of genuine opportunity, where all hardworking newcomers can prosper, contribute to the country's rich cultural mosaic, and eventually join the Canadian "family." Such portraits of Canada as a place where everyone can be both "different" and "equal" ignore the fact that, as Tania Das Gupta and I observed elsewhere, Canadian immigration and refugee policy have long been exclusionary and discrimina-tory with regard to so-called "undesirables." But I want also to take the point further. The liberal "we are an immigrant nation" discourse (which perhaps only the U.S. has more aggressively promoted) also ignores or downplays the more invidious aspects of gatekeeping efforts to remake into something else even those newcomers ostensibly "welcomed" into the nation.

In addressing this theme, my article shifts the focus from the present to the recent past, and from the exclusionary practices described above to the immigrant and refugee reception and citizenship campaigns of the early post-war and Cold War decades before 1965. More specifically, it examines the gendered nature of reception activity, and nation-making after 1945. And rather than addressing forms of outright exclusion—such as screening for Communists or deporting newcomers deemed politically or morally suspect, or deemed potential burdens on the state—I adopt an analytical framework central to the emerging social and gender histories of Cold War capitalist societies—domestic containment. By focusing on women, nutrition, food, and gender and family ideals, I explore here how the dominant gender ideologies of liberal democracies in the early Cold War—including a bour-geois model of home-making and food customs and family life—informed reception work and social service activities among immigrant and refugee women. By domestic containment, I mean, of course, both state-sanctioned and volunteer efforts within western countries to police not only the political but also social, personal, moral, and sexual lives of its citizens—a process that, ironically, involved the repression in liberal western democracies of individual rights and freedoms in the name of democratic rights and freedoms. The Cold War, as U.S. scholars such as Elaine Tyler May and Canadian historians such as Gary Kinsman have documented, witnessed the resurgence of a conservative and hegemonic family ideology that "normalized" an ide-alized bourgeois Anglo-Celtic nuclear family, and that in turn served as an (unrealistic and oppressive) standard against which "non-conformists" were harshly judged, harassed and punished.

I have documented elsewhere that even as Canada's social welfare elite boldly declared the birth of the brave new world, they also debated at length the fragility of postwar democratic society and swore to attack all threats— from within and without—to democratic "decency." The threat of the atomic bomb, the Soviet Empire, and homosexual spies were marked features of the Cold War, as were working mothers, juvenile delinquents, (especially but not exclusively gang girls), women deemed sexually promiscuous, and male "sex perverts," and they legitimated a "corrupted democracy" in which the state, and its civilian accomplices, was obliged to censor its citizenry. Historian Geoffrey Smith has effectively used the metaphor of disease to describe how the U.S. state waged a dirty war against all those considered sources of contamination—godless communists, gay civil servants, marginal African-American welfare mothers, and others. Similar patterns obtained in Canada; indeed, recent research on the domestic side of the Cold War, made possible in part because of recent access to security intelligence materials (such as RCMP case files), has begun to challenge the conventional wisdom that Canada's Cold War was essentially, or comparatively, benign.

Mariana Valverde's *The Age of Light, Soap and Water: Moral Reform in English Canada 1885-1925* showed how Canadian nation-building in earlier era required more than protective tariffs, backroom political deals, and a transcontinental railway. It also involved various moral campaigns aimed both to encourage middle-class white Canadian women to procreate (or face "race suicide") and to ensure the moral "uplift" of working-class immigrants and racialized Canadians deemed inferior on both moral and mental health grounds. The desire for a healthy body politic, both literally and figuratively, also fueled nationalist boosters and social and psychological experts commit-ted to national reconstruction after the Second World War. While hardly the sole cause of these post-1945 agendas, the arrival of the Cold War did impart a particular kind of political and moral urgency to campaigns meant to ensure the long-term physical, mental, and moral health of Canada's current and future citizens. Both men and women were targeted by such campaigns, but women, as in the past, were more vulnerable to moral assessment and branding.

My research on immigrant and refugee women and families offers another lens through which we can explore some of these key issues. Here, I take one thematic slice—nutrition and food campaigns and what front-line health and welfare workers called "family life" projects intended to improve poor and immigrant children's lives and remake their mothers. In tackling this topic, I have considered a wide range of players and activities. They include, on the one hand, a variety of gatekeepers, from front-line settlement house workers, citizenship activists, adult literacy workers, and women's organizations to professional social workers, psychologists, and government bureaucrats; and, on the other, the more than two million women, men and child immigrants and refugees, especially but not exclusively, from Europe. Taken together, the activities under scrutiny were many and varied: from the more explicitly ideological work of the Citizenship Branch and the RCMP, both of whom engaged in the political surveillance of the left ethnic press and organizations, to the numerous English classes, social agency services, and neighbourhood "projects for newcomers" undertaken in these years, particularly those aimed at low-income immigrant mothers and children in inner-city neighbourhoods in Toronto.

"Selling" Canadian abundance and modernity to Europe's "backward" women

As the Second World War ended, the media alerted Canadians to the widespread hunger, starvation, and health disasters affecting people from around the world. Canadian newspapers, for instance, contained graphic and heartbreaking images and tales of emaciated Holocaust survivors, flood and disaster victims in Europe and beyond, and malnourished mothers and children from towns ravished by war. Indeed, a central theme emerging in these early years stressed the great gap between Canada as a land of modest affluence and a devastated Europe.

With the coming of the Cold War, this theme also served ideological ends. Among the most popular texts of the day were what I call "iron-curtain escape narratives"[1] published in newspapers and magazines. Highly dramatic, these stories featured the trials and tribulations of those who had escaped "Red" countries, risked health and death to trek across frontier border towns, and eventually reached the western zone in Europe, finally settling in countries like Canada. A *Toronto Star* front-page story (23 Sept.1950) that told about the escape of a "pretty little Czech girl" who "outwitted" Soviet Police," and "waded mountain snows" to reach Canada is emblematic. A PhD student from Prague, 23-year-old Irene Konkova had been arrested "for not conforming to Communist dictates." After escaping jail, she gave the Soviet police the slip at a remote inn and finally reached safety in west Germany. There, she worked in the U.S. zone as a physical education director with the YWCA-YMCA until taking a YWCA job in Winnipeg. Though worried about her parents, Konkova told reporters she was "looking forward to the Canadian way of life," which she associated with western modernity and affluence. When asked what most impressed her about Canada, she noted the "smart clothes and immaculate appearance" of Canadian women and abundance of food. She loved it all: "hot dogs and potato chips impressed her as much as steaks, cakes and candy."

Both U.S. and Canadian propaganda material contrasted the good fortunes of mothers in North America, where liberal capitalism permitted them to raise and nurture well-fed and moral children, with those mothers working far away from their children and in other ways struggling under the exploitation and scarcity prevailing in "Iron Curtain" countries. From stoves to one-stop grocery stores, boosters sang the praises of Canadian modernity. In the Displaced Persons and refugee camps, on ships sailing overseas, and in locales across Canada, women newcomers confronted these messages of Canadian

209
TESTED RECIPES
A NEW COMPLETE COOKBOOK

Chatelaine

Dr. Hilliard helps
teen-age girls meet
their biggest problem

What to do if you're lonely

Chatelaine cover, October 1956

affluence and modernity everywhere: in films, pamphlets and newspapers, in English and citizenship classes, and in settlement house mothers' clubs and YWCA meetings. Cooking lessons, sermons, and health "interventions" sought to reform both Canadian and New Canadian women's cooking regimes and food customs, household management, and child welfare. Indeed, health and welfare experts offered their version of the postwar, bourgeois homemaker ideal, with their middle class and sexist denunciations of married women and wives who worked for pay—among them, huge numbers of refugee and immigrant women. Canadians were encouraged to embrace the newcomers but also teach them the superior values of democracy, "freedom," and, not least of all, the well-balanced Canadian meal.

Post-1945 Canadian nutritionists, food writers, and health and welfare "experts" focused much of their attention on the hundreds of thousands of Europeans who figured prominently among the more than two-and-one-half million newcomers who had entered the country by 1965. Food and health campaigns aimed at immigrant women and their families were varied and numerous. They were part of larger campaigns intended to "improve" the homemaking skills of all women in Canada, and also a piece apart. When, for example, British war brides were offered health lectures and cooking classes, both in England and Canada, they were not only taught to measure ingredients the Canadian way (i.e., the British measured dry ingredients by weight, North Americans by volume) but were deliberately being "trained" for their new role as wives and mothers of Canadian husbands and children. Media coverage of the war brides' resettlement in Canada, a major government undertaking in which the military and Canadian Red Cross played important roles, garnered enormous public attention, and was everywhere punctuated by the image of the fresh faces of young, white British women and their ruby-cheeked children. By contrast, the non-British war brides, including Dutch and Italian women, and their children never attracted as much attention.

Central to these health and welfare campaigns were certain over-riding concerns: preaching the value of a well-balanced diet, efficient shopping and household regimes, planned menus, and budget-conscious shopping. Much of the food advice prioritized middle class ideals regarding preparation and consumption—clean and uncluttered homes, formal dining rooms or kitchen "dinettes," and a stay-at-home wife and mother. This was a far cry from the crowded and sub-standard flats, low and vulnerable incomes, and harried and tired working mothers that were the hallmarks of many newly arrived immigrants and refugees in Toronto and other urban locales.

Canadian culinary ways

As Valerie Korinek's important book, *Roughing It in the Suburbs: Reading Chatelaine in the Fifties and Sixties* well illustrates, Canada's top-selling

Chatelaine, January 1948

woman's magazine offers us an excellent source about postwar food and health campaigns. In saying this, I am not suggesting a direct causation between immigrant women, *Chatelaine* magazine, and changed habits. Rather, the magazine's food features and recipes provide valuable glimpses into the images, assumptions, messages, recipes, professional advice, and other features of postwar health and homemaking campaigns. Korinek persuasively argues that the magazine, despite its image as a conventional woman's magazine, was not composed exclusively of "happy homemaker" images. She also cautions against simple and reductionist theories that assume women readers are passively duped by bourgeois women's magazines. Still, as she adds, the food advertisements and features did provide many conventional images of traditional middle class femininity—including images of mothers who showed their love in part by baking bread, shopping well, and producing a grand variety of cheap but well-balanced meals, nicely presented on tableclothed tables. The ads that delivered such messages also reflected the interests of food corporations whose much-

Chatelaine, August 1981
Photo: Ken Mulveney

needed funds kept *Chatelaine* afloat. Central images emerged in these food features. For example, the "Canadian way" (as Korinek and I detail elsewhere) was usually portrayed by attractive, white, middle-class Canadian women pushing overflowing grocery carts down aisles with well-stocked shelves, or cooking meals in modern and well-appointed kitchens using canned, frozen and other ingredients from their well-stocked pantry shelves, freezers, and refrigerators. Recipes featured affordable meals using cheap cuts of meat— hamburger, for example, in the ever ubiquitous casserole (though by the 1960s curry chicken casseroles actually hit the pages!) and on occasion, fancy hors d'oeuvres and brunches.

By the early 1960s, the magazine began to feature more "ethnic" recipes and even discuss the plight of working wives and mothers, but these were very modest concessions. A case in point is Italian food. U.S. food historians such as Harvey Levenstein and immigration historians such as Italian specialist Donna Gabaccia have documented both that Italians were among the most resistant of the immigrants in the U.S. when it came to pressures to change their food customs and that Italian foods, including pasta, were among the most successfully "mainstreamed" ethnic foods in the U.S. diet. For the U.S., the conflicts and accommodations involving immigrant and particularly Italian foods occurred in particularly dramatic ways during the inter-war decades, following the mass migration of Southern and Eastern Europeans to the U.S. during the period from the 1880s to the 1920s. Levenstein and Gabaccia trace the promotion of Italian and other ethnic foods that were inexpensive, nutritious, and filling—in food magazines, food corporation ads, and also the military, where large numbers of young American men were first introduced to Italian foods. That process invariably involved modifying "foreign" or "exotic" foods for the more timid palates of North American consumers by removing pungent cheeses, or other offensive ingredients, and perhaps including more recognizable ones (cheddar cheese instead of parmesan, for instance). Similar developments occurred in Canada especially though not exclusively during the post-1945 era, when the country witnessed its mass migration of incoming newcomers. Yet, it is also clear that Canadian women did experiment with ethnic recipes, particularly by the 1960s. By then, *Chatelaine* also began featuring (white) "ethnic" women, including working mothers, and their recipes, although this did not preclude a reliance on "cute" and patronizing racial-ethnic and sexual stereotypes.

Nursing inner-city kids, pathologizing immigrant mothers

In contrast to media depictions of ethnic foods, the records of Canadian health and welfare experts from the 1950s and 1960s are less ambiguous with respect to the "problems" posed by the huge influx of immigrant and refugee mothers and their families. Indeed, they are replete with examples of the ways in which Canadian experts singled out immigrant women for special attention or blame, particularly those from more impoverished and "peripheral" rural regions of

Southern Europe. Invariably the "experts" stereotyped these humble immigrants and low-income mothers (and fathers) as too ignorant, isolated, backwards, stubborn, and/or suspicious to access "modern" health care, secure their children's health needs, and otherwise raise their children appropriately as future Canadians.

Such themes emerge in a popular postwar food guide, *Food Customs of New Canadians*, (1959, revised 1967), that was prepared by professional home economists and nutritionists for use by health and welfare personnel working with newcomers. Although presented as a scientific and objective assessment of the food customs of racial-ethnic groups, the guide sought to equip front-line activists with ways of encouraging immigrants to adapt their food patterns to Canadian foods, recipes, equipment, and eating regimes. Some recommendations—drink more milk, for instance—were intended for everyone. Overall, however, the guide reflected middle class, pro-capitalist, North American assumptions such as the wisdom of a three-meals-a-day pattern because it was well-suited to Canadian school and work hours. It also reflected the superiority of Canadian utensils, equipment, and modern appliances.

The guide isolated particular problems for each group under review and assigned teaching suggestions for eliminating them. No group received an entirely negative (or positive) evaluation. For example, while the Chinese scored poorly in hygiene on what the experts considered insufficient cleaning of pots and shared use of chopsticks, they scored well overall on their use of fresh foods, including vegetables. Overall, North-Western Europeans, such as Austrians and Dutch, generally fared much better, though there was room for improvement here too. The guide also referred to the propensity of "Czechs" to be overweight because of their love of dumplings, and the Austrians were cited for consuming too many sweets, and so on.

More problematic were the Italians and Portuguese. Italian immigrant women emerged in the guide as uneducated and primitive peasant women forced to cook on outdoor clay or brick ovens and whose homes lacked the necessary equipment of a modern household: a gas or electric stove, a refrigerator, and storage space. Although praised for their ability to "stretch" meats through use of pastas and other starches, Italian women in Toronto were chastised for spending too much of their modest family income on purchasing specialty foods from Italy such as fine-grade olive oil when cheaper Canadian substitutes were available! (Curiously, only the Italian entry refers explicitly to the possibility that the high rate of female labour participation meant that, after migration, Italian women had less time to produce food.) Similarly, Portuguese women were criticized for buying fresh fish from the market because it was more expensive than the frozen variety. Professional nutritional experts appear to have prioritized their professional repertoire over the values and cultural preferences of their clients. Italian mothers, I should add, were also singled out for their "bad" habit of serving their children a bit of wine with dinner. Their advise, of course, ran counter to that of today when we are told to more closely emulate various features of the continental European diet.

Many of the recommendations contained in the guide reflected the concern of nutrition experts to determine the capacity of immigrant women in low-income families to produce well-balanced meals. Since family economic need pushed many of them into the paid force, these women had even less time for "improving" homemaking skills. Thus, even while public and professional campaigns intended to raise homemaking standards were aimed at the entire female population, class distinctions, which over-lapped with racial-ethnic ones, accounted for some differing remedies. Regrettably, home economists have long assumed that poor people's diets were more the result of their ignorance of nutrition and food preparation than material scarcity. Proposed solutions usually meant imposing austere diet and meal plans on the poor, while the approved diets and advertised meal plans for middle class families permitted various frills and luxuries. In postwar Toronto, experts serving immigrant neighbourhoods were routinely asked whether people in the area seemed aware of general health rules such as Canada Food Rules, cod liver oil for children, hours of sleep, and so on. School nurses and child welfare workers held differing expectations for the mother and children of bourgeois and poor families. On one level, this was a reasonable response: as Cynthia Comacchio observed for an earlier period, it was insulting to teach the finer points about child personality training, or food fussiness and toy fetishes, to poor immigrant mothers who could not even afford "decent" housing. Yet, rather than attack class inequities, the experts focussed on teaching mothers the fundamentals of health—cleanliness, nutrition, fresh air—as though mothers alone could prevent ill health.

Toronto provides a valuable case study for considering how low-income immigrant and refuge women were both given some critical assistance by front-line social workers and health and welfare personnel keen to improve health care among struggling working-class immigrants— and also pathologized by the experts.[2] Front-line social and welfare personnel identified several major problems. They worried about the ill effects of crowded and substandard housing on low-income immigrant families and the special burdens that inadequate wages imposed on women who, whether housewives or working mothers, had to stretch inadequate pay checks to cover rent, food, drugs, clothing, furniture and other necessities. If the family had purchased larger ticket items like furniture on credit (which became more accessible to low-income people in these years) there was the burden of additional bills to pay and collection agencies that would demand payment. The lack of proper cooking facilities in many substandard rental flats encouraged unhealthy eating. Furthermore, the budget item that invariably appeared most flexible was food. To pay the bills, women, it was feared, turned to cheap, usually starch-heavy, foods while cutting out comparatively more expensive and healthy alternatives. The result, claimed nutrition experts, was malnutrition, which might not be detected for years but would nonetheless take its toll on the mental and emotional as well as physical health of immigrant adults and children. An additional concern was that as more middle-class Canadians abandoned the urban core for the suburbs, cities like Toronto would become host to "decaying" inner-city neighbourhoods. In response, experts basically applied old remedies to the current context—home visits, family budgets, meal plans—and tried to attract particularly stay-at-home immigrant mothers into their cooking and nutrition programs. Some modest successes were scored, but the main response recorded is continuing frustration with absenteeism.

A related problem earmarked by health and welfare experts was that the immigrants' seeming ignorance of Canada's social services, combined with their needless suspicion or distrust of outsiders, meant that many immigrant parents, especially mothers, were unwittingly neglecting their children's health. When both parents worked, mothers were unavailable or too exhausted to tend to their children's needs. Settlement House social workers referred to the "tremendous job" required to educate the newcomers about the value of nursery school, summer camps, parent education, and other valuable services "new" and "strange" to them.

Once again, rural non-English-speaking immigrants transplanted to major urban centres were considered most pathetic. In the heavily Portuguese neighbourhood of Parkdale, the International Institute of Metropolitan Toronto (IIMT), the city's largest immigrant aid society, opened up an extension office in 1961 to reach these sorts of women. The project supervisor, veteran social worker Edith Ferguson, collected field work notes and produced case histories meant to illustrate the value of social work interventions. One such case involved a mother who told the visiting caseworker that her daughter had infected tonsils but could not afford to have them removed. Although the family had been registered with the Ontario hospital plan, the mother, who had recently undergone an operation, erroneously assumed that time had to elapse before they could return to hospital. They could not afford a private surgeon's fee because they held a heavy mortgage on a recently purchased house and the husband was sidelined by a workplace injury. A 17-year-old daughter was the only income earner.

In response, the IIMT caseworker contacted the girl's school nurse, who, wrote Ferguson, saw the child immediately, determined her tonsils were badly infected, and referred her to Toronto Hospital for Children. Having secured the parents' trust, Ferguson added, they could assist with other things—completing the husband's workman's compensation application, enroling him in a training course, and checking out job possibilities for a nephew wishing to come to Canada. They also found the daughter, who had been earning a dismal factory wage, a better-paying clerical job in a new local pharmacy interested in a Portuguese-speaking employee.

Like the *Food Customs* manual, front-line workers also stressed the lack of pre-natal instruction for immigrant and refugee women. While the guide focussed on the absence or inadequate pre-natal education in the women's homelands, front-line caseworkers dwelt on a continuing widespread ignorance about modern childfeeding and childrearing methods among immigrant women. Immigrant women, they argued, suffered needless "complicated pregnancies" for lack of doctor appointments. Those convinced to go to out-patient clinics or pre-natal courses learned very little as the lectures and mimeo-graphed diet and instruction hand-outs were in English. When "costly vitamins or medicines" were prescribed, women "seldom" took them "because of a lack of understanding of their worth." Too often, community social workers had had to convince parents to rush a sick child to hospital.

In response, experts searched for better ways to reach immigrant women; translating information pamphlets, more systematic home visiting. Public health workers also began enrolling in Italian and Portuguese language classes, while others lobbied for more local pre-natal and child nutrition clinics. However, the evidence best captures the frustrations of professional nutrition and health experts determined to reshape immigrant behaviour. For example, city settlement records in the early 1960s commented on the high rates of absenteeism among recently arrived newcomers, including Chinese mothers.

Health and welfare personnel also frowned on what they dubbed the inadequate, makeshift daycare arrangements of immigrant working mothers who reportedly left babies and toddlers in the care of grandparents, siblings, and others sitters incapable of providing proper supervision, nutritious meals, healthy recreation, or moral guidance. While all working mothers were vulnerable to such criticism, non-English-speaking immigrant and refugee women were considered particularly prone to bypassing modern daycare centres for informal, often kin-based arrangements. The result in downtown areas was "an epidemic of inadequate child care arrangements." Home visitors had reported on a range of inappropriate sitters: an old age pensioner who lived next-door, a six-year-old child in charge of a two-year-old, and harried mothers with their own children.

Determined to raise the standard of child care in the community, St. Christopher House (SCH), along with the neighbouring Protestant Chil-dren's Home and the Victoria Day Nursery, began experimenting in 1962 with small day care programs "in specially selected family settings." Like other social welfare programs, including progressive ones intended to support low-income working mothers, a carrot-and-stick approach characterized this scheme: all participating mothers had to attend House sessions on child care and home-making.

By the early 1960s efforts aimed at inner-city immigrant mothers included downtown experiments intended to "strengthen family life" by addressing "part of a complex of problems of family living," namely, meal planning, food purchasing on limited funds, and child and adult eating habits. In 1961, St. Christopher House (whose neighbourhood was bounded by Queen St., Bathurst St., College St., and Spadina Avenue) participated in a hot lunch program in a local school, Ryerson Public School, a program launched by the Toronto Board of Education, and the Metro Toronto Social Planning Council. An important program that deserves praise for addressing the needs of low-income children, the hot lunch project nevertheless came with its own carrot and stick: a dozen "undernourished" children from the neighbourhood were given money subsidies (donated by the Rotary Club) to purchase nutritious hot lunches at school provided that their mothers agreed to attend fortnightly classes at St. Christopher for "help in nutrition and meal planning." The children were selected in consultation with school and St. Christopher staff, who could supply "knowledge of family conditions," and a family life worker hired by SCH conducted some follow-up visits. The hot meals were not described but likely consisted of conventional cafeteria fare of this era, such as hot roast beef sandwiches with peas and carrots or cooked ham with (canned) pineapple and (canned) vegetables, and, of course, milk.

According to St. Christopher staff, the hot school lunch produced positive results for both children and mothers. Within a year, they reported a general increase in the number of students buying hot lunches at Ryerson P. S. Meanwhile, the mothers of the subsidized children had shown much "enthusiasm" for their meetings and their "excellent" instructor, a nutritionist from the Visiting Homemakers Association who used a good mix of films, kitchen demonstrations, and lectures. Two years later, a report claimed that teachers had "observed improvement in the health of the children and in the quality of their work in school," while their mothers had "gained practical knowledge through their contact with a nutritionist and a social worker." Furthermore, the classes had provided the women with "their only social experience in an otherwise drab existence" and given them "the feeling that somebody cared." On a more negative note, nutritionists expressed "some concern about finding methods to ensure that the families are taking full advantage of the subsidy to purchase the lunches at school"—suggesting that some immigrant mothers, by choice or circumstance, were spending the money on other items.

The Hot Lunch campaign quickly became incorporated into a more intrusive two-year Family Life project launched at SCH in 1962. With funds from the Laidlaw Foundation, this project too aimed to "reach" rural immigrant women now transplanted to an urban centre and provide them with "a very basic type of adult education for adults eg., consumer buying, citizenship etc." The primary target was the growing number of Portuguese newcomers in the Kensington market area, though Italian, Chinese, Caribbean and other newcomers were also contacted. A full-time Family Life worker and a Portuguese-speaking nutritionist with experience in Home Economics education in Angola were hired. The IIMT also collaborated on the project.

Like other community experiments with inner city immigrants, the Family Life Project produced mixed results. Also, like other front-line work with newcomers, it reflected and perpetuated the marginal status of women from rural, impoverished, and formally uneducated Old World backgrounds.

Immigrant and refugee women's recipes for "Canadian" living

Although anecdotal, the available evidence suggests that refugee and immigrant women also responded selectively to postwar health and homemaking campaigns, even if they could not control the terms of their encounter with social welfare personnel. Like surviving written sources, oral testimonies[3] attest to the critical importance of food to immigrants and refugees and to women's efforts to negotiate a complex culinary terrain. Immigrant and refugee women had their own versions of European scarcity and Canadian abundance: their recollections contain horrific tales of starvation in Nazi camps and heroic ones of gentiles and partisans who risked their lives to get food to hungry prisoners across Europe. Some testimonies offer us humourous recollections of the joys of eating Canadian bread and fruit upon arrival in Halifax, while others record the serious complaints and protests of refugees clearly disgusted by what they saw as over-indulgence and the (sinful) throwing out of leftovers. In addition, immigrant women's cooking and their families' food-eating patterns varied greatly during these years and thus defy easy categorization: some immigrant mothers steadfastly stuck to "traditional" meals in the home while others were keen to experiment with Canadian recipes or convenience foods. The example of Polish Jewish survivors who responded differently to Canadian food customs and the availability of many commercial products suggest too the importance of individual choice. One woman explained her insistence on cooking traditional "Jewish food" in part as a concrete way of continuing to defy Hitler's Final Solution; the other embraced Betty Crocker and other U.S. as well as Canadian products because these newfangled things offered her one of several ways of putting behind the past and moving forward.

While these briefly summarized testimonies are highly suggestive, the gender and generational dynamics involved still require more research and closer scrutiny. Here again, my research sheds some light on various intriguing patterns. For example, some immigrant and refugee husbands definitely pressured their wives to stick to familiar meals and insisted that their children eat their homeland foods at home. In some cases, this gender dynamic overlapped with political as well as ethnic or cultural tones. During the early Cold War years, for instance, left-wing Ukrainian Canadians who belonged to the Farm-labour Temple in Winnipeg evidently insisted on eating Ukrainian as a sign of their continuing resistance to a repressive Canadian state—but they also left it to women to do the time-consuming labours involved to prepare the food. By the same token, certain immigrant or ethnic Canadian men deliberately encouraged their wives to incorporate some Canadian foods because they wished to "embrace" Canada; other times, the opposite pattern emerged. Children also played a role, usually by pressuring their mother to "try" or "buy" Canadian goods—with hot dogs, hamburgers and pop being favourites. In short, the evidence, though fragmentary, points to a seemingly endless number of permutations of hybrid diets in the households of working-class and middle-class immigrants who increasingly combined familiar foods with Canadian foods and "ethnic" foods from other homeland origins.

Particularly for cities like Toronto, immigrant foods (and ethnic restaurants) have clearly changed the city's culinary landscape even as the immigrants' own food customs have themselves been modified. But we still need to trace more closely and to develop a sharper analysis of what some have called the "yuppification" of ethnic foods. I find it especially ironic that the foods that had caused me much embarrassment as a child—spicy and pungent salami, prosciuto, strong and smelly cheeses, dense and crusty bread —have become markers of middle-class taste. But they have also been embraced by people from diverse racial-ethnic and class backgrounds, many of whom, in my view, are not merely using food to affect a certain sophisticated, worldly, or snobbish big city style. Rather, they (we) clearly value the sensuality involved in eating a range of foods, of experimenting with new smells and tastes, of embracing food practices that see eating as a social and cultural practise, not merely a biological function, during which people talk, laugh, argue, debate, and in this and other ways spend hours making and re-making community.

Equally important, we cannot deny the power politics embedded in food wars and customs—to make only brief mention of the so-called "wok wars" that recently received media attention in Toronto, when a WASP Canadian couple complained bitterly and publicly against their Chinese neighbour's cooking habits and "smells." Nor can we omit the role that food corporations, saturation-advertising, and capitalist imperialism have played in shaping women's cooking and shopping habits and family eating customs—how else can we explain what I have called the post-war Dole Pineapple conspiracy? As suggested by the New Left scholars of the late 1960s and the 1970s, who exposed the insidious links between U.S. imperialist ambitions in Latin America, the creation of so-called banana republics, and multi-national food corporations' aggressive promotion of their various tinned and packaged citrus fruits to (North) Americans, the political economy of food must inform our analysis of the social and gender practises surrounding the purchase, production, and consumption of food.

So too do people matter; their curiosity, willingness to experiment, in short their agency—should also figure in our efforts to discern key changes in food customs, including the recent rise of "multicultural" eating in Canada. Nevertheless, when we focus on the immigrant and refugee women and families who encountered Canadian nutrition and food experts on their door steps or in their children's schools, health and welfare offices, hospitals or settlement houses during the early post-1945 decades, a particularly strong theme looms large: working-class immigrant women residing in inner-city neighbourhoods bore the brunt of professional discourses that attributed women's failure to conquer the kitchen and ensure "quality" food and family life to ignorance and distrust of modern standards and distrust of social service interventions.

I am indebted to Valerie Korinek for sharing her research materials and ideas with me. We have co-authored a lenghty article on related themes, entitled, "Jello Salads, One-Stop Shopping, and Maria the Homemaker: The Gender Politics of Food," Marlene Epp, Franca Iacovetta, Frances Swyripa, eds., Sisters or Strangers? Immigrant

Women and the Racialized Other in Canadian History. *Very warm thanks to Cynthia Wright for inviting me to submit this piece and to her and Ian Radforth for their speedy and valuable feedback. Finally, thanks to CWS/cf editor Luciana Ricciutelli and staff for their patience with a scholar who refuses to install the latest information technology at her cottage!*

Originally published in CWS/cf's Summer 2000 issue, "National Identity and Gender Politics" (Volume 20, Number 2): 12-21.

[1]The oral testimonies were selected from a larger data base of more than 100 interviews with post-1945 immigrants culled from the Oral History Collection, Multicultural History Society of Ontario), my sample here is of 28 interviews, most of them conducted in the 1970s, with immigrant women and couples asked about food customs, with the following breakdown: European (18), including European Jewry (4), Asian (2), Carribean (1), and South Asian (India) (3). I also drew on a few anecdotes collected from numerous colleagues and members of audiences who have heard me speak about this research. I thank them for sharing their stories with me.

[2]See, for example *The Toronto Star* from 1945-65.

[3]Sources listed in order of appearance in the text: Toronto City Archives: Social Planning Council (SC) 40, Box 53 File 3 A-International Institute Parkdale Branch (IIPB)1961-63, Report on School Principals at Grace, Alexander Muir, Old Orchard, Charles E. Fraser, and Lansdowne Public Schools; SC 24 D Box 1 University Settlement House, Executive Director's Reports, 1939-1975, Head Resident's House Report, 14 Feb 1952; Executive Director's Monthly Report, 28 May 1956 on Housing and Suburbs: National Federation of Settlements Conference; St. Christopher House, SC 484 IA1, Box 1, Folder 5, Minutes 1951-1952: Annual Report 8 Feb 1951; SC 484 IA1 Box 2 St. Christopher House Folder 1 Minutes 1959, dated 23 April 1959; Box 1 Folder 7 Minutes 1955; Folder 8 Minutes 23 May 1956; SC 40, Box 53, File 3 A-IIPB 1961-63, Report from Parkdale Branch, International Institute (Edith Ferguson) to School Principals at Grace, Alexander Muir, Old Orchard, Charles E. Fraser, and Lansdowne Public Schools; SC 484 IB2 Box 1 Folder 6 "Briefs and Reports 1962-1970," St. Christopher House to the Select Committee on Youth. Oct 1964; Box 2 folder 4 Minutes 1962; Folder 6 "Briefs and Reports 1962-1970," Draft Presentation of the St. Christopher House to the Select Committee on Youth. Oct. 1964 (description of School Lunch Committee, Child and Family Section, Social Planning Council of Metropolitan Toronto, May 1964; Box 2 Folder 5 Minutes 1963, 24 Jan 1963; Report filed by Family Life worker Miss Spadafore regarding Visiting Homemakers Nutritionist.

References

Adams, Mary Louise. *The Trouble With Normal: Postwar Youth and the Making of Heterosexuality*. Toronto: University of Toronto Press, 1998.

Archives of Ontario, International Institute of Metropolitan Toronto Collection, MU6410, File: Cookbook Project, Booklet: Toronto Nutrition Committee, *Food Customs of New Canadians* (2nd ed., 1967, 32 pages). Published with funds from Ontario Dietic Association.

Belmonte, Laura A. "Mr and Mrs America: Images of Gender and the Family in Cold War Propaganda." Paper presented at Berkshire Conference on the History of Women, Chapel Hill, North Carolina, June 1996.

Brienes, Wini. *Young, White, and Miserable: Growing Up Female in the Fifties*. Boston: Beacon, 1992.

Comacchio, Cynthia. *Nations Are Built of Babies*. Montreal and Kingston: McGill-Queen's University Press,1993.

Gabaccia, Donna. *We Are What We Eat: Ethnic Food and the Making of Americans*. Cambridge: Harvard University Press,1998.

Gleason, Mona. *Normalizing the Ideal: Psychology, the School and the Family in Postwar Canada*. Toronto: University of Toronto Press,1999.

Iacovetta, Franca. "Gossip, Contest and Power in the Making of Suburban Bad Girls, Toronto 1956-60." *Canadian Historical Review* 80 (4) (Dec 1999).

Iacovetta, Franca. "Making Model Citizens: Gender, Corrupted Democracy, and Immigrant Reception World in Cold War Canada." *Whose National Security? Canadian State Surveillance and the Creation of Enemies*. Eds. Gary Kinsman, Dieter K. Buse and Mercedes Steedman. Toronto: Between the Lines, 2000.

Iacovetta, Franca and Tania Das Gupta, editors. "Whose Canada Is It?" *Atlantis* 24 (2) (Spring 2000).

Kingston, Anne. *The Edible Man: Dave Nichol, President's Choice and the Making of Popular Taste*. Toronto: McFarlane, Walter and Ross,1994.

Kinsman, Gary. *The Regulation of Desire*. Montreal: Black Rose Books,1987. Revised edition 1996.

Kinsman, Gary and Patrizia Gentile *et al.* "'In the Interests of the State': The Anti-gay, Anti-lesbian National Security Campaign in Canada." A Preliminary Research Report. Laurentian University, April 1998.

Korinek, Valerie. *Roughing It in the Suburbs: Reading Chatelaine in the Fifties and Sixties*. Toronto: University of Toronto Press, 2000.

Levenstein, Harvey. *Revolution at the Table: The Transformation of the American Diet*. New York: Oxford University Press, 1988.

Levenstein, Harvey. *Paradox of Plenty: A Social History of Eating in Modern America*. New York: Oxford University Press, 1993.

May, Elaine Tyler. "Gender, Sexuality, and Cold War: For the U.S." *Homeward Bound: American Families in the Cold War Era*. New York: Basic Books, 1988.

Myerowitz, Joanne. "Beyond the Feminine Mystique: A Reassessment of Postwar Mass Culture, 1946-58." *Journal of American History* 79 (March 1993).

Meyerowitz, Joanne, ed. *Not June Cleaver: Women and Gender in Postwar*

America, 1945-1960. Philadelphia: Temple University Press 1994.

Parr, Joy, ed. *A Diversity of Women: Ontario, 1945-1980*. Toronto: University of Toronto Press, 1995.

Smith, Geoffrey S. "National Security and Personal Isolation: Sex, Gender, and Disease in the Cold-War United States." *The International History Review* 54 (2) (May 1992).

Valverde, Mariana. *The Age of Light, Soap and Water: Moral Reform in English Canada, 1885-1925*. Toronto: McClelland and Stewart, 1991.

Visser, Margaret. *Much Depends on Dinner*. Toronto: McClelland and Stewart, 1986.

Whitaker, Reginald and Gary Marcuse. *Cold War Canada*. Toronto: University of Toronto Press, 1994.

It's Time for Change!

The World March of Women 2000

Pam Kapoor ➤

In solidarity with women from 157 countries, Canadian women are marching to demand that our federal government adopt immediate and effective
measures to end poverty and violence against women in the year 2000.
Across Canada, in all languages, communities, cultures, races, and sectors,
women are calling on the Canadian government to radically change its way
of governing, and to actively promote the public interest and adopt specific
measures that will move us forward in the progressive realization of women's
rights.

The World March of Women 2000 is a global campaign initiated by the
strong vision of the Fédération des Femmes du Québec (FFQ), and has united
over 5000 organizations across the planet around the goals of the March. The
actions of the World March will culminate with a World Rally at the United
Nations Building in New York on October 17th, 2000 in conjunction with
solidarity events around the world. In recognition of the significance of this
global movement, Secretary General Kofi Annan and leaders of both the
World Bank and the International Monetary Fund have agreed to meet with
an international delegation of Women's March participants.

The Canadian Women's March Committee

In Canada, the March has been coordinated by the Canadian Women's
March Committee (CWMC), a diverse coalition borne out of several ad-hoc
gathering of representatives from a variety of national organizations during
the fall of 1998. Formal meetings of this committee began in January of 1999,
and have continued on a regular basis since then. Currently, the CWMC is
comprised of 36 women representing 24 national organizations that work
directly on issues pertaining to women's equality, justice, and rights.

Statistics demonstrate that in all spheres of Canadian society, men
have been allowed to discriminate, oppress and exploit women. Sexual
harassment has been the unspoken norm of our working conditions. Public
and professional institutions have collaborated in the subordination of
women, allowing doctors, clergy, and teachers to abuse positions of power
and sexually assault women and girls. Women with disabilities have been

particularly vulnerable to sexual assault and abuse within families and public institutions. Racism has intensified the oppression of Black women, women of colour and Aboriginal women. Racist biases in public services and in the justice system wind up protecting abusers and further punishing victims. Achieving social justice and the elimination of discrimination will ensure women's access to, and equitable treatment within, Canada's judicial system. It will also enable women to access appropriate health and social services, and to lead in the restoration and reform of valued social programs. This would also include the participation of Aboriginal women in the self-government process.

Given the current climate of economic globalization, international trade, and transcontinental treaties, women are facing a new set of obstacles in our struggle for equality and social justice. To counteract this powerful global tide, all levels of government in Canada must live up to commitments that have been made at the national and international levels to protect human, workers', and women's rights. Women in Canada and elsewhere have a difficult road ahead to achieving true equality. There is a strong desire amongst women in Canada to work more closely with one another and with women around the world on issues of relevance in today's society. To that end, the CWMC has been focused on the broad participation of women in all the March initiatives. The CWMC is committed to the broadening of the collective voice, having prioritized an outreach initiative to facilitate the participation of all women, including Aboriginal, Black, immigrant, refugee, disabled, and rural women, women of colour, young and older women.

Wanting to see Canadian women participate in the World March of Women 2000 in a significant and meaningful way, the CWMC is committed to bridging geographic and organizational gaps within the Canadian women's movement in order to generate as broad a participation base as possible. The CWMC has worked actively to link Canadian women to one another as well as to the international activities of the March, including the global support card campaign.

Women's lives today: How the new global order hurts women

The history of women's rights is one of struggle and hard won victories. Women have long joined together to fight injustice, poverty, violence and war. Because of this, women's lives over the past century have improved in many ways. The strength and tenacity of women everywhere brought us the right to vote. The adoption of the *Canadian Charter of Rights and Freedoms* in 1982 directs Canadian and provincial governments to respect and promote women's equality rights, in particular our right to life, liberty and security of the person without discrimination. More recently, women through feminist organizing struggled for and won state-funded maternity benefits.

Despite these victories, women's basic security and dignity continues to be threatened and denied. Indeed, in Canada, our federal government has radically altered social policies and programs across the country. Cutbacks and the erosion of programs in the areas of health care, education, social assistance, child care, (un)employment insurance, and social housing have directly impacted women. Rape crisis centres, transition houses for women, second-language training and specialized services to immigrant communities are some of the essential resources that have been attacked.

Creating more free markets, cutting taxes, reducing the size of government, privatizing public institutions, deregulating work, removing or ignoring rules that protect the environment, privatizing health care, opening our schools to big corporations—none of these policies imposed around the world by the new global order benefit women. On the contrary, they force women into non-standard and precarious jobs, push our wages down, erode our health and safety, increase the number of poor and condemn us all to much more unpaid work in the home.

68 steps on the march to women's equality

The CWMC has worked with individuals and groups across Canada to develop and present a set of demands to the federal government pertaining to the overarching themes of poverty and violence. Everywhere in the country, Canadian women are demanding that our government take immediate measures to eliminate poverty and violence against women. "It's Time for Change" is the Canadian Women's March Committee's blueprint for broad legislative reform. The document, which contains 68 demands, takes into consideration the needs of women from all communities across Canada, and proposes concrete measures that must be implemented in order to achieve justice and equality for all women, as well as the universal respect of our human rights. These measures are organized around eight themes: protecting and promoting women's social, economic and cultural rights, women's work, the human rights of immigrant women, Aboriginal women, and lesbians, supporting the human rights of women around the world and encouraging women's active citizenship.

The Committee has identified 13 urgent demands to which we are requesting a positive response from the federal government by 15 October 2000. The national lobbying campaign directed at Members of Parliament has been a major strand of the March in Canada. On October 17, 2000 the National Women's Lobby will allow an opportunity to meet and, in many instances, follow up with Cabinet Ministers and MPs to further discuss our demands. The Committee also expects to meet with the Prime Minister.

The World March of Women 2000 is an unprecedented global campaign calling for the recognition of women's lives, the prioritization by national and international governing bodies of our dignity and security, and the incorporation of a broad range of perspectives of women from every community into all decision-making bodies. These are not extraordinary goals —but they do require extraordinary effort—and the participation of all women, both here in

Canada and around the world.

Originally published in CWS/cf's Fall 2000 issue, "Women 2000: Eradicating Poverty and Violence in the 21st Century" (Volume 20, Number 3): 12-21.

Author's Postscript: The Canadian events during the World March of Women 2000 were a tremendous success, by any standard.

Twelve months of organizing in communities in every province and territory culminated in a National March and Rally in Ottawa on October 15th, a Women's "SpeakOUT" on October 16th, a National Women's Lobby on October 17th, 2000 on Parliament Hill, and complementary events in communities across Canada.

By the end, 1,000 individual groups and organizations "signed-on" to the campaign, March-themed activities were carried out in over 200 communities nation-wide, and nearly a quarter-million Canadians signed the international support card directed to the United Nations in the name of this campaign.

Perhaps most significantly, in what some have called the largest mobilization in the history of the Canadian women's movement, upwards of 35,000 people marched onto Parliament Hill on October 15th, 2000 in support of the goals of the campaign, demanding that poverty and violence against women be eradicated immediately.

The international March movement forges on, linking dynamic inter-hemispheric networks in an ongoing effort to advance the "Women's Global Charter for Humanity," created and agreed upon by 6,000 women's organizations world-wide. The Charter is based on five core values: equality, freedom, solidarity, justice, peace.

After 2000, the Canadian Women's March Committee reported on its efforts to the Canadian women's movement. It exists informally today as the Canadian Women's March 2005 Coalition, working towards the elimination of poverty and violence in Canada and making links between local and global actions. The Coalition is committed to continuing the work to meet the 13 demands developed in 2000.

THE FEMINIST DOZEN
13 IMMEDIATE DEMANDS TO THE FEDERAL GOVERNMENT
TO END POVERTY AND VIOLENCE AGAINST WOMEN

1. Restore federal funding to health care and enforce the rules against the privatization of our health care system, beginning with Alberta.

2. Spend an additional one per cent of the budget on social housing.

3. Set up the promised national child-care fund, starting with an immediate contribution of $2 billion.

4. Increase Old Age Security payments to provide older women with a decent standard of living.

5. Use the surplus from the Employment Insurance Fund to increase benefits, provide longer payments periods, and improve access, as well as improve maternity and family benefits.

6. Support women's organizing for equality and democracy by:

a. allocating $50 million to front-line, independent, feminist, women-controlled groups committed to ending violence against women, such as women's centres, rape crisis centres and women's shelters;
b. recognizing and funding the three autonomous national Aboriginal women's organizations to ensure full participation in all significant public policy decisions as well as provide adequate funding to Aboriginal women's services, including shelters, in all rural, remote and urban Aboriginal communities;
c. funding a national meeting of lesbians to discuss and prioritize areas for legislative and public policy reform;
d. providing $30 million in core funding for equality-seeking women's organizations, which represents only $2.00 for every woman and girl child in Canada—*our Fair Share*.

7. Fund consultations with a wide range of women's equality-seeking organizations prior to all legislative reform of relevance to women's security and equality rights, beginning with the Criminal Code, and ensure access for women from marginalized communities.

8. Implement progressive immigration reform to: provide domestic workers with full immigration status on arrival; abolish the "head tax" on all immigrants; include persecution on the basis of gender and sexual orientation as grounds for claiming refugee status.

9. Contribute to the elimination of poverty around the world by: supporting the cancellation of the debts of the 53 poorest countries; increasing Canada's international development aid to 0.7 per cent of the Gross National Product.

10. Adopt national standards which guarantee the right to welfare for everyone in need and ban workfare.

11. Recognize the ongoing exclusion of women with disabilities from economic, political and social life and take the essential first step of ensuring and funding full access for women with disabilities to all consultations on issues of relevance to women.

12. Establish a national system of grants based on need, not merit, to enable access to post-secondary education and reduce student debt.

13. Adopt proactive pay equity legislation.

Excerpted from "It's Time for Change: Demands to the Federal Government to End Poverty and Violence Against Women," published by the Canadian Women's March Committee.

Differences and Identities

The Boundaries of Identity at the Intersection of Race, Class and Gender

Didi Khayatt ➤

Moment one:

The year was 1981. A graduate student at the Ontario Institute for Studies in Education, I was working on my Ph.D., I was a novice feminist, listening to the words of my professors and of my fellow students, and absorbing the ideas that were changing my life and my thoughts. We were being taught to attend to the words of other women, and to locate ourselves in our research. That day, in class, the discussion centred on immigrant women. Students were attempting to grapple with the new (to us) sociological methodology which began from the standpoint of the oppressed, in this case, "immigrant women," and not from a defined sociological category. The debate was raging for close to an hour when finally the Professor was asked to give her opinion regarding what constituted an "immigrant woman." The Professor smiled, looked in my direction, and said: "We have an immigrant woman in our midst, why do we not ask her what she thinks?" Following the Professor's example, the whole class focused on the space where I was seated, and, likewise, I, too, glanced behind me, trying to find the "immigrant woman" to whom the Professor was referring. In my astonishment at being included in that category, I was rendered speechless. It had never occurred to me that I could be perceived as an "immigrant woman," a category which, to be precise, did include me because I had emigrated from Egypt in 1967, but one which did not fit me any more than it did our "immigrant" British Professor.

Why did I reject being included in the category "immigrant woman?" Why did I feel the label did not fit? We had just been told that people who originated from white, western, industrialized countries were not considered "immigrant." I came from Egypt. Why did I think I did not qualify?

The term "immigrant" technically refers to any individual who has a legal status in Canada of "landed immigrant" or "permanent resident" as opposed to being a "citizen." It is a temporary category intended as a period of adjustment, but also an interval during which those who are being considered as potential citizens are being evaluated. Individuals are given the rights and privileges in areas of work and education but are not yet able to vote or to carry Canadian passports. Indeed, historically, immigration policies were traditionally tied to labour needs and the political and economic imperative of populating certain areas of Canada with various skilled and unskilled labour. However, currently, as Roxana Ng suggests, the term is used in government documents to suggest all persons who are "foreign-born," regardless of their citizenship status. She continues:

> In common sense usage, however, not all foreign-born persons are actually *seen* as immigrants; nor do they see *themselves* as 'immigrants'. The common sense usage of 'immigrant women' generally refers to women of colour, women from Third World countries, women who do not speak English well, and women who occupy lower positions in the occupational hierarchy (29).

I agree with Roxana Ng that there is a disjunction between the legal government definition and the commonsense notion of what comprises an "immigrant woman."

Moment two:

I was recently going up the elevator with one of the cleaning staff of my building. Since I often saw her, smiled, and always greeted her previously, it was appropriate that in the time we had to go up nineteen floors we would engage in a short conversation. I asked her where she was from. She answered: "Me from Korea." I informed her that I was from Egypt. She smiled at me and said: "No, you Canadian, me Korean." I laughed and insisted that I was from Egypt. She was adamant. She kept shaking her head and repeating: "You Canadian, me Korean" right up to the floor where I got off.

What had this woman seen in me that was Canadian, that denied my assurance to her that I came from Egypt? Evidently, she perceived me as assimilated, as having power, and, in her eyes, as undifferentiated from those people who fit her notion of "Canadian." Although not all immigrant women are "visible minorities"[1] (another state-originated term) like this Korean woman, and neither are all "visible minorities" foreign-born, often both categories are *perceived* as almost interchangeable. Frequently, as Roxana Ng points out, the situation of Canadian-born "visible minorities" and that of "immigrants" are similar in many respects because of the race and class biases inherent in the social structure (29).

In her analysis of theories of race and class oppression, Caroline Ramazanoglu argued against the notion that racism can often be reduced to class. She rightly points out that black women and, I add, women of colour, "are not uniformly oppressed and they can have contradictory interests in which race, class, ethnicity, and nationality cut across each other." Furthermore, she asserts that colour "is not a static or universal category of disadvantage that transcends all other sources of social difference which determine the quality of people's lives" (134). Although I agree with Ramazanoglu's position, I suggest that colour is *perceived* to be a category of disadvantage, as are other labels, such as "immigrant," "visible minority," "refugee," "person from a developing or Third World country," and so on. This perception does not just stem from bigotry, but is in keeping with official government ideology which currently has designated individuals who fit into state categories of gender and/or of multiculturalism[2] as disadvantaged minorities who should be protected from discrimination and assisted in maintaining equal access to Canadian standards of living. The state, for the most part, has defined these categories, and as such, they have entered the currency of institutional language. They each have a state-produced definition which is designed to signal difference, but, at the same time to protect those included in these classifications from social and economic discrimination in this society. It is precisely because of the perception that these categories are of disadvantage that I am concerned with indiscriminate labelling of individuals. To call me an "immigrant woman" or a "woman of colour" is to trivialize the very real oppressions of those who are within these categories and who are disadvantaged. Moreover, those "benign" categories themselves, although useful for state-supported policies of affirmative action or legal bases for human rights complaints, are not as effective for the individuals themselves who are named within them. They often do not locate themselves in that manner precisely because the categories emphasize what seems to be an inalienable difference between themselves and the rest of the population. Where these classifications are significant is when they are appropriated to provide a feeling of belonging to a community, where this self-labelling may develop into an accepted identity, or whenever these terms are taken up by the women so identified and transformed into a political identity. For instance, being referred to as a "woman of colour" because a person merely belongs to a particular ethnic group, regardless of whether this individual shares any common concerns, becomes more a means of slotting people to force containment, rather than self-labelling, where, even if the same term is applied, it is used by the people themselves to achieve a cohesive community of support based on shared concerns or political perspectives.

In this article, I want to use my own experience to discuss the intersections of sex, race, class, and ethnicity. I am interested in examining how, in the process of assimilating into a new culture, one finds the self definitions which will eventually comprise one's identity. I shall also investigate the distinctions made between the various expressions of dominant white culture and minority groups within the social contexts of Canada. Finally, I shall demonstrate how the categories used to describe race and ethnicity operate differently to keep certain groups oppressed when particular elements are present. These include such factors as sex, religion, sexuality, class, language, financial situation, education, relative darkness of skin, combined with an individual's particular history.

I came to Canada in the late sixties to do graduate work. At the end of my first year in this country, I decided I wanted to stay and I applied for immigration status. At that time, the process included an application form, a set fee, and, most important, an appointment with an immigration officer who would assess, based on a predetermined point system, whether I, as a candidate, was suitable to become a landed immigrant. According to Alma Estable, this hurdle consisted of assigning points to different categories, the most significant of which were employment skills and professional qualifications. Immigrants were also "assessed on the basis of their personal characteristics (such as age, and professional qualifications), education, possession of a skill in demand"[3] (28). Because it was quantifiable, this system was supposed to be neutral and equitable. However, it should be noted that the linking of citizenship with occupation points to a system which is located within the dynamics of capitalism. Canada needed (and still needs) young, skilled immigrants therefore practical training and work experience comprised the category which yielded the highest points. For my appointment with the immigration officer, I dressed up and made a special effort to look "good," not that I had any idea what would really make a difference. I presented myself at the appointed time, and we proceeded with the interview. On the one hand, my age, my very fluent English, my education, as well as my knowledge of Canada's second official language, French, gave me a certain number of points. On the other hand, my chosen field of anthropology did not rate at all on the priority list of needed skills, neither did I gain any points because of professional capacity. I had never worked in my life, not even at a summer job. The education officer questioned me regarding sponsorship by a relative, an organization or a company. I had none. Did I currently have a job? No. What kind of work was I capable of doing? I was a cultural anthropologist, my choices were limited. The poor man obviously wanted to give me the points, but I was clearly ten short of the required number and no amount of prodding into my professional experience could produce one single point more. Finally, he just looked at me, smiled, and said: "I know. I shall give you ten points for charm."

Would I have obtained these points had I spoken English haltingly? Would he have had the same measure of patience with my lack of skills and work experience had he perceived me as a "visible minority?" The accredited "charm" that the education officer appreciated relied on a combination of social relations which are not quantifiable, nor were they meant to be. Points were based on very practical state-defined occupational categories as well as potential characteristics which would eventually lead to job proficiency. I was assigned ten points based on nothing more functional than class and gender. I was located as a woman with no colour. My different-ness was invisible. I was perceived as posing no threat to the ruling white system. As a woman, my potential for work was trivial when compared with my youthfulness, and thus my procreational capacity. Therefore, I would suggest, what he saw was a woman of the right age and class to marry well, after which my assimilation would eventually be complete.

The assumptions implicit in the categories of "immigrant woman," "woman of colour," and "visible minority" conceal real differences in experience and do not account for nor distinguish between the various levels of oppression. They assume a homogeneity of background amongst all people who fall into those various groupings. As Linda Carty and Dionne Brand point out, these terms are "void of any race or class recognition and, more importantly, of class struggle or struggle against racism" (39). Who is entitled to determine who we are? How are those labels made to apply to various people? What do the labels really signify and how does that translate itself in the experiences of the individuals to whom they are applied? The question becomes, not who we are, but who are we perceived to be. It is not my identity which is of concern but the appropriate label that can be attached to me and which can decipher what I represent. The labels are applied by those in power to differentiate between themselves and those they want to exclude, and they accomplish this on the basis of race, class, ethnicity, and other factors. Or, as Linda Carty and Dionne Brand suggest: "State policy around issues of race, class, or sex can be characterized as policy of containment and control" (39).

Moment three:

Several years after I obtained my landed immigrant status, I was finally granted citizenship. By that time I had qualified as a secondary school teacher and had been gainfully employed by a northern Ontario Board. The day I was supposed to be sworn in was finally at hand and I presented myself at the local courthouse. The judge had come all the way from Toronto for just this occasion, to oversee the transition from immigrant to citizen of several people. There were only five of us: a Chinese family of three, an Italian man, and myself. After the ceremony, we were all invited to attend a tea given by the I.O.D.E. (the Imperial Order of the Daughters of the Empire) where they were to present us with a few mementoes, a Bible and a Canadian flag, to commemorate the occasion. I crossed the street from the courthouse to the church basement and found myself surrounded by older women bent on making me feel "welcome to Canada," my new land. Since the other four people had great difficulty with English, I became the centre of attraction, the one queried about conditions of my "old" country. The gist of the conversation was to make me articulate how I had left behind a dreadful situation to come to this land of plenty. The questions revolved around how we dress in Egypt, what and how we eat, do we have cars or is our public transportation based on camel power. I thought they were joking. I believed that they spoke in stereotypes on purpose and I played along. I laughed at their references and exaggerated differences, all in the name of fun, until the moment I left. Since I was the only Egyptian for miles around in that northern Ontario town, people often made humorous allusions to pyramids and camels in order to tease me. It never occurred to me that these women were deadly serious. I did not take offence at the conversation.

I did not translate the exchanges as a level of racism. I knew my background and therefore I did not perceive their presumptions about Egypt as anything more than lack of information. It was many years later when I understood the language of racism that this incident fell into place, that I recognized their benevolent attention, not as welcoming me, but as relegating me to my "proper" place as grateful immigrant. Racism is not about colour, it is about power. Racism is power. It is not only a recognition of difference, but is the explicit emphasis on difference to mediate hierarchy based on colour, ethnicity, language, and race. Those women would probably not have seen me as particularly distinctive if I had met them socially without mention of my cultural background. Within the framework of my class, they had no power over me, which is why I took no offence at their words. I was neither destitute, nor was I essentially dependent on Canada for my well-being. I had emigrated for personal reasons which had more to do with the necessity of finding myself than the urgency of earning my living.

In a recurrent discussion with my friend Marian McMahon (where she plays devil's advocate) she suggests that just because I am not conscious of racism does not mean that I am not the brunt of racist attitudes and remarks. When I interject that racism serves to place an individual in a vulnerable position, that, like sexism, it is flagged as a fundamental difference to highlight hierarchy and therefore justify discrimination, she agrees, but argues that as with those women who say they are not oppressed, my inability to feel oppressed is a denial of my status as a woman of colour, indeed, is in itself a form of internalized racism on my part. I take up her discourse seriously. However, I see that because of my privileged background, I can hardly qualify as "a woman of colour" and it would be inconsistent with the spirit of the common-sense usage of the word for me to assume that label when I have never been submitted to the anguish of discrimination, the alienation of being slotted without my consent, or the experience of being silenced.

Moment four:

In 1967 I came to Canada to do graduate work at the University of Alberta, Edmonton. I was 23. My entire formal education had been in English up to this point, and I spoke French and Arabic as well. Shortly after my arrival, the Chair of the department in which I was enrolled invited all new graduate students and faculty to a party at his house to meet the rest of the department. I attended. I mingled. I exchanged pleasantries with many people. I answered innumerable questions about my country, our traditions, our ways of eating and dressing. When I thought it was appropriate to leave, I went to my host who promptly accompanied me to find my coat and boots, scarf and gloves. It was late October in Edmonton. At the front door, in full view of a room full of his guests, after he turned and winked at them in collusion, he offered me his hand to wish me goodnight. Since I was already dressed to go out, I tended my gloved hand toward him, and following the rules of formal social conventions I had been taught, I said, with all the dignity of youth: "Please excuse my gloves." At which point, the entire room full of people who had been watching our exchange, burst into laughter. I looked at them in surprise, and left without bothering to give or receive any explanation. To my youthful naive eyes, these people proved to be boors without redemption. Not for a single second did it occur to me that my behaviour was inappropriate, or that I needed to feel self-conscious. To me, they were simple amiss in their manners.

Laughter and humour, when aimed at a certain person or is at the expense of someone, when the individual is not "in the know" because she is new to a culture, when she is different from the rest of the group in some way(s), is a method of ridicule or mockery. It is particularly so when the person being laughed at is not included in the jocularity. If I had not the assurance of privilege, the knowledge that my manners were impeccable, the assumption that my class background transcends most western cultures, I would have withered in shame, wondered at my possible "faux pas," and wilted from the insensitivity of these, perhaps, well meaning strangers. However, I did not give them a second thought. Consequently, in the same way that, in the first account, I knew that the term "immigrant woman" did not quite apply to me, I did not experience this incident as humiliating nor as a negative comment on my race or ethnicity. Even though I had just arrived from Egypt, a country considered "Third World," even though as a new graduate student I was at the bottom of the intellectual hierarchy within the context of that department, and even though I was probably perceived as non-white, I had the composure of class and the confidence of privilege to protect me from the exclusion to which I may have otherwise been subjected and of which I may have been made an object.

From a very young age I was taught that I was the daughter of such a family, from a certain class, a particular city in the south of Egypt. Managing class is not just the knowledge that one is born to privilege, but the understanding that this privilege may transcend different social and cultural changes. For instance, it did not come as a surprise to me when one day, as I was shopping for a sofa-bed in Eaton's department store in Toronto, the salesman recognized my family name. He came from Egypt and asked me the inevitable question to verify whether I came from that certain city in Upper Egypt and whether I was a Copt. Even though I was living on the limited means of a graduate student, he was immediately deferential. It was not me personally that he recognized, but how class operated in Egypt. The major discount he gave me was, perhaps, a reflection of his acknowledgment that, even in this new country, he had not forgotten the conventions of our past lives, that we both belonged—if differently—to a distant past, that in the vast sea of Canadian foreignness, we shared a common history.

The formation of my identity includes my class, my colour, my ethnicity, my sex, my sexuality, and my religion. These factors seem constant since I have been old enough to identify myself. They are my location. However, other elements which are as important are variable, their relevance modified by changes in personal politics, circumstances, age, career, current ideologies, the general political climate.

I came to this country over two decades ago. I could speak both official languages very fluently and with minimum accent. The relative lightness of my skin colour combined with my privileged class background have spared me from experiences of discrimination or prejudice. At best, I intimidated people around me, at worst, they found me exotic. Even though "exotic" is, broadly speaking, a form of racist categorization, the word is often used to imply a kind of difference which is coveted rather than scorned.

Although I claim not to have suffered racism, I am often made to feel aware of my different-ness. Strangers regularly mispronounce my name but then people in North America often stumble over most names which are not simply spelt or are uncommon. When I refuse to use my first name, Madiha, it is because of the way it is frequently butchered, and because it is seldom remembered (even when people comment on "what a pretty name" it is). Moreover, as a result of its foreignness, if my name is being called out to take my turn at being served, it is often presumed that I do not understand English (especially if I hesitate before answering); therefore, I am addressed in that loud, over-enunciated diction which assumes that volume will make up for language. But it takes only a moment to set people straight.

I would maintain that those incidents are very minor, that if they constitute racism they, essentially, do not have any recognizable consequence on my life. I have been assimilated well. I do not stand out. I have had to adjust to Canadian cultural significations, not to prevent discrimination against me, but to avert feelings of inadequacy which may spring from lack of communication. I have had to alter my British accent, to tone down my formal manners, to adapt to many Canadian customs and traditions. I have learned to use cultural referents to project the messages I want to convey. Consequently, I become visible because I am recognizable. What is concealed is my history, what is hidden is my Egyptianness. However, I am in a position to produce my history when it suits me, when it adds a new dimension to my qualities, and certainly not when it can be held against me.

Can it be said that my very insistence on assimilating is itself a response to levels of internalized racism? Is the invisibility of my foreignness precisely an indication of racism? I have argued that I do not suffer racism because of class and skin colour. This does not deny that racism exists, but it does suggest that, given certain other factors, I am not touched by its virulence. My assertions contain elements of contradiction because they stem from an issue which is complicated. The fact remains that I am spared, that in the ability to define my own identity, to convey a specific persona, to contain these contradictions, I can manage to control how I am perceived. I choose to make myself invisible only in that I want to blend; I do not want to stand out. Consequently, although I can be heard, a part of me is silenced.

Rigid definitions of race and ethnicity which do not account for the fluidity of the categories are not useful in that they mask the differences of class and location. They fail to respect individual identities or to take into account lived experiences. Conversely, gender as a category, when considered a basis for discrimination without accounting for class or for race, conceals distinct and intelligible levels of oppression within the category. And yet, Catharine

MacKinnon reminds us, "to argue that oppression 'as a woman' negates rather than encompasses recognition of the oppression of women on other bases, is to say that there is no such thing as the practice of sex inequality" (20). It is also difficult to forget an early comment by Audre Lorde who informs us succinctly that: "Black feminists speak as women because we are women" (60). Feminism transcends yet recognizes difference. As a feminist, I bring to the discussion of race and gender the specifities of colour and class. Unless the boundaries of race, gender, class, and sexuality intersect to make visible the various nuances of each category, the usefulness of each becomes lost in a hierarchicalization of oppressions. In other words, if we isolate each characteristic in an attempt to make it visible without taking the whole framework into consideration, we are, in effect, rendering invisible the significant factors which combine to produce situations of oppression and discrimination. We are reduced to piling one oppression on another to show the extent of discrimination, or we attempt to debate which form of oppression—race or gender or class or sexuality—is more potent. Gender, race, class, sexuality have to be considered together and at the same time. They must each convey specific location without denying the distinctiveness of individual experiences.

Finally, if I have personally ever felt the alienation of national identity, it is not in Canada but in Egypt. Egypt, situated in what the Europeans called "the Orient," is anchored in people's minds as "a place of romance, exotic beings, haunting memories and landscapes," but, as Edward Said continues: "The Orient was almost a European invention" (79). In Egypt where colonization by French and English have reworked class structures to incorporate western notions of "culture" and "education," upper class society demands an understanding and consideration of and an affinity with the conquerors, with their locus of power. Some of the questions Said addresses in his book are appropriate:

> What...sorts of intellectual, aesthetic, scholarly, and cultural energies went into the making of an imperialist tradition...? What is the meaning of originality, of continuity, of individuality, in this context? How does Orientalism transmit or reproduce itself from one epoch to another? (15)

I am a product of his problematic. Despite my pure Coptic origins, each one of my family sports European names, my father Andrew, my uncles Albert, Maurice, Robert and my aunts Edna, Margaret, Dora. My generation was defiantly christened with Arabic names, another conqueror, but closer in geography and culture. It is in Egypt where I have never properly learned my native tongue that I feel like a foreigner. I have never read Egyptian literature except in translation. The imagery that filled my formation is that of distant lands. I recited poems on daffodils when I had never set eyes on one. I described fields, streams, and forests while living in a land of intensive agriculture and wasted deserts. I knew of snow but had never experienced it. I enjoyed western toys, bought real estate in London playing British *Monopoly*, and donned clothes made in Europe. I attended French and English schools, and an American university. I walked the streets of Cairo and felt I did not belong because I spoke my own language with the exaggerated enunciation of one who is not using it continually; my idioms are out-dated, my expression forgotten. When I return to my native land, I stand as foreign, am perceived as alien. I was never assimilated because class demanded a perceived difference from the masses. In Canada I am integrated because my survival depends on my being like everybody else.

The author gratefully acknowledges the support and ideas of Marian McMahon, Frieda Forman, Linda Carty, Peggy Bristow, and Dina Khayatt. They should get the credit of refining my thinking, although I take the responsibility of my words.

A version of this article was published in Encounters: Culture, Values and Identity. *Eds. Carl E. James and Adrienne Shadd. Toronto: Between the Lines Press, 1994. This article has been reprinted with permission from Between the Lines Press.*

Originally published in CWS/cf's Spring 1994 issue, "Racism and Gender" (Volume 14, Number 2).

[1]"Visible minority" is a comprehensive term which describes any person who is non-white, including South Asians, Blacks, Chinese, but also, broadly speaking, Native Canadians. The term is not currently utilized because its use has proven limited.

[2]"Multiculturalism" is a term which expresses the varied ethnic heritages of Canadians. *The Collins Dictionary of Canadian History, 1867 to the Present* (by David J. Bercuson and J.L. Granatstein), states that the term was first heard in the 1960s "as a counter to the emphasis on Bilingualism and Biculturalism that characterized the Liberal Government." The authors explain that the "ethos of multiculturalism is that every Canadian, whatever his or her origin, has the right to honour his or her heritage in Canada." However, the dictionary also notes that government policies of multiculturalism were subsequently perceived to be a political tool to remove francophone concerns from the limelight by introducing those of other rapidly growing ethnicities. This strategy promoted politics of divide and rule by using federal funds. Marjory Bowker distinguishes between two versions of multiculturalism, in the first of which "all cultures are allowed to prosper and flourish amongst their followers; that nothing in the law be allowed to impede the personal enjoyment and enrichment to be derived from one's ethnic heritage." The other version, like the above, "concerns government funding for ethnic programs which tend to divide rather than unite, resulting in a loss of cohesiveness and eventually a fragmented Canadian culture" (87).

[3]Alma Estable mentions that the Immigration Act was revised considerably

although the point system continues in effect, and where practical training and experience continue to be assigned the greatest number of points.

References

Bercuson, David J., J.L. Granatstein, eds. *The Collins Dictionary of Canadian History, 1867 to the Present.* Toronto: Collins, 1988.

Bowker, Marjorie. *Canada's Constitutional Crisis. Making Sense of It All.* Edmonton, Alberta: Lone Pine Publishing, 1991.

Carty, Linda, Dionne Brand. "'Visible Minority' Women—A Creation of the Canadian State." *RFR/DRF.* 17(3) (1988).

Estable, Alma. "Immigration Policy and Regulations." *RFR/DRF.* 16(1) (1987).

Lorde, Audre. "Sexism: An American Disease in Blackface." *Sister Outsider.* Freedom, Ca.: The Crossing Press, 1984.

Ng, Roxana. "Immigrant Women in the Labour Force: An Overview of Present Knowledge and Research Gaps." *RFR/DRF.* 16(1) (1987).

MacKinnon, Catharine. "From Practice to Theory, or What is a White Woman Anyway?" *Yale Journal of Law and Feminism,* Fall (1991).

Ramazanoglu, Caroline. *Feminism and the Contradictions of Oppression.* London and New York: Routledge, 1989.

Said, Edward. *Orientalism.* New York: Vintage Books, 1979.

Biting the Hand that Feeds Me

Some Notes on Privilege from a White Anti-Racist Feminist

Nancy Chater ━

It is a particular challenge when speaking from a position of privilege to advocate a complete transformation of the ideologies, structures, and everyday practices which re/produce that very privilege. How does one account for the contradictions of one's own location in the process? How do I, as an anti-racist white feminist writer? I believe that those of us who identify as white anti-racist feminists must examine these contradictions as we name, and act on, our stake in dismantling white supremacy. Articulating our examination of these contradictions to other white women (and men) in a politicizing and mobilizing way is an important component of the contribution we can, indeed must, make to anti-oppression movement which necessarily includes anti-racist struggle.

White feminist writers and activists, myself among them, have to confront the ready potential of speaking or acting in ways that are based on or slide into arrogance, moralizing, self-congratulation, liberal politics, appropriation, careerism, or rhetoric when conceiving of and expressing our stake in fighting racism. Each of these un/consciously preserves power—in this case, white power—and none contributes to revolutionary change in terms of how access to and use of power are re-distributed.

Understanding and naming our motivations to "bite the hand that feeds" privilege also forms the foundation on which political alliances with women (and men) of colour and other anti-racist whites can be built. For this reason, they need to be rooted in a clear, strong, and tenacious ethics and politics.

By the term "anti-racist feminist" I mean feminist theory which takes into account the interaction of race, class, gender, ability, sexuality, imperialism, and colonialism in capitalism. This analysis must be credited to the Asian, Black, First Nations, and Latina feminists, and self-named feminists of colour who have managed, despite barriers, to have their voices heard.[1] While feminism must be grounded in this integrative analysis, that is not always the case when gender-based feminism is taken as the norm. Therefore I consciously place an integrative, anti-racist feminist framework at the center of feminism.

***

In response to the question, *why is fighting racism something white feminists need to do*, I want to summarize a few key feminist concepts, noting that it is feminists of colour who have put this question on the table. One answer is that racism is a form of oppression, and all oppression is wrong, unjust, brutal, deadly. A second reason is that feminism is defined as a collective struggle, open to all women, whose goal is the liberation of all women from all forms of oppression. It follows that because some women are oppressed by racism, while others are privileged by it, racism is a feminist issue. Related to this is the understanding that all forms of oppression reinforce each other. A third reason is that in a racist society, all people are *racialized* and are located, with unequal power, in relation to each other. So racism involves and affects all women. A fourth reason is that the survival of all peoples and the earth itself are interdependent: the way a society is willing to exploit and waste those it has relegated to the bottom speaks of the future conditions for everyone except the few at the top, unless fundamental systemic and cultural transformations that benefit those with the least social power are fought for and won.

While each of these is plenty reason enough, the point has also been made, by both feminists of colour and white feminists, that a system built on relations of dominance impacts profoundly and destructively on those who also in other very real ways benefit. Reaping rewards is destructive to those who gain at the expense of others. This is a difficult but critical concept, particularly for anti-racist white feminists to address. I say "particularly" because I think it is racist to look to feminists/people of colour to attend to the destructiveness of privilege *for white people*.[2] To speak of the personal and social distortions and loss of humanity for those who dominate is indeed a major cultural and political task. It is not easy to accomplish when social status, identity, and success are grounded in consumer capitalist values that are individualistic, materialistic, hierarchical, and competitive.

To convince those in, or those seeking, positions of power and privilege of the cost to them requires a fundamental cultural transformation. It requires a reclaiming and re-investing with meaning of concepts that to many in North America have come to sound lame and rhetorical. These concepts include genuine collectivity, respect, including self-respect, connectedness to all life, honesty, sharing, honour, and inter-dependence. Each of these terms has been used hypocritically for so long by spokespeople of the institutions of the dominant society that their meanings have been trivialized. This dilemma of language and meaning points to the need for cultural revolution which is absolutely vital to the transformation from a racist culture to a truly social democratic one.

***

I have already named a few of the potential pitfalls of challenging racism from a position privileged by it. There are certainly others. Minnie Bruce Pratt, for example, identifies four roles taught her as a white, Southern U.S., Christian-raised woman which she struggles not to fill in doing anti-racist work: judge, martyr, peacemaker, and preacher (31). Another feminist activist with white-skin privilege, Melanie Kaye/Kantrowitz, identifies two problematic models: the missionary and the crusader (277).

Being self-reflexive and engaged are two important elements. Pratt notes that there are "interior questions I have asked myself about my understanding of anti-Semitism and racism," and then "raise[ed], out loud, with other women" (31). In this way she engages herself in the issues about which she speaks, sharing her own process of change, and her stake in individual and societal change. I have taken a valuable lesson from Pratt and from African-American activist and writer June Jordan, who describes her self-reflexive strategy in the following way:

> What I try to do in a political essay is, whatever the problem is, I try to show people how I am part of the problem. And then as I try to articulate how I'm working my way *out* of being part of the problem, I need to persuade people to join me. And I think this is a way of making allies, rather than making people feel a we/they formulation (Christakos 1992, 33).

***

I want to raise three contradictions of white privilege that I confront in speaking or writing about racism and the social construction of whiteness to other white people.

One such contradiction emerges in the tendency of anti-racist whites to assume an edge of moral or intellectual superiority over and distance from other white people, especially those displaying a lack of politicized awareness of racism. This has been termed the "flight from white" (AWARE workshop). This position establishes a false separation between oneself and those with whom one actually continues to share access to inequitable benefits, regardless of divergent consciousnesses.

A second contradiction of white privilege arises if one unconsciously claims a speaking stance, or occupies a cultural space which is itself created by the privileged access to resources—white exclusivity—which one at the same time critiques. Let me illustrate this from my own experience. In 1985 a co-worker and I sought to publicize the murder of a young Black woman in Toronto whose death, we argued, could have been avoided had the police taken seriously the previously assaultive behaviour (only the day before) of the man who killed her. At that time, I was not conscious of how my racialized white identity figured into my assumptions that I was "a woman speaking out for a woman who couldn't" (Chater 102). I meant "the woman who couldn't" because she was silenced by death. I have since reflected on my unequal power and unexamined racist attitudes toward the Black friend and co-worker with whom I worked on this publicity campaign. Because of her apparent "shyness" and seeming timidity in the face of authorities, I saw it as a matter "of course" that I did the interviews and public speaking at a (white feminist) rally we linked up with. We did not discuss the possibility of her taking up that public space and empowering herself and Black women in the process. Then, by publishing an account of this experience in a predominantly white feminist journal, my voice again occupied a cultural space organized by racism, i.e., white exclusivity. I am not saying that I should not have done or said anything as a white woman in white-dominated spaces. My point is that in the process of anti-racist transformation, decisions about who speaks, about whom, and how, and where, involve issues of privilege which need to be examined.

The third issue involves the times when I do *not* speak out or confront racism, yet am aware of wanting to. (This does not include the ways and times in which I unconsciously accommodate myself to white-skin privilege.) For me this involves instances with actual persons or groups, as well as not completing and seeking publication of writing that deals with racism. I have witnessed and heard about white women not speaking out when they were conscious of something wrong numerous times. This pattern is created by contradictions between power and powerlessness within individuals.

What stops me in such moments? A sense of powerlessness. Which then propels fear of conflict. This sense of powerlessness is a double impediment to my politics and my ethics. Not only does it silence and derail my capacity to fight back, but it also allows me to obscure the always-relative power I do have as a white woman. Since part of white-skin privilege is the "freedom" not to be aware of it, conceding to feeling powerless in the face of actual confrontations with racism serves only to reproduce racism.

My sense of powerlessness is real and painful. It arises from the emotional and physical violence to which I have been subjected as a child and woman; growing up working class; and from living as bisexual. It stems from the ways in which I am objectified and silenced. However, after reflecting on areas of both power *and* powerlessness in my life, I have realized that when what drives my powerlessness is allowed to take the front seat and determine the course of my actions, it keeps me from figuring out how to use the always-relative power I do have to fight back, to resist. It renders me speechless and compliant to my privilege, which also includes being university educated, English speaking, Canadian born, Anglo Saxon, not visibly disabled, young, Christian-raised, born in and residing in a capitalist centre in the west/global north. So, my battles against being rendered powerless and my striving toward empowerment are motivated partly by my commitment to be *accountable to my access to power.*

Of course, there are many external barriers to speaking out and being heard, such as access to public space and the power to determine meaning. Before, or while, confronting those barriers one needs first to overcome many internalized blocks.

***

What is privilege? How is it defined or measured?

Privilege can be a problematic term, it seems to me, because material conditions that all peoples inherently deserve, have a right to, when not available to all, become a privilege. Food, housing, health care, education, bodily autonomy, love, respect, and self-determination as peoples can be termed privileges because of their inequitable distribution. Having access to them, however, is not necessarily experienced as a privilege. Nor would I advocate that basic human and civil rights and responsibilities be understood as privileges. Privilege, like power, is relational and so constantly shifting. Although privilege and power have historically sedimented along lines mediated by class, caste, nation, race, gender, sexuality and so on, many, if not most, people have a complex and contradictory relationship to power and powerlessness, to privilege and oppression.

Given the relational nature of privilege, from one social context to another, and over a lifetime, balances can shift. For example, in my previous paid work as a waitress the balance of power differed in each of the following cases: when I ejected a white homeless man from the restaurant; when I took an order from a customer who dehumanized me through his gaze and manner, yet I was coerced by the economic relations into being "polite"; when I went into the kitchen and made a request of a young male working-class Tamil dishwasher; when I was ordered around by a ten-year-old child already familiar with authority over service workers; when I trained a new staff member with less "seniority," and so on.

As well, we all move from being children to adults. Often this entails early experiences of being dominated and of wide-spread neglect and abuse. Many, especially women, encounter blocks when it comes to exercising their power as an adult in situations of conflict because early-instilled patterns of feeling paralyzed in the face of fear are triggered and take centre stage. This can create a sense of powerlessness that overshadows awareness of access to social power.

I raise the question of these fluctuations because I think they are important to consider when asking for individuals or groups to "acknowledge privilege" and "give up privilege." In the context of sometimes-contradictory relations to privilege, what does that really mean; and how will it be done? I am aware that revolutionary change occurs primarily through subjugated groups *taking* and exercising power, not through those who have it "giving it up." To the extent that privilege can be consciously given up, what strategies are workable? Nobody wants to give up what they experience as subsistence or even as necessary. The question then arises as to whose definition of "necessary" counts, individually or between groups and nations.

Regarding questions of necessity, the problem is not, for example, that some have food but rather that some do not. Of course, we all need food. The degree of the *disparities* between people, between groups, and between nations with regards to access to resources—where some throw vast amounts of food away while others starve or barely survive picking through and consuming garbage—is a function of unequal patterns of distribution. The political economy of resource distribution is a critical framework within which to analyze the disparities that create "privilege," and then determine courses of action to change inequitable distribution.

***

More than one white feminist writer has argued that white women need to understand the struggle against racism as *our own fight*. In fact, this is something which most of the still-small number of white feminists (see Kaye/ Kantrowitz; Pratt; Ramazanoglu; Rich; Spelman; Warland; Ware; Christakos, 1991) taking up racism and the construction of whiteness/white supremacy have grappled with. Adrienne Rich writes that "our stake as women in making those connections is not abstract justice; it is integrity and survival" (304). Kaye/Kantrowitz critiques the shortage of this understanding and finds evidence to "suggest ... how little the [gender-based feminist] movement has taught [white women] to see struggles against racism as life-giving, nourishing; as our own" (277). Vron Ware points out that, historically, the alliances white gender-based feminists have made with various groups, including Black people, have often "emerged or disappeared depending on whether or not they were very useful to the women making them at the time" (239). This illustrates the need for lasting and ethical grounds on which white feminists attempt to build alliances with peoples of colour. Otherwise, tokenism, exploitation, and expediency can be, and are, practiced by white feminists.

The shortage of gender-based feminist commitment to anti-racism is particularly significant in light of the fact that the abolitionist movement of the 1830s and the civil rights movement of the 1960s gave rise to and deeply influenced the first and second wave of the North American women's movement (see Ware 30–35, 239–241, Davis 148). Involvement in these two movements led many white women "from an awareness of injustice against [B]lack people to a sense of their own struggle for equality" (Ware 32). Yet it is clear that making the links in what can be described as the reverse direction, from gender-based feminism to anti-racist feminism, continues to meet with much resistance from many contemporary white feminists. This can be attributed to the erasure of histories of resistance in North American education and culture, and the extent to which gender-based feminism replicates this; to the basic denial of racism which "is so central to the way in which modern racism works" (Razack 148); to the way whiteness itself is rendered invisible to white people as a racialized identity; and to the euro-and white-centrism that gender-based feminist discourse has continually reinscribed. There continues to be a need, therefore, for white feminists to produce work that intentionally addresses why and how the struggle against racism is indeed life-giving and ours, too.

At the same time, it is crucial for those of us who are white anti-racist feminists to recognize the long tradition of white women challenging racism (see Pratt, Rich), and being, as Adrienne Rich puts it, "disloyal to civilization." Though small in numbers, they are an important source of knowledge and strength for white anti-racist feminists today.

A culture founded on racism means that for white people "a part of ourselves will remain forever unknown to us" (Rich 308). Salish-First Nations writer Lee Maracle asserts that acquiescence to racism "condemns white folks to being half-smart, half human" (172). Racism impacts white people in such a way that we do not usually feel, identify, or desire the missing "half" of our smarts and our humanity. The apparent disconnection from yet dependence on privilege is a major barrier to working towards our own critically conscious wholeness.

While on the one hand, speaking of a need for "wholeness" of white people pales in relation to the ongoing brutality marshaled by racist imperialism against peoples of colour in Canada and everywhere, on the other hand white feminists committed to "biting the hand that feeds us" the bitter pill of supremacy must attend to such fracturing contradictions of privilege. By doing so we can forge and sustain the ethical grounds on which we can and must contribute to revolutionary feminist change.

The author would like to thank Tiss Clark, Robert Gill, and Nicole Hosten for their comments as I developed this article.

Originally published in CWS/cf's Spring 1994 issue, "Racism and Gender" (Volume 14, Number 2).

[1]To cite some of the writers who have critically informed my thinking since my exposure, then active seeking, began in 1987: Audre Lorde, bell hooks, June Jordan, Patricia Hill Collins, Beth Brant, Lee Maracle, Paula Gunn Allen, Chrystos, Linda Hogan, Linda Carty, Dionne Brand, Himani Bannerji, Nourbese Philip, Chandra Mohanty, Swasti Mitter, Trinh T. Minh-ha, Gloria Anzaldua, Sky Lee; anthologies such as Gloria Anzaldua, ed., *Haciendo Caras: Making Face, Making Soul*, San Francisco: Aunt Lute Books, 1990; Makeda Silvera, ed., *Piece of My Heart: A Lesbian of Colour Anthology*, Toronto: Sister Vision Press, 1991; Shabnam Grewal *et al.*, eds, *Charting the Journey: Writings by Black and Third World Women*, London: Sheba Feminist Publishers, 1988; Beth Brant, ed., *A Gathering of Spirit: A Collection by North American Indian Women*, Toronto: Women's Press, 1988.
[2]Even though it is a painful irony that most of what I have learned to date about this effect has come from writers of colour.
[3]Both Minnie Bruce Pratt and Adrienne Rich make this point and provide examples.

References

Alliance of Women Against Racism etc. (AWARE). Workshop on "unlearning racism." Conducted in Toronto in 1989. (AWARE is a mixed-race feminist collective from Vancouver).

Chater, Nancy. "waitress in linguiform." *Room of One's Own.* 12 (2/3) (1988).

Christakos, Margaret. "The Craft that the Politics Requires: An Interview with June Jordan." *Fireweed.* 36 (1992).

Christakos, Margaret. "Axioms to Grind." *Room of One's Own.* 14(1) (1991).

Davis, Angela. *Women, Race and Class.* New York: Vintage Books, 1983.

Kaye/Kantrowitz, Melanie. "To Be a Radical Jew in the Late 20th Century." *The Issue is Power.* San Francisco: Aunt Lute Books, 1992.

Maracle, Lee. "Ramparts Hanging in the Air." *Telling It: Women and Language Across Cultures.* Ed. Telling It Book Collective. Vancouver: Press Gang Publishers, 1990.

Pratt, Minnie Bruce. "Identity: Skin Blood Heart." *Rebellion: Essays 1980-1991.* Ithaca, NY: Firebrand Books, 1991.

Ramazanoglu, Caroline. *Feminism and The Contradictions of Oppression.* London: Routledge, 1989.

Razack, Sherene. "Racism in Quotation Marks: A Review of Philomena Essed's Work." *Resources for Feminist Research.* 20 (3/4) (1991).

Rich, Adrienne. "Disloyal to Civilization: Feminism, Racism, Gynephobia." *On Lies, Secrets, and Silence: Selected Prose 1966-1978.* Ed. Adrienne Rich. New York: Norton, 1979.

Spelman, Elizabeth V. *Inessential Woman: Problems of Exclusion in Feminist Thought.* Boston: Beacon Press, 1988.

Ware, Vron. *Beyond The Pale: White Women, Racism, and History.* London: Verso, 1992.

Warland, Betsy. "the white page." *Proper Deafinitions: Collected Theorograms.* Vancouver, Press Gang, 1990.

An African Child Becomes a Black Canadian Feminist
Oscillating Identities in the Black Diaspora

Notisha Massaquoi ━

The Black Diaspora is a place where the points of departure and the points of arrival are constantly shifting and the search for certainty, stability, and fixidity are overshadowed by the dynamic nature of transnational flows. Diasporas have come to be associated with resistance to the nation-state within which they are located, and in this vein, transnationalism and Diaspora are best discussed through the politics of culture, identity, and subjectivity (Grewal and Kaplan). Where transnationalism and Diaspora often become interchangeable, referencing the cross-border migration and flows of capital, the Black Diaspora is an environment that fosters the invention of tradition, ethnicity, kinship, and other identity markers. It is a place where multiple African communities become a monolithic entity and ethnic differences are replaced with national pride. It is also a place where it becomes more advantageous to identify with the homogenous group, "Black people," as opposed to ethnic or national identities; and regional differences become less important than our shared experience of immigration, racism, and search for belonging in Canadian society.

As African women living in the Diaspora, we are not only sustaining the Canadian nation, we are supporting a nation we left behind. We are also part of creating new nationalities and identities. This paper situates a discussion of the rearticulation and reinventing of African identities diasporically and the impact of transnational factors on gendered African identities as they appear globally. My personal project has been to make sense of my own lived experience as an African woman with multiple identities living in Canada through the exploration of a collective past and lived experiences of others who both reflect and contradict me. Through this process I have come to understand that academic engagement and theoretical analysis are necessary exercises in the exploration of the varied experiences of African women in Canada. This exploration needs to be framed in the concepts of otherness, resistance, reclamation, and reconstitution of identity, all while exploring concepts and language which do not always support and in fact frequently oppress (Massaquoi). The lived experiences of African women are highly complex and require analytic strategies that take into account their experiences with multiple oppressions. A discussion which reflects the realities of

African women in Canada must be grounded in the specific materiality of African women's lives while acknowledging placement, displacement, and movement and while interrogating the dominant racialized and gendered discourse of the Canadian nation.

The nature of our arrival in Canada clearly articulates many things about how we will be perceived to be, our place in the nation-state, and our entitlement to what the nation state has to offer. For those of us arriving in Canada as African people from former British, French, and Portuguese colonies, the very concepts of identity, sovereignty, and entitlement were already eroded and our cultural traditions as colonized people have created and maintained the ideal situation of otherness prior to and upon arrival at Canadian borders. Without the concept of the "other" the Canada we know would not exist, nor would Canadian concepts of self- image be shaped, mirroring the imperialistic thoughts that shaped the self- image of Europe and Europeans (Said 1993).

Our identity as African people in Canada is predominantly one of oscillation. To be African is to be in a state of constant negotiation between our minority status in the nation state and our majority status in the country of origin; and, to complicate matters even further, our affiliation with African-American culture which is just south of our border (Hess; Gilroy1993). For many of us, our identity is based on a constant longing for the imagined home, the one that no longer exists, that many of us were too young to remember, that we have infrequently visited, and the one which became frozen in time and romanticized at the moment of arrival in Canada.

The understanding of transnational identity cannot be separated from the way selves are narrated. Every self is a storied self and every story is grouped within the realities of others so that each subject consists of both the stories we tell about ourselves and the stories told by others. Theories that support the subjectivity of African women in Canada need to interrogate responses to racialized and gendered discourses of nation, movement, and democratic citizenship (Spivak) There needs to be an amplification of how African gendered bodies negotiate their identities and politics across dynamic spaces. This, for me, translates into how we begin to understand transnational identities as reconstructed subjectivities that have been altered by the external forces associated with migration and reconstitution in new locales.

Subjectivity is constituted by reference to discursive practices and shaped by the effects of power operating through individuals. The relation between the marginalized subject and the other is framed in terms of oppositions and exclusions (Venn). It is not sufficient to note that the subject emerges in relation to an "other;" rather, the marginalized subject is necessary since her or his narrative becomes a measure of power. The theorization of resistance, revolution, and change cannot be separated from the theorization of the formation of subjects and selves.

The transformation of subjectivity is a combination of the cognitive, affective, and embodied experiences and none of these dimensions can be privileged. However, there also needs to be an engagement in geographically bound self-discovery which involves the conventional understanding of what it means to be an individual whose identity has been created by acts of refusal, imposed upon as a subordinate other, or premised on exclusion. I am originally from the south currently living in the north. I immigrated to Canada as a child with my parents which reduces my "authenticity" in either locale significantly. My parents are African immigrants and I am their diasporic child. Let's see: if I scan the "Are you an authentic African immigrant?" checklist, I fail miserably. English is my first language and my authentic African accent is long gone. I did not flee war. I did not need to be saved by feminist advocates from the horrible knife of FGM practices. I do not need assistance navigating the Canadian system by well-meaning social workers. I have a Canadian education and, most importantly, a Canadian passport. I am not considered African by most and, ironically, I am viewed by few as Canadian.

Identity, I believe, becomes a necessary component of agency, resistance, and survival in the Black Diaspora and for me has been attained through an ongoing process of self-analysis and interpretation of social position and the meanings given to those positions through discourse. Who are we as African women? What is written about us? What is our experience in Canada? Identity can also be viewed as the folding of the outside inside oneself (Venn), a folding that changes the aesthetic of the self. The Black Diaspora is both a contested space where identities are being constructed, and a subversive space where we are free to explore our multiple identities as African women as opposed to those imposed upon us by the dominant culture. It is also a space that brings different groups in direct contact with one another both materially and symbolically and pulls competing and conflicting discourses onto a shared terrain for examination.

These sites of recognition in the formation of identity acquires its specific content from the transnational narratives of belonging and ancestry (Gilroy 1995). It is the route to our roots, the understanding of identity which cannot be separated from the conceptualization of who we are as narrated identities dependent on geographical location. I remember vividly being pinched in a department store by my mother for being rude to a stranger. A woman had asked me what my name was. I responded and then proceeded to spell it for her. She was astounded that a five-year-old could spell such a long and unusual name. I asked her if she couldn't spell hers and hence the pinch. I remembered this story as I stood in front of a bank teller some 30 years later in Sierra Leone. "What is your name?" she asked me as I was attempting to make a bank transaction. "M-A-S-S-A-Q-U-O-I," I replied. "I can spell!" the bank teller snapped. I was very embarrassed. Of course she could spell Massaquoi. It is a common name in Sierra Leone.

Upon reflection, I can say in my defence that I have spent most of my life in Canada having to spell my name, spell out my identity, so that when asked I don't even say it, I automatically spell, clarify it, so we can end the interaction as quickly as possible instead of listening to the poor attempts at pronunciation and misspelling; and fielding responses such as "very unusual, where are you from?" Then explaining where Sierra Leone—not Surinam, not Senegal, not Sri Lanka—is in the world. This is usually followed by a 15-minute discussion of how and when I got here, the last five minutes of which I am praised for my wonderful English. Learning to navigate these diasporic transactions is also what creates distance and disconnection from my imagined "home." Upon reflection, these very geographically-based experiences confirm for me the notion that the validation of cultural identification in one context and the negation in another is what contributes to the oscillation of identities in the Diaspora. Our immovable and relatively unchanging characteristics such as racial identity, physical attributes, and our names continue to connect us to an African identity while we experience life in a locale which can not fully validate this identity. We move between the space of identity validation and the space of identity negation with the Diaspora and country of origin oscillating in between, acting as sites of endorsement and sites of exclusion.

Imagined homelands and frozen recollections

Due to physical distance we are often removed from the natural evolution of our countries of origin—the culture, the struggles of the people, the country's interplay with development and modernity—making it impossible to maintain cultural authenticity in the new home where we are now located. What we develop is cultural hybridity which is a combination of the frozen recollection of the home we left behind and our interactions with the one within which we currently exist. Journeys across the borders of regions and nations create concepts of home, community, and identity shaped by histories and memories we often inherit, and the political choices we make.

My parents, despite their choice to raise their children in Canada, were intent on raising us within an African context and with an African sensibility. The values, traditions, customs, and practices that were bestowed upon us were those that my parents had personally experienced up until the point of departure from Sierra Leone. What they did not factor into this upbringing was that culture is dynamic and ever changing and as a result of this innocent oversight we were raised more traditionally and less progressively than our counterparts in Sierra Leone. We were also in constant conflict with our adopted Canadian culture which often expressed itself as contrary to the beliefs within the walls of my home. And, we had to contend with the fact that as children we were quicker to adapt to and understand the new cultural context than our parents who were still in that state of frozenness. That is the cold space upon arrival in our new home where we are suspended in uncertainty, caught between the culture we left behind and the new one we don't quite yet understand, and the transgenerational stability of knowledge that can no longer be assumed (Appadurai). It is in this state that home as we remember it becomes that ideal place, a warm place, the romanticized place. Home for me became the imagined home of my parents, the romanticized home I had created from vague memories and vivid stories of our past. The past being not a land which I can authentically return to but essentially a mental warehouse of memories framed within the collective historical imaginations of individuals and communities distributed globally throughout the Black Diaspora.

As groups migrate and regroup in new locations and reconstruct their narratives, claiming identities based on history, social location, and experience is always a matter of collective analysis and politics. "Home" becomes a crucial concept for immigrants and how one understands home, community, belonging, and citizenship is profoundly complex and personally political. The concept of home is intrinsically tied to identity, which is something we hold dear in the Diaspora. The way in which home is often experienced is tied to loss (of what has been) and to the imagination of what is to come. It is the thing that connects us to something larger than ourselves. It is a space that can embrace us when this Diasporic space fails. What does it mean to connect psychologically to the majority in Africa while physically being the minority and racialized other in Canada? What does it mean to be an African living in Canada? As groups migrate across borders they collectively reconstruct their homes and histories and fine tune their identity politics which no longer have the same meaning in these different geographical and political contexts.

Exploration of traditional African Diasporic notions of flight to an imagined homeland have been less often geographic than psychological and introspective. From the perspective of many of us currently living in the Black Diaspora, this notion is literal and based on physical geographic movement and locality shifting. Halie Gerima visually and metaphorically captures the essence of this concept in his prolific film *Sankofa*, named for a philosophical, mythological bird found in the folklore of the Akan people of Ghana. It means to move forward, and reclaim the past. In the past, we find the future and understand the present. The film deals with the contemporary reality of the Diaspora and how we as Diasporic Africans harness our collective memory and learn from our collective experience. From a Foucauldian perspective, we are looking at the notion of time-span, space and histories. We are living in the now as a movement from the past and coming towards the consciousness of the present. It is a combination of the memory of having been and an anticipation of what is to come, the loss of what has been and the imagination of what is to come. This leads to the question: Who are we at the present (Foucault)? Imagined homelands become homes only in memory, homes that we cannot return to. They become homes that are historically situated in the imaginations and cultural storage rooms within the imaginations of individuals spread out over the world.

For some, home is an idealized womb of nurturance and safety; for the realist, the imagined home is a dynamic, persistently changing entity which is impossible return to in any authentic sense (Said; Gilroy 2000); and for others, home is the Canadian context in which we currently exist despite the inhospitable climate we must often navigate as African women. What we essentially have are multiple imaginings of home which influence and are influenced by identity, perceived freedom, and the political strength to affect change. If we are to say that geographic space provides historical and cultural anchors, I must analyze how my Africaness becomes embedded in me and how racism, sexism, homophobia, and classism are involved in my relationship with the Canadian nation.

African roots + live aid = feminist development

As an African woman living in the Diaspora, I am fighting a different kind of gendered and racialized struggle, but one which is very much tied to the struggles of women on the African continent. I feel that having such a voice is not only a bridging mechanism but one which provides the grounds for the amplification of a unified experience of Black Women globally. We must encompass new definitions, paradigms, and understandings of political, cultural, and ethical issues of the Black Diaspora (Mohan and Williams; Gilroy 2000). We must also interrogate the experiences of women of the south living in the north who meaningfully oppose roles imposed on them by white feminist movements, such as third world models, or cultural interpreters, or poster children for the benevolency of the Canadian state. I don't quite cut it as an African woman in mainstream Canadian feminist circles. I am far from the model native informant or an authentic third world subject. I spend far too much time supporting, engaging and researching Black women in Canada, particularly considering how race, class, and gender intersect to impact their current existence in the Canadian context, as opposed to focusing my efforts on the impact of imperialism, colonization, and globalization which have been the burden of my sisters in Africa.

For those of us raised in North America during what I term the Live AID[1] era, the images of Africa, poverty, and its starving, primitive people are etched in our psyche with no other images to replace the carefully constructed media view of the Continent and its people for the past 18 years. This has become how Africa is imagined and constructed in western discourse and intellectual spheres. What we have is a modern version of the us/not us, west vs. the rest polarization that followed colonization and the foundation for contemporary biases of academic readings of gender, race, class, and identity in the west (Razack). Identifying myself as being a woman of African origin had a profound effect on the formation of a Feminist consciousness while growing up in a Canadian context.

In this imagining of Africa, my role as African Woman then comes to serve as a point of contrast between definition of modernity and primitivism (Mohanty). With further interrogation, we understand that the dominance of the west in the global system, the legacy of colonialism and imperialism all imagine African Women as passive victims, as being unable to escape traditional practices which are harmful or unhealthy, unable to care for their children, uneducated, and pawns of war (Agger; Amadiume; Byrne). For many of us living in Canada at this time, the ability to facilitate movement toward the so-called advanced west symbolized passage from this "primitive" image to one of "civilization." Those that we left behind subconsciously, or even consciously, were viewed as being in a state of inferiority (Brennan).

I truly became a feminist when I was able to look at those negative, racist images of African women and identify myself within them, despite my overwhelming desire to distance myself from any connection; when I was able to interrogate what was real and what was a controlling image (Collins), and what was an empowering symbol; when I was able to hold my head up and say that those women are me, my aunties, and my grandmother and that I will create my own version of their story, contrary to what the west believes us to be.

Through this exercise of articulating who I am as an African women living in the Black Diaspora, I have come to understand that, possibly more than any other grouping, we are very much an imagined community and in effect foster complex imagined identities. Both politically and economically, Diasporic people have an important role to play in contemporary social processes operating at an increasingly global scale, and any theory which reflects the realities of Diasporic people must account for complex, dynamic, overlapping geographies and oscillating identities while interrogating the relations between Diasporic subjects, nation-states and and cultural dynamics. The process of displacement, movement, and replacement to a new locality fosters a unique form of political consciousness which has been central to my development as an African Woman and as a Black Canadian feminist.

Originally published in CWS/cf's Winter 2004 issue, "Women and the Black Diaspora" (Volume 23, Number 2): 140-144.

[1]A Global musical benefit organized by Bob Geldof, held on July 13,1985, to raise funds, aid relief and awareness to support the victims of the Ethiopian famine.

References

Agger, Inger. *The Blue Room, Trauma and Testimony Among Refugee Women: A Psychosocial Exploration.* London: Zed Books, 1992.

Amadiume, Ifi. *Reinventing Africa: Matriarchy, Religion and Culture* London: Zed Books, 1997.

Appadurai, Arjun. 1996). Disjuncture and Difference in a Global Cultural Economy in *Modernity at Large: Cultural Dimnersions of Globalization.* Minneapolis: University of Minnesota Press, 27-65.

Brennan, Timothy. *At Home in the World: Cosmopolitanism Now.* London: Harvard University Press, 1997.

Byrne, Bridget. "Towards a Gendered Understanding of Conflict" *IDS Bulletin* 27 (3) (1996): 31-41

Collins, Patricia Hill. *Black Feminist Thought: Knowledge, Consciousness and the*

Politics of Empowerment. New York: Routledge, 1990.

Foucault, Michel. "Politics and the Study of Discourse." *The Foucault Effect.* Eds. Graham Burchell, Peter Mill and Colin Gordon. Chicago: University of Chicago Press, 1991. 53-72.

Gilroy, Paul. *Against Race: Imagining Political Culture Beyond the Color Line.* Cambridge: Harvard University Press, 2000.

Gilroy, Paul. "Roots and Routes: Black Identity as an Outernational Project." *Racial and Ethnic Identity.* Ed. Herbert W. Harris. London: Routledge, 1995. 15-30.

Gilroy, Paul. *The Black Atlantic: Modernity and Double Consciousness.* Cambridge, Massachusetts: Harvard University Press, 1993.

Grewal, Inderpal and Caren Kaplan. "Global Identities: Theorizing Transnational Studies of Sexuality." *GLQ: A Journal of Lesbian and Gay Studies* 7(4) (2001): 663-679.

Hess, Barnor. *Un/settled Multiculturalism: Diasporas, Entanglements, Transruptions.* New York:Zed Books, 2000.

Massaquoi, Notisha. "Writing Resistance." *Our Words, Our Revolutions: Di/verse Voices of Black Women, First Nations Women, and Women of Colour in Canada.* Ed. G. Sophie Harding. Toronto: Inanna Publications and Education Inc, 2000. 83-88.

Mohan, Gilles. and A B Zack-Williams. "Globalization from Below: Conceptualizing the Role of the Black Diaspora in Africa's Development". *Review of African Political Economy* 92 (2002): 211-236.

Mohanty, Chandra. *Feminism Without Borders: Decolonizing Theory, Practicing Solidarity.* Durham and London: Duke University Press, 2003.

Razack, Sherene. *Looking White People in the Eye: Gender, Race, and Culture in Courtrooms and Classrooms.* Toronto: University of Toronto Press, 1998.

Said, Edward. *Culture and Imperialism.* New York: Vintage Books, 1993.

Sankofa. Halie Gerima and Shirikiana Aina (Producer). Gerima Halie (Director). Mypheduh Films Inc., 1993. 125 min. Video/C 999: 1596.

Spivak, Gayatri. "Diasporas Old and New: Women in the Transnational World." *Textual Practice* 10 (2) (1996): 245-269.

Venn, Couze. *Occidentalism: Modernity and Subjectivity.* London: Sage Publications, 2001.

"The Queen and I"
Discrimination Against Women in the *Indian Act* Continues

Lynn Gehl ⟿

How would you answer the question, "What is your cultural identity?" There are many people living in Canada today who struggle with issues of identity in terms of their culture, ethnicity, minority status, sexuality, and race. Many people have relocated to Canada against their will, while others, for many reasons, made a conscious choice. These dislocated and relocated people at some point in their lives, if not all their lives, will wrestle with their identity and their sense of belonging. However, for many Aboriginal[1] women and their children, this is not a question of belonging and being but rather a question of law. The oppression of Aboriginal women is of a particular nature as their cultural identities are entangled with legislation.

In Canada, federal legislation known as the *Indian Act* determines who is and who is not an Indian. Legislation titled the *Indian Act* was first formalized in 1876. In 1869, "patrilineage was imposed" on Aboriginal peoples and *Indianness* was defined as any person whose "father or husband was a registered Indian" (Stevenson 67). Eventually, the *Indian Act* underwent one of its infamous amendments known as section 12 (1) (b). Here the *Indian Act* dictated that Indian women who married non-Indian men were no longer Indian. The goal of the *Indian Act* was one of assimilation and the arduous task of civilizing the savages—a national agenda. Ironically, what this type of policy did was subjugate women to the status of "chattel of their husbands" (Voyageur 100). It stripped women of their rights socially, politically, and economically and made them dependent people. By European standards, this was the proper location for women on the social evolutionary scale (Stevenson).

The struggle to have the gender inequalities removed from the *Indian Act*, which continues today, has been a difficult journey. The paternalism is so well entrenched in Aboriginal communities that Native women have been struggling externally as well as internally to have their rights acknowledged. The oppressed have often proven to be the oppressor.

One of the first women to speak out publicly about section 12 (1) (b) was Mary Two-Axe Early in the 1950s (Bear). Legally, the first women to argue the discrimination set out in 12 (1) (b) were Jeanette Lavell and Yvonne Bedard (Bear). In 1973, the Supreme Court of Canada determined that the *Indian Act* was exempt from the Canadian Bill of Rights. Part of the problem in the fight to remove the discrimination was the lack of unity and support the women had from the National Indian Brotherhood (NIB, now known as the Assembly of First Nations). The NIB feared changes to the *Indian Act* would jeopardize the federal government's legal responsibility to status Indians (Bear).

In 1977 Sandra Lovelace took her complaint against 12 (1) (b) to the United Nations Human Rights Committee and in 1981 they found that Canada was "in breach of the International Covenant on Civil and Political Rights over sexual discrimination" (Bear 210). And in 1979, the Tobique Women's Group of New Brunswick[2] organized a grassroots march from Oka, Quebec to Parliament Hill in Ottawa[3], the country's capital, to raise awareness of Aboriginal human rights specific to women.

In 1985, the *Indian Act* was apparently amended to conform to the equality provisions of the *Canadian Charter of Rights and Freedoms*. I add "apparently" to this statement because, despite what many people think, much of the gender discrimination still exists. Myself, my family, and many other First Nations people[4] continue to be excluded from registration as Indians.

Aboriginal people who wish to pursue registration as a status Indian[5] with the Department of Indian and Northern Affairs Canada (INAC) must have extensive knowledge of their family history, great determination, as well as awareness of the continued discrimination against women and their descendants perpetuated by section 6 of the current *Indian Act*.

In the remainder of this paper I will take you on a genealogical journey of five generations of my family history. Then I will discuss the difficulties I encountered when forced to fulfill the documentation requirement of the application process for registration with INAC. Finally, I will explain how INAC exercises section 6 of the *Indian Act* to my application for registration and how it continues to discriminate against me and my family on the basis of gender and marital status.

I am often asked, "Why is registration as a status Indian so important?" This question is difficult to answer because, as my understanding of my identity and my right to identify with the Aboriginal First Nations has evolved, so has my reply. Most people living in Canada are fortunate enough to identify with their place of origin. This is not true for many Aboriginal people, including myself. One can argue that identity to Native people is not a subjective process but rather something that legislation provides. For Native people, registration as an Indian with INAC is an important component of their cultural identity. For example, the denial of Indian status has excluded many Aboriginal women and their descendants from residing on the reservation and from sharing in the benefits available to the community. Further, registration as an Indian in Canada is required to participate in rights to land, education, health care and, most importantly to share in similar cultural values. Larry Gilbert articulates this challenge well in the preface to his book,

> As an Algonquin Indian from Ontario and as an aboriginal person who has lived and worked outside of the aboriginal community all of

my life, I am acutely aware of the identity crisis suffered by many aboriginal people separated from their homeland, their tribe or clan, their language and their culture. Seeking and protecting one's identity is a personal and a very human aspiration. It is seldom that the state intervenes and declares persons are not who they really are. That is the legacy and the reality of the *Indian Act*. (Gilbert iii)

On January 2, 1945, my great-grandmother wrote a letter to Ottawa. She explained that she was having some difficulty with her nationality and was wondering if they could help in any way. "I would like to know if I am counted as an Indian. Please let me know soon." Four weeks later, she received a reply which read as follows:

Dear Madam:

I am in receipt of a copy of your letter recently sent to Indian Affairs Branch, Ottawa, with regards to your status as an Indian. In reply I wish to inform you that you are not an Indian as defined by the *Indian Act*. At the time of your marriage to Joseph Gagnon, a white man, any rights you had as an Indian of the Golden Lake Band ceased, (section 14 of the Indian Act), and you became a white woman.

Yours very truly,
H.P. Ruddy,
Indian Agent

Prior to the implementation of Bill C-31, the *Indian Act* discriminated against Indian women by revoking an Indian woman's status upon her marriage to a non-Indian man. "She was stripped of her *Indian identity* and not able to live on the reserve with her extended family." (Voyageur 101, my emphasis). However, an Indian man was allowed to retain his status and pass it to his non-Native wife. This inequity prevented Indian women from passing Indian status on to their children in their own right, while permitting Indian men to do so. This is how my great-grandmother lost her entitlement to status and, as a result, so did my kokomis[6] Viola. Of particular interest is that my great-grandmother's husband was also a Native person through his mother (my great-great-grandmother), not his father. Hence, because of the male lineage criteria he too was deemed a *white* person. His mother Angeline married a *white* man and became *white* as well.

My kokomis was born and raised on the Golden Lake reservation (now known as the Algonquins of Pikwàkanagàn). In 1927, at the age of 16, she and her parents were "escorted off" the reservation by the Royal Canadian Mounted Police. They lost their home, most of its contents and, from what my kokomis tells me, they were given nothing to start their new lives as free people. Welcome to civilization. After all, this was the intent of the *Indian Act*, to protect the Indians until they had assimilated into white society and then to set them free[7] (Jamieson).

Consequently, when my father was born, Viola recorded her racial origin as French despite the fact that both of her parents, Annie and Joseph, were Native. By this time, it had been deeply ingrained in her soul that she was French. My kokomis gave birth to my father where she was born, on the reservation, were she felt most at home. He was born of unknown paternity. The midwife who attended my kokomis was my father's great-aunt Maggie, and this is the person with whom he spent his early years. His life on the reservation came to an end, just as his mother's before him, when his Aunt Maggie was also escorted off by the RCMP.

When one considers the legacy of the oppressive legislation, the effects of residential schools, and the poverty, it should not be difficult to understand the deleterious effects on Indian women and their children materially, culturally and psychologically (Jamieson). These effects leave people lacking confidence and self-esteem, which makes them vulnerable to illiteracy, hostility, alcohol, and suicide. For example, in 1992 Health and Welfare Canada reported the suicide rate as "at least three times the national average..." (cited in Norris 205). This scenario is a reality all too familiar for Native people. For myself this also proved to be the legacy of the *Indian Act*. My father died suddenly in 1988. I know that this was the direct result of the oppressive nature of the *Indian Act* and the forced assimilation process. A few years later, I proved his eligibility for registration; however, I was too late.

When Bill C-31 came into effect, I was aware that the major changes were to reinstate women previously enfranchised because of whom they married. My kokomis and her mother, Annie, would regain their status. I was also aware that Annie's husband, Joseph, was entitled through his mother, Angeline. This was where the challenge presented itself. In order for me to have my father entitled, I had to prove that both of his grandparents were entitled. Alternatively, I had to prove that both Annie and Joseph were entitled to be registered with INAC, so that status could be passed to my grandmother in such a manner that she, in her own right, could pass it to my father; otherwise, he would be affected by what is known as the second generation cut-off rule, which results in the loss of Indian status after two successive generations of parenting by non-Indians (Wherrett).

I started by spending many hours with my kokomis learning my family history via the oral tradition. Without this opportunity, I would not have been successful, and for this I am eternally grateful. It was difficult, though, because she was bitter and often sad about her life on the reserve. She did remember our family history well. She told me about her mother Annie, and her father Joseph. I was most interested in finding more information about Joseph's mother, Angeline. My kokomis did not know much about Angeline, although she did repeatedly say that, "Angeline was a black Indian from the Lake of Two Mountains who adopted two French boys whose mothers were unwed."

After the family history lesson, I constructed a family tree and began the formidable task of searching for the documents to prove my ancestral link to a past band member. This proof is required to fulfill the Registrar's demands that "...the applicant connect the ancestor to an existing band as the basis of his [sic] entitlement regardless of the date of evidence" (Gilbert 16). I sent away to the Office of the Registrar General for birth certificates of my father, my kokomis, and myself. I also sent away for the marriage certificate of Annie and Joseph as well as the death certificate of Angeline. The Registrar General holds the records of births, marriages, and deaths for 95 years, 80 years, and 70 years respectively. After this time period, the records are microfilmed and then held at the Archives of Ontario located in Toronto.

When I first entered the Archives of Ontario library, I was overwhelmed. The library essentially consists of numerous filing cabinets stuffed with microfilm. There are archivists on staff to assist in your research, from 9:00 a.m. to 5:00 p.m. Needless to say I was discouraged, especially when I read an outline that was prepared by the archives which discussed Aboriginal sources. The outline explained the difficulty with Native surnames and how they vary widely in records written by people who did not speak their languages. An additional blow was a caution that read: "Aboriginal ancestors more than three generations away from you may be hard to document and therefore very difficult to claim status from" (Archives Ontario 3). I had an enormous task ahead of me with having to research back five or possibly six generations to Angeline's male family members.

A person requires a variety of skills in order to do this type of work, many of which I acquired on the job. I spent many hours using microfilm readers searching, compiling, and analyzing documents. I had to be very organized in my research and, as a result, made many purchases along the way such as a filing cabinet, a large magnifier, and many reference books on how to do genealogical research. I also had to spend hours becoming proficient on the microfilm readers, printers, and learning how the actual microfilms are organized. When I would find birth, marriage, death, or census records that I felt might have significance, I would photocopy them. I would then take everything home and construct and reconstruct my extended family tree in an attempt to look for clues as to where I could find Angeline's male family members. It became such a difficult task that at times I would stop for weeks or even months at a time. I had stopped for a period of several months when I once again began to act on my desire to be a registered Indian.

This turned out to be the day that I found what I needed. It appeared that Angeline was at the home of the birth of her brother's child. The date of the birth was August 20, 1882. For unknown reasons, the child's birth registration was delayed until December 1934, 52 years later. It seems his mother was missing and, since Angeline was present at the time of his birth, she was the only person qualified to sign the declaration. This declaration of delayed birth stated her brother's name as the father and herself as the child's aunt. This document was the "patrilineal link" that tied the two surnames together— Angeline's married name with her brother's—and which could connect her to a band member. I knew that what I held in my hand was the necessary document, and I quickly sent all the documents and necessary affidavits along with several applications to INAC.

By this time I was familiar with section 6 of the *Indian Act*. I was certain my great-grandmother, my great-grandfather, my grandmother, and my father would all be reinstated or registered. I was uncertain about myself because I did not know how my father's unknown paternity would be interpreted.

How INAC applies section 6, the main entitlement section of the current *Indian Act* is summarized in Tables A and B.

Table A[8]

6(1) = a person with two Indian parents
6(2) = a person with one Indian parent
N = a non-status or non-Indian parent
UP = Unknown/Unstated Paternity = N

Table B

6(1) + 6(1) = 6(1)
6(1) + 6(2) = 6(1)
6(2) + 6(2) = 6(1)
6(1) + N = 6(2)
6(2) + N = N

INAC applied section 6 to my family in the following manner: Angeline was reinstated as 6(1) status, her son who was also Annie's husband was registered as 6(2) status. Annie was reinstated as 6(1). My grandmother, the child of a 6(1) parent and a 6(2) parent, was registered as a 6(1) as above. My father's combination of parents was applied as 6(1) + N, and registered as a 6(2). The Registrar, when applying section 6, assumed a negative presumption for my father's unknown paternity as being a non-status or non-Indian person. This means that he cannot confer status to myself in his own right, because a 6(2) + N (my mother is a non-status person) = N.

All previously registered Indians in the Indian register as of April 16, 1985 were granted 6(1) entitlement (Wherrett). This was also the situation when reinstating women who lost status through marriage "…however, their children are entitled to registration only under section 6(2)" (Wherrett 10). In contrast, the children of Indian men who married non-Indian women, whose registration before 1985 was continued under section 6(1), are able to pass on status if they marry non-Indians (Wherrett). Alternatively, the new rules of section 6 were being applied retroactively to Indian women and their children, which creates an inequity, because 6(1) registration permits a person to pass on status to their children yet 6(2) does not.

I became acutely aware of the continued discrimination within the amended *Indian Act* and how it was affecting me. I was denied registration. With this denial it became evident to me that, if my female ancestors had been male, I would be entitled to Indian status today. Had they been male, they would never have lost registration and they could then pass it to me. Since all previous entitlement continues, I would be a 6(1) in my own right and I could therefore pass status onto my children. Thus, the present day *Indian Act* continues with the theme of discrimination on the basis of gender (Gilbert). Furthermore, the *Indian Act* continues to violate section 15 of the *Canadian Charter of Rights and Freedoms*. Section 15(1) provides that all individuals are equal before and under the law.

The 1985 amendments to the *Indian Act* (Bill C-31) corrected only part of the discrimination against women who lost their status upon marriage to non-Indian men. However, these amendments failed to address the discriminatory aspect which does not allow Indian women, who married non-Indian men, to pass their status to their grandchildren. The result is that the current *Indian Act* continues to discriminate against the children and grandchildren of Indian women who lost their status. Alternatively, the children of Bill C-31 Indian women are treated differently than children born to Indian men. The former are granted status under section 6 subsection (2), whereas the latter are granted status under section 6 subsection (1).

My application was denied entitlement on February 13, 1995. I submitted a letter of protest on March 16, 1995 and on February 4, 1997 I received a letter from the Registrar which concluded that my name was correctly omitted from the Indian Register. I filed an appeal claiming discrimination on the basis of gender and marital status. INAC denied my appeal in April 1998.

I am now content with my identity, partly because of my new understanding of these huge issues as well as my realization, achieved in the process, that legislation cannot tell me who I am. It is, as a matter of principle, that I continue to appeal to the appropriate court as outlined in section 14.3 of the *Indian Act*.

In conclusion, I would like to suggest a very simple, fair, logical and equitable remedy to eliminate the continuum of discrimination within the *Indian Act*. All children, including their descendants, born prior to 1985 to an Indian man or an Indian woman regardless of who they married should be entitled registration under 6(1). The new rules of entitlement should then, and only then, be applied to all births equally after 1985. This would resolve the continued inequities in the current *Indian Act* between men and women, and would then bring it in accord with the *Charter*. This would also resolve the issue of unknown paternity before 1985 as unknown paternity is also being interpreted in an unequal manner.

With this said, it is important for me to note that the biggest challenge to having my family members reinstated or registered with INAC was the Registrar's demand that I connect my ancestors to an existing band member as the basis of my family's entitlement. I found two official documents in which Angeline was recognized and recorded as an Indian: her death certificate and her marriage certificate. This though was not enough. I had to further my search until I could prove a link. This is grossly unfair and an unreasonable request when one considers that "...there are countless historical records of Indians who never belonged to a band" (Gilbert 15). Angeline was an Indian, regardless.

After reading this paper, one should be more aware of the research and analytical skills required to prove Aboriginal ancestry; in particular, being able to prove a link to an existing band member. It is an enormous task. Individuals require time, money, stamina and great determination to fulfill the Registrar's requirements. Many of Canadas[9] Aboriginal people are poor, illiterate, or unemployed as a result of the forced assimilation process. When the *Indian Act* was amended, assistance in the form of guidance from genealogical researchers should have been made available to the non-status communities to help them in their quest for their identity as well as registration.

Finally, I will never see myself as a Canadian first, but rather as an Aboriginal person. My ideologies of who I am and who my ancestors were will always extend beyond national policies and boundaries of control and assimilation. Neither identity nor human behaviour can be constructed through rigid definitions such as the *Indian Act*. My identity as an Aboriginal person was partially achieved through political struggle and the need to realize the potential of my genetic memory. I feel this way despite the fact that I am not a "legal" Indian.

The support and guidance of Dr. Eva Mackey, Dr. Naomi Adelson, and Jacquelyne Luce at all stages of preparing this paper were greatly appreciated. Questions regarding this paper and the subsequent court challenge can be directed to the author at lynngehl@trentu.ca.

An earlier version of this paper was published in CWS/cf's Summer 2000 issue, "National Identity and Gender Politics" (Volume 20, Number 2): 64-69.

[1]In this paper I am primarily talking about Aboriginal women who at one time were considered Indian and who, thus, may have had status registration or may have been entitled to it. Further, in this paper, I use the terms Indian, Aboriginal and First Nations interchangeably when in fact they are not interchangeable. For example, it must be appreciated that many Aboriginal peoples did not have status and never lived on a reservation. This in itself does not deem them any less Aboriginal.

[2]For the complete story see Silman.

[3]It is interesting to note that Parliament Hill is located on unsurrendered Algonquin territory. This is my Nation's traditional territory.

[4]Interestingly, by 1991, 69,593 individuals did regain status registration (Dickason). Also keep in mind here that women marrying non-Indian men was not the only reason for enfranchisement, although they did make up the majority (Voyageur).

[5]Meaning a person who is registered as an Indian under the *Indian Act*, as defined by the *Indian Act*.

[6]This is the Algonquin word for grandmother. In this paper, I use kokomis and grandmother interchangeably.

[7]The author originally used the word enfranchised, but I substituted it with free. Enfranchisement was a goal of the *Indian Act* as a measure of civilization and could be achieved both voluntarily of involuntarily as in the case of Indian women marrying non-Indian men. This *freedom* was imposed on them.

[8]Tables A and B are adapted from Brizinski.

[9]The apostrophe is intentionally left out as it implies ownership.

References

The Archives of Ontario. "Aboriginal Sources at the Archives of Ontario." Toronto: Ministry of Citizenship Culture and Recreation.

Bear, Shirley with the Tobique Women's Group. "You Can't Change the Indian Act?" *Women and Social Change: Feminist Activism in Canada*. Eds. Jeri Dawn Wine and Janice L. Ristock. Toronto: James Lorimer and Company, 1991. 198-220.

Brizinski, Peggy. *Knots in a String: An Introduction To Native Studies in Canada*. Second ed. Saskatchewan: University Extension Press, 1993.

Dickason, Olive Patricia. *Canada's First Nations: A History of Founding Peoples from Earliest Times*. Second ed. Toronto: Oxford University Press, 1997.

Gilbert, Larry. *Entitlement to Indian Status and Membership Codes in Canada*. Scarborough: Carswell Thomson Canada Ltd., 1996.

Jamieson, Kathleen. *Indian Women and the Law in Canada: Citizens Minus*. Ottawa: Minister of Supply and Services, 1978.

Minister of Supply and Services. *Canadian Charter of Rights and Freedoms: A Guide for Canadians*. Ottawa: Minister of Supply and Services, 1992.

Minister of Supply and Services. *Impact of the 1985 Amendments to the Indian Act (Bill C-31)*. Ottawa: Minister of Indian Affairs and Northern Development, 1990.

Native Women's Association of Canada. *Guide to Bill C-31: An Explanation of the 1985 Amendments to the Indian Act*. Ottawa: Native Women's Association of Canada, c1986.

Norris, Mary Jane. "Contemporary Demography of Aboriginal Peoples in Canada." *Visions of the Heart: Canadian Aboriginal Issues*. Eds. David Alan Long and Olive Patricia Dickason. Toronto: Harcourt Brace and Company, Ltd., 1996. 179-237.

Silman, Janet. Ed. *Enough is Enough: Aboriginal Women Speak Out (as told to Janet Silman)*. Toronto: The Women's Press, 1987.

Stevenson, Winona. "Colonialism and First Nations Women in Canada." *Scratching the Surface: Canadian Anti-Racist Feminist Thought*. Eds. Enakshi Dua and Angela Robertson. Toronto: Women's Press, 1999. 49-80

Voyageur, Cora J. "Contemporary Indian Women." *Visions of the Heart:*

Canadian Aboriginal Issues. Eds. David Alan Long and Olive Patricia Dickason. Toronto: Harcourt Brace and Company, Ltd., 1996. 92-112.

Wherrett, Jill. *Indian Status and Band Membership Issues*. Ottawa: Research Branch, Library of Parliament, 1996.

Others in Their Own Land

Second Generation South Asian Canadian Women, Racism and the Persistence of Colonial Discourse

Angela Aujla ⟶

"Go back to where you came from!"
"Where are you *really* from?"
"*Paki!*"

Though born and raised in Canada, the national identity of multigenerational South Asian Canadian women is subject to incessant scrutiny and doubt, as reflected in the phrases above. They are othered by a dominant culture which categorizes them as "visible minorities," "ethnics," immigrants, and foreigners—categories considered incommensurable with being a "real" Canadian, despite the promises of multiculturalism. Never quite Canadian enough, never quite white enough, these women remain "others" in their own land. Not only are they excluded from national belonging, they are haunted by a discourse which has historically constructed non-white women as a threat to the nation-state. Contemporary constructions of South Asian Canadian women are situated in a larger racist, sexist, and colonial discourse which cannot be buried under cries of "unity in diversity."

In this article, I focus on how the gendered racialization of multigenerational South Asian Canadian women excludes them from national belonging and pressures them to assimilate. The literary production of these women reflects the deep repercussions of this exclusion, and provides a location where issues of identity, otherness, and racism may be articulated and resisted. I will look at poetry and personal narratives by multigenerational South Asian Canadian women as points of intervention into these issues. Beginning with a brief overview of racism against South Asians in Canada, I will discuss how racist and colonial discourses of the past continue to influence dominant discourses and perceptions of South Asian Canadian women today.

Unity against diversity

Despite the many differences among multigenerational South Asian Canadian women, similar experiences can be identified. These include experiences of racism, feelings of being "other" and not belonging, colonialism, patriarchy, sexism, and living in a diasporic culture. I use the term "South Asian" because it challenges the geographical locatedness of cultures and identities through its wide scope of reference. Generally, the category "South Asian" refers to those who trace their ancestry to places including India, Pakistan, Sri Lanka, Bangladesh, Bhutan, Tanzania, Uganda, South Africa, and the Caribbean (Henry *et al.*; Agnew). Terms such as "East Indian" and "Indo-Canadian" are problematic because of their narrow reference. Both refer directly to the Indian subcontinent, excluding other South Asian regions. They also refer to nation states and nationalities, implying the idea that ethnicity, identity and "race" are neatly confined within the borders of homogenous states.

Much in the same spirit as colonial cartography, South Asians have been "mapped" and inscribed by the dominant culture through racialized discourse and state practices since they began immigrating to Canada in the late nineteenth century (Buchnigani and Indra). Surrounded by an imposed mythos of being deviant, threatening, undesirable and inferior to the white 'race', South Asians were constructed as 'other' to the dominant Canadian culture who could not even bear to sit beside them on trains (Henry *et al.*). This attitude is evident in the contemporary phenomena of "white flight" in certain B.C. municipalities where some white residents have chosen to move rather than live alongside the South Asians who are "ruining the neighbourhood." In the early 1900s, they were not permitted to participate as full citizens, the Canadian state controlled where they could live, where they could work, and even what they could or could not wear. Though they were British subjects, they could not vote federally until 1947 (Henry *et al.*). Though in a less overt form, the traces of this mapping continue to effect South Asian bodies today. Dominant representations of South Asian Canadians are largely stereotypical and impose static notions of culture and identity on them, whether they are immigrants or multigenerational.

The history of media images of South Asians attests to this. In the early nineteenth century, the South Asian presence in British Columbia was referred to as "a Hindu Invasion" by the news media; a proliferation of articles in B.C. newspapers stressed the importance of maintaining Anglo-Saxon superiority[1] (Henry *et al.*). Negative media portrayal of South Asians still persists. As Yasmin Jiwani states,

> ...even contemporary representations cohere around an "us" versus "them" dichotomy that ideologically sediments a notion of national identity that is clearly exclusionary. (1998: 60)

Canadian Sikhs for example, have been depicted as over-emotional religious extremists predisposed to violence. Used repeatedly, these images reinforce prejudice against all South Asians, both male and female. The *Vancouver Sun* headlines "Close Watch on City Sikhs" and "Sikh Militancy Grows" have not strayed very far from the cry of "Hindu Invasion" in the early part of the twentieth century. Representations of South Asian Canadian women in the media portray them as the meek and pitiful victims of arranged marriages and abusive husbands or uses them as colourful, orientalized exotica to be fawned over (Jiwani 1998). Such media images subtly exclude South Asian Canadians from national belonging. Their cultures are represented as barbaric and backwards, as "clashing" and "conflicting" with civilized and modern Canadian society. These portrayals imply that South Asians do not "fit in" here, and that they are certainly not "real" Canadians. Edward Said states,

> [The] imaginative geography of the "our land/barbarian land" variety does not require that the barbarians acknowledge the distinction. It is enough for "us" to set up these boundaries in our own minds; "they" become "they" accordingly, and both their territory and their mentality are designated as different from "ours." (54)

Said describes how the us-them boundary and its accompanying mythos about "others'" mentalities has historically been constructed by the dominant culture and imposed onto "others" regardless of their consent. Though Said was referring to relations between colonizer and colonized, his idea remains just as relevant when applied to contemporary relations between South Asian Canadians and the dominant Canadian culture.

Feel-good, multicultural goals of unity in diversity and ending racism are simplistic and certain to fail because they do not acknowledge the deeply rooted racist, sexist, and colonial discourse that has constructed Canada and "Canadian identity." As Ann Laura Stoler argues, "the discourse of race was not on parallel track with the discourse of the nation but part of it" (93). Historically, Canadian identity has not been a First Nations identity, or even a French identity. It has been, and continues to be a white, British, Anglo-Saxon identity. As in other white-settler colonies, and in Britain, the civility and superiority of blood and nation was constructed against the "backwardness" and inferiority of the "darker races" (Stoler; Jiwani 1998; Dua). For example, the modernity of the Canadian state was juxtaposed to the pre-modern South Asian woman, the blood of the superior Anglo Saxon race was juxtaposed to the degenerate blood of non-white races (Henry *et al.*). White, Anglo-Canadian unity was constructed in opposition to non-white "diversity." But now, with the introduction of multiculturalism, we are suddenly expected to make the very unrealistic leap from unity against "diversity," to unity *in* diversity.

The persistence of colonial discourse

South Asian women have been both sexualized and racialized through colonial discourse as oppressed, subservient, tradition-bound, and pre-modern (Dua). They are also constructed as seductive, exotic objects of desire. In another construction they are considered overly-fertile, undesirable, smelly, and oily-haired (Jiwani 1992; Brah). The legacy of colonial discourse is evident in contemporary racialized and sexualized constructions of South Asian women. In a *Guardian* article published September 5, 1985, a 19-year-old South Asian woman in London recounts the sexualized racist comments she faces walking home from college:

...if I'm on my own with other girls it's, "Here comes the Paki whore, come and fuck us Paki whores, we've heard you're really horny." Or maybe they'll put it the other way around, saying that I am dirty, that no one could possibly want to go to bed with a Paki.... (qtd. in Brah 79)

These co-existing sentiments of desire and revulsion can be seen as remnants of British colonial attitudes towards South Asian women. While their colonizers considered non-white women savage, and backwards, they were also thought to possess a "sensual, enticing and indulgent nature" (Smits 61). According to Yasmin Jiwani, in British imperialist fiction by authors including Rudyard Kipling, the Indian woman was characterized by her rampant sexuality and her abundant fertility (1992). As can be inferred from the comments yelled at the 19-year-old South Asian woman walking home from college, contemporary stereotypes of multigenerational South Asian women remain deeply rooted in the colonial tradition.

Race, blood, and nation have historically been deeply interconnected and overlapping concepts in the West. Historically, the immigration and presence of women of colour in Canada, and other western countries was seen as a threat to the nation-state. They brought with them the danger of increasing the non-white population and the possibility of miscegenation—a danger all the more immanent given their "overly fecund" nature. Dua comments that "In Canada, as well as other settler colonies, racial purity was premised on the Asian peril—the danger of Anglo-Saxons being overrun by more fertile races" (252). Non-white women endangered western "civility" and national identity; the prolif-eration of non-white babies was not just a threat to the racial purity of western societies, but to their dominance and very existence. It was thought that miscegenation and too many non-white births could lead to the demise of the Anglo-Saxon race, and therefore, the demise of the nation state itself. As Dua writes,

...the submissiveness of Hindu women was linked to a decline into pre-modern conditions. While white bourgeois women were racially gendered as mothers of the nation, colonized women were racially gendered as dangerous to the nation-state. (254)

Similarly, in everyday the racist/xenophobic discourse of this country, the "real" Canadians complain that immigrants are invading their neigh-bourhoods, cities, and the country itself. The *Globe and Mail* warns "that soon there will be more visible minorities than whites in Vancouver and Toronto", and that their number "is the highest in history." Feeding into fears of non-white women's limitless fertility, they also report that the number of visible minorities born in Canada is rising steadily and that they are younger than "the total Canadian population" (Mitchell). Such articles reflect the persistence of colonial discourse; while the white woman's regulated fecundity was supposed to ensure the reproduction of the social body, the non-white woman's "limitless fertility" was seen as endangering the reproduction of the social body. Non-white and "mixed race" bodies signalled a danger to the State.

I am Canadian?

"Are you Fijian by any chance?" the stranger asked.
    "No," I replied.
    "Are you from India?"
    "No."
During this brief encounter on Vancouver's Robson Street in 1997, various thoughts quickly ran through my head: do I reply with the answer that I know he wants to hear? Or do I explain that I'm Canadian only to be met with the standard reply of "Where are you *really* from?" or "But where are you from *originally?*" I walked away frustrated, glad I didn't give him the answer he expected, but upset that I didn't take the opportunity to challenge his preconceptions further by stating that not all brown people are immigrants, or saying "why do you ask?" taking the spotlight off me and hopefully inciting him to question the motivation behind his intrusive inquiry. Kamala Visweswaran states,

> Certainly the question "Where are you from?" is never an innocent one. Yet not all subjects have equal difficulty in replying. To pose a question of origin to a particular subject is to subtly pose a question of return, to challenge not only temporally, but geographically, one's place in the present. For someone who is neither fully Indian nor wholly American, it is a question that provokes a sudden failure of confidence, the fear of never replying adequately. (115)

Even in "multicultural" Canada, skin colour and ethnicity continue to act as markers of one's place of origin, markers which are used to ascertain traits and behaviours which are associated with certain "races." It is a question that left me with an acute sense of being out of place and being "other"—if I seemed out of place to the man who asked the question, I must appear so to the people around me. Underlying such (frequently asked) questions are racist assumptions about what a "real" Canadian looks like. In that brief encounter, the stranger automatically linked me to a far away land that I have never seen, a place where I would surely be considered an outsider, and certainly not be considered Indian. His question served as a reminder of my "visible minority" status, and that I was not quite Canadian and could never be so.

The "other" does not necessarily have to be "other" in terms of exhibiting strange or "exotic" language and behaviour. Time and time again, the dominant culture reduces identity down to imaginary racial categories. The fact that multigenerational South Asian Canadians are treated as Other, as not-quite Canadians, attests to this. At what point do multigenerational South Asian Canadians cease being seen as from somewhere else? As Himani Bannerji comments, "[t]he second generation grows up on cultural languages which are not foreign to them, though they are still designated as foreigners" (1993: 186). South Asian Canadian women are in a predicament of perpetual foreigness—constantly being asked where they are from and having stereotypical characteristics assigned to them despite their "Canadianness." Though they are in their country of origin, they are not *of* it.

Presentation of self is one way in which we demonstrate our personal identities and recognize those of others. This holds true if we encountered someone who had inscribed her body with tattoos, multiple body-piercings, and blue hair. However, it is quite a different situation when a South Asian Canadian woman tries to ground her personal identity in this way; regardless of whether her hair is covered by a *hijab* or is short and chic, regardless of whether she is wearing a *salwaar-kameez* or jeans, she is still subject to an otherization based on an imaginary "South Asian other" constructed through racist ideology. Her own body inscriptions are ignored, as the only signifier needed for recognition from the dominant culture seems to be phenotypical. These phenotypical characteristics stand, as they have in the past, though perhaps to a lesser extent, as signifiers of difference and inferiority.

In Farzana Doctor's poem "Banu," the narrator traces her changing responses and attitudes towards racism at different stages throughout her life. During childhood and as a young adult, assimilation is her response. Eventually she rejects assimilation in favour of resistance. In "Banu," the racist interpellation, "Paki go home" (218) is directed at the little girl in the poem. According to the Oxford English Dictionary, "Paki" is an abbreviation for Pakistani, and is also described as a slang word. In "Banu," however, the common use of the term does not reflect its literal or etymological meaning. The term has become imbued with racist emotions and signifies detest, hatred and intolerance towards all South Asians, regardless of their geographical place of origin.

A generically used term in places such as Canada, Great Britain, and the United States, "Paki" is a common racist insult directed toward those who appear to be of South Asian ancestry (Bannerji, 1993; Sheth and Handa). Unlike racist insults against South Asians that are based on food or dress such as "curry-eater" or "rag-head," the insult "Paki" is based simply on one's "foreign/other" appearance. Being brown is enough to warrant a racist insult. The insult "Paki" does not simply express disgust at aspects of South Asian cultures as the previously mentioned insults do. Rather, it expresses disgust or hatred based directly toward one's "race" or ethnic background. For a multigenerational South Asian Canadian to be told "Paki go home" is particularly disturbing because she is told that Canada is not her home, but that home is a far away land which she may have never set foot on. Regardless of being Canadian by citizenship and birth, she remains, under racist eyes, simply a "Paki." When the South Asian *Canadian* girl in the poem is told to "go home," she is not only told that she does not belong in Canadian society, but is also told that she should leave. The man who uttered the slur obviously felt he was a "real" Canadian with the right to tell the "foreigner" what to do. The popularity of this term in racist discourse not only reflects an ignorance about South Asian cultures and their diversity, but also reinforces the opinion that Canada does not have room for non-white "others."

Others in their own land

In looking at Canadian multiculturalism and its promotion of diversity and tolerance, one would not find any overt pressures promoting assimilation. If anything, it seems that assimilation is not an issue—they tell us that we can all co-exist harmoniously within our respective tile of the mosaic. Yet, unstated, implied, and subtle pressures to assimilate remain a powerful force. As Michel Foucault stated, "[t]here is no need for arms, physical violence, material constraints, just a gaze" (155). While official Canadian multiculturalism may promote the acceptance of diversity, the lived experience of multiculturalism is quite a different thing. For many South Asian Canadian women the strong desire to "fit in," as a result of being discriminated against, culminates in an internalization of the gendered racism they receive. Frantz Fanon argues that the consequence of racism from the dominant group to the minority group is guilt and inferiority. The inferiorized group attempts to escape these feelings by "proclaiming his [sic] total and unconditional adoption of the new cultural models, and on the other, by pronouncing an irreversible condemnation of his own cultural style" (38-9).

This is a process multigenerational South Asian Canadian women undergo in their in their attempts to reject South Asian culture and assimilate. Assimilation has often been used as a coping mechanism not only by South Asian Canadians, but by all visible minorities where the majority of the dominant culture is white. Obvious forms of assimilation include speaking English and wearing western-style clothing. A less obvious form is the desire to change one's physical appearance (Bannerji 1990; Sheth and Handa; James; Karumanchery-Luik). Based on personal experiences and literature by multigenerational South Asian Canadian women, the desire to be white or possess typically western features is, unfortunately, quite common. The impact of this is compounded for multigenerational South Asian Canadian women who have been socialized into the western beauty ideal.

Internalized racism is a theme common to much of the literature by multigenerational South Asian Canadian women. One manifestation of this is the hierarchy of skin colour in South Asian communities, illustrated by the use of "Fair and Lovely" skin cream and skin bleaches by South Asian women, and the desire expressed in matrimonial ads for light skinned wives. Anita Sheth comments that light skin is so desirable in India that "The cosmetics industry continually pitch skin-lightening products to women" (Sheth and Handa 86). Various cosmetic products promising to do this are also found in Vancouver and Surrey's South Asian shops.

The desire for whiteness is demonstrated in second generation South Asian Canadian activist and theatre artist Sheila James' personal narrative about how she unnaturally became a blond because "All the sex objects on TV, film and magazines were blond-haired and blue eyed. I figured I could adjust the colour in my head to fit the role" (137). Underlying the desire for "whiteness" is a racist ideology which interprets the world associated with the dark skin of Indian and African people with danger, savagery, primitiveness, intellectual inferiority, and the inability to progress beyond a childlike mentality. Meanwhile whiteness is equated with purity, virginity, beauty, and civility (Ashcroft *et al.*; Arora).

Assimilation pressures and internalized racism experienced by the second generation are captured quite forcefully in Himani Bannerji's short story "The Other Family" (1990: 140-145) in which the second-generation South Asian protagonist of the story draws what is supposed to be a picture of her family for a school project. The picture, however, bears very little resemblance to her own family. She draws her family as white with blond hair and blue eyes, and herself as having a button nose and freckles. The drawing can be interpreted as an illustration of the little girl's desire to belong and to be like the other children—to fit in at the cost of the negation of her own body, of her own physical appearance. An essay by a multigenerational South Asian Canadian woman, Nisha Karumanchery-Luik, reflects a similar theme:

> When I was younger, I hated my brown skin. I had wished that I was not so dark, that my skin would somehow magically lighten. When I was younger, I was ashamed and embarrassed of my Indian heritage and the "foreigness" that my skin betrayed. I developed creative strategies of denial and pretense to cope with and survive in a racist environment. (54)

Her choice of phrase that her skin "betrayed" her "foreignness" and Indian heritage is a significant one. It speaks to the circumstance that many multigenerational South Asian Canadian women and other multigenerational visible minorities are in—though they may act "Canadian" in the mainstream-white-Anglo-Saxon-Protestant sense of the word (language, clothes, behaviour), their skin colour and phenotypical characteristics, signifying them as "other," never fail to give them away. Being different from the mainstream is, of course, not a problem in and of itself. The reason it becomes one is the resulting othering, gendered racism, and exclusion that multigenerational South Asian Canadian women are subject to. In the following excerpt of a poem by Reshmi J. Bissessar, she reveals the shame she felt over being Guyanese:

I was there last in '86
At age fourteen
Eleven years ago
When I would say
Thank you
If someone told me
that I didn't look
Guyanese.
My, how loyalties change. (22)

Often, multigenerational South Asian Canadian women try to hide and mask what it is that singles them out for racist taunts and prying gazes. For example, in another poem, the parent of a young South Asian Canadian woman asks the daughter "why do you cringe when seen by white folks in your sari?/ why are you embarrassed when speaking Gujurati in public?" (Shah 119). Thus the pressures to assimilate and "belong" result in denying aspects of South Asian culture—even to the point of internalizing the dominant ideology and seeing themselves as inferior. Thinking that their food "stinks,", that their physical characteristics are less beautiful and undesirable according to western standards, embarrassment over being seen in Indian clothing, or by the accents of their parents, are all aspects of their inferiorization.

At the borders of national belonging

Multigenerational South Asian Canadian women's efforts at masking their ethnicity are, of course, in vain. The closest they come is to be mistaken for a less marginalized ethnic group or to be bestowed with the status of "honorary white," through comments to the effect of "you're different.... you're not like the *rest* of them." I was given this status when deciding where to go for dinner with a group of people. One white woman asked me if I ate meat, implying that I must have "strange" eating habits as a South Asian. Before I could answer, another white woman exclaimed, "Oh of course she does, she's *just like us!*" But despite the "acceptance" of being just like them, I was still othered by the initial curiosity of "do you eat meat?" If I was "just like them" why was I the only one to whom that question was posed? Thus, even the "honorary white" status given to some South Asians fails to appease a sense of not belonging. Suparana Bhaskaran outlines the limiting typology of the "assimilated South Asian" and the "authentic South Asian" which can be applied to the phenomena of the "honorary white" discussed above:

The logic of purity allows South Asians to be conceptually defined in only two ways: as authentic South Asians or assimilated South

Asians. The "authentic South Asian" may range from being conservative, lazy and poor to being spiritual, brilliant, non-materialistic
and religious. By this definition, the assimilated South Asian...pursues
the promise of the "postcultural" full citizenship of Anglo life. (198)

Though some multigenerational South Asian Canadian women may, by
the above typology, be considered "assimilated South Asians" and therefore
subject to the discrimination faced by the "authentic South Asian," we see in
the literature by South Asian Canadian women that seeking this identification and inclusion into "Anglo-life" is, for the most part, unattainable and
continues to be fraught with othering and a sense of exclusion.

Being singled out as "other" and the consequent pressures to assimilate has
a particularly strong effect on multigenerational South Asian Canadian
women. They have been socialized in Canadian society from birth and have
thus, unlike their parents, lived their entire lives as "ethnic/other," and
different from the dominant culture. For the second generation, the assimilation process begins much earlier and in the more formative years. Therefore,
racism and being otherered by the dominant culture has a deeper, more
detrimental impact on multigenerational South Asian Canadians than it does
on their parents who did not grow up in Canada. Though the parents of second-
generation South Asian Canadians may be more "othered" due to their
accents, the fact that they wear Indian clothing, and from having been
socialized in a non-western culture, they have come to Canada with some pre-
established sense of identity (though it changes through their experiences in
their new country), which is not the case for their children.

It is likely that many Canadians would be quite content if South Asian
Canadians and other "visible minorities" simply integrated into Anglo-
Canadian society instead of making a fuss about racist immigration policies, or
their right to wear *hijabs*. Of course, assimilation can no longer be overtly
legislated, although it continues to be suggested in more subtle ways, as
reflected in the literature by South Asian women. Because of "subtle" pressures
to assimilate, many South Asian Canadian women have interiorized the
inspecting gaze of the dominant culture to the point that they are exercising
surveillance over themselves. Foucault argues that physical violence and
constraints are no longer needed to control a population once they have
interiorized the inspecting gaze,

a gaze which each individual under its weight will end by interiorizing
to the point that he is his own overseer, each individual thus
exercising this surveillance over, and against himself. (155)

The inspecting gaze in this context, are the judgemental eyes of the
dominant culture—state officials, journalists, neighbours, teachers, and peers.
The pressure to assimilate is no longer over, it is embedded in everyday
language and stereotypes used to describe and "other" South Asian Canadian

women, in popular culture and media depictions, and in structures such as institutional racism. The content of the literature by multigenerational South Asian discussed earlier reveals that they have interiorized the inspecting gaze of the dominant culture, though it is a gaze which many of them have come to reject. Over and over again, these writers express the desire they have or once had to belong, to be accepted, and to "fit" into the dominant culture.

Conclusion

Though I have concentrated on how multigenerational South Asian Cana-dian have been "raced" and gendered through the dominant ideology, it is important to note that those constructed as other are not merely the passive recipients of power. In many cases, they are remapping themselves by challeng-ing dominant representations of "their kind" through subversive forms of literary production. I would argue that in the tension between imposed identities and those asserted by multigenerational South Asian Canadian women, spaces of resistance have formed in the anthologies and other venues in which they publish, and in the act of writing itself. These venues provide a forum for South Asian Canadian women to creatively express their insights, anger, pain, and reflections. It is a textual space created by and for multigenerational South Asian Canadian women in which their marginalization and repression is both articulated and resisted.

Multigenerational South Asian Canadian women's literature is consid-ered a new, diasporic form of cultural production. It is new in that these women are writing as both insiders and outsiders to Canadian society. Their literature demonstrates an ongoing negotiation of two intertwined cultural contexts and influences. The positionality of these women allows for a unique vantage point from which to comment on Canadian racism, sexism, and other repressions. Their writing poses an important challenge to the idea that culture and identity are fixed within certain national borders.

Originally published in CWS/cf's Summer 2000 issue, "National Identity and Gender Politics" (Volume 20, Number 2): 41-47.

[1]*The Daily Colonist* wrote: "To prepare ourselves for the irrepresible conflict, Canada must remain a White Man's country. On this western frontier of the Empire will be the forefront to the coming struggle.... Therefore we ought to maintain this country for the Anglo-Saxon and those races which are able to assimilate themselves to them. If this is done, we believe that history will repeat itself and the supremacy of our race will continue" (Henry *et. al.* 71).

References

Agnew, Vijay. *Resisting Discrimination: Women from Asia, Africa, and the Caribbean and the Women's Movement in Canada.* Toronto: University of

Toronto Press, 1996.

Arora, Poonam. "Imperilling the Prestige of the White Woman: Colonial Anxiety and Film Censorship in India." *Visual Anthropology Review*, 11 (2) (1995): (36-49)

Ashcroft, Bill, Gareth Griffiths and Helen Tiffin. *Key Concepts in Post-Colonial Studies*. London: Routledge, 1998.

Bannerji, Himani. "The Other Family." *Other Solitudes: Canadian Multicultural Fictions*. Eds. Linda Hutcheon and Marion Richmond. Toronto: Oxford University Press, 1990.

Bannerji, Himani. "Popular Images of South Asian Women." *Returning the Gaze*. Ed. Himani Bannerji. Toronto: Sister Vision Press, 1993.

Bhaskaran, Suparna. "Physical Subjectivity and the Risk of Essentialism." *Our Feet Walk the Sky: Women of the South Asian Diaspora*, Eds. Women of South Asian Descent Collective. San Fransisco: Aunt Lute Books, 1993.

Bisessar, Reshmi J. "Struggle." *Shaktee Kee Awaaz: Voices of Strength*. Eds. Shakti Kee Chatree. Toronto: Shakti Kee Chatri, 1997.

Brah, Avtar. *Cartographies of Diaspora: Contesting Identities*. London: Routledge, 1996.

Buchnigani, N. and D. Indra. *Continuous Journey: A Social History of South Asians in Canada*. Toronto: McLelland and Stewart, 1985.

"Close Watch on City Sikhs." *Vancouver Sun* 20 October 1985a.

Doctor, Farzana. "Banu." *Aurat Durbar*. Ed. Fauzia Rafiq. Toronto: Second Story Press, 1995.

Dua, Enakshi. "Beyond Diversity: Exploring the Ways In Which the Discourse of Race Has Shaped the Institution of the Nuclear Family." *Scratching the Surface: Canadian Anti-Racist Feminist Thought*. Eds. Enakshi Dua and Angela Robertson. Toronto: Women's Press, 1999.

Fanon, Frantz. *Toward the African Revolution*. New York: Grove Press, 1967.

Foucault, Michel. *Power/Knowledge*. New York: Pantheon, 1980.

Henry, Frances, Carol Tator, Winston Mattis and Tim Rees. *The Colour of Democracy*. Toronto: Harcourt, Brace and Co., 1995.

James, Sheila. "From Promiscuity to Celibacy." *Aurat Durbar*. Ed. Fauzia Rafiq. Toronto: Second Story Press, 1995.

Jiwani, Yasmin. "The Exotic, Erotic, and the Dangerous: South Asian Women in Popular Film." *Canadian Woman Studies/les cahiers de la femme* 13 (1) (1992): 42-46

Jiwani, Yasmin. "On the Outskirts of Empire: Race and Gender in Canadian TV News." *Painting the Maple: Essays on Race, Gender and the Construction of Canada*. Eds. Victoria Strong-Boag et al. Vancouver: University of British Columbia Press, 1998.

Karumanchery-Luik, Nisha. "The Politics of Brown Skin." *Shaktee Kee Awaaz: Voices of Strength*. Eds. Shakti Kee Chatree. Toronto: Shakti Kee Chatri, 1997.

Mitchell, Alanna. 1998 "Face of Big Cities Changing." *Globe and Mail* 18 February 1998: A1, A3.

Said, Edward W. *Orientalism*. New York: Vintage, 1994.

Shah, Susan. "The Interrogation." *Shaktee Kee Awaaz: Voices of Strength*. Eds. Shakti Kee Chatree. Toronto: Shakti Kee Chatri, 1997.

Sheth, Anita and Amita Handa. "A Jewel in the Frown: Striking Accord Between India/n Feminists." *Returning the Gaze*. Ed. Himani Bannerji. Toronto: Sister Vision Press, 1993.

"Sikh Militancy Grows." *Vancouver Sun* 7 November 1985b.

Smits, David. "Abominable Mixture." *The Virginia Magazine of History and Biography* 95 (2) (1987): 227-61.

Stoler, Ann Laura. *Race and The Education of Desire: Foucault's History of Sexuality and the Colonial Order of Things*. Durham: Duke University Press. 1995.

Visweswaran, Kamala. *Fictions of Feminist Ethnography*. Minneapolis: University of Minnesota Press, 1994.

Regulated Narratives in Anti-Homophobia Education

Complications in Coming Out Stories

Gulzar Raisa Charania ❦

What does it mean to come out? This, to me, was the central question that I was forced to negotiate and renegotiate in framing and telling my coming out stories.[1] As David Eng and Alice Hom state, coming out is about "the ways in which social groups and categories organize, stage and discipline the naming of our desires" (qtd. in Lee 3). As Ruthann Lee argues in relation to Asian queers,

> by declaring who we are, we are trying to express what we are, what we believe and what we desire. However, these beliefs, needs and desires are often contradictory—not only amongst different communities but also within ourselves. (3)

In this paper, I explore the function of coming out stories in anti-homophobia education.[2] The coming out story in the context of anti-homophobia education required a certain coherence that made it difficult to be or speak myself as a subject in process or a subject becoming (Venn 56, 58) or as Lee suggests, a subject with contradictory desires and beliefs. It also required, by its very form, a primacy and linear telling of sexual identity, ending with a "fully realized 'gay' subject" (Gopinath 268). In excavating some of the assumptions in coming out stories, Gayatri Gopinath elaborates that a commitment to visibility in very specific and public ways as well as a focus on the individual gay or lesbian subject presupposes "Euroamerican social and historical formations" (272) that may or may not be commensurate with South Asian and I would add, other non-white contexts and experiences. While I was being asked to come out, to disclose who I was, in a sense, it was a story and subject that I participated in producing in relation to the requirements of the coming out story, the school system, interpretations of my own experiences, and the particulars of the school in which I was working (Gubrium and Holstein 164). Often, I felt compelled to speak myself into existence as a coherent, fixed and finished subject—a lesbian and Muslim. That I don't comfortably or uniformly identify as a lesbian, that being Muslim is a complicated set of religious and cultural practices, fell outside the purview of what it was possible to speak. That being Muslim for me is inseparable from being non-white seemed beyond the frame of the story, as a complication to my coming out story, rather than integral to what constituted it, or at least my understandings of it.

The context, the framework, the questions

I locate coming out stories as part of what Michel Foucault termed subjugated knowledges (1972: 82), to refer to knowledges that are present but excluded and disqualified from dominant knowledges. As a long tradition of feminists and critical pedagogues have argued, the sharing of experiences of variously marginalized groups can provide important insights, both to the individuals themselves, as well as to movements of social resistance and change. Far from individual experiences being of little political consequence, an examination of personal experiences can provide an entry point to explore the organization of social relations of power (Smith 154). In the context of anti-homophobia education, the coming out stories of lesbians, gays, and bisexuals attempt to enlarge the spaces of the sayable (Foucault 1991: 59) by naming the homophobia of school practices and insisting on our visibility. This work seeks to challenge the assumptions of who students are/are not, what and how students are/are not taught, and the behaviours and attitudes that are/are not permissible. In fact, even the naming of homophobia and acknowledgment of lesbian, gay, and bisexual people in some school contexts can be seen to be profoundly destabilizing to established heterosexual norms. At stake are not only symbolic practices but material ones, as lesbians, gays, and bisexuals attempt to (re)constitute them/ourselves as subjects with rights and entitlements within school communities. These rights, while formally recognized,[3] continue to be elusive. I start out by acknowledging the importance of anti-homophobia education in schools. These programs were secured after much advocacy and activism on the part of community members and educators. While I do want to critically challenge the function of coming out stories in anti-homophobia education, I do so in a way that acknowledges the commitment and risks of individuals who continue to do this difficult work—difficult because of the homophobia and other forms of violence that continue to operate in schools in pervasive and insidious ways and the ongoing difficulty in naming and addressing these violences.

The desire for coming out stories was quite persistent during this work and it is this desire for student stories of oppression and struggle, specifically in relation to coming out, that I explore in this paper. I focus primarily on the dilemmas I faced in framing and telling my coming out stories as well as some of the responses to them. I suggest that some of these dilemmas have resonances beyond my own stories of coming out and are relevant in thinking critically about aspects of anti-homophobia education as well as anti-racism and equity education more broadly speaking. Acknowledging this work to be crucially important, I am curious to explore how it is that I constituted myself as a particular subject in order to claim a place of inclusion in school communities.

My main questions can be summarized as follows: what are the conventions of the coming out story in anti-homophobia education? How do coming out stories in classrooms produce both stability and instability? Why the desire for stories? And how do storytelling and the constraints imposed by the classroom context flatten and freeze complicated social relations and subject positions? I attempt to problematize the practices in which I participated, as well as the dilemmas I negotiated. I also evaluate my coming out stories from multiple perspectives, including what seemed to be politically effective in practice, the simplifications in which I engaged, and the contexts which I negotiated. As Foucault explicates, in relation to power, his concern is not to understand power as only, or primarily, repressive and individualized but also productive, occurring through the entire social body and in its external practices and mechanisms (1994: 120; 1972: 97). I rely primarily on Foucault's understanding of power as repressive and productive as it allows me to expand my analysis and understanding of power in coming out stories as part of anti-homophobia education in interesting and challenging ways. Rather than seeing anti-homophobia education, and coming out stories in particular, as only oppositional and part of marginal or subjugated knowledges (McHoul and Grace 15), I also begin to formulate an analysis around how the stories themselves become techniques of normalization and what counts as truth (McHoul and Grace 25), in sometimes troubling and problematic, as well as strategic ways.

I also want to acknowledge something that risks falling outside the frame altogether in my focus on coming out stories and that is the extent to which the individuals most at risk and with the most to lose, are doing the bulk of the work in addressing homophobia. How does this let everyone else, particularly heterosexual or straight-identified school administrators, teachers, and other educational leaders, "off the hook" for taking responsibility for addressing homophobia? While I was a reluctant participant in what often felt like a show and tell routine, it is true that other LGB people might find telling their coming out stories to be empowering in ways that I did not. However, I do remain concerned about how a focus on telling and consuming coming out stories comes to stand in place of examining how heterosexism and homophobia are organized, sustained and produced in policies and practices throughout the school. For example, I have observed that rather than being seen as part of wider anti-homophobia efforts to address systemic violence, lack of curricular representation and unsafe school environments, presentations of coming out stories have become the exclusive focus of some teachers and administrators. At times, such presentations are in response to homophobic incidents but rarely are they part of much larger and sustained school or system wide anti-homophobia initiatives. I would argue that this is also the case with "one-off" presentations or assemblies to deal with racist and other forms of systemic violence in schools. While often initiated by well intentioned teachers and school leaders, sometimes with little support, such interventions are of limited use if they are the primary vehicle through which to acknowledge and address persistent and systemic inequities within our schools.

Regulated narratives: A story of samenesss

My initial story was not recognizable as a coming out story, leading me to consider how it was that an audience came to recognize a "proper" coming out story. At the start, I told a story less about personal experiences with oppression and more about privileges I had not experienced, of whiteness, straightness and economic security. I came to an understanding of my sexual identity through complicated processes, including my relationship to my body as a non-white, working-class young woman and the kinds of meanings I had made and those made for me in relation to my body. The feedback I often received was that I needed to simplify my story and focus more on what it meant to be a lesbian and to try and connect with students emotionally, in terms of the hardships I had experienced. If I wasn't explicit in saying "I am a lesbian" in the story, students often asked at the end of my story, "so what are you?" However, the fact that I am perceived to be sufficiently feminine means that my body does not come into question in the same way as a body perceived to be outside the bounds of accepted gender norms. Calling on these norms, some students informed me that "I don't look like a lesbian." Ambiguity in the story was not well tolerated, particularly in relation to assigning a familiar or recognizable name to my sexual orientation. In schools with Muslim students, I was often asked questions about what kind of Muslim I was, whether I prayed regularly or fasted during Ramadan. Some students insisted that I was not in fact Muslim as I did not follow certain rituals and ceremonies while others insisted that it was impossible to claim that I am Muslim and lesbian as these are incompatible identities. That Islam is a faith of great diversity of traditions, interpretations, and practices was lost in translating my behaviour to familiar rituals observed by some. That my relationship with Islam and as a Muslim has and continues to change and is also something deeply personal as well as connected to a larger community felt quite impossible to engage or explicate. As Thomas King writes in relation to stories, "we trust easy oppositions. We are suspicious of complexities, distrustful of contradictions, fearful of enigmas" (25). As "coming out" suggests, there seemed to be a desire for me to come out and be recognizable in particular ways and in many cases, I felt that I was not intelligible, either as a Muslim or a lesbian.

I was constantly negotiating Judith Butler's insight that "no subject is its own point of departure" (9) with the recognition that no subject is wholly produced by this point of departure. However, it is this desire for me to be recognizable that I explore, in relation to what I speculate is at stake for dominant bodies and the resulting production of myself in ways that were at times, barely recognizable to me. As time went on, I spoke less of relations of power and more of oppression and more specifically, homophobic oppression. I spoke less of ambivalences and more of certainties; less of difference and more of sameness. I displaced much that was not considered relevant to my coming out. In short, I attempted to make myself recognizable and respectable as a Muslim lesbian in order to more effectively do the work of addressing homophobia, or so I thought. I was very careful about presenting the homophobia I experienced as a Muslim within my family and community in ways that I hoped would not reinforce the prevailing racism and stereotypes of Muslim communities as more homophobic, conservative, and traditional. My strategies of respectability included mentioning my long-term relationship, talking about the challenges I faced but emphasizing survival and support from family and friends, and presenting myself as a healthy and productive person. That I am well educated formally, with multiple degrees, and speak English "without an accent," or at least without the wrong accent, all bolstered my claims to respectability. I tried to get as close as I could to "normal."

My analysis of the world as a complicated place in which oppressions work together and that people, including myself, respond to in messy and contradictory ways got packaged into a story that often flattened this analysis. While there were certainly still traces of these understandings, they were often barely perceptible. Himani Bannerji's insight that living "is always like that, this being in society, it lacks neatness, a proper compartmentalization" (11) was not only difficult to speak in my story, as time went on it seemed to me that it was difficult to be heard, at times quite literally. Responses in classrooms ranged from ongoing homophobic comments during which it was difficult to even speak to quiet condemnation and refusal to engage, struggles to understand, moments of recognition, disclosure, and quiet affirmation. As Jaber Gubrium and James Holstein suggest, "stories are not complete prior to their telling" (166) and certainly these range of responses had an impact on what I was able or willing to say and the levels of risk that felt endurable. I struggled with compartmentalizing myself, and in particular with the difficulty I had of speaking about myself as a racialized person in ways that have and continue to so profoundly shape my life. I often felt that I was talking about race and whiteness as complications to coming out or as footnotes in my story. I was accused many times of having a hierarchy of oppressions, in which race was firmly on top, when it was homophobia that needed to be addressed and centred in coming out stories. I was often told, subtly and by exclusion, that I did not actually do anti-homophobia education. I understood such feedback and comments about simplifying my story and focusing on coming out as a lesbian to be about the displacement of what were understood to be peripheral identities, primarily of race. I understood this pitting of oppressions against each other as the need to secure for ourselves "our own place on the margin" (Fellows and Razack 339) in order to make claims of belonging and inclusion. Often, I did not want to risk complications that might jeopardise my claim. However, it is easier for some LGB people, particularly those who are white, to simplify their story as their privileges make this possible and even desirable. It became clear to me that I did not understand or locate my coming out only or primarily in relation to my sexual orientation and it was not just this that I was attempting to name and centre. However, given all of the other constraints and the dominant framing of the coming out story that I was constantly negotiating, in terms of other people's demands and expectations, as well as the political project at hand, I often complied but uneasily.

Why a story of sameness? Empathy, accountability and other things along the way[4]

While I have alluded to it above, in this section, I attempt to more thoroughly excavate some of the assumptions about what constituted an effective coming out story and I speculate on the investments in telling and hearing certain stories and performing myself as a certain kind of subject, rather than others. What is at stake in this particular way of doing anti-homophobia education? From my own reflections on my experiences of coming out, I suggest that the story that is solicited and desired in coming out is a story of sameness, the story that we are just like you, or at least almost like you, and in fact it is this near sameness that makes us as LGB people recognizable. However, for racialized LGBs, the performance of sameness can only go so far as we are already Othered in complicated and sometimes contradictory ways. Where we are/I am different, I certainly attempted to generate empathy on the part of the audience, asking them to imagine what it might mean to come to school everyday and experience homophobic violence and exclusion.

I suspect for the dominant bodies, straight, white students and staff, my story was more palatable and less threatening when it was a story of oppression and sameness. What might it mean to shift my story from one of asking for inclusion to questioning its formation and terms? What might it mean to rely not on generating empathy but responsibility as a political project and would it be an effective political intervention in schools to advance anti-homophobia education? As Craig Womack, a self-identified Indian gay man[5] writes in relation to the desire for stories,

> I'm always being asked by, well, for lack of a better term, white people, to come to various gatherings and tell stories. I get the feeling that they already have a certain type of story in mind ... a story, in short, that mirrors their own culture back at them and makes them feel good, unimplicated. (31)

I suggest that the "put yourself in my shoes" approach to talking about difference, while politically expedient, reproduces problematic dynamics, including the ones that Womack suggests, that in fact often undermine claims to social justice.

I rely on Sherene Razack to demand an interrogation of the interpretive structures and spaces between the narration of experience and its reception and investments in hearing stories in ways that demonstrate the "dominant group's refusal to examine its own complicity in oppressing others" (40). As Joan Scott suggests, while exposing the different experiences of marginalized groups reveals repressive mechanisms, it does not help us to understand difference as relationally constituted (25). Without speaking about this relationality between homophobia and heterosexism, there is an obscuring of how homophobia is organized relationally to benefit people who are heterosexual at the expense of those who are not. Rather than trying to only align themselves with the suffering of LGB peoples, what might it mean to suggest that straight staff and students are all too familiar with homophobia as they enact and benefit from it, either directly or through the heterosexual privileges they incur? Applying Razack's insights to anti-homophobia education, how is accountability replaced by feeling? How might the frame of anti-homophobia education be expanded to include race, not as a complication but also as part of the way in which homophobia and heterosexism are lived and organized? If as Megan Boler contends, "these 'others' whose lives we imagine don't want empathy, they want justice" (255), do coming out stories move us towards justice and if so, which stories and how heard? Womack articulates the possibilities and pitfalls of storytelling in this way: "Storytelling, it now seems to me, is a vast terrain with many possibilities for getting lost, as well as for finding one's way, and not enough folks talking about better maps that represent the real territory in question" (33). I suggest that the real territory includes questions of domination, oppression, and injustice that are often displaced or peripheralized in coming out stories, including my own.

While some LGB people willingly see and story themselves as the same, I participated in this story very reluctantly and anxiously. This connection between myself and the audience that I attempted to make was one in which I could make myself a person with a family, feelings, likes, dislikes—a story in which I could make myself human in the hopes that students and staff with homophobic ideas and attitudes might reconsider their ideas and behaviours about who they presumed me to be. If I had a face, a name, a body and a story, perhaps their homophobia would be tempered or challenged by my humanness, by my story. In cases where students, as well as staff, continue to believe that LGB people do not deserve protection, rights, and entitlements in the schools, sometimes as basic as the right to be alive, the possibility of seeing me and other LGB people as human is a radical political project. For those students and staff who are LGB or questioning and not out in schools, I can only speculate what the workshops and our presence might mean. In some cases, as I came to know, it meant that people, students as well as teachers, did not feel hopelessly alone, despondent or totally isolated. For those students who contacted me after workshops or through teachers to whom they were out, the need for support and visibility and to know that they were not alone was critically important.

Playing the respectable subject

As Paul Passavant argues, "rights are given meaning within a discourse that embodies subjects who can make legitimate right claims" (115). He traces the liberal subject who is authorized to make and benefit from such claims, not as disembodied (117), but as civilized, meaning bourgeois and "racially white" (118). Drawing on Passavant, Kari Dehli elaborates that the "possibility of becoming and being recognized as a subject with rights or a subject who knows is constituted through discourses of reason, morality, decency and civility" (136). In the context of coming out stories, I see traces of my efforts to perform myself as respectable so as to be admitted to the category of those entitled to rights, despite the provisional and tenuous nature of this status, given my non-white, lesbian, Muslim identities and the differing meanings and impacts of these identities. While my performance might be strategic, I am also instructing others, both LGB and non-LGB audience members about what it means and looks like to be a lesbian. I am produced and participate in producing myself as a particular subject, in order to be recognizable and deserving of rights. However, how am I reproducing the very terms of regulation and repression that I am attempting to challenge through these "forms of self-governance" (Passavant 122) that are required in order to be recognizable? How, for example, might we read my own efforts to expand the category "normal" to include myself and other lesbian, gay and bisexual individuals under very specific terms of inclusion, as implicated not only in undermining or challenging heteronormativity, but also in reproducing it?   Sara Ahmed cites Butler in relation to problematizing efforts for gay marriage while also recognizing what it means to have one's relationship recognized by others. Following Butler, Ahmed asks how efforts to secure gay marriage might actually "strengthen the hierarchy between legitimate and illegitimate lives" (Ahmed 150). I want to ask a similar question of my efforts to produce myself as respectable and recognizable in my coming out story. How do I attempt to secure legitimacy for myself, however tenuous and incomplete, at the expense of those who cannot be seen as legitimate, or refuse to do so, while also recognizing the importance of the political project at hand and the contexts in which I am coming out? As Foucault argues,

> there are two meanings of the word *subject*: subject to someone else by control and dependence and tied to his own identity by a conscience or self-knowledge. Both meanings suggest a form of power which subjugates and makes subject to. (1982: 212)

It is much apparent to me how LGB people are subject to control outside of ourselves and live lives in conditions not of our making. What is less clear is how my own understanding of who I am, my identities, are also forms of power that I sometimes take up as a way of producing myself, not outside of identities to which I am subjugated, particularly in my efforts to gain access to rights. As Mary Louise Fellows and Sherene Razack argue, "respectability is a claim for membership in dominant groups; attaining it, even one aspect of it, requires the subordination of Others" (352). How might partial and complicated bids for inclusion also be connected to broader movements for social justice that extend beyond our investments in particular subjects and not others? Is it possible as a short term strategy to fight for respectability while also attempting to question the terms and relationality on which respectability is constructed? Foucault's work on how subjects constitute themselves "through the exclusion of some others" (1994: 403-404) I have found helpful, not only in relation to how heterosexuals construct themselves through the exclusion of LGB peoples but also about how we, as marginal Others, engage in these dividing practices in our political work as a result of our bids for inclusion. While I do want to qualify that the impacts of these exclusionary practices are not the same, I also want to draw attention to how anti-homophobia and equity efforts are involved in these complicitous practices.

Disparate thoughts—wrapping up

As Mariana Valverde observes, "we have not developed practices of truth telling that acknowledge power differences" (86). In the framing, telling and taking up of coming out stories in ways that do not centre asymmetrical relations of power but rely on emotions, primarily empathy, to move the audience to rethink their homophobia, I am suspicious of what remains unnamed and unchallenged. Echoing Womack, I suspect that the great desire for particular coming out stories is in part due to the fact that the audience, in this case teachers, administrators, staff, and students, can remain innocent and unimplicated. I also suggest that the desire for coming out stories in which sexual identities are almost exclusively focused is due in part to the fact that white lesbians, gays, and bisexuals can continue to avoid questions of white privilege and complicities with racism. While coming out stories may be an important strategy in seeking rights, representation, and protection for LGB students and staff, it is not without risks. Coming out stories, and certainly my coming out story, did not only speak back to power but was a practice embedded in power in particular ways. David Scott's insight that we come to understand and perform freedom and resistance not only in ways of our making but in appropriate ways (52, 81) is, to me, both disturbing and illuminating. Following Scott, Dehli asks "about the terms in which it is possible (or not) to 'fashion' a self that can legitimately be recognized as a speaking subject" (137). For me, one of the tasks becomes to investigate how, in part, I produced and am produced as a subject that I also contest, participating in problematic practices of normalization (Dehli 135) despite my own efforts to advance equity. This article is an effort to supportively challenge and trouble this particular approach to doing anti-homophobia work in order to think more critically about our interventions for social justice and what they conceal and illuminate. While every analysis and intervention is partial and problematic, not all are equally so and I want to be able to continue asking which are better and more effective in relation to the goals and contexts in which I/we locate our interventions while keeping a focus on the mechanisms of power.[6]

194 *Gulzar Raisa Charania*

I would like to thank Kari Dehli for her detailed and insightful engagement with the initial paper on which this article is based. I would also like to acknowledge the many people with whom I worked at the Toronto District School Board. In particular, I would like to thank Ken Jeffers for his support over many years as well as Jamie Berrigan and Nadia Bello for their ongoing engagement with the issues in this paper.

Originally published in CWS/cf's Winter/Spring 2005 issue, "Lesbian, Bisexual, Queer, Transsexual/Transgender Sexualities" (Volume 24, Numbers 2/3: 31-37).

[1]I use the term coming out stories, in plural, to reflect the many and varied stories I told.

[2]A number of preoccupations bring me to this inquiry. During my time as an equity worker at the Toronto District School Board (TDSB), my responsibilities included participating in, supervising and sometimes leading various equity efforts, including the collaborative oversight of the anti-homophobia speakers' bureau. Anti-homophobia workshops were usually requested from teachers or school administrators in response to incidents of homophobia or as one time educational sessions.

[3]Despite the adoption of a broad equity policy that is inclusive of class, race, gender, sexual orientation, and ability, the gap between policy and reality in TDSB schools is difficult to miss, not only in relation to anti-homophobia but all equity areas. See www.tdsb.on.ca for details of the full policy. This policy was secured as a result of the advocacy of a broad range of community organizations, educators and activists.

[4]I rely on ideas and insights about storytelling developed in an M.A. thesis that was collaboratively researched and theorized with my colleague Tabish Surani. These insights were also collaboratively written in the theoretical framework sections of both theses. For a fuller discussion of this point, see Surani; Charania.

[5]Womack identifies as being of Creek, Cherokee, Irish and German descent. Throughout the article, he variously refers to himself as Native American, a Creek trickster, a warrior, mixed blood, a queer Indian and a gay Indian man.

[6]At the time of writing this article, my position as a Student Program Worker at the TDSB remains vacant. It was not reposted when I left the board. Cuts to equity positions, lack of accountability for anti-homophobia, anti-racism and equity policies as well as deep cuts in services and funding to public education and a corresponding rise in punishing equity seeking youth and communities continues.

References

Ahmed, Sara. *The Cultural Politics of Emotion.* New York: Routledge, 2004.
Bannerji, Himani. *Thinking Through: Essays on Feminism, Marxism and Anti-Racism.* Toronto: Women's Press, 1995.

Boler, Megan. *Feeling Power: Emotions and Education.* New York: Routledge, 1999.

Butler, Judith. "Contingent Foundations: Feminism and the Question of 'Postmodernism.'" *Feminists Theorize the Political.* Eds. J. Butler and J. W. Scott. New York: Routledge, 1992. 3-21.

Charania, Gulzar Raisa. "Encounters with Northern Development Workers: Reflections from the 'Field.'" Department of Curriculum, Teaching and Learning, Ontario Institute for Studies in Education of the University of Toronto, Toronto, 2001.

Dehli, Kari. "'Making' the Parent and the Researcher: Genealogy Meets Ethnography in Research on Contemporary School Reforms." *Dangerous Encounters: Genealogy and Ethnography.* Eds. M. Tamboukou and S. J. Ball. New York: Peter Lang, 2003. 133-151.

Fellows, Mary Louise and Sherene Razack. "The Race to Innocence: Confronting Hierarchical Relations Among Women." *The Journal of Gender, Race and Justice* 1 (1998): 335-352.

Foucault, Michel. "Two Lectures." *Power/Knowledge: Selected Interviews and Other Writings 1972-1977.* Ed. C. Gordon. London: Harvester Press, 1972. 78-108.

Foucault, Michel. "The Subject and Power." *Michel Foucault: Beyond Structuralism and Hermeneutics.* Eds. H. Dreyfus and P. Rabinow. Chicago: University of Chicago, 1982. 208-226.

Foucault, Michel. "Politics and the Study of Discourse." *The Foucault Effect: Studies in Governmentality.* Eds. G. Burchell, C. Gordon, and P. Miller. Chicago: University of Chicago, 1991. 53-72.

Foucault, Michel. "Truth and Power." *Michel Foucault: Power, Essential Works of Foucault, Volume 3.* Ed. J. D. Faubion. New York: The New Press, 1994. 111-133.

Gopinath, Gayatri. "Nostalgia, Desire, Diaspora: South Asian Sexualities in Motion." *Theorizing Daspora.* Eds. J. E. Braziel and A. Mannur. Malden, MA: Blackwell Publishing Ltd., 2003. 261-279.

Gubrium, Jaber F. and James A. Holstein. "Narrative Practice and the Coherence of Personal Stories." *The Sociological Quarterly* 39 (1998): 163-187.

King, Thomas. *The Truth About Stories: A Native Narrative.* Toronto: House of Anansi Press, 2003.

Lee, Ruthann. "'Coming out' as Queer Asian Youth in Canada: Examining Cultural Narratives of Identity and Community." M.A. Thesis, Sociology and Equity Studies in Education, OISE/University of Toronto, Toronto, 2003.

McHoul, A. W. and Wendy Grace. *A Foucault Primer: Discourse, Power, and the Subject.* New York: New York University Press, 2003.

Passavant, Paul. "The Governmentality of Discussion." *Cultural Studies and Political Theory.* Ed. J. Dean. Ithaca, NY: Cornell University Press, 2000. 115-131.

Razack, Sherene. *Looking White People in the Eye: Gender, Race, and Culture in Courtrooms and Classrooms.* Toronto: University of Toronto Press, 1998.

Scott, David. *Refashioning Futures: Criticism After Postcoloniality.* Princeton: Princeton University Press, 1999.

Scott, Joan W. "Experience." *Feminists Theorize the Political.* Eds. J. Butler and J. W. Scott. New York: Routledge, 1992. 22-40.

Smith, Dorothy E. *The Everyday World as Problematic: a Feminist Sociology.* Toronto: University of Toronto Press, 1998.

Surani, Tabish. "Shaping the North-South Encounter: The Training of Northern Development Workers." Department of Curriculum, Teaching and Learning, Ontario Institute for Studies in Education of the Univeristy of Toronto, Toronto, 2001.

Valverde, Mariana. "Experience and Truth Telling in a Post-Humanist World: A Foucauldian Contribution to Feminist Ethical Reflections." *Feminism and the Final Foucault.* Eds. D. Taylor and K. Vintges, 2004. 67-90. Chicago: University of Illinois Press.

Venn, Couze. "Refiguring Subjectivity After Modernity." *Challenging Subjects: Critical Psychology for A New Millenium.* Ed. V. Walkerdine. Houndmills, Baskingstoke: Palgrave, 2002. 51-71.

Womack, Craig. "Howling at the Moon: The Queer But True Story of my Life as Hank Williams." *As We Are Now: Mixblood Essays on Race and Identity.* Ed. W. S. Penn. Berkeley: University of California Press, 1997. 28-49.

 **Work/Economy**

The Feminization of Poverty

An Old Problem With a New Name

Lesley D. Harman ━━

Just as things are starting to look better for women, in what many have come to call the "post-feminist" era, the feminization of poverty is being spoken of as a new social problem. In fact, it is an old problem with a new name. Women's poverty, while not new, is taking a new shape. Women have always been poor, but through their dependent roles as wives, mothers, and daughters, their poverty has been concealed as only a potential plight, or as something that only happened to other women, women who did not have a man. But as more and more women live without men, either by choice or by necessity, women's poverty becomes more visible, and their dependency is transferred from the male breadwinner to the state (Harman).

The apparent gains of the women's movement, including a general shift of women's presence from the domestic ghetto to a growing visibility in the public sphere, have been accompanied by a general complacency, as well as the recently noted backlash against feminism (see Faludi). One often hears that "things have changed"—the battles have been won, equality is here. What implications does this have for the young women about to enter the workforce? Many of these women have been encouraged to be independent and to develop their own careers, a path which they believe will ensure them a good life, in which they will avoid the dependency and potential poverty of their mothers and sisters who had followed the previous generations' role prescriptions. The current mythology is precisely that this life will be possible and attainable. The prospect of being unable to succeed is foreign; the idea that they might be susceptible to poverty, remote. The reality, however, is that in 1996, 58 per cent of poor Canadian adults were women—just one per cent lower than in 1975 (National Council of Welfare 1998: 1). In Canadian society today, 84 per cent of all women will spend part of their adult lives without husbands, supporting themselves as well as their children (National Council of Welfare 1990: 15). At every stage of their lives, women are more likely to be poor, and are more likely to be trapped in a life of poverty.

What is meant by the feminization of poverty? Simply put, it means that without the support of a man, a woman is likely to be poor. This fact of life is not new. Women's economic dependency on men has been essential to the perpetuation of the system of masculine dominance. Economic dependency produces and is reproduced by women's subordination and powerlessness, which ensures that females conform to role prescriptions around reproduction (motherhood) and labour (both unpaid domestic labour and work in the paid labour force). As more and more women enter the paid workforce, work and family obligations result in conflicts and often economic difficulties for women.

Reproduction factors heavily into women's material existence. As our society is currently organized, women have very little control over their reproductive potential. Women have the children, and childbearing and childrearing are the least valued of all occupations. If we can judge the social value of an occupation by how much those performing it are paid, we will quickly notice that those who get paid for caring for children (domestics, nannies, babysitters, and daycare workers) are among the lowest paid of all members of society, and 97 per cent of those holding these jobs are women (Harder 6). Indeed, the pay for most typically "female" jobs (clerical, service, teaching, nursing, and caregiving), reflects the fact that women's work in general is devalued and trivialized in our society. In 1993, 86 per cent of women in the paid labour forced worked in the service sector (Harder 5). By 1996, women still earned 73.4 per cent of what men earned in the paid labour force in Canada (Canadian Social Trends). This work is essential and must be done. However, as long as it is assumed that it will be done, gladly and even gratefully, by women for no money or recognition, then the fundamental structures which reproduce women's dependency will continue to go unchallenged.

In addition to being assumed as women's natural role and ultimate route to fulfillment (which it may in fact be for many women), reproduction is used to legitimize women's inferior position in the paid labour force. Because it is generally assumed that most women in our society will eventually marry and have children, it is also assumed that their aspirations for career advancement are selfish. It is taken for granted that women will take several years from their careers to spend in full-time mothering. While it is true that over half of all married women in our society are in the paid labour force, and most of them are there because they need the income, it is also true that pregnancy and childbirth guarantee a minimum six-week absence from the workforce. With recent revisions to maternity leave provisions, new mothers can now leave their paid positions for up to six months (or more as unpaid leave). While the new leave provisions are long overdue and should be applauded, we must be careful not to overlook some of the possible implications of women's protracted absence from the paid workforce. It stands to reason that one or more lengthy absences from a career will put a woman "off time" in her own career (Burman).

The resumption of a career after childbirth usually means employing another person to do the caregiving, although with the current economic recession often hitting male breadwinners, an increasing number of fathers are taking on full-time caregiving roles. Given the gross inequities between salaries in traditional dual-income families, it is usually the woman who receives less money for her work in the paid labour force. Whether or not to go back to work is, therefore, sometimes a difficult decision. It is not unusual to hear a woman say, "I can't afford to work." What does this mean? It means that after taxes, work-related expenses (transportation, wardrobe, and lunches), many women find that having another person look after their children ends up costing them more than they earn. If they cannot afford to leave their jobs, they may then be heard to say, "I can't afford to have children."

The economic difficulties produced through work and family conflicts have serious implications for women's poverty. On the one hand, this situation can be used to argue that a woman's place is in the home and that we should return to the 'family wage,' an arrangement in which the male breadwinner is seen to be earning enough money through his one paycheque to support the entire family. This idea precludes the necessity of women working for income to share in the support of the family. It also puts the final nail in the coffin of the feminization of poverty, ensuring that women do not have any opportunities for economic independence. Women's poverty thus becomes a self-fulfilling prophecy.

While a return to the family wage would seem to be unlikely in these times of dual-income families, of concern is that paid employment for women has itself become a poverty trap. The prevalent myth that women can compete in the paid labour force, offered equal opportunities to succeed in their careers, and make adequate incomes, is shattered when it is understood that for many women it is economically impossible to work in the paid labour force and have children. Economic dependency on either the male breadwinner or the state becomes a necessity, rather than a choice.

The above discussion has assumed a traditional, nuclear familial arrangement in which there are no adult caregivers to stay home during the day with the children, a paid male breadwinner, and a mother who is forced to give up her job in order to look after the children during the day because she cannot afford to work. This is perhaps one of the least visible manifestations of the feminization of poverty because by returning to the private sphere, the women in question are no longer considered to be on the job market and are not categorized as "unemployed" (Burman). Instead, they have resumed their so-called 'natural,' dependent roles in the family. As long as women are economically dependent on men, the opportunities for change are very few.

While female economic dependency is not new, some of the manifestations of what happens when women live in ways other than traditional dependency arrangements, are becoming gradually more visible. Such visibility confirms that the more things change, the more they stay the same. As recent statistics reveal, women's poverty is most striking among those living without men. According to the National Council of Welfare, in 1996 61.4 per cent of female lone parents, 45.4 per cent of unattached women over the age of 65, and 39.5 per cent of unattached women under 65, were living in poverty in this country (National Council of Welfare, 1998: 85).

Teenage pregnancy is often a direct path to early and long term poverty for women. For young women who give birth and keep their babies, the label "single mother" is inevitable. Even when they marry the fathers of their children, the majority of such unions end in early divorce, with the mothers usually taking custody of the children and often ending up as Family Benefits recipients. Family Benefits is another expression of economic dependency on the state. Along with never-married or divorced teenaged mothers, all mothers of young children who find themselves "alone" (read: without a man) may eventually find it necessary to turn to the state for financial support.

Aging and poverty are historically related in our society, particularly for women. Because women tend to outlive men by an average of seven years, it is likely that women will spend at least some portion of their last years alone. Recently, the aged have become more affluent, perhaps due to increases in universal pensions and the tendency for more employed citizens to finance their own retirement through registered retirement pension plans. However, a woman who has spent her adult life bearing and rearing children and doing unpaid domestic labour in the home may have had little opportunity to save, and is not entitled to the Canada Pension Plan in her old age.

The bleak reality of being old and female is that there is very little hope of ever emerging from a life of poverty. Poverty is more like a life sentence: as long as you are alive, you will be poor. When women are young, the myth of equal opportunity seems more believable. As we have seen, however, myths can be the most insidious traps of all. The myth of equality of opportunity extends to other minority groups as well. If the dominant, privileged, and wealthy group in our society is comprised of white, able-bodied, heterosexual, Anglo Saxon males somewhere in their middle years with a university education, then we can see that not only is our society sexist and ageist, but it is also classist, racist, heterosexist, and ableist.

In our racist society, "women of colour"[1] are made to feel as if they are "other" to white women. Immigrant women face difficulties upon arriving in Canada, such as language barriers, lack of education, and racial discrimination in the job market. Domestic workers are one of the most exploited groups of immigrant women. Not only do they perform the most devalued roles in our society, but they are subject to low pay, low status, cruelty, and harassment by their employers. Finally, the double impact of gender and race is nowhere more evident than in the lived experiences of Aboriginal women, who belong to the poorest and most discriminated against group in Canadian society.

Discrimination on the basis of sexual preference exists for lesbian women. The Canadian state offers tax advantages to those who marry and have children, resulting in relative economic disadvantage for women who do not. Subtle and not-so-subtle heterosexism may result in lesbian women having to conceal their sexual orientation for fear of losing their jobs or not being hired.

Physical disability is an almost guaranteed route to poverty for women. Disabled women are less likely to be married than are disabled men or able-bodied women; if they are alone, they are less likely to be employed and will therefore have to depend on the state for their material existence. Disabled single mothers often find it difficult to find affordable, accessible housing (National Council of Welfare 1990: 117).

Perhaps the most visible indication of the breadth and depth of the feminization of poverty is the growing phenomenon of homelessness among women (Harman). Women who become homeless have basically lost, or never had, the means to support themselves. This is a tragic but inevitable outcome of the feminization of poverty. Homelessness occurs among women from all social classes and a variety of racial and ethnic backgrounds. It is very difficult to gather reliable data on homeless women because they are the group of women in our society which is the most difficult to locate. Their abject poverty, entitling them to membership in the 'underclass,' places them both outside and below the class system, and disenfranchises them from citizenship in this society.

The web of relations that constitutes the rights and duties of citizens (home ownership, taxation, employment, familial relations) also necessitates a series of controls over citizens, in the form of numbers: address, phone, bank account, social insurance, credit card, health insurance, driver's license, passport—the list seems endless. While many such identifiers have taken on the rather perverse connotations of freedom and privilege in our society (the American Express Card), they are really ways of locating and potentially controlling the "homeful." When women are "homeful" they can always be found ("May I speak to the lady of the house, please?"). When women are homeless, what they "lack," the source of their "deficiency," is precisely a place within these relations of dependency.

The plight of homeless women points to certain contradictions in Canadian society which affect the lives of all women, "homeful" or not. To be a woman in Canada today is to face a strong likelihood of being poor at sometime in her life. The myth of equality of opportunity conceals the fundamental inequalities which continue to keep women economically dependent on men and the state. While appearing to guarantee women's economic security, the traditional roles of wife and mother in fact only serve to mask how close all women are to a life of poverty. When women attempt to break free of dependency relations, their inferior position in the paid workforce, and the liabilities they will face if they have children, they have a greater likelihood of being economically disadvantaged and of seeking social assistance. Women who are older, non-white, lesbian, or disabled, will find their experiences of poverty compounded.

What is the price of freedom? With all of the courage that it takes to be free of masculine dominance in one's personal life, is it inevitable that it will be replaced by the domination of the state through some form of social assistance? The structural conditions that might guarantee women's financial independence are simply not in place. Does this mean the ultimate freedom is to simply opt out? As Thelma and Louise chose their own death above subjugation to male brutality and the violent state, so it seems that homelessness and abject poverty are the ultimate end for those women who do not have a conventional place within the patriarchy. Is this horrific observation far from the truth? It seems that as long as reproduction and labour power remain in the hands of the patriarchy, so will the material existence of women.

For there to be a glimmer of hope on the horizon, we must look to ways in which women can enrich their own lives. Like all powerless groups, women have found strength in numbers, and empowerment in revaluing what their oppressors devalue. Perhaps the feminization of poverty exists because 'feminine' is defined as impoverishing. Finding our wealth in the very traits which make us poor in this society may be a rewarding path on the road to true equality.

Originally published in CWS/cf's *Summer 1992 issue, "Women and Poverty" (Volume 12, Number 4). This article was subsequently reprinted in a volume entitled,* Gender in the 1900s: Images, Realities, and Issues, *edited by E.D. Nelson and B. W. Robinson, published by Nelson Canada in 1995.*

[1]I use this term reluctantly because the term itself is implicitly racist. The language lumps all "women of colour" together as being "not white," thus implying that the only normative is white.

References

Burman, Patrick. *Killing Time: Experiences of Unemployment.* Toronto: Thompson Educational Publishing, 1988.

Canadian Social Trends. "Social Indicators." Canadian Social Trends (Spring 1999): 27.

Faludi, Susan. *Backlash: The Undeclared War Against American Women.* New York: Crown, 1991.

Harder, Sandra. Women in Canada: Socio-Economic Status and Other Contemporary Issues. Ottawa: Minister of Supply and Services Canada, 1996.

Harman, Lesley D. *When a Hostel Becomes a Home: Experiences of Women.* Toronto: Garamond, 1989.

National Council of Welfare. *Women and Poverty Revisited.* Ottawa: Ministry of Supply and Services Canada, 1990.

National Council of Welfare. *Poverty Profile 1996.* Ottawa: Ministry of Supply and Services Canada, 1998.

Solidarity and Pride

Sue Genge ⟶

The CLC clearly understands that sexism, racism, ableism and heterosexism share common roots. We acknowledge that we can change attitudes and behaviour if we stand united. We know we will fail if we allow ourselves to be divided. We believe that we can be unified without uniformity and that we can celebrate our diversity without divisiveness. We will strive to achieve a truly inclusive union movement that is representative of all its members. (CLC 1994a)

Over the last few years the Canadian Labour Congress (CLC) and the labour movement as a whole have taken a number of major steps towards recognizing and fighting for the rights of lesbian and gay trade union members. Beginning in 1980, the CLC made a formal amendment to its own constitution to include sexual orientation as a prohibited ground of discrimination. The same convention also passed a general resolution in support of gay rights and the inclusion of sexual orientation in human rights laws across the country.

Prior to this convention, there had been some preliminary organizing among lesbian and gay union activists. The Canadian Union of Postal Workers (CUPW) for example, bargained language prohibiting discrimination on the basis of sexual orientation in their collective agreement in the late '70s. Several library locals represented by the Canadian Union of Public Employees (CUPE) were also active in bargaining protection and in raising the issue in federations of labour and at the CLC.

After this convention, activists within labour concentrated their efforts in several areas, including education and bargaining protections and equal access to workplace benefits. As well, during this period a number of significant arbitration cases and court challenges were launched by lesbian and gay trade unionists with the moral, political, and financial support of their unions. Perhaps the most well known are Karen Andrews's fight to have the Ontario Health Insurance Plan recognize her partner and their children as eligible for benefits and Brian Mossop's fight to gain recognition of his bereavement at the death of his partner's father.

A key legal victory spearheaded by trade unionists concerns private pension plans. Nancy Rosenberg and Margaret Evans as employees of the Canadian Union of Public Employees challenged the federal income tax regulations that only recognized opposite sex spouses for survivor benefits. CUPE as the employer in this case fully supported the court challenge. In April 1998, the Ontario Court of Appeal unanimously ruled that the federal income tax act is unconstitutional and must be read to include coverage for same-sex partners.

This victory opened the doors for the successful campaign for equal access to workplace benefits—such as health and dental, bereavement leave, family leave, survivor benefits—for same-sex partners and families. The CLC and other unions made numerous presentations to federal House of Commons and Senate Committees in support of amending federal legislation to remove discrimination on the basis of sexual orientation and family status. Similarly, unions were involved in the recent campaign to win access to civil marriage rights for gay and lesbian couples. The CLC was one of the founding groups of Canadians for Equal Marriage, the coalition of churches, social justice groups, professional associations, community associations which lead the fight for equal legal rights in this area. The support of Canada's unions was stronger than ever in this campaign and saw union leaders across the country take public stands in support of equal marriage.

One of the most important early areas of activity was the beginning of self-organizing among gay and lesbian people within the labour movement. From informal caucuses meeting in hotel rooms and hallways, activists organized committees and working groups and demanded formal recognition from their unions. In CUPE, a Pink Triangle Committee was formed with representatives from across the country. Similarly, gay and lesbian members of the Public Service Alliance of Canada (PSAC) organized into officially recognized gay and lesbian support groups. These early forms of self-organization were concentrated in public-sector unions.

In May 1994, delegates at the CLC convention overwhelmingly endorsed a major policy paper on sexual orientation that ends with the statement quoted at the beginning of this article. This policy paper, passed along with a policy on "Confronting the Mean Society," links the oppressions faced by women, people of colour, Aboriginal people, people with disabilities, and lesbian and gay people. The two policies have helped to define the work of the labour movement and of equality-seeking union activists over the last few years.

The statement called on the CLC and all affiliated unions to develop anti-harassment policies to include sexual orientation, for the workplace and the unions; make bargaining protection for lesbian and gay workers and recognition of same-sex spousal relationships for benefits a priority; actively oppose homophobia in the workplace and unions; participate in public campaigns to win human rights for lesbian and gay members of society; prepare and distribute educational material for union members; and establish a Lesbian, Gay, and Bisexual Working Group as part of the Human Rights Committee of the CLC.

Since then, the CLC and a number of unions have carried work forward in all of these areas. Notably, the Canadian Labour Congress decided to intervene in support of Jim Egan and John Nesbit in their fight for same-sex spousal pension benefits before the Supreme Court *(Egan and Nesbit* v. *R.)*. The CLC also supported Delwin Vriend's case at the Supreme Court to ensure that the Alberta *Human Rights* Act provided protection against discrimination on the grounds of sexual orientation. Vriend was fired for being gay and had no access to legal remedies under the current law in Alberta.

> The Canadian Labour Congress has intervened ... because it is committed to combatting and eliminating discrimination and preju-dice against gays and lesbians in the workplace and in Canadian society. From the perspective of the CLC, the discrimination expe-rienced by gays and lesbians in the employment context is directly and integrally related to the fact that, in society at large, gays and lesbians have historically suffered exclusion, prejudice and discrimi-nation. (Factum of the Intervenor, *Egan and Nesbit v. R.*)

This CLC statement to the Supreme Court explains the importance of these cases for the work of unionists in combatting discrimination. The Congress also pointed out to the Court that as the senior union organization in Canada with over 90 affiliated trade union organizations, representing over two million Canadians, the position of the CLC represented a significant segment of society.

The CLC was also involved in the ultimately successful campaign to amend the *Canadian Human Rights Act* to prohibit discrimination on the basis of sexual orientation. We helped mount pressure on the government of Newfoundland and Labrador to similarly amend their human rights legisla-tion. The CLC also worked closely with activists in Alberta to ensure that the Klein government did the "right thing" in response to the successful Supreme Court challenge launched by Delwin Vriend. The Supreme Court ruled that the Alberta human rights law must be read to include protection on the grounds of sexual orientation. The Klein government spent a week deciding whether to accept the Court's decision—a week full of a vicious, ugly, anti-gay, right-wing backlash. The homophobia was so shocking that Premier Klein was forced to state unequivocally that it is "morally wrong to discriminate on the basis of sexual orientation" and that his government would respect the Court's ruling.

Unions are increasingly involved in supporting and participating in lesbian and gay pride day events across the country. The CLC has produced posters and pins highlighting "Solidarity and Pride," the two critical slogans of the two movements. Leaders of unions and the CLC, presidents of federations of labour, and labour councils now regularly speak at pride day events across the country, bringing greetings from labour and pledging solidarity.

As well, many unions provide courses to help educate union members about the discrimination faced by gay and lesbian trade unionists and ways to combat it. These courses are constantly being evaluated and developed to meet the needs of human rights activists and lesbian and gay members. Several unions have developed videos. One example is an anti-harassment video produced by the Canadian Auto Workers (CAW), which focuses on the harassment experienced by a lesbian factory worker.

The formation of the national Lesbian, Gay, and Bisexual Working Group (subsequently renamed the Solidarity and Pride Working Group), mandated by the 1994 Convention, was a very significant development for Canadian labour. The Working Group began meeting in the fall of 1994 and has been growing continually. Representatives come from the Public Service Alliance of Canada, the Canadian Union of Public Employees, the Canadian Auto Workers, Communication, Energy, and Paperworkers, the Canadian Federation of Nurses' Union, the Canadian Union of Postal Workers, the Telecommunications Workers Union, the United Steelworkers, Service Employees International Union, the Ontario English Catholic Teachers Association, the National Union of the Canadian Association of University Teachers, the International Association of Machinists and Aerospace Workers, United Food and Commercial Workers and the Ontario, Saskatchewan, North West Territories and Quebec Federations of Labour. Other unions are also moving to appoint representatives. The group is increasingly representative of workers in both the public and private sectors and of the various areas in the country.

The first "campaign" the group undertook in the labour movement we called a "visibility campaign." There were two major points we wanted to make: (1) lesbians and gay men are everywhere at the workplace and in every union; and (2) our issues are central and legitimate union issues, which we expect our unions to address. The campaign included the production of "Solidarity and Pride" posters and buttons. The Group also conducted a political, consciousness-raising intervention into the 1996 CLC convention. One morning every tenth delegate was presented with the then-new "Solidarity and Pride" button and flyer which proclaimed "Congratulations—you have been selected as Gay for a Day. Like the rest of us, your selection was entirely random. And you are now entitled to experience the following aspects of our oppression." Convention delegates took this all in good spirits and many who weren't "selected" came to ask for a button.

At the 2005 CLC Convention, the Group distributed a flyer called "Until," which thanked unionists for their support and reminded them that "until" equality was achieved in some 20 areas "we will continue to phone, fax and email you" for support. Some of the lines are:

Until we're considered equal, and not simply "tolerated."
Until we don't have to justify, explain and expose our private lives.
Until we can express our gender without fear of reprisal or ridicule.
Until the cure for homophobia is discovered.
Until we can love and be loved, with joy and gay abandon.

A general questionnaire was also prepared for the attention of unions, federations of labour and labour councils asking them to outline the activities they have undertaken to support gay and lesbian issues. Entitled "Defending Gay and Lesbian Members: Our Record to Date," the questionnaire sparked discussion throughout the labour movement about the issues, about what had been done, and about other initiatives that could be undertaken.

A major project of the Working Group came to fruition in the next year. The CLC held the first ever Solidarity and Pride Conference for Lesbian, Gay, Bisexual Trade Unionists and Our Allies in Ottawa in October 1997. Over 300 participants, from across the country, representing many unions, gathered to discuss issues such as homophobia, legal decisions, contract provisions, negotiating strategies, and creating a safe place in workplaces and communities for gay, lesbian, and bisexual trade unionists. To our knowledge, this conference was a world first. Not that there haven't been other conferences of lesbian, gay, bisexual, transgender unionists before. There have been—in the United States and in Europe. These earlier conferences, however, were organized by independent groups of trade unionists, rather than by the official trade union structures. Our conference as an official CLC conference, sponsored and financed by the Canadian trade union central.

For conference participants the experience was a breakthrough in many ways. For those active in the labour movement, it was a place to be where we could be absolutely comfortable about our sexual orientation and could exchange our ideas and experiences with others who share a class location and perspective. It was refreshing, to say the least, to be able to be both working-class and gay with hundreds of brothers and sisters.

The conference generated much enthusiasm and many challenges. Primarily, delegates wanted to see an even deeper commitment by the labour movement to confronting homophobia and fighting for the rights of lesbian and gay members—as workers and as citizens. We wanted to be able to organize more widely at the local and regional level. One sister returned to Saskatchewan and persuaded the Federation of Labour to establish a provincial Solidarity and Pride Committee. A very successful Prairie regional trade union conference was held in Premier Klein's town of Edmonton, just to let him know we aren't going away. And the Ontario Federation of Labour held a similar conference in 1999. Activists at the conference raised the issue of inclusion of the discrimination faced by transgendered workers within the ambit of the CLC'S Working Group.

Since this first conference, the CLC has organized two more cross-Canada Solidarity and Pride Conferences: in BC in 2001 and in Quebec City in 2005 and another regional conference, the "East Coast Gathering of Lesbian, Gay, Bisexual and Transgender Unionists and Our Allies" in Nova Scotia in 2003.

Following the 1997 conference, the Solidarity and Pride Working Group broadened its mandate to include discrimination on the basis of gender identity and gender expression. We organized a cross-country consultation on the issues facing transgender workers. Over the course of several years, the

Group met with trans unionists and activists and developed a guiding document for trade unions: "Trans Issues for the Labour Movement."

Another focus of concern is to see lesbian, gay, bisexual, and transgender people in positions of leadership. It is amazing to see the numbers of delegates in leadership positions in the labour movement. At our conferences, over half the delegates stand when asked how many hold elected positions in their unions.

In Ontario—another first. At the Ontario Federation of Labour convention in November 1997, delegates supported the creation of a position on the Federation executive for an out lesbian or gay trade union vice president and a lesbian was elected to the executive at that convention. The Canadian Labour Congress followed suit with the establishment of a CLC Executive Council LGBT Vice President position in 2002, which ensures that issues for this community are raised in the highest decision-making body of the CLC.

The Solidarity and Pride Working Group continues to promote labour support and activity. Plans are in the works to develop information and educational material and to share the news about what is happening on sexual orientation and gender identity issues in various unions. Building networks to reach out and involve more lesbian, gay, bisexual, and transgender members in the labour movement and in the activities of the Working Group is a critical task. Working in solidarity with other equality-seeking groups and building links between lesbian and gay organizations and unions is also high on our list of priorities.

> Solidarity means listening to and supporting each other, encouraging unity in diversity, and finding common ground. There is no room in our ranks for ideologies and prejudices which pit worker against worker. The leaders and activists in the Canadian labour movement have a difficult but rewarding job ahead of them. Our members—all our members—our unions and ultimately our society will reap the benefits. (CLC 1994b, Paragraph 33)

An earlier version of this article was originally published in CWS/cf's Spring 1998 issue, "Women and Work" (Volume 18, Number 1).

References

Canadian Labour Congress (CLC). Sexual Orientation Policy Paper. Ottawa: CLC, 1994a. Online: www.canadianlabour.ca.

Canadian Labour Congress (CLC). "Confronting the Mean Society." Ottawa: CLC, 1994b. Online: www.canadianlabour.ca.

Canadian Labour Congress (CLC). "Trans Issues for the Labour Movement." Ottawa: CLC, 2003. Online: www.canadianlabour.ca.

"Until: A Message from the CLC Solidarity and Pride Working Group." Ottawa: CLC, 2005. Online: www.canadianlabour.ca.

Thinking it Through

Women, Work and Caring in the New Millennium

Pat Armstrong and Hugh Armstrong ━

The American feminist Deborah Stone, an eloquent analyst of women's caring, talks about being a "'lumper' rather than a 'splitter'" (91). For "lumpers," the emphasis is on what is common about women's work, on what women share. At the same time, there remains in her publications a clear recognition of tensions and differences. Miriam Glucksmann's revealing analyses of British women's work speaks of "slicing" data, theory and concepts to create multiple and complex pictures of particular peoples in particular places (16). Her purpose is to look at the various ways work is divided up within what she calls the "total social organization of labour."

This paper is about both lumping and slicing. It attempts to explore what is common, not only among women but also across time and space. At the same time, it seeks to examine different slices of the same questions. Such slices are meant to help expose the complex and contradictory nature of the concepts we use in considering women's work and of the current state of women's work. It assumes that contexts and locations matter, and that while women face considerable pressures from forces outside their immediate control, they also are active participants in shaping their own lives.

Why lump?

Everywhere throughout recorded time, there has been a division of labour by gender. Every society we know about has defined some work as men's and some as women's. And every society we know about has made distinctions between what women can and should do. Women have primary daily responsibilities for children and for the sick or disabled, as well as for much of the other work in domestic domains. They do most of the cooking, washing, cleaning, toileting, bathing, feeding, comforting, training for daily living, shopping and planning for domestic consumption and care. And it is women who bear the children.

This division of labour is combined with a gap between average male and female wages. Jobs mainly done by men pay more than those mainly done by women. Women are much more likely than men to work part-time or part-year and to have interrupted career pattems or casual, temporary jobs. When self-employed, they are much less likely than men to employ others. And much of the work women do pays no wage at all.

Feminists have long been struggling to make the full range of women's work both visible and valued. Lumping has allowed them to do this. They began in the early 1960s by focussing on domestic labour, understood as the unpaid work women do in households, and by revealing the institutional and social arrangements that combine to produce systemic discrimination in the paid workforce. Initially, the emphasis was on what was termed the reproduction of labour power on a daily and generational basis. This meant having babies and providing for their needs, along with those of their breadwinning fathers. As the research on women's work expanded, the picture of this work became both more refined and more complex. More categories of work, such as care for the elderly, the sick and the disabled, appeared in the literature. Then this care category, too, was further refined to include care management, assistance with daily living and personal as well as medical care, and it came to be seen as a relationship rather than simply as a work category. Similarly, the picture of women's work in the labour force was further developed to encompass the detailed division of labour found within occupations and industries and the nature of workplace relationships. Within the formal economy outside the home, working in the public sector was distinguished from the private sector, and then this private sector itself divided between the for-profit and the not-for-profit, or what came to be called the third sector. Within this not-for-profit sector, women's work as volunteers was distinguished from their paid employment. Locations in the underground economy, where women worked for pay as cleaners, prostitutes, babysitters and secretaries, and in formal economy jobs that they did in their own homes, also have been exposed.

Lumping also allows us to explore the social, economic and institutional arrangements as well as the policies and practices that contribute to these patterns in women's work. But lumping is not only about processes remote from the individual lives of most women, about abstract concepts or far-away decision-makers. It is also about how women's work is shaped at the level of the hospital, day-care, community centre, clinic, home and office; about the fine divisions of labour; the ways policies are played out in daily lives and the ways women act to create spaces in their own lives or to limit those spaces. So, for example, lumping allows us to ask what kinds of caring work women and men do, and what kinds of government funding support or undermine this work.

Lumping, then, is appropriate because there are so many common patterns in women's work. Lumping allows us to see what women, as women, share, in terms of the nature of both the work and the work relationships. It also helps us to expose the forces that keep these patterns in place and change them.

Why slice?

Although there is a division of labour by sex everywhere, there is also no common division of labour across time and space and often not even within countries during a particular period. What is defined and practised as men's work or women's work varies enormously, and most cultures have at least some women who do men's work. Moreover, the actual division of labour can contradict the prescriptions or accepted practices. Equally important, there are significant differences among women related to class, race, culture, age, marital status, sexual orientation and spatial locations, as well as for the same women over time.

Once, those paid to do secretarial and teaching work were mainly men; now, most are women. Those paid as chefs are mainly men, while women do most of the unpaid cooking. However, in Canada at least, if the unpaid cooking is done outside on the barbeque, it is men who do the work, but the unpaid kitchen jobs are still primarily left to women. In the USSR, most doctors were women at the same time as North American medicine was dominated by men. The care provided by women in a Bosnian refugee camp differs fundamentally from that provided in a household in Ottawa's exclusive Rockcliffe neighbourhood. While care work is women's work, there are multiple forms of women's paid and unpaid caring. There are also considerable variations in what is defined as women's caring work. Our grandmothers, for example, did not clean catheters, insert needles or adjust oxygen masks as part of the care work they did at home.

There may also be large gaps in both places between what women and men think they should do and what they are able to do. There is, in other words, often a gap between practices and ideas about appropriate practices. For example, while most Canadian and British men think they should equally share the domestic labour, there is little evidence that such sharing actually happens in practice. Yet many men who think care is women's work find themselves providing care for ill and aging partners. Many women who provide care do not necessarily think that it is their job, nor do they necessarily have the skills to do the work. At the same time, many women who think they should provide care cannot do so because they have too many other demands on their time, because they do not have the skills, because they do not have the other necessary resources or because they do not have the physical capacity. Many who do provide care, providing services such as meal preparation, comforting and cleaning, may not even see this as care because it is so much a part of their daily lives.

Not only within countries at particular times, but also within workplaces, there may be significant differences among women. A hospital, for example, may have women working as managers and women working as housekeepers. The managers are more likely to be white, Canadian-born, with English or French as a first language and relatively young, while the housekeepers are more likely to have migrated to this country, to have neither English or French as their mother tongue and to be older than the female managers. And, of course, there are significant differences between these groups in terms of power, pay and ideas about work, and in their political, material and symbolic resources related not only to their positions in the paid work force, but also to their positions in their households and neighbourhoods.

But slicing is not only necessary to draw out the differences related to women's various spatial, physical, social, psychological, economic, work and age locations, it is also necessary in order to see the different ways of understanding the evidence, different ways of developing evidence and different views on the same processes. It is, for example, possible to look at care from the perspective of the care provider or from that of those with care needs, or to examine care as a relationship. Furthermore, the family as a group may see care issues one way, and the government, the agencies and the paid providers in other ways. Indeed, each household member may have a specific way of slicing the situation. Equally important, the tensions among these may not be possible to resolve but possible only to recognize and handle. By beginning with a recognition of contradiction, by taking this slice, it is possible to base and develop policies and practices that seek to accommodate such tensions rather than setting out single solutions based on notions of harmony.

Analysis can begin from a number of different questions: asking, for example, what does this mean in the short term and what does it mean in the long term? What does it mean for those immediately involved, and what does it mean for the country or the world? It can also begin by acknowledging that some practices, conditions and situations are contradictory. Women, for example, may at one and the same time want to provide care and find it impossible to do so. They may love the person for whom they provide care but, precisely because of this love, hate to provide care.

Slicing can expose the different kinds of care work involved in providing for children with and without disabilities: for teenagers who join gangs and for those unable to attend university because there is no money, for adult neighbours with chronic illness and for those with marital problems, for healthy elderly and severely ill old people. It can also reveal what it means to provide this care at home or in an institution and what different kinds of institutions and homes there are.

It is also possible to begin with quite different purposes. For example, most policies are about helping households and families adapt to the demands of paid work and services. It is also possible, as some Norwegian policy analysts make clear, to start by figuring out how paid work can adapt to family lives (Brandth and Kvande). Instead of asking what resources the growing number of elderly require, the questions could be about the resources they bring and the services they provide. Rather than asking how care can be made an individual responsibility, we can ask what conditions make it possible to care without conscripting women into caregiving. Rather than assuming, as we do in Canada, that public care is what supplements family care done mainly by women, we could assume that families supplement public care.

Slicing adds both a recognition of difference and the possibility of developing different views of the same issues, circumstances and evidence.

Why women?

On the one hand, we have a universal pattern in terms of a division of labour by sex and women embracing caring work. One the other hand, we have an incredible range of labour done by women and defined as women's work. We also have women resisting caring work. Indeed, American historian Emily Abel argues that some nineteenth century women "complained bitterly that caregiving confined them to the home, caused serious physical and emotional health problems, and added to domestic labour, which was gruelling even in the best of times" (Abel 5). What factors, ideas, structures and processes contribute to this universality and difference, this embracing and resistance? More specifically, why do women provide the care but in so many different ways? There are no simple answers to these questions. Rather there are a number of answers that help contribute to a better understanding of care as women's responsibility.

We do know that only women have babies. But we also know that the meaning, experience and consequences of having babies varies enormously, not only across time and with location and culture, but also for individual women from one baby to another. Having a baby is fundamentally different for Celine Dion than it is for an Aboriginal woman who must leave her northern Quebec community if she is to receive medical assistance. Moreover, there is no necessary connection between having babies and rearing them; that is, to providing care. Bodies, then, are a factor in all of women's lives, but these bodies themselves are embedded in social, economic and political structures that are continually influencing how bodies work, as well as how they are defined and valued. They cannot provide much of the explanation for why women provide most of the care, not only for the babies they bear, but for other people as well.

Although there is plenty of evidence to suggest that women are more likely than men to identify with the emotional aspects of caring, there is very little evidence to suggest that this is connected to the way women's bodies or minds are physiologically constructed or that men are physiologically incapable of such caring emotions. There is also evidence to suggest that girls are taught and expected to exhibit such caring, and they are also more likely than their brothers to be assigned the caring jobs in the home. What sociologists call early socialization obviously contributes to women's skills in and attitudes about care, as well as to their brothers' notions of who is responsible for care and knows how to care. However, the pressures on women to provide care do not end and perhaps are not primarily created by early learning. Just as children are born and formed within a social context, so too are women carers daily created and shaped within social relationships, processes and structures. At the same time, women are active in creating these same relationships, processes and structures, albeit often from a weaker position than that of men.

These relationships, processes and structures are about power, not only in the sense that governments, employers, community organizations and husbands have specific powers and protect specific rights, but also in the more general sense of whose preferences, ways of acting and ideas prevail in daily practices. And they are about resources and the principles, as well as the mechanisms for their distribution. Power and resources in the formal and underground economies, in community organizations and households are often mutually reinforcing and are definitely linked. They are also unequally distributed, not only between women and men, but also among women. Women do have resources and are active participants in creating caring work. However, most women have fewer resources than most men, and the resources, as well as the means of participating they have, are frequently different from those of men.

There is, then, very little that is "natural" about women's work in general or their caring work in particular. Contexts matter much more than bodies in creating and maintaining women's caring work. Caring can be understood only as women's work within unequal relationships, structures and processes that help create women as carers and undervalue this caring work.

Thinking globally: The largest context

Globalization has become a familiar term in recent years. While familiar, though, teasing out its meanings and its implications for women in different locations is a complicated task.

Globalization implies a process that is drawing the world and its occupants closer together on what is often seen as an inevitable and undirected path. At the core of this process are giant corporations centered in one, usually Northern, country but operating throughout the globe. These transnational corporations (TNCs) helped create the technologies that have themselves contributed both to the corporation's multinational form and their power. Such technologies make it possible to move money rapidly around the globe, thus allowing these corporations to avoid or at least threaten to avoid any particular government's taxes and regulations by moving their investments. The technologies also make it possible to move work around the world, thus allowing the corporations to avoid or threaten to avoid demands from workers or restrictions on the use of labour imposed by governments. In order to facilitate this movement of goods, money and work, the giant corporations have been central in promoting what is often called free trade. Free trade is far from new, and traders have always enjoyed considerable freedoms as well as considerable power. It may well be, however, that the speed of transactions has altered along with the size of the corporations directing them. As a result, their power may be greater than ever before.

Instead of combining to resist this pressure, many governments have come together to support the process of achieving greater and easier movement of goods, services and money. At the international level, the First World countries (also called northern, developed or industrial countries) in particular, have worked through the International Monetary Fund, the World Bank and the World Trade Organization to promote the removal of restrictions on trade, a process which entails both de-regulation and re-regulation. Countries owing enormous debts have been required to introduce structural adjustment programs that involve the removal of many restrictions on foreign investment and labour practices, as well as the sale of public corporations to private ones, cutbacks in public services and the adoption of market strategies within the public sector that remains. The impact on women has been mixed and contradictory, both within and across nations.

Some women have been able to get new jobs on the "global assembly line," producing goods and even services previously produced mainly by women in the highly industrialized countries. Precisely because firms have relocated in these countries in order to avoid high wages and restrictions on working conditions, these jobs for women have rarely been good jobs. But they have offered some new possibilities for work, income, shared locations and minimal protections. More common has been the expansion of paid work for women outside the factory walls within the underground or informal economy where few, if any, rules apply. Women have been drawn into small-scale retail and service work, into domestic and homework, or simply into semiclandestine enterprises (see Ward). Here the boundaries between household and formal economy, between public and private space, and between employment time and non-employment time are blurred and protection along with visibility absent. At the same time, the withdrawal of public services has meant that women have had to do more of this work without pay or support within the confines of their private worlds, where the work is less visible and less available. For many women within these countries, there is no paid work at all. The poverty and unemployment that follow in the wake of structural adjustment policies push many to search for jobs in those First World countries that have created these policies. Women, in particular, have sought work as what Grace Chang calls "disposable domestics." Separated in time and space from their children, these women often do the domestic and caring work for First World women under conditions supported in the First World by the combination of government regulations, women's working conditions, and the failure to provide care services. Like free trade, the movement of women to do such work is not new, but the scale has altered. The result is a growing gap among women within and between countries, a gap that is frequently linked to racialized categories, as well.

In addition to imposing structural adjustment programs on Third World countries (or what are often called southern or developing countries), First World countries have entered into trade agreements that promise to support the movement of goods, services, money and, to a lesser extent, people across borders. This has not necessarily meant less government, but it has meant more measures to allow corporations to operate with less regard to national practices and preferences and fewer taxes or other contributions to national economies. It has also meant less local and democratic control as more decisions are being made by these international trading groups. Facing debt pressures themselves, these countries have adopted strategies similar to those imposed on the Third World. First World countries have acted more like entrepreneurs at the same time as they have handed over more of the services previously provided by governments to private, for-profit firms.

These shifts have had critical consequences for women. The expansion of the public sector had provided many, and often quite good, jobs for women. Indeed, "in 1981, between 65 and 75 per cent of college-educated women in Germany, Sweden and the U.S. were employed in the 'social welfare industries'" (Pierson 130). Many of these jobs disappeared or their character changed in the wake of the global reforms. Trade agreements did allow some women to move to other countries in search of work. Registered nurses, for example, left Canada in large numbers when hospitals closed, acquiring jobs in the United States. But those women from Third World countries seeking work in Canada found it more difficult to gain full citizenship status, providing just one example of how free trade has not worked in the same way for everyone.

As public services have declined, more of the services have been provided for sale in the market.

This process, often described as commodification, determines access primarily on the ability to pay rather than on need. More of the women in First World countries, as compared to those in the Third World, have had the means to pay for commodified services. However, women in both Worlds have continued to earn less than men, and women have continued to bear primary responsibility for care and domestic work. Faced with fewer public services and relatively low pay, but still in need of income to purchase these services, women in the First World have sought the cheapest means of paying for care or other supports. These means have often involved the even poorer women from the Third World. This is not to suggest that most First World women have completely escaped unpaid work or that the majority of women could afford to pay for services. Indeed, the reduction in public services has meant that a considerable amount of this work, formerly done by women for pay in the market, is now done by women without pay in the home. In other words, it has been de-commodified but not eliminated. Rather, it is to stress the linkages among women created by globalization and the growing gaps among women that these linkages often entailed.

Globalization does not simply refer to economics, however. It also refers to the ways people, ideas and cultures are brought closer together around the world. This has, in many ways, meant the spread of First World, and especially U.S., practices. Along with music, movies, fashions and food have come ideas about all aspects of social life, including women's work. This dissemination of ideas is also linked in many ways to the corporations, both through their ownership of companies that produce these goods and through their influence over the media. In these global sources, the emphasis is increasingly on the individual as a consumer with choices being based on the capacity to purchase.

Like the relocation of jobs, the spread of ideas is a mixed blessing. On the one hand, feminist ideas have spread rapidly around the world. On the other hand, the First World version of feminism was what has spread most rapidly, and this version too often fails to take context and difference into account.

This notion of shared international perspectives is not particularly new. Indeed, after the Second World War there was much talk of a postwar consensus. This consensus was based on a commitment to expanded government-provided services to a mixed economy that combined public and private enterprise, and to policies of full-employment along with sustained economic growth (Pierson 125). Redistribution of goods and services was part of the package, as were collective responsibility and shared risk. Now, this consensus seems to have fallen apart, only to be replaced by a new, and quite different, one. Public rights are replaced by private ones, with markets rather than states as the preferred means of allocating jobs, goods and services. But markets are unable to respond to many human needs and are especially ill-equipped to promote equity and full employment or to avoid long-term problems like pollution or other health consequences. Instead, they result in greater inequality, especially for women. As British theorist Ian Gough puts it, "Markets paradoxically require altruistic, collective behaviour on the part of women in the household in order to enable men to act individualistically in the market" (16).

Globalization has allowed much more than money, people, goods, and services to move quickly around the world. Diseases, too, face more permeable borders. New epidemics, such as HIV/AIDS, are transported along with old ones, like tuberculosis and hepatitis, around the globe with relative ease, transported in and by airplanes, as well as by service workers. Increasing inequality, not only in the Third World but also in the First, encourages their development and prevents their treatment. Diabetes has become much more common, especially among marginalized groups in large urban centres and on reservations. At the same time, protections under free trade rules for pharmaceutical patents frequently leave treatments beyond the reach of many.

One way, then, to slice globalization is to reveal the increasing dominance of transnational corporations, the converging of governments around market strategies, the declining democratic controls and the growing gap for and among women. Another way to slice it is to expose the counter tendencies. The same technologies that support corporate power allow various kinds of social and labour movements to organize around their interests. We see evidence of this not only in the "battle of Seattle" and in the streets of Quebec, but also in the Beijing Conference on Women that reached a consensus around means of promoting women's equality and in the attempts to protect sweat shop workers encouraged by the success of Naomi Klein's book *No Logo*. The movement of people around the globe has meant that many of us are more familiar with other cultures and practices.

We also see counter tendencies in the escalation and power of terrorism. Although many governments have adopted strategies taken from the for-profit sector, there is still an incredible variety in the ways these governments operate. Important public programs that reflect a continuing commitment to social rights and collective responsibility remain in many countries. Others have taken a route that emphasizes family values while still others have turned to religion and ethnicity. Moreover, the trade alliance among members of the European Union has served to improve working conditions for many women and help improve services for others. Instead of de-regulation, we see on occasion the extension of regulation. Britain, for example, has been required to provide protections for part-time workers and to introduce both minimum wage and equal pay legislation, all of which improve women's market jobs. Several countries are resisting the high drug prices that prevent them from treating mothers with HIV/AIDS, a sign that not all countries are willing to put property rights above people's right to life. And perhaps most importantly, there is ample evidence to demonstrate that spending on social programs can enhance rather than prevent trade, and that gender-based analysis linked to effective programs is essential to economic development.

Contradictions within global developments, as well as those among particular kinds of developments, are important in understanding where and how change may occur or is occurring. It is equally important to examine the details of how global agreements and patterns are played out within specific locations, because practices may well defy or transform intentions.

In short, globalization is about processes that result from actual decisions and practices rather than about forces beyond human control. While there is strong evidence to demonstrate that corporations are powerful players that are often supported by governments, there is also evidence to suggest that there are both limits on this power and contradictory patterns. There are choices to be made. These choices can have important consequences for women and their work and have to be considered in developing strategies for care.

Excerpted from "Thinking it Through: Women, Work and Caring in the New Millennium" published by "A Healthy Balance," a research program located in the Atlantic (formerly Maritime) Centre of Excellence for Women's Health. Reprinted with permission of the authors. The original version of this paper was funded by the Healthy Balance Research Program, through the Canadian Institutes of Health Research, Maritime Centre of Excellence for Women's Health (MCEWH) and the Nova Scotia Advisory Council on the Status of Women (NSACSW). It expresses the views and opinions of the authors and does not necessarily reflect the official policy of the MCEWH or NSACSW, or any of its sponsors.

Originally published in CWS/cf's Spring/Summer 2002 issue, "Women, Globalization and International Trade" (Volume 21/22, Numbers 4/1): 44-50.

References

Abel, Emily K. "A Historical Perspective on Care." *Care Work: Gender, Labour and the Welfare State*. Ed. Madonna Harrington Meyer. London: Routledge, 2000.

Brandth, Berit, and Elin Kvande. "Flexible Work and Flexible Fathers." Paper presented to the conference on "Rethinking Gender, Work and Organization." Keele University, England, June 2001.

Chang, Grace. *Disposable Domestics: Immigrant Women Workers in the Global Economy*. Cambridge, MA: South End Press, 2000.

Glucksmann, Miriam. *Cottons and Casuals: The Gendered Organization of Labour in Time and Space*. London: British Sociological Association, 2000.

Gough, Ian. *Global Capital, Human Needs and Social Policy*. New York: Palgrave, 2000.

Klein, Naomi. *No Logo: Taking Aim at the Brand Bullies*. Toronto: Knopf Canada, 2000.

Pierson, Christopher. *Beyond the Welfare State: The New Political Economy of Welfare*. Second Edition. Oxford, Blackwell, 1999.

Stone, Deborah. "Caring by the Book." *Care Work: Gender, Labour and the Welfare State*. Ed. Madonna Harrington Meyer. London: Routledge, 2000.

Ward, Kathryn. Ed. *Women Workers and Global Restructuring*. Ithaca, NY: Cornell University Press, 1990.

Unpaid Workers

The Absence of Rights

Marilyn Waring ~~

The key impediment to recognition of rights has been the restriction of the words "work" and "worker" in international human rights texts, to those who are in paid work. The definition of the "economically active population" is "all persons of either sex who furnish the supply of labour for the production of economic goods and services" (ILO 32). It's patently obvious that unpaid work furnishes the supply of labour for "the production of economic goods and services," yet those doing the defining mean that there is only economic activity if there is a market transaction.

Unpaid work is the predominant form of labour in four sectors: subsistence production, the household economy, which includes unpaid productive, reproductive and service work, the informal sector, and in voluntary and community work. The informal sector includes large numbers of people who are marginal to the "modern economy" and often invisible. Lourdes Beneria speaks of its "clandestine character ... often involving activities that are bordering on the illegal" and "its unstable, precarious and unregulated nature" (290-291). But it's not all like that: a lot of the regular "babysitting" arrangements people make in their communities fall into this category.

The United Nations System of National Accounts (SNA) rules of 1993 expanded the boundary of production so that the accounts should include subsistence and informal sector work. It recommended that all production of *goods* in households for their own consumption be included, but it still excluded own-account production of *services*. This means that (subsistence) agriculture and non-market production of goods for household consumption now fall inside the production boundary as recommended by the SNA, but that household work (including meal preparation), child and elderly care and other family-related services are still excluded. This leads to the remarkable feats accomplished with one bucket of water: wash the dishes, wash the child, cook the rice—not production. Use the same water spray the corn and wash the pig—this is productive. The boundary has effectively shifted only theoretically, and not in practice, and the demarcations are increasingly blurred.

In this article I would like to focus on those in the unpaid, or underpaid, or differently paid full-time caregiving role, and the ways in which legulations and regulations continue to compromise their rights.

The UK Census 2001 was the first to include a question on health, disability, and the provision of care. It showed more than a million people working more than 50 hours a week unpaid to care for family members, friends, neighbours or others because of long-term physical or mental ill health or disability, or problems related to old age. More than 175,000 children under 18 were acting as caregivers, of which 13,000 were providing more than 50 hours care a week! Let's reflect on the question of the rights of these workers, and imagine the compromised rights of these children—to leisure, to education, to full enjoyment of life.

Who does the bulk of unpaid work?

Since I finished the first edition of *Counting For Nothing* in 1988 (Waring), there have been some extraordinary changes in the economic environment in which we live. Changes in technology, in women's paid labour force participation, in government provision of social services, and the impact of structural adjustment policies and globalization agreements are all of enormous significance. So just how resistant and entrenched have the patriarchal rules around unpaid work been?

Michael Bittman writes that "Finland represents an instance of a country that combines a high level of expenditure on the public provision of social services and a remarkably high proportion of the female population in full-time employment". Yet women spend 25.78 hours and men spend 15.17 hours a week in unpaid work (Brittman 37). In a situation where the majority of women are in full time as opposed to part time paid employment, men in Finland seldom take parental leave. There are major divisions of labour by gender in the paid work force, more so than anywhere else in Europe. Women are paid on average 80 per cent of the male wage for full-time work. Men still occupy most managerial positions in the public and private sectors, and only two per cent of the top managers in big enterprises are women (CEDAW Finland Fourth Country Report).

Bittman reports that almost regardless of their position at any time in their life, Finnish men's weekly hours of unpaid work tend to be a fixed quantity, while the amount of time women spend in unpaid work varies.

A reduction in men's paid work hours generally results in greater leisure time, so that men literally can choose between (paid) work and leisure. The best predictors of the hours men make available for leisure are the hours they must commit to paid work. For women, however, it is statistically more likely to be a choice between paid and unpaid work. (28)

In Australia the gap between men's and women's average time spent in unpaid work has decreased, but because of a sharp reduction in women's hours of work in the kitchen, and in laundry, ironing and clothes care, rather than because of any large change in men's hours. The major reason for the change was attributable to increased reliance on market substitutes for women's domestic labour" (Bittman 27). Women have also increased their activity in home maintenance and car care.

While men have increased the hours they devote to child care, their share of this responsibility has not grown because women's time spent in child care has increased at the same rate. Parents have been devoting an ever increasing amount of time to primary face-to face child care despite falling family size. (Bittman 30)

In New Zealand, 60 per cent of men's work is paid, but almost 70 per cent of women's work is unpaid. The New Zealand time use survey of 1998-1999 demonstrated how economically valuable the contribution of this work is to the nation's economy. "In a year, the time spent by men and women on unpaid work in New Zealand as a primary activity equates, at 40 hours per week, to two million full-time jobs. This compares with the equivalent of 1.7 million full-time jobs in time spent in labour force activity" (*Around the Clock: Findings from the New Zealand Time Use Survey 1998-99* 17-18).

A combination of the most advanced collection of national data on unpaid work by Statistics Canada, and the use of this data by advocates and scholars, makes it possible to track the effects of unpaid work on the lives of men and women in Canada.

The *Canada Year Book 2001* reported that in 1998 women spent 15.2 hours on unpaid housework (not counting child care) per week compared with 8.3 hours for men. Mothers aged 25-44 who were working full time spent nearly 35 hours a week at unpaid work (Statistics Canada 2001).

Data from the 1995 Statistics Canada General Social Survey reveals that between married couples, few husbands take over their wives' unpaid work responsibilities when wives' paid work hours increase (cited in Phipps, Burton and Osberg 2). At the same time there's a market premium rather than a penalty associated with being a father (the ratio of income for fathers who worked full-time in the paid labour market to men who had never had children was 133.6 per cent in 1996) (Phipps *et al.* 412). My own suspicion is that this is a marriage premium rather than a child premium

Any woman who has ever had a child earns less than women who have never had children. For example, in 1996 mothers in Canaada (aged 24 to 54) who worked full-time in the paid labour market received 87.3 per cent of the income received by women who had never had children (Phipps, Burton and Lethbridge 412). Research results suggest a "human capital depreciation" for each year of absence from the paid labour market. The magnitude of the depreciation is substantial (what is lost in one year out is equal to about 37 per cent of what is gained by one year in) (Phipps *et al.* 420). For women, the finding of a child penalty is consistent regardless of whether or not we control for marital history. Thus, the "child penalty" is not actually a "marriage penalty" for women, though the "child premium" may be a "marriage premium" for men (Phipps *et al.* 416-417).

Canada's method of assessing the value of unpaid activities is one of the more conservative approaches, but even that gives a result of the value of unpaid work being one third of Canada's Gross Domestic Product (GDP).

What does that mean? If you take a look at the monthly GDP figures for Canada in March 2004, unpaid work was equal to the total production from agriculture, forestry, fishing, hunting, mining and oil and gas extraction, manufacturing, and the construction industries utilities—and at that point it was still $20 million short.

Have we ever made progress?

In reviewing where the feminist movement needs to go with respect to unpaid work, its important to ask if we ever made some headway in achieving recognition of unpaid work and the rights of the workers in that sector. In 1975 when I was elected to the New Zealand parliament our issues and situation were very different. In a country that had gained full suffrage in 1893, I was only the thirteenth woman elected. There were no women Cabinet Ministers, no women judges, no women editors of major daily newspapers, or jockeys or firefighters or Air New Zealand pilots. There were no rape amendments, no matrimonial property changes, no domestic protection legislation, no reproductive freedom, no Human Rights Commission, little formal quality childcare provision for working parents, no parental leave, and an even larger pay gap between men and women.

But there was a consciouness about unpaid work. In a formal international context the first references on unpaid work were at the first United Nations World Conference on Women held Mexico City in 1975. I was on the floor in the New Zealand delegation in Copenhagen to extend those paragraphs, and references continued in other major UN conferences in Nairobi (1985), Beijing (1995), Copenhagen (1995), Vienna (1993), and Rio de Janeiro (1992). Through publications such as the United Nations Development Program's *Human Development Reports* and *The World's Women*[1] commentary and statistics and research kept up the pressure.

But the ideology of the New Right swept through our national and international movement post Nairobi. The women's movement was caught between Structural Adjustment Policies and the World Trade Organization agendas. The market ruled our economic lives and the energy required for activism in the face of its power dominated the movement's activities. The feminist response and focus was to allow itself to be restricted to activity and energy around that debate—fostered in part by the old left approach about exploitation of women only happening in the market.

Isabella Bakker has written that "researchers have argued that gender-neutral macro-economic policy will only address women's needs and experiences to the extent to which they conform to male norms" (1). And feminist advocates were overwhelmingly co-opted to work primarily on analysis and criticism of the dominating economic paradigms in their political and academic work too, and far from proposing alternatives, addressed women's needs and experiences in the realms in which women conformed to male norms, and could be measured against them. There have been a number of exceptions to this framework in Canada: Carol Lees, Evelyn Drescher, Beverly Smith, Meg Luxton, Isabella Bakker, Shelley Phipps, Lynn Lethbridge, Peter Burton, Ron Coleman, Mark Anielski, and others.

I don't want to set up an either/or or dichotomous debate here: we have always needed both/and approaches to the issues of women in paid and unpaid work, but that has simply disappeared. For feminists actively concerned with the both/and approach, this has made us very wary of the kind of support we attract. In Canada, Meg Luxton wrote:

The absence of much of the feminist movement from these debates was reflected in the discussion about whether or not unpaid work would be included in the 1996 Canadian census. With the notable exception of Mothers Are Women (MAW) and the Work is Work is Work coalition, the women's groups lobbying for its inclusion were non-feminist or explicitly antifeminist and represented women who were primarily homemakers themselves, or whose political activities focused on what they call "the family." (436)

Statistics Canada reported this advocacy as follows: "Proponents for inclusion indicated that recognizing unpaid work promotes the status of those who choose to stay at home to look after young children, seniors or other family members" (cited in Luxton 436).

Note the use of the word "choose" which is of key importance to issues raised a little later in the paper. But, in addition, Luxton focused attention on the double work situation of significant numbers of the paid work force:

Missing was any recognition that most women, including those with paid employment, do domestic labour and would benefit from having is (and therefore their) status promoted. A bias in favour of women "who choose to stay at home" could have serious implications for policy development. (436)

The consultation for the 2006 Canadian Census resulted in 42 comments on unpaid work. Fifty-five per cent of these asked for the question to be removed or asked only every ten years. Among the reasons given were that there was no widespread need for unpaid work data. The estimates were not reliable enough because "some respondents might confuse family and friendship support with a broad range of volunteer activities" (Statistics Canada 2004: chapter 14). (So that means it's not work?)

So many of the key policy agenda items for the feminist movement have just made it easier for women to do two jobs more effectively, becoming the cohort group who work the most hours of any in the nation's economy. For example, when social policy suggests "family-friendly" alternatives, from childcare to flex-time to family leave, the implementation of these policies is often skewed by patriarchy and the marketplace. Since women's market wages are, on average, lower than men's, and women's traditional role has been that of caregiver, the burden of using family-friendly policies is often shifted, as an implicit cost, to women, further restricting their labour market options. Almost all the recent CEDAW reports from the Scandanavian countries reflect this position.[2] In addition, wherever there are policy provisions for unpaid leave, or parental leave at a reduced salary, it is clearly biased in favour of high income, dual-earner families who can more easily absorb a cessation one member's income; in Canada, up to 12 months combination of paid maternity and parental leave are available.

In Canada a range of policies discriminate against the unpaid worker and alternative arrangements. The child care expense deduction under the *Income Tax Act* is restricted to receipted daycare or nanny care and excludes recognition of market costs and social capital benefits of other forms of care of children. Unpaid caregivers are ineligible to contribute to their own registered retirement savings or pensions under the Canada Pension Plan. New mothers who are self-employed, or unpaid caregivers are ineligible for maternity benefits under the *Employment Insurance Act*. Unpaid caregivers in the home are also excluded from parental benefits under the *Employment Insurance Act* (Smith).

The policies of most OECD-member countries to try and persuade men to accept an equal share of unpaid work rely on round-about ("soft") measures such as education and information. An additional disadvantage of this strategy is the presupposed presence of someone with whom to share your household chores. Lone mothers and singles of all ages and sexes lack a "sharing partner" (Swiebel 17).

Specific cases

In New Zealand, I have been following the Human Rights decisions and complaints of the full time caregivers of members of their immediate families who are not remunerated, or remunerated on a different basis from other caregivers. This situation was first covered in *Hills v IHC*. Two parents of a disabled child were found to have been discriminated against on the ground of family status (they were the child's parents and therefore related to him) because the IHC (New Zealand's largest provider of services to people with intellectual disabilities and their families) would not pay them to care for him in the same way they would pay caregivers not related to him to take care of him.

More recently complaints have been made in regard of the government policy of not contracting or paying parents to provide residential care to their disabled children. Although the complainants receive some income replace-ment from the government (in the form of NZ superannuation—the retire-ment pension paid to every person aged over 66—or the Domestic Purposes Benefit [DPB] for care at home of sick or infirm, they are discriminated against in the government's disability services purchasing policy of not contracting/employing/paying parents for the provision of residential care services to their disabled children.

The New Zealand government currently has no idea how many families are currently "justifiably" subject to discrimination. As at July 25, 2003, there were 3,260 people in receipt of the DPB (caring for sick and infirm). No one knows how many people in receipt of NZ superannuation are full-time caregivers of family members who are sick and infirm. If the majority of these older caregivers are women they are likely to have fewer resources with which to carry out their care. Indeed, even Finance Minister Michael Cullen has spoken of a "hugely pronounced" bias existing in relation to women and retirement in New Zealand (*New Zealand Herald*).

The rules and regulations governing any "assistance" for caregivers have been a series of knee jerk responses to differing circumstances over time, that were sufficiently highlighted to demand political response. Caregivers are subject to different levels of funding and different assessment criteria. The sickness community (distinguished in New Zealand as separate from those who are infirm as a result of an accident) is not identified as part of the disability community. The rules are different depending on whether the person being cared for is a partner, a parent, or a child. There are also regional differences in the subsidies allowed and in the regionally-available budgets, which will impact on the benchmarks of assessors. Subsidies can range from $260 per week to $670 per week. Benchmarks are not about the quality or amount of care, but about the nature of the disability of the person being cared for. But full-time care is not about the amount of time the caregiver works. It is about the patient having access to 24-hour care. The Ministry of Social Development rules for the administration of the DPB state that "a caregiver can be away from the home for a few hours per week." And, it is recognized that when the patient needs 24-hour continuous care, "it is not reasonable to expect one person to manage. However, there is no provision to pay more than one Domestic Purposes Benefit in respect of the same patient" Home help might be available temporarily and in an emergency to some carergiver, but "generally home help should not be approved if able relatives other than primary or secondary school students live in the home." Home support services are different again, and may be available from a District Health Board Assessor to provide relief for a caregiver. Those who don't qualify for a Domestic Purposes Benefit might qualify, under special circumstances, for an Emergency Benefit, but if the person who is ill is their partner there will be more stringent tests applied before the Emergency Benefit can be received.

In Ontario, Canada the situation is also variable, but let me present one example. If I was extremely ill or lived with a severe disability and I was not being cared for by an immediate family member, I would be able to gather receipts for full-time attendant care, for supervision if I was residing in a home with a prolonged impairment, and for sign language interpreter fees if I was deaf. The attendant care component would cover health care, meal preparation, housekeeping, laundry, a transportation driver, and security services where applicable. Now when my mother or father or my sister or brother or my daughter or son are doing this work full-time for months if not years, they are allowed to deduct reasonable expenses associated with the cost of training required to care for me. They might get a disability credit, as a caregiver, which varies according to whether I am under 18 years of age and which can be claimed with other expenses to a maximum of $5,808. If the family income of my caregiver was less than $33,487 in 2003, they might have received another $1,600. Then, there are also personal tax credits for caregivers of relatives over 17 years old of up to $587. This is an extraordinary exploitation (Ontario Government).[3]

But, a recent ruling on a case tried in British Columbia this past summer will have significant implications for the unpaid work of family members providing care for relatives that are severely disabled. On June 29, 2004, the B.C. Human Rights Tribunal ruled that the Ministry of Health had discriminated against a 34-year-old woman with severe cerebral palsy by denying her the right to pay her father as her caregiver (*C & P Hutchison v. HMTQ*). Phillip Hutchinson, who is 73 years old, had been caring for his daughter Cheryl since she was 13. Cheryl Hutchinson suffers from cerebral palsy and requires 24-hour attendant care. She receives services under B.C.'s Choices in Supports for Independent Living (CSIL) program, an individualized funding program that allows people with disabilities to arrange their own caregiving according to their needs and to hire the caregiver of their choice. However, the CSIL program prohibits people with severe disabilities from hiring relatives as personal care attendants. Ms. Hutchison challenged that policy arguing she could not find a reliable caregiver to meet her most intimate needs that she trusted as much as her own father. The government was ordered to pay Mr. Hutchison $105,000 in wage loss for the services he provided (B.C. Association for Community Living). The provincial government has, however, filed an appeal of the decision, and it will be interesting to watch what happens.

The introductory speech to Parliament of Chris Bentley, Ontario Minister of Labour, in moving the *Employment Standards Amendment Act* (Family Medical Leave) 2004 on April 13, 2004 is revealing in terms of the motivations for enactment of such legislation. The bill is intended to provide up to eight weeks of job-protected, unpaid time off work for those taking care of seriously ill family members. He said:

It is clear that an aging population and significantly increasing workplace demands have contributed to growing levels of employee stress due to work-family conflict.... A recent Ipsos-Reid poll found that almost 32 per cent of Canadian adults were now responsible for the care of older relatives.... Most of our work life schedules do not include the additional time to provide the necessary care and support for seriously ill dependents

(I love it when men use "we" in situations in which they would never find themselves!)

...Employees making the impossible choice are less productive. They are often forced by circumstance into unplanned absences. When employees are forced to quit their job, the employees lose their skills, training and experience as well as their work. The costs to business are massive."

And finally, "the availability of Family Medical leave will support our existing health services. In some cases, it might reduce the demand on these services." At last came the admission that the unpaid work is relieving expenditure by the state.

Unlike some of the other supposedly women-friendly leave policies in Canada, this applies to all employees including those working part-time. Seniority and credit for length of service and length of employment will count as if they had been at work. Employer contributions to the premiums for pension plans, life and extended health insurance plans, accidental death plans, and dental plans will have to be kept up. But for those in the full-time unpaid workforce in the same circumstances, there is nothing.

Rights questions

These cases raise questions about many more potential complaints for lack of access to fundamental human rights. What of the family members who care full-time for someone who does not fit into the current operative definition of "disability" for the sake of a benefit? Should rights extend only to those full-time caregivers whose work continues for years and years without ceasing? Is there some time consideration which would mean that a parent stopping work to care for a child accident victim or terminally-ill parent for six to nine months is in a different category from one who undertakes caring for five years?[3] What about grandparents who are full time caregivers for grandchildren, in a situation where the child might otherwise be placed in foster care?[4] Do we think that their capability and freedom to function effectively might be compromised? Do we think that the payment differential between their eligibility for assistance and that of foster parents might be discriminatory? Do we think that the rights of children who work long hours in unpaid work might be losing out on access and opportunities—to education, to leisure and enjoyment of life? Should day care subsidies flow to institutions, or with the child to the person who carries out the care? Unpaid caregiving of the sick is a critical part of the healthcare system which compromises the well being of the caregiver who is then further penalized by the system in terms of loss of earnings, or no recognition at all.

Canadian research has found evidence that women in dual-earner households are more time-stressed than men, apparently as a result of the continued gendered division of housework, despite high levels of paid work by wives (Phipps, Burton and Osberg 1).

In respect of a right to leisure, having a pre-school aged child in the household is important for men. A pre-schooler in the family reduces husband's satisfaction with time for self by a small amount (about seven percentage points); *any* child in the family reduces wife's satisfaction with personal time by a much larger amount (almost 20 percentage points). For women, there is no difference between having a pre-schooler and having an elementary-school-aged child; having *any* children is the key variable. The researcher's note that for men, making "leisure time for one's spouse is a poor substitute for having such time for oneself" (Phipps, Burton and Osberg 18).

> Women's opportunities to take an equal part in civil and political life is compromised. In bolstering ... civil society ... strategies of increased civic participation and engagement rest on sufficient leisure time. [This is not possible when] women's unpaid work is intensifying not easing (Bakker 17).

In terms of a rights-based approach to those in the unpaid workforce, and for example for those in the unpaid or underpaid or differently paid full-time caregiving role we have to ask: to what extent does the discrimination and different treatment of family members in long term care giving (in terms of the legislation and regulations surrounding this) compromise or inhibit their capacity to participate effectively in political or community life, to attain the highest possible standard of physical and mental health, to exercise their right to opportunities of lifelong education, to enjoy safe and healthy working conditions, etc? It's time the rights debate encompassed and included (again) the exploited unpaid work of women.

Originally published in CWS/cf's Spring/Summer 2004 issue, "Benefiting Women? Women's Labour Rights" (Volume 23, Numbers 3/4): 109-115.

[1]These reports can be accessed on the UNDP's website: http://hdr.undp.org/reports/view_reports.cfm?type=1.

[2]CEDAW Country Reports are available online: http://www.un.org/womenwatch/daw/cedaw/reports.htm

[3]The Federal Government of Canada has now introduced a compassionate leave policy which allows those paid workers who have put in at least 600 paid hours and who have a doctor's certificate to prove their relative is dying, the chance to spend six months at home caring for that person on partial salary. Of course the unpaid full-time caregiver remains unpaid.

[4]Under s.3 of the *Children Young Person's and their Families Act* 1989, payments received by people in receipt of a social security benefit and providing foster care under the Act have all payments disregarded as income for benefit abatement purposes, but no one has been able to tell me what the position is in respect of superannuation.

References

Around the Clock: Findings from the NZ Time Use Survey 1998-99. Auckland: Statistics New Zealand, 2001.

Bakker, Isabella. *Unpaid Work and Macroeconomics: New Discussions, New Tools for Action*. Ottawa: Status of Women Canada's Policy Research Fund, 1998.

Bell, David N. F. and Robert A. Hart. "Unpaid Work." *Economics* 66 (1998): 271-290.

Benería, Lourdes. *The Enduring Debate Over Unpaid Labour. International Labour Review* 138 (3) (1999): 290-291.

Bittman, Michael. "Parenthood Without Penalty: Time Use and Public Policy in Australia and Finland." *Feminist Economics* 5 (3) (1999): 27-42.

Bond, Sue and Jill Sales. "Household Work in the UK: An Analysis of the British Household Panel Survey 1994." *Work, Employment and Society* 15 (2) (2001): 233-250.

British Columbia Association for Community Living. Online: http://www.bcacl.org/issues/family/updates.shtml

CEDAW Finland Fourth Country Report. CEDAW/FIN/4 Online: http://daccess-ods.un.org/TMP/5854976.html

Hills v IHC 6HRNZ 213.

International Labour Organization (ILO). *International Recommendations on Labour Statistics*. Geneva; ILO, 1976.

Luxton, Meg. "The UN, Women, and Household Labour: Measuring and Valuing Unpaid Work. *Women's Studies International Forum* 20 (3) (1997): 431-439.

Ministry of Social Development, New Zealand. Online: http://www.msd.govt.nz/media-information/benefit-fact-sheets/benefit-fact-sheets-index.html*New Zealand Herald* 28 July 2003.

Ontario Government. Disability Tax Credit. Online: http://www.children.gov.on.ca/CS/en/programs/SpecialNeeds/disabilityTaxCredit.htm. Date accessed: June 22, 2004.

Ontario Human Rights Commission Online: http://www.ohrc.on.ca/english/guides/hiring.shtml.

Phipps, Shelley, Peter Burton and Lynn Lethbridge. "In and out Labour Market: Long-term Income Consequences of Child-related Interruptions to Women's Paid Work." *Canadian Journal of Economics* 34 (2) (2001): 411-429.

Phipps, Shelley, Peter Burton and Lars Osberg. "Time as a Source of Inequality

Within Marriage: Are Husbands More Satisfied With Time for Themselves Than Wives?" *Feminist Economics* 7 (2) (2001): 1-21.

Smith, Beverly. Personal communication, June 21, 2004.

Statistics Canada. *2006 Census Content Consultation Report*. Ottawa, 2004. Catalogue no. 92-130-X1E. Online:
http://www12.statcan.ca/english/census06/products/reference/consultation/contentreport-unpaidwork.htm

Statistics Canada. *Canada Year Book 2001*. Ottawa: Statistics Canada, 2001. 11-402-XPE.

Swiebel, Joke. *Unpaid Work and Policy-Making: Towards a Broader Perspective of Work and Employment*. Discussion paper No.4, ST/ESA/DP.4. DESA. New York: United Nations, 1999.

System of National Accounts. New York: United Nations, 1993.

UK Census 2001. Online: http://www.statistics.gov.uk/census2001/default.asp

Waring, Marilyn. *Counting for Nothing*. Auckland: Bridget Williams Books, 1988. [published under the title *If Women Counted* in the UK and US.]

Farm Women

The Hidden Subsidy in Our Food

Wendee Kubik ◄—

On February 8th 2005, Canadians were able to observe Food Freedom Day. This is the calendar date that represents the point in the year at which time the average Canadian has earned enough income to pay her or his individual grocery bill for the entire year. In 2005 it was 39 days into the 365 day year ("February 8 is Food Freedom Day."). Although food prices for consumers have gone up over the years, the percentage of disposable income Canadians spend on food has steadily decreased. According to Statistics Canada, in 2003, Canadians spent 10.6 per cent of their disposable income on food, a small percentage when compared to other fixed costs such as housing, utilities, or taxes.

Between the years 1997 and 2003, the price Canadian consumers paid for food increased by 13.8 per cent. By contrast, the average price received by farmers for their produce increased by only 2.1 per cent (Statistics Canada). This means that the price paid by consumers increased over six times more than the prices received as a return for farmers. The following graph illustrates how the price of bread has gone up between the years 1975-2002 and how the price paid to the farmer for wheat has remained relatively stable.

Other examples of the difference between the costs of the processed end product and the income of the primary producers are the price of milk, corn, and beef. In 2003, the average retail price of a litre of milk was $1.66, but farmers received only $0.64 a litre. A box of corn flakes in the stores cost approximately $3.50 but the farmer who grew the corn received only $0.11 while the prime rib sirloin steak that costs $14.00 returned $1.83 to the beef rancher ("Compare the Share").

How do farmers in Canada survive? The simple answer is many of them don't! There has been a large exodus of people leaving the farm over the last few decades because, for many, it has not been possible to make a viable living by farming (Stirling 2004). Others remain farming but at a cost to themselves, to their family, and to their health. The graph below illustrates the decline of the total number of farms in Saskatchewan since 1951.

We often hear in the news and read in the papers about how the government or Canadian tax payer is subsidizing farmers in Canada. I would contend that our food is being heavily subsidized by farmers. In particular,

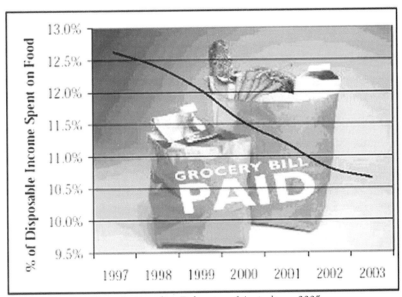

Figure 1. *Canadian Federation of Agriculture, 2005*

much of the labour of farm women enables Canadians to purchase quality food at low prices, contributing to the high standard of living we enjoy in Canada today.

This paper will attempt to link some of the structural changes that are occurring in agriculture to the (often unrecognized) contributions of farm women to the economy. It is based on a qualitative and quantitative study on the *Changing Roles of Farm Women* that I conducted on the Canadian prairies in 2002 (see Kubik 2004). The study (n = 717) utilized an exploratory, multi-strategy, multi-stage approach combining qualitative and quantitative methodologies directed by a feminist standpoint perspective to systematically explore the lived experience of farm women in the province of Saskatchewan. Eighteen preliminary interviews were conducted with individuals who worked with and represented farm women. The findings were then employed in the development of a 20-page questionnaire focusing on ten subject areas 1) healthcare; 2) health status; 3) social support; 4) well-being; 5) lifestyle and activities; 6) stress; 7) work; 8) female and male roles; 9) demographics; 10) farm issues. Subsequently 20 in-depth interviews with 20 farm women from across the province were undertaken. The Farm Stress line and Saskatchewan Women in Agriculture (SWAN) were the community partners in the research.

Women's unpaid labour on the farm

Contributions to the farm economy by farm women has increased over the last 20 years for a number of reasons. In order to remain viable most farms have

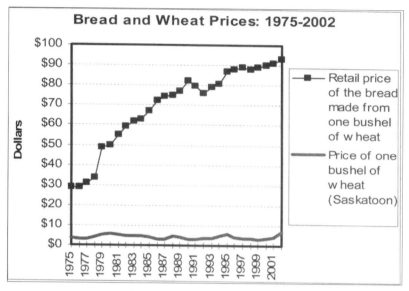

Figure 2.National Farmers Union

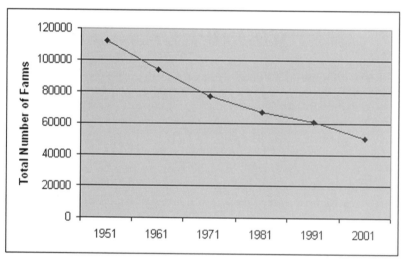

Figure 3.Total number of farms in Saskatchewan (1951-2001)
Data from Statistics Canada

increased in size over the last few decades, however, even with larger and more efficient (and expensive!) machinery this generally translates into more work for the farm family (Jaffe). Because of the low prices farmers receive for their products it is not viable for most families to hire extra help. Consequently, extra help comes from members of the farm family. More women are doing more farm work today than in previous times (Smith). The number of women who engage in farm field work tasks on a regular basis has increased by an average of 12 per cent while the number engaged in farm management tasks on a regular basis has increased by 22 per cent from 1982 to 2001-2002 (Martz and Brueckner).

It is difficult to count the work that farm women do. Such labour is often viewed as "helping out" and not seen or counted by their spouses or themselves as farm work at all. Women are often viewed as the "on-call" labour particularly around seeding and harvest time. Many times, especially if there are children in the family, a farm women will be multi-tasking, doing work for the farm and home simultaneously (e.g., driving for parts for the tractor, groceries for the household, and taking her children to hockey practice). This obscures the farm work she is doing. Her work is contributing to the farm but because she is doing other things as well, it is hidden labour (Reimer; Wiebe; Cohen; Fox)

Sandra,[1] one of the farm women interviewed in the study, illustrated the work expected of farm women and the resulting stress that she incurred:

> *Farm women are labour. Even when they have children they are used for trucking, they are used for taking meals to the field, they often do the books, they are the "go-fers", whatever needs to be done they are the ones that do it. Farm wives also have the family and the home and that's a major one. That is a job within its self. Often they would have the farm, the family, the finances, the accounting end of it, and sometimes even to the extent of it that they would work off the farm and so they have major stress.*

Household work

In spite of their increasing workload on the farm, and for many, their work off the farm, farm women generally remain responsible for the majority of household tasks such as cooking, cleaning, and childcare (NPHS). The *Changing Roles* study documented that farm women were responsible for at least 80 per cent of the household labour with the rest being completed by various other family members. Women continue to do the majority of housework regardless if they have an off-farm job or if they are increasingly contributing to the farm labour. Forty per cent of the farm women interviewed in the study indicated that their average work day was over 13 hours long.

Many of their household "jobs" overlap the home and farm (e.g., bookkeeping, looking after livestock, growing and preserving produce from a large garden, etc.). Typically, women farmers are not paid for this work even though it subsidizes the farm and frees up a large portion of the farm's consumption costs. I suggest that their unpaid labour, in the home and on the farm, also subsidizes the low prices we pay for food when we go to the store. Carrie describes a typical day during harvest:

> *I have to make dinners and suppers all at breakfast time before I go to the field so I would get up early. If I happen to have some of that done or had leftovers, I would be unloading grain and then I would go to the field and*

I'd be in the field until about seven o'clock or eight o'clock at night. Then I would come in, put on the supper and do whatever I have to do around the house that I can get done, and then when the men come in, feed them or else I take meals out to the field at night. If it's seeding time then I'm moving equipment around or maybe going for fertilizer, or going for grain and trying to help. In calving time, we could be up all night.

The majority of labour on a family farm that supports the farming activity is not wage-labour, it is the labour of family members. Family farmers are independent commodity producers, that is they own some of the productive resources (land and machinery), however they and their families work for profit on the farm without re-numeration in the form of a salary. Bill Reimer shows that the tendency to focus on "productive" labour has caused women's indirect contribution to the farm to be overlooked. This concept of separate productive and domestic spheres then has the tendency to make women's work in the home invisible. For farm women, whose work is characterized by an intertwining of household and farm work, both work in the home and the work contributing to the agricultural enterprise has often been overlooked (Shortall; Wiebe; Smith).

Many women felt that a lot of their farm or household work was not acknowledged or recognized as making a major contributor to the farm. Pat summed it up by noting:

Women work hard making a living for themselves and their family and out of that I think most women would like some recognition. I think a lot of women, even if they are not active out in the field or with the animals, are still playing a large role by having meals and raising the family, gardens and yard work and on and on, accounting, going for parts and those kinds of things that I feel they don't get recognized for.

Women's paid labour and off-farm work

In order to make a viable living on the farm, more women are working off the farm than in any other time in history. The *Changing Roles* study found that 51 per cent of the farm women worked off the farm in order to have the money necessary to cover household expenses, while the labour of 32 per cent of the women working off the farm contributed to farm operating costs and repairs. By paying for household expenses and helping with farm costs with money earned on off-farm jobs, farm women are continuing to subsidize the farm, and by extension, the food we buy in our grocery stores. Mary, who was juggling off-farm, on-farm, and household work described what it was like for her.

I work off the farm in a job that is very stressful and very demanding. You come back and there is so much to do. A woman's work is never done is very true. You've got your housework, you've got your yard work and plus we have cattle and a mixed farm.... you can only stretch yourself so thin and you are always running around and there is always loose ends and you can never be a totally organized person. There is just too much expected and I think we are a generation so close to the generation where the women stayed home and they were able to fulfil all these duties and it is a real flip-flop because our generation can't. I think that is where there is the biggest change in farm women and their roles.

Women who have off-farm jobs often need to commute long distances, in all types of weather, often in isolated areas with poor roads. Extra money is needed for gas and car upkeep. More often than not it is difficult to find a job that utilizes one's skills or pays well (Kubik 1996) However, in spite of these difficulties, for a lot of farm families it is an economic necessary to have off-farm work.

Conflict and pressures of being a traditional farm wife

In the quantitative portion of the *Changing Roles* study the farm women were asked if they felt there were any particular expectations placed on them because they were farm women. Thirty-six percent of the women said the largest expectation they felt was to be a "traditional farm wife." When asked in the interviews what this meant to them, several offered descriptions similar to this one given by Erin.

The traditional farm wife is going to cook and clean and raise the kids and do all the yard chores basically. If you have chickens, they are your responsibility. The garden is your responsibility. Chasing after your husband whenever he snaps his fingers, like run, that to me is a traditional wife. You are there 24 hours a day to dote on them and your life revolves around the children, your house and husband. You're strictly expected to be here and do everything and that's it.

Even though the women had a view of what constituted a traditional farm wife and experienced pressure or expectations from various sources to try and fulfill this role, they felt they did not measure up to it. Women on the farm have expanded and increased their work on the farm as well as off-farm work, while continuing to be responsible the majority of household work and childcare. The structure of the traditional farm family is perpetrated today even when farm women are working off the farm in record numbers and doing more on-farm work than in the past (Statistic Canada 1999). Since this is seen as the "normal" farm family relationship, expressions of dissatisfaction with the arrangement are viewed as atypical or as not being a "good" farm wife.

When asked about what job title they would give themselves only 17 per cent of the women in the questionnaire placed themselves in the category of farmer, rancher, manager, owner or boss. Darlene explained why many farm women are reluctant to do this.

Most of the time they see themselves as homemakers and that's so ironic because they are out there running the equipment and stuff. But you sit and talk to a circle of women and they are not saying.... [she speaks here in a deep voice] yeah, I got to get out and plow that back forty. *What they are saying is their kid was sick last night and they are busy sewing Halloween costumes. They are not going to take that away from their husbands... that wouldn't look proper.*

Forty-two per cent of the women in the quantitative portion of the study reported that they had experienced conflict in the household over sharing of available resources. The issue that caused the most conflict was the necessity of the "farm always coming first" in terms of monetary decisions. Farming is a business and in order for the business not to "go under" many farmers exploit themselves by working harder and longer hours, and cutting expenses wherever they can. This means any available surplus is put back into the farm and because the household is interlocked with the farm it often suffers. Suzi described her situation:

In the spring, when the crop is going into the ground, don't ask for anything. Buy groceries, that's it. Because all of the money is going into the land. Well, actually it is from April until the end of September when harvest is done, that is the priority. Anything else takes a backseat and that's been ever since we've been married. In fact, my husband has gone so far as to say playfully, but with a grain of truth to it, "women who ask things of their husbands during harvest become statistics," meaning don't ask me, I've got lots on my mind, you know, I'll talk to you, I'll do that later. So yeah, those decisions are, everything for the farm first and then secondly, the household. But the farm always comes first.

Doing without within their own households—in order to ensure the ongoing operation of their farms—is yet another way that farm women subsidize their farms, and our food.

It is not surprising then that the many hours that farm women spend working, the lack of income they encounter, and the pressures they experience in their everyday lives cause them to experience a great deal of stress. The *Changing Roles* study documented the amount of stress women reported and compared it to the National Population Health Survey conducted by Statistics Canada. Fifty-five per cent found their lives "somewhat stressful" compared to 37 per cent in the NPHS; 29 per cent said their lives were "very stressful" (comparable to the NPHS's 28 per cent). Only 16 per cent said their lives were "not very stressful", far less than the 35 per cent in the NPHS. The most frequent stress symptoms were difficultly sleeping, having trouble relaxing/ feeling anxious, and feeling sad or depressed. One of the most common major

Audrey Dixon who farms near Rocanville, Saskatchewan Photo by Wendee Kubik

stressors for farm women is economic hardship (Fromback; Martz and Brueckner; Women on Farms Initiative)

Conclusions

The essential role that women play in the production of food and the survival of the key institution of food production —the family farm—has often been overlooked. The *Changing Roles of Farm Women* study has demonstrated that women are key to the production of the food on which society relies and, ironically, their labour plays an important role in maintaining the patriarchal system.

Definitions of farm work are often narrow and many times work that does contributes to the farm (e.g., book-keeping, running errands for the farm) is not defined as farm work SIMPLY because it is a woman who does it. The dominant view surrounding women's farm work is an example of how women's subordination in the farm family is structured and perpetuated, making women our society's "invisible farmers."

Farm women illustrate the nature of the social relations that characterize socio-economic systems that are both capitalist and patriarchal. The relationship of independent commodity producers to both the input and output side has been well documented by Robert Stirling (2001) and Murray Knuttila. As larger and larger multinational corporations dominate each side of the process, farmers are forced to pay more for inputs while, very often, the same corporations, are the major players on the output side, paying farmers very little for their product. As a result, family farmers, as independent commodity producers, are squeezed to the margin and beyond. In terms of gender relations and practices, Canadian farm families are typically organized as patriarchal institutions. As a result farm women are required to work within structures and ideologies that typically undervalue their work and contributions, regardless of the actual existing realities of the situation.

The long hours of work (off-farm, on-farm, and household) done by these invisible women farmers does not result in a larger paycheck for farm women. Instead, the many hours of work contributed by farm women in Canada enable us to observe Food Freedom Day earlier and earlier each year. I have agued that their labour thus subsidizes the farm economy and the food produced by farm families. While we pay less and less of our total income for food, farm women's outcomes are exceptionally high levels of stress linked to physical and psychological problems.

The incorporation of the concept of patriarchy into the study of health and farm women is sorely needed as patriarchal attitudes are prevalent in rural areas. New models of work that accounts for the diverse interlocking work that farm women contribute in the home and on and off the farm would make visible the many contributions made by farm women.

We are at a crossroads at the present time regarding the type of food production we are willing to support in Canada. Do we want our food to be produced by corporate farms? Do we develop alternative ways to produce and market our food products that recognize philosophically and monetarily the people (particularly the large role of women) who produce the food?

Originally published in CWS/cf's Summer Fall 2005 *issue, "Rural Women in Canada" (Volume 24, Number 4): 85-90.*

[1]All quotes are from interviews conducted for the *Changing Roles* study. Names have been changed to ensure anonymity.

References

"Compare the Share." *Canadian Federation of Agriculture Food Freedom Day Fact Sheet.* 2005. Online: http://www.cfa-fca.ca/upload/ffdayfacts-2005.pdf

Cohen, Marjorie. "Capitalist Development, Industrialization, and Women's Work." *Perspectives on Canadian Economic Development.* Ed. G. Laxer. Toronto: Oxford University Press, 1991. 311-332.

"February 8 is Food Freedom Day." *Canadian Federation of Agriculture Food Freedom Day Fact Sheet.* 2005. Online: http://www.cfa-fca.ca/upload/ffdayfacts-2005.pdf

Fox, Bonnie "Women's Role in Development. *Perspectives on Canadian Economic Development.* Ed. G. Laxer. Toronto: Oxford University Press, 1991. 332-352.

Fromback, Hannalore. *Stress in Farm Women: A Multivariate Approach.* Unpublished Master's thesis, University of Regina, Regina, Saskatchewan.

Jaffe, JoAnn. "Family Labour Processes, Land, and the Farm Crisis in Saskatchewan." *Farming Communities at the Crossroads: Challenge and Resistance.* Eds. Harry P. Diaz, Joann Jaffe and Robert Stirling. Regina: Canadian Plains Research Centre, 2003.

Knuttila, Murray. "Globalization, Economic Development and Canadian Agricultural Policy." *Farming Communities at the Crossroads: Challenge and Resistance.* Eds. Harry P. Diaz, Joann Jaffe and Robert Stirling. Regina: Canadian Plains Research Centre, 2003.

Kubik, Wendee. *The Study of Farm Stress: A Critical Evaluation.* Unpublished Master's thesis, University of Regina, Regina, Saskatchewan, 1996.

Kubik, Wendee. *The Changing Roles of Farm Women and the Consequences for their Health, Well-Being, and Quality of Life.* Unpublished Dissertation, University of Regina, 2004.

Kubik, Wendee and Robert Moore. "Women's Diverse Roles in the Farm Economy and the Consequences for Their Health, Well-being, and Quality of Life." *Prairie Forum* 27 (1) (Spring 2002): 115 – 129.

Martz, Diane and Ingrid Brueckner. The *Canadian Farm Family at Work: Exploring Gender and Generation.* Centre for Rural Studies and Enrichment, 2003. Online: http://www.nfu.ca/epff/documents/The_Canadian_Farm_Family_at_Work.pdf

National Farmer's Union. "Recent income data highlights market failure." 2003. Online: http://www.votenga.ca/Common per cent20Pages/BackgrounderTextFiles/Farm_Income.htm

National Population Health Survey (NPHS). (Cycle 3). Ottawa: Statistics Canada, Health Statistics Division. 1999. Online: www.statcan.ca/english/survey/household/health/health.htm.

Reimer, Bill. "Women as Farm Labour." *Rural Sociology* 51 (2) (1986): 143-55.

Shortall, Sally. "Canadian and Irish Farm Women: Some Similarities, Difference and Comments." *The Canadian Review of Sociology and Anthropology* 30 (2) (1993): 172-190.

Smith, Pamela. "Beyond 'Add Women and Stir'." *Canadian Rural Society Rural Sociology in Canada.* Eds. D. A. Hay and G. S. Basran. Toronto: Oxford University Press. 1992. 155-170.

Stirling, Robert. (2004) "Introduction." *Prairie Forum* 29 (2) (Fall 2004).

Stirling, Robert. "Transitions in Rural Saskatchewan." *Saskatchewan Politics.* Ed. Howard Leeson. Regina: Canadian Plains Research Centre, 2001.

Statistics Canada. *Food Statistics and Farm Product Price Index.* 2003. Online: www.statscan.ca

Statistics Canada. *For Farm Women, Agriculture is Just a Beginning. Excerpts from Canadian Agriculture at a Glance.* 1999. Online: www.statscan.ca/english/kits/agric/work.htm

Wiebe, Nettie "Farm Women: Cultivating Hope and Sowing Change." *Changing Methods, Feminists Transforming Practice.* Eds. S. Burt and L Code. Peterborough, Ontario: Broadview Press,1995. 137-162.

Women on Farms Research Initiative 2001. Online http://agwomen.aers.psu.edu/research.htm

Provisioning
Thinking About All of Women's Work

Sheila Neysmith, Marge Reitsma-Street, Stephanie Baker Collins, Elaine Porter

Local and transnational firms search for flexible workforces, cheaper goods, and more consumers and profits. Women in Canada and elsewhere find they are expected to respond to rising demand for flexible part-time, contract, and insecure jobs. At the same time they must also meet the demand for consistent contributions to parenting, household, mutual aid, and community work. "Women's work is never done" expresses the reality for all too many women, especially poor women. Invisibility adds to the tyranny of this endless work. Much of what women do is not considered work or not counted as valuable.

Seeing, counting, and valuing all the work women do is an important way to resist the invisibility yet endlessness of women's work. This article presents several ways of conceptualizing and accounting for the work women do. Each of these approaches highlights aspects of women's labour. Each comes from different disciplinary practices and address concerns that have arisen in that tradition, while uncovering other problems. The article ends by proposing the concept of provisioning as a way to think about all the work that women do in more nuanced, complex ways, that attends to the time, purpose, diversity, claims and possible entitlements. The concept of provisioning, used to date by some feminist economists (Nelson) may open up a more comprehensive understanding of what women actually do to acquire resources for meeting the responsibilities they carry for the well-being of themselves and others, and for imagining different policy and practice possibilities. Our research intends to examine the multiple dimensions, costs and implications of provisioning in ways that extends the contributions that have been made to understand the paid, unpaid, caring and volunteer labour performed by women.

Paid employment

Paid employment is the way that individuals and households are expected to acquire the resources they need to purchase the necessities of life. The majority of poor women have for centuries engaged in farm or market employment to bring money into the household. In the past few decades, however, girls and women of all classes are increasingly expected to do paid work in addition to fulfilling traditional female work expectations. Today, welfare policy, pension policy, daycare policies, and virtually all social and educational policies and benefits are designed to ensure that women participate in paid employment, promise rewards if they do, and make life difficult if they do not.

Yet paid employment is but one avenue used for achieving the goal of acquiring resources for life's necessities. There has been considerable research carried out in the '90s that document the multiple income strategies used by those who live in low-income households (Barndt; Goode and Maskovsky; Razavi). When considering these data it is important to remember that such strategies are commonly used in high-income households—it is just that the latter have more choice, more options available to them. For low-income households, like their high-income counterparts, patterns of employment changed during the '80s and '90s, under the powerful regulation of a new economic discourse of global economy, local restructuring, and the need for a flexible workforce that allows industry to quickly respond to changing international conditions (Beneria, Flora *et al.*). In many countries, Canada being no exception, this process was marked by massive layoffs across many different types of employment sectors (Cohen). New hires were for short-term contract jobs. This was key to ensuring that the workforce was flexible but it also marked the end to the ideas of a stable job or a career ladder—key assumptions in post WW II labour market policies (Bakker). People became contingent workers, moving from contract to contract as firms adapted a just-in-time approach to inventories. Although this new labour force has been billed as particularly attractive to women, giving them some time and work location flexibility (Gardiner), as well as work/non-work options, the majority of these jobs are dead-end, as well as short-term. Thus, frequently women are faced with the additional work of constantly looking for new contract jobs and reorganizing their caring responsibilities (de Wolff).

The speed and scope of globalization, it is argued, was possible because of the advent of information technology which meant that even if workers were not mobile, their labour was. This did mean that those with certain technical skills could command good salaries but, as in the "old economy," information technology also spun off bad jobs—many of which were taken up by women (Anderson). Another result was that certain types of work could now be done in the home. The advantages of this needs to be counterbalanced against the costs that women carry in terms of balancing yet another type of work carried out in the home, along with its attendant isolation, and lack of benefits. Not surprisingly, the incomes women make continue to be low, while sources and amount of income are unstable (Luxton; Saraswati). The expectations placed on women to be employed, and the insecurity of the types of jobs available to them, are important for understanding why women negotiate responsibilities and build community in the ways that they do.

The underground economy and informal work

The existence of an underground economy is well-documented (Donath;

Himmelweit) albeit it is associated in the minds of many with Third World economies. An underground economy, and its associated informal labour market, thrives in Canada; for obvious reasons its size and scope are difficult to estimate. Attempts made to document it tend to be associated with studies of low-income households, but such economic activity occurs across all income levels. However, as in other areas of research, upper-income households have not been scrutinized under the research lens as closely as those living in poverty. With that reservation in mind, the limited data that do exist suggest that in Canada the underground economy, estimated at two to three per cent of Gross Domestic Product, takes the form of such activities as skill exchanges and bartering, as well as informal arrangements amongst women for services such as babysitting (Waring).

Paid work accounts for the financial value of women's work but leaves out diversity of work and suggests a very narrow purpose of work. The informal economy begins to account for more diverse types of women's work and broader purposes, but it is often invisible. Nor is it clear how much time it takes up, especially when conducted inside the home. Moreover its invisibility means it cannot serve as a basis for claims on public service such as pensions or social insurance.

Household and domestic work

The household and domestic work done by women has been the site of a rich and diverse scholarship, as well as political debates (Matthews; Porter and Kauppi). Some took the form of documenting the tasks done, the time devoted to these tasks, the skills required to do them, their value when translated into monetary terms, and their contribution to GDP. The sheer amount and dollar worth of this work is no longer questioned. However a reservation frequently noted, even by those promoting a research approach that documents the dollar value of unpaid work, is that the labor market value of such work is low (Waring). Thus, the translations, while high in terms of hours, are consistently low in terms of the monetary market worth of the work. The critique arising from this debate is what is pertinent to this paper. Namely, work that is associated with the household, the private realm, is undervalued.

Another thread in domestic work scholarship stems from its historic connection with labour policies and immigration regulations designed to bring into Canada people, mainly women, who are able to fulfill the local demand for domestic servants (Anderson). Historically, in the Canadian context, these women came disproportionately from the Caribbean and, more recently, from South Asia. Such domestic work policies are one arena within which anti-racist critiques have developed. Through such policies and practices Canada traffics in a global care chain of women migrants whose wages are important sources of foreign exchange to their home economies and whose labour meets the domestic demands of Canadian households. Feminist scholars as well as childcare advocates have connected this to Canada lack of a national childcare policy (Arat-Koc; McWatt and Neysmith).

Caring work

Since Janet Finch and Dulcie Groves published their much-quoted volume *A Labour of Love: Women, Work and Caring* in 1983, research and theory on caring labour has expanded (Armstrong and Armstrong). The literature now addresses the range of activities, working conditions, relationships, tasks and difficulties when caring labour is performed by paid and unpaid carers in households and community (Neysmith; Perrons).

One of the initial distinctions about caring work is still fundamental to current debates, namely, they argued that a distinction needs to be made between caring for and caring about. Caring *for* speaks to physical and concrete activities including feeding, cleaning, and attending to needs of others, while caring *about* captures the relational and emotional work. The importance of this distinction lies in the challenge it raises for assumptions that equate the expectation that women will care for others if they care about them. It is this assumption that undergirds social policies and practices that center women as responsible for ensuring the care of dependents. At the same time the state, as well as men, eschew such responsibilities, while reaping the benefits of putting their time, energy and capital resources elsewhere. This critique is not limited to Canada. It has proved to be an important lens when examining a range of social policies whether these be in progressive countries such as Sweden or welfare laggards such as the U.S. (Gottfried and Rees). The provision of services to children and old people have been particularly critiqued by feminists for their gender bias about caring labour.

Some of the analytical strength in the literature on caring stems from the fact that it has also been developed simultaneously in several disciplines (Williams). Unfortunately, it seems from the shape of debates arising in various aspects of this scholarship, that these streams have not been talking much to each other. For instance, although social policies concerned with social justice and health services are dominated by healthcare professionals, both the ethics of healthcare practice and home-care policies continue to be little influenced by the now sophisticated literature on the ethics of care and/ or the feminist critiques of caring labour (Neysmith).

Two aspects from this rich body of literature we find particularly useful: (1) Caring research has highlighted the importance of social relations in the production of quality care work. Whether paid or unpaid, the work is accomplished through social relationships. If, as Foucault argued, such relations are the capillaries of power, research on caring suggests that they are also the arteries of care. Feminist scholars have taken pains to point out that these arteries are not exclusively embodied in female kin which, as noted above, seems to be an assumption in current social policies around care of dependents. Political scientist Nancy Fraser's universal care-giver model elucidated what a gender neutral policy might look like. (2) The examination of caring labour has exposed assumptions about definitions of time. Most jobs are defined in terms of hours of work and frequently are paid accordingly. "Time is Money" is a colloquialism that highlights the connection between the two in industrialized society. The clash has been documented in development literature (Adam), frequently invoking the idea that adherence to clock time is an indicator of progress while other concepts of time are remnants of old cultural practices. In Canada the time clash is visible in home-care services where the care work has been broken down into a series of tasks. For instance, a bath is allocated 20 minutes. The in-joke status of this referent in home-care circles works as humour because everyone knows that giving a bath, its very possibility and the time required to accomplish it, is dependent upon the quality of the caregiver care/recipient relationship. Clock time and caring work are not necessarily compatible. They may not always be contradictory but to bind the two together into a job description conflates the market economy with what some have called the "other economy" of caring (Donath).

Volunteer and community work

These terms are considered together because they are frequently conflated. Volunteering is considered an important avenue for making a contribution to one's community. In 1997 Statistics Canada released an important document that estimated the amount of time that Canadians contributed to various types of volunteering. The results supported those found in earlier less systematic studies, namely, that the patterns between men and women differed; higher-income groups undertook voluntary work that was quite different from that of lower income Canadians, older people volunteered more than people of working age, among others. The critique of the survey was that it only captured formally structured volunteer activities (Neysmith and Reitsma-Street 2000). People who work irregular hours, have childcare responsibilities, work multiple jobs in order to make ends meet, who are recent immigrants etc. seldom belong to formal volunteer organizations. They also frequently do not define the volunteer work that they do as volunteer work. The language does not capture how they see this work

In research done by the authors of this paper, even when participants clearly understood that the work they were doing could be classified as volunteer work, the amount of work was consistently underestimated (Reitsma-Street and Neysmith). The authors emerged from this foray into volunteer work with the concern that the concept rendered invisible much of the work that women in poor communities were doing. As a result, such work would never appear on surveys such as that done by Statistics Canada. Indeed these women would fall into that category of not doing volunteer work and, by default, not contributing to community well-being. Thus once again a concept, and the tools used to operationalize it, fail to capture an important dimension of women's lives.

The critique goes beyond noting that the concept of volunteering is a poor fit for the work that women do outside of their family and paid work commitments. Another dimension that arises is around the concept of community. On the one hand, the term can be rather ethereal. On the other, it can be almost prosaic, limited to understandings of geography and local groups. At the time of writing community is a contested concept. The point to be made here is that whatever the debates about how to identify community, who belongs, or where the boundaries are drawn, community does not exist without people making it happen. Women, poor and wealthy, put much time, energy, and resources into their community work. They care for and about others beyond the household based on a collective, historical sense of what is important to preserve and struggle for.

The third shift

This term is frequently invoked to capture the multiple work demands that women juggle (Hochschild). It stands in counterpoint to definitions that categorize people as being in the labour force (employed or unemployed) or not. Women might work one shift of a day in a paid job and another shift at home, but at any given time while visibly in any of these named options, at the same time they are caring for children, elderly members of the family, maintaining an irregular contract job and participating in community work. The scope and time commitments, as well as the organization of these different aspects of a woman's life, also change over time. Thus, the word "shift" captures the dynamics as well as the flow and shuffling of work demands. The work and its conditions in one shifts affects that of others. Furthermore, the work is not sequenced. Frequently shifts are occurring at the same time, making different demands and requiring different sets of skills.

The term captures the dimension that some of the other concepts do not. For instance, very different and multiple types of activities can be occurring within one unit of time. Research and theorizing about work need to account for this. Secondly, there is work involved in negotiating among the demands made of women within and between the different shifts.

Provisioning

Each of the foregoing ways of thinking about the work that women do is useful in addressing some aspects of the problem and each has been successful in opening up hitherto unexplored dimensions of work. However, working with a variety of strands from different traditions presents a challenge to weaving a coherent explanation of the meaning of women's work with the explanatory power that can become the foundation for resistance and transformation. Provisioning is a concept we are introducing into research on women, poverty and communities to see if it opens new doors to thinking comprehensively yet succinctly about all the work women do. Provisioning refers to the multiple tasks, time required and relational dimensions of women's work in the context of the purposes for which the work is done. Debates on provisioning aims to explicate how the work women do is valued, and by whom, and what impact these value decisions have on claims for the resources required to perform adequate provisioning for households, community and society.

The following short case summary captures some of the multi-dimensionality of women's work that demands description, interpretation and explanation. The woman, named Ms. A., has been employed and aims to get a job again. She is continuously engaged in household and caring work, and wishes to give back volunteer work to the communities that have helped her. Her current limited financial resources constrain her options and make it necessary for her to take far more time and energy to garner resources for herself, her children, and others she cares for. Her poverty increases the difficulty of all the work she, and the many other poor women like her, do. As the case highlights, living in poverty also increase the invisibility of the work of women like Ms A. because it robs them of a language for describing this work with words that are valued:

Ms. A, is in her 30s and mother of three children. She left her last husband following years of abuse and now claims welfare. She had been an educational assistant before and wants to do similar work after upgrading her education. She is also seeing a counsellor about the abuse and her addictions because "I've got to be able to function properly." For the past year her children had to live with relatives but she sees them "all the time," and she visits the relatives and workers who are taking care for her children. With the help of an agency working with abused women, she recently became eligible for a place in public housing and now has more space so her eldest child can live with her half time. Ms. A receives a single persons shelter allowance and monthly welfare of just over $500 per month as if she is single and employable and as if "her kids still do not count" even though she directly provides for them part of the time.

It is a "long climb back" she says to establish a household. She spends careful, anxious hours trying to figure out what she is eligible for and negotiating with her various counsellors and welfare workers—eight in the last year, as well as teachers, parents, and volunteers from various churches and food banks. It takes skill to do "what is needed to be done": to get adequate food and clothing for herself and the children; to find furniture for the bedrooms; to obtain medical care coverage for her children; to accompany her son to a friend's birthday party and watch daughter play ball on the street as "that doesn't cost anything"; to find free dental care. She is paying for a phone that she can't afford but needs so she can call her children, welfare and various workers, and pursue leads to paid work.

Besides setting up a new household and working to get her children back to live with her full-time, Ms. A is finishing high school. She is also thinking about the future, and trying to put money away for her children so they can have the opportunity to do "whatever they're gifted at." Yet, she worries that she cannot provide. She hears "the clock is ticking" and is worried that she may be one of those in British Columbia who will be cut off welfare because of the two-year limits in the new laws and she won't find a job that pays enough to provide for herself or her children. Thus she wonders if it is right to have children if she cannot afford them, stating "If I don't have enough food for them, and I can't support them that way then I wonder if I'm doing the right thing. But we've really gotten really close again. And you know they want to come around so it's kind of a drag." Ms. A. also hopes to volunteer at a thrift shop for women and for another organization that helped her over the years as she says: "I'd like to give some back you know."

In our research we are using the concept of provisioning in furthering the goal of exposing and documenting the complexity and sheer amount of different types of work that women like Ms. A. do on a daily basis (Neysmith and Reitsma-Street 2005). We define provisioning as the work of securing resources and providing the necessities of life to those for whom one has relationships of responsibility. This definition speaks to a range of specific activities that are never finished, must be performed regularly, and require energy and attention. Provisioning includes paid employment and unpaid household and caring work. It takes place in the three spheres of market, household, and community, and shifts between them. Provisioning activities cannot be isolated or separated from the context of social relationships in diverse times and spaces because provisioning consists of those daily activities performed to ensure the survival and well-being of oneself and others. Both the activities and the relationships may be voluntary or prescribed. The point is that the activities are necessary; without them people would not survive.

Preliminary analysis (Reitsma-Street, Neysmith, Aronson, Baker Collins and Porter) of 67 qualitative interviews conducted with women living on low or insecure incomes in five communities indicate women engage in a complex pattern of provisioning for a variety of relationships using a range of activities including:

- Domestic household services
- Caring labour especially for kin, but also ex-spouses, friends, and others
- Employment and bartering
- Claims making for services from family, agencies, and the state
- Innovative, manipulative and illegal pursuits including not telling the truth and creating stories to account for poverty
- Creation of time as a resource through multi-tasking and using time rather than money as a resource.

A key finding is women on low, insecure incomes face many contradictions and nearly impossible situations as they try to provide. They report they could not fulfill their provisioning obligations without the support of informal community and formal state resources. The community and others, however, also become a site of obligations and responsibility for provisioning as well. Our future research agenda is to understand the dimensions and costs of provisioning; to identify relationships between provisioning and community; and to account for conditions that affect the relationships between women and their communities as they engage in provisioning work.

Concluding comments

Dominant understandings of women's work are limited to the two solitudes of family and the market. If it occurs in the former it is named caring; if in the latter, it is employment. Theories of social networks that are depicted as pathways to connect the two solitudes and build social capital have been limited to formal engagement in organized voluntary activities or leisure activities such as sport. Feminists have critiqued such gender-blind depictions of work and social capital (Rankin). Missed were, for example, the networks that women develop to meet the multiple demands of caring for children. These are face-to-face relationships of relative equality that foster trust as well as forming the basis for collective action.

However, the private/public split continues to mark both research and theory about the many types of work that women do. Within such discourses Ms. A. is silenced. Because she at this moment is not the primary caregiver of her children, and not holding a full-time job, she gets categorized as "not working" on both counts. Yet her days are filled with the work of provisioning for herself with part-time employment and welfare assistance, attending to the multiple tasks that need to be done before the children come home, reciprocating in-kind some of the resources made available to her by others, and planning for the future of those for whom she has responsibility.

We argue that the concept of provisioning is more robust than other available terms for revealing aspects of the work performed by Ms. A and all women. Articulating the community and policy implications of provisioning has a particular urgency to those who live in the midst of the increasing poverty, instability, regulations, and penalties that accompany decreases in public supports in Canada and elsewhere (Goode and Maskovsky; Luxton; Neysmith). Frequently employment and dependent-care policies have actually pitted differentially located groups of women against each other (Fraser). The concept of provisioning is useful in laying out the dynamics of the options and strategies used by women to secure resources for themselves and others. Women who live on limited, insecure incomes need a more solid conceptual basis that makes visible all the work they do, and values it. Without provisioning, women cannot provide for themselves and others, nor accumulate what is required to sustain households and community in the future.

We acknowledge the financial support of SSHRC Initiatives New Economy Development Grant #503-2002-0017 and SSHRC Standard Research Grant #410-2004-0233.

Originally published in CWS/cf's Spring/Summer 2004 issue, "Benefiting Women?
Women's Labour Rights" (Volume 23, Numbers 3/4): 192-198.

References

Adam, B. "The Gendered Time Politics of Globalization: Of Shadowlands
and Elusive Justice." *Feminist Review* 70 (2002): 3-29.

Anderson, B. *Doing the Dirty Work? The Global Politics of Domestic Labour.*
London, Zed Books, 2000.

Armstrong, P. and H. Armstrong. "Thinking it Through: Women, Work and
Caring in the New Millennium." *Caring for/Caring About: Women, Home
Vare, and Unpaid Baregiving.* Eds. Karen R. Grant, Carol Amaratunga, Pat
Armstrong, Madeline Boscoe, Ann Pederson and Kay Wilson. Aurora:
Garamond Press, 2004. 5-44.

Arat-Koç, S. *Caregivers Break the Silence: A Participatory Action Research on the
Abuse and Violence, Including the Impact of Family Separation, Experienced
by Women in the Live-in Caregiver Program.* Toronto: Intercede, 2001.

Bakker, I., Ed. *Rethinking Restructuring: Gender and Change in Canada.* Toronto: University of Toronto Press, 1996.

Barndt, D. *Tangled Roots: Women, Work and Globalization on the Tomato Trail.*
Aurora: Garamond, 2002.

Beneria, L., M. Flora, et al. "Introduction: Globalization and Gender." *Feminist
Economics* 16 (3) (2000): vii-xviii.

Cohen, M. *Training the Excluded for Work: Access and Equity for Women,
Immigrants, First Nations, Youth, and People with Low Income.* Vancouver:
University of British Columbia Press, 2003.

de Wolff, A. "The Face of Globalization: Women Working Poor in Canada."
Canadian Woman Studies/les cahiers de la femme 20 (3) (2000): 54-59.

Donath, S. "The Other Economy: A Suggestion for a Distinctively Feminist
Economics." *Feminist Economics* 6 (1) (2000): 115-125.

Finch, J. and D. Groves. Eds. *A Labour of Love: Women, Work and Caring.*
London: Routledge and Kegan Paul, 1983.

Fraser, N. *Justice Interruptus: Critical Reflections on the "Postsocialist" Condition.*
New York: Routledge, 1997.

Gardiner, J. *Gender, Care and Economics.* London: Macmillan, 1997.

Goode, J. and J. Maskovsky, eds. *The New Poverty Studies.* New York: New
York University Press, 2002.

Gottfried, H. and L. Rees. "Gender, Policy, Politics and Work: Feminist
Comparative and Transnational Research." *Review of Policy Research.* 20
(1) (2003): 3-20.

Himmelweit, S. "Making Visible the Hidden Economy: The Case for Gender-
Impact Analysis of Economic Policy." *Feminist Economics* 8 (1) (2002): 49-
70.

Hochschild, A. R. *The Time Bind: When Work Becomes Home and Home
Becomes Work.* New York: Metropolitan Books, 1997.

Luxton, M. *Getting By in Hard Times: Gendered Labour at Home and on the Job.* Toronto: University of Toronto Press, 2001.

Matthews, G. *"Just a Housewife": The Rise and Fall of Domesticity in America.* New York: Oxford University Press, 1987.

McWatt, S. and S. Neysmith. "Enter the Filipino Nanny." *Women's Caring* (Rev. Ed). Eds. C. Baines, P. Evans and S. Neysmith. Toronto: Oxford, 1998.

Nelson, J. "Labour, Gender and the Economic/Social Divide." *International Labour Review* 137 (1) (1998) : 33-46.

Neysmith, S. Ed. *Restructuring Caring Labour: Discourse, State Practice and Everyday Life.* Toronto, Oxford University Press, 2000.

Neysmith, S. and M. Reitsma-Steet "Valuing Unpaid Work in the Third Sector: The Case of Community Resource Centres." *Canadian Public Policy* 26 (3) (2000): 331-346.

Neysmith, S. and M. Reitsma-Street. "Provisioning: Conceptualizing the Work of Women for 21st Century Policy." *Women's Studies International Forum* 28 (2005): 381-391.

Perrons, D. "Care, Paid Work, and Leisure: Rounding the Triangle." *Feminist Economics* 6 (1) (2000): 105-114.

Porter, E. and C. Kauppi. "Women's Work is (Almost) Never Done...(By Anyone Else)." *Changing Lives: Women in Northern Ontario.* Eds. By M. Kechnie and M. Reitsma-Street. Toronto: Dundurn Press, 1996. 162-173.

Rankin, K. "Social Capital, Microfinance, and the Politics of Development." *Feminist Economics* 8 (1) (2002): 1-24.

Razavi, S. Ed. Shifting Burdens: Gender and Agrarian Change Under Neoliberalism Bloomfield, CT: Kumarian Press, 2002.

Reitsma-Street, M. and S. Neysmith. "Restructuring and Community Work: The Case of Community Resource Centres for Families in Poor Urban Neighbourhoods." *Restructuring Caring Labour: Discourse, State Practice, and Everyday Life.* Ed. S. Neysmith. Toronto, Oxford University Press, 2000. 142-163.

Reitsma-Street, M., S. Neysmith, J. Aronson, S. Baker Collins and E. Porter. "Redefining Boundaries and Crossing Borders: Implications of Women's Provisioning Work in Community." Paper presented at the Global Social Work Congress. Adelaide, Australia, Oct. 3, 2004.

Saraswati, J. "Poverty and Visible Minority Women in Canada." *Canadian Woman Studies/les cahiers de la femme* 20 (3) (2000): 49-53.

Statistics Canada. *Caring Canadians, Involved Canadians: Highlights from the 1997 National Survey of Giving, Volunteering and Participating.* Cat. No. 71-542XIE. August 1997.

Waring, M. *Counting for Nothing: What Men Value and What Women are Worth.* Wellington: Allen and Unwin, 1988.

Williams, F. "In and Beyond New Labour: Towards a New Political Ethics of Care." *Critical Social Policy* 21(4) (2001):467-493.

Freedom for Whom?

Globalization and Trade from the Standpoint of Garment Workers

Roxana Ng ⟶

"Globalization" and "restructuring" are buzz words of the new millennium. They are seen in positive and negative lights. On the one hand, governments and corporations see globalization as a positive process enabling businesses to move around the globe in search of markets and "flexible" labour, thereby augmenting profits. Predicting the world in 2001, Dudley Fishburn, editor of this special issue of *The Economist*, states:

> 2001 will be a year in which the world becomes a richer and sharply more decent place. Europe expand its wealth at the fastest rate for a decade.... the 2.3 billion people of China and India will organise their societies so as to double their prosperity every ten years.... Globalisation will raise the standards of human rights, law, ethics and corporate governance around the world, even in dismal Africa. The revolution in communications lies behind this imperative.... No pollution, no barriers, no dogmas, no sweatshops exist in the freer exchange of information. (9)

On the other hand, organized labour in Canada, as well as elsewhere, argue that globalization has led to work restructuring, job loss, and depression of wages, thereby impoverishing the livelihood of working people. Who is right? How do we see and understand the manifestation of these abstract, macro processes as concrete and actual relations that shape people's everyday lives? This paper will examine aspects of globalization in relation to the changing working conditions of garment workers in Canada. I will first explain what I mean by globalization and restructuring. I will then describe briefly the changing reality of the garment industry in Canada. I will focus on trade agreements as one component in the conglomerate of processes that shape the working conditions of garment workers against the backdrop of globalization and work restructuring.

Globalization, which should be called more appropriately "economic globalization," refers to the integration of national economies around the world into an international, global economy and market. It signals a stage of capitalist development where capital, embodied in multi- and transnational corporations, has developed the capacity to move across national boundaries. This capacity is partly facilitated by the electronic revolution (*vis-à-vis* the industrial revolution, which was an earlier stage of capitalist development that began in the nineteenth century), by computers and telecommunication systems that have the ability to "capture" and direct the market (the exchange of commodities and services virtually) simultaneously through cyberspace.[1] The movement of capital globally has also led to a corresponding movement of people around the world, either in search of employment, a better liveli-hood, or through the displacement of their homes by the lack of secure economic and social opportunities, or by warfare. This latter phenomenon often is not considered part of globalization. However, it *is* economic globali-zation and colonization that have led to the displacement of people from their indigenous livelihood (Sassen).

In some ways, globalization is not new. Some argue that colonization, especially European colonization of the rest of the world, has been with us for several hundred years. What is new in this era of globalization is the ability of capital to move sites of production across national borders with relative ease, and the virtual and instantaneous character of exchange (e.g., through stock market activities). Thus, it is worth investigating how the current processes of globalization affect us because the forms of profit augmentation and labour exploitation are changing.

Closely related to globalization is a process called "work restructuring," or restructuring. However, I don't want to posit a direct, causal relationship between restructuring and globalization, because things are more complicated than that. Restructuring is quite unique, depending on local conditions, and how those involved in particular sectors respond to and innovate around local, regional, national, and international changes. The restructuring of the Cana-dian garment industry in the last two and a half decades, for example, presents an interesting and complicated case of Canadian manufacturers' responses to pressures imposed by the various processes related to globalization. Indeed, some analysts suggest that one of the effects of globalization is intense localization (Murphy). The varied responses within the garment sector in Canada seem to bear out this hypothesis.

What is happening to the Canadian garment industry?

The garment industry is a predominantly Canadian-owned industry and a major employer of immigrants and women. Historically it occupied a secure position in Canadian manufacturing. It is the eighth largest provider of manufacturing jobs, and an important employer of women and immigrants. The garment work force is comprised of about 50 per cent immigrants and 76 per cent women (Gunning, Eaton, Ferrier, Kerr, King, and Maltby,). Histori-cally and presently, the industry has relied on low wages for competitive advantage, and makes use of immigrants as a pool of inexpensive labour. The industry is internally differentiated by gender and ethnicity. In the period immediately after the war, many garment workers were immigrant men from Europe. As they acquire skills and seniority and move up the production hierarchy (e.g., by becoming cutters, who are seen to be more skilled than sewing machine operators), women replace them as sewing machine operators at the bottom of the garment production hierarchy. It is noteworthy, although not surprising, that in employing immigrant women as sewing machine operators, the skills they have acquired in domestic settings (such as mending and sewing) can be readily transferrable to the industrial context; thus these workers are seen by employers as unskilled or semi-skilled (*vis-à-vis* cutters who are seen to be skilled).

Historically, homeworking and sweatshop operation were an integral part of the garment trade. With the formation of the International Ladies Garment Workers' Union (ILGWU), first in the U.S. and later in Canada, garment workers became the few unionized female work force that enjoyed decent wages and employee benefits. Unlike some other sectors with heavy concentration of female immigrant workers, garment workers were protected by labour standard legislation and rights to collective bargaining since the 1930s.[2]

Since the 1980s, however, the garment industry has been undergoing dramatic and contradictory changes. For instance, according to Industry Canada between 1989 and 1993 the sector experienced a staggering loss of 800 plants and over 33,000 jobs, leading to the prediction that it was a "sunset" industry. But since then the industry has been growing. From the mid-1990s on, both shipments and employment have been increasing (Gunning *et al.*). Some segments of the industry (e.g., private label manufacturing) are booming. Control within the industry has shifted from manufacturers to large transnational retail chains, such as Wal-Mart. Manufacturers have responded to their slip in control in different ways. Some retired and got out of the business altogether. Some become importers or contractors to retailers and sub-contract out work to plants in low-waged countries through a vast and expanding global production network, taking advantage of trade agreements between/among governments, and of the establishment of free trade zones in third world countries (Yanz, Jeffcott, Ladd and Atlin). Some reorganize production locally by sub-contracting to smaller shops and jobbers to lower cost and increase productivity, for example by scaling back on their plants and by using home-based workers for the bulk of their production (Ng 1999b). The effects of this restructuring are job loss and the re-emergence of home-based work and sweatshop operations in the Canadian context.

To illustrate, my 1999 study on homeworkers and their working conditions (Ng 1999a) found that the wages of sewing machine operators have not arisen since the 1980s. In her classic study in *The Seams Allowance: Industrial Home Sewing in Canada*, Laura Johnson reported that the piece rate for skirts was two dollars (Johnson and Johnson). Today, workers also make two dollars for a skirt. A shirt is around three dollars, and a dress pays four to five dollars. These are clothing that are retailed for up to 200 dollars. For section work (that is, sewing on pockets or collars), workers make between 20 to 50 cents per piece. Based on the piece rate and number of items completed per hour, the average hourly rate can be estimated at between six dollars and eight dollars. The highest hourly rate reported is 17 dollars per hour for evening gowns. The lowest is two dollars per hour. What is more critical to note is that as home-based workers become skilled at what they are sewing and begin to make more than minimum wage (about seven dollars per hour), the employers drop the piece rate so their earning is effectively reduced. For example, one woman reported that depending on the complexity of the design, she used to get three to four dollars per skirt; now she is paid two dollars and 80 cents to three dollars. This finding concurs with a larger study on the garment trade, which reported on a decline in the piece rate (Yantz *et al.*). Some of the other problems mentioned by the women in the study include: the employer will not give information on piece rate until the garments are completed; late payment or being paid less than the agreed upon amount; no vacation pay but employers include vacation pay on the T4A issued at year end to give the appearance of conforming to employment standards. In these situations the women feel that their only recourse, after pursuing the employer repeatedly, is to discontinue work with a particular employer. The story of this worker illustrates non- or late payment:

> *I don't have very serious problem with getting paid. What may happen sometimes is getting late payment. One time there was this employer who owed me about $500-600. He admitted to it and kept saying sorry. But I still haven't got any pay from him. It was six to seven years ago. He later referred me to another sub-contractor, who sent the fabric from Montreal to his place. So I would go to his place to pick up the fabric and my pay. Another time, he asked me to lend him money. I did. And he has never paid me back. I still see him from time to time, but I do not work for him any more.*

In addition to the low pay rates and non-payment of benefits, liberalization of provincial employment standards and government cut-backs across the country also mean that health and safety regulations may not be adhered to in the smaller shops. The overall picture, from the standpoint of garment workers, is one of decreasing protection and lower wages; that is, deepening exploitation.

The new regime of ruling in the era of globalization

Elsewhere, I have argued that what we witness in terms of increasing competition among employers and workers, and decreasing security for jobbers and workers alike, are not inevitable. They are the result of what I call a "globalized regime of ruling" that produce, in part, the local conditions we find in centres of garment production in Canada and around the world (Ng 1998; 2001). I use the term, "regime" after George Smith, to indicate that these are not accidental processes. They are planned and effected by actual people in their actual everyday activities, working toward the integration of markets, including labour markets, on a global scale. With regard to garment production, I have identified four sets of processes that work in concert to produce the phenomenon we see around the world. I will mention them briefly, but will focus on trade agreements in this paper.

First of all, the increasing concentration of capital through corporate mergers and takeovers have had a tremendous impact on the present-day configuration of the garment industry. The shift of control away from manufacturers to large retail chains such as the Hudson's Bay Company (which also owns Zellers) and increasingly to transnational retail chains such as Wal Mart has centralized control of the industry while production is progressively fragmented. By fragmentation I am referring to the sub-contractual nature of most garment production, especially in sub-sectors such as ladies and children wear. In response to their slip of control, manufacturers scale down production by reducing plant size, retaining a couple of cutters, thereby becoming *contractors* to retailers. The making of garments is contracted out to a network of *sub-contractors*, called jobbers, who may use home-based workers or sweatshop operations to minimize operating costs and maximize profit margins. In Canada, we also witness the increasing penetration of large U.S. chains into the retail sector, pushing local retailers and manufacturers out of business. Apart from deepening class exploitation and creating new classes of workers, these kinds of shifts produce further inequalities between men and women because of women's location at the bottom of the production hierarchy.

Secondly, under the ideology of neo-liberalism (that is, the mentality of "letting the market decide"), many governments at all levels have cut back on or privatized social provisions, deregulated industries and services, and "liberalized" employment standards. For example, in spite of the increasing phenomenon of home-based work, the Ontario government has consistently resisted reforming labour legislation to enable home-based workers such as domestic and garment workers to unionize across work sites (Mirchandani). Furthermore, in Ontario the legal working hours for the work week have been extended to 60, effective lengthening the work week of workers without giving them protection against possible employer exploitation. This development works in concert with coercive regulation of worker mobility, for example by tightening immigration and refugee policies, especially since the September 11, 2001 terrorist attacks on the U.S. Accompanying this move, in Canada, is the increasing use of workers on work permits, effectively restricting the mobility and citizenship rights of groups of workers, frequently from third world countries (Sharma). What we see here is not only the international division of labour between the economic North and South, but also the creation of third world enclaves within the North and the maintenance of existing racial hierarchy worldwide.

Closely related to this phenomenon of deepening the exploitation of citizens as workers is the increasingly coordinated international networks of human trafficking across national borders. Indeed, analysts monitoring this situation assert that human trafficking is the number one illegal activity across the globe, surpassing the illegal traffic of drugs and firearms (Kwong; Murphy). Illegal migrants are used to supply industrialized countries such as Canada and the U.S. with a cheap labour force, thus creating a new category of workers called "undocumented workers." Undocumented workers and illegal migrants are seen frequently as a third world phenomenon arising out of the appalling economic, social and political conditions of southern countries.[3] In reality, we have to interrogate the way in which demand for cheap and docile labour in the developed and industrialized countries creates the impetus and incentive of illegal migration and for people to act as intermediaries for this activity. Illegal migration is often seen as an accidental phenomenon. In fact, it is an activity that requires a great deal of planning, coordination, and cooperation among groups of people (the intermediaries, those working in transportation companies and border control, to name only a few players). It is therefore through and through an integral part of the present condition we call globalization.

Finally, the forging of trade agreements between Canada and the U.S., not to mention internationally, has had a profound impact on the garment industry in Canada. It is to this that I will now turn.

Trade agreements and their impact on garment workers

I mentioned in the beginning of this paper that what distinguishes this period of globalization from previous colonizing efforts by western powers is the increasing capacity for capital to move across national borders. This capacity is facilitated by trade negotiations between and among nations and international trade organizations such as the World Trade Organization (WTO). These negotiations, leading to the signing of trade agreements, govern trade and investment between and among countries. The Canadian government has taken a progressively active role in these trade agreements for over 15 to 20 years, beginning notably with the negotiation and implementation of the Canada-U.S. Free Trade Agreement (the CUSFTA or simply the FTA) in 1989. It is not possible to outline all the trade agreements negotiated between Canada and other countries.[4] I will only highlight the major agreements that concern the garment industry directly. I will then look at the implications of these agreements for the industry and for workers' security and conditions.

Until the 1980s, Canada's garment industry was relatively protected by tariffs and quotas.[4] Trade liberalization in the garment sector began with the signing of the FTA in 1989. The FTA is a bilateral agreement between Canada and the U.S. Before the FTA, Canada's major apparel suppliers were China, Hong Kong, and Korea. Since the signing of the FTA, there has been a huge jump in the value of U.S. garments imported to Canada. According to Industry

Canada statistics, between 1988 and 1995 apparel imports from the U.S. increased at an average rate of over 25 per cent (cited in Yanz *et al.* 79). Although as a bilateral agreement, the scope of the FTA was limited, it is an important piece of legal document because it set precedents for future trade negotiations, such as negotiations around the North American Free Trade Agreement (NAFTA).

Trade liberalization was accelerated with NAFTA, released on September 6, 1992 and implemented in January 10, 1993. It played a major role in the re-configuration of the garment sector because this agreement enables the movement of production and goods more freely between/among Canada, the U.S. and Mexico. Specifically, it enables manufacturers to invest in, set up, or out-source to garment plants in Mexico where labour costs are much lower relative to U.S. and Canadian wages. Indeed major Canadian manufacturers such as Nygard International, which manufactures women's wear, and Gildan, the largest T-shirt manufacturer in Quebec, now have plants in Mexico, Latin America, and the Caribbean Basin. This has led directly to job loss, depression of Canadian wages, and the restructuring of garment manufacturing in the Canadian context (MSN). One strategy used by U.S. manufacturers, for example, is to ship U.S.-produced textile to Mexico, where garments can be made much more cheaply, and then import the finished products back to the U.S. market taking advantage of the free tariff and quota agreement of NAFTA (Vosko).

Since the signing of NAFTA, Canada's apparel export to the U.S. has also increased. However, the advantage of NAFTA to Canadian manufacturers is contradictory. According to Vosko, the "rules of origin" in NAFTA limit Canadian manufacturers in two ways.[5] First, these rules stipulate that duty is only exempted for products containing textile made in North America. The high-end clothing produced in Canada, however, is made mainly with textile imported from Europe. Since much Canadian-made clothing would be considered non-originating, the work of Canada's apparel manufacturers and their employees are effectively devalued. Thus, NAFTA sets unfair export limits and duties on Canada's most competitive garments. Second, the same rules also force Canada and Mexico to import yarn from the U.S., thus giving U.S. textile and apparel manufacturing an unfair advantage.

In terms of international agreements, Canada first participated in the Multi-Fibre Agreement (MFA) negotiated through the WTO in 1974. The MFA involved negotiation, country by country, bilateral quotas concerning the quantity of garments that exporting countries from the South could send into Canada and other northern countries. This has protected the Canadian industry from southern countries that have a competitive edge in terms of lower labour costs, lower labour standards, and fewer work place health and safety requirements. In 1995, a new agreement, the Agreement on Textiles and Clothing (ATC) came into effect, which replaced the MFA. Under the ATC, worldwide apparel and textile quotas will be phased out by 2005. This will enable countries such as China to dramatically increase apparel and textile exports to western markets, thus significantly affecting garment production within Canada.

Although the effects of the ATC is unclear at this point, taken as a whole, we can begin to pinpoint certain trends in garment production in Canada and globally. It is clear that globalization, through the negotiation of trade agreements, has led to increasing competition among workers across national borders. For example, Canadian workers, who historically received protection through unionization and strict tariffs and quotas, will now face intense competition from workers in countries such as Mexico and China, who are paid much less. This has led and will lead to further depression of wages and erosion of labour protection for Canadian workers. To keep existing manufacturers and investors and attract new ones, provincial governments will likely respond by further de-regulating labour standards. This has indeed been the strategy of the Conservative Ontario Harris and the Alberta Klein governments. This strategy is being valiantly pursued by the Liberal government in British Columbia. We will thus see the increasing use of sweatshops and home-based work, as manufacturers and jobbers compete in the international market for garment production. Another logical extension of this trend is to use even more undocumented workers, thereby augmenting the demand for illegal migration and human trafficking. Canadian garment workers will face increasingly similar working and living conditions as their third-world counterparts. I have argued elsewhere that immigrant garment workers from third world countries are undergoing re-colonization in the first world (Canadian) context (Ng 1998). This trend has been and will continue to be exacerbated with the trade agreements we examined above. Workers everywhere will face more adverse working conditions as manufacturers compete for price advantage *vis-à-vis* their buyers—the transnational retail chains.

What can be/is being done?

Giving the tremendous odds faced by garment workers in Canada and globally, it is clear that drastic measures are needed to ameliorate increasing labour rights violations. In addition to the efforts of unions and labour rights groups, there are at least three areas in which concerned citizens can be involved, and these are: *research, public education, and activism.* While I have separated them for the purpose of identifying areas of action, in fact they work in concert with each other.

First of all, we need more and better research done on tracking the global production and organization of apparel and textile. Due to the private nature of ownership and the secretive character of garment production, it is very difficult to trace the extensive network and chain of garment production in Canada and globally. Tracking the global inter-connections between/among garment plants therefore requires researchers with different knowledge and skills. For example, statistical analysis of export and import figures of garment manufacturing coupled with interviews with garment workers illuminate the multi-faceted and contradictory nature of garment production. Tracking investment patterns of manufacturers indicates the movement and places of garment production across national borders. It is only through collaboration and partnership among researchers in different locations (e.g., in the academy, in unions, in the community) that we will begin to unravel the complex nature and organization of garment production in Canada and elsewhere.

Second, we need to bring to public awareness the complex system of exploitation of workers and the strategies used by retailers and large manufacturers to augment profit. Instead of de-regulation, governments need to put in better protective and monitoring legislation and regulation. But governments will only become more accountable with tax-payers' forceful insistence. Thus, research and public education need to be bolstered by activism on the part of citizens. For example, as a result of lobbying by students and other concerned citizens, the University of Toronto developed, in 1999, a Code of Conduct for Trademark Licensees to ensure that suppliers of the university's trademarked merchandise (such as T-shirt, sweatshirts, and souvenirs), meet minimum employment standards regarding such issues as wages and benefits, working hours, and overtime compensation. When the University learned about the allegations directed at Gildan Activewear, mentioned above, regarding their unethical treatment of workers in the third world through the CBC-TV program called "Disclosure," aired on January 22, 2002, the administration asked Gildan to account for allegations about poor working conditions in its factories. This is the kind of pressure that can keep manufacturers and retailers as accountable and responsible employers.

Finally, we need to develop alliances and multi-pronged strategies, not only to work with workers in Canada, but to make linkages with workers and groups in the South. Given the intimate connection of garment production between northern and southern countries, gains by one group of workers will have a ripple effect on other groups. An example of an organization that combines these three areas of action I identified above to show the feasibility of this approach is the Maquila Solidarity Network (MSN). This Toronto-based non-profit network of 400 plus organizations concerned with labour issues worldwide has been at the forefront of research and advocacy on garment production. It traces Canadian manufacturers' involvement in garment production in Mexico, Central America, the Caribbean Basin, and more recently Asia. In addition to research, MSN is also collaborating with women's and labour rights organizations in the economic South, for example by advocating the development and implementation of codes of conduct governing garment production. Working in coalition with labour and other social action organizations, the network has initiated and organized campaigns in Canada to bring to light the situation of garment workers worldwide, and what Canadians can do to ameliorate the plight of these workers. Their latest disclosure and no sweat campaigns are an innovative, multi-pronged strategy that integrates research, public education, and worker education. The disclosure campaign, mounted by the Ethical Trading Action Group, is trying to get the federal government to amend the Textile Labelling Act so that the "CA number" on clothing labels would have to reveal where the article is actually made. This would enable researchers and activists to trace the global network of garment production by Canadian manufacturers.[6] It is also a way of educating Canadians the nature of garment production.

Eliminating inequity is the responsibility of us all. It is by working together in solidarity and cooperation that we can push back or push away the detrimental effects of globalization, and work toward a global system that would benefit the majority of the world population.

The research, on which this paper is based, is funded by the Social Sciences and Humanities Research Council of Canada. Thanks are due to Patty Simpson and Ann O'Connell for research assistance, and to Jonathan Eaton for feedback.

Originally published in CWS/cf's Spring/Summer 2002 issue, "Women, Globalization and International Trade" (Volume 21/22, Numbers 4/1): 74-81.

[1]Some analysts and lay people use the term "globalization" to refer exclusively to the electronic and communication revolution. While this is not inaccurate, I insist that this development must be understood in the context of the transnational movement of capital. Technological innovations in communication should be seen as an integral part of economic globalization.
[2]The International Ladies Garment Workers Union (ILGWU) was formed in 1900, and the Amalgamated Clothing Workers of America (ACWA) was founded in 1914 to organize the men's clothing industry in the U.S.. While both unions quickly moved into Canada, workers did not win labour laws such as the Industrial Standards Act in Ontario and the Decree Law in Quebec until the 1930s. Thus, there was a time lag between unionization and when workers gained legislative protection. I thank Jonathan Eaton for providing this detail.
[3]I am using the terms "third world" and "the economic South" or southern countries here interchangeably to refer to the common sense understanding between the developed and developing world. I recognize that these terms are problematic, because they reinforce, rather than name, power differential between and among nations. Indeed, elsewhere I have argued for a re-thinking of these categories with the advent of globalization (see Ng 1998).
[4]The Multi-Fibre Agreement (MFA), an international agreement negotiated through the World Trade Organization (WTO), is an example that offers Canadian clothing manufacturing some protection against cheaper imports. How the MFA worked is explained later on in the paper.
[5]For an outline of the trade agreements being negotiated up to 1998, consult *Review—The North-South Institute Newsletter*. Since 1998, trade negotiations have been accelerated, with the FTAA held in Quebec City in 2001 being one instance of this activity.
[6]For the work of the MSN, which is also the secretariat of the Ethical Trading Action Group, see their website, www.maquilasolidarity.org.

References

Ethical Trading Action Group www.maquilasolidarity.org.

Fishburn, Dudley. "Editorial." *The Economist-The World in 2001.* 9 (2001).

Gunning, J., J. Eaton, S. Ferrier, M. Kerr, A. King, and J. Maltby, *Dealing with Work-Related Musculoskeletal Disorders in the Ontario Clothing Industry.* Report submitted to the Research Advisory Council of the Workplace Safety & Insurance Board. Toronto: The Union of Needletrade and Industrial Textile Employees (UNITE), November 3, 2000.

Johnson, Laura and Robert Johnson, *The Seam Allowance: Industrial Home Sewing in Canada.* Toronto: The Women's Educational Press, 1982.

Industry Canada. *Clothing Industry Statistical Data.* 1996.

Kwong, Peter. *Forbidden Workers: Illegal Chinese Immigrants and American Labor.* New York: The New Press, 1997.

Maquila Solidarity Network (MSN), *A Needle in a Haystack: Tracing Canadian Garment Connections to Mexico and Central America.* Toronto: MSN, October 2000.

Mirchandani, Kiran. "Shifting Definitions Of The Public-Private Dichotomy: Legislative Inertia On Garment Homework In Ontario." *Advances in Gender Research.* (3) 1998. 47-71.

Murphy, Brian. "International NGOs and the Challenge of Modernity," *Development in Practice.* 10 (3&4) 2000. 330-347.

Ng, Roxana. "Homeworking: Home Office or Home Sweatship? Report on Current Conditions of Homeworkers in Toronto's Garment Industry." Toronto: The Ontario Institute for Studies in Education, 1999a. (Available online http://www.nall.ca)

Ng, Roxana. "Homeworking: Dream Realized Or Freedom Constrained? The Globalized Reality Of Immigrant Garment Workers." *Canadian Woman Studies.* 19 (3) Fall 1999b. 110-114.

Ng, Roxana. "Work Restructuring and Recolonizing Third World Women: An Example From The Garment Industry In Toronto." *Canadian Woman Studies/les cahiers de la femme* 18 (1) Spring 1998. 21-25.

Ng, Roxana. "Exploring The Globalized Regime Of Ruling From The Standpoint Of Immigrant Women," Public Lecture delivered at the University of Victoria, February 13, 2001.

Review–The North-South Institute Newsletter 2 (1) 1998.

Sassen, Saskia. *Globalization and Its Discontents: Essays on The New Mobility of People and Money.* New York: The New Press, 1998.

Sharma, Nandita. "The Social Organization of 'Difference' and Capitalist Restructuring in Canada: The Making of 'Non-Immigrants' and 'Migrant Workers' Through the Formation of the 1973 Non-Employment Authorization Program." Unpublished Ph.D. dissertation, Department of Sociology and Equity Studies, OISE/University of Toronto, 1999.

Sharma, Nandita. "The True North Strong and Unfree: Capitalist Restructuring and Non-Immigrant Employment in Canada, 1973-1993." Unpublished MA thesis, Department of Sociology and Anthropology, Simond Fraser University, Burnaby BC, August 1995.

Smith, George. "Accessing Treatments: Managing the AIDS Epidemic in Ontario" *Knowledge, Experience, and Ruling Relations*. Eds. M. Campbell and A. Manicom. Toronto: University of Toronto Press, 1995. 18-34.

Vosko, Leah F. *The Last Thread: Analysis of the Apparel Goods Provisions in the North American Free Trade Agreement and the Impact on Women*. Ottawa: The Canadian Centre for Policy Alternatives, February 1993.

Yanz, Lynda. Bob Jeffcott, Deena Ladd, Joan Atlin, *Policy Options to Improve Standards for Garment Workers in Canada in Internationally*. Ottawa: Status of Women Canada, January 1999.

The Politics of Sustainable Development

A Subsistence View

Ana Isla ——

Over the past ten years sustainable development has been proposed as a means to confront the environmental and social crises that we are currently experiencing around the world. The environmental crisis is evidenced by, among other things, the effects of green house gas emissions, acid rain, and global warming; oceans rising and hurricanes; higher temperatures; toxic chemicals, soil erosion and depletion; decertification, acidification, and the depletion of ground water. The social crisis has resulted in increased poverty and destitution; sexism; ethnicism, and racism; environmental and economic refugees; terrorism, trafficking, imperialism, neo-colonialism and the spread of violence.

This paper links the United Nations Conference on Environment and Development (UNCED), or the Earth Summit, held Rio de Janeiro in 1992 with the Johannesburg Summit in 2002. At both conferences, sustainable development was offered as a cure for social and environmental crises.

In Rio, development and environment were linked together as sustainable development under *Agenda 21*, a plan of action negotiated during the Summit. Sustainable development was defined as "development that meets the needs of the present without compromising the ability of future generations to meet their own needs" (WCED 8). The discourse of sustainable development was thus equated with economic growth and promised that globalization of the economy would rescue poor countries from their poverty, even in the most remote areas of the world (Pearce and Warford). Since then, the WB's Global Environmental Facility (GEF), established in 1991 to fund projects and programs in developing countries that protect the environment, has been financing the Global Resource Managers (GRM), a special category of functionaries who broker the industry involved in corporate globalization and economic restructuring.

The Earth Summit held in Johannesburg in 2002 marked the ten-year anniversary of the original Earth Summit in Rio. While at the Rio conference, government/states were seen as responsible for organizing sustainable development, in Johannesburg, responsibility for sustainable development was transferred to corporations and their shareholders. According to the United Nations, the Summit in Johannesburg will be remembered not for the treaties, the commitments, or the declarations it produced, but for the first stirring of a new way of governing the global commons ... [by] oriented partnerships that may include non-government organizations, willing governments and other stakeholders. ("The Johannesburg Summit Test: What Will Change?")

As industrial production is led by transnational corporations (TNCs), their impact on the environment was disregarded throughout the United Nations Conference on Environment and Development (UNCED) process although a voluntary code of conduct was adopted. Instead, proponents of economic growth portrayed the poor of the world, *campesinos*/peasants and Indigenous populations as the prime enemies of the rainforest in order to legitimize the expropriation of their commons and their exclusion from those commons (Hecht and Cockburn). Michael Goldman states:

As long as the commons is perceived as only existing within a particular mode of knowing, called development, with its unac-knowledged structures of dominance, this community [GRM] will continue to serve the institution of development, whose *raison d'être* is restructuring Third World capacities and social-natural relations to accommodate transnational capital expansion. (47)

The ten years between Rio and Johannesburg have thus been a triumph of corporate-driven globalization that resulted in the imposition of global control on the commons—land, water, biodiversity, rivers, lakes, oceans, atmosphere, forest, and mountains—at the national, regional, and municipal levels. For women and men who depend on the local commons, the assault on their surroundings means loss of dignity and independence, security, liveli-hood, health, and, sometimes, loss of their lives. Nevertheless, as governments and corporations seek to expand the economic growth of globalized capitalist accumulation by appropriating the everyday commons of women, households, Indigenous people and peasants, a new ecological-gendered-class-ethnic-struggle is emerging over the use of ecological resources for livelihood.

This paper will apply a socialist ecofeminist perspective to review the social practice of sustainable development and the social responses to it during the ten years between Rio and Johannesburg. Ecofeminists, in coming to terms with the causes and consequences of the social and environmental crises, delegitimized and contested the dominant concepts of sustainable develop-ment. Eco-feminists value nature and the knowledge and experience of women as sources of the reproduction and sustenance of individual and community life. They note the intimate connection between the ways women, peasants, Indigenous people, and nature are treated, and argue that it has been possible to sustain the illusion that economic growth is a positive and benign process only because the costs have been borne by Third World peasants, Indigenous peoples, nature, and women (Mies; Shiva; Merchant; Salleh 1994, 1997; Agarwal).

Divided into two sections, this paper also examines local-resistance to the discourse/project that has revived colonization and sees the environment as an adjunct to economic growth. In the first section, I illustrate the politics of the state-based sustainable development advocated at UNCED in Rio de Janeiro in 1992 through a critical examination of Plan Puebla Panama (PPP) project. In the second section, I illustrate the logic and consequences of the private-side of sustainable development advocated at the Summit in Johannesburg in 2002 through an examination of the struggles that have emerged around private mining initiatives in Tambogrande, Peru.

Rio's state-based development and the politics of the global commons

At the Earth Summit in Rio, economists proposed that the ecology must be embedded in the economic system through the price system, that is, the economy requires a fully monetized world in order to be protected. This meant that atmosphere, oceans and seas, land, forest, mountains, biological diversity, ecosystems, fresh water etc. need to be priced. Following this logic, the WB developed "genuine" saving measures that "broaden the usual national accounts definitions of assets to include human capital, minerals, energy, forest resources and the stock of atmospheric CO_2," (Hamilton), thus legitimizing the enclosure of the common. Robert Smith and Claude Simmard subsequently expanded the concept of natural capital into three categories: *natural resource stocks*, the sources of raw materials (priced or unpriced) used in the production of manufactured goods; *land*, essential for the provision of space for economic activity to take place; and *environment systems* (or ecosystems), necessary for the services that they provide directly and indirectly to the economy, including purifying the air and water, providing biodiversity, stabilizing climate, providing protection from solar radiation, and providing stable flows of renewable natural resources. However, using an ecological economics perspective, Juan Martinez-Alier questions translating environmental values into monetary values, because there is no common unit of measurement. He argues that economic incommensurability arises not only from the fact that prices depend on the endowment of property rights and on the distribution of income; or on how to give present values to future uncertain and irreversible changes, but the fact that most environmental resources and services are not and cannot be in the market. Further, money is not the relevant standard of comparison for people who are not yet wholly immersed in the generalized market system.

At the NGO Global Forum that was taking place at the same time as the official conference in Rio, women's organizations, however, were proposing to work for cancellation of Third World countries' foreign debt and advocated reparation for the damage caused by 500 years of colonization, despite the fact that it was clear that cancellation of the debt itself would not solve the problems of inequality and injustice unless the systematic and institutional patterns of inequality are also changed. The suffering of subsistence producers, women, peasants, and Indigenous people in the indebted world at the hands of commercial banks, the International Monetary Fund (IMF) and the World Bank (WB), and their stabilization and Structural Adjustment Programs (SAPs) activated women's solidarity from all corners. A proposal was approved by the NGOs that put pressure on the UN to:

> work for the international recognition of ecological debt and commit to the recognition of the ecological creditors (ethnic groups, communities, countries and regions affected by the exhaustion of resources), the ecological debtors (responsible for environmental and social deterioration) and the necessity of applying measures of ecological adjustment (modifications and changes in the present patterns of production and consumption) so that actions of devastation and contamination do not continue to be taken (Debt Treaty).

However, despite the Debt Treaty signed in 1992, and the subsequent Debt Treaty Movement (DTM)[1] which raised the profile of the debt and the problems arising from development, and which by the end of the 1990s were identified with sustainable development in particular, indebtedness, rather than being reduced has expanded and has led to ecological destruction and legitimated ecological appropriation of indebted countries' nature, particularly in Latin America.

Since the late 1980s, the commercial banks and the multilateral institutions such as the International Monetary Fund (IMF) and the World Bank (WB), who previously made loans to Third World countries, have been replaced by an inflow of private portfolio funds and debt-for-nature investments or "debt swaps."[2] Debt swaps are financial mechanisms that offer repayment of loans held by creditors (commercial banks, governments) in return for handing over ownership of national industries, public enterprises, bank assets, and natural resources. Particularly since 1988, capital accumulation relies on debt-for-nature investments. Debt-for-nature investments, one of the major outcomes of the UNCED, are the core sustainable development mechanisms of choice for the WB, the IMF, UNESCO, and large environmental corporations. Since UNCED, the Global Environmental Facility (GEF) under World Bank management has established funding for numerous NGOs involved in debt-for-nature swaps to "protect" the global environment. The sustainable development framework is thus not different from economic development (Isla 2002a, 2002b).

As the price mechanism becomes over-extended with respect to the natural environment, and economic growth has as an inherent objective the capture of the local commons, locality has become a site of confrontations, where the new forms of domination, exploitation, and oppression encounter responses (Escobar). However, resistance is no longer only at the local level, it has brought international political mobilization and solidarity, particularly among women.

Plan Puebla Panama

The Plan Puebla Panama (PPP), also called the Mesoamerican Biological Corridor, has been regarded as the principal initiative of sustainable development of the Central American region arising from *Agenda 21* (WB). Proposed and accepted by eight countries of Central America (Mexico, Guatemala, Belize, El Salvador, Honduras, Nicaragua, Costa Rica, and Panama), PPP, involving an area of 1,026,117 square kms and 62,830,000 inhabitants, is aimed at poverty reduction and environmental reparation. As a development project, PPP comprises eight initiatives: a) roads and highways integration; b) human development; c) hydro-electric production; d) promotion of eco-tourism; e) partnership for sustainable development; f) prevention and mitigation of disasters; g) building of functional customs houses; and, h) development of a telecommunications network. As it is presented, PPP complements the neo-liberal programs of privatization of public resources, such as water, energy, and public services with the expansion of commercial markets, highways and transport infrastructures, direct investments in *maquiladoras* (sweatshops) and transnational businesses, wage work, and electricity (Ornelas). As an environment project, the World Bank presents the PPP as a project aimed at identifying and quantifying the biodiversity of the area. WB Director of Environment, Kristalina Georgieva, declared that the PPP was necessary as "there are over 45 million people in the region, of which 60 per cent live on less than $2 a day" (WB). Poverty defined as the absence of western consumption patterns, cash incomes and industrialization (Mies and Shiva), is thus the excuse for the new assault on Central America commoners.

Despite capital's global reach, corporations still depend on nation states and ruling elites. They expect PPP to benefit them by extending the boundaries of their economic activity by bringing more land into development and evicting the locals. None of the inhabitants living in these eight countries involved were consulted about PPP (Ornelas). Eucebio Figueroa belongs to an organization called *"Por la Vida y por la Gente"* (For Life Itself and People's Livelihood) that represents a large network opposing PPP. In the words of Figueroa, the main goal of PPP is to use what is left of Indigenous peoples' land and cultural domains as the new frontiers for global capital's colonization project. In this way, Indigenous communities are targeted for disintegration. To the resisters, which include Indigenous people, local poor and rural women, PPP is a war against "our culture and ways of life, because we live from subsistence agriculture" (Figueroa). To defend the threatened commons, in 2001 more than 300 organizations of local communities and thousands of Indigenous people met in Xelaju Forum, Quetzaltenango, Guatemala and wrote a document in which participants reject this "forced globalization" … and denounced the fact that PPP's main goal is to create an infrastructure to facilitate the export of goods, the exploitation of our natural resources, biodiversity and labour of our people; but which does not answer in any way [our] social problems … [further] we were not consulted … as a result it violates the autonomy of our countries. (Bartra cited in Saldivar 80)

Since the arrival of "development" in the 1950s, millions of peasants and Indigenous families have been impoverished as calculated acts of development policy have dismantled, degraded, and corrupted their cultures (*The Ecologist*). This is clearly evident in Central America.

In Mexico, roads and highways have been built as part of the PPP project in order to increase industrial transportation and mobilize commodities produced in the area. PPP makes Oaxaca and Chiapas central areas of development by building the Trans-Isthmus Megaproject and superhighways along the Pacific and Gulf coasts of the country, through the lands of the Indigenous peoples, the Choles, Zoques, Tojolabales, Tzotziles, Mames and Tzeltales. The human development component of sustainable development is reduced to people's value as labour. Peasants and Indigenous peoples' "integration" into the global market system underlies the break-up of rural families and the forced mobility of women. Sustainable development claims to increase the equality of women by providing low-waged labour for labour-intensive *maquiladora* (sweatshop) production.[3]

In Guatemala, to produce hydro-electricity for *maquiladoras* and for U.S. consumption, PPP proposes to build 72 dams, 38 between Chiapas in Mexico and Peten in Guatemala over Rio Usumacinta. The building of the dams will displace more than 100 communities and cooperatives that belong to these Indigenous communities by flooding approximately 400 square kms in southern Mexico and 300 square kms in Peten (in northern Guatemala). Indigenous communities of Chole, Chontales and Lacandones have shared this river for millennia. They are campaigning against dams based on their experience. In 1985, Chixoy dam in Baja Veracruz displaced around 5,000 people, killing 900 Indigenous women and children in the surrounding area of Cano Negro, and flooding sacred Mayan land (*Usumacinta, lugar del mono sagrado-video*). The communities that will be affected by the proposed new dams are *Piedras Negras* (Mayan sacred temple, *El Cayo and Macabillero* (land of the Lacandon people), *La Pasadita* (Mayan ceremonial centre) and others (Figueroa).

In Costa Rica, eco-tourism has had a significant impact on vulnerable species and their habitats as increased deforestation to build cabins and resorts has resulted in an irreparable loss of diversity in species, and endangered wildlife habitat by provoking mudslides, biotic impoverishment, and species-forced migration. Ecotourism can also radically alter ownership claims. Around the Arenal Volcano in La Fortuna de San Carlos, entire communities have been forcibly evicted. While the majority of the land around the volcano is not arable or adequate for cattle ranching, small farms had existed in the area. In

1994, this land was expropriated by the government Ministry of Environment and Energy (MINAE) to expand the National Park. Peasants who had organized their lives by clearing land for agricultural production and pasture around the Arenal Basin were thrown off the land. Former property owners have become hut renters (*ranchos*) or slum inhabitants (*tugurios*). The personal effects of the *campesinas/os*, such as cars and small electrical appliances, were taken by the commercial banks when they could not afford to repay their loans acquired for economic development. When in desperation some of them returned to their land to plant yucca, beans, corn, and other subsistence foods, they were declared to have broken the law and some were thrown in jail. Their lands, pastures, homes and roads have been converted into expensive resorts with access limited to tourists who can afford recreational activities (Isla 2003c).

As the commons are "enclosed" and commoners access to nature is curtailed, it becomes a "national security" issue. Land enclosure legitimizes a military presence and assaults on any groups who want to reclaim their right to use nature for their livelihood or differently than capital circumscribes.

In Mexico, for example, an intensive militarization of the South of Mexico started with the Zapatista uprising. On January 1, 1994, the *Ejercito Zapatista de Liberacion Nacional* (EZLN),[4] declared war on the Mexican federal government by occupying seven municipalities/cities in Chiapas. On that day, *Zapatistas* demanded:

- a new pact between Indigenous Peoples and the national society in search for a new state project and a new constitution that includes ethnic diversity and recognition of Indigenous Peoples as part of the nation;
- land restitution, because lands were commons rather than state property; and
- expulsion of the municipal officers that have been deepening poverty by enforcing neo-liberal social and economic policies expressed in the Free Trade Agreement (FTA). (Munoz 3)

Indigenous people know that they have no other recourse to resist state and international development except direct action. The Zapatistas, therefore, argued that "This [war declaration of war] was a last resort against misery, exploitation and racism, basically, it was a last resort from oblivion" (Munoz 3).

To break their courage, Indigenous communities that resist are confronted with paramilitary organizations in alliance with the regular army, rich landowners, and *narcotrafico* (Salazar Perez). The Truth and Reconciliation Commissions in Guatemala and El Salvador has reported that since the arrival of development in the 1950s, more than 200,000 Guatemalans and 65,000 Salvadoreans have been murdered.

Further, the Central America PPP is connected to Plan Colombia in Colombia, and Plan Dignity in Chapare, Bolivia.[5] The three Plans justify their interventions using the same objectives: strengthening of democracy, poverty reduction, anti-drug efforts, elimination of drug trafficking, sustainable development, and support of the U.S. anti-terrorism struggle. In each of the plans, important members of society have been implicated in counter-insurgency practices, stirring up paramilitaries that attack civilians. The impact on the lives of rural women is significant. Women in the South of Mexico, for example, are unable to work and forced to remain in their homes in order to avoid being raped by soldiers (AWID 2002a). In the northern part of Mexico, women's transition from farm woman to an "independent *maquila*" worker continues to exact a high-price. In Ciudad Juarez, on the Mexican-U.S. border, over 800 women working in *maquiladoras* have been kidnapped, raped and murdered with seeming impunity (AWID 2002b; Amnistía Internacional-Uruguay).

Indigenous people, peasants, and all women in these communities want to continue with the time-tested ways of life that depend on them keeping their land. As a consequence, in association with environmentalists, they are fighting each of these projects embedded in PPP and are building international solidarities. They are forging an international campaign of *hermanamiento* (in Spanish this means accompaniment by sisterhood and brotherhood) of individuals, organizations and universities, by making permanent their physical presence in the areas threatened by sustainable development. They believe that an international presence will force the democratization of their societies, and will support their collective rights to land integrity, where impunity of women's rape and leadership assassination is expanding and the threat of social and environmental collapse by development as enclosure is daunting.

Ten years later in Johannesburg : The private side of sustainable development

The Earth Summit in Johannesburg resulted in the launch of 60 voluntary partnerships to support efforts to implement sustainable development, reflecting the success of neo-liberal corporate campaigns for a voluntary approach instead of government regulation. These voluntary, non-negotiated partnerships, were an outcome of this Summit. This voluntary approach actually means the privatization of the implementation of jobs that are under the category of sustainable development. The justification for this approach was that state/government actions during the last ten years have been so inadequate that by encouraging voluntary partnership initiatives "Type-II outcomes"[6] might bring new impetus to the implementation of the various commitments. The logic behind the multi-stakeholder model is that by bringing together the "Major Groups"[7] identified by the UN, consensus can be reached on certain outcomes, which are in turn easier to implement and more legitimate. Behind this approach were: The International Chamber of Commerce (ICC), the World Business Control for Sustainable Development (WBCSD), and Business Action for Sustainable Development (BASD).

BASD submitted for formal consideration as sustainable development various initiatives, among which were the Energy and Biodiversity Initiative, the Marine Stewardship Council, the Chemical Industry Responsible Care Program, and the Global Mining Initiative. One result of such initiatives was the official acceptance of "Mining and Minerals as Sustainable Development,"[8] at the Earth Summit in Johannesburg. The actual outcome of the politics of partnership promoted in Johannesburg can be seen in the case of Tambogrande, in Peru and its struggle against Manhattan Minerals Inc. of Canada.

Tambogrande and the politics of partnership

Mining is a fundamentally unsustainable activity because it is based on extraction of non-renewable concentrations created during millions of years. Once extracted, the destruction is permanent and the costs are always assumed by the locals. As mining and mineral extraction have been declared sustainable development, and as economic growth plans its entrance into local commons though the front door, Tambogrande has become a site of encounters where the new forms of domination, exploitation, and oppression meet resistance.

Tambogrande is an agricultural area located in San Lorenzo Valley in Piura, Peru. The San Lorenzo valley region produces 25,000 tons of mangoes, and many more in limes. Its products are sold nationally and internationally. In the past, the area was owned by cotton plantation landowners, but since the early 1970s, land reform turned peasants into landowners of small and medium size plots. As Peru is one of the most indebted countries, in order to pay its debt many corporations were given concessions by the Fujimori government from 1990 to 2001.[9] Fujimori, following IMF and WB policies, intended to make mining a top priority in the country as mining in Peru provides about 40 per cent of export revenues. Manhattan Minerals, a Vancouver-based corporation, is one of ten mining companies with concessions in and around Tambogrande. Under Tambogrande lies a deposit of a million ounces of gold and silver, and 64 million tonnes of rock rich in copper and zinc that the company wants to excavate. To extract these ores and minerals would affect 180 villages, demolish 80 per cent of the houses, displace more than 100,000 inhabitants, and eliminate the production of limes, mangoes and avocados that sustain their life. According to the partnership initiative, once the Manhattan mine opened for business, CENTROMIN—the national mining centre—would own 25 per cent of the operation, making it both a regulator and stakeholder (Boyd). Fujimori granted Manhattan ten concessions in the region totaling 89,000 ha. for an open pit. The Global Aware Cooperative, a Canadian NGO, made it known that the first mine, TG-1, will require the relocation of 8,000 people, while the second pit, TG-3, will require the deviation of the Piura River. Further, the tailings pond will occupy 200 hectares and various stages of mining will require the use of deadly poisons like cyanide and involve the disposal of heavy sulphide contaminated tailings.

The Peruvian government and the mining company, using the concept of sustainable development, claim that agriculture and mining can harmoniously coexist. But the affected communities understand that minerals are located deep beneath the earth's surface, and to get them forests, rivers, landscapes, wildlife, and people's homes, farms, livelihood, health and heritage are inevitably destroyed. Farmers who prefer working the land of their family homes to the lure of gold (Boyd) fear that a mining operation would compete with the water needed for agriculture, consume farm land, contaminate the fruit with cyanide and mercury, destroy the forested and mountainous ecosystem with the use of explosives and heavy machinery, and force them into mining jobs they know nothing about.

The community in Tambogrande has actively campaigned against open pit mining arguing that it could damage the homes of 8,000 inhabitants; destroy the fertile valley of San Lorenzo, the heart of Peru's mango and lime production, valued at US$110 million a year; contaminate the San Lorenzo Irrigation Project with cyanide, mer-cury and other heavy metals; and break their spirit, hopes, and customs. Over 70,000 people in the area earn their living from agriculture. In contrast, the mine would provide a maximum of 500 jobs. An open-pit mine would compete for scarce water reserves or contaminate the groundwater; alter flora and fauna, in particular the quality of *cortarrama*, one of the most important medicinal plants of the area; pose health risks; legitimize unde-mocratic takeovers of peasant lands; and exterminate the *algarrobo* forest as it will be exposed to toxic, acid rain and suffocation due to the dust produced by plant processors.

When disagreements, between the locals and the mining corporation began, Mayor Alfredo Rengifo collected 28,000 signatures from Tambogrande's 36,000 eligible voters on a petition calling for Manhattan's immediate departure. This petition was presented to Peru's Congress. Manhattan accused him of using improper methods and the government refused to act (Boyd). Despite the multiple ways that women, men, and children of Tambogrande have said "no" to the project, the company has embarked on a confrontational path.

In 1999, a local coalition of mango producers and concerned citizens opposing the mine—the Tambogrande Defence Front—was organized. The movement includes peasants, Indigenous communities, small landowners, the Catholic Church, local politicians, environmental activists, and artists. Soon after, in November 1999, a group of unidentified persons set fire to Manhattan's machines.

The climate of hostility erupted into full-scale battle on February 27 and 28, 2001, when a peaceful two-day strike turned violent: "About 150 protestors stormed Manhattan's walled, high-tech compound at the edge of town, burning and sacking offices, trucks and machinery and wounding 30 police officers" (Boyd 1).

The collective protest also torched the first section of "model homes" that the company planned to give to 1,600 families displaced by the first phase of its project (Munoz).

On March 31, 2001, one month after the expulsion of the mining company from Tambogrande, the main leader of the Defence Front, Godofredo Garcia, was killed in his organic lime grove farm by two hooded men. The killer was taken into custody and then released. "Up until now the murderer has not been caught, in spite of being completely identified" (Garcia). Since then, persecution has increased against the leadership of the Defence Front and their families. In 2002, the daughter of Francisco Ojeda, President of the Tambogrande Defence Front, was kidnapped by five individuals and paraded through the streets of Tambogrande's with a knife stuck in her back. Further, she was threatened with the death of her two-year-old nephew, Ojeda's grandson, if her father continued in the Front before she was released. This human rights violation was taken to London Amnesty International which sought a government guarantee for her life. The Peruvian government has ignored this request (Ojeda).

The confrontation attracted activist supporters from Piura and Lima. Later, anti-globalization and solidarity NGOs from Canada, U.S. and Europe went to advise the people of Tambogrande in their fight. For instance, Oxfam (America) spent an estimated US$20,000 in the community studying environmental consequences and legal costs for several people facing charges for destroying Manhattan's property.

Supported by Oxfam (UK), Mayor Alfredo Rengifo, again hoping to channel local tensions and frustrations, proposed a referendum on the mine. On June 2, 2002, despite the Peruvian government's objection, the Tambogrande municipality held the referendum on whether or not to allow mining in the area. It was the first referendum of its kind on the continent. About 36,936 people on a municipal voters' list cast ballots in the referendum. Of those who voted, 25,381, or 94 per cent said "No" to the mine proposal.[10] Nine in ten voters made it known that the mining company, Manhattan Minerals, was not welcome (Munoz).

Peru's Ministry of Energy and Mines has said that the referendum was held without appropriate information on mitigation measures and compensation or benefits. Further, the Peruvian president, Alejandro Toledo, made clear that a municipal referendum does not have legal weight in any decision of the central government. In response to government intransigence, the people of Tambogrande in an act of self-determination elected as mayor of the city Francisco Ojeda, President of the Tambogrande Defence Front.

In October 2003, Manhattan presented its first Environmental Impact Study (EIS). Manhattan's previous EIS was criticized by hydrologist and geochemist Dr. Robert Moran, in a report sponsored by Oxfam America.[11] In addition, another independent study produced 119 cases against Manhattan's EIS which Peru's Ministry of Energy later declared were satisfactorily resolved by the corporation (Huilca).

On November 5, 6 and 7, 2003, the Ministry of Environment convoked three public hearings in Tambogrande, Piura and Lima intending to publicize positive findings of Manhattan's EIS which concluded that mining would not adversely affect agriculture in the area. But, the public hearings were forced to be cancelled due to a national mobilization of communities affected by mining supporting the Tambogrande cause. On the first day of the hearings, members of the Second National Congress of Peruvian Communities affected by Mining (CONACAMI) stood in front of the Engineers College in Piura where the public hearing was scheduled to take place. The Ministry had planned to thwart the protest by staging support for the mine.

Three hundred unemployed young people were taken to an audience where they pretended to be agriculturalists that supported the mining; but the inhabitants who had been alerted to the situation went to the police to request the legal ousting of the impostors. As the police acted indifferent, the inhabitants put the fakers out of the town using stones. (Huilca 4)

Tambogrande responded with a statement position declaring once again its opposition to mining and demanding that Manhatan's EIS not be approved. This call was endorsed nationally and internationally (Ardito Vega). Despite the powerful partners involved, Manhattan and the Ministry of Energy of Peru, Tambogrande's resistance is bolstered by national and the international solidarity from Amnesty International; Rights and Democracy, Canada; Belen Mission, Switzerland; World Campaign for Forestry; Oilwatch; SEEN, USA; Equipo Nizkor, Spain; Friend of Heart, Netherlands; Serpaj Europe; Barcelona Parliament; Oxfam (America); Oxfam (U.K); and Mining Watch of Canada.

On December 11, 2003, it was publicly announced that Manhattan Minerals had lost its main concessions under Tambogrande on a technicality. The Peruvian government looked for a politically viable way out of a highly charged situation and used the fact that the corporation had not yet collected from their shareholders the US$100 million requested by the government ("Victory in Tambogrande").

Conclusion

Plan Puebla Panama in Central America and the community of Tambogrande in Peru reveal the neo-colonial relations of sustainable development in the politics of the global commons and the politics of partnership respectively. In both cases, there is a clear connection between global capital and nation/states. Sustainable development of the neo-liberal regime cannot be expanded without the direct intervention of the nation/state over local inhabitants and their commons.

What distinguishes these stories is that their local struggles reach across borders, involving activists around the world in a truly "globalized" campaign against the worst aspects of sustainable development and corporate globalization. In the ecological, gendered, ethnic, class struggle, local communities are building resistance. Their struggle is internationalized by democratic forces from Europe, Canada, and the U.S., made up of individuals, grassroots groups and NGOs. This new feature of resistance in this period is the result of the internationalization of productive and financial capital, which is showing clearly its tendency for dispossession of the very means of survival of people who follow the rhythm of nature. The awareness of this new context is developing an international class struggle, drawing massive solidarity and support to local struggles led by women, Indigenous people, and the local poor.

Rural women, Indigenous people and peasants have shown that the politics of sustainable development are not separated from their everyday life. As economic growth of capitalist priorities are emphasized, not only are women's livelihoods jeopardized, but the natural world is equally externalized and annihilated. Maria Mies and Veronika Bennholt-Thomsen (1996, 1999) proposed subsistence economies for women's equality and local sustainability, in order to stop the rapacious dependence of developed societies on the resources and labour of the underdeveloped other. This perspective championed by many eco-feminists is a necessary basis to defeat the neo-liberal development pursued by state and corporate "partnerships" in the name of sustainable development.

Originally published in CWS/cf's Fall/Winter 2003 issue, "Women and Sustainability: From Rio de Janeiro (1992) to Johannesburg (2002)" (Volume 23, Number 1): 6-16.

[1]By 1993, the DTM involved representatives from six regions of the world— South America, Caribbean, North America, Europe, Africa and Asia. Among the members of this international coordinating group were the 50 Years is Enough Campaign from the US; Eurodad, from England, Freedom From the Debt Coalition, from the Philippines, Women for a Just and Healthy Planet, from Toronto; and the Social Justice Committee of Montreal. In 1994, in Spain, more than 300,000 anti-debt members were mobilized, including the churches that later produced Jubilee 2000 Campaign calling for cancellation of the debt (Chomsky).

[2]Debt-for-nature investments are based on a negative assessment of the debt country's ability to pay the debt. Debt titles can thus be sold at a fraction of their value in the secondary market. Debt-for-nature investment was proposed by several environmental corporations as a way of capturing some benefits of debt-reduction efforts. For environmental organizations, the main objectives of this type of investment have been to identify and gain access to ecologically-sensitive areas for the purpose of protecting and negotiating them as sites for research and scientific data collection (Dawkins).

[3]At the Association for Women in Development (AWID) conference in Guadalajara in 2002, Central American women's advocates as well as peasant daughters working in *maquiladoras* denounced that fact that as the economy of Central America changes from agriculture to assembly plants for *maquiladoras*, women's low wages in *maquiladoras* and the tax exemptions in the export

manufacture zones are yet another advantage that the elites of Latin America can offer to foreign investors (Konojel). According to the presenters, in *maquiladoras* women work an average of 14 hours a day, and are often forced by managers to take amphetamines to work longer hours. They do not receive overtime. The conditions are deplorable and result in countless occupational illnesses that are not recognized in government legislation. Generations of women are becoming ill due to work-related repetitive movements or, worse, chemical hazards, and are returning home poorer than before.

[4]The EZLN was organized as a regular army in 1983 by Indigenous peoples of choles, zoques, tojolabales, tzotziles, mames and tzeltales (Munoz).

[5]Plan Colombia is publicly justified under the "War on Drugs." Established in July 2000, it is the largest foreign aid package ever sent to a Latin American government, making Colombia the third largest recipient of U.S. aid in the world (only Israel and Egypt surpass this amount) and the number one recipient of military aid (two million dollars per day). Plan Colombia will displace 10,000 rural people, mostly Afro-Colombians and Indigenous populations as a result of military presence. According to Colombians, however, it is a response to more than 50 years of struggle between large landowners and small peasants, between cattle ranching and subsistence agriculture. Plan Dignity, initiated in 1998 to eradicate coca production in Chapare, Bolivia, involves the building three new military bases in the region. To be built with six million dollars in U.S. assistance, the bases will permanently deploy 1,500 troops in the area, a move bitterly opposed by local residents and many human rights groups.

[6]"Type-II outcomes are UN-branded voluntary projects carried out in partnership between different 'stakeholders' such as governments, NGOs and business" (CEO 1).

[7]Major groups are identified as women, youth and children, Indigenous people, NGOs, local authorities, workers and trade unions, scientific and technological community, farmers, and business and industry (CEO).

[8]"Mining, Minerals and Sustainable Development (MMSD) initiative is a partnership project between the World Business Council for Sustainable Development (WBCSD), the Institute for International Environment and Development, and the Global Mining Initiative (GMI)" (CEO 3). This initiative was sponsored by 30 mining companies and large environmental NGOs, among them the International Union for Nature Conservation (the mother organization of the World Wildlife Fund), Nature Conservancy, the Smithsonian Institution, and Conservation International. All of them have recently joined British Petroleum, Shell and Chevron Texaco in the Energy and Biodiversity Initiative (http://www.theebi.org/).

[9]Former president Alberto Fujimori fled to Japan in 2001 and currently faces charges in Peru ranging from corruption to murder.

[10]Voting took place in six schools in the area. Canadian observers, such as the International Centre for Human Rights and Democratic Development, a Montreal-based group, and Groupe Investissement Responsable, were present.

A report on the referendum is available online: http://www.ichrdd.ca
[11]A copy of this report is available online: <http://www.oxfamamerica.org/
pdfs/tambo_eng.pdf >

References

Agarwal, Bina. "Environmental Management, Equity and Ecofeminism: Debating India's Experience." Ed. Kum-Kum Bhavnani. *Feminism and Race.* New York, Oxford University Press, 2001. 410-455.

Amnistía Internacional-Uruguay. *Revista N. 63* (octubre-noviembre 2003).

Ardito Vega, Wilfredo. "Un Liston Verde por Tambogrande." *La Republica* October 17, 2003.

Association for Women in Development (AWID) Workshop: *In Solidarity with the Independent Movement of Women in Chiapas: Resistance to Neoliberal Globalization.* AWID's Nineth International Forum: Reinventing Globalization, Guadalajara, Mexico, October 3-6, 2002a.

Association for Women in Development (AWID) Workshop: *Globalizing Actions Against Impunity of Feminicides in Ciudad.* AWID's Nineth International Forum: Reinventing Globalization, Guadalajara, Mexico, October 3-6, 2002b.

Boyd, Stephanie. "Miner Sins, loved eco-activist dies while battling Canuck outfit." *Now Magazine* 20 (33) (April 18-24, 2001).

Chomsky, Noam (1998) "Jubilee 2000." 1998. Retrieved Online: http://www.lbbs.org/jubilee2000.htm

Corporate Europe Observer (CEO). "Rio + 10 and the Privatization of Sustainable Development." 11 (2002).

Dawkins, Kristin. "Debt-for-Nature Swaps." *Debt Swaps, Development and Environment.* Ed. Maria Clara Cuoto Soarez. Rio de Janeiro: Instituto Brasileiro de Analises Sociales e Economicas, 1992. 31-46.

The Debt Treaty. 1992.

The Ecologist. Whose Common Future: Reclaiming the Commons. New Societies Publishers, Philadelphia, PA, Gabriola Island, BC in cooperation with Earthscan Publications Limited, 1993.

Escobar, Arturo. "Culture Sits in Places: Reflexions on Globalism and Subaltern Strategies of Localization." *Political Geography* 20 (2001): 139-174.

Figueroa, Eucebio. (2003) "Plan Puebla Panama". Guatemalan-Maya speaker at Brock University, St. Catharines, Ontario, October 8, 2003.

Garcia, Ulises (son of Godofredo Garcia). Personal communication, 2002.

The Global Aware Cooperative. *Manhattan Minerals Corporation vs the People of Tambogrande, Peru.* Retrieved Online: http://www.globalaware.org

Goldman, Michael. "Inventing the Commons: Theories and Practices of the Commons' Professional." *Privatizing Nature: Political Struggles for the Global Commons.* Ed. Michael Goldman. New Brunswick, NJ: Rutgers University Press, 1998.

Hamilton, Kirk. "Genuine Savings, Population Growth and Sustaining Economic Welfare." Paper presented at the Natural Capital, Poverty and Development Conference, Toronto, 5-8 September, 2001.

Hecht, Susana and Alexander Cockburn. *The Fate of the Forest: Developers, Destroyers and Defenders of the Amazon.* London: Penguin Books, 1990.

Huilca, Flor. "Tambogrande en la Hora Cero." *La Republica* October 19, 2003.

Isla, Ana. "A Struggle for Clean Water and Livelihood: Canadian Mining in Costa Rica in the Era of Globalization." *Canadian Woman Studies/les cahiers de la femme* 21/22 (4,1) (2002a): 148-154.

Isla, Ana. "Enclosure and Micro-enterprise as Sustainable Development: The Case of the Canada/Costa Rica Debt-for-Nature Investment." *Canadian Journal of Development Studies* 22 (2002b): 935-955.

Isla, Ana. "Land Management and Ecotourism: A Flawed Approach to Conservation in Costa Rica." *Natural Capital, Poverty and Development.* Eds: Adam Fenech, Roger Hansell and Kirk Hamilton. Amsterdam: Kluwer Publishing, 2003c.

"The Johannesburg Summit Test: What will Change?" U.N. Feature Story, Johannesburg, Summit 26 August-4 September, 2002. New York, 25 September. Online: http://www.johannesburgsummit.org/

Konojel, Kichin. "Condicion de la Mujer en la Maquila." Association for Women in Development (AWID) Workshop: *Protecting the Labour Rights of Women Workers: The Maquila Situation in the Globalized Economy.* AWID's Nineth International Forum: Reinventing Globalization, Guadalajara, Mexico, October 3-6, 2002.

Martinez Alier, Juan. "Ecological Economics and Ecosocialism." *Is Capitalism Sustainable? Political Economy and the Politics of Ecology.* Ed. Martin O'Connor. New York: The Guilford Press, 1994. 23-36.

Merchant, Carolyn. *The Death of Nature: Women, Ecology and the Scientific Revolution.* New York: Harper and Row, 1990.

Mies, Maria. *Patriarchy and Accumulation on a World Scale: Women in the International Division of Labour.* London: Zed Books Ltd., 1986.

Mies Maria and Veronika Bennholdt-Thomsen. *The Subsistence Perspective: Beyond the Globalized Economy.* London: Zed Books, 1999.

Mies, Maria and Vandana Shiva. *Ecofeminism.* London and New Jersey: Zed Books, 1993.

Ojeda, Francisco "Tambogrande's Struggle." Ontario Institute for Studies in Education of the University of Toronto, May 6, 2002.

Ornelas, Jaime. "El Plan Puebla Panama y la Globalizacion Neoliberal." *Lectura Critica del Plan Puebla Panama.* Eds. Robinson Salazar Perez and Eduardo Sandoval Forero. Buenos Aires: Libros en Red, Insumisos Latinoamericanos, 2003. 19-54.

Pearce. W. David and Jeremy J. Warford *World Without End: Economics, Environment and Sustainable Development.* New York: Oxford University Press, 1993.

Salazar Perez, Robinson. "El Vinculo Militar del Plan Colombia y el Plan Puebla Panama." *Lectura Critica del Plan Puebla Panama.* Eds. Robinson

Salazar Perez and Eduardo Sandoval Forero. Buenos Aires: Libros en Red, Insumisos Latinoamericanos, 2003. 135-165.

Saldivar, Americo. "El Plan Puebla Panama: Una Locomotora sin Vagones de Segunda." *Lectura Critica del Plan Puebla Panama*. Eds. Robinson Salazar Perez and Eduardo Sandoval Forero. Buenos Aires: Libros en Red, Insumisos Latinoamericanos, 2003. 75-110.

Salleh, Ariel. "Nature, Woman, Labour, Capital: Living the Deepest Contradiction." *Is Capitalism Sustainable? Political Economy and the Politics of Ecology*. Ed. Martin O'Connor. New York: The Guilford Press, 1994. 106-124.

Salleh, Ariel. *Eco-feminism as Politics*. New York: St. Martins Press, 1997.

Shiva, Vandana. *Staying Alive: Women, Ecology and Development*. London: Zed Books, 1989.

Smith, Robert and Claude Simard. "A Proposed Approach to Environment and Sustainable Development Indicators Based on Capital." Paper presented at the Natural Capital, Poverty and Development Conference, Toronto, 5-8 September, 2001.

United Nations (UN). *Rio Declaration on Environment and Development and Agenda 21: Program of Action for Sustainable Development*. 1992. New York: United, 1994.

UNESCO. "Effects of Structural Adjustment Programs on Education and Training." General Conference of UNESCO, Twenty-eighth Session, Paris, 25 August 1995. 28 C/14.

Usumacinta, lugar del mono sagrado. Video produced by Frente Petenero Contra las Represas.

"Victory in Tambogrande." *Mining Watch Canada Newsletter* 14 Autumn 2003.

World Bank (WB). "Briefing." *Shareholders and Donors of Mesoamerican Biological Corridor Conference from 12-13 December, 2002, at Conference Center of the World Bank in Paris*. 2003.

World Commission on Environment and Development (WCED). *Our Common Future*. New York: Oxford University Press, 1987.

Policy

Hidden in the Past

How Labour Relations Policy and Law
Perpetuate Women's Inequality

Anne Forrest ⟶

"A woman's place is in her union" is the colloquial expression of the research finding that unions are good for women. Many studies have documented this advantage: by comparison with equivalently qualified women in the non-union sector, organized women earn significantly higher wages, have better fringe benefits, and greater job security. However, this does not mean that union women are equal to union men; they are not. Collective bargaining has narrowed but not eliminated the gender gap in pay, which remains substantial. On average, union women earned $2.77 (13.4 per cent) less per hour than equivalently qualified union men in 1997 (Drolet 2001) plus an unquantified difference in fringe benefits (Currie and Chaykowski).[1]

The persistence of this gap is generally attributed to women's unequal status in the labour movement. There is no doubt that unions co-operated with employers in the past to ensure male privilege and that the legacy of those discriminatory practices continues to affect the economic prospects of union women today. But this limited analysis heaps too much weight on union shoulders. Of greater significance to women is the industrial relations system within which unions function.

Canadian industrial relations policy and law, which date from 1944 but remain little changed today, were shaped in response to a war-time crisis in traditional men's work; hence, the very structure as well as the application of the law embody this purpose. The particular features of this system—highly regulated right to organize, fragmented union representation, decentralized collective bargaining, and restricted right to strike—reflect the compromise between organized labour and capital that simultaneously acknowledged and constrained the right of (male) workers to bargain collectively through unions of their choice. For men—at least for those employed in manual occupations in large primary and secondary sector firms—the result was an acceptable, if diminished, version of "free" collective bargaining. Not so for women, who were and continue to be systematically disadvantaged by a labour relations system that assumes a "male" and "industrial" model of both work and unionism (Forrest 1997).

A gender analysis of labour relations policy and law has been overlooked by most critics of labour-management relations.[2] Because the system is ungenerous to all workers its one-sidedness is usually framed as a class rather than a gender problem. There is ample evidence that the right to organize was wrenched from an unwilling government and subsequently protected only to the extent necessary to minimize work stoppages. The result is policy and law that fix the balance of power in favour of employers whose managerial prerogative is carefully protected in unionized workplaces. Yet, within this intentionally restrictive framework men have fared better than women. The strongholds of traditional men's work—capital-intensive manufacturing, natural resource extraction, construction, and transportation—are better organized than women-dominated manufacturing and service industries. Union men also have privileged access to the better paying, more secure jobs in organized workplaces and earn more than equivalently qualified union women. All are logical outcomes of Canada's industrial relations system.

Organizing women-dominated industries

Industrial relations law and policy have failed women, most particularly those employed in traditional women's work in the private sector. In the women-dominated industries of banking, insurance, retail, and services union density falls below 15 per cent (Akyeampong), not because these employees do not wish to be represented by unions or because unions have ignored these industries, but because the law allows employers to avoid collective bargaining. Problems with the law were evident as early as the 1950s, following the high-profile failures to organize Eaton's and the chartered banks, and remain uncorrected today. Over the last 20 years, worker-initiated organizing drives in retail (e.g., Sears, Walmart, Eaton's), the banks (e.g., CIBC, TD, Canada Trustco), and fast-food restaurant chains (e.g., MacDonald's, Wendy's) have failed to establish on-going collective bargaining relationships.

The Canadian system of collective bargaining requires unions to be legally recognized as exclusive bargaining agents; yet, the certification procedure imposes a myriad of rules that afford employers legitimate ways to delay and avoid collective bargaining. Among other things, labour boards are called upon to determine whether a union's proposed bargaining unit is appropriate for collective bargaining and which jobs should be excluded from the union because the employees exercise managerial functions, have access to confidential information, or perform jobs that put them at arm's length from their co-workers. Inevitably, these questions are more complex in industries where there is a limited history of collective bargaining and few established protocols.

Labour board definitions of appropriate bargaining units developed for manufacturing and resource industries do not always fit the service sector. The less certain dividing line between managerial and non-managerial employees and the many forms of "non-standard work" (e.g., part-time, casual, and limited term contract) characteristic of service industries are but two issues that often require labour relations boards to hear detailed evidence about who does what in the workplace and with what degree of authority. As a result, workers often wait months for the outcome of certification. Even if the issues are resolved in the union's favour, these delays sap workers' support for the union, especially in small bargaining units[3] where managers and employees work side-by-side and labour turn-over is often rapid. In the worst cases, the long delays between application and certification allow employers time to undermine workers' confidence in the union's ability to protect their interests, as a number of studies have shown.[4]

In all jurisdictions,[5] the law requires an employer to bargain in good faith and make every reasonable effort to conclude a collective agreement with a certified union. However, the reality often falls short of the theory. An employer who wishes to evade its legal obligations may do so by simply refusing to come to terms with the union. A "no-concessions" bargaining strategy is often lawful and effective, as the Eaton's case demonstrates. After months of negotiations, the company offered its newly organized workers nothing more than they already had: no increase in wages, no improvement in benefits, no job security, and contract language "so outmoded as to be more relevant in the 1940s" (Forrest 1989: 195). "Hard bargaining" of this sort was lawful, the Ontario Labour Relations Board ruled, because Eaton's was prepared to sign a collective agreement, if only on its own terms (Forrest 1989).

Labour boards draw the line at employer demands that lack "any semblance of business justification" (Forrest 1989: 198). But Eaton's and other large-scale employers of women's labour have legitimate, even pressing, business reasons for maintaining labour costs at the industry norm that in service industries is often little above the minimum required by law. Thus, despite the company's admission that it was unwilling to improve wages and benefits because to do so would only encourage further union organizing, the Ontario board detected no "anti-union animus." So long as an employer participates in the bargaining process—its negotiating committee meets the union regularly, provides the necessary information, and exchanges proposals—and does not undercut the bargaining authority of the union by unilaterally changing the terms and conditions of employment, bargaining directly with employees, or engaging in other forms of anti-union conduct, labour boards are unlikely to find a violation of the duty to bargain in good faith. George Adams describes the purpose of the law as bringing the parties to the table; there is an expectation but no requirement that they come to agreement (10/91-4). Labour boards do not ask whether an employer's offer is fair and are careful to guard against union efforts to use the duty to redress an imbalance in bargaining power.

Frustrated by their employer's intransigence, the Eaton's workers struck. But there, again, the law failed them. On the picket line, they confronted the full economic power of an employer with "deep pockets." In general, the law permits employers to draw on the full extent of their managerial prerogative and financial resources to resist union bargaining demands. Eaton's responded by assigning managers to perform bargaining unit jobs, hiring replacement workers, and removing pickets from mall entrances. It could also have shifted work to other locations, eliminated jobs, or even closed a store down. Workers, by contrast, can only stop working, a sanction that has little import in the service sector where struck firms offer the same services in many locations. It is almost impossible for a small group of workers—in the Eaton's case, less than four per cent of its employees at only six of its 110 stores (Forrest 1989: 202)—to inflict a meaningful economic penalty against a national/multi-national employer within the law. Union actions to bridge the gap in bargaining power such as sympathy strikes by other unions, working to rule in supplier or client firms, picketing that blocks access to the struck location, and other workers' refusals to cross a picket line are almost always unlawful and so expose unions to fines and individual workers to industrial discipline.[6] In the service sector, striking workers are often forced to rely on public support, which is uneven and unreliable at best. Thus, despite the Eaton's strikers *cause célèbre* status in Toronto, positive press coverage, and a six-month work stoppage, collective bargaining did not take root. Not long after the strikers returned to work, their unions were decertified or lost their bargaining rights as a result of inactivity (Forrest 1989: 210).

Policy changes designed to remedy this obvious structural imbalance of power in private-sector services have been short-lived or rendered ineffective by timid application. Pro-worker legislation such as the ban on hiring replacement workers during strikes, implemented by the New Democratic Party (NDP) in Ontario, was immediately overturned by the subsequent Conservative government in response to employers' threats to relocate to more accommodating jurisdictions. Longer-lived but no more effective is the availability of final and binding arbitration to end first agreement disputes. In place for 20 years in some jurisdictions, the imposition of first agreements is a remedy that is sparingly (except in Quebec) and conservatively applied. Newly certified unions should not expect radical improvements from the arbitration process. In first agreement situations, arbitrators impose terms and conditions of employment similar to those in comparable workplaces (Labour Law Casebook Group 413-20), which could mean not much at all in predominantly non-union industries. In any event, the imposition of a first collective agreement through arbitration does not ensure a second, which unions, however small and isolated, must bargain on their own. No surprise, then, that first agreement arbitration has not led to organizing breakthroughs in the service sector.

Institutionalized job segregation by gender

Labour relations policy and law establish gender as a legitimate basis for union representation and collective bargaining. The result is that job segregation by gender is as sharp in the union as in the non-union sector[7] and has the same negative consequences for union women. Study after study has demonstrated that women earn less than men primarily because they are women and tend to be employed in undervalued "women's work." Using data for the economy as a whole, Marie Drolet (2002) concluded that 46.8 per cent of the gender gap in hourly wages is explained by women's over-representation in low wage industries and occupations, 38.8 per cent by gender discrimination,[8] and only 10.6 per cent by differences in personal characteristics. There are no studies of the gender gap in wages for the union sector on its own; however, there is no reason to believe the results would be significantly different.

Job segregation by gender and low pay for traditional women's work are facts of life in unionized workplaces, in part, because workers are divided by occupation during the certification process. Depending on the jurisdiction, one or all of blue-collar/manual, office/clerical, professional, sales, security, part-time, casual, contractually limited, self-employed, and home workers are routinely separated from each other. These distinctions are based more on employers' than employees' needs, Judy Fudge argues. However, even when labour boards take workers' interests into account they often rely on out-dated and sexist assumptions about their community of interest. In many jurisdictions, the social construction of women and "women's work" as essentially different from men and traditional men's work is affirmed by the labour board construct of appropriate bargaining unit.

The Ontario board has been particularly rigid in its approach, assuming, for example, that pink-collar and part-time workers have economic interests different from—even in conflict with—full-time, blue-collar/manual workers in the same establishment. Although it is now rethinking its approach to part-time (but not office and clerical) workers (Adams 7/43-6), the legacy of this policy legitimates the different/inferior terms and conditions of employment attached to this form of traditional women's work. In the union sector, part-time workers are almost always paid less for doing the same jobs as full-time employees in the same establishment in the union sector. Their "Other"/lesser status is also affirmed by their more limited rights for promotion or in the event of cutbacks. Where full- and part-time workers are both organized, the latter are commonly prevented from moving into the full-time jobs for which they are qualified, even when their accumulated seniority is greater than their full-time competitors.

Where labour relations policy and law institutionalize the gender division of labour they reify small differences among workers that benefit employers more than workers and men more than women. Why differences between "non-standard" and "regular" employees are more fundamental than other potential conflicts of interests, for example, between skilled and unskilled or junior and senior workers, has never been explained. In practice, community of interest is a political, not a "natural" construct. Knitting together the diverse sectional interests related to occupation, department, seniority, skill level, race/ethnicity, and gender is an essential aspect of union education that begins but does not end with an organizing drive. Unions that fail to take on this project leave their members vulnerable to employer whipsawing.[9]

Labour relations policy and law can perpetuate job segregation by gender and inferior terms and conditions of employment for traditional women's work within bargaining units, as well as between them. It is standard bargaining practice, and not unlawful, for employers and unions to negotiate seniority clauses that restrict workers' mobility within a bargaining unit, even when the result is to lock women out of higher paid, male-dominated job categories. Moreover, in the absence of pay equity legislation, it is neither uncommon nor unlawful for employers and unions to evaluate female-dominated jobs by different criteria than male-dominated jobs and so "reproduce, rationalize, and legitimate" lower pay for jobs historically performed by women (Steinberg 388-90).

Consider the case of Beatrice Harmatiuk, who was employed as a house-keeper at Pasqua Hospital where she earned less than her co-workers employed as caretakers. Although similar in skill, responsibility, and working conditions, the all-male caretaker job scored ahead of the all-female housekeeper job in the negotiated job evaluation scheme because of its marginally greater physical demands. By contrast, the extra mental effort required of housekeepers who interacted with patients went unrecognized. Ms Harmatiuk lost two appeals to her employer and union before she won her point at the Saskatchewan Human Rights Tribunal.

Ms Harmatiuk was forced to take her complaint to the Tribunal because, by the standards labour relations policy and law, she had incurred no wrong. There was no violation of the collective agreement—she was paid the established rate for her job—and had she filed a grievance alleging gender discrimination it could not have succeeded without her union's support. There was no violation of the union's duty of fair representation—her union took her concerns seriously and investigated the matter fully (Christian)—and no violation of the employer's duty to bargain in good faith. In theory, Ms Harmatiuk's and other housekeepers could have used Saskatchewan's labour relations legislation to hold their employer and union to account if they subsequently failed to correct the discriminatory elements of the job evaluation scheme; however, this would be a novel use of a law that was never intended to promote gender equality.

Decentralized wage bargaining

Inferior terms and conditions of employment for traditional women's work are all but ensured by the long-standing policy preference for decentralized wage determination. Originally intended to control wage growth in unionized "men's work," this policy preference now weighs more heavily on union women. The gender gap in wages is largest in countries where wage bargaining is fragmented and decentralized (Kidd and Shannon; Reiman), that is, where workers in female-dominated bargaining units generally bargain on their own or with other female-dominated groups. In Canada, women are more often located in the smallest and lowest paid bargaining units (Currie and Chaykowski) and establishments (Drolet 2002) where they are poorly positioned to close the gender gap in wages, even when their unions are solidly behind the demand.

For workers in women-dominated bargaining units and establishments closing the gender gap in pay necessitates bargaining in alliance with workers in male-dominated bargaining units and establishments; yet, labour relations law and policy make this all but impossible. Unlike other OECD countries, the majority of collective bargaining in Canada involves only one bargaining unit in one establishment. This high degree of fragmentation is the consequence of what H. D. Woods and Sylvia Ostry called a "bias" (270) in labour law that originates in the certification process. Single-establishment certification is the norm in Ontario and within establishments separate bargaining units are generally created for blue-collar, white-/pink-collar, sales, craft/professional employees, and others. Bargaining units are not so narrowly described in every jurisdiction, however. Both the Canada and British Columbia boards prefer employer-wide bargaining units where collective bargaining is well established (Adams 7/19-23). But whatever the practice, bargaining rights follow certification rights. In all jurisdictions, the law requires each union/bargaining unit, no matter how small, to negotiate its own collective agreement.

Though not unlawful in itself, it is a violation of the duty to bargain in good faith for a union to make its desire for broader-based bargaining a strike issue. Accordingly, it is impossible for company-, industry-, or even establishment-wide bargaining to emerge unless it would be in the interests of the employer. But fewer and fewer firms are willing to negotiate on this basis. Economic restructuring and globalization have heightened competitive pressures among workers within and between firms. The consequence is that well-established, broader-based bargaining has broken down in many industries as more and more unions are pressured to settle for wages and working conditions that reflect the profitability of each establishment (Chaykowski 2001: 241).

Many labour relations experts such as Paul Weiler defend the existing fragmented, gender-segregated system of union representation and collective bargaining as essential to workers' right to self-organize. In Weiler's view, efforts to promote women's economic equality that disrupt established collective bargaining practices should be avoided. Addressing the federal Pay Equity Task Force, Weiler argued that any "equal pay or pay equity statute which allows comparisons of the value of work regardless of bargaining unit boundaries would wholly undermine the notion of free collective bargaining" (10).

Elevating the structures that perpetutate male privilege to immutable principles of labour law is incompatible with women's right to equal pay for work of equal value, as the case of *Canadian Union of Public Employees* v. *Canadian Airlines/Air Canada* (1998) demonstrates. In this situation, flight attendants in a female-dominated bargaining unit were denied access to their logical, and only, male comparators in the male-dominated ground crew and pilot unions on the grounds that each bargaining unit constituted its own, unique system of labour relations. This was the employer's position in bargaining, later affirmed by the Canadian Human Rights Commission. Taking note of the differences in negotiated terms and conditions of employment in the three collective agreements, the Commission ruled that each of the three bargaining units was a functionally separate establishment, notwithstanding the fact that all work out of the same locations.

This result is a classic catch-22. First, labour relations law imposes gender-segregated patterns of union representation and decentralized wage bargaining, then, when different/inferior terms and conditions of employment are negotiated for female-dominated bargaining units, the result is interpreted as differences in workers' bargaining preferences and priorities, not as evidence of systemic gender discrimination.

This interpretation was rejected by the federal government's Pay Equity Task Force. Members of the Task Force identified the fragmented and gender-segregated structure of union representation and collective bargaining as obstacles to gender equality (Canada 448, 462), even as they acknowledged the important role unions have played in advancing the rights of women. Their recommendations include a new structure—the "pay equity unit"—that would span all of the operations of a single employer and so ensure equal pay for work of equal value for workers across all bargaining units (Canada 206). If implemented, this form of broader-based bargaining would blunt the "male/industrial" bias in labour relation law while protecting workers' right to organize into gender-segregated, occupation-based unions.

Conclusion

Union women have put the issue of gender equality on the bargaining agenda of a reluctant labour movement. Pushing and prodding their way forward, feminist activists have insisted that unions address systemic barriers to women's economic equality such as sexual harassment, family responsibilities, and low pay for traditional women's work. The results are impressive. Limited at first to collective agreements negotiated by the most progressive unions, the fruits of these initiatives are now widespread. Sexual harassment polices and procedures, paid maternity/parental leave with no loss of seniority, family leave with pay, and pay equity legislation now benefit all or, in the case of pay equity legislation, hundreds of thousands of women (and men) in the non-union as well as in the union sector.

These gains have been made against the grain of an industrial relations system that is "male" and "industrial" in structure and purpose. But much of this is hidden in the past. Present-day collective bargaining policy and law, though rooted in the sexist norms and mores of the 1940s, appear to be nothing more than the workings of a system that sets the balance of power in favour of employers. It takes a feminist analysis to reveal the subtle ways that these norms and practices discriminate against women workers in particular. More importantly, it takes feminist activists to press for change.

The author wishes to acknowledge the helpful criticisms of Rena Isenberg.

Originally published in CWS/cf's Spring/Summer 2004 issue, "Benefiting Women?
Women's Labour Rights" (Volume 23, Numbers 3/4): 64-71.

[1]In 1997, non-union women earned an average of $4.19 (23.5 per cent) less per
hour than equivalently qualified non-union men (Drolet 2001: 28).
[2]But see Fudge and Forrest (1997).
[3]The average size of newly certified unions in private-sector services in Ontario
between 1981 and 1999 was 28 employees (Yates).
[4]See Thomason and the references cited therein. Using certification data for
Ontario during the 1980s, Thomason concluded: "An employer who insists on
a hearing, commits an unfair labour practice, and extends the period between
the application and final disposition of the certification by 100 days ... can
reduce the proportion of employees supporting the union by almost 15 per cent
and the probability of certification by nearly 20 per cent" (223).
[5]Labour relations falls within provincial jurisdiction. The consequence is a
multiplicity of statutes that differ one from the other in small rather than large
ways.
[6]The consequences for participating in an unlawful strike vary by circumstance
but can include dismissal.
[7]Using collective agreement data from Ontario for the years 1980-1990, Currie
and Chaykwoski estimated that almost two-thirds of women workers in the
union sector would have to change jobs in order to eliminate gender segregation. This is higher than the Duncan indexes estimated for the economy as a
whole (Fortin and Huberman).
[8]Most researchers accept that the portion of the gender gap in wages not
accounted for by differences in worker or workplace differences should be
labelled gender discrimination.
[9]Whipsawing occurs when an employer seeks to impose the inferior terms and
conditions of employment negotiated with one group of workers on better-
paid workers. The tactic is most successful when the better-paid group is fearful
that it may lose jobs to the lower paid group. The tactic can be used in reverse
by unions in a tight labour market.

References

Adams, George W. Canadian Labour Law. 2nd ed. Aurora: Canada Law Book,
    2003.
Akyeampong, Ernest B. "Fact-Sheet on Unionization." *Perspectives on Labour
    and Income* 13 (3) (2001): 46-54.
Canada. *Pay Equity: A New Approach to a Fundamental Right. Pay Equity Task
    Force Final Report 2004*. Ottawa: Pay Equity Task Force, 2004.
Canadian Union of Public Employees v. *Canadian Airlines International/Air
    Canada* (1998). 34 C.H.R.R. D/442 (C.H.R.T.)
Chaykowski, Richard P. "Collective Bargaining: Structure, Process, and
    Innovation." *Union-Management Relations in Canada*. 4th ed. Morley

Gunderson, Allen Ponak, and Daphne Gottlieb Tara, eds. Toronto: Addision Wesley Longman, 2001. 234-71

Christian, Timothy J. "The Developing Duty of Fair Representation." *Labour Arbitration Year Book* 2 (1991): 3-30.

Currie, Janet and Richard Chaykowski, 1995, "Male Jobs, Female Jobs, and Gender Gaps in Benefits Coverage in Canada." *Research in Labor Economics* Solomon W. Polachek, ed. Greenwich, CT: JAI Press, 1995. 171-210

Drolet, Marie. The *"Who, What, When and Where" of Gender Pay Differentials.* The Evolving Workplace Series. Ottawa: Statistics Canada, Human Resources Development Canada, 2002.

Drolet, Marie. The Persistent Gap: *New Evidence on the Canadian Gender Wage Gap.* No. 157. Ottawa: Statistics Canada, Business and Labour Market Analysis Division, 2001.

Forrest, Anne. "Securing the Male Breadwinner: A Feminist Interpretation of P.C. 1003." *Relations Industrielles* 52 (1) (1997): 91-113

Forrest, Anne. "Organizing Eaton's: Do the Old Laws Still Work?" *Windsor Yearbook of Access to Justice* 8 (1989): 190-213

Fortin, Nicole M. and Michael Huberman. "Occupational Gender Segregation and Women's Wages in Canada: An Historical Perspective." *Canadian Public Policy*, 28 Supplement, S11-39 (2002): S23.

Fudge, Judy. "Rungs on the Labour Law Ladder: Using Gender to Challenge Hierarchy." *Saskatchewan Law Review* 60 (1996): 237-263.

Harmatiuk v. Pasqua Hospital, 4 CHRR 239, D/1177-81.

Kidd, Michael P. and Michael Shannon. "The Gender Wage Gap: A Comparison of Australia and Canada." *Industrial and Labour Relations Review* 49(July) (1996): 729-46.

Labour Law Casebook Group. *Labour and Employment Law: Cases, Materials and Commentary.* Sixth ed. Kingston: IRC Press, 1998.

Reiman, Cornelis A. *"Has Enterprise Bargaining Affected the Gender Wage Gap in Australia?"* Canberra: The National Centre for Social and Economic Modelling, University of Canberra, 1998.

Steinberg, Ronnie. "Gendered Instructions: Cultural Lag and Gender Bias in the Hay System of Job Evaluation." *Work and Occupations* 19 (4) (1992): 387-423.

Thomason, Terry. "The Effect of Accelerated Certification Procedures on Union Organizing Success in Ontario." *Industrial and Labor Relations Review* 47 2 1994: 207-226.

Weiler, Paul. 2002, "Presentation by Professor Paul Weiler, Harvard Law School to the Federal Task Force on Pay Equity." 2002. Online: payequityreview.gc.ca/4400-e.html.

Woods, H. D. and Sylvia Ostry. *Labour Policy and Labour Economics in Canada.* Toronto: Macmillan of Canada, 1962.

Yates, Charlotte. "Staying the Decline in Union Membership." *Relations Industrielles* 55 (4) (2000): 640-74.

Sponsoring Immigrant Women's Inequalities

Sunera Thobani ➤

Immigration has been central to the historical production (and reproduction) of the Canadian nation since its inception. The nation was founded through the colonization of Aboriginal peoples, the subjugation of their sovereignty, and the erosion of their traditional and customary rights (Culhane; Green; Maracle). Aboriginal women were subjected to white, male domination, as well as to a strengthening of patriarchal relations within Aboriginal communities by the Indian Act (Fiske; Goodleaf).

Along with this colonization, the immigration of European settlers, particularly that of European women, was critical for nation building and capitalist development (Stasiulis and Jhappan). Designated "preferred races" by the Canadian state, European settlers and their descendants have been integrated into the Canadian nation, their citizenship the measure of this integration (Thobani).

In this racialized project of nation building, immigration policy sought to strictly control, and often halt, the entry of third world immigrants. Designating them "non-preferred races," the state organized the provision of their labour to the economy, but discouraged their permanent settlement (Bolaria and Li). Women from third world countries were expressly targeted for exclusion. They were defined as posing a two-fold threat to the nation: the presence of these racially "inferior" women was seen as "polluting" the nation, and their ability to reproduce future generations of "non-preferred races" was perceived as a threat to the whiteness of the nation (Thobani). This overt racialization of immigrants was maintained into the 1960s and 1970s.

Racializing and gendering immigration

The Immigration Act 1976–77 emphasized labour market needs and family relations. It removed overt references to "race" and included a specific "non-discrimination" clause on the grounds of "race, national or ethnic origin, colour, religion or sex" [Section 3(f)]. The Act organizes immigration into two main categories: (i) the family class (which makes immediate family members eligible for sponsorship and requires sponsors to assume financial responsibility for their dependents for upto ten years), and; (ii) the independent class (whose eligibility is based upon the allocation of points for education, skills and qualifications).[1]

The *Act* has allowed a major shift in immigration patterns, significantly increasing the presence of third world peoples, in particular women, and helping to make their labour available to the economy. Immigration under the family class has been greater than under the independent class, and while women represent over half of all immigrants, they are more likely to enter under the family class (Boyd 1988).

A number of scholars have defined the point system as a neutral, non-discriminatory one (Green and Green; Hawkins). Feminist and anti-racist scholars, however, dispute this claim. They argue that while the *Act* made a commitment in principle to ending racist and sexist discrimination, it did not do so in effect. Discrimination remains ongoing on two counts. Firstly, the unequal allocation of resources for immigration processing favours "developed" countries with large white populations. Secondly, the discriminatory powers granted to immigration officers allows their subjective prejudices to influence the allocation of points in immigration selection (Abu-Laban; Das Gupta; Jakubowski; Ng and Sprout). Immigration officers tend to process the applications of women under the family class. Men, on the other hand, are more likely to be processed under the independent class as heads of household (Boyd 1998, 1992; Das Gupta; Ng and Sprout).

With sponsorship regulations making sponsored relatives financially dependent upon their sponsors, this processing of women under the family class increases their vulnerability to increased control by sponsors (Abu-Laban; Boyd, 1998, 1992; Das Gupta). While this analysis has played an important role in our understanding of the workings of immigration policy, the *Act* in fact does much more: it organizes the ongoing racialization of the nation and immigrants, as well as the gendering of immigration.

One of the stated objectives of the *Act* is "to enrich and strengthen the cultural and social fabric of Canada, taking into account the federal and bilingual character of Canada" [3 (a) and (b)]. This definition of the "character" of Canada as bilingual, of course, refers to English and French. In committing itself to strengthening the "cultural" and "social" fabric of Canada, whose character is specifically defined as "bilingual," the *Act* becomes complicit in perpetuating a particular colonial construction of "Canadian-ness." Thus, the *Act* does not seek—even in principle—to end the racialization of the nation which had been the specific objective of preceding immigration policies. It sought instead to strengthen this "bilingual" character of the nation, as well as its attendant "cultural and social fabric." In this objective, the *Act* represents a historical continuity in the racialized distinction of immigrants: immigrants who are defined as compatible with the nation—on the basis of their cultural, social, and linguistic characteristics—become ideologically constructed as future citizens, to be integrated into the nation as Canadians; immigrants who are defined as incompatible—on those same grounds—become constructed as immigrants, outsiders to the nation.

Further, in organizing immigration into the categories of the independent and family classes, the *Act* organizes the gendering of immigration. The very naming of the independent class ideologically constructs it as a masculinized category. In western patriarchal terms, men are defined as independent economic agents, as heads of households, because they are men, whereas women are defined as the dependents, as the "family," of men (MacDonald; Mies). The *Act* reinforces this patriarchal definition and ideologically constructs the independent class as masculine, while constituting the family class as a feminized one. The very naming of this category organizes it as a feminized class, a construction which is further reinforced by its designation as a category of "dependents," thereby associating it with everything which is not "masculine." Where men are defined as independent economic agents, women and children are defined only by their relation to these "independent" male actors—as their "dependent" family members. By organizing immigration into these categories, and in specifying unequal conditions for each, the *Act* in effect genders immigration, denying immigrant women autonomy and independent status once they enter the country. This distinction masculinizes the independent class as a self-sufficient, economically productive category, while feminizing the family class as one of "non-economic" "dependents" who must be sponsored. Further, and most significantly, this ideological category of "dependent" is made actionable by imposing upon immigrant women a literal dependency on their sponsor for ten years through the sponsorship regulations. Whereas earlier immigration policies sought to keep women of the "non-preferred races" (see Bolaria and Li; Thobani) out of the country, the *Immigration Act* allows them entry, but on the condition of making them dependent on sponsors, and making invisible their very "economic" contributions to the Canadian nation.

These ideological practices mean that men who enter under the family category are able to escape their "dependent" status because they are men. In the capitalist economy, men are defined as workers and economic actors. Socially, they are defined as heads of households. This "maleness" of immigrant men—some of whom might be sponsored—allows them to overcome their "dependent" status once they are in the country. For sponsored women, on the other hand, their actual status as women reinforces their "dependent" status even after they enter paid work. A number of studies demonstrate that most sponsored immigrant women enter the paid labour-force relatively soon after their arrival into the country (Boyd 1992; Das Gupta; Ng and Estable; Samuel), but this reality is ignored by the *Act*. Nor is the unpaid labour of immigrant women, which reproduces immigrant families including future generations of workers for the "national" economy, recognized as an "economic" contribution. Thus, despite the reality that sponsored immigrant women make very tangible contributions-through their paid and unpaid labour-immigration categorization renders this reality invisible.

The *Act's* separation of the independent and family categories also makes a ranking of the worth of these categories inevitable. This categorization ensures that, in the ranking of the "value" of immigrants to the nation, the family class comes up short in capitalist terms which define individuals by their financial and "economic" worth. The *Act* allows, quite literally, applicants under the independent category to "score" points for their economic measure. Applicants under the family class, on the other hand, are ranked largely on the basis of their family relationship.

Immigration regulations also institutionalize the unequal access of sponsored immigrant women to social entitlements such as social assistance, old age security, social housing and job training programs. Although sponsored immigrants are eligible for citizenship after a three year residency, the sponsorship regulations remain in effect for ten years. Therefore, immigration policy continues to organize unequal citizenship rights for sponsored immigrant women even after they become tax-payers and *de jure* citizens. The welfare state's underlying principle-that members of a society, as tax-payers, have a legitimate right to access programs collectively funded by their taxes-does not apply to these women. The taxes paid by immigrant women into "national" revenues becomes yet another form of their economic contribution to the welfare of "citizens" who have greater access to these programs. Likewise, sponsors themselves become discouraged from making claims to social security programs—even if they have legal entitlement. In order to qualify for sponsorship, sponsors have to demonstrate their ability to be self-supporting and to provide financial support to their sponsored relatives (EIC). The result is that both sponsor and sponsored immigrant are made subject to a lesser citizenship through the sponsorship agreement, further reinforcing the ideological construction of immigrants as "lesser" than Canadians-as-member-of-the-nation.

In short then, the *Immigration Act* organizes the nationalization of white immigrants on the basis of their social, cultural, and linguistic compatibility with the nation. Indeed, they become defined as essential to the nation's reproduction. The racialization of these members of the nation mean that they become distinguished from immigrants of colour, even when both groups enter the country under the same legal category. To compound this racialization, the gendering of immigration further defines the family class, and immigrant women, as not making economic contributions to the nation. And whereas Canadian-born women of colour have *de jure* citizen status, their racialization on the basis of their cultural, linguistic and social "diversity" associates them with immigrant women of colour. As a result both are made to assume the ideologically constructed status of "outsider-to-the-nation." Therefore, it is women of colour who have come to be most strongly associated with "costs" to the nation; we have come to personify this category as outsiders to the nation and a burden on its resources. The race/gender/class nexus embedded in the *Act* borders all immigrant women as a most potent threat to the "nation."

Sponsoring inequalities for the twenty-first century

The *Immigration Act, 1976–77* remained in effect into the 1990s. However, immigration policy is undergoing significant changes with the current restructuring of the Canadian economy, and a strategy for immigration for immigration for the twenty-first century has been outlined by the state. This strategy seeks essentially to increase restrictions upon future third world immigration for permanent settlement into Canada, as well as further limiting the grounds upon which claims to Canadian citizenship can be made (Thobani). A number of the recommendations outlined in this strategy have been implemented by the federal government (the re-introduction of the head tax on immigrants and reduction of overall immigration levels being among the chief ones); further changes which will also include a new *Immigration Act* continue to be proposed by the government.

Recent changes proposed in the document *Building on a Strong Foundation for the Twenty-First Century: New Directions for Immigration and Refugee Policy and Legislation* state that the objective of "enriching through immigration the cultural and social fabric of Canada" remains "still supported by Canadians" (CIC). In this, the state has signaled its intention of maintaining the racialization of the nation and immigrants for the foreseeable future. Indeed, the official definition of the nation as bilingual and bicultural—English and French—is being given even greater currency as the federal government seeks to contain the sovereigntist aspirations of the Quebec separatist movement.

These proposals also call for the "reinforcement of the family class as the traditional cornerstone of Canada's immigration program" (CIC 1998). Specific changes proposed include: reducing the sponsorship period; increasing the enforcement of the sponsorship agreement; suspending the sponsorship agreement in cases where sponsored immigrants or sponsors are convicted for violence, and; recognizing common law and same-sex couples for sponsorship.

In maintaining the family class as a separate class with sponsorship requirements, the current proposals will maintain the feminization of this category. Likewise, the proposals will continue to render invisible the economic contributions of this class. Acknowledging the economic contributions of the family class would challenge its construction as a "dependent one." This would undermine the legitimacy of the sponsorship agreement and would reveal the intensification of patriarchal control immigrant women are made subject to. In maintaining the sponsorship relation, the state's intentions are to continue rendering immigrant women's economic worth and work invisible, while continuing to construct us as a burden on the nation's resources.

The proposal to reduce the sponsorship period from the current ten year is certainly a step in the right direction. However, in simultaneously proposing the strengthening of the enforcement of sponsorship regulations, any progressive move is undermined. Even if the sponsorship period is reduced, the unequal social entitlements of sponsored immigrants to social assistance programs and their dependency on the sponsor will be maintained. Indeed, it will be policed even more closely. The proposals call to "expand Citizenship and Immigration Canada's power to undertake collection action against defaulting sponsors and share proceeds with the provinces" (CIC 1998). In doing this, the federal government is increasing the incentive of provincial governments to police more closely claims by sponsored immigrants to social assistance, and to use the provincial social service system for this increased surveillance. With most people of colour in Canada being racialized as outsiders to the nation regardless of our legal status or the length of our residency in the country, it is safe to anticipate that the claims of most people of colour (and most particularly of women of colour) to social security programs will be policed more closely as one consequence of this specific proposal.

Another significant change proposed to the sponsorship agreement is the suspension of sponsorship if either the sponsor or the sponsored immigrant is convicted for perpetrating violence. The state currently intensifies the dependency of sponsored immigrant women on their sponsors through the sponsorship regulations, making these women more vulnerable to violence and abuse. Therefore, the change necessary to protect these women from violent sponsors is to do away with the sponsorship relation which creates (or increases) this dependency and women's vulnerability. Instead, this proposal seeks not to reduce women's dependency and vulnerability to violence, but attempts to intervene after the violence is committed, and even then, only with the involvement of the criminal justice system in the stipulation that sponsorship will be suspended only after conviction. This proposal means the state will continue to make sponsored women vulnerable to violence, as well as make them even more reluctant to move out of the power of their sponsor. The criminal justice system has repeatedly failed to protect women who have experienced violence and have gone to the police, as the recent case of the murder of Rajwar Gakhal and her family tragically demonstrated (Jiwani). Studies on violence against women reveal that even when women are experiencing violence in intimate relationships, their priority is to end this violence, not to prosecute perpetrators (DeKeseredy and MacLeod). This is particularly true of sponsored women who rely on their sponsors to sponsor other members of their family. To demand that these women engage with a racist and sexist criminal justice system, secure convictions against their sponsors, and only then will their dependency upon sponsors be revoked, is to condemn the women to continue living with violence. Sponsored immigrant women who leave violent sponsors, and who do not necessarily want to engage with the criminal justice system, will thus be more effectively denied claims to social security programs if the only condition upon which they can do so is the conviction of their sponsor.

Simultaneously, this proposal will increase the incentive of violent sponsors to control their sponsored relatives more effectively. The fear that sponsored family members might pursue criminal charges may increase the sponsor's incentive to control their actions even more strongly than is currently the case. Rather than lessen the vulnerability of sponsored immigrant women to violence at the hands of their sponsors, this proposal will only serve to increase the control which sponsors currently assert over their "dependents," and could potentially lead to an escalation of violence against immigrant women.

The proposal that common law and same-sex partners be covered under the family class could also potentially be of benefit in challenging homophobic attitudes and practices. However, even as the state proposes legitimizing same-sex relationships, doing this through the family class means that same-sex couples will also become subject to the sponsorship agreement that increases the power of the sponsoring partner over that of the sponsored partner. Therefore, rather than this change working to transform the patriarchal, heterosexual family within Canada, this proposal would subject same-sex relationships to the same relations of domination within the heterosexual relationship by increasing the control of one partner over the other.

Conclusion

The family class has already been subjected to numerous restrictions in the 1990s. The re-introduction in 1995 of the head tax of $975 per immigrant has placed a disproportionate financial constraint on immigrants from the third world, and particularly third world women who have relatively lesser access to financial resources. The head tax places an onerous burden upon families who await reunification. Additionally, annual levels for the family class were reduced in the five year plan tabled by the federal government in 1995 (CIC 1994). In light of these changes, the new proposals which seek to strengthen the sponsorship agreement and to penalize sponsorship default can be anticipated to restrict further the immigration of all except the most financially solvent immigrants from the third world.

The current *Immigration Act* organizes the racialized nationalization of white immigrants on the basis of their cultural, linguistic, and social affinity to a colonial definition of Canadian-ness. On the other hand, the racialized/gendered bordering of third world immigrant women is organized on the basis of their social, linguistic, and cultural diversity, and through the non-recognition of their contributions to the nation. The current organization of the family class and the sponsorship regulations effectively make immigrant women subject to increased patriarchal control through increased dependency on sponsors. As long as immigrant women are allowed into the country on unequal terms, and are made subject to a lesser citizenship, the race/class/gender nexus will continue to be reproduced. These social relations, organized by the Canadian state, result in the construction of immigrant women in particular as an economic "burden" to the nation, and as a "threat" to the nation's social and cultural cohesiveness.

Originally published in CWS/cf's *Fall 1999 issue, "Immigrant and Refugee Women" (Volume 19, Number 3): 11-16.*

[1]Canada also allows in refugees, whose eligibility is assessed under the United

Nations definition of Convention refugees. Additional categories under which migration is organized are the Non-Immigrant Employment Authorization program (Sharma) and domestic workers (Bakan). For the purposes of this paper, however, I will concentrate on the family class.

References

Abu-Laban, Y. "Keeping 'em Out: Gender, Race and Class Biases in Canadian Immigration Policy." *Painting the Maple: Essays on Race*. Eds. J. Anderson, A. Eisenberg, S. Grace. and V. Strong-Boag. Vancouver: University of British Columbia Press, 1999.

Bolaria, P. and P. Li. *Racial Oppression in Canada*. Toronto: Garamond Press, 1985.

Boyd, M. "Foreign-Born, Female, Old ... and Poor." *Canadian Woman Studies/ les cahiers de la femme* 12 (4) (1992): 50-52.

Boyd, M. *Migration, Human Rights and Economic Integration: Focus on Canada*. York University: Centre for Refugee Studies, 1998.

Citizenship and Immigration Canada (CIC). *Building on a Strong Foundation for the Twenty-First Century: New Directions for Immigration and Refugee Policy and Legislation*. Ottawa: Minister of Public Works and Government Services Canada, 1998.

Citizenship and Immigration Canada (CIC) *A Broader Vision: Immigration and Citizenship Plan 1995-2000, Annual Report to Parliament*. Ottawa: Minister of Supply and Services Canada ,1994.

Culhane, D. *The Pleasure of the Crown: Anthropology, Law and First Nations*. Burnaby: Talonbooks, 1998.

Das Gupta, T. "Families of Native Peoples, Immigrants and People of Colour." *Canadian Families: Diversity, Conflict and Change*. Eds. N. Mandell . and A. Duffy. Toronto: Harcourt Brace and Co., 1995.

DeKeseredy, W. and L. MacLeod. *Woman Abuse: A Sociological Story*. Toronto: Harcourt Brace and Co., 1997.

Employment and Immigration Canada (EIC). *Canada's Immigration Law: An Overview*. Ottawa: Minister of Supply and Services Canada, 1983.

Fiske, J. "Political Status of Native Indian Women; Contradictory Implications of Canadian State Policy." *American Indian Culture and Research Journal* 19 (2) (1995): 1-30.

Goodleaf, D. "Under Military Occupation: Indigenous Women, State Violence and Community Resistance." *Still We Rise: Feminist Political Mobilizing in Contemporary Canada*. Ed. L. Carty. Toronto: Women's Press, 1993.

Green, J. "Towards A Détente With History: Confronting Canada's Colonial Legacy." *International Journal of Canadian Studies* 12 (1995): 85-105.

Green, A. A. and D. A. Green. "The Economic Goals of Canada's Immigration Policy, Past and Present." Paper presented at the British Columbia Centre for Excellence on Immigration, 1997.

Hawkins, F. *Canada and Immigration: Public Policy and Public Concern*. Montreal: McGill-Queen's University Press, 1972.

Immigration Act, 1976-77. Ottawa: Queen's Printer for Canada.

Jakubowski, L. *Immigration and the Legalization of Racism*. Halifax: Fernwood Publishing, 1997.

Jiwani, Y. "Culture, Violence and Inequality." Vancouver: Conference Proceedings, *Meeting the Cross-Cultural Challenge*, 1998.

MacDonald, M. "What is Feminist Economics?" *Beyond Law* 5 (14): 1996: 11-36.

Maracle, L. *I Am Woman*. Vancouver: Press Gang Publishers, 1996.

Mies, M. *Patriarchy and Accumulation on a World Scale*. London: Zed Books, 1986.

Ng. R. and Estable, A. "Immigrant Women in the Labour Force: An Overview of Present Knowledge and Research Gaps." *Resources for Feminist Research* (1987): 29-33.

Ng, R. and J. Strout. *Services for Immigrant Women: Report and Evaluation of a Series of Four Workshops Conducted in the Summer, 1977*. Vancouver: Women's Research Centre 1977.

Samuel, T. J. *Family Class Immigrants to Canada, 1981-1984: Labor Force Activity Aspects*. Ottawa: Employment and Immigration Canada, 1986.

Stasiulis, D. and R. Jhappan. "The Fractious Politics of a Settler Society: Canada." *Unsettling Settler Societies: Articulations of Race, Ethnicity, Gender and Class*. Eds. N. Yuval-Davis and D. Stasiulis. London: Sage Publications, 1995.

Thobani, S. "Nationalizing Citizens, Bordering Immigrant Women: Globalization and the Racialization of Women's Citizenship in Late 20th Century Canada." Vancouver: Doctoral Dissertation, Simon Fraser University 1998.

Globalization and the Erosion of the Welfare State

Exploring the Experience of Chinese Immigrant Women

Guida Man ~~

Since the 1980s, the Canadian neoliberal state has been rapidly undergoing economic restructuring. The dominant discourse argues for the natural and inevitability of the mechanisms of globalization, structural adjustment, and privatization, thus closing off challenges and debates for possible alternative strategies and action. The withdrawal of the state and the erosion of welfare programs (such as daycare, elderly care, women's shelters, psychiatric hospitals, etc.) changes concretely the everyday lives of Canadian citizens, particularly for women and other disadvantaged groups. Previously state-subsidized programs such as childcare, elderly care, mental care, and healthcare are either downsized or privatized. The work of caring is being pushed back into the home and downloaded onto women who are expected to be the primary caregivers due to their gender. The shutdown or downsizing of public institutions causes many women to lose their jobs, since they are over-represented in the public sector. Those women who seek employment are being channelled into the private sector as part-time, flexible labour, with no benefits or job security. The hollowing out of the welfare state means that the state no longer provides a social safety net for its citizens. Unemployment is seen as an individual, private problem, rather than a public responsibility.

In recent years, feminist scholars have addressed the impact of globalization on women in general (Bakka; Brodie; Evans and Wekerle), and on immigrant women of colour in particular (Ng 1999; Das Gupta 1999; Lee). Many of the studies shed light on the experience of "unskilled"[1] immigrant women. This paper examines how globalization and economic restructuring affect immigrant women who are "skilled" or professionals. I will focus on the Chinese immigrant women who have immigrated from Hong Kong and China to Canada in recent years. I will present empirical data to elucidate how their experiences have been affected by institutionalized policies as a result of the globalization of trade and commerce, and the neoliberal state's valorization of private enterprise over public welfare. I will demonstrate the contradictions of the rationale of the state to actively recruit highly skilled labour to bolster the labour market on the one hand, and the concurrent problem of unemployment, underemployment and deskilling experienced by the highly educated and skilled Chinese immigrant women on the other.

Canadian immigration policies

Prioritizing highly educated, skilled immigrants and business personnel has historically been the objective of the Canadian state (see Man 1995b; 1998), although it was not always made transparent. The privileging of these immigrants was explicitly stated in 1967when the supposedly non-discriminatory points system of the immigration policy was introduced. With the globalization of trade and the concomitant consequences of economic restructuring, privatization, and deregulation, the Canadian neoliberal state in the 1980s and the 1990s further intensified its restrictive measures in their selection of highly skilled professionals and business immigrants as immigration priorities. The rationale behind these economically driven policies was that these highly skilled new immigrants would benefit Canada in the new economic order. They would provide Canada with a "comparative advantage" (Brecher and Costello), propelling the Canadian economy into the twenty-first century with global competitiveness, despite criticisms of the state's strategy to skimp off "la creme de la creme" from immigrant-sending countries, rendering a brain-drain of their skilled labour and crippling their economies.

During the 1980s, migration from Hong Kong to Canada has increased rapidly. Since 1987, Hong Kong has been the number one source country for immigrants to Canada (see EIC 1989-1993; CIC 1994-2001). This is coincidental with the events occurring in Hong Kong in the 1980s. The uncertainty of the reversion of Hong Kong from British to Chinese sovereignty in 1997 has prompted many Hong Kong residents to seek a safe haven abroad. The signing of the Sino-British Joint Declaration in 1984, the subsequent political developments in China, and the violation of human rights suggesting China's disrespect for the rule of law, eroded Hong Kong residents' confidence. Consequently, a mass exodus of emigrants to foreign countries started in the mid-80s. The Tiananman massacre in 1989 further exacerbated people's uncertainty of the future of Hong Kong, prompting more citizens to emigrate. Not surprisingly, some changes in the Canadian immigration policy coincided with the developments of events in Hong Kong. In January 1984, Canada adopted new procedures in the business immigration program designed to attract highly qualified entrepreneurs. In January 1986, the investor component was introduced to further attract eligible immigrants with excess money for investments (see Borowski and Nash).

The privileging of business class immigrants does not favour women, who comprise of a small proportion of business immigrants. According to two surveys conducted by Employment and Immigration Canada (EIC), only 10.7 per cent[2] of entrepreneur immigrants in 1984, and 12.7 per cent in 1986/87 were women.[3] It is evident therefore that male and female Chinese immigrants occupy different locations in Canadian society, and it does not offer an optimistic and encouraging view of the status of Chinese immigrant women in Canada.

From 1987 to 1997, Hong Kong became the leading immigrant group to

Canada (EIC 1989-93; CIC 1994-2001). In the post-1997 period, immigration from Hong Kong started to dwindle as a result of the seemingly smooth transition of power from British to Chinese sovereignty, generating increased confidence of Hong Kong people in the political stability of Hong Kong. Furthermore, the unemployment and underemployment of many Hong Kong immigrants in Canada has prompted a stream of returned migration. At the same time, since the 1990s, the number of Chinese immigrants from Mainland China to Canada has been increasing steadily. By 1998, Chinese immigrants from Mainland China became the single largest group of immigrants coming to Canada (CIC 1994-2001), and has remained so ever since. Many of these new immigrants were highly educated professionals in their home country.

The Chinese are not a homogenous group. They differ in gender, class, and sexual locations, and they come from diverse social, cultural, political and geographical sites (see Man 1995b) although they belong to the same "ethnic" group, the Chinese immigrant women from Hong Kong and those from Mainland China are vastly different in many ways. For example, they have lived in diversely different social, political and economic systems. While Hong Kong immigrants have lived in a capitalist system under colonial rule for 99 years, people from Mainland China have lived under a communist regime since 1949. In general, the Hong Kong immigrant women are more affluent and have personal assets prior to immigrating to Canada vis-a-vis their counterparts from China. The selective immigration policy, however, ensures only the highly educated and "skilled" professionals are admitted, regardless of whether they are from China, Hong Kong or elsewhere. Other discriminatory processes such as employer's reluctance to hire new immigrants without "Canadian experience" and the lack of recognition of foreign degrees by professional organizations also have a homogenizing effect on the new immigrants, rendering the new immigrants' previous experience in the home country obsolete, and their education and training irrelevant. For those immigrant women who have insufficient English language skills to practice in their profession, English language training courses are inadequate to meet those needs. Only those immigrants who have the material resources to be retrained can dream of eventually re-entering their original professions. The employment opportunities for immigrant women who often have to take primary responsibility for housework and childcare are drastically hampered.

In the following analysis, I will draw upon data from two research projects. The data for Chinese immigrant women from Hong Kong is based on in depth interviews with 30 Chinese immigrant women from Hong Kong who came to Canada between 1986 and 1992. The data for the immigrant women from China is based on in depth interviews and focus groups with 20 women who have immigrated to Canada between 1995 and 2000. The latter research is part of a larger project on the Mandarin-speaking Chinese immigrants in Toronto, conducted for the South East Asian Service Centre (see George, Tat Tsang, Man and Wei Da; Man, George, Tat Tsang and Wei Da). All the women in both studies were married.

In my analysis of the research data, I have used a feminist methodology which addresses the intersections of gender, race, class, and other discourses of inequality and which places women as the subjects of the study (see Ng 1982; 1993; hooks; Smith). My goal was to link the Chinese immigrant women's accounts of their situations to the larger structures of society, to the social, economic, and political processes where their experiences are embedded. By making visible the processes which are organized extra-locally, and which have tremendous impact on their everyday lives, I hope to bring about policy changes which would improve these women's lives.

The deskilling of Chinese immigrant women

In the paid labour market, women's household and childcare responsibilities have always been seen by management as too cumbersome for an efficient and low-cost labour force (Kerr). The gender segregation of the labour market has ghettoized women into jobs with lower pay and fewer benefits. The globalization of trade, economic restructuring, and downsizing in recent years have significant impacts on women's employment. The erosion of funding for social and community services undermines women's labour market participation that is concentrated in these sectors (Armstrong). The labour force is becoming increasingly feminized. As full-time secure employment dwindles, women, along with some men, are being channelled into part-time, flexible, insecure employment.

The situation has an adverse effect on immigrant women's employment. In the last decade, the labour force participation of immigrant women in Canada has been drastically reduced. In comparison to immigrant men, immigrant women's labour market participation is even more disadvantaged. According to Statistics Canada, while the employment rate for immigrant men between 25 and 44 fell from 81 per cent to 71 per cent between 1986 and 1996, for immigrant women of the same age group, their employment rate fell from 58 per cent to 51 per cent in the same time period; while for Canadian-born women, it rose 8 per cent to 73 per cent (Carey). Similarly, previous studies have found that immigrant women have higher unemployment rates than Canadian-born women and they are concentrated in poorly paid and insecure service, sales and production jobs (Boyd; Badets and Howaston-Lee). Immigrant women generally have a higher educational attainment than their Canadian-born counterparts. Unfortunately, it does not improve their chances of employment (Mojab). Although immigrant women who come to Canada as adults are twice as likely as Canadian-born women to have some university training, they are less likely to hold professional jobs once in Canada (Travato and Grindstaff).

The employment opportunities for immigrant women of colour in a gender segregated, racialized, and globalized labour market are even more seriously jeopardized. It has been demonstrated that being foreign-born, a member of a visible minority group, or female, has a cumulative effect such that foreign-born women of colour received the lowest wages and salaries of all workers (Boyd). Immigrant women from developing countries who do not have English or French language skills, nor the "appropriate" educational background are ghettoized in low-paid menial labour (Ng 1993; Das Gupta 1996).

The Chinese immigrant women I interviewed, whether they were from China or Hong Kong, were highly educated. The majority had university degrees or post-secondary education (21/30 of Hong Kong women, and 20/20 of women from China). Despite their high level of education, the majority of them came to Canada under the family class immigrant status as dependents of their husbands, the principal applicants (Man 1996; Man et al). As dependents immigration officers see them as being "not destined for the labour market," despite the fact that many have participated in the paid labour market in their home country as skilled workers and professionals. Women in China have always participated alongside their male counterparts in productive processes. Recent studies of the employment patterns and work decisions of married women in Hong Kong also confirm the centrality of women's monetary contributions to the livelihood of the families concerned (Association for the Advancement of Feminism). But institutionalized racist and sexist practices embedded in the immigration process discriminates against these women, treating them as if they were "non-productive" labour.

Both groups of women spoke of the extreme pressure they felt for both monetary and emotional reasons to find employment as soon as possible, particularly for the women from China, who felt extremely vulnerable economically. Although most of the Hong Kong women had some financial assets, they feared they would soon deplete their savings. They also did not want to be dependent on their husbands financially.

The climate of globalization has a downward levelling effect by lowering wages, fostering part-time, unstable employment, and generally contributing to the feminization of the labour force (Armstrong). Under such circumstances, immigrant women of colour looking for work are vulnerable to employers' discriminatory practices towards them. A contentious issue many immigrant women of colour have experienced, which were reiterated by Chinese immigrant women in my study, was the employers' requirement for "Canadian experience," and their reluctance to recognize immigrant women's qualifications and experience from their own country. These practices pose a significant barrier for the Chinese immigrants and other immigrant women, hampering their participation in the labour market, and relegating them to underemployment or unemployment (Preston and Man; Man 1995b; 1997; George).

In order to make a living, and to acquire "Canadian experience," these highly qualified women professionals had to take whatever employment they could find. These jobs were usually low-paying, low-status, entry-level menial positions, often exploitative, and that did not utilize their skills, education, or experience. Due to the long hours they spend on the jobs, and the demands of their household responsibilities, some of the women from China were not able to continue with their ESL courses. As a result, these immigrant women were unable to extricate themselves from the menial positions they are ghettoized into. Their experiences are typified by one woman who was a teacher in Beijing prior to immigrating to Canada, and found a job in Canada as part of a hotel's cleaning staff:

The first job I had was babysitting, that was one month after I arrived. I found this job from a newspaper. My husband helped me prepare the interview. At that time, I knew very little English, but the woman hired me because she thought I have a good heart and would be kind to her children. I was very happy to get this job. ... I worked there for over one year. I have very good relationship with that family. Now I work in a hotel as a cleaner, full-time. It's hard work. My English is not good, I want to improve it, so I attended English classes in the evening at first while I was working during the day. But I couldn't keep doing so as I felt too tired. I couldn't concentrate on my study, so I have to give it up.

Some women, particularly those from China, felt that their lack of fluency in the English language affected their employment opportunities. At the same time, most of the women found the Language Instruction for Newcomers (LINC) program for ESL classes to be too elementary, and it did not help them in gaining the vocabulary they needed to find employment that would be commensurate with their qualifications. The racialized and gendered labour market also made them ineligible for the Labour Market Language Training (LMLT) program, an advanced language training program targeting those whose labour market skills are most in demand (EIC 1992). Furthermore, neither of these programs provide a living allowance, and both are restricted to new immigrants who have been in Canada for less than a year. The elimination of a living allowance discriminates against the most disadvantaged immigrants who cannot afford to forgo wage work to attend language classes full-time. It is in this way that inequality in race, gender, and class practices in Canadian society is reproduced and perpetuated.

Even though some of the women did find employment, the poor condition of the work environment, the discriminatory practices, the irregular hours, and the unstable and insecure nature of the work made it difficult for them to survive on the job. The women's underemployment and unemployment in the new country undermined their sense of stability and well-being. The difficulties some of them encountered in communicating in English also exacerbated their feelings of isolation and depression. Some women from China talked about friends or acquaintances that had experienced depression or had even committed suicide after immigrating to Canada. The class privilege of the immigrant women from Hong Kong did allow them relatively more choices, affording some the option of not participating in the paid labour force.

Childcare

Although childcare is a primary concern for women, the state has not responded to their needs. There are no public policies to ensure the availability of adequate childcare facilities (Luxton and Reiter). The hollowing out of the welfare state and the dismantling of social safety net have foisted healthcare and childcare onto the family and the unpaid work of women. In Ontario, restructuring and severe government cutbacks of social services (Friendly; Kitchen and Popham; Evans and Wekerle). Feminist gains in the last decade in such areas as childcare services and employment equity have also been drastically undermined (Brodie; McQuaig).

Previous studies have found that immigrant women bear the bulk of the day-to-day housework and caring responsibilities, while their husbands are only marginally involved in such tasks (Weber; Gelfand and McCallum). Predictably, most of the women interviewed bore primary responsibility for housework and childcare. They also found childcare services inadequate in meeting their needs. One immigrant woman from Hong Kong voiced her criticism of the inadequacy of daycare in Canada:

> I have a five-year-old and a two-year-old. I'm finding that daycare is a serious problem. Daycare is not flexible enough to accommodate working parents. Their hours of operation don't fill our gaps. We have to choose between quality or service. Sure, there are a few daycare centres now that run from 7:00a.m. to 6:00p.m. They are all privately run. They offer the service, but not necessarily the quality. So sometimes you don't want to put your child at risk....

The lack of subsidized daycare, coupled with the women's marginalized position in the labour force, relegates them part-time menial work with irregular hours. Their household and childcare responsibilities in turn hampers their opportunity for obtaining full-time positions. The racialized and gendered labour market structures in Canadian society intersect to further marginalize their everyday experience, compounding their difficulties in the new society (Das Gupta 1994; Ralston).

Some of the immigrant women from China who had to negotiate several part-time jobs in order to make ends meet, and who had difficulty obtaining subsidized childcare, resolved to send their children back to China to be taken care of by grandmothers or other family members. Some of the children were babies when they were sent away. The long-term effect of this prolonged separation from their parents is not known. Anecdotal evidence, however, shows that it can be detrimental. Some of the children who grew up separated from their parents subsequently disowned their parents. Some Chinese immigrant women from Hong Kong have become "astronaut" wives (see Man 1995), staying in Canada with their children while their husbands returned to Hong Kong to work. However, their stories of isolation and loneliness were harrowing. Although not found in my study, some women from Hong Kong who were discouraged by their underemployment and unemployment in Canada resolved to return to Hong Kong to find work along with their husbands, leaving their children alone in Canada.[4] While outside of the scope of my research, the long-term effects of "parachute children" warrants serious investigation.

Conclusion

As the process of globalization deepened in recent years, the Canadian state, in an effort to take full advantage of the fluidity and flexibility of human capital, launched new initiatives to actively recruit skilled immigrants to the country. However, institutionalized racist and sexist practices embedded in Canadian society continues to marginalize the highly educated and skilled Chinese immigrant women. The retrenchment of the state in providing an adequate social safety net, the lack of adequate childcare services and subsidies, coupled with immigrant women's diminished earning power makes it even more difficult for immigrant women to be able to afford childcare for their children. Their household and childcare responsibilities in turn prevents them from engaging in full-time positions, and in some cases, deters them from taking ESL courses which, in any case, do not meet the employment needs of these professional and highly skilled women. Thus, the "brain drain" occurring in developing countries has become the "deskilled" labour force in the new country. As one disillusioned woman from China commented indignantly:

I think Canada needs labourers, but not professionals…. Now they use professional people to do menial labour. How do you expect us to function well psychologically?

For these women to become equal and active participants in Canadian society they must be able to have access to the resources required to help them develop to their full potential. To bring about changes in state policies and institutional support for new immigrant women we have to first unmask the rhetoric of globalization and reveal that it is an unnatural and socially constructed process. When we move away from hegemonic thinking about the market as a natural and inevitable force we can begin to imagine how women can play a role in shaping markets and economies (Beneria). It is only through the implementation of inclusive programs and policies that Chinese immigrant women will be able to enjoy equal opportunity and outcomes in an anti-racist and anti-sexist environment.

Originally published in CWS/cf's Spring/Summer 2002 issue, "Women, Globalization and International Trade" (Volume 21/22, Numbers 4/1): 26-32.

[1]It should be noted that "skill" is in fact socially constructed and is imputed

with gendered and racialized meanings.
²The figures of 10.7 per cent and 12.7 per cent for female entrepreneur immigrants were lower than the female figures for the Canadian entrepreneur population as a whole (Thompson 1986, 6-8).
³See EIC PPDB 1985, Tables 2.6, 3.5, 3.6; EIC Strategic Policy and Planning 1990, 27.
⁴Preliminary data analysis of the study "Transnational Citizenship and Social Cohesion: Recent Immigrants from Hong Kong to Canada" by Audrey Kobayashi, David Ley, Guida Man, Valerie Preston, and Myer Siemiatycki found that such occurrences are not uncommon among recent immigrants from Hong Kong.

References

Armstrong, Pat. "The Feminization of the Labour Force: Harmonizing Down in a Global Economy." *Rethinking, Restructuring: Gender and Change in Canada*. Ed. Isabella Bakker.. Toronto: University of Toronto Press, 1996.
Association for the Advancement of Feminism (AAF). "The Hong Kong Women's File." Hong Kong: Association for the Advancement of Feminism, 1993.
Badets and Howaston-Lee. "Recent Immigrants in the Workforce." *Canadian Social Trends* (Spring 1998): 16-22.
Bakka, Isabella. Ed. *Rethinking, Restructuring: Gender and Change in Canada*. Toronto: University of Toronto Press, 1996.
Beneria, Lourdes. "Globalization, Gender and the Davos Man." *Feminist Economics* 5 (3) (1999): 61-83.
Borowski, A., and A. Nash. 1992. "Business Migration to Canada and Australia." *Immigration and Refugee Policy: Australia and Canada Compared*. Vol. 1. Eds. Howard Adelman, Allan Borowoski, Myer Bursterin, and Lois Foster. Toronto: University of Toronto Press, 1992.
Boyd, Monica. "Gender, Visible Minority and Immigrant Earnings Inequality: Assessing an Employment Equity Premise." Ed. Vic Satzewich. *Deconstructing a Nation: Immigration, Multiculturalism and Racism in 1990s Canada*. Halifax: Fernwood Press, 1992. 279-321.
Brecher, Jeremy and Tim Costello. *Global Village or Global Pillage: Economic Restruction from the Bottom Up*. Boston: South End Press, 1994.
Brodie, Janine. *Politics on the Margins: Restructuring and the Canadian Women's Movement*. Halifax: Fernwood Publishing, 1995.
Carey, Elaine. "Immigrants Faced Tough Job Search in 1990s: Statscan, Less Likely to Get Work Than Those Who Come in '80s." *The Toronto Star*. 12 March 1999: A19.
Citizenship and Immigration Canada (CIC). "Citizenship and Immigration Statistics 1992-99." Ottawa: Public Works and Government Services Canada, 1994-2001.

Das Gupta, Tania. "Political Economy of Gender, Race and Class: Looking at South Asian Immigrant Women in Canada." *Canadian Ethnic Studies* 26 (1) (1994) 340-54.

Das Gupta, Tania. *Racism and Paid Work.* Toronto: Garamond Press, 1996.

Das Gupta, Tania. "The Politics of Multiculturalism: 'Immigrant Women' and the Canadian State." *Scratching the Surface: Canadian Anti-Racist Feminist Thought.* Eds. Enakshi Dua and Angela Robertson. Toronto: Women's Press, 1999.

Employment and Immigration Canada (EIC). Immigrant Regulations, 1978 as amended by SOR/92-214, P.C. 1992-685, April 1992.

Employment and Immigration Canada (EIC). *Immigration Statistics 1987-91.* Ottawa: Minister of Supply and Services, 1989-93.

Evans, Patricia M. and Gerda R. Wekerle. *Women and the Canadian Welfare State.* Toronto: University of Toronto Press, 1997.

Friendly, Martha. "What is the Public Interest in Child Care?" Eds. L. Ricciutell., June Larkin and Eimear O'Neill., *Confronting the Cuts: A Sourcebook for Women in Ontario.* Toronto: Inanna Publications and Education Inc., 1998.

Gelfand, D. and J. McCallum. "Immigration, the Family and Female Caregivers in Australia." *Journal of Gerontological Social Work* 22 (3-4) (1994): 41-59.

George, Usha. "Caring and Women of Colour: Living the Intersecting Oppressions of Race, Class and Gender." *Women's Caring: Feminist Perspectives on Social Welfare.* Eds. Carol Baines, Patricia M. Evans, and Sheila M. Neysmith. Toronto: Oxford University Press, 1998.

George, Usha, Ka Tat Tsang, Guida Man and Wei Wei Da. "Needs Assessment of Mandarin-Speaking Newcomers: A Project of South East Asian Services Centre." OASIS-CIC and SEAS unpublished report. Toronto: South East Asian Services, 2000.

hooks, bell. *Feminist Theory: From Margin to Center.* Boston: South End Press, 1984.

Kerr, Joanna. "Transnational Resistance: Strategies to Alleviate the Impacts of Restructuring on Women." *Rethinking Restructuring: Gender and Change in Canada.* Ed. Isabella Bakka. Toronto: University of Toronto Press, 1996.

Kitchen, Brigitte with Rosemarie Popham. "The Attack on Motherwork in Ontario." Eds. L. Ricciutelli, June Larkin and Eimear O'Neill. *Confronting the Cuts: A Sourcebook for Women in Ontario.* Toronto: Inanna Pub. And Education Inc, 1998.

Lee, Jo-Ann. "Immigrant Women Workers in the Immigrant Settlement Sector." *Canadian Woman Studies/les cahiers de la femme.* 19 (3) 1999: 97-103.

Luxton, Meg and Ester Reiter. "Double, Double, Toil and Trouble...Women's Experience of Work and Family in Canada 1980-1995." Eds. Patricia M.Evans and Gerda R. Wekerle. *Women and the Canadian Welfare State.* Toronto: University of Toronto Press, 1997.

Man, Guida. "The Astronaut Phenomenon: Examining Consequences of the Diaspora of the Hong Kong Chinese." *Managing Change in Southeast Asia: Local Identities, Global Connections.* Calgary: University of Alberta: Quality Color Press Inc., 1995a: 269-281.

Man, Guida. "The Experience of Women in Recent Middle-Class Chinese Immigrant Families from Hong Kong: An Inquiry into Institutional and Organizational Processes." *Asian and Pacifica Migration Journal* 4 (2-3) (1995b): 303-325.

Man, Guida. "Women's Work is Never Done: Social Organization of Work and the Experience of Women in Middle-Class Hong Kong Chinese Immigrant Families in Canada." *Advances in Gender Research.* 2. Greenwich: JAI Press Inc., 1997: 183-226.

Man, Guida. "Effects of Canadian Immigration Policies on Chinese Immigrant Women (1858-1986)." *Asia-Pacific and Canada: Images and Perspectives,* Tokyo: The Japanese Association for Canadian Studies. 1998: 118-133.

Man, Guida, Usha George, Ka Tat Tsang, Guida Man and Wei Wei Da. "Settlement Experiences of Mandarin-speaking Immigrant Women in Toronto: An Investigation in the Relations of Gender, Race and Class." Paper presented at the Fourth National Metropolis Conference, Toronto, March 22-25. 2000.

McQuaig, Linda. *The Cult of Impotence.* Toronto: Penquin Books, 1999.

Mojab, Shahrzad. "De-skilling Immigrant Women." *Canadian Woman Studies/ les cahiers de la femme.* 19(3) (1999): 110-114.

Ng, Roxana. "Immigrant Housewives in Canada/" *Atlantis.* 8 1982:111-117.

Ng, Roxana. "Immigrant Women and Institutionalized Racism." *Changing Patterns: Women in Canada.* Eds. Sandra Burt, Lorraine Code and Lindsay Dorney. Toronto: McClelland and Stewart, 1993: 279-301.

Ng, Roxana. "Homeworking: Dream Realized or Freedom Constraint? The Globalized Reality of Immigrant Garment Workers." *Canadian Woman Studies/les cahiers de la femme.* 19 (3)(1999):110-114.

Preston, Valerie and Guida Man. "Employment Experiences of Chinese Immigrant Women: An Exploration of Diversity." *Canadian Woman Studies/les cahiers de la femme.* 19 (3)(1999):115-122.

Ralston, Helen. "Race, Class, Gender and Work Experience of South Asian Immigrant Women in Atlantic Canada." *Canadian Ethnic Studies.* 23 (2) (1991): 129-139.

Smith, Dorothy. *The Everyday World as Problematic: A Feminist Sociology.* Toronto: University of Toronto Press, 1987.

Travato and Grindstaff. "Economic Status: A Census Analysis of Thirty-Year-Old Immigrant Women in Canada." *Canadian Review of Sociology and Anthropology* 23 (4) (November 1986): 569-587.

Weber, G. *Celebrating Women, Aging and Cultural Diversity.* Toronto: The Arthur Press, 1994.

Trafficking in Women for Purposes of Sexual Exploitation

A Matter of Consent?

Monique Trépanier

Trafficking in women for purposes of forced prostitution and other exploitation within the commercial sex industry is recognized as a pressing global problem. International and domestic laws, regulations and instruments relating to trafficking issues have been created not only to prevent and combat trafficking in persons, but also to protect the rights and meet the needs of those who are victimized and exploited. Their successful application to this latter objective, however, is in part contingent upon the identification of a victim. This essay will explore recent Canadian and international legal responses to trafficking issues. The nature of trafficking in persons will first be examined, followed by a discussion of whether choice or consent can be exercised within the realm of trafficking in women for sexual purposes. Finally, the way in which current laws and initiatives may be viewed either as perpetuating gender inequality or as promoting an end to women's subordination, depending on one's conclusions with respect to the consent or coercion of trafficked sex workers, will also be discussed.

Trafficking in persons defined

Trafficking in persons occurs both within and between countries, and is generally understood to involve the recruitment or transportation of persons for profit (Chuang). Although historically, international recognition of trafficking in persons focused on the forced recruitment of women for prostitution purposes, a much broader conception of the problem has emerged in recent years to include such aspects as forced domestic labour (see Connor), commercial marriages (see Kelly), organized begging, and other forms of exploitative labour and services extracted from men, women and children.[1] Complex social, cultural, economic and political factors are deemed to contribute to women's vulnerability to such deception and abuse (Derks; see also Chuang). Women are "victims of poverty, of the social practice of marginalizing women, [and suffer because]of the failure of some cultures and societies to place value on traditional women's work, and of the lack of education and employment opportunities for women in developing and transition countries" (Tiefenbrun 208).

Despite knowledge of the factors contributing to trafficking, the actual extent of the worldwide phenomenon is still not known. This has been attributed to a lack of available and reliable statistics (IOM),[2] the underground and illegal nature of trafficking, and the lack of a precise, modern and internationally recognized definition of trafficking, which was only recently addressed by the United Nations (Doezema; see also Derks).

A definition encompassing a wide range of aspects of trafficking in persons emerged from United Nations (UN) negotiations on transnational organized crime (Blackell). The *Protocol to Prevent, Suppress and Punish Trafficking in Persons, Especially Women and Children* (Trafficking Protocol), that accompanies the UN *Transnational Organized Crime Convention*, was adopted by the General Assembly in November 2000 and defines trafficking in persons as follows:

> Trafficking in persons shall mean the recruitment, transportation, transfer, harbouring or receipt of persons, by means of the threat or use of force or other forms of coercion, of abduction, of fraud, of deception, of the abuse of power or of a position of vulnerability or of the giving or receiving of payments or benefits to achieve the consent of a person having control over another person, for the purpose of exploitation. Exploitation shall include, at a minimum, the exploitation of the prostitution of others or other forms of sexual exploitation, forced labour or services, slavery or practices similar to slavery, servitude or the removal of organs. (Art. 3 (a)).[3]

The Trafficking Protocol also specifies that the consent of a trafficked victim to the intended exploitation will be deemed irrelevant (Art. 3(b)). The elaboration of such a definition is the result of much debate between various state representatives and non-governmental organizations, over the significance of consent and coercion to the trafficking realm. With the entry into force of the Trafficking Protocol on December 25, 2003,[4] this definition raises the question of whether the debate surrounding a woman's potential consent to being trafficked, particularly for the purposes of working in the sex industry of another country, has been quelled.

Sex worker as victim or agent? Applicability of the prostitution debate to the trafficking realm

Can women who worked in the sex industry in their home countries "agree" to be trafficked to do similar work in Canada? Scholars, experts and activists have disagreed over the issue of whether all trafficking, particularly that of sex work, is by definition coercive. Closely related to this debate is the issue of whether sex work or prostitution *per se* is always exploitative or whether a woman can choose to sell her body and/or consent to being trafficked in order to achieve a better life for herself in another country.

Attempts to achieve a working definition of trafficking, particularly in the last several years, have challenged traditional assumptions regarding viola-tions to women's rights (Chuang). Prior to, and during negotiations on the draft Trafficking Protocol, representatives from two discrete camps lobbied vigorously over the definition of trafficking to be adopted within this docu-ment (Goldscheider).

On one side of the debate, representing a traditional prohibitionist/abolitionist approach towards prostitution and spearheaded by the Coalition Against Trafficking in Women (CATW), were those who believe that consensual prostitution does not exist and that prostitution itself is a form of sexual exploitation that reduces women's bodies to commodities (Leidholdt). Similar in focus to aspects of Catherine MacKinnon's views on gender inequality and the male pursuit of control over women's sexuality, proponents of this school believe that prostitution victimises all women and that even if women themselves claim to have consented to such work, their consent is meaningless. Social inequities (economic and social marginalisation) experi-enced by women in society, as well as past exposure to sexual and/or other physical abuse, are believed to propel the majority of women into the sex industry to begin with. Women are left without any other valid work options, and often what they believe they have consented to do, does not include the slavery-like situation in which many later find themselves. For this reason, the CATW argues, any definition of trafficking should make consent of the victims immaterial (Leidholdt).

The other side of this debate was represented in the international arena by the Global Alliance Against Trafficking in Women (GAATW). This group, as well as "pro-sex work governments,"[5] drew a distinction between "forced prostitution" and "voluntary prostitution." They argued that such a distinction within the Trafficking Protocol's definition was crucial in order to acknowledge women's rights to freely choose prostitution as a way to make a living, and by extension, to choose to migrate for sex work. Supporters of this view identified the problem of trafficking largely within the context of forced labour, not prostitution, and condemned trafficking only where elements of coercion were at play. To do otherwise would risk treating women as hapless victims and would deny many women the means to survival, thus violating their human rights (Goldscheider).[6] By treating women as independent agents, capable of making rational decisions with respect to their own bodies, women are deemed to be able to overcome powerlessness and oppression. This viewpoint echoes less recent arguments made by feminist scholars and support-ers of legalised prostitution, such as Margaret Radin, who believe that women might understandably prefer to sell their sexual services given the conditions of poverty in which some too often live.

So-called "Third World" and anti-racism scholars also subscribe to views that coincide with those within the "pro-sex-worker" camp. In much the same way as scholars such as Angela Harris have criticized Catherine Mackinnon's work for employing a grand theory that fails to take into account the realities of non-white women, scholars such as Kamala Kempadoo, and Chandra Mohanty identify aspects of gender and race essentialism inherent to the position of some radical feminist scholars writing on trafficking and prostitution issues. Mohanty criticizes western feminists for positioning non-western women in their work as "religious (read 'not progressive'), family-oriented (read 'traditional'), legal minors (read 'they-are-still-not-conscious-of-their-rights'), illiterate (read 'ignorant'), [and] domestic (read 'backward')" (18). In this way, non-western women are perceived as being faithful to "traditions" of female subservience, and as victims incapable of making decisions as to whether to work in the sex industry (Doezema). Kempadoo elaborates on this view noting that certain feminists, "in true colonial fashion" apply a particular definition to sex itself which is not necessarily shared by women the world over:

> Subaltern understandings and lived realities of sexuality and sexual-economic relations, such as found in various African or Caribbean countries for example, where one can speak of a continuum of sexual relations from monogamy to multiple sexual partners and where sex may be considered as a valuable asset for a woman to trade with, are ignored in favor of specific western ideologies and moralities regarding sexual relations. (12)

By focusing on sex work in particular, and arguing that migration for prostitution whether forced or "voluntary" is a human rights violation, some feminists thereby deny the voice and experience of non-western women who may not share the same view.

Southern women themselves have criticized those who view prostitutes or migrant sex workers as helpless victims who can only be "rescued" through the support of their western sisters (see Kotiswaran).[7] One cannot, however, identify one distinct Southern voice with respect to these issues. In contrast to those who advocate reforms that highlight the agency of sex workers, a voluntary Indian organization called Prerana, for example, works to abolish all commercial sexual exploitation, and believes that women, at least those from India, cannot consent to work in the sex trade. Prerana's executive secretary argues that "where gender-based, class-based, and caste-based inequalities conspire against women and children, it is inhuman and exploitative to state that girls and women join and continue in this 'profession' out of their own 'free will'" (Patkar).

Scholars of international law have also focused on issues of cultural relativism in relation to trafficking and prostitution. Di Otto's criticisms of earlier UN trafficking instruments such as the *Convention for the Suppression of the Traffic in Persons*, rest on the fact that measures contained within them, such as prohibitions against consensual prostitution, limit women's opportunities to achieve economic justice and equal rights. She notes that women are often constructed in such documents, "in procreative and heterosexual terms as mother and wife…" based on western ideas that are upheld as international feminist goals and strategies, but that reflect an exclusion of identities (Otto). Finally, sex workers themselves are also held to have influenced the work of those who condemn trafficking only where coercion is involved (Kempadoo 14). As Jo Doezema notes, however, while the GAATW's view of trafficking has promoted significant legal advances for those "forced" into prostitution, women who choose sex work are still marginalized by a moralistic approach that reinforces the innocent victim / bad woman dichotomy. According to Doezema, the "whore" who decides to do sex work is still deemed to deserve the treatment she receives when the issues are framed in such a way (cited in Kempadoo 14).

Given the UN's adoption of a definition that will not allow traffickers to use consent as a defence against prosecution, the question posed at the outset of this essay has effectively been answered in the negative. Not only do the elements of coercion, deception and force that are the focus of this definition, vitiate any free and informed consent, but the provision explicitly states that consent to being trafficked is considered irrelevant. Despite this development, however, the prostitution/sex work aspect to this debate appears to be alive and well. A woman may not be able to consent to trafficking, but it is still arguable whether she can consent to prostitution or sex work, and by extension, consent to migrate for work in the sex industry.

The debate today

Both sides to the trafficking for sexual services debate still actively pursue their respective stances on the prostitution issue, focusing at the moment on domestic governmental implementation of the Trafficking Protocol. Significantly, delegates attending the UN negotiations agreed to leave the key phrase "exploitation of prostitution of others or other forms of sexual exploitation" undefined while clarifying the omission in a note further along in the text. The *travaux préparatoires* thus indicate that this phrase was not defined so as not to prejudice the way in which States Parties choose to address prostitution within their respective domestic laws (Crime Prevention and Criminal Justice; see also, Blackwell). GAATW's comments with respect to the final definition chosen reflect satisfaction that states are not required to treat all adult participation in prostitution as trafficking (2). In their view, the international community has acknowledged that while one may not agree to being trafficked, consenting to the provision of sexual services is no longer necessarily seen within a context of victimisation.

The CATW's view of the post-UN negotiations on the other hand, is cautious but equally laudatory of the results achieved. According to Janice Raymond, the group's Co-Executive Director, the CATW and its proponents won a key international battle over the definition of trafficking. Nevertheless, she believes that some governments and NGOs are currently undermining this achievement, by "only emphasising the provisions of the Protocol that suit them and ... [by] focus[ing] only on forced trafficking" (7). In her view, trafficking and prostitution are intrinsically linked and should not be dealt with as two separate issues within domestic legislation just because some countries have legalized or regulated prostitution. On the contrary, she contends that prostitution exploits women in the same way as does trafficking for prostitution purposes. Governments, she believes, must therefore place prostitution on their legislative policy agendas and address it as a human rights violation (8).

Where does this leave the issue of trafficking for prostitution purposes? Scholars such as Kamala Kempadoo argue that many cases involving migration for work in the sex industry still fall within a grey area. She argues that there are extreme cases where women are held against their will and suffer serious human rights abuses, but that there are numerous cases that cannot be as clearly defined (Gardiner). A November 2000 study conducted on behalf of Status of Women Canada confirms such a view. In an extensive report on migrant sex workers from Eastern Europe, scholars from the University of Toronto found that only half of the migrant sex workers they interviewed could be considered to have been trafficked. Nine out of 18 women were brought to Canada either under totally false pretences, or knew they were destined for the sex trade, but were not aware of the coercive work conditions they would encounter upon their arrival. The other nine women were classified by the researchers as non-trafficked sex workers, who ended up in the industry because they could not obtain gainful employment elsewhere (McDonald, Moore and Timoshkina).[8] Classification of migrant sex workers as either victims or agents has significant implications for the women involved. Nevertheless, regardless of whether or not the women's experiences fit neatly into the Trafficking Protocol's definition, reports with respect to Canada's response to these women and to trafficking in general, point to a large scale denial of women's basic human rights.

Canada's response to trafficking and "trafficked" women

Canada's criminal justice system faces significant challenges in combating trafficking and in providing services to victims of this offence. It is well known that enforcement of international treaties and conventions can only be effective if countries enact the domestic legislation required to implement the international standards, and devote the financial resources required to achieve these aims. Canada's treatment of traffickers and victims of trafficking in past years has not been deemed effective or respectful of the rights of victims. Police raids of massage parlours in Toronto between 1998 and 2000, which involved the arrest of several women from abroad (primarily Thai and Malaysian) on prostitution-related charges, were heavily criticised for treating the women involved as criminals instead of as victims of trafficking (Blackell). Canadian law enforcement officials had publicly announced that the raids were conducted to "rescue" Asian women from "traffickers," yet despite this rhetoric, the women were treated as criminals and illegal migrants, and were given little if any assistance from government authorities (The Toronto Network Against Trafficking in Women). The sentences meted out to those responsible were based on existing criminal code provisions for procuring sex workers[9] or operating a common bawdy house.[10] These were also criticized as lenient and ineffective since fines of $15,000 represented a pittance in comparison to the amount of money generated from a few trafficked women in one day (McClelland).

Despite having signed the UN *Convention Against Transnational Organized Crime* as well as the Trafficking and Smuggling Protocols on December 14, 2000 (Blackell), the vulnerability of trafficked and of migrant sexual workers in Canada appears to have not been lessened to any significant extent. The *Immigration and Refugee Protection Act*, which was passed by the government of Canada on November 1, 2001 includes fines of up to $1 million and the possibility of life imprisonment for those convicted of trafficking.[11] It remains to be seen, however, whether prosecutors will be successful in attaining such penalties, given the necessity of having victims testify at trial against their traffickers. An October 2001 British Columbia case involving the trafficking of women for sexual services indicates that much remains to be done to ensure convictions are attained against the perpetrators of trafficking as well as to ensure that protections are afforded to its victims. Police in that case infiltrated a prostitution ring in Vancouver involving 11 Malaysian women who fall under the Trafficking Protocol's definition of a victim. At least five of the women had been duped by traffickers prior to their departure for Canada, and all were later subjected to slavery-like abuses upon their arrival. Despite these facts, Canadian authorities deported the women back to Malaysia when none agreed to testify (McClelland).

Trafficking victims' reluctance to testify is not remarkable considering what they stand to lose. They, and often their families are vulnerable to further exploitation and victimization if their traffickers are charged with lesser offences and released. Furthermore, many victims may not understand their role or the implications of their involvement in the legal process and fear stigmatisation as well as potential legal action being taken against them personally. Despite existing initiatives for victim assistance and witness protection in Canada,[12] it is questionable whether they are sufficient to meet the needs of victims of trafficking, if women such as the Malaysians noted above choose not to testify against their abusers. Indeed, if Canada's budgetary planning is any indication, the billions earmarked for security purposes in the aftermath of the September 11th terrorism attacks in the United States, leave open to question whether serious and effective measures to protect victims of trafficking will be implemented as per Canada's commitments under the Trafficking Protocol.

Conclusion

The international community, through its adoption of the UN Trafficking

Protocol has clearly stated that it is not possible to consent to being trafficked. The same community, however, by allowing individual states to address prostitution according to their own policies and to the beliefs of their citizens, has recognized that adult participation in migrant sex work cannot necessarily be seen as trafficking. Although some women who migrate to Canada to work in the sex industry will therefore be subject to penalties and likely deportation if they arrive illegally or are found to be engaging in any prostitution-related offences, the recognition of voluntary prostitution represents a victory to those who believe that migration for work in the sex industry is a way of expanding women's life choices and of acknowledging their rights.

Canada's approach to migrant sex workers as well as to victims of trafficking has been ineffective in distinguishing between these two groups, and in ensuring that the rights of both of these group's members are not abused. An uneasy balance has been achieved where neither side appears to come out on top. Women who are legitimate trafficking victims are not always considered and treated as such, and migrant sex workers who are leading a fight to be recognized as labourers may resort to claiming victimhood, in order to avoid the risk of being prosecuted and deported. Is it questionnable whether decriminalising Canada's prostitution-related laws would remedy this situation. At least in some respects, women who migrate for the sex industry might be freed of violations to their rights, and actual victims of trafficking could potentially benefit from better focused and more effective measures to protect theirs.

Originally published in CWS/cf's *Spring/Summer 2003 issue, "Migration, Labour and Exploitation: Trafficking in Women and Girls" (Volume 22, Numbers 3/4): 48-54.*

[1]For a historical review of trafficking, see Derks.

[2]Although it is has been estimated that hundreds of thousands of people are trafficked all over the world every year, most countries have only limited statistics available on the scale of trafficking within their boundaries, and calculations used to arrive at these figures are not always clear(IOM).

[3]Note that a second instrument, the "Protocol Against Smuggling of Migrants by Land, Sea and Air" was also negotiated at the same time.

[4]As of June 20, 2003, there were 117 signatories and 100 ratifications to this instrument. For current ratifications, see the UN Office for Drug Control and Crime Prevention Online: <http://www.odccp.org/crime_cicp_signatures_trafficking.html>.

[5]Such as the Netherlands, Germany and Australia where prostitution has been legalized and where, according to the Network of Sex Work Projects, prostitution is seen as a legitimate form of labour.

[6]Goldscheider is quoting Ann Jordan, the Director of the Initiative Against Trafficking in Persons, International Human Rights Law Group, based in Washington, D.C.

[7]Although a S. J. D. candidate at Harvard Law School at the time she wrote

her article, Kotiswaran was previously involved in an Indian law student initiative to recognise prostitution as a form of labour. See also M. Pal *et al.* and Tandia. The contributors to Kempadoo and Doezema's collection highlight the personal narratives of various Third World prostitutes and sex workers rights groups. Common to all is the theme of being recognized as women who choose to be seen not as victims of patriarchy, but as actors who have made economic choices to supply a commodity for which there is global market—albeit a market which is due to the uneven distribution of wealth and discrimination against women in society.

[8]The authors note, however, that any change with respect to the legal status of these women—such as the expiry of a working visa, might be used by their employers to exploit them, thereby rendering them more clearly "victims" of trafficking.

[9]*Criminal Code*, R.S.C. 1985, s. 212. Re: Procurement, including transporting foreign women for the purposes of prostitution, living off of the avails of prostitution for the purpose of gain and exercising control over the movement of the individuals procured.

[10]*Criminal Code*, R.S.C. 1985, s. 210 (1) and (2) Re: Keeping a common bawdy house, and being found in any place used for the purpose of prostitution or the practice of acts of indecency.

[11]S.C. 2001, c. 27. Online: Citizenship and Immigration Canada <http://www.cic.gc.ca/english/irpa/key-ref.html>.

[12]Such programs are hailed by Blackell as being significant in comparison to most countries. Interestingly, in May 2006, the Canadian federal government announced that it had adopted new measures to assist victims of human trafficking. Immigration Officers can now issue temporary residents permits to victims of human trafficking for up to 120 days, and these victims are also eligible for temporary health care benefits (see Citizenship and Immigration Canada). It is too early to judge the success of such an initiative.

References

Blackell, G. "The Protocols on Trafficking in Persons and Smuggling in Migrant.s" Paper presented at The Changing Face of International Criminal Law Conference, Vancouver, Morris J. Wosk Centre for Dialogue, June 9, 2001. *The Changing Face of International Criminal Law: Selected Papers.* Ed. The International Centre for Criminal Law Reform and Criminal Justice Policy, 2002. Online: www.icclr.law.ubc.ca/publications.

Citizenship and Immigration Canada. "Assistance for Victims of Human Trafficking." News release, May 11, 2006. Online: www.cic.gc.ca/English/press/06/0602-e.html

Chuang, J. "Redirecting the Debate over Trafficking in Women: Definitions, Paradigms, and Contexts." *Harv. Hum. Rts. J.* 11 (1998):65-107.

Connor, J. Rapporteur, Council of Europe, "Report on Domestic Slavery," submitted to the Committee on Equal Opportunities for Women and Men (Doc. 9102, 17 May 2001). Online: http://stars.coe.fr/doc/doc01/ EDOC9102.htm. Date accessed: 23 November 2001.

Crime Prevention and Criminal Justice, *Report of the Ad Hoc Committee on the Elaboration of a Convention against Transnational Organized Crime.* 55th Sess., UN Doc. A/55/383/Add.1, 2000.

Derks, A. "Combatting Trafficking in South East Asia: A Review of Policy and Programme Responses." International Organization for Migration Research Series, 2000. Online: <http://www.iom.int/index2.htm> Date accessed: 17 November 2001.

Doezema, J. "Loose Women or Lost Women? The Re-emergence of the Myth of 'White Slavery' in Contemporary Discourses of 'Trafficking in Women'." *Gender Issues* 18 (1) (2000) 23-50.

Gardiner, S. "The Gray Area of Prostitution: Can it be an Opportunity or is it Always Exploitative?" *Newsday* (15 March 2001) Online: www.newsday.com/news/local/newyork/ny-smuggled-grayarea.story. Date accessed: 9 December 2001.

Global Alliance Against Traffic in Women. "Protocol to Prevent, Suppress and Punish Trafficking in Persons, Especially Women and Children, Supplementing the UN Convention Against Organized Crime." 2001. Online: www.inet.co.th/org/gaatw/SolidarityAction/HRSLetter. htm

Goldscheider, E. "Prostitutes work—but do they consent?" *The Boston Globe* January 2, 2000. Online: www.catwinternational.org/bgcon.htm. Date accessed: 9 December 2001.

Harris, A.. "Race and Essentialism in Legal Theory." *Women, Law and Social Change: Core Readings and Current Issues,* 3d ed. Ed. T. B. Dawson. Toronto: Captus Press, 1998. 322-332.

International Organization for Migration (IOM). "New IOM Figures on the Global Scale of Trafficking." *Trafficking in Migrants Quarterly Bulletin* 23 (April 2001): 1-6.

Kelly, L. "Marriage for Sale: The Mail-Order Bride Industry and the Changing Value of Marriage" *Journal of Gender Race and Justice* 5 (2001): 175-195.

Kempadoo, K. "Introduction: Globalizing Sex Workers' Rights." Eds. K. Kempadoo and J. Doezema. *Global Sex Workers: Rights Resistance and Redefinition.* New York: Routledge, 1998. 1-28.

Kempadoo, K. and J. Doezema, Eds. *Global Sex Workers: Rights Resistance and Redefinition.* New York: Routledge, 1998.

Kotiswaran, P. "Preparing for Civil Disobedience: Indian Sex Workers and the Law." *B.C. Third World Law Journal* 1621 (2001): 161-242.

Leidholdt, D. "Position Paper for the Coalition Against Trafficking in Women." Special Seminar on Trafficking, Prostitution and the Global Sex Industry, United Nations Working Group on Contemporary Forms of Slavery, Geneva Switzerland, June 21, 1999. Online: www.catwinternational.org/ posit1.htm. Date accessed: 9 December 2001.

MacKinnon, C. "Feminism, Marxism, Method and the State: An Agenda for

Theory." *Women, Law and Social Change: Core Readings and Current Issues*, 3d ed. Ed. T. B. Dawson. Toronto: Captus Press, 1998. 317-319.

McClelland, S. "Inside the Sex Trade." *Maclean's* December 3, 2001: 20, 6pp.

McDonald, L., B. Moore and N. Timoshkina. *Migrant Sex Workers from Eastern Europe and the Former Soviet Union: The Canadian Case* Ottawa: Status of Women Canada, 2000.

Mohanty, C. "Under Western Eyes: Feminist Scholarship and Colonial Discourses." *Fem. Rev.* 30 (1988): 61-88.

Network of Sex Work Projects. "Commentary on the Draft Protocol to Combat International Trafficking in Women and Children." 1999. Online: <http://www.walnet.org/csis/groups/nswp/untoc-comment.html> (Date accessed 10 December 2001).

Otto, D. "A Post-Beijing Reflection on the Limitations and Potential of Human Rights Discourse for Women." *Women and International Human Rights Law*, Vol. 1. Eds. K. D. Askin and D.M. Koenig. Ardsley, NY: Transnational Publishers, 1999.

M. Pal *et al.* "The Wind of Change is Whispering at Your Door: The Mahila Samanwaya Committee." Eds. K. Kempadoo and J. Doezema. *Global Sex Workers: Rights Resistance and Redefinition.* New York: Routledge, 1998. 200-203.

Patkar, P. "Consolidating Protection against Ever-escalating Violation: The Case of Prerana's Intervention for Protection of Rights of Victims of Commercial Sexual Exploitation in India." *Women in the Criminal Justice System: International Examples & National Responses.* Eds. N. Ollus and S. Nevala. (Proceedings of the Workshop held at the Tenth United Nations Congress on the Prevention of Crime and the Treatment of Offenders, Vienna, Austria, 10-17 April 2001). Helsinki: HEUNI, 2001.

Protocol to Prevent, Suppress and Punish Trafficking in Persons, Especially Women and Children, supplementing the United Nations Convention Against Transnational Organized Crime. 2000. Online: www.odccp.org/crime_cicp_convention.html#final.

Radin, M. "Market-Inalienability." *Harvard Law Review* 100 (8) (1987): 1849-1937.

Raymond, J. "Guide to the New UN Trafficking Protocol." 2001. Online: www.catwinternational.org/transcr.htm. Date accessed: 9 December 2001.

Tandia, O. "Prostitution in Senegal." Eds. K. Kempadoo and J. Doezema. *Global Sex Workers: Rights Resistance and Redefinition.* New York: Routledge, 1998. 240-245.

Tiefenbrun, S. "Sex Sells But Drugs Don't Talk: Trafficking of Women Sex Workers." *Thomas Jefferson Law Review* 11 (2001): 199-226.

The Toronto Network Against Trafficking in Women. *Trafficking in Women, Including Thai Migrant Sex Workers, in Canada.* Ottawa: Status of Women Canada, 2001.

Women and Risk

Aboriginal Women, Colonialism, and Correctional Practice

Patricia Monture ⟶

I often feel that the stories I have to tell begin outside of the words and ideas that have been placed on pages. There is no where that this is more true than when the issue is the contact and experience that Aboriginal people, and especially Aboriginal women, have with the Canadian criminal justice system. Given the thousands of pages of government reports which examine the issue of Aboriginal overrepresentation in he Canadian criminal justice system, this may come as a great surprise to many people. However, the truth remains that much of what I have read about Aboriginal people and Canadian criminal justice is not what I have experienced and been taught were the central issues.

The most recent report on Aboriginal people and the Canadian justice system, is the *Report of the Royal Commission on Aboriginal Peoples*. The justice materials were compiled in a separate report, titled *Bridging the Cultural Divide*,[1] released in 1996 just prior to the Commissioner's six-volume final report. This most recent report is an excellent example of the gap that still exists between Aboriginal understandings of our justice struggles and the words that have been written on the page. It is also essential to note that this report will not be helpful in examining the questions which come to the fore regarding Aboriginal women and the administration of their prison sentences including the issues of risk assessment, risk management, and security classification.[2] The *Report*, in fact, is silent on how to remedy the negative experiences of Aboriginal women in prison (see Monture-Angus 1999). This is troubling.

It is important to note the nature and scope of the discussion in the RCAP report. Their first justice recommendation states:

> Federal, provincial and territorial governments recognize the right of Aboriginal nations to establish and administer their own systems of justice pursuant to their inherent right of self-government, including the power to make laws, within the Aboriginal nation's territory. (RCAP 1996a, 312)

Although I do not disagree in principle with this statement, it is not very realistic in practical terms. As a result of the colonial legacy of Canada, Aboriginal nations are not represented as nations in the way our political organizations have been structured. Rather, these Aboriginal nations are organized around the classifications which arise out of the *Indian Act* regime either because of registration as an "Indian" or the lack of such a legal recognition. This must be seen as a demonstration of the degree to which colonial policy and practice has fragmented and re-structured Aboriginal governing structures. For example, the Assembly of First Nations is an organization which represents *Indian Act* Chiefs while the Congress of Aboriginal People represents those who are not entitled to be registered or maintain off-reserve residency which disentitles them to many of the benefits of the *Indian Act*. If the power to have justice relationships is not maintained at the community level but at the nation level, as the Royal Commission on Aboriginal Peoples (RCAP) endorses, then the power for Aboriginal persons to exercise their jurisdiction in justice matters is seriously compromised if not fully limited. Although this first recommendation is an eloquent statement of principle, it means very little in practical terms as our nations no longer remain significantly organized in this political way. Therefore, celebrating the wisdom of the Royal Commission which saw fit to acknowledge the self-governing power of Aboriginal nations must be cautiously undertaken. The impact of colonialism was discounted by the Commission, if not fully ignored, and as a result no real opportunity exists to transform the recommendations from mere words into reality.

It is equally important to note that the justice recommendations of the Royal Commission did not significantly focus on the circumstances and experiences of Aboriginal people in prison. The rate at which Aboriginal women are overrepresented in Canadian institutions of incarceration is higher than the rate of overrepresentation for Aboriginal men if national figures are used as the base.[3] So if the silence of the Royal Commission on prison circumstances is noted, the double silence regarding the situation of Aboriginal women in prison is of greater consequence as their experiences are often based on the denial of their race/culture and concurrently their gender.[4] Granted, I do believe that it is essential that we look to the future when reclaiming Aboriginal justice practices. I do not agree that this task can be allowed to force us to sacrifice the current generation housed in federal, provincial, and youth institutions of confinement for the mere hope that future generations will not have to face the imposition of Canadian criminal justice law and practices. Hope after all guarantees nothing.

Turning to the six-volume final *Report of the Royal Commission on Aboriginal Peoples* to understand more about the manner in which the Commissioners included Aboriginal women in their work, identifies further problem areas. The Commission believes that we, as women, hold "perspectives"[5] and neatly identifies two issues which are of (by implication) special concern *only* to Aboriginal women.[6] This is an insufficient way to characterize the position of Aboriginal women in our nations. These two issues are violence and loss of status under former section 12(1)(b).[7] Although I do believe that these are important issues, they do not reflect the full diversity of concerns that

Aboriginal women possess. They do not reflect my "perspective" on being an Aboriginal (more accurately, Mohawk) woman. Some deconstruction of these ideas and the way they limit my race/culture-based knowledge of gender is necessary.

First, section 12(1)(b) is just one small example of the way our government has been interfered with by the imposition of Canadian ways of and ideas about governing. This includes the way that women's roles were diminished in the government forms that were brought to the Aboriginal territories now known as Canada. This is not a correct construction of the gender-balanced roles in Aboriginal societies. Second, to suggest that the place of Aboriginal women is a "perspective" is to do serious harm to the governing structure of Aboriginal nations that would be described as matrilineal. Gender in these governments is a fundamental part of the way that government responsibilities are distributed.[8]

Both the fact that Aboriginal governments have been interfered with and the specific manner that this interference was gender-based is important to understanding the justice obstacles Aboriginal people now face. Logically then, it can be easily surmised that as women were and *are* central to the structure of Aboriginal governments, women also played a significant role and possessed authority in matters of (criminal) justice. I have heard from Aboriginal people all over the continent: "Grandmother made the rules and Grandfather enforced them." If this is the case, then Aboriginal women had (and still have) a fundamental responsibility with and to justice relations in our communities. The imposition of foreign forms and relations of governance must be seen to have significantly interfered with Aboriginal justice traditions. This does not mean that traditions have been destroyed or that they no longer exist. It simply means that colonialism has had, and continues to have, a negative impact on the ability of Aboriginal people to maintain peaceful and orderly communities.

Since the Task Force on Federally Sentenced Women in 1990, the direction that First Nation[9] communities have taken with justice matters is also of importance to this discussion. The Task Force recommended the building of a Healing Lodge for Aboriginal women. This recommendation was realized with the opening of Okimaw Ochi Healing Lodge at the Nekaneet First Nation in 1995. Since then at least two more Lodges[10] have been opened in the prairie provinces with negotiations occurring in other areas of the country as well.[11] Little research[12] has been completed on the introduction of these new institutions and they are institutions no matter how much Aboriginal culture and tradition inspires their contour, shape, and form. This direction demonstrates the degree to which Aboriginal communities have been willing to embrace conventional correctional practice.

The government of the Nekaneet First Nation understood that the Healing Lodge was a part of the legal and bureaucratic structure of the Canadian prison system. In their negotiations, the community addressed this concern by recognizing that the building of the Lodge was only a first step and *not* a final step. Their vision was that as time passed the Lodge would move more and more toward community control and administration. This was also the vision of the Aboriginal women who participated in the Task Force. Anecdotal evidence clearly suggests that this is not what has happened. Rather, as time passes, the philosophical foundation of the Lodge has shifted toward the Canadian correctional mentality. Chief Larry Oakes of the Nekaneet First Nation had at least one meeting with the Commission of Corrections in the fall of 1998 to discuss the community vision and further community involvement. There are no negotiations underway based on this community vision (Oakes) and, in my view, this is unacceptable.

As a result of the willingness of some prairie (primarily Saskatchewan and Alberta) First Nations to embrace at least as a starting point, conventional correctional practice, determining risk predictors is especially important to have from a First Nations stand point. A "stand point" is different from a "perspective." The women's facility is designated as a medium-security facility. The federal male institution at Hobemma is a minimum-security facility. This is despite the fact that it has been known for some time that Aboriginal men and women are overrepresented within the maximum-security classification. This is very frustrating.

As a member of the Task Force on Federally Sentenced Women, I believe that my contributions and values have been profoundly disrespected by the Correctional Service of Canada.[13] These "Aboriginal" institutions are based on the borrowed notion of security classification. Therefore, work on developing better risk scales undertaken by Corrections Canada has a direct, but generally invisible, impact on the institutions that were envisioned by First Nations. Unfortunately, this impact has not been expressed in any of the literature that I have seen on the development of risk predictors or on the new Aboriginal institutions. The isolation in which Aboriginal initiatives are developed in this federal bureaucracy has a profoundly negative impact on the amount of Aboriginal visioning that is possible. As many First Nations communities do not have access to the professionalization of justice relationships, I worry that these consequences are not necessarily always visible. Our dreams are limited by correctional expectations that we will accept certain ideas such as risk management and risk prediction scales. This must be seen for what it is. It is a clear form of systemic discrimination.

An idea such as risk management is one that is contrary to how I was raised as an Aboriginal person to think about relationships. As I have noted in other writings, relationships are the central construct in "Indian" law as I understand it (see "Roles and Responsibilities" in Monture-Angus 1996a). People (or any "thing" with spirit) were not intended to be managed but rather respected. The conclusion is that one of the foundational ideas of current correctional philosophy is, in my opinion, incompatible with Aboriginal cultures, law, and tradition. This incompatibility is a greater obstacle than simple theories of cultural conflict. This opinion is a substantive criticism that is much larger than questioning the cultural relevance of programming within correctional institutions which has been a significant preoccupation in the many justice reports that address Aboriginal experiences and concerns.

This discussion has now brought me to the place where I can make some comments about the idea popular among prison administrators regarding their ability to determine risk. These risk scales are all individualized instruments. Applying these instruments to Aboriginal people (male or female) is a significant and central problem. The individualizing of risk absolutely fails to take into account the impact of colonial oppression on the lives of Aboriginal men and women. Equally, colonial oppression has not only had a devastating impact on individuals but concurrently on our communities and nations (see Monture-Angus 1996b). This impact cannot be artificially pulled apart as the impact on the individual and the impact on the community are interconnected.

For example, in the *Report of the Aboriginal Justice Inquiry of Manitoba*, it is noted that Aboriginal "women move to urban centres to escape family or community problems. Men on the other hand, cite employment as the reason for moving" (485). Once in the city, many Aboriginal women face issues that they had not expected from systemic and overt to subtle forms of racism as well as lack of opportunities. The Manitoba Justice Inquiry notes that "what they were forced to run to is often as bad as what they had to run from" (485). And often, what they experience in the city (from shoplifting to prostitution, drug abuse to violence) as a result of poverty and racism, leads them into contact with the criminal justice system. Yet, a criminal court is not interested in hearing about this long trail of individualized and systemic colonialism which leads to conflict with the law. Courts are only interested in whether you committed a wrong act with a guilty mind. This is a clear example of how the individualized nature of law obscures systemic and structural factors. This is a problem that exists within the court process but also in other justice decision-making practices and bodies such as security classification, risk assessment, penitentiary placement, parole, and so on.

Examination of the risk prediction scales identifies many common considerations taken into account to predict risk. For example,

[t]he Case Needs Identification and Analysis protocol identifies seven need dimensions, including *employment, marital/family, associates, substance abuse, community functioning, personal/emotional and attitudes*. (Motiuk 19; emphasis added)

Several of these dimensions are particularly problematic for Aboriginal "offenders." Aboriginal people do not belong to communities that are functional and healthy (and colonialism is significantly responsible for this fact). Therefore, constructing a "community functioning" category ensures that Aboriginal people will not have access to scoring well in this category. This is not a factor for which individuals can be held solely accountable. Rather than measuring risk this dimension merely affirms that Aboriginal persons have been negatively impacted by colonialism. The same kind of assessment can be put forward for the dimensions of "marital/family" and "associates" as the incidence of individuals with criminal records is greater in Aboriginal communities. It has been frequently noted that the issue of substance abuse in Aboriginal communities is a symptom[14] of a much larger problem. Therefore, this simple analysis demonstrates that scoring higher on these categories is predetermined for Aboriginal prisoners because of the very structure of the instruments. What is being measured is not "risk" but one's experiences as part of an oppressed group.

The work that assesses the validity of these risk prediction scales is also a problem because it does not do race (Aboriginal) and gender (female) as categories that are inclusive (see Motiuk; Blanchette; Bonta; and Collin). The studies tend to examine the validity of these scales for Aboriginal people but not for Aboriginal women. Despite this fact, prison administrators and senior bureaucrats remain committed to applying these "tests" and concepts to the structure of individual Aboriginal women's prison sentences as well as to the manner in which the prisons in which Aboriginal women serve their sentence are structured. In my opinion, this is a violation of the *Canadian Charter of Rights and Freedoms*' section 15 equality provisions. It also strains the common sense interpretation of section 28 of the *Corrections and Conditional Release Act* which provides that persons confined in a penitentiary shall be confined in the least restrictive environment. If risk prediction scales are not valid for Aboriginal women (and I have not seen convincing documentation that they are), then security decisions based on these scales cannot be reasonably applied to Aboriginal women.

Enough has been said and written about the devastating effects of the Canadian criminal justice system on both Aboriginal citizens and our nations. Despite this fact, little has been accomplished to do more than accommodate Aboriginal persons within the mainstream system. There has been no systemic change of Canadian justice institutions. As we approach the tenth anniversary of the report of the Task Force on Federally Sentenced Women, perhaps it is time to revisit the work of the last decade and see how true it has remained to the original vision of the women who were asked to participate in this project. This project should take place within some formal structure. I am quite confident that I am not the only former Task Force participant who is bitterly disappointed.

This paper was originally presented at the Inter-disciplinary Workshop on Risk Assessment, Risk Management, and Classification organized by Professors Kelly Hannah Moffat (Brock University) and Margaret Shaw (Concordia University) held in Toronto, Ontario on May 21–23, 1999. The support of Status of Women Canada is gratefully acknowledged.

The author would like to acknowledge the guidance of the late Elder, Dr. Art Solomon and the many Aboriginal women who have served federal sentences who have demonstrated their patience and understanding when teaching her. Any errors are the author's and not the teachers'.

Originally published in CWS/cf's Spring/Summer 1999 issue, "Women and Justice" (Volume 19, Numbers 1/2): 24-29.

[1]It is my understanding that the justice materials were released early as a way of noting the seriousness with which the Commissioners saw this topic.

[2]Pages 139–147 of *Bridging the Cultural Divide* discusses the experiences of Aboriginal women in prison. This discussion does not move beyond the descriptive and no recommendations made. The Commissioners did attend a special hearing at the Kingston Prison for Women, and the women shared their stories (often very painful stories) with them. The end result is that the Commission "borrowed" the pain of Aboriginal women prisoners and gave nothing beyond a few pages of descriptive discussion back to the women. This fails to meet the standards of responsibility that I was raised with as a Mohawk woman. If you take from a person, you are obligated to give back at least what you took. The irony that this is what occurred in a Commission that was meant to be Aboriginal-specific and Aboriginal-focused has not escaped me.

[3]The national figures do disguise some of the circumstances that Aboriginal men who are incarcerated experience. Although the national rate of overrepresentation is a figure lower than 20 per cent (depending who counts and how the counting is being done) for Aboriginal men, this figure hides the fact that Aboriginal men make up approximately 80 per cent of the population at Saskatchewan Penitentiary.

[4]My point is not numerical and I realize that there are far fewer women incarcerated in Canadian prisons than men.

[5]The section on Aboriginal women is titled, "Women's Perspectives" and appears as Chapter 2 of the volume titled, "Perspectives and Realities." The chapter devoted to women begins on page 7 and the discussion ends on page 96 (totaling 90 pages). Not including introductions and conclusion, the discussion appears under the headings: "Historical Position and Role of Aboriginal Women: A Brief Overview" (3.5 pages); "Reversing a Pattern of Exclusion—Women's Priorities for Change" (less than a page); "Aboriginal Women and Indian Policy: Evolution and Impact" (31 pages); "Health and Social Services: A Priority on Healing" (9.5 pages); "The Need for Places of Refuge" (6.5 pages); "The Rise of Aboriginal Women's Organizations" (3 pages); "the Need for Fairness and Accountability" (12 pages); and, "The Family" (12 pages). The longest discussion deals with issues of status and membership under the *Indian Act*. The relationship between violence in communities and the overrepresentation of Aboriginal women in corrections institutions is not made.

[6]The way the Commission has constructed gender is highly problematic. Violence against women is not a women's problem. It is a community problem. Further, the section on "family" appears in the women's section. Are men no

longer part of our families with particular gender-based responsibilities? [7]This section of the *Indian Act* stripped Indian women of their status if they "married out." The same prohibition was not extended to women who "married in." I am not familiar with any research which examines if there is a relationship between being stripped of your status and contact with the criminal justice system. The idea that such research might yield interesting results occurs because many Indian women who go to the city do not have and have not had access to educational opportunities or employment. This is another example of the gaps that exist in the written record.
[8]See, for example, *The Report of the Aboriginal Justice Inquiry of Manitoba*, Volume 1, pages 475–477.
[9]The change of language from Aboriginal to First Nations is intentional. It indicates that my comments focus on the experiences of "Indians" to the exclusion of Metis and Inuit peoples.
[10]The Prince Albert Grand Council operates a facility on the Wahpeton (Dakota) First Nation near the city of Prince Albert, Saskatchewan. This facility holds only male offenders primarily serving provincial sentences with five federal beds. The Pe'Sakastew Centre is located on the Hobemma (Cree) First Nation in Alberta. It is a federal minimum security facility.
[11]This is one of the ways that First Nations have chosen to participate in reclaiming traditional justice practices.
[12]The most significant research was completed by Connie Braun (Cree) in her M.A. thesis (1998). In this work she documents the experiences of Aboriginal men at the Hobemma facility against their experiences of conventional prisons.
[13]Please see Chapter 2 of the Task Force Report, *Creating Choices*, for a discussion of the hesitations the Aboriginal women had with regard to participating in the Task Force. I do understand that the degree to which I feel violated in this process arises out of my Aboriginal values and teachings about respect.
[14]Further research, research that is conducted with the primary involvement (meaning control) of Aboriginal persons (including women) is needed in this area.

References

Aboriginal Justice Inquiry of Manitoba. *Report of the Aboriginal Justice Inquiry of Manitoba*. Winnipeg: Queen's Printer, 1991.

Blanchette, Kelly. "Classifying Female Offenders for Correctional Interventions." *Forum (on Corrections Research)* 9 (1) (January 1997): 36–41.

Bonta, James. "Do We Need Theory for Offender Risk Assessment?" *Forum (on Corrections Research)* 9 (1) (January 1997): 42–45.

Braun, Connie. "Colonization, Destruction, and Renewal: Stories from Aboriginal Men at the Pe'Sakastew Centre." M.A. Thesis. University of Saskatchewan, 1998.

Collin, Jeannette. "Legal Aspects of Inmates's Security Classification." *Forum (on Corrections Research)* 9 (1) (January 1997): 55–57.

Monture-Angus, Patricia. "The Justice *Report of the Royal Commission on Aboriginal Peoples*: Breaking with the Past?" Pres. at "Building the Momentum: A Conference on Implementing the Recommendations of the Royal Commission on Aboriginal Peoples." Osgoode Hall, Toronto, Ontario. 22–24 April 1999. Online. Internet. Available at www.indigenousbar.ca.

Monture-Angus, Patricia. *Thunder in My Soul: A Mohawk Woman Speaks.* Halifax: Fernwood Books, 1996a.

Monture-Angus, Patricia. "Lessons in Decolonization: Aboriginal Over-Representation in Canadian Criminal Justice." *Visions of the Heart.* Eds. David Long and Ovide Dickason. Toronto: Harcourt Brace, 1996b.

Motiuk, Larry. "Classification for Correctional Programminmg: The Offender Intake Assessment (OIA) Process." *Forum (on Corrections Research)* 9 (1) (January 1997): 18–22.

Oakes, Chief Larry. Personal interview. 27 April 1999.

Royal Commission on Aboriginal Peoples (RCAP). *Bridging the Cultural Divide.* Ottawa: Supply and Services, 1996a.

Royal Commission on Aboriginal Peoples (RCAP). *Report of the Royal Commission on Aboriginal Peoples.* Ottawa: Supply and Services, 1996b.

Same-Sex Rights for Lesbian Mothers

Child Custody and Adoption

Jennifer L. Schulenberg

Family life as an individual experience and as a social institution is in transition. In highly industrialized countries, such as Canada, families have been undergoing changes especially since the early 1970s. Some of these changes include increased birth rates to unmarried women, higher rates of divorce and remarriage, decreased fertility, and altered household composition (see Eichler). The predominant gender role pattern during the 1960s was that women would drop out of the labour market either upon marriage or upon giving birth to their first child. In contemporary times, the pattern is that women stay within the labour force throughout marriage and motherhood. This creates a new division of labour and necessitates a new perspective of the meaning of gender within couple relationships. For example, a heterosexual couple can think about having a child in the knowledge that society, in most cases, is fully supportive of their desire to be parents. This holds true except for "those couples whose sexuality is marked as deviant. [They] obtain little recognition of, or protection of their desire to become or *remain* parents" (Zicklin 56). The manner in which the term parental "fitness," "family," and "the best interests of the child" are conceptualized in the justice system greatly affects the outcome of custody cases involving a homosexual parent.

In Canada, judges have discretionary leeway in determining what the best interests of a child are in custody disputes. It can be argued that lesbian mothers are facing formidable obstacles. "A lesbian mother's likelihood for success is no more than 50 per cent compared to the standard maternal custody award of 90 per cent" (Causey and Duran-Aydintug 57). With approximately 250,000 lesbian parents in Canada this has a profound effect on the children of our nation (Epstein). Not all of the cases that appear before the courts are reported in legal journals. Child custody disputes in which the mother is a lesbian seldom appear in case law reports. As Arnup notes, it is commonly seen in cases with homosexuality or lesbianism being a factor "to seal the records ostensibly to protect the privacy of the individuals involved" (1995, 341). This practice presents a problem as the cases that *are* reported and made accessible to judges and lawyers for their use in future cases are thereby given an importance beyond their individual significance.

Historical evolution of family law

Many of our laws, especially since the 1930s, relied on legal realism not in the sense of a philosophical theory, but as an attitude. It calls for an instrumental utilitarian use of law. Law is seen as a social tool. Legal realism attempts to create laws that are for the greatest good for the majority of people. Historically, family law has been the least amenable to legal realism and has been the most preoccupied with conscious creation of the symbolism of *normal* family life (Rosen).

Until the nineteenth century, English common law gave the father virtually unlimited rights to the custody of his minor, legitimate children. "Custody law considered children as pieces of property in which their father had a vested interest rather than as individuals whose welfare and interests were legitimate legal issues" (Arnup 1988, 246). In the middle of the nineteenth century, the process of industrialization created the separation of the home from the workplace. The roles of women and men became sharply differentiated. Men were expected to become the breadwinners of the family unit and the women were to be the wives and mothers. "The reduction in the autocratic powers of the father over his children was not so much a reflection of the improved status of women as a recognition of the social value of adequate mothering" (Arnup 1988: 246).

"The cult of motherhood" (Mason and Quirk 220) developed during this time. It focused on the superior moral and nurturing characteristics of women that naturally suited them for the rearing of children. In the twentieth century, power over who has the children shifted from individuals to legislation. In other words, "real power shifted to family court judges who had the authority to determine whether a mother *deserved* to have custody of her children" (Arnup 1989, 24). The problem arises in what is the criterion that judges a mother's worthiness to have her children? The problem "is not motherhood in isolation that is revered by the courts, but mother hood within a familial structure" (Arnup 1989, 25). Societal attitudes, prevalent norms and how the family is defined influences the decision on whether the familial structure is adequate or appropriate for the granting of custody. This distinction can have disastrous consequences for lesbians seeking custody of their children.

Conceptions of the family

The definition of the family is ambiguous in the legal, social, and linguistic conceptualizations used. It is now recognized among researchers and policy makers that a monolithic definition[1] of the family is no longer adequate to reflect the complex reality that exists today. For example, if we define the nuclear family "as a working husband, housekeeping wife, and two children, and ask how many Americans actually still live in this type of family, that answer is seven per cent of the total United States population" (Ricketts and Achtenberg 83). According to the Vanier Institute, "we need a notion of family that accurately reflects the real experiences of individuals and the intimate relationships that they establish and attempt to sustain over time" (5). Narrow definitions, built on legally verifiable relationships (i.e. marriage), provide only a partial representation of the family. These descriptions tend to be judgmental by indicating that a family consists of a husband and a wife living in a neolocal residence, more commonly refered to as the nuclear family. This conjugal family has become *the family* which does not merely represent an ideal type but an overarching conceptualization where this ideal is feasible for the majority of the population. Within this given environment where the family is defined as an ideal type, "other family living arrangements are considered to be somehow deficient in familial content, or more radically, not familial at all" (Bould 133).

The variability of the treatment of the "the family" has implications in the area of family law. "It is the state, both the legislatures and the courts, and not individuals, which decides who is *in* and who is *out* of the *family*" (Findley 133). Notions of "fit parents," such as those deemed to provide a stable home environment, are grounded in societally-accepted definitions of the family. Yet, the conventional notion of heterosexual marriage as the legal foundation and the building block of our social fabric is weakening. Statistics indicate that "50 per cent of first marriages and 60 per cent of second marriages are likely to end in divorce" (Cherlin 32; Martin *et al.* 38). Homosexuals are living a lifestyle that is in defiance of societal norms and values concerning sexuality and maternity (Arnup 1995, 341). They are not seen as participating in a family structure that is based upon a recognizable legal union, marriage, or a co-habitation for the purpose of procreation.

If a lesbian mother living with another woman is not part of the accepted definition of the family, the issue of child custody becomes that much more complex. Katherine Arnup stipulates that, "to judges, the lesbian feminist in particular seems to pose a double threat. She represents a refusal to abide by traditional sex roles, as well as a rejection of heterosexual nuclear family life" (Arnup 1995, 341). Her argument is collaborated by Rachel Epstein:

> ... A lesbian mother who is prepared to accept the traditional values of society in creating a stable facsimile of a nuclear family, may, in the future, be permitted to retain custody of her children. In so far as she represents a fundamental and ongoing challenge to the structures of heterosexuality and the nuclear family, however, the existence of the lesbian mother must be denied. (112)

David Rosen, however, suggests a more cultural definition of the family that would enable alternative family structures, such as the ones of lesbian mothers, to be recognized in family law. He states that the family is "a group of people united by certain convictions or common affiliation or as a collective body of persons who live in one house under one head or management" (37–38). If this form of a definition of a stable home environment became part of legal statute, the rights of the co-parent[2] would be recognized.

Methodology

The data for this article came from interviews conducted with seven lesbian mothers. The interviews occurred between May and July of 1998 and took place in private settings in Toronto, Kitchener, Hamilton, and Guelph. The lesbian mother's ages ranged from 29 to approximately 55. Their children ranged in age from three to 26 years old. All of the respondents but one are the biological mothers of the children they are raising. The one respondent who was not the biological mother was the co-parent of a child biologically related to her partner that she had successfully legally adopted. Four of these women had adopted a child within their partnership. There are seven lesbian mothers that I interviewed. Of those seven, four of them had children with their lesbian partners through artificial insemination with an unknown donor. The other three lesbian mothers conceived their children while involved in a previous heterosexual union (be that marriage or common-law) prior to identifying themselves as lesbians. All the lesbian mothers interviewed had only one child. Out of the seven women only two were single at the time of interviewing. Their professions ranged from a lawyer, psychologist, public health nurse, and employees of lesbian/gay associations. Overall, the lesbian mothers that were interviewed are only representative of a small segment of the lesbian mother population. They were primarily white, middle-class lesbian feminists that had completed post-secondary education or further.

The analysis that follows seeks to highlight any patterns and themes that arose out of the interviews conducted. These women spoke as feminists, as lesbians, and as mothers. The themes which emerged from the data involve the importance of the education of the judiciary in lesbian custody cases, the awareness that motherhood has political significance, redefinition of motherhood as an experience and an institution in society, and the re-creation of the term family to include the patterns of lesbian biological mothers and co-parents.

Findings, analysis, and discussion

The court treatment of lesbian mothers has been motivated by three dominant fears. Firstly, there is the myth that the child(ren) will become homosexual. The available research on the psychosexual development of children raised by lesbian mothers uniformly demonstrates that these children are as psychologically healthy as those that are raised by a heterosexual mother. Dr. Richard Green[3] and the traditionalist, Dr. Benjamin Spock,[4] agree. Indeed, "there is no evidence that homosexual parents are more apt to raise homosexual children. Most homosexuals are children of conventionally heterosexual parents" (Gross 520). Another concern is the fear of inappropriate gender socialization. The role of parents as models of gender-related behaviour was initially thought to be important in social learning theory. This theory's premise is children that are exposed to role models of both sexes from an early age through the media, siblings, peers, and parents ensures proper gender identity development. Currently gender development is conceived as a process in which the child learns that he or she belongs to a category of male or female. Through exposure to cultural notions of what constitutes male and female behaviour and socialization with peers the child gradually develops a sense of gender identity and roles that are connected with that gender. Several studies that compared lesbian and heterosexual mothers and their children concluded, "that there is virtually no difference among the children with regard to gender identity, gender role behaviour, psychopathology or homosexual orientation" (Epstein 110–111; see also Gottman; Green *et al.*; Kirkpatrick *et al.*; Patterson 1992a, 1992b). Studies have shown that, "lesbian couples are more flexible in social roles, more egalitarian and less oriented toward traditional gender divisions of labour than are heterosexual couples" (Brophy 490). And, finally, there is the fear that the children will suffer embarrassment and/or teasing by their peers and the community as a whole because of the social stigma attached to the sexual identity of the mother (see Arnup 1988; Epstein; Ferris; Findley; Hall; Kaufman and Dundas; Sanders). These concerns were not supported by research findings which suggest that, "being homosexual is clearly compatible with effective parenting and is not a major issue in parents' relationships with their children" (Harris and Turner 130). A summary of the findings of 30 studies of the children of lesbian and gay parents was published in the October 1992 issue of the journal *Child Development* that were unanimous in their findings that the children raised in homosexual households had developed normally (Sanders). Yet, despite the overwhelming research to the contrary a 1996 survey of undergraduate students had disturbing conclusions. It found that the students rated a homosexual couple more likely to "create a dangerous environment for the child, be more emotionally unstable, and to be less likely to be awarded custody of the child than the heterosexual couples" (Crawford and Solliday 63).

Laurie Pawlitza, a lawyer working with a law firm in Toronto clarifies many of the issues that lesbian mothers face today. Lawyers need to change their strategy when dealing with cases of child custody that involve a lesbian mother. "We have to educate the judiciary about the impact of *or the lack of impact* of homosexuality and child rearing." Pawlitza feels there are judges today that look at homosexuality *per se* as detrimental to the best interests of the child.

Some judges, particularly, I would think older judges, just have not a lot of sense of what ramifications there are if any … they may still believe that homosexuality is something that is taught and that a gay or lesbian parent might try to influence the kid.

She warns that while claimants and lawyers must be careful not to offend any of the judges, they also want to ensure that judges are aware of the current research, and what the possible implications are of awarding custody to the lesbian mother, which are minimal.

As Katherine Arnup (1995) noted, many cases are sealed when an issue of homosexuality is involved. Laurie Pawlitza agrees but suggests there are a myriad of other situations that occur in these cases which make them difficult to research for other lawyers and academics. Many heterosexual couples that separate where one spouse is lesbian or gay settle all their disputes before trial. She indicates that this is not uncommon and occurs when the spouses are very good friends, but she is quick to add that if one spouse has a personal vendetta they can make life very miserable for their spouse when a personal vendetta enters into litigation. However, in the event they do, she confirms that it is definitely not uncommon to seal records so that statistics are hard to come by. Nevertheless, according to Pawlitza, 90 per cent of all family law cases are settled before trial and for many of them a court action is never started.

The voices of lesbian mothers

Brenda,[5] a financial consultant points out that most women that she knows have had kids as "out" lesbians except for one.

> She is the only one I know that has a father in the picture. Everyone that the child knows is aware that her mother is a lesbian, he knows that she is a lesbian, the lawyers know that she is a lesbian, but she would be hard pressed to go into court as a lesbian because she fears for the custody of her child.

Brenda reiterates that most people she knows are open about their sexual orientation as lesbians.

Rebecca, an accountant in her mid-40s, is an identified lesbian mother with a child from a previous heterosexual marriage. She comments that the women she knows that have a connection with the father of their children were in previous heterosexual relationships. Rebecca states that she, like the others, are very careful:

> … lots of written agreements and lots of documentation and a good relationship with [my] lawyer where [I am] constantly dealing with child rearing stuff, visitation stuff, how much time in the summer stuff and it is really onerous.

When asked whether Rebecca knew of any lesbian mothers that have suffered homophobic reactions from the father she was quick to respond that it is always a threat whether it is spoken or not. "*I don't know any lesbian who will boldly take the father, drag him into court because the father has that trump card … yeah, but she's a dyke*"! Rebecca expressed her desire for her partner to be legally recognized as a co-parent, however, the adoption and joint custody laws do not currently allow her any legal options.[6]

Sarah, a civil servant is the co-parent of a child that was born to her partner through artificial insemination by an unknown donor. When their son was two, they decided to pursue legal protections for them and their child. The first step was to secure joint custody. Sarah obtained this with relative ease. The next step was to pursue an adoption. Other members of the birth mother's family can challenge custody. Her partner gave birth to him so her partner's biological family had more legal claims to her son than she did because they had a biological connection that she did not. In order to erase that or supercede it they decided to go forward with the adoption where each parent is given the full bundle of parental rights physically and legally. In doing so, they ran into the problem that according to the *Child and Family Services Act of Ontario*, spouse was defined as someone of the opposite sex. They therefore did not qualify and in the interview with the Children's Aid Society they were turned down.[7] At this stage, the only alternative that was open to Sarah and her partner was to go to court and challenge the piece of legislation that stipulated a spouse was of the opposite sex. They did so with three other lesbian couples who had gone through the same process. Sarah explains,

> ... We decided that there is a certain strength in numbers and that if we all went together it would be much more difficult for a judge to consider this as such an isolated and one-off kind of incident. If you are sitting there before eight women and seven kids that it would be harder than if you are just dealing with one couple and one kid.

The eight women and seven kids sat through a day and a half of court. Expert testimony was provided on what kind of families lesbians form, their longevity, "what the impact is on children having two loving parents versus having one loving parent or parents who don't love them" (Sarah) and so forth. The judgment concluded that the definition of spouse should be changed and amended to reflect this diversity. This ruling allowed them to be examined on a per case basis as would occur with the adoption by a heterosexual married or common-law couple in Ontario.

The Honorable Judge James P. Nevins makes the following statement in his judgment of *Re K.*:

> What is crucial to the children of lesbians and gay men, as to the children of heterosexual men and women, is loving, stable parenting. The opportunity for a lesbian or gay male parent to adopt a biologi-cally unrelated child whom they parent provides a socially and legally recognized structure for an emotional relationship of great impor-tance to the child. Such a structure recognizes the role and authority of the non-biological parent in both ordinary activities ... and in times of transition or crises such as illness, disability, or death. Such

a structure also helps to ensure arrangements which fully recognize parenting relationships of importance to the child in the event of relationship breakdown and/or separation. Although many lesbian and gay male parents are able to make fair and orderly decisions about issues of child support and custody in the absence of a legal framework, the emotions associated with relationship breakdown can make this process difficult if not impossible for some. Where a child has been legally adopted by a non-biological parent, this structure may assist in clarifying the needs of the child and parental responsibilities. (16–17)

Thus, to legally sanction the agreement between the two people is to validate their partnership and establish their clear intent to parent together, and even upon the demise of their relationship to have access and a certain degree of influence and responsibility for the child. The laws across Canada need to be re-examined with this intent and purpose in mind. Unfortunately, the heterosexual world of parent-teacher interviews, pediatrician visits, birth-day parties, and permission slips rarely recognizes that these women are lesbians *and* mothers. Vanessa, a lesbian mother comments,

> ... the [lesbian] community as a whole would say without question that the lesbian mother community is facing an easier task to legitimize their duality in society. But even within the lesbian community we often feel like an invisible minority. We may not have to make surreptitious agreements and make wills that could be overturned anymore to get our custody and adoption orders but if we have been in a hetero relationship before and the natural father is not prepared to consent to an adoption then ultimately, in the end, if the lesbian relationship ends as a result of death or separation, the death of the bio-mum, for example, the non-bio mum could lose a custody dispute with the natural dad even after ten years of co-parenting the child.

Organizations such as PFLAG (Parents, Families, and Friends of Lesbians and Gays) help support lesbian mothers and their friends and family. Today, with more lesbian mothers choosing to have or adopt children there are many organizations and resources become available to help support lesbian mothers and the children of lesbian and gay parents to cope with the institutionalized homophobia and the heterosexual assumption that is still prevalent in many institutions in Canada. As Laurie Pawlitza states, "the bio-mum community, at least, insofar as ideal in adopting (*being fit to adopt*) [is] well on its way."

Conclusion

It is easy to see how a court might legitimately be concerned about how the larger community as a whole receives the children of lesbian mothers and co-parents. Violent crimes against homosexuals and the rejection of Bill C-167[8] in the Ontario Legislature in 1994 are only two overt examples of how homophobia and stigmatization affect lesbians and gays despite the hetero- sexual public's growing acceptance of gay and lesbian unions.

The intent of this research was to determine if any barriers existed for lesbian mothers in obtaining custody of their children and/or adoption in Canadian society. Through an extensive review of the available literature and the research conducted within this study the importance of how terms such as "family," "spouse," "dependent," "parental fitness," and the "best interests of the child" are conceptualized in the justice system greatly affects the outcome of custody cases involving a homosexual parent. The majority of lesbians that have biological children from a previous heterosexual union are not *as* concerned as their peers were 5 to15 years ago. As a result of the landmark decision in *Re: K. et al.* in Ontario that allows co-parents to adopt their partner's biological children a process of change has begun. However, lesbian mothers still feel that their sexual orientation plays a role in determining the best interests of their children. Some still live in fear of losing custody of their children because of their lifestyle choices. As with lesbian mothers, current research does not indicate that there is a reason to believe that gay men are unfit parents as a result of their sexual orientation. According to Charlotte Patterson, the "protection of the best interests of children in lesbian and gay families increasingly demands that courts and legislative bodies acknowledge realities of life in nontraditional families" (1992b: 1037).

A great majority of the research conducted on lesbian motherhood centres around debunking the myths and stereotypes associated with lesbian and gay relationships and their lack of effect on parenting ability. One area for further research is the comparison of the commonalties and differences among lesbian families without the comparison to the heterosexual alternative. There appears to be an absence of longitudinal studies on children that were raised in lesbian families and the longevity of lesbian partnerships. Furthermore, there is a need for accurate documentation of alternative family structures that exist in Canada. The next Statistics Canada census needs to include questions that are mutually exclusive and exhaustive and which would allow for same- sex households, with or without children, to be accurately documented. Finally, research is needed that deals specifically with Canadian custody disputes of lesbian mothers from 1995 onwards. From the academic writings that have been published to date, it is not entirely clear whether the factors that judges claim are most important in determining custody have much to do with the final result. The interviews that were conducted in this research have indicated that there has been a considerable amount of progress in the redefinition of the family and lesbian mother's quest for custody within family law. In the author's opinion, this has not been clearly identified in the literature available. Through the education of the judiciary and further research that explores, supports, and reflects the structural changes within the institution of the family and the effect of judicial process on women, we will hopefully see a more even application of the law and court rulings. Further research, education, and law reform are mandatory, as homosexuality *per se* is not and should not be a barrier to child custody or adoption.

The author wishes to acknowledge the help and guidance of Dr. Belinda Leach and Dr. Nora Cebotarev.

Originally published in CWS/cf's *Spring/Summer 1999 issue, "Women and Justice" (Volume 19, Numbers 1/2): 24-51.*

[1]A monolithic bias or structure has an emphasis on uniformity of experience and universal structure and functions rather than on diversity of experiences, structure, and function.

[2]The term co-parent refers to the non-biological mother in a lesbian relationship.

[3]Dr. Richard Green is the best known authority on homosexuality and its effects on children. He has been quoted with approval by numerous judges in the United States and was extensively quoted in *Barkley v. Barkley*.

[4]Benjamin Spock's child rearing books are well-known and read in North America. It is particularly interesting that he takes this position, since he is generally considered to be "conservative in his views" (Gross 1986, 521).

[5]Names and identifying information have been changed to ensure the confidentiality that was assured to all participants.

[6]In Rebecca's case, there is a known father from a previous heterosexual relationship. For her lesbian partner to be able to legally adopt her child would require the birth father to completely abdicate any legal, physical responsibility for that child. Rebecca's ex-husband is not willing to do this, therefore her partner cannot be legally recognized as a co-parent.

[7]Interviews with the Children's Aid Society are standard practice in adoption cases. Questions include what your aspirations and goals are, what you do for a living, what kind of income you earn, what kind of home you live in etc. Sarah and her partner did not have to undergo a home visit as they were not applying for a strange baby adoption but a partner adoption where the child had resided with both parties since birth.

[8]Bill 167 "aimed to amend 56 provincial laws to equate same-sex couples with heterosexual couples. This was the first North American attempt to move from *ad hoc* changes to systematic reform" (Sanders 122–123). One of the Bill's intentions was to allow gay and lesbian people the legal right to adopt children. The Bill was defeated on second reading by nine votes in June 1994.

References

Arnup, Katherine. "Lesbian Mothers and Child Custody." *Gender and Society: Creating a Canadian Women's Sociology*. Ed. Arlene Tiger McLaren. Toronto: Copp Clark Pitman, 1988.

Arnup, Katherine. "Mothers Just Like Others: Lesbians, Divorce and Child Custody in Canada." *Canadian Journal of Woman and the Law* 3.1 (1989): 18–32.

Arnup, Katherine. "Living in the Margins: Lesbian Families and the Law." *Lesbian Parenting.* Charlottetown: Gynergy Books, 1995.

Barkley v. Barkley (1980), 16 R.F.L. (2d) 7 (Ont. Prov. Ct.).

Bould, Susan. "Familial Caretaking: A Middle Range Definition of Family in the Context of Social Policy." *Journal of Family Issues* 14.31 (1993): 133–151.

Brophy, Julia. "New Families, Judicial Decision Making and Childrens Welfare." *Canadian Journal of Women and the Law* 5 (1992): 484–497.

Causey, Kelly A., and Candan Duran-Aydintug. "Child Custody Determination: Implications for Lesbian Mothers." *Journal of Divorce and Remarriage* 25.1–2 (1996): 55–74.

Cherlin, Andrew J. *Marriage, Divorce, Remarriage.* Cambridge: Harvard University Press, 1992.

Crawford, Isiaah and Elizabeth Solliday. "The Attitudes of Undergraduate College Students Toward Gay Parenting." *Journal of Homosexuality* 30.4 (1996): 63–77.

Eichler, Margrit. "Lone Parent Families: an Instable Category in Search of Stable Policies." *Single Parent Families.* Eds. Joe Hudson and Burt Galaway. Toronto: Thompson Educational Publishing, Inc., 1993.

Epstein, Rachel. "Lesbian Families." *Voices: Essays on Canadian Families.* Toronto: Nelson Canada, 1996.

Ferris, Kathryn. "Child Custody and the Lesbian Mother." *Resources for Feminist Research* 12.1 (1983): 106–109.

Findlay, Barbara. "All in Family Values." *Canadian Journal of Family Law* 14.2 (1997): 129–196.

Gottman, Julie Schwartz. "Children of Gay and Lesbian Parents." *Marriage and Family Review* 14.3–4 (1989): 177–196.

Green, Richard, Jane B. Mandel, Mary E. Hotvedt, James Gray, and Laurel Smith. "Lesbian Mothers and their Children: A Comparison With Solo Parent Heterosexual Mothers and their Children." *Archives of Sexual Behaviour* 15 (1986): 167–184.

Gross, Wendy. "Judging the Best Interests of the Child: Child Custody and the Homosexual Parent." *Canadian Journal of Women and the Law* 1.2 (1986): 505–531.

Hall, Marny (1978). "Lesbian Families: Cultural and Clinical Issues." *Social Work* 23 (1978): 380–385.

Harris, Mary B., and Pauline Turner. "Gay and Lesbian Parents." *Journal of Homosexuality* 12 (1985): 101–113.

Kaufman, Miriam and Susan Dundas. "Directions for Research about Lesbian Families." *Lesbian Parenting.* Ed. Kathrine Arnup. Charlottetown: Gynergy Books, 1995.

Kirkpatrick, M., C. Smyth, and R. Roy. "Lesbian Mothers and their Children:

A Comparative Study." *American Journal of Orthopsychiatry* 51 (1981): 545–551.

Martin, T. C., R. B. Jacobson, and J. J. Bigner. "Recent Trends in Marital Disruption." *Demography* 26 (1989): 37–51.

Mason, Mary Ann and Ann Quirk. "Are Mothers Losing Custody?: Read My Lips: Trends in Judicial Decision Making in Custody Disputes—1920, 1960, 1990, and 1995." *Family Law Quarterly* 31.2 (1997): 215–236.

Patterson, Charlotte J. *Children of Lesbian and Gay Parents.* Charlottesville, VI: University of Virginia: 1992.

Patterson, Charlotte J. "Children of Lesbian and Gay Parents." *Child Development* 63 (1992): 1025–1042.

Pawlitza, Laurie. Personal interview. 8 June 1998.

Re K. (1995), 15 R.F.L. (4th) 129 (Ont. Prov. Div.).

Ricketts, Wendall and Roberta Achtenberg. "Adoption and Foster Parenting for Lesbians and Gay Men: Creating New Traditions in Family." *Marriage and Family Review* 14.3–4 (1989): 83–118.

Rosen, David M. "What is Family? Nature, Culture and the Law." *Marriage and Family Review* 17.1–2 (1991): 29–43.

Sanders, Douglas. "Constructing Lesbian and Gay Rights." *Canadian Journal of Law and Society* 9.2 (1994): 99–143.

Vanier Institute of the Family. *Profiling Canadian Families.* Ottawa: The Vanier Institute of the Family, 1994.

Zicklin, Gilbert. "Deconstructing Legal Rationality: The Case of Lesbian and Gay Family Relationships." *Marriage and Family Review* 21.3–4 (1995): 55–76.

The Social Policy Snare

Keeping Women Out of University

Jennifer Nicole Hines ⟶

My daughter is playing; She is seating her dolls around the kitchen table. She is pretending they are eating breakfast and that she is their mother. With the innocent bliss of a three-year-old, she mimics me. I am moved knowing that I am her biggest influence, that I have such a part to play in her destiny, but I am troubled.

She does not know that we use the food bank and that our clothing is not new. She does not see that we live in a cramped apartment with musty carpets and that we do not own a car. Unlike me, she has not yet learned the shame and hopelessness that can accompany being raised on social assistance, and I am determined that she never will.

Soon I will enter my fourth year of university, where I hope to complete an honours degree in sociology. I dream of becoming a social justice lawyer and providing my daughter with everything I never had. Yet, at 22 years of age my aspirations continue to be threatened. I am currently facing a discriminatory policy, which states that I cannot attend university and have access to social assistance benefits at the same time.

Prior to April 1998, single parents who needed social assistance could receive benefits to cover living expenses as well as access student loans to cover educational expenses. But, on April 1 1998 the government of Nova Scotia implemented changes to the social assistance and employment support policy (*Social Assistance and Employment Support Policy Manual*). The new policy which was again ratified on November 1, 2000 as part of the new, *Employment Support And Income Assistance Act* now states: "A person attending a post-secondary education program of more than two years shall not receive assistance unless the person is funded to attend by the Employability Assistance for Persons with Disabilities Program" (67(1)).[1]

I was informed of this decision in the summer of 2002. As a newly unemployed single parent I applied for social assistance benefits. I told the caseworker I was planning to return to university for my second year of studies. She informed me that as a student I would have access to student loans and, therefore, I was ineligible for social assistance. The logic behind the legislation seems to be that since student loans provide for living expenses and childcare, students do not need social assistance. But student loans do not provide enough money for single parents to live on.

While students who do not have children can share housing costs with roomates, a single parent must single-handedly pay all rent and utilities for a family-sized dwelling. Single parents must also pay for all of her child's expenses including childcare, food, clothing, and medicine. A single person can usually walk to most places, while a woman with a child cannot avoid transportation costs. For example, I could not attend class without bringing my daughter to and from daycare. Since there is no public transportation I am often obliged to use taxies. These costs are calculated in a student aide assessment, but since there is a ceiling on the amount that can be allocated to each student, these costs are not actually fully covered.

The budget for my second year of university illustrates what a student with one child might expect to spend and receive for her eight-month study period, assuming that she receives the maximum allocation from Student Assistance and the National Child Benefit.

Budget of Single Parent Student In Nova Scotia

Income		Expenses	
Student Loan	9210	Tuition and Fees	5500
Canada Study Grant	1300	Books	300
Canada Child Tax Benefit	2048	Rent (With Utilities)	5560
		Child Care	3920
GST Rebate	_500_	Taxies	_400_
	13,058		15,680
			-2,622

I had a $3,000 deficit that did not include the cost of food, clothing, medicine, or other basic necessities. *The Employment Support and Income Assistance Act*, ironically subtitled "An Act to Encourage the Attainment of Independence and Self-sufficiency through Employment Support and Income Assistance," thus works to effectively deny the very people who are most likely to overcome poverty access to education that will provide them opportunities for long-term self-sufficiency.

The Family Mosaic Project recognizes the importance of education for young women who are single parents. The project asserts that the incidence and depth of poverty are increasing in Nova Scotia and that 92 per cent of single parents between 20-24 years of age live below the poverty line (9). It also demonstrates that women who have less education tend to be marginally employed and employment layoffs and heath issues are a trend in marginal jobs. Thus, women who are employed in marginal trades are likely to return to using social assistance over a period of time (25). But, the report also shows that those who had access to education have a better chance of being able to support their families and, in fact, that education is the key to reducing intergenerational poverty (24).

It would be logical to assume then that if single parents are permitted to receive social assistance benefits for the four years they are in university, it is likely they will never need social assistance again. Yet, less than two years after the report was published, the Nova Scotia Department of Community Services decided to discriminate against single parents.

In February of my second year I found myself with only eleven dollars to live on. I knew that I did not qualify for social assistance but I hoped that the Department of Community Services would make an exception, given my desperation. Together with an advocate from the Antigonish Women's Resource Center, I explained my situation to a caseworker. He explained that in light of the recent policy changes that there was absolutely nothing he could do for me.

"But what if I dropped out of school today?" I asked, "Then would I qualify?"

"Yes," he responded." "You would. But as long as you are attending university we are not allowed to do anything for you."

At that moment I realized I was trapped by the whims of social policy. Yet I stubbornly held on to the conviction that I had the right to my education and I managed to get through the rest of the year with the help of hard-earned bursaries and assistance from some charitable organizations.

During the summer break, however, I expected to receive social assistance. After all, student loans are only meant to cover expenses during the school term. When I asked my caseworker why I could not access benefits during the summer he informed me that as a student I qualified for government work grants and therefore would not need social assistance. Do policy makers actually believe that a single parent who has just spent eight months balancing university course work and children by herself, can immediately set herself to applying for grants, and that she would indeed receive a grant that could cover the costs for herself and her child? At the end of my second year, I was an unskilled worker, so even if I worked full-time I could not afford to pay for childcare. A year of parenting while in university, anxiously scrambling for sources of income and feeling hopeless about ever reaching my goals, drove me into a major depression. I received letters from two separate doctors stating that I was not fit to work. Yet when I presented these letters to the Community Services Office I was denied once again. They told me that the only way I could access benefits was if I could prove that I would not return to university in the fall. A letter from the registrar stating that I was not currently a student did not qualify as proof. I had to prove that I had actually *quit* school. I then had to plead to the registrar's office to remove me from their records. I was literally forced to drop out of school in order to survive.

I was furious. Under Canada's *Constitution Act* of 1982 I have an equal right to opportunities. A university education should be considered one of these opportunities. I called the Human Rights Commission and complained about having to drop out of school. The person that I spoke with told me that I didn't have a case because I was arguing against legislated policy. I explained to them that if I returned to school in September that I could be charged with fraud. The only advice that he could give me was to reapply anyway.

That August I applied to be readmitted. I had to write a letter to the university stating why I had "changed my mind" about quitting school and I had to send in a new application including the customary application fee. I returned to the ongoing game of "which bursary do I qualify for now." For those single mothers who can achieve high grades, bursaries and scholarships can provide more money than working a part-time job. If I had worked part-time during the school year most of my wages would have gone to childcare. I would not have had time to have a relationship with my daughter and I would have been too tired to do well in my studies. Instead I studied hard so that I could apply for bursaries. In my second year I received over $2,000. But I was under constant stress to maintain above-average marks without any certainty of receiving a bursary as there are only a limited number available.

Frustrated by a number of attempts to raise awareness about this unjust policy, I wrote a letter to the Minister of Community Services, the Hon. David Morse, and asked him what the government planned to do to help single parents in university. He responded in writing stating that the government of Nova Scotia was helping by adding a supplement to the Canada Child Tax Benefit. He also mentioned that the province supports subsidized housing and childcare. I wrote Mr. Morse again to inform him of the housing crisis in Antigonish, and to tell him that there were not enough subsidized childcare spaces to go around. He did not respond this time.

I grew tired of explaining to the social assistance office that I was indeed poor. Few people acknowledged my complaint as valid. As a student I needed to be well-dressed, confident, and articulate. But these assets made me appear *undeserving* when I mentioned that I needed help. At the student food bank I was only given enough food for one person, and at the town food bank I was lectured for not using the student food bank. I spent so much time adjusting to and arguing against peoples' attitudes that I began to lose a sense of myself.

My fourth major battle with depression came at the end of my third year. I could not find a job and it was summer vacation. I did not bother with social assistance because I knew that they would deny me. I decided that the best way to survive would be to go to school full-time over the summer. But after spending a month on a distance education course I was denied a student loan because of a minor technicality. According to Student Assistance, I was not a summer student for a long enough period to be considered for a full time student loan, and a part-time loan would only cover tuition and books. I spent weeks on the phone, begging for an exception to no avail. Eventually, I had to ask the university to refund part of my tuition so that I could afford to live, and I set out to find a job.

I wanted to shout. "Why am *I* not allowed to get my degree? I am in the top ten per cent of my class, so what makes me less deserving than anyone else? Should I be punished just because I love and raise my child?"

Every time I opened my medicine cabinet through the dark weeks of a severe depression, I saw sleeping pills, antidepressants, and tranquilizers. I had fantasies of swallowing whole bottles. If my life was always going to be this all-encompassing exhausting task of just staying alive, with no dreams, no security, and no hope, then I did not want to live. My daughter became my only purpose for living.

Then I got a bursary from the Antigonish Women's Resource Center. I began to see a psychologist. Later that week I was offered a job at the Women's Center. My mind slowly became clear and I was able to see that I had achieved a great deal in my two years as a single parent student. With my new-found sense of security I was able to recollect the people and systems that supported me.

In my apartment building there are other single-parent students. This past school year one of them drove my daughter and me to daycare every day in exchange for a little bit of gas money. It was she who realized I was depressed and directed me to the help I needed. My best friend is also a single mother in university. When our children play together we have some time to socialize. Through her support I learned that it is all right if my life follows a different pattern than my peers. Although my mother does not have any money to offer me, she does all that she can to help me achieve my goals. She drives me places that I need to go, and she and some of my other relatives pitch in to babysit or do housework when I am too busy or too tired. I am now also fortunate enough to finally have a subsidized childcare space.

The Antigonish Women's Resource Center has an important impact on my life. There I was able to learn that poverty was a situation, not an identity, and I that I could have big dreams for myself. When I struggled to achieve my education the staff were always there to listen and offer advice. They helped organize meetings and marches against this unfair policy. They invited me sit in on meetings where I learned about the government and social policy. They even asked me to give a speech about my struggle in university which subsequently turned into this article. I didn't realize they were working to empower me. Because they recognized the potential in me, a poor single mother, I became able to see the potential in myself.

Many women have dreams like mine, of having careers and good lives. We should never be asked to choose between these dreams and loving and raising our children. Some people say that a woman can do anything she wants as long as she puts her mind to it. Instead, I would like to offer that a woman can do anything she wants as long as she has a support system. Not all women have the benefit of a support system like mine. Nonetheless, they still deserve to pursue the kind of education and careers they want and their children also deserve to escape from the cycle of poverty. This is why Canadians need to improve support bases for women, rather than continue to diminish them.

Since writing this article, Jennifer Hines and her daughter havei moved into a nice low-rental apartment where they are both happy and healthy. Jennifer plasn to graduate in 2006 with a BA Honours from St Francis Xavier University.

Originally published in CWS/cf's Spring/Summer 2004 issue, "Benefiting Women? Women's Labour Rights" (Volume 23, Numbers 3/4): 138-141.

[1]The Employability Assistance for Persons with Disabilities Program, which is a program for adults with vocational handicaps funded by Human Resources Development Canada in partnership with the Government of Nova Scotia.

References

Canada *Constitution Act*, Paragraph 15 section 1 and 2, 1982.Online: http://www.canlii.org/ca/const_en/const1982.html

The Family Mosaic Project. Nova Scotia Department of Community Services 1999. Online: http://www.gov.ns.ca/coms/files/fm.asp.

Province of Nova Scotia. *Employment Support and Income Assistance Act*, Chapter 27 of the Acts of 2000, Bill No.62

Social Assistance and Employment Support Policy Manual. Department of Community Services, Nova Scotia, April 1, 1998.

— **Violence**

Commemoration for the Montreal Massacre Victims

Ursula Franklin

The events in Montreal certainly and surely upset all of us deeply. As somebody who has taught for the last two decades in the Faculty of Applied Science
and Engineering and who has tried to encourage young women to enter our
profession, as somebody who is a pacifist and a feminist, the events in Montreal
deeply trouble me. They trouble me because any one of these young women
could have been one of my students; could have been someone I encouraged
by saying: "Look, you can do it. It's a tough turf alright, but there are others.
Nothing will change if we aren't there."

But these fourteen women are not there anymore. And many say what
happened to them was an act of a madman, something more or less like a
random printing error that had nothing to do with anything except the state
of Marc Lépine's mind. I'm one of those who say, yes, it was the act of a
madman, but it is not unrelated to what is going on around us. *That* people get
mad may happen in any society, any place, every place. But *how* people get
mad, *how* that escalation from prejudice, to hate, to violence occurs, what and
who is hated, and how it is expressed, is not unrelated to the world around us.
When a madman uses easily-available weapons and easily-available prejudices, it is not totally his problem, which will go away when he does. At another
time, it could have been Jews who were lined up, it could have been black
people, but in Montreal it was women—women in an engineering faculty—
killed by somebody who wanted to be an engineer.

In remembrance what is it that we are called upon to reflect? We
remember the fourteen students in Montreal. But we also remember that they
were abandoned. Our memory should not block out the fact that Marc Lépine,
at one of the killing stations, went into a classroom in which there were men
and women. He asked them to separate into two groups, and when this didn't
happen, he fired a shot to the ceiling. Then it did happen. The men left.
Fourteen women were killed, and Marc Lépine could leave this classroom. It
is not as much a question of how he got in, but it is a question of how he got
out. In our memory and reflection, we have to include the fact that these
women were abandoned by their fellow students. We have to face it.

We men and women have to ask: What does it take to make solidarity real?
Is one shot to the ceiling or its verbal equivalent enough to abandon the

victims? You may wish to think on what you would have done, maybe even what you are doing in less lethal situations. Is a joke enough to condone harassment? There's a lot to be reflect upon. Many of the comments after the massacre were comments on what was called a "senseless killing." Are there killings that are not senseless? Are there sensible killings? Are there people who can be abandoned? If reflection shows that all killing is senseless, we may ask why then do we have tools of killing around—if we agree that all killing is senseless. We may wish for a second to reflect how we, as a community, would have felt if the identical massacre had taken place in a bank, in a post office. Maybe, heaven forbid, in a hotel where the young women were prostitutes. How would we react?

We speak on occasion with fair ease about all of us being brothers and sisters. And maybe finally I could urge you, in memory of these our young colleagues, to reflect on what it means that someone is your sister, someone is a member of that human family. That doesn't mean you have to like or love her, but it does mean you have to respect her presence as the right to be there on her own terms, not by gracious permission of the dominant culture, not only as long as she keeps her mouth shut and goes through the prescribed hoops; but because we are members of one family and each of us has an inalienable right to be, and to fulfill our potential. And if the grief we feel, the remembrance we must continue, and the reflections we have to share, bring us into a world in which it is not empty rhetoric when we speak of each other as brothers and sisters, then, I think, the memory of the students in Montreal will serve us well.

The author gave this address at a commemorative service for the fourteen women murdered at the École polytechnique, Montreal. Her address, given on 19 January 1990, was also read to the Senate by Senator Roy Firth on 21 February 1990 as part of the request for a Senate Committee inquiry into violence against women.

Originally published in CWS/cf's Summer 1991 issue, "Violence Against Women" (Volume 11, Number 4).

Some Reflections on Violence Against Women

Radhika Coomaraswamy

The following statistics indicate the extent of the problem of violence against women. In the United States a rape occurs every six minutes and violence occurs once in two-thirds of all marriages (Carillo 5). In Papua, New Guinea, 67 per cent of rural women and 56 per cent of urban women are victims of wife abuse (APDC 15). In Santiago, Chile, 80 per cent of women acknowledge being victims of violence in their homes (Carillo 6). In Canada, one in every four women can expect to be sexually assaulted at some point in her life (Carillo 5). In France 95 per cent of its victims of violence are women, 51 per cent of the above at the hands of a husband (Carillo 5).

In Bangladesh assassination of wives by husbands accounts for 50 per cent of all murders (Carillo 5). In India there have been 11,259 dowry-related murders in the last three years (APDC 15). In Pakistan 99 per cent of housewives and 77 per cent of working women are beaten by their husbands (Carillo 6). Given the number of men in India and China, there should be about 30 million more women in India and 38 million more women in China (Carillo 6). In Korea two-thirds of all women are beaten periodically by their husbands (Carillo 6). According to the World Health Organization more than 80 million women have undergone sexual surgery (female circumcision) in Africa alone (Schuler 400). Every minute and a half a woman is raped in South Africa, totalling approximately 380,000 women raped each year (Schuler 322).

Violence against women is a latecomer to the world of international human rights. In the 1970s, women's issues focused on discrimination in political and economic benefits and an equitable development process for women of the third world. The major international convention which dealt with women's rights, The Convention on the Elimination of All Forms of Discrimination Against Women (CEDAW), which came into force in 1979, adopted the "non-discrimination" model; women's rights were violated only if women were denied the same benefits as men. Though there were sections on custom and traditional practices, the Convention was silent on the issue of violence against women. At the World Conference celebrating the Women's Decade in Nairobi in 1985, the problem of violence against women was raised but in a marginal manner, as an afterthought to the other provisions dealing with discrimination, health, economic, and social issues.

This neglect of the issue of violence against women generated a great deal of non-governmental organization (NGO) activity in this regard, especially during the '80s and '90s. This activity struck a responsive chord within the United Nations system and the process culminated in the Declaration on the Elimination of Violence Against Women by the United Nations General Assembly in 1993 and the appointment of a Special Rapporteur on violence against women in 1994.

Approaches

There are in effect three approaches to the issue of violence against women (Omvedt). The radical feminist approach locates the discussion in an understanding of patriarchy. According to this approach violence is intrinsic in the relationship between men and women and manifests itself in sexuality as well as in the social and political institutions of society. This leads to a focus on problems of domestic violence, and rape as a manifestation of the initial inequality in the relationship between the sexes (Firestone). Violence is therefore pervasive and inherent in women's daily interaction with men (Brownmiller).

Socialist feminism approaches the question of violence against women in a fundamentally different way. Violence is seen as a part of the social and economic forces which operate in society, forces which make women one of many victims. The struggle against violence is therefore not a struggle against men and male domination alone but against systems of exploitation which disempower women. Violence is a result of economic exploitation and only secondarily a function of the male-female relationship. Third world socialist feminists see female workers in certain industries as being victims of violence. There is also a concern with the commodification of women as sexual objects in prostitution and the international trafficking of women (Mitchell).

Eco-feminism also deals with violence against women in a significantly different way. It sees relationships between women and nature, between subsistence production engaged by certain women and violent accumulation engaged by certain men and the state. Violence is seen as part of the military-industrial complex, an attempt to destroy both women and nature. As is often said in these circles, "There is no essential difference between the rape of a woman, the conquest of a country, and the destruction of the earth" (Omvedt 15). The issues that are relevant to these groups are a concern with the destruction of the lifestyles of women living in the rural areas of the third world along with those who live in tribal homelands. Violence is seen as a by-product of the industrial age.

The human rights paradigm, on the other hand, privileges a certain type of human personality, namely, the free, independent woman as an individual endowed with rights and rational agency (Coomaraswamy 1992a:3). The core concept of the human rights approach centres around the issue of empowerment. Violence against women involves the use of force or the threat of the use of force to prevent the necessary empowerment of women within society. The state is therefore under an obligation to ensure that women are given full opportunity to be independent and empowered without being abused. In the past, the human rights approach has centred on empowering women through access to education, equal employment, adequate health care, and equal civil and political rights. CEDAW, for example, is structured along these lines. The more modern approach, however, is that the right to be free and independent includes the right to be free from fear and the right to be secure in the family and in the community.

In addition, violence was initially seen as an act of private individuals and the human rights model was not structured to hold states accountable for the acts of private citizens. But in recent times there is a growing understanding that state responsibility includes the duty to prevent the rights of individuals from being violated by private actors, whether they be individuals or corporations. The emergence of state responsibility for violence in society has been one of the most important contributions of the women's movement to the issue of human rights.

The human rights approach to violence, therefore, is based on the rights of individuals to be free and independent without being threatened by the use of force. If force is not strictly construed to mean only the actual use of physical force, the mandate is a broad one. It implies the right to investigate all forms of action which disempower women because of the fear of violence, whether that fear is instilled by the state, by actors in the community or by members of the family. This broad approach appears to have been adopted by the General Assembly in its Declaration on the Elimination of Violence Against Women.

Categorization of violence

To be understood and confronted, violence has to be categorized. Gail Omvedt in her article on violence appears to believe that violence can be categorized in terms of violence and sexuality, violence and economic exploitation, and violence and culture. The first includes violence which is the result of the sexuality of the victim whether it be rape, sexual harassment, or domestic violence, although the latter does not completely fit the category. Violence and economic exploitation refers to aspects of a woman's life which are related to her labour. This includes labour in sweat shops as well as prostitution and trafficking. It also includes violence against women as bonded labour or agricultural workers. Finally, violence and culture refers to cultural practices devised by different societies, such as female circumcision.

One may also categorize violence in terms of women's relationships to men and society. Women are subject to violence because of being female. In this capacity, they are subject to rape, female circumcision, genital mutilation, and female infanticide. These relate again to the construction of female sexuality. A woman is also subject to violence because of her relationship to a man. Examples include domestic violence, dowry murder, and/or *sati*. Finally, a woman is subject to violence because of the social group to which she belongs. In times of war, riots or ethnic and caste violence a woman may be raped or brutalized as a means of humiliating the community to which she belongs (Coomaraswamy 1992b).

In recent times violence has been categorized by the location of the violence: violence in the family, in the community, and by the state. The UN Declaration on the Elimination of Violence Against Women categorizes violence in this manner and recent social science writing has also accepted this categorization (Schuler).

The General Assembly Declaration on the Elimination of Violence Against Women defines violence as:

> any act of gender-based violence that results in or is likely to result in physical, sexual or psychological harm or suffering to women, including threats of such acts, coercion or arbitrary deprivation of liberty whether occurring in public or private life. (Article 2)

This definition appears to envision individual victims at the receiving end of individual acts of violence. Women from the third world would want to expand the interpretation of this section for a broader reading of violence. As Govind Kelkar has written:

> A narrow definition of violence may define it as an act of criminal use of physical force. But this is an incomplete concept. Violence also includes exploitation, discrimination, unequal economic and social structures, the creation of an atmosphere of religio-cultural and political violence. While violence against women is part of general violence found in the social structures such as class, caste, religion and ethnicity, and in the way the state controls people, it also encompasses aspects of structural violence and forms of control and coercion exercised through hierarchical and patriarchal gender relationships in the family and society. (qtd. in Schuler)

For an international consensus on violence, it is important that a broader reading is accepted by the international community.

Causes of violence against women

A large majority of women writers link violence against women with a lack of economic independence. David Levinson studied 90 societies and found wife-beating to be prevalent in 75. The four cultural factors that are strong predictors for wife abuse are sexual and economic inequality, a pattern of using violence for conflict resolution, male authority and decision-making in the home, and divorce restrictions for women (Schuler). Omvedt writes:

the basic economic dependence of women, their propertylessness and resourcelessness, renders them fearfully weak in standing up and challenging violence and power that is used against them in society. (5)

Women's economic dependence disempowers them and makes them not only susceptible to violence but also unable to challenge and fight against violence.

Linked to the notion of economic dependency are other sorts of legal, political, and social dependency which make it difficult for women to assert their independence when confronted with violence. Legal systems which do not permit women to divorce, for example, or which do not support women when they are in a situation of violence aggravate the problem. Women are expected to remain in situations where violence is being used against them and therefore the nature and extent of the violence increases.

An undemocratic society which uses the military as the tool of repression is likely to have a great deal of violence directed against women. This militarization develops a culture of violence in society and violence against women is only one of the many manifestations of the resolution of conflict through the use of force.

Patterns of socialization which disempower women with regard to responsibility and decision-making whether in the home or in society also create an atmosphere where violence against women appears to be more legitimate. Patterns of conduct in the home and in educational institutions are extremely important in this regard, as is the media.

Violence against women is also the result of a society which wants to control the expression of female sexuality. Violence is often directed against a woman to ensure that she is "chaste" and virtuous. It is argued that this is to ensure that the children she gives birth to are the children of the correct father and therefore the lawful heirs to his property. Allegations of adultery were the major reason for wife beating in Papua, New Guinea (APDC 17). Sexual harassment of free trade zone workers is often excused by the fact that they dress "provocatively." And of course, it is always a defence for rape and harassment that the woman in her demeanor "asked for it." The fear of violence is an important part of women's reality and it conditions women's behaviour in many aspects of their day-to-day lives.

Male alcoholism is also one of the major reasons for violence in the family, along with woman's refusal to perform her "wifely duties," a euphemism for sexual intercourse (APDC 17). Although social workers have to take these causes into consideration, it is imperative that the legal system not recognize any of these excuses for violence as legitimate. Whatever the causes for violence against women, they should not be understood as justifications for the use of violence against women. Women's right to be free from violence is an absolute right which cannot be mitigated by empirically discovered social causes.

The role of the state

In the past strict judicial interpretations of international law only held the state responsible for its own actions, for example, in relation to women in custody or detention and women during armed conflict. Domestic violence, rape, and sexual harassment, for example, were not seen as state action but only as the acts of individuals. This narrow interpretation has been recently challenged. A state which tolerates violence against women at the community and family level and which does not take effective measures to prevent this violence or hold accountable those who are responsible for the violence is as guilty as the individual perpetrators.

This gives rise to a debate as to whether violence in the family should be "criminalized" or whether the state should adopt measures of "conciliation" and "mediation." In my view, there are elements of criminality in the actions of private citizens when they engage in violence in the family and those elements have to be reflected in the law. The seriousness of these acts must also be acknowledged. The scope of the law should not prevent experimentation with new strategies that may be more effective in confronting this violence. The manner in which the "criminalization" of acts of violence is tempered by a "conciliation" process for effective results is up to individual states as long as there are sincere and meaningful efforts to ensure that violence against women in the family and in the community is eliminated.

International standards

Until recently, there has been no real set of international legal standards which relate to violence against women. The approach during the early stages was to make violence an aspect of discrimination and therefore central in spirit to CEDAW. Violence against women was seen to violate Articles 2, 3, 5, 6, 11, 12, and 16 of CEDAW. These articles deal specifically with prohibition of discrimination by public and private actors, the obligation to ensure full development and advancement of women, the need to eliminate traditional practices which discriminate against women, the need to eliminate trafficking in women, and the need to promote employment, health, and equality in the family (Sullivan). Though none of the provisions deal directly with the issue of violence, it was argued that the eliminating the problem of violence is part of the elimination of discrimination. The Committee in charge of implementing the CEDAW stated clearly in General Recommendation 19 that violence is a form of discrimination. The attempt to stretch the Convention to include violence has been somewhat successful but more specific international standards are necessary. Those standards have been clearly spelled out in the UN Declaration on the Elimination of Violence Against Women passed by the General Assembly in December 1993.

The preamble to the Declaration locates the problem of violence against women in unequal power and in women's structural subordination. It also identifies particularly vulnerable groups of women who are at the receiving end of violence. These include minority women, indigenous groups, refugee women, migrant women, women living in rural or remote communities, destitute women, women in detention, female children, women with disabilities, elderly women, and women in situations of armed conflict.

The Declaration defines violence broadly to include physical, sexual, and psychological violence. It is categorized according to whether it occurs in the family, in the community, or by the state. Under each category the types of violence which are prevalent are enumerated. In the family, these include: battering, sexual abuse of female children, dowry-related violence, marital rape, female genital mutilation, traditional practices which are harmful to women, non-spousal violence, and violence relating to exploitation. In the general community, types of violence include rape, sexual abuse, sexual harassment, intimidation, trafficking, and forced prostitution. State violence is clearly defined not only as acts that are perpetrated but also those which are "condoned." The obligations of the state are further spelled out in Article 4. The state is obligated to condemn violence and cannot invoke custom, tradition, or religion to avoid the obligation. States are expected to pursue all "appropriate means" "without delay" to adopt a policy for eliminating violence against women.

Other specific state obligations outlined in Article 4 of the Declaration include the ratification of CEDAW, the exercise of due diligence in preventing and investigating violence against women, in accordance with national legislation, and the punishment of acts of violence by the state or by private persons. There are specific directives for developing legal and administrative mechanisms to ensure effective justice for victims of violence and to ensure that there is support and rehabilitation for women victims of violence. The Declaration recommends training judicial and police officials, reforming educational curricula, promoting research in this area, and engaging in full reporting of the problem of violence against women to international human rights mechanisms.

The Declaration sees the international community as an essential actor in the process of eliminating violence against women. UN agencies are responsible for promoting awareness of the issues in their program, collecting data on the problem, periodically analyzing the trends, formulating guidelines and manuals on the issue, and cooperating with NGOs in addressing the issue.

The UN Declaration is not a binding document but it sets out international standards in a clear and comprehensive manner. The Declaration should be an integral part of the mandate of the Special Rapporteur on Violence Against Women and provide her with guidance in her work.

The issues

The issue of violence in the family raises issues relating to the privacy of the home. Many will argue that the state should be cautious in invading the sanctity of the marital home. Dealing with violence in the family differently from other types of violence, however, is not in keeping with international standards. The doors of the family should be wide open for scrutiny if there is violence, but the strategies for dealing with this violence are left to national legislation as long as the legislation is in accordance with international norms.

Violence in the community raises different issues. Although the Declaration states that states should not invoke cultural or religious factors as an excuse for condoning violence against women, these identities are extremely powerful, especially in the third world. A purely legalistic approach to these issues will not suffice and in fact may raise the argument that the Declaration is a "western" draft not related to the situation in the east or other parts of the third world. If international action can link with NGOs in putting forward an argument that violence against women is never a part of an essentialist national "culture," only a man-made practice which distorts that culture, then the likelihood of making an impact in these societies is greater.

Violence by the state also raises particular issues. In repressive states, the problem of women in custody and detention is significant. In this context the thrust to make the state answerable for violence against women is part of the general struggle for human rights and democratization. In pursuing these issues it is important to work with NGOs and other groups who are interested in the general problems of democracy and human rights. The women's issue cannot be seen in isolation.

State responsibility for the general violence in society directed against women is perhaps the most important principle to emerge in this context. The assertion of this principle is perhaps the primary vehicle for making it clear to government that it is responsible if effective action is not taken to prevent, investigate, and to punish acts of violence directed against women.

In addition, states are responsible for ensuring that victims of violence are given humanitarian assistance. This humanitarian aspect should not be lost in a strict legal approach. It is an important component of any program aimed at eliminating violence against women. These social structures should be seen as part of the legal package—the positive duty to provide assistance. The UN Declaration has made it clear that this humanitarian concern is also part of international legal standards.

Originally published in CWS/cf's Spring/Summer 1995 issue, "Women's Rights are Human Rights" (Volume 15, Numbers 2 & 3).

References

Asia and Pacific Development Centre (APDC). *Asia and Pacific Women's Resource and Action Series: Law*. Kuala Lumpur: APDC, 1993.

Brownmiller, S. *Against Our Will*. New York: Simon and Schuster, 1975.

Carillo, R. *Battered Dreams*. New York: UNIFEM, 1992.

Committee on the Elimination of Violence Against Women. General Recommendation no. 19. CEDAW/C/1992/L.1/Add.15.

Convention on the Elimination of all Forms of Discrimination Against Women (CEDAW). UN Doc. A/34/46 (1979).

Coomaraswamy, R. "To Bellow Like A Cow." Paper presented at the University of Toronto Workshop on *Women's Rights Are Human Rights*. Toronto, 1992a.

Coomaraswamy, R. "Of Kali Born: Women, Violence and the Law." *Freedom From Violence*. Ed. M. Schuler. New York: UNIFEM, 1992b.

Firestone, S. *The Dialectic of Sex*. London: Women's Press, 1979.

Kelkar, G. "Stopping the Violence Against Women: Fifteen Years of Activism." *Freedom from Violence*. Ed. M. Schuler. New York: UNIFEM, 1992.

Levinson, David. *Family Violence in Cross Cultural Perspective*. Newbury Park: Sage Publications, 1989.

Mitchell, J. *Women: The Longest Revolution*. London: Virago, 1984.

Omvedt, G. *Violence Against Women*. New Delhi: Kali, 1990.

Schuler, M, ed. *Freedom From Violence*. New York: UNIFEM, 1992.

Sullivan, D. *Violence Against Women: The Legal Framework*. New York: The International League for Human Rights, 1992.

United Nations Declaration on the Elimination of Violence Against Women. GA Res/104/UN GAOR 48th Session (1993).

Judging Women

The Pernicious Effects of Rape Mythology

Janice Du Mont and Deborah Parnis

We live in a culture characterized by both pervasive violence against women and a mistrust of those who have been violated. For many women, the horrifying experience of having been raped[1] may be compounded by a criminal justice system which responds with suspicion and disbelief. In reality, the woman who has been sexually assaulted frequently finds that both she and the accused are being judged. At the heart of this systemic bias is a long tradition of rape myths that have permeated not only the legal system, but that are pervasive in society. Here we review some of the key research literature centred around the nature and prevalence of these broadly held myths. We highlight their insidiousness through an examination of *R. v. Ewanchuk* (1999) and the response of Alberta's Appeal Court Justice John McClung to a judgment delivered by Madam Justice Claire L'Heureux-Dubé to a Supreme Court of Canada ruling which overturned his decision in this case. His response and the ensuing public debate reveal that rape myths may be the tip of the iceberg with respect to broader negative attitudes toward women. We argue that measures be taken to eliminate gender-based stereotyping within the criminal justice system and in society.

How rape myths hurt women

Rape myths underlie and fuel violence against women and inform the negative societal reactions to those who have been sexually assaulted (Ward 1995; see also Briere, Malamuth, and Check; Brownmiller; Torrey; Weis and Borges). Defined as "prejudicial, stereotyped, or false beliefs about rape, rape victims and rapists" (Burt 1980, 217), these myths serve to trivialize, justify and deny sexual assault (Burt 1991; Lonsway and Fitzgerald). Some common myths include:

> women mean "yes" when they say "no"; women are "asking for it" when they wear provocative clothes, go to bars alone, or simply walk down the street at night; only virgins can be raped; women are vengeful, bitter creatures "out to get men"; if a woman says "yes" once, there is no reason to believe her "no" the next time; women who

"tease" men deserve to be raped; the majority of women who are raped are promiscuous or have bad reputations; a woman who goes to the home of a man on the first date implies she is willing to have sex; women cry rape to cover up an illegitimate pregnancy; a man is justified in forcing sex on a woman who makes him sexually excited; a man is entitled to sex if he buys a woman dinner; [and] women derive pleasure from victimization. (Torrey 1015)

Rape myths perpetuate the belief that women are responsible for their own victimizations (Burt 1980; Kopper).

These false beliefs and negative stereotypes about rape and women who are raped are pernicious and widespread (Giacopassi and Dull). They have been linked to the likelihood of labelling rape "rape" (Burt and Albin; Norris and Cubbins), stereotyped expectations of women's behaviour (Burt 1980; Check and Malamuth; Costin; Hall, Howard and Boezio; Truman, Tokar and Fische), stereotyped notions of male sexuality (Cowan and Quinton), sexual conservatism (Check and Malamuth), beliefs that sexual relationships are inherently adversarial (Burt 1980; Caron and Carter; Check and Malamuth; Quackenbush; Ward 1988), the acceptance of interpersonal violence (Burt 1980; Check and Malamuth; Quackenbush), the self-reported likelihood of raping (Bohner, *et al.*; Briere and Malamuth; Check and Malamuth; Quakenbush), self-reported sexual aggression (Koss, Leonard, Beezley, and Oros; Muehlenhard and Linton), and higher rates of reported sexual assault (Muir, Lonsway, and Payne). In experimental situations, these beliefs have been associated with an unwillingness to convict an assailant of rape (Burt and Albin) and to sentence offenders strictly (Quackenbush). Martha Burt (1980) found that more than 50 per cent of the 598 Minnesota residents whom she surveyed endorsed rape myths regarding the woman's moral character and her propensity to lie. Of 122 West Virginian adolescents aged 14 to 19 surveyed by Ruth Kershner, over half strongly agreed that some women fantasize about being raped (52 per cent) and provoke men into sexually assaulting them (53 per cent).

The questioning of women's credibility within the criminal justice system

A woman known legally as Jane Doe was sexually assaulted on August 24, 1986. She was the fifth victim of a serial rapist who stalked women within a five-block radius of inner-city Toronto. She sued the local Board of Commissioners of Police, alleging that the police had used her as "bait" to apprehend the perpetrator. After eleven years of litigation, she was awarded $220,000 in damages on July 3, 1998. Ontario Court Justice Madam Jean MacFarland concluded at that time that "the police failed utterly in the duty of care they owed Ms. [Doe]" (*Jane Doe* v. *Toronto [Metropolitan] Commissioners of Police*, para 174). She stated,

[the] investigation and the failure to warn in particular, was motivated and informed by the adherence to rape myths as well as sexist stereotypical reasoning about rape, about women and about women who are raped. (*Jane Doe v. Toronto [Metropolitan] Commissioners of Police*, para 162)

Although feminists like Susan Brownmiller have been writing about this problem for years, few research studies have systematically examined law enforcement and legal personnel views on rape. Of those that have, many are dated, and some findings may be not be generalizable to Canada as they have drawn largely on small samples and American data. Nonetheless, their results indicate that some police, prosecutors, and judges hold the same negative attitudes and stereotypes that also pervade society.

John LeDoux and Robert Hazelwood surveyed 2,170 police officers in the United States about their attitudes and beliefs toward rape and reported that overall these officers viewed rape as a serious crime and were generally sympathetic to women who had been sexually assaulted. However, at the same time, the respondents agreed with a psychopathological view of rapists as sexually frustrated and out of control. Furthermore, they tended to believe that women provoke rape by dressing or behaving seductively. Appearance, previous sexual contact with the assailant, and age were factors they agreed influenced the legal resolution of rape cases.

Examining American police officers' definitions of rape, Rebecca Campbell and Camille Johnston found that 51 per cent of the 91 officers surveyed gave definitions of rape heavily influenced by rape myths. Their examples included:

Sometimes a guy can't stop himself. He gets egged on by the girl. Rape must involve force—and that's *really* rare; [and]

Men taking what women really want at that moment but decide they didn't the next morning when they sober up. (268)

Among this group, sexual assaults that did not conform to the stereotypical rape scenario (e.g., an armed stranger leaping out of the bushes at night) were discounted. Beyond their difficulties regarding the veracity of women raped by acquaintances, these officers had the least positive views of women and were most accepting of interpersonal violence.

Research findings have suggested that women police may also share some of the same negative perceptions about rape and women who are raped. David Lester, Fred Gronau and Kenneth Wondrack compared attitudes toward rape in female college students and female police recruits. They found that the recruits were more likely than the students to believe that women provoke rape and should resist an assailant vigorously. They were also more likely to view rape as a sex crime and to believe that women with good reputations do not get raped. Neither group of women tended to agree that rape was a crime of power.

There is evidence to suggest that prosecutors have also been considerably concerned with assessing the credibility of the sexually assaulted woman. In a study of prosecutorial decision-making (Law Enforcement Assistance Administration), 145 American prosecutor-respondents stated that the use of physical force, injury to the raped woman, her resistance and promptness of report, and proof of penetration were important in securing a conviction. The authors noted that force and injury "[were] ... related to the credibility of the victim, ... [and were not] necessary elements of the crime" (19). In fact, prosecutors reported that they sometimes requested that the woman take a lie detector test.

Eighteen prosecutors in Winnipeg were similarly queried about the factors required for conviction (Gunn and Minch). The use of physical force or a weapon, injury to the raped woman, and the interpersonal context of the offence were among the top five factors ranked. In fact, 17 of the prosecutors stated that one of the difficulties in securing a guilty verdict was the perceived credibility of the woman who had been sexually assaulted. As well, concerns about her veracity included references to her lifestyle and personal characteristics.

In a larger study, Lisa Frohmann examined the prosecutorial rejections of sexual assault cases over a two-year period (1989 to 1990) in two California jurisdictions. After observing over 300 case screenings and interviewing the investigating officers and prosecuting district attorneys involved in those cases, she reported that negative stereotypes and false beliefs about women who had been raped were used to discount sexual assault complaints or determine the cases as being unconvictable. Women with "criminal connections," whose stories were inconsistent, who did not report immediately to the police or appear upset during the interview, and who continued to see the assailant after the assault were more likely to have their cases screened out of the legal system by prosecutors.

Carol Bohmer examined judicial attitudes toward raped women, with seemingly similar results. Her interviews with 38 Philadelphia judges in 1971 revealed that "their central orientation in trying rape cases [was] to evaluate the credibility of the victim's allegation that forcible rape ... [had] occurred" (304). These judges tended to rank cases by the level of credibility ascribed to the woman. A complainant was perceived as "genuine" (i.e., assaulted by a stranger in a park at knife point), "asking for it" (e.g., met the assailant in a bar), or simply "vindictive" (i.e., wasn't raped or the sex was consensual). They also placed significant weight on circumstantial evidence during rape trials. This evidence included whether the woman was willing to cooperate, her reason for filing the complaint, and the promptness of her report.

Hubert Feild investigated the attitudes toward rape of 1,448 American police, citizens, rape crisis counsellors, and rapists. Overall, police officers were more similar to rapists than crisis counsellors with respect to their attitudes toward the etiology of rape and raped women. The law enforcement officers and rapists tended to agree that rape is a crime of sexual passion not power, that sexual offenders are mentally ill, and that women who have been raped are somehow less desirable. These officers were also the group most likely to believe that women may precipitate rape by how they dress and behave.

In a similar study, Shirley Feldman-Summers and Gayle Palmer examined the attitudes toward rape of 83 American police officers, prosecutors, and judges and compared them to rape crisis centre employees. The authors found that the law enforcement and legal professionals were more likely than the rape crisis workers to endorse rape myth-laden statements about the causes (e.g, women dress seductively and say "no" when they mean "yes") and prevention of rape (e.g., women should change the way they behave). They were also more likely than the social service personnel to believe a complaint was false. The authors found no differences between the groups regarding what constituted a "real" rape. A report was believed to be false if a woman was not injured, did not report the assault promptly, was unwilling to take a lie detector test, had engaged in pre- or extra-marital sex, knew the assailant, accompanied him willingly, or gave more than one account of the offence.

More recently, Colleen Ward (1988, 1995) surveyed the attitudes toward rape of 510 police officers, doctors, lawyers and counsellors in Singapore. All four professional groups endorsed a wide range of rape myths. More than 70 per cent of the overall sample agreed that women provoke rape by how they dress. Nevertheless, the police held the most stereotypical negative views of raped women. More than 50 per cent of these officers agreed that accusations of rape by bar girls, dance hostesses and prostitutes should be viewed with suspicion; many women claim rape if they have consented to sexual relations but changed their minds afterwards; the extent of a woman's resistance should be the major factor in determining if a rape has occurred, [and]; a healthy woman can successfully resist rape if she really tries.[2]

Ward and other social scientists have argued that the acceptance of rape myths by law enforcement and legal professionals prejudices the treatment of women within the judicial system (e.g., Bohmer and Blumberg; Edwards; Mack; Schwendinger and Schwendinger; Torrey; Weis and Borges). Indeed, many studies suggest that a sexually assaulted woman may be "twice trauma-tized" (e.g., Bohmer and Blumberg; Busby; Hendricks; Renner and Parriag). Her veracity may be challenged both during the police investigation and the prosecution (LaFree; Robin). Later, "she becomes the focus of the trial, and it is her actions, not those of the alleged offender, that are dissected and debated" (Andrias 3). The results of a recent Alberta Court of Appeal ruling are illustrative.

How some judges judge women: The case of Mr. Justice John McClung

On February 13, 1998, Mr. Justice John McClung of the Alberta Court of Appeal upheld a lower court's acquittal in a sexual assault case. His decision, which was later appealed to the Supreme Court of Canada, sparked a frenzied media reaction and a spate of controversy and public debate. It is clear evidence of the persistence of rape myths at a senior level of the criminal justice system.

On a summer evening in 1994, Steve Brian Ewanchuk, who had previously been convicted of three rapes, sexually assaulted a 17-year-old girl after what was ostensibly a job interview for a position in his woodworking business. Following the interview in Mr. Ewanchuk's van, which was parked outside an Alberta mall, he asked the woman if she would like to see a sample of his work in the attached trailer, to which she agreed. Once in the trailer, Mr. Ewanchuk proceeded to initiate

> a number of incidents involving touching each progressively more intimate than the previous, notwithstanding the fact that the complainant plainly said "no" on each occasion. He stopped his advances on each occasion when she said "no" but persisted shortly after with an even more serious advance. Any compliance by the complainant was done out of fear and the conversation that occurred between them clearly indicated that the accused knew that the complainant was afraid and certainly not a willing participant. (*R. v. Ewanchuk*)

Following the incident, the young woman contacted the police and Mr. Ewanchuk was charged with sexual assault. He was acquitted, however, by an Alberta trial judge who accepted the defence of "implied consent" concluding, despite the fact the sexually assaulted woman had clearly stated she did not want Mr. Ewanchuk to touch her and submitted to the sexual activity only out of fear that resistance would provoke a more violent reaction from him, the accused's perception of the complainant was that she had been agreeable to his increasing advances. This acquittal was upheld in the provincial Court of Appeal where it was concluded that the Crown had failed to prove that the "accused posed the requisite criminal intent" (*R. v. Ewanchuk*, para 18) and that "the onus [was] not on the accused to prove implied consent ... [but] on the Crown to prove beyond a reasonable doubt that there was an absence of consent" (qtd. in *The Globe and Mail* 14).

Although the ruling was problematic in legal terms, it was Mr. Justice McClung's attack on the character and behaviour of the sexually assaulted woman that revealed biases rooted in rape myths. He commented on her clothing: "the complainant did not present herself to [the accused] ... in a bonnet and crinolines" (qtd. in *R. v. Ewanchuk*, para 88); her past sexual history and her lifestyle: "she was the mother of a six-month old baby and ... along with her boyfriend, she shared an apartment with another couple" (qtd. in *R. v. Ewanchuk*, para 88); and the way in which she reacted to both the perpetrator and the assault: "in a less litigious age, going too far in the boyfriend's car was better dealt with on site—a well chosen expletive, a slap in the face or, if necessary, a well-directed knee" (qtd. in *R. v. Ewanchuk*, para 93). He also described Mr. Ewanchuk's behaviour as an expression "of romantic intentions ... far less criminal than hormonal" (qtd. in *R. v.*

Ewanchuk, para 90, 92). Furthermore, he was quoted later as saying that the complainant "was not lost on her way home from the nunnery" (qtd. in Saunders A4).

Both the acquittal and Mr. Justice McClung's statements elicited a strong response from the Supreme Court, which unanimously reversed the Alberta Court of Appeal's decision and stipulated a conviction. The Court's decision firmly upheld the principle of "no-means-no." Writing on behalf of five of the nine judges, Mr. Justice John Major stated that "the trial judge relied on the defence of implied consent ... a mistake of law as no such defence is available in ... Canada" (*R. v. Ewanchuk*, para 1). Madam Justice Claire L'Heureux-Dubé further stated, "[t]his case is not about consent since none was given. It is about myths and stereotypes" (*R. v. Ewanchuk*, para 82).

> That any woman could successfully resist a rapist if she really wished to; that the sexually experienced do not suffer harms when raped...; that women often deserve to be raped on account of their conduct, dress, and demeanor. (Archard qtd. in *R. v. Ewanchuk*, para 82)

Mr. Justice McClung took this judgment personally and launched a scathing and highly personal attack on Madam Justice L'Heureux-Dubé. In a letter published by the National Post, he implied that the Supreme Court judge was responsible for the high rate of male suicide in her home province of Quebec (McClung). Although his words stunned many in the legal community and the public, he found a sympathetic constituency among those who saw this highly publicized confrontation as an opportunity to challenge both legal definitions of sexual assault and the experiences of sexually assaulted women, and to attack feminists and women in general.

In identifying the Court's decision as a feminist ruling, defence lawyer Alan Gold told the *Toronto Star* that Madame Justice L'Heureux Dubé's judgment "turns (human sexuality) into a business-like formalistic affair where everything must be absolutely clear" (qtd. in Hoy A19) ... "and 'puts complainants on a pedestal' by absolving them of any responsibility for their conduct" (Hoy A19). Toronto lawyer Edward Greenspan asserted that L'Heureux-Dubé was "intemperate, showed a lack of balance, and a terrible lack of judgment" and incorrectly claimed that she had called McClung "the male chauvinist pig of the century... [and the] ultimate sexist jerk" (qtd. in Kozinski). Perhaps the coup de grace, Barbara Amiel's column in the National Post, equated feminists with communists and fascists and argued that L'Heureux-Dubé's judgments were "relentlessly anti-male, illiberal and anti-equality" and implied that she was herself a "'victim' ... [and as a] high-achieving wom[a]n ... living beyond her intellectual means" (Amiel). We believe that comments such as these reflect the pervasiveness of negative attitudes toward women in Canada. It remains to be seen if Mr. Justice McClung's words and actions have inadvertently served a valuable function by bringing these negative attitudes to the fore, where they may be clearly and decisively rebutted.

Conclusions

Numerous changes have been made to the sexual assault legislation in Canada since the early 1980s. Many of these were designed to eliminate biases in the legal system that worked against women who had been raped. Their partial success is evident in the Supreme Court's ruling on the Ewanchuk case which has established a benchmark precedent for the future. Nevertheless, attitudes such as those expressed by Mr. Justice McClung, Mr. Greenspan, and Mr. Gold suggest that our criminal justice system remains replete with anti-woman sentiment. Perhaps Quebec Court Justice Mr. Denys Dionne's comment in 1989 best exemplifies this bias: "rules are like women, made to be violated" (qtd. in Picard A4).

Clearly, there is still need for progressive change in the criminal justice system. Some have suggested that the use of expert educational testimony in courtrooms would help dispel the common misconceptions surrounding rape for jurors (e.g., Tetreault). Exposure to the same information for lawyers and judges could also be effective in reducing harmful attitudes toward women (Andrias), as could training programs that include modules on rape mythology.[3] Furthermore, there is a dearth of Canadian research studies which document the myriad ways that rape myths shape the legal response to women who are raped.

On a societal level, it remains incumbent upon us all to address the prejudicial views of these women. Studies have shown that the tolerance of rape is linked to stereotypical expectations of women's behaviour, beliefs that sexual relationships are inherently adversarial, and the acceptance of interpersonal violence (Burt 1980). Because these attitudes may be acquired at a very young age (e.g., Kershner), we believe that a long-term strategy to address and prevent violence must be to strengthen and extend community- and school-based educational campaigns aimed at eradicating gender-based stereotyping and inequities. There is evidence to suggest that educational programs can change negative attitudes toward women who are sexually assaulted (Ward 1995); the commitment for change need only be there.

Background sections of this paper were drawn from the first author's doctoral dissertation that was supported in part by the Social Sciences and Humanities Research Council of Canada and the Atkinson Foundation. The authors gratefully acknowledge Robin Badgley and Alison Morrow for their helpful comments on earlier drafts of this paper.

Originally published in CWS/cf's Spring/Summer 1999 issue, "Women and Justice" (Volume 19, Numbers 1/2): 102-109.

[1] We use the terms "rape" and "sexual assault" interchangeably throughout this paper.
[2] Items from the "Attitudes Toward Rape Victims Scale" (Ward 1995, 60).

[3]The effectiveness of any educational initiatives must be periodically evaluated.

References

"A Touch is Just a Touch: The Definition of Sexual Assault Needs Refining." *Globe and Mail* 26 Feb. 1999: 14.

Amiel, B. "Feminists, Fascists, and Other Radicals." *National Post* 6 March 1999: B7

Andrias, R. T. "Rape Myths. A Persistent Problem in Defining and Prosecuting Rape." *Criminal Justice* 7 (1992): 3-7, 51-53.

Archard, D. *Sexual Consent.* Boulder, CO: Westview Press, 1998.

Bohmer, C. "Judicial Attitudes Toward Rape Victims." *Judicature* 57 (1974): 303-307.

Bohmer, C., and A. Blumberg. "Twice Traumatized: The Rape Victim and the Court." *Judicature* 58 (1975): 391-399.

Bohner, G., M.A. Reinhard, S. Kutz, S. Sturm, B. Kerschbaum, and D. Effler. "Rape Myths as Neutralizing Cognitions: Evidence for a Causal Impact of Anti-Victim Attitudes on Men's Self-Reported Likelihood of Raping." *European Journal of Social Psychology* 28 (1998): 257-268.

Briere, J., and N. Malamuth. "Self-Reported Likelihood of Sexually Aggressive Behavior: Attitudinal Versus Sexual Explanations." *Journal of Research in Personality* 17 (1983): 315-323.

Briere, J., N. Malamuth, and J. V. P. Check. "Sexuality and Rape-Supportive Beliefs." *International Journal of Women's Studies* 8 (1985): 398-403.

Brownmiller, S. *Against Our Will: Men, Women and Rape.* New York: Simon and Schuster, 1975.

Burt, M. R. "Cultural Myths and Supports For Rape." *Journal of Personality and Social Psychology* 38 (1980): 217-230.

Burt, M. R. "Rape Myths and Acquaintance Rape." *Acquaintance Rape. The Hidden Crime.* Eds. A. Parrot and L. Bechhofer. New York: John Wiley, 1991. 26-40.

Burt, M. R., and R. S. Albin. "Rape Myths, Rape Definitions, and Probability of Conviction." *Journal of Applied Social Psychology* 11 (1981): 212-230.

Busby, K. "Discriminatory Uses of Personal Records in Sexual Violence Cases." *Canadian Journal of Women and the Law* 9 (1997): 149-177.

Campbell, R., and C. R. Johnson. "Police Officers' Perception Of Rape. Is There Consistency Between State Law and Individual Beliefs?" *Journal of Interpersonal Violence* 12 (1997): 255-274.

Caron, S. L., and D. B. Carter. "The Relationship Among Sex Role Orientation, Egalitarianism, Attitudes Toward Sexuality, and Attitudes Toward Violence Against Women." *The Journal of Social Psychology* 137 (1997): 568-587.

Check, J. V. P, and N. Malamuth. "An Empirical Assessment of Some Feminist Hypotheses About Rape." *International Journal of Women's Studies* 8

(1985): 414-423.

Costin, F. "Beliefs About Rape And Women's Social Roles." *Archives of Sexual Behavior* 14 (1985): 319-325.

Cowan, G., and W. J. Quinton. (1997). "Cognitive Sstyle and Attitudinal Correlates of the Perceived Causes of Rape S cale." *Psychology of Women Quarterly* 21 (1997): 227-245.

Edwards, S. "Sexuality, Sexual Offenses and Conceptions of Victims in the Criminal Justice Process." *Victimology* 8 (1983): 113-130.

Feild, H. S. "Attitudes Toward Rape: A Comparative Analysis of Police, Rapists, Crisis Counsellors, and Citizens." *Journal of Personality and Social Psychology* 36 (1978): 156-179.

Feldman–Summers, S., and G. C. Palmer, "Rape as Viewed By Judges, Prosecutors, and Police Officers." *Criminal Justice and Behavior* 7 (1980): 19-40.

Frohmann, L. "Discrediting Victims' Allegations of Sexual Assault: Prosecutorial Accounts Of Case Rejections." *Social Problems* 38 (1991): 213-226.

Giacopassi, D. J., and R. T. Dull. "Gender and Racial Differences in the Acceptance of Rape Myths Within a College Population." *Sex Roles* 15 (1986): 63-75.

Gunn, R., and C. Minch. *Sexual Assault: The Dilemma of Disclosure, the Question of Conviction.* Winnipeg: University of Manitoba Press, 1988.

Hall, E. R., J. A. Howard, and S. L. Boezio. "Tolerance of Rape: A Sexist or Antisocial Attitude?" *Psychology of Women Quarterly* 10 (1986): 101-118.

Hendricks, J. E. "Criminal Justice Intervention With the Rape Victim." *Journal of Police Science and Administration* 11 (1983): 225–232.

Hoy, C. "A Feminist Hijacking of Justice." *The Toronto Star* 3 March 1999: A19.

Jane Doe v. Toronto (Metropolitan) Commissioners of Police (1998) O.J. No. 2681 (Ontario Court of Justice, General Division). Online. Internet. Available at www.blaney.com/janed.htm

Kershner, R. "Adolescent Attitudes About Rape." *Adolescence* 31 (1996): 29-33.

Kopper, B. A. "Gender, Gender Identity, Rape Myth Acceptance, and Time of Initial Resistance on the Perception of Acquaintance Rape Blame And Avoidability." *Sex Roles* 34 (1996): 81-93.

Koss, M. P., K. E. Leonard, D. A. Beezley, and C. J. Oros. "Nonstranger Sexual Aggression: A Discriminant Analysis of the Psychological Characteristics of Undetected Offenders." *Sex Roles* 12 (1985): 981-992.

Kozinski, A. "An Unfair Attack on a Decent Judgment." *National Post* 8 March 1999: A18

LaFree, G. D. *Rape and Criminal Justice. The Social Construction of Sexual Assault.* Bellmont, CA: Wadsworth, 1989.

Law Enforcement Assistance Administration. *Forcible Rape. A National Survey of the Response by Prosecutors (Vol I).* Washington, DC: U.S. Government

Printing Office, 1977.

LeDoux, J. C. and R. R. Hazelwood. "Police Attitudes and Beliefs Toward Rape." *Journal of Police Science and Administration* 13 (1985): 211-220.

Lester, D., F. Gronau, and K. Wondrack. "The Personality and Attitudes of Female Police Officers: Needs, Androgyny, and Attitudes Toward Rape." *Journal of Police Science and Administration* 10 (1982): 357-360.

Lonsway, K. A., and L. F. Fitzgerald. "Rape Myths. In Review." *Psychology of Women Quarterly* 18 (1994): 133-164.

Mack, K. "Continuing Barriers to Women's Credibility: A Feminist Perspective on the Proof Process. *Criminal Law Forum* 4 (1993): 327-352.

McClung, J. "Right of Reply." *National Post* 26 Feb. 1999: A19.

Muehlenhard, C. L., and M. A. Linton. "Date Rape and Sexual Aggression in Dating Situations: Incidence and Risk Factors." *Journal of Counseling Psychology* 34 (1987): 186-196.

Muir, G., K. A. Lonsway, and D. L. Payne. "Rape Myth Acceptance Among Scottish and American Students." *The Journal of Social Psychology* 136 (1996): 261-262.

Norris, J., and L. A. Cubbin. "Dating, Drinking, and Rape. Effects of Victim's and Assailant's Alcohol Consumption on Judgments of Their Behavior and Traits." *Psychology of Women Quarterly* 16 (1992): 179-191.

R. v. Ewanchuk. Supreme Court of Canada. 1999. File No.: 26493. Online. Internet. Available at http://scc.lexum.umontreal.ca/en/1999/1999rcs1-330.pdf.

Renner, K.E. and A. Parriag. "Documenting the Outrageous for Adults." Unpublished Manuscript, 1998. Available at www.napasa.org/ORASA.htm.

Picard, A. "Jews Didn't Suffer, Quebec Judge Says." *Globe and Mail* 9 December 1995: A4.

Quackenbush, R. L. "A Comparison of Androgynous, Masculine Sex–Typed, and Undifferentiated Males on Dimensions of Attitudes Toward Rape." *Journal of Research in Personality* 23 (1989): 318-342.

Robin, G. D. "Forcible Rape. Institutionalized Sexism in the Criminal Justice System." *Crime and Delinquency* 23 (1977): 136-153.

Saunders, J. "McClung Calls Letter, Interview a Mistake." *The Globe and Mail* 2 March 1999: A4.

Schwendinger, J. R., and H. Schwendinger. "Rape Myths: In Legal, Theoretical, and Everyday Practice." *Crime and Social Justice* 1 (1974):18-26.

Tetreault, P.A. "Rape Myth Acceptance: A Case For Providing Educational Expert Testimony in Rape Jury Trials." *Behavioral Sciences and the Law* 7 (1989): 243-257.

Torrey, M. "When Will We Be Believed? Rape Myths and the Idea of a Fair Trial in Rape Prosecutions." *U.C. Davis Law Review* 24 (1991): 1013-1071.

Truman, D. M., D. M. Tokar, and A. R. Fischer. "Dimensions of Masculinity: Relations to Date Rape Supportive Attitudes and Sexual Aggression in

Dating Situations." *Journal of Counseling and Development* 74 (1996): 555-562.

Ward, C. "The Attitudes Toward Rape Victims Scale. Construction, Validation, and Cross–Cultural Applicability." *Psychology of Women Quarterly* 12 (1988): 127-146.

Ward, C. A. *Attitudes Toward Rape. Feminist and Psychological Perspectives*. London: Sage, 1995.

Weis, K., and S. S. Borges. "Victimology and Rape: The Case of the Legitimate Victim." *Issues in Criminology* 8 (1973): 71-115.

Linking Violence and Poverty in the CASAC Report

Lee Lakeman ───

CASAC (Canadian Association of Sexual Assault Centres) Links is a project in which ten anti-rape centers each allocated one staff and gathered ten callers to participate in a five-year research and development project. In examining the application of legal and feminist concepts of equality to the legal cases of women complaining of violence, we found ourselves up against not only the law but also the regressive changes to our country's social safety net and to global economic relations. We have tried here to connect our crisis calls to those other grave considerations. What follows is several small parts of our national CASAC Links report: *Canada's Promises to Keep: The Charter and Violence Against Women.*

Some effects of restructuring Canada on the nature, severity and incidence of violence against women

"The poor will always be with us," "prostitution is the oldest profession," and "men are just naturally that way." These stereotypical assumptions and essentialist positions or attitudes are not promoted in CASAC centres.[1] Rather, we see that each corporate move, social policy, and interaction of the state with its subjects moves us toward or away from the desired future. Class, race, and gender division and domination are social and economic construc-tions always in the making, as is equality.[2]

The end of the welfare state and the social welfare it sometimes provided is part of the globalization process in which Canada has played a role and that has engulfed women living in Canada. We have rarely had the opportunity to express, in our own way, the connections we live daily between those international economic forces, federal laws and policies, and what is happen-ing in anti-rape centres. Rare indeed is our opportunity to express the *link* between global/federal forces and our advocacy supporting women, especially those violated women trying to engage the power of the state against the power of their male abusers.

The CASAC Links project offered possibilities for renewing our alliances with other anti-rape centres and for speaking out together about the lives of women; but in any case we were compelled to do so by the changes in our daily work brought by the changes in Canadian society.

We are not the best ones to articulate, and there isn't space in this report to fully express, the devastating impact on Canadian women of the loss of public sector jobs and services.[3] But from our point of view, it is clear that there are few women who have not been made more vulnerable to criminal sexual assault. Every form of criminal violence against women in Canada has been aggravated. There is no liberatory and/or ameliorative process affecting violated women that has not been damaged and undermined.

CASAC's goal of a social economy that values women's labour and fairly shares wealth with women has been drastically set back. The trajectory of reforms toward those ends that had been won by our grandmothers, mothers, and ourselves—from the vote to unemployment insurance, from pensions to childcare, from self-determination to settling land claims, from welfare to more humane immigration policies, from criminalizing sexist violence to the inclusion of women in a living Charter of Rights and Freedoms—has been reversed in the service of grotesque individualism and corporate wealth.

CASAC wishes to express our understanding of those effects which we have encountered *most often* in our crisis work during this five-year research and development period (1998-2003), and which affect anti-violence work most profoundly: the loss of women's welfare, the promotion of prostitution and the use of the *Divorce Act* in such a way as to uphold the permanence of the patriarchal family, and the restructuring of Canada (from the shape of the justice system to the structure of civil society). These effects appear to CASAC to amount to a refusal by our national government to apply the Charter of Rights and Freedoms. To apply the Charter would require a diligent application of the current knowledge of women's oppression and an appropriate commitment to women's advancement.[4]

There are those who see it differently.[5] We have had to defend our positions rather rigorously in the last few years. The government has applied only formal equality when attending to equality at all. It has sometimes ignored both the Supreme Court rulings against formal equality and the reverse impact of the application of these polices. Huge economic and political forces have been mounted to oppose any government role beyond armies and prisons. Sometimes we have found ourselves reeling from many simultaneous blows.

At the same time, there was a big push, supported by government, to promote the rights of victims, even a possible new national victim's association. (The government was referring here to the rights to information about upcoming hearings, the rights to be notified if an offender is released from jail, etc.; what might in general be considered politeness and consideration.) The government promotion of the notion of "victim" as a legal policy category plus the changes to community policing, sentencing changes, to confinement in the home rather than jails, and the promotion of prostitution, opened up a number of key questions within criminal justice: for instance, who defines community and how? And who is considered part of the community? What is the relationship between the state and the community? What is the relationship between women's antiviolence groups, social change, and the state?[6]

We were interested in those conversations that might affect our under-standing of our options as the nature of the Canadian state changed.

The bottom line: The loss of the women's welfare

Most members of the community realize that we are contending with mean-spirited welfare reductions and restrictions that make life more difficult for the poor. Although it is difficult to keep track of the specifics, some changes have been publicized. In B.C., for instance, we know that "women with children will lose one hundred dollars a month from their already inadequate cheques by April 1, 2004" (Duncan).

No government declared honestly to its citizens before election either the nature of welfare cuts it intended or the further feminization of poverty that would be imposed by those cuts. It is simply not true that Canadians voted for those attacks on the poor.

And no government within Canada has been given a mandate to end welfare. Any such mandate would be legally questionable in any case, given the Charter and human rights law and conventions. This is perhaps why no government makes public those whom it is refusing subsistence. But CASAC women are witness to the fact that women across the country have no guaranteed, or even likely, access to a promised minimum standard of living. No matter how poor, women have no guarantee of welfare in any form. As women consider their options for improving their lives they certainly learn this, and so do we.

We have lost a small but significant recognition and amelioration of the historically disadvantaged economic condition of women's lives. But as predicted in feminist accounts of the end of Canada Assistance Plan (CAP) funding and as recorded in our alternate reports to the oversite committee of the United Nations Convention on the Elimination of All Forms of Discrimi-nation Against Women (CEDAW), women in Canada have also lost what application we had of this encoded economic human right. (Brodsky and Day). CASAC is most concerned that we are losing this benchmarked recognition of the economic oppression and redistribution of income toward equality.

In each province and community the attacks and erosion have been different, ranging from workfare to "man in the house" rules, age limitations, rate decreases, time limited access, lifetime bans, immigration and settlement restrictions, punishment bans after and through criminalization, to bans based on health requirements.

Not only has the formal policy been degraded, but the positive discretion-ary power in applying procedures and enforcing regulations has also been curtailed. Management and sometimes the remaining staff too often interpret rules with the same anti-entitlement attitudes.

The abdication of the federal role in assuring women and others who need a guaranteed dignified income is plain and it is Canada-wide. This includes the downward pressure of shrinking transfer payments and block funding without national standards (Brodsky and Day). That abdication encourages provinces to set social welfare, education, and health needs of the community against the needs of business for roads and bridges, to ship goods, and transport tourists. We don't win.

Transition houses too were funded under the same mechanisms of the CAP program. They were one of the permissible ways that social welfare dollars could be spent by the provinces.

Transition houses in Canada emerged partly to deal with the limits that existed in the welfare policy of the 1970s. Welfare departments would refuse to grant women welfare cheques when they came to the state for assistance in dealing with abusing husbands. Welfare workers were directed to tell women that the state could not be responsible "for the break-up of families" (Lakeman). If a woman left and established residency on her own, then welfare might be granted since it was an assumed economic right of Canadians to not starve or be homeless. Since they usually had no money, women moved to transition houses, where they didn't need rent or deposits, not only for immediate safety, but to establish a separate residence to prove to the state that they had left the marriage/family/couple. During their stay with us, they qualified for welfare.[7]

Women still come. Transition houses are full. Shelters for the homeless and other emergency facilities are also full. But now these women "qualify" for welfare less and less often, and they do not ordinarily receive benefits without aggressive advocacy from someone independent of government. They are told constantly that it is not a right and cannot be relied on. Welfare, they are told, can be reduced, withdrawn, and denied temporarily. A woman could be banned for life.[8]

While we are focused here particularly on social welfare payments to single and single-parent women, the colloquial understanding of the women who call us and the women who work in our centers is of a human right to a dignified minimum income that might be delivered as unemployment insurance, minimum wage, old age or disability pension or welfare but was in their minds entitlement by law to every resident to an economic share that could ensure survival and dignity.

Women, especially poor women, have always had to make extra-legal deals with the men in their lives. When ex-husbands or lovers are taking a kind of responsibility by sliding women money under the table for childcare, we are all glad. But in women's position of extra dependence created by the state withdrawal, sometimes those deals are dangerous underground contracts, which the women cannot enforce, and which subjugate them to the very men they are trying to leave for the sake of themselves and their children.

Any welfare granted currently is so inadequate and insecure as to force the women into subsidizing it with an informal economy: house work for others, childcare for others, personal health care for others, food preparation and production for others, drug sales, and/or prostitution.[9] Subsidizing legally is either clawed back through mechanisms that "allow" recipients to keep only pittance earnings above the welfare check or the subsidizing activity itself is illegal. To be poor is to be criminalized.

In our CASAC report we are most concerned with what happens to women under these conditions trying to report sexual violence. Women who complain to the state of rape, sexual harassment, incest, sexual exploitation, and trafficking face the denial of security: no exercisable right to welfare. If by some cleverness, accident, or kindness a woman gets welfare and is subsidizing it to get by, she is vulnerable to blackmail by her attacker. If she reports criminal sexual abuse, she will quickly be threatened (directly and indirectly) by the defence bar. Exposure can cause either a loss of informal income or the loss of her credibility as a complainant. She can and will be painted as a liar, thief, con, drug dealer, prostitute, unworthy of the protection of the law.

The 14 or 18-year-old incest victim leaving home, the worker on minimum wage or making her way in the informal economy, the dislocated woman pulled from her small town or reserve into the city for work or education, the immigrant woman struggling to survive or trying to transition into lawful citizenship and a reasonable life.—all are frustrated. If the normalcy of male violence against women were not known, one might think this was something other than state collusion with violence against women.[10] Access to the rule of law and equal protection under the law become meaningless.

In anti-rape centres we now face daily many women who judge that they simply cannot leave or escape men who criminally abuse them: husbands, fathers, bosses, pimps, johns, landlords, and sometimes social or welfare workers.[11] Since they cannot afford to actually leave, they cannot afford to effectively stand up to their abusers either. Those that do leave those economic positions are on their own with their children, and they know it.

A global economy: The promotion of prostitution

Can anyone still believe that there is no connection between the economic redistributive functions of the state, including within the social safety net, and the staggering increase in the informal economy? The economic division of the peoples of the world is staggering. The economic division among Canadians is growing exponentially.

Child and street-level prostitution and the so-called "adult entertainment" industry are booming. This is globalization being brought to Canada. Drug trafficking and prostitution are replacing welfare, health care, and education as the hope of the destitute.

Professor Dara Culhane at Simon Fraser University describes "a process that moves women farther and farther out from under whatever small protections working people and women have been able to construct within the state."[12] While they have been for many years prey to the law-and-order agenda and remain so, at the same time some are now moving out past the reach of law to the no-woman's land of the urban and suburban informal economies.

Aboriginal women have been talking about this for years as a factor in violence against women on and off reserve. We remember Teresa Nahanee at an Ottawa Legal and Education Access Fund (LEAF) conference in the early 1990s describing the condition of Aboriginal women in many parts of Canada as having to live without any basic rule of law. Now these are the conditions for many women in every major Canadian settlement.

Many women are being driven into the hands of global traders in labour, flesh, and drugs. They are trafficked into and throughout Canada by those global traders on the one hand and, on the other, within Canada by Canadian gangs, particularly the motorcycle gangs.[13] As protection we are offered racist immigration practices that jail the people trafficked and legalization of the prostitution industry. Of course, we don't want the criminalization of the victims, including all those at the bottom of these rigid hierarchies.[14] But surely we are all aware now that this multi-billion dollar prostitution industry is actively involved not only in the trade itself, but also in the promotion of the legalization of the trade in women and drugs.[15]

As with our struggles against the rest of the inhumane multinational trade agenda, we must expose, confront, and interfere with the managers, owners, profiteers, and consumers. The leadership of Sweden in this matter of human rights and women's rights is impressive and hopeful.[16] Sweden has criminalized the seller and begun to protect the victimized.[17] It regards prostitution as violence against women. It is no accident that Sweden is not building an economy on tourism or the sex tourism that goes with it.

To ignore women's equality aspirations and the current unequal status of women in Canada and in the world will undermine any progressive efforts to protect prostituted women from criminalization. Naive good intentions to protect the individual women should not be used to tolerate the development of this grotesque industry. In our efforts to address the needs of women trafficked into and throughout Canada, CASAC has come to the conclusion that we can only serve them by protecting their gender rights, their status as women, and the status of all women. No one is disposable or worthy of any lesser rights.

In our centres we are contending with women trafficked from abroad as indentured labour, mail order brides, domestic workers, and street-level prostitutes. Sometimes we are asked to support beaten and raped exotic dancers, as well as women working in "escort" services and "massage" parlours. Daily we are dealing with women dislocated from remote territories within Canada and trying to make their way in the cities. We are taking calls from, housing, and referring women who have been supplementing their incomes with prostitution and who want protection, both legal and political, from their pimps, johns, boyfriends, lovers, and fathers, and sometimes from the government officials to whom they try to report incidents of violence.

The public provision of exit services to women leaving prostitution is inadequate. From our centres in the early 1980s we supported the development of both The Alliance for the Safety of Prostitutes (ASP) and Prostitutes and Other Women for Equal Rights (POWER) networks.[18] Both were spin-offs, in both membership and politics, of anti-rape centres that wanted to specialize in serving women prostituted.

During this project we participated in Direct Action Against Refugee Exploitation (DAARE)[19] and have supported financially and politically Justice for Girls[20] and many other initiatives across the country. But we remain convinced that to use the easier provision of services as an argument for legalization is misguided. As Cherry Kingsley says:

> If we want to set up areas to protect women, to give women dignity and police protection, appropriate childcare, housing, and job train-ing, and so on, then we should do that. Why should women have to service men sexually to be offered those things needed by all women?[21]

Certainly among the women who call us and come to us, most do not choose prostitution except as a highly available way to survive. We speculate that the few women in the world who do choose it are short-time participants with privileges that allow them to leave. The provision of services specific to women trapped in or wanting to leave prostitution is inadequate everywhere. But to think that such services alone will curtail the harm of prostitution in the midst of this economic agenda is ridiculous. And for the federal government to refuse to try to curtail the domestic and international prostitution of women is barbarous.

The recognition of the so-called "rights of prostitutes" or the new talk of decriminalization (meaning legalization) is a self-serving policy ploy.[22] It legitimizes men's right to abuse women and also legitimizes Canada's refusal to redistribute income to women, some of whom are the most needy women, both within her borders and in the international community.

Predictable access to welfare was a power used by more than the destitute. It was a power in the hands of all women: the knowledge that we could (in a very modest amount) pay for food and shelter for ourselves and our kids by right. It was a power used to fend off attackers and to take advantage of opportunities. It was a basis on which to build one's self respect. The organizing in the 1930s, resulting in the legislation of welfare rights, had declared that everyone in Canada was entitled to at least this minimal share in the community and in the commonwealth.

We have no romantic memories of the days when welfare was great. We learned early in our herstory, and as we discussed our lived experiences, a critique of the welfare state as social control, especially of women.[23] We needed much more income redistribution and much less regulation of women's lives (Sidel). Still, we share with many second and third-wave feminists[24] a critique of the dismantling of the welfare state and the social safety net that it sometimes provided.[25]

Canadians have been deceived and manipulated to achieve this reversal of social policy. Clearly national standards are necessary as are achievable protections for women across the country.

When we redesign "welfare," as we surely will, we must start by acknowledging everyone's right to an adequate income. We must revive the Guaranteed Annual Income concepts that generated welfare reforms from the 1930s to 1975. Feminists must not tolerate going back to notions of family income or of the worthy and unworthy poor, to disentitling immigrant workers, divisions of minimum wages from disability rights, disassociated child poverty, or to mothers' allowances, Aboriginal disentitlement, forced work camps, or age restrictions even when disguised as age entitlements. We will certainly not tolerate going back to the intrusive state supervision of the private lives of women.

In this desperate time for so many women, perhaps we should take heart that most Canadians have not yet realized our loss of welfare and will surely rise to the occasion.

The CASCA Links Report, Canada's Promises to Keep, is available at www.casac.ca and will soon be available in book form by Black Rose Books.

Originally published in CWS/cf's Spring/Summer 2004 issue, "Benefiting Women? Women's Labour Rights" (Volume 23, Numbers 3/4): 57-62.

[1] We are saying that there is nothing intrinsically different about the women and children who end up poor or violated. And the men who violate them are not biologically compelled; they make choices to do so.

[2] Professor Dorothy Smith's work has helped us to keep seeing this. Her early analysis of the United Way struggle in Vancouver from the 1970s to 1990s was followed by conversations with us about class and the women's movement over the years.

[3] We have learned a lot from Penni Richmond, Madelaine Parent, Sharon Yandel, and Linda Shuto, and suggest their bodies of work as a source of that history and its importance to women.

[4] According to our Supreme Court Rulings that support both substantive equality approaches rather than merely formal equality (a notion that sometimes treating unequal groups exactly the same way causes more inequality) and support contextual understandings.

[5] The Social Union Framework Agreement has not been an improvement on the Meech Lake Accord or the lost CAP and Health regimes. It has left women totally vulnerable in every way. The process has barred non-government involvement. We have no reassurance either that our particular identities will be recognized or that our collective or universal needs and entitlements will be met. While there seems to be some consensus that the framework can be adjusted to serve us as citizens and specifically as women, we should not be satisfied with less than the language that encodes those promises in enforceable national standards and oversight mechanisms.

[6] In their 1992 book, *Women, Violence and Social Change*, Dobash and Dobash present the results of a respectful examination of the ways in which anti-

violence groups have analyzed and affected the state by comparing the movement in Britain where a welfare state was in place to the U.S, where a constitutional rights-based approach was more common.

[7] Between 1975 and 1995 it was rare for women to have trouble getting welfare after living in a transition house.

[8] In both B.C. and Ontario, lifetime bans have been imposed. Temporary refusals have been instituted. Time limits—for instance, of only being eligible for two years out of five—have been imposed. Health criteria have been imposed. Rate reductions have been imposed.

[9] All welfare rates as well as minimum wage rates in the country are below the poverty line.

[10] Federal-Provincial-Territorial Ministers Responsible for The Status of Women, 2002.

[11] Welfare workers and social workers are sometimes reported to us as abusers of their clients. They have much more power to abuse if the women know they have no enforceable right to welfare: they are dependent on the discretion in his hands.

[12] Personal communication, October 2001.

[13] In our work we have become aware of the ownership and prostitution dealings of (at least) The Hell's Angels in every province except the Maritimes, the Big Circle Boys gang, the Lotus gang, Fukianese, the Russians, the Mafia-related gangs, and the Vietnamese gangs.

[14] Most of the Canadian women's movement has agreed that prostitutes and low-level drug dealers should not be jailed or even criminalized. We have also agreed that those women trafficked as indentured labour or sex slaves should not be criminalized or deported. Our debates are about how to deal with the men and how to interfere with the trade.

[15] Gunilla Eckberg, personal communication, September 2003. She is special advisor to the government of Sweden on prostitution.

[16] For instance, see online <http://www.naring.regeringin.se/fragor/jamstadlldhet/aktuellt/trafficking.htm>.

[17] And here we mean the pimps. We rarely see the women as the sellers.

[18] See online: <http://wwwrapreliefshelter.bc.ca/herstory/rr_files86.html>.

[19] The extra A is because the cookie company DARE threatened women organized under that name with lawsuits if we used their trademark name, although the police have a drug abuse program with the same name.

[20] Justice for Girls is a group focusing on feminist intervention against the exploitation of young women.

[21] Cherry Kingsley, personal communication, October 2001. Cherry Kingsley escaped prostitution and often speaks as a woman who has experienced these conditions. She works in the International Centre to Combat Exploitation of Children.

[22] Decriminalization used to mean preventing charges against the women. Now it is shorthand for the legitimating of the trade. We continue to stand with the women and against the trade.

[23]See CASAC newsletters (1978-1982) available at Vancouver Rape Relief library.
[24]Such as the member groups of FAFIA and the B.C. CEDAW group.
[25]See online <http://www.fafia-afai.org/index_e.htm>

References

Brodsky, G. and S. Day. *Canadian Charter Equality Rights for Women: One Step Forward or Two Steps Back?* Ottawa: Canadian Advisory Council on the Status of Women, 1989.

Dobash, E. and R. Dobash. *Women, Violence and Social Change.* London and New York: Routledge, 1992.

Duncan, C. "Raging Women: Fighting Cutbacks in B.C." Paper presented at the Raging Women's Conference by Vancouver Women's Health Collective. Vancouver, Canada, October, 2003.

Lakeman, L. *99 Federal Steps Toward an End to Violence Against Women.* Toronto: National Action Committee on the Status of Women, 1993.

Sidel, R. Keeping Women and Children Last: America's War on the Poor. New York: Penguin, 1996.

Women Under the Dome of Silence

Sexual Harassment and Abuse of Female Athletes

Sandra L. Kirby, Lorraine Greaves and Olena Hankivsky

Sexual harassment and abuse in sport is a significant and often hidden problem for female athletes. Sport remains a complex cultural phenomenon and, in an effort to understand the nature and scope of the problem of sexual harassment and abuse, it has been necessary for researchers to consider "not just the athlete and her coach but also sport organizations, the police, child protection and legal agencies, other coaches, peer athletes, siblings and parents" (Brackenridge 2001: 44). The research started with Crosset's study on male coach/female athlete relationships and Brackenridge's (1986) article on codes of practice for coaches. By 2001, some 26 pieces of research had been completed by 33 different researchers in eight countries and WomenSport International had formed a Task Force of Sexual Harassment in Sport to inform governments and sport practitioners around the world. Canadian researchers such as Lenskyj, Holman, Kirby and Greaves, Kirby, Greaves and Hankivsky, and Donnelly figure prominently among them.

Research findings reveal consistancy on four points. First, they all agree that sexual harassment and abuse affects significantly more female athletes than male athletes and that for male athletes, there is even more of a problem of under reporting than for the female athletes. Second, all agree that like sexual abuse in other institutions, sexual harassment and abuse is debilitating, shaming, isolating and traumatic to its victims (Kirby *et al.*). Third, all agree that athletes do not know what to do about abuse they experience and, if they do lay a complaint, are unlikely to be satisfied with the outcomes or with the penalties for the abuser. And fourth, all agree that sport organizations and practitioners are not doing enough to identify the problem areas and people and to protect their participants from harassment and abuse. With those results in mind, we argue here that a "dome of silence" exists to keep athletes complacent in sport and that seven imperatives (patriotism/nationalism, militarism, competition, media sport, the work ethic, heterosexism/hypersexuality and familism) dictate the shape and strength of that "dome of silence."[1]

The experience of female athletes

In the original survey of 1200 Canadian national team athletes (Kirby and

Greaves), the authors addressed four questions about sexual harassment and abuse: did athletes think these were important issues; what had athletes seen and heard; what had they experienced; and what did they think needed to be done about the problem. In this article, we use the voices of the female athletes to fill in the picture and thus, it is from their perspective that we carefully draw out how female athletes live under the "dome of silence" in the complex sport world.

The female athletes who responded to this survey averaged 25.8 years of age and 5.4 years of experience on the national team. We specifically did not ask what sport they participated in to avoid any individual identifiers. However we did ask who they had been coached by while on the national team and 66 per cent reported being coached by males, 17 per cent by females and 17 per cent by both males and females. Half of the athletes were single and/or lived alone and another eleven per cent had children. On average, they reported being sexually active on or about 18 years of age. The majority had already completed college or university degrees, including graduate degrees. This makes them among the more educated of Canada's population. Because their average income was less than $10,000 in 1996 dollars, they are also among the poorest.

First, did female athletes think these were important issues? There is a difference between knowing about and issue and being informed about it. We can comfortably conclude that many athletes, particularly female athletes, are well aware of instances of sexual harassment and abuse. And, while it is heartening to know that female athletes are generally aware of the issues, they appeared to get the majority of their information about the issues from outside of sport. Only one-third of the athletes heard about these issues specifically within the sporting context. Also, female athletes are much more likely to feel vulnerable, unsafe or fearful in sport than are male athletes, with 45 per cent of female athletes feeling "less than very safe" in sport. Female athletes are likely to fear, in order of priority, rape/sexual assault, sexual harassment, child sexual assault, and physical harassment. These results show that feelings of vulnerability, feelings of safety and fear of sexual violence are a very real part of the experience of many female athletes. Here are some examples:

> ... when a coach said to my team, "Boy, you look great in those sex suits. You look like sex." Another coach that same week told a girl to "suck my dick" while the athletes were changing positions during training.

> ... It had gotten to the point where we heard this language everyday, we were desensitized to it. But charges [the man was charged] opened our eyes to the serious wrongdoing.

In addition, the athletes complained about a thriving sexist environment where verbal abuse went unchecked, sexual jokes and sexual allusion to what athletes must do to make the team were commonplace and there was a high tolerance for homophobic and sexist attitudes among the coaches. In spite of the female athletes' feelings of being informed, they were not, or at least not to the point where they knew what to do in situations like the above.

Second, what had female athletes seen and heard, that is, what was the extent and content of the rumour mill about sexual harassment and abuse? What we found was that the rumour mill was alive and well and functioned to warn female athletes about potentially dangerous situations. About twice as many female as male athletes report hearing rumours or actually seeing sexual harassment or abuse take place. While some athletes related personal accounts of harassment and abuse, many reported the ongoing nature of these activities. They happened in a number of places (on team trips, during training or in private locations like the home or vehicle of a coach or older athlete) rather than restricted to a single and predictable site. The female athletes wrote four times as many accounts involving coaches (48) than about others. Medical doctors or personnel, physiotherapists (5), strangers (5), national team committee members, or site managers (2) are also implicated in these reports but in far fewer accounts. Here are some typical examples of their accounts:

A 30-year old coach I know was sleeping with a 15-year old team members while on road trips. She was his girlfriend at the time.

A coach who used his authority to take advantage of students, during regular training and also at his home. A long-time coach with a close and trusting relationship with a student began inviting her to his home for "extra" training-related sessions. He subtly began to sexually harass/molest her in such a way that she was afraid to speak up about the issue for a long period of time.

The sexist coach of the women's team was … too touchy during regular training. He was also verbally abusive, sexist and he liked to get too close to the women during "private" coaching.

Not to be allowed to say anything because you're a female or public arguments about girls not being capable of operating power tools to work on equipment or of operating a van. The coach and the male athletes concurred.

All these accounts of sexual harassment and abuse, we believe are testimony to the culture that exists in sport which pressures female athletes to put up with the sexist environment and gives the impression that those in positions of authority, who have sexual motives, have little or no difficulty in selecting vulnerable athletes upon whom they prey. These results confirm that the issues are not secret but apparently cannot be spoken about outside of sport, or perhaps even outside the team. We have asked ourselves whether this is because of apathy on the part of the female athletes or because they fear the consequences of speaking out. The latter is the more likely case.

Third, what had these athletes actually experienced in the way of sexual harassment and abuse? Here, we asked athletes to share their personal histories of sexual harassment and abuse and to describe the situations which upset them the most.

Many athletes report experiencing put-downs or insults based on their being female, or gay or for some other reason or characteristic. Over half (55 per cent) of female athletes experienced put-downs or insults which are serious enough to upset them. And female athletes who experience such comments are also more likely to be upset if the comment is made by a coach rather than by team-mates or some other person in the sporting context. This is testimony to the effect coaches can have on athletes, particularly male coaches on female athletes, when the communication is both negative and a cross-gendered put-down.

In addition, 43 per cent of the female athletes reported sexually suggestive comments and nine in ten comments came from males, usually older male coaches or athletes. The following are typical of the comments:

It varied. Nothing serious enough to be the "most upsetting"; just constant comments re: issues of attractiveness, looking feminine, being flat-chested, good or bad in bed because of being an athlete, etc.

I was called a dyke basically because I was athletic.

Female athletes also report receiving obscene phone calls, being stalked on training runs if they are alone, in corridors of training centres if they have a regular pattern of activity or when they are at home, being flashed (someone exposing their genitals).

We also found an abuse of power by some of those in positions of authority occurring in Canadian sport. Coaches and others must know where to draw the line, and what is foul play, behaviours crossing the line between responsible behaviour and abuse of authority. For example, 15 female athletes felt that an authority figure in a sporting situation had made them afraid by being sexually interested in them. The authority figures were always male. Some who were made afraid because of this attention from male authority figures and because of that fear, experienced sexual intercourse with them.

Even more damning is that one in five athletes (90 per cent of them female) had sex with a person in a position of authority over them in the sporting context. The authority figures were almost always older males, sometimes much older males. In addition, a quarter of those abused athletes experienced physical and/or emotional abuse during the encounter or encounters. This shows that these people in positions of authority have abused the trust given to them by the sport system and by the athletes to gain sexual access to those athletes based on the presence of that fear. Here is an account in one athlete's words:

> One of my teammates had slept with the coach (43 years old when it started) since she was 13. She felt awful because she couldn't say anything to anybody. The sexual abuse happened on team trips, in his trailer, in his vehicle, in the hotel and in many other places. The coach said how special she was and he took her on as his special project ... he slept with her until she was 18. He completely isolated her from the rest of us.

Further, child sexual assault, like the situation above, was experienced by two per cent of the female athletes in the sporting context. A further ten per cent of female athletes reported experiencing attempted or forced sexual intercourse after the age of 16 years:

> I was 20 he was 34. At a training camp, after the training in the evening, only once, he forced himself on me. After that I trained only with others present.

> A male athlete on another team forced me. I was 18 and he was 26. It was in an hotel room after the championship competition. There was drinking involved. It was sexual intercourse from behind. I was basically asleep. I told no one.

This introduces a new relational context, almost an incestuous one, into our understanding of sexual harassment and abuse. Team-mates are like family and as such, should be safe confidants and supports.

Fourth, and finally, we asked what did they think needed to be done about the problem. An overwhelming majority of harassed and abused athletes did not lay an official complaint, particularly when the perpetrator was someone the athletes knew well and trusted like members of the family. This introduces a whole new dynamic into our understanding of the issue. Fellow athletes are like family and coaches, and perhaps other authority figures, are somewhat like parental figures for the national team female athletes. For the few who did lay a complaint, not only was the process a difficult one, but the athletes were generally unsatisfied with the outcomes. Thus, the athletes do not appear to have faith in the existing complaint process or outcomes, and they describe strong pressure from teammates and authority figures in sport not to "rock the boat" if they wish to continue to be successful.

Thus, from this section on female athletes' experiences, we can conclude that not only are the above accounts alarming, but also they are a clarion call for education for the athletes. They have a right to enjoy sport free from sexual harassment and abuse and education can give them some of the skills in recognizing the discriminations and abuses—an important first step to eradicating them. At this time, female athletes are uncertain about what supports are around them, many feel maligned if they complain and sport organizations have not yet developed effective ways of handling complaints and communicating these processes to the athletes. It is not a very encouraging picture.

The dome of silence

These reports are extremely disturbing, revealing patterns of systematic sexual harassment and abuse of athletes often by authority figures and requiring further investigation on a sport by sport basis, and at all levels of sport competition. The harasser is most often male, the victim most often female. However, there may be harassment by a member of the same sex, or a female harassing a male. The harassment can happen on the playing fields, tracks, rinks, pools or waterways. It can happen in change rooms, on buses, in cars, in hotel rooms and in elevators. It can occur on team trips or training courses, at conferences or team parties. It can happen to any member of the public using sport facilities or any member of a sport organisation before, during, or after the regular sport participation. It usually happens repeatedly over a short or long period of time. Most often, it happens in private. Not only does sexual violence diminish the quality of sport performance but it negatively affects the quality of the experience for all concerned; the athletes, coaches, administrators, and officials alike.

We can clearly see: 1) The shift from private to public has been noticeable and dramatic. Practices that were previously secretive and shameful have become publicly deplored and increasingly criminalized. 2) An increased awareness of the dynamics of violence in relationships, and a growing respect for victims' rights to disclose and seek help and compensation have also been developed. 3) There is a strong similarity between sport and other institutions in the unveiling of the private agony of sexual abuse and harassment, institutions such as churches, schools and the military.

Another powerful social institution to come under scrutiny is the media. There are numerous critiques of the impact of portrayals of violence (McLelland; Brink) for their role in socialization by perpetuating violence through the use of violent imagery. For example, in the sport of ice hockey, commentator Don Cherry's "Rock 'Em Sock 'Em" videos focus on the hardest, most aggressive "hits" in the sport and encourage young players to make the hits but to stay within the rules while doing so. Television, print, film and recently, the Internet and video games have been challenged for endorsing violent behaviours in youthful audiences (Larkin). The linkage between pornography and sexual violence has been much discussed over the past two decades. Research on the quality of the link between violent media imagery and violent behaviour is not fully conclusive.

The most profound changes, however, have occurred in the family. Traditionally the most private of places and ideally the sanctuary of emotional support and love has been transformed into a site of intense public interest. Physical, emotional and sexual abuses of women and children within family life have become exposed, publicized, analyzed and often criminalized. The characterization of these abuses as either private, justifiable or insignificant has been largely rejected in Canadian life. The confounding context of love and security, contaminated by violence and abuse has deterred many from disclosure. Even with disclosure, the spectre of re-victimization by the perpetrator or "the system" looms large.

For a variety of reasons, sport has evaded the same level of scrutiny and exposure.

Explaining this delay in applying the relationship violence lends to sport prompts us to assess the ideological underpinnings of sport and the structure of the sporting context. What are the values that are paramount in the institution of sport, and how have they affected disclosure and scrutiny of sexual abuses within it? What are the structures in place that affect the sport experience, and how have these contributed to this delay, or the reaction to abuse when it does arise?

Ultimately, these are questions about values. What is the place of sport in our culture, and how has this insulated sport from analyses of sexual violence?

The Imperatives: Seven values appear to have a huge impact on sport. These imperatives or main drives in sport are both positive and, when taken to extremes, negative. Briefly, the seven are:

1) *Patriotism/nationalism:* Patriotism is the love for and devotion to one's country. Nationalism is the specific support for the well-being of the country (supporting the culture and collective interests on the nation).

2) *Militarism:* The identification with the ideals of the professional military. Both patriotism/nationalism and militarism are overlapping concepts characterized by athletes' loyalty to team (community, nation), ambassadorial roles (opening ceremonies, media appearances), wearing of uniforms and hence, a "uniforming" of athletes (elimination of diversity), and adherence to rules, unquestioning obedience and commitment to "toe the line"and "be like the rest." However, shared values and preparedness for competition also reinforce long standing discriminatory attitudes and behaviours (race, class, sex, language are enshrined as bases for discrimination and race and ethnicity) almost disappear from the winner's podium. The patriotism is also gendered, where females in sport are still living and training in a paternalist, patriarchal environment filled with institutional sexism.

The next three of the seven have to do with upward mobility.

3) *Competition:* Competitive sport is filled with ideologies of liberalism and individualism. Competition, or doing well in sport, is seen as being successful against others, against a standard, or against "the mountain," but not as many female athletes describe competing with one's competitors to bring out the best of performances for all. Skill and prowess are seen as equivalent to health, and are often seen as morally good. Competition is further characterized by a pecking order that exists among athletes. And, although sport is seen as liberating for the human body, extreme training can often compromise health. The liberation expected of the human body in sport is manifested in the notion that athletes have supreme control over their bodies and have trained long and hard to perfect their strength and endurance. This is very much at odds with the serious loss of control involved in being sexually abused or sexually harassed. As a result, a complex rejigging of self, identity and team

participation is required to absorb the experience of abuse in the sport context.

So too, the gendered valuing of the outcomes persists. In Canada, sport remains a place where men's outcomes are of higher value and according greater space in public accounts. Recently, Canada's women's and men's team won gold medals at the Olympic Games in Salt Lake City. While the media commentators tried very hard to remember that the women had also won gold, they clearly spent more time on the build-up, games and outcome analysis for the men's team. More critically, for the analysis of abuse within sport, it is a site of creating the male and defining masculinity. Men who succeed in sport are deified and granted high status and prestige. This sets the stage for the use of power as a way to control others, the absolute underpinning of interpersonal violence.

4) *Media sport:* This is the creation of sport as a virtual reality (larger than life, records, valour, and more recently, one of extremes). The media frames how sport is viewed (as "news" of the Olympics rather than the actual events themselves). However, the sport media have been both excellent for bringing the issue forward and poor in how they have framed the issues of sexual harassment and abuse.

5) *Work ethic:* This is "a good day's work for a good day's pay" resulting in success and rewards. The promise is that if athletes work hard and follow the plan, they will be successful. If they are not successful, they must *not* have worked hard enough. There are no unions or workplace safety and health organizations to ensure the quality of the athletes workplace.

When competition and media sport are added to work ethic—we still see that sport is *not* available on an equal basis (race, sex, disability, language, age and so on).

And the last two:

6) *Heterosexism/Hypersexuality:* Heterosexism is discrimination based on heterosexual privilege and in sport, heterosexuality is the sexual norm. Athletes are directed into heterosexuality, a stylized heterosexuality, where, for the female athletes, appropriate feminine behaviour is part of sport performance (eg. figure skating). For women and girls in sport, success often includes sexual attractiveness, sexual suggestiveness and conformity to a heterosexual image of femininity. Positive heterosexual role models are front and centre in the media coverage. On the other hand, there is limited room for not masculine enough men, androgynous or masculine women and if sexual harassment or abuse occurs, it is most often from males to females and to some extent is normalized as "boys will be boys." Hypersexuality is a word we are using for the stereotype of excellent male athletes as also highly virile and superactive sexually. Together these link to form the violent underbelly of sport (trash talk, sex talk, sexual and physical hazing/initiation and dangerous sexual practices (such as unsafe sex). These also tell us that we must consider the intersectionality of sex and other forms of harassment is we want to understand and eradicate it.

7) *Familism:* This is the replication of the nuclear family model in sport.

The family unit is paralleled in the sports team (male head = coach, children = athletes, relatives = teammates and other persons in authority). Familism adds an aura of democracy to sport. But also, as in all families, the "dirty laundry is not to be aired in public." The family has always been a fertile ground for abuse and the incest model of sexual abuse, particularly child sexual abuse, is applicable to sport. Abusers, as we have seen, can abuse with some impunity.

Together these imperatives are woven tightly over sport and work together to keep athletes from speaking out about any unhappy or negative conditions in which they train and perform. We call this the *Dome of Silence*. We think that if we emphasize the positive aspects of these imperatives and eliminate the negatives then we have gone a long way to eliminating the fertile ground for sexual abuse in sport.

Changing an institution as resilient and resistant as organized sport takes time and re-orienting those in sport to this new focus takes considerable effort. It is not just poor personal decisions made by individual harassers and abusers which explains the existence of sexual abuse. So too, the environment in which people engage in sporting activity influences what behaviours and attitudes are developed and encouraged. Thus, we reject the notion that sexual harassers or abusers are just "individuals gone bad" and accept that organized sport has a responsibility to ensure that a culture of harassment and abuse do not thrive in the sport environment. This is challenging because of the dedication of generations of young athletes who embrace the powerful "win at all costs" imperative that pervades sport.

Sexual abuse and harassment of athletes are significant problems that have been under-acknowledged to date. We have proposed some explanations for this, focusing on the values and imperatives that underpin sport, and illustrating the power of these features in securing and perpetuating the silence surrounding sexual abuse and harassment. We have argued that these features have led to sports being among the last major social institutions to be scrutinized and exposed with respect to sexual abuse issues.

Over the past few years, several incidents of sexual abuse and harassment, child molestation and sexual assault in the sporting context have come to light. As in all interpersonal and relationship violence, it can be safely assumed that these reported cases are only the tip of the iceberg and most cases remain hidden. Some of the individuals who have been victims have participated in criminal or civil suits against their perpetrators. Some have settled for public exposure in the media. The public and sport communities have reacted with typical, initial responses of shock, denial, anger, and disbelief. As can be seen in the comments of the athletes surveyed in this study, the personal emotional costs can be life-long and serious. Even so, early responses from many sport organizations often focused mainly on risk management and reducing liability by instituting screening training and protocol development for staff and volunteers. Some sport organizations or assocations have focused on particular elements within their sport, such as coaching or inter-athlete behaviour. More recently, some sport organizations have responded with more comprehensive foundational codes of ethics on which to build codes of conduct and behaviour. It is clear that the issues of sexual abuse, harassment and assault are important to athletes, sport organizations, their governing bodies and the public. Indeed, abusive behaviours in sport are important and of concern to the nation.

Originally published in CWS/cf's *Winter/Spring 2002 issue, "Women and Sport" (Volume 21, Number 3): 132-138.*

[1]Note: The quotes used in this article have been previously published in Kirby, Greaves and Hankivsky (2000).

References

Brackenridge, C. H. *Spoilsports: Understanding and Preventing Sexual Exploitation in Sport.* London: Routledge, 2001.

Brackenridge, C. H. "Problem? What Problem? Thoughts on a Professional Code of Practice for Coaches." Unpublished paper presented to the Annual Conference of the British Association of National Coaches, Bristol, England, 1986.

Brink, P. J. "Violence in TV and Aggression in Children." *Western Journal of Nursing Research* 23 (1) (Feb. 2001): 5-8.

Crosset, T. "Male Coach/Female Athlete Relationships: A Case Study of the Abusive Male Coach." Unpublished paper, 1985.

Donnelly, P. "Who's Fair Game? Sport, Sexual Harassment and Abuse." *Sport and Gender in Canada.* Eds. P. White and K. Young. Toronto: Oxford University Press, 1999.

Holman, M. "Female and Male Athletes' Accounts and Meanings of Sexual Harassment in Canadian University Athletics." Unpublished PhD dissertation, University of Windsor, Ontario, 1995.

Kirby, S. L., L. Greaves and O. Hankivsky. *The Dome of Silence: Sexual Harassment and Abuse in Sport.* Halifax: Fernwood, 2000.

Kirby, S. L. and L. Greaves. "Foul Play: Sexual Abuse and Harassment in Sport." Paper presented to the Pre-Olympic Scientific Congress, Dallas, U.S., 11-14 July, 1996.

Lenskyj, H. "Unsafe at Home Base: Women's Experiences of Sexual Harassment in University Sport and Physical Education." *Women in Sport and Physical Activity Journal* 1 (1) (1992):19-34.

Larkin, M. "Violent Video Games Increase Aggression." *Lancet* 355 (9214) (April 29, 2000): 1525-1532.

McLelland, F. "Do Violent Movies Make Violent Children?" *Lancet* 359 (9305) (Feb. 9, 2002): 502-503.

Taking off the Gender-Lens in Women's Studies

Queering Violence Against Women

Janice Ristock ⟶

Women's Studies Programs have generally been important sites within Universities where lesbians/queers have found room to theorize our experiences. In Canada, many universities are claiming severe budgetary restraints and have been reluctant to fund the establishment of autonomous Gay and Lesbian Studies Departments. Therefore, Women's Studies Programs remain as one of only a few key academic disciplines (Sociology, History and English departments being the other three) where new courses in the burgeoning field of lesbian and gay or queer studies are able to be established (see Ristock and Taylor for more on the development of lesbian/gay/queer studies in Canada). Women's Studies is enriched by housing developments in Queer Studies; similarly Queer Studies is enriched by the interdisciplinary focus of Women's Studies, with its emphasis on understanding interrelated systemic conditions (such as racism, sexism, classism, heterosexism) and its many different strains of feminist theorizing (such as postmodernism). That said there are certain areas in Women's Studies that remain steadfastly understood through an exclusionary and limiting gender-based lens. Violence against women is one such area where the overwhelming focus in the field has remained male violence against women and where topics such as abuse in lesbian/same-sex relationships have been more difficult to bring forward.

In this paper I explore the ways that I have re-designed and developed a course entitled "Feminist Perspectives on Violence Against Women" that I teach within a Women's Studies program. I discuss some of ways that I have conceptualized the course so that it can and must include an exploration of same-sex domestic violence that cannot be accounted for by an oversimplified (and at times essentialist) gender-based analysis. I was compelled to re-conceptualize my course, in part, because of a large scale research project that I completed on violence in lesbian relationships (see Ristock). I describe the process of doing this project and present some of the research findings that in fact show how our theorizing of violence against women can be furthered if we adopt a queer lens: one trained on the areas where lines are blurred, categories uncertain, boundaries challenged. Queer theory interrupts a focus on binaries such as male/female, straight/gay where we define our understandings against another and instead works to disrupt the establishment of authentic, totalizing, and normative positions. This lens offers a different view from the strong beacon of a gender lens that illuminates its own subject powerfully (for example exposing the workings of patriarchy and male privilege) but makes it difficult to see anything beyond its scope.

How women's studies currently talks about violence against women

Violence against women is now more publicly acknowledged as a human rights issue demanding worldwide attention. For example the international lobbying organization, The World March of Women presents a broad definition of violence against women and recognizes its intimate and systemic forms as well as its diverse expressions that include behaviour, imagery, legislation and the media. The various forms and expressions of violence against women are seen as locally different but universally linked because they are identified as "springing from an imposed hierarchy of men over women that is reflected in the political structures of countries" (World March of Women).

This strong gender-based analysis reflects the dominant discourse in the political arena that has been arguing for over 30 years that more action must be taken to stop male violence against women. Numerous studies support this need and have documented a strong pattern of male violence over women— including a recent report by Statistics Canada which found in 2001 the largest increase in spousal homicides was wives killed by their husbands-69 wives were killed in 2001, 17 more than in 2000 (Statistics Canada). Given this urgent context it is not surprising that Women's Studies has been a leading force in researching and theorizing this issue. And while there is certainly agreement in this academic field that violence against women is unacceptable there are differences over what constitutes violence, what causes violence and hence, what should be done about violence. So what then does Women's Studies have to say about same-sex relationship violence? How are queer peoples' experiences of violence taken up?

When examining the way Women's Studies talks about same-sex domestic violence there are two predominant streams. One is a gender-based discourse that essentially ignores same-sex relationship violence or sees abusive women as having internalized misogyny in order to present them as male-like and preserve a focus on women being victimized because of their gender in a patriarchal context (see, for example, Radford, Friedberg and Harne). The other is a structural discourse that identifies marginalized women as being more vulnerable to violence because of other aspects of their social location. Within this discourse a space is opened up for the recognition of lesbian domestic violence as well as the violence experienced by other marginalized populations such as disabled women, indigenous women, and visible minority women who are seen as having heightened powerlessness in society which then translates into increased victimization in public and private spheres (Duffy and Cohen). While a gender-based analysis can be criticized for oversimplifying and universalizing women's experiences, a structural analysis can also be criticized for treating marginalized women's experiences as separate, special, homogeneous cases while ultimately keeping the experiences of white, heterosexual western women as the norm and at the forefront. Thus a gender-based analysis is still preserved. There are other discourses on violence that reflect postmodern and postcolonial influences (see, for example work, by Lamb; Razak) but the gender and structural approaches remain as the strongest overarching frameworks within the area of violence against women in Women's Studies because of their politically strategic value of uniting women.

Teaching violence against women: Pedagogical confessions

As a professor in Women's Studies who teaches a course on violence against women while also engaging in research on violence in lesbian relationships, I have often found myself caught between these two limiting discourses and their tendency to oversimplify stories of violence in their efforts to be all-explanatory frameworks. While leaning more to the structural discourse that allowed me to at least include topics such as same-sex domestic violence, gay bashing, and violence in/towards Aboriginal communities, I often felt these issues became the sensationalized side-shows, add-ons to the more familiar forms of violence that we were studying in the course. In addition I found I had to counter the sometimes homophobic or racist reactions about these pitiable "other" groups of marginalized women as well as curtail the anti-feminist reactions that wanted to see any example of women's violence as being far worse than men's. At these times I would find myself countering with the solid gender-base discourse as a pedagogical way of reasserting a shared stance as oppressed women.

What concerned me is the way that each of these discourses on violence against women ends up positing truth claims that oversimplify, obscure, delegitimize or subjugate certain knowledges in order to legitimize or normalize others. I found myself asking "What are the ethical implications of this simplification of the spaces of violence and what are the subject positions that they create?" I was better able to understand the effects of a gender-based analysis as a "regime of truth" through my research on violence in lesbian relationships.

Researching violence in lesbian relationships: Differing truths

I recently completed a cross-Canada study that involved interviewing 102 lesbian/queer women who had experienced abuse. The women that I interviewed reported many different experiences of abuse including physical, emotional, verbal and sexual abuse. Beyond the different forms of abuse that women experienced, their accounts suggested different patterns of intimate violence arising from various societal roots and interpersonal dynamics, indicating that not all violence is the same. Efforts to understand violence in lesbian relationships that ignore the differing social contexts run the risk of treating all cases of relationship violence as equivalent and interchangeable when that does not seem to be the case. The blanket homogenizing categories of a structural analysis such as working-class, lesbian, Latina, are not subtle enough to illuminate the local context.

In fact, both the research process and the results confirmed the need to constantly interrogate the language, categories and assumptions that we currently have available to us to talk about and theorize violence against women. I provide a few examples to make this more concrete.

Language

One of the first women that I interviewed asked me if she was qualified for the study since she did not identify as lesbian and was in fact married to a man but had been in a relationship with another woman for several years and it was that relationship that was physically abusive. This is a reminder that woman-to-woman abuse itself is a challenge to the feminist focus on male violence against women. Further this example not only caused me to change my own language so that the study more clearly included lesbian, queer, bisexual, transgendered and/or straight women involved in intimate relationships with other women, but it also served as an important example of the limits of our binary categories for defining sexual and gender identities.

Another woman that I interviewed felt the limits of our language categories when she explained to me why she never sought any help for the violence that she was experiencing:

> *I feel like I can't talk about it, I mean how many therapists/social service providers are going to understand queer, s/m, abuse, intersexed, interracial [all features of her abusive relationship]—it's too complicated, there is too much explaining that I'd have to do.*

Categories of violence

What also became clear when I was concentrating on relationship violence was the fact that I was just illuminating one aspect of women's lives when in fact many women had experienced multiple forms of violence. For example, one woman spoke to me about her experiences of being sexually abused as a child, of working as prostitute, being beaten by johns, using drugs and alcohol, getting involved in an abusive relationship with a woman, and then she herself becoming abusive in another relationship with a woman.

> *As I look back my mom's physically abusive to me and my brother, I was sexually abused by my grandfather and that was huge for me ... plus I'm from Alberta and there is a lot of racism towards Natives. People running people over and not caring. What I seen is what I thought was acceptable.*

She spoke with out offering excuses. Her account reflects a context of violence in which the neat categories of victim and abuser no longer seem to hold. Her account also shows us the way stories are linked to social contexts that influence and shape people lives and further reveals the way racism, sexism, and homophobia interact and affect one another in contexts of sexual abuse, child abuse, domestic violence, and so forth. Seeing the various and differing contexts in which relationship violence takes hold and recognizing the multiple subject positions that they in turn create became a significant finding of my research (Ristock).

Power

So much of feminist theorizing on violence has focused on violence as a form of power and control—universally men's power over women and secondarily the greater powerlessness of vulnerable, marginalized women. As Aysan Sev'er asserts:

> in feminist explanations, the gender, power and control triangulation determines relations in work, politics, law, health, and education, as well as, the domination pattern within coupled relationships. (51)

Yet, this binary model of power and control/victim and perpetrator cannot account for an unemployed waitress who is abusing a woman who is a prosperous chartered accountant. Nor can it account for dynamics where power shifts and a victim retaliates with physical violence. And it cannot capture those incidents in which a woman might be both a victim and a perpetrator; for example a victim of emotional abuse while a perpetrator of physical violence in her relationship. These differing power dynamics were all evident in my research.

A feminist service provider that I interviewed acknowledged that certain layered relational power dynamics are often ignored in anti-violence organizations because they do not seem to fit with a dominant feminist understanding of power:

> *I think racism is another thing we don't talk about—the ways white women might use power over their partner who is a woman of colour—there is power and control there … how do we talk about that and then also talk about other power complexities in the relationship?*

The image of a victim

Finally, the example of women fighting back, sometimes in self-defense sometimes as a form or resistance and sometimes in retaliation as an intentional act to cause harm, was another finding from my research that challenges dominant essentialist constructions of what it means to be a victim of violence. Most often we are presented with the image of a victim as female, passive and innocent. Yet 38 of the women that I interviewed described physically fighting back within their abusive relationships with another woman. For example:

The next thing you know we were in fisti cuffs.

(Interviewer) *And both of you were physically fighting?*

Yeah, yeah, well I wasn't going to stand there and let her beat on me you know, I mean I was a street kid myself you know, and you protect yourself.

Overall then the findings from my research challenge the either/or binaries within which we most often work, challenge constructions of what a victim looks and acts like, and demand that we develop more localized and contextualized understandings of people's experiences of violence rather than seeking to posit all-explanatory grand narratives.

Queer(y)ing violence against women

The differing experiences of women in abusive same-sex relationships serve as powerful examples that concretely show the complexities of violence and remind us of the need to disrupt any normalizing and totalizing truth claims. I now use these examples in my course on violence against women as a way to open up an examination of the differing spaces of violence. While we still remain concerned about the strong pattern of male violence against women, the knowledge that women can be violent requires us to look at our own complicity in different forms of violence (for example, in racialized violence between women, in the history of colonization, etc.). The knowledge that gays, lesbians, transgender persons can both experience and perpetrate violence reminds us that we must examine the multiple subject positions that people hold. Queering a feminist lens for studying violence requires an ongoing reflexive analysis of the multiplicity of individual identities and the interlocking nature of systems of privilege and oppression (Crenshaw; Razack) while disrupting simplistic, normative binary thinking (Hawley). Even though we are examining local and specific contexts our analysis remains political/ feminist in focus. We see the ways that larger systems of inequality support and encourage violence.

In the course we are raising a set of critically reflexive questions as part of our quest for deeper understandings and responses to violence. These questions include: Who benefits from the way we currently talk about relationship violence? What difference does that make? Who is telling the story and from what social location? Who voices are heard and not heard when we tell the story using the category lesbian relationship violence, heterosexual relationship violence, family violence, violence against women etc.? How else can this story be told? What difference would that make? (Ristock). These questions help make us more accountable, not only because they acknowledge our limited and partial perspectives but because they provoke us to imagine what we do not understand. Students are at times resistant to this less seamless and unifying pedagogical approach but for most students it also opens up more spaces in which to see themselves and their experiences. I share some examples of comments from students' writings in the course:

> I was at first very defensive of the gender-based system. My initial reaction was to defend centering our analysis on gender and my thoughts were if we open the category up to everything than what does that mean anymore? I questioned whose purposes does it serve that the gender-based analysis stays at the core of our understanding of oppression and also who becomes silenced when we do this. It is quite obvious from the readings that when we work from a gender-based analysis then the voices of lesbians, gays, and transgendered persons become invisible in the dialogue.

> As a man in a group of women examining a lesbian's account of lesbians' relationships, I have a special sense of privilege (in the kinder sense) and responsibility to be careful about what I do with this experience. And as a student breaking from the conventions of academia and declaring my learning as a (gasp) personal process, I sense a measure of reciprocating that trust. As you explore in the book, these simultaneous and dissonant power dynamics have too often been oversimplified.... Your analysis of exceptions and limitations of the gender based power analysis made it possible for me to explore more specificity and context to heterosexual relationships as well.... Men who use abuse are still typically constructed as an anonymous and uniform group of oppressors. Their identities are typically described in ways that bind them with their maleness, and all of their behaviours are linked back to their oppressive position. In effect, the binary categories have had one polarity expanded upon, but not the other. Intersectional analysis of power can be safely applied to women, but can we also see men as lying within, rather than on top of, power structures?

> I am reminded of Take Back the Night which happened this past fall. Women, queer, straight, transgendered people and allies walked together to demonstrate our strength, agency, and support for one another and our struggles. I hope that feminist theory will take the hint and embrace the hardships that are hard to name or figure out, the problems that challenge our own understandings of what it means to be a woman, lesbian or victim of abuse.

My hope is that, despite the difficulties, work on violence against women within Women's Studies, like students in my course, can embrace the ethical challenge of queering violence against women. It is a move that in fact broadens the field of Women's Studies by requiring a more complex, non-binary understanding of violence, gender, and sexuality which can only help to enhance our efforts to end all forms of violence and to keep Women's Studies Programs as important spaces for lesbian/queer work in universities.

Originally published in CWS/cf's Winter/Spring 2005 issue, "Lesbian, Bisexual, Queer, Transsexual/Transgender Sexualities" (Volume 24, Numbers 2/3): 65-69.

References

Crenshaw, K. W. (1994). "Mapping the Margins: Intersectionality, Identity Politics, and Violence Against Women of Color." *The Public Nature of Private Violence.* Eds. M. A. Fineman and R. Mykitiuk. New York: Routledge, 1994. 93-118.

Duffy, A. and R. Cohen. "Violence Against Women: The Struggle Persists." *Feminist Issues: Race, Class and Sexuality.* Ed. Nancy Mandell. Toronto: Prentice-Hall, 2001. 134-166.

Razack, S. *Looking White People in the Eye.* Toronto: University of Toronto Press, 1998.

Hawley, John C. Ed. *Post-Colonial Queer: Theoretical Intersections.* Albany: SUNY, 2001

Lamb, S. Ed. *New Versions of Victims: Feminists Struggle with the Concept.* New York: New York University Press, 1999.

Radford, J. M. Friedberg and L. Harne. Eds. *Women, Violence and Strategies for Action: Feminist Research, Policy and Practice* London: Open University Press, 2000.

Ristock, J. L. *No More Secrets: Violence in Lesbian Relationships.* New York: Routledge, 2002.

Ristock, J. L. and C. G. Taylor. Eds. *Inside the Academy and Out: Lesbian/Gay/Queer Studies and Social Action* Toronto: University of Toronto Press, 1998.

Sev'er, A. *Fleeing the House of Horrors: Women Who Have Left Abusive Partners.* Toronto: University of Toronto Press. 2002.

Statistics Canada. Centre for Justice Statistics. Juristat. Vol. 22 no. 7 September, 2002.

Women on the March. April 2002. Online: www.ffq.qc.ca/marche2000.

 **Representations**

Out from Under Occupation

Transforming Our Relationships
with Our Bodies

Carla Rice ⟶

I have often experienced a distressing physical sensation which I know is
related to my sense of my body and self in the world. It stems from an
overwhelming desire to escape my skin. Of literally wanting to eject myself
from my body—to flee a shameful, painful presence. The need is to deliver
myself from some unexpressed, wordless reality which threatens to invade and
consume me. When I think about the sensation of wanting to escape my own
skin, of detaching myself from my body, I wonder if I am alone in this feeling.
When I look around and observe many women silently hurting, I realize these
private feelings are not solely personal ones.

Everyday, everywhere, millions of women are engaged in chaotic, controlled, ritualized, and routine acts of self-harm. We are quietly depriving ourselves, starving ourselves, weighing and judging ourselves, bingeing, purging,
and exercising excessively, equating emotional well-being with meeting an
unattainable ideal. We are also numbing ourselves with drugs or alcohol, cutting, bruising and burning ourselves, or dissociating, in an attempt to survive
by escaping our bodies entirely. Most of us bear this suffering silently, afraid of
being labeled crazy or sick. Why do so many of us punish our bodies? From what
sources do these feelings of inadequacy, this striving, this pain, stem?

I believe these feelings stem from personal life experiences which have left
legacies of self and body loathing. At the same time, I believe such personal
experiences have deep political meaning; that these feelings stem from a
collective displacement of much that is wrong with this culture onto the terrain
of women's bodies; and that such feelings have their roots in an age-old attempt
to control and colonize women. I believe these collective feelings of loathing,
shame, and alienation are the fall-out of a war—a conflict waged on the
landscape of our bodies. This conflict, played out on the terrain of that which
defines us as female, is fought through the regulation, control, suppression, and
occupation of virtually every aspect of our physical being—sexuality, dress,
appearance, deportment, strength, health, reproduction, shape, size, space,
expression, and movement. The effects of such struggle on our bodies, minds,
and spirits are similar to the effects of violence on the landscape of a war—
suffering, chaos, starvation, mutilation, devastation, and even death.

If this notion seems too extreme, too drastic, too radical, too rabid, think about our shared cultural and personal legacies as women. Think about the numbers of women who feel the yoke and fall-out of violence everyday, those who are held down by the weight of shame and self-loathing, those unable to live freely and fully in the boundaries of their skin, who are alienated from their bodies, and living outside themselves.

Remember the 38 per cent of women who walk with the scars of sexual abuse, the 25 per cent who bind and stem the wounds of rape, the 80 per cent of us cut and bruised by daily acts of sexual violation, and the countless women in this country who are being raped, abused, and coerced as you read this sentence. And think about the hostility that surrounds us, the degrading and dehumanizing images, the documentation of our violation and powerlessness and our private responses, the endless, intimate acts of self-harm in which we engage, and the shame we carry in our bodies like a heavy load that binds and chains us to an unknown enemy.

Remember those of us for whom food is poison, who cannot live in our bodies, who are depriving ourselves, starving ourselves—despising ourselves— and doing everything in our power to achieve an impossible, increasingly artificial, ever-changing and ever-shrinking ideal. Consider the women who have found refuge from the battle in a bleak and somber haze of alcohol and drugs, lost in a downward cycle of self-deception and destruction; and those of us who have escaped our consciousness, who are fragmented, dissociated, split off, cut off, and who are driven, literally, out of our minds. And think about the woman who cuts her own skin, who bruises and burns herself in rage and fear, because she lacks the words to speak her torment. Think about the woman who binges, purges, and starves herself because she knows no other means of expressing the pain and despair she feels. And remember the woman who has survived the abuse but is lost to this war, who has ended the nightmare in the definitive act of ending her life.

Remember these women, your sisters, friends, neighbours, classmates, acquaintances, relatives, co-workers, mothers, daughters, yourself. Remember these women and think again about the metaphor of occupation. Hatred of women—expressed both in images and everyday acts of violence—drives us out of our bodies. It also drives us out of our minds. Hatred of women, which is played out on the terrain of our bodies, is directed towards us precisely because of these bodies. In other words, such hatred finds its roots and its home in the female body. The female body becomes the battleground of the war against women, and the battleground itself, our own worst enemy.

Taking up space

The war waged on women's bodies is first a conflict over size and shape, over the terrain and territory of our bodies, played out in deeply entrenched cultural taboos and a powerful patriarchal dictate against women taking up space and claiming room of our own.

Ironically, as women have moved more and more into the public realms of life in the twentieth century, in western culture, we have desperately, urgently, and often hopelessly, tried to take up less and less actual, physical space. In fact: 90 per cent of us dislike and are trying to reduce the size of our bodies; 70 per cent are continually dieting; up to 20 per cent of us develop serious struggles around food and weight. With a shocking 50 per cent of girls in Canada dieting before the age of nine, and many girls as young as three already expressing dissatisfaction with their bodies, we are passing our struggles onto a new generation of women and witnessing them bare our most intimate pain (Hutchison, Canadian Gallup Poll; Holmes and Silverman).

We have been raised in a culture where body size is of paramount importance, where thinness is equated with health, attractiveness, morality, sexuality. Where, in fact, a woman's essential value is based on her ability to attain a thin body size. Marilyn Monroe, the icon of female attractiveness in the 1950s, would probably be considered 20 pounds overweight by today's standards. The emaciated ideal of beauty for women gained prominence in the 1960s, with the explosion of the super model Twiggy onto the international fashion scene. At the peak of her fame, Twiggy was reported to be 5'8" and weigh 97 pounds. Today, the ideal of beauty is embodied in waif-like models such as Kate Moss, who is reported in the popular media to be 5'7" or 5'8" and weigh anywhere from 98 to 105 pounds.

Messages about the importance of achieving thinness are rife in popular advertising, particularly in advertisement campaigns for the beauty, and weight loss industries. These are multi-billion dollar industries in North America, with markets that can be sustained and expanded only through the spread of body insecurity among larger and larger numbers of female consumers. It doesn't take a trained eye to note that popular magazine, newspaper, and television advertising promotes an ideal of beauty that is young, white, able-bodied, flawless, and above all, thin. Women especially are continually assaulted by advertisements which claim "you can never be too rich or too thin," "I'm afraid I'll lose him if I don't lose weight," and "get the shape that guys love in 14 days."

Research supports these observations. One study found that almost 70 per cent of the female characters on 33 top-rated TV shows were slender; while only 17 per cent of the male characters were thin (Silverstein *et al.*). A study of three women's magazines reported that the percentage of thin female models rose from three per cent in the 1950s to 46 per cent in the 1980s (Gagnard). Another study of five women's magazines found the degree of fatness of female models decreased by 55 per cent from the 1950s to the 1980s, while the space devoted to weight-loss articles increased five-fold (Snow and Harris). Finally, research has shown that the ideal of beauty became 23 per cent lighter over a twenty-year period while women in general actually became four per cent heavier (Garner *et al.*). This suggests a growing disparity between actual body sizes and the cultural standard.

How does this focus on thinness affect women? An increase in the prevalence of anorexia and bulimia has been closely linked to socio-cultural pressures on women to reduce the size of their bodies. Anorexia was rare until this century, when its incidence increased dramatically. The related problem of bulimia was virtually unknown until the last three decades. Not only do anorexia and bulimia appear to be culturally and historically specific problems, but they also seem to be gendered ones; 90 to 95 per cent of those with a serious eating problems are women. Early research suggested anorexia and bulimia were primarily problems of upper middle class, white women. However, these statistics were often collected in treatment centres, school districts, and geographic areas which were not accessible to or representative of low income and non-white women. Research is now documenting increases in the numbers of Black and Asian women struggling with eating problems (Rosen *et al.*, Hsu). These new findings reflect my own work experience. I have found that some of the most devastating food and weight struggles are experienced by doubly marginalized groups of women.

Many women who are not anorexic or bulimic struggle with related problems such as yo-yo dieting, compulsive eating, or a constant preoccupation with food and weight. In the last ten years, researchers have begun to address the negative effects of the diet craze and look critically at the claims of diet programs. The most glaring problem is that virtually all weight loss programs have dismal results. Studies show that up to 95 per cent of dieters will regain all weight lost at the end of one year (Polivy and Herman 1983). Not only are diets ineffective in the long-run, but it is now clear they have their own set of hazards. In addition to inadequate nutrition, dieting has been implicated in the development of weakness, fatigue, binging, bulimia, weight gain, obesity, and sudden death from damage to the heart (Ciliska). Dieting may also be associated with diabetes and heart disease.

Regardless of age, ethnicity, race or class, most women growing up in North America learn we are unworthy, unhealthy, and even immoral, if we cannot maintain a low body weight. The irony of this is profound. Historically and cross-culturally, many societies have associated fatness with desirable social status, as fat is a symbol of wealth where food is not abundant. Approximately 25,000 years ago, goddess figures were revered throughout much of the world. In many cultures, fatness has been viewed with admiration as a sign of fertility, strength, and prosperity, all of which are related to human survival (Sheinin). Even in western culture, fat has been associated with youth and beauty as demonstrated in the nineteenth-century paintings of fleshy, plump women, depicted by artists such as Renoir. While it may be difficult for us to believe today, advertisements from the 1930s actually promoted weight gain. Advertisers for weight enhancement products attracted women consumers with enticing slogans such as "Dangerous to be Skinny," and "No Skinny Woman Has an Ounce of Sex Appeal."

Despite these values, we have learned to despise fat. Fat people, especially fat women, are the butt of jokes by many comics and cartoonists and are vulnerable to public humiliation and ridicule. Health professionals rate fat people as more "disturbed" than thin people and have an insulting tendency to blame all health conditions on fat. Fat people have lower rates of acceptance to university, reduced likelihood of being hired for jobs, and lower rates of pay (Bray; Canning and Maye; Karris; Gortmaker *et al.*).

Why has our culture declared a war on fat? Hatred of fat is justified by health reasons. Fat is despised because it is seen to be under an individual's voluntary control. Yet, fatness is not a disease or a symptom of weakness and moral decay. It is a genetically inherited trait, much like height. Fat women may be as healthy as those who are thin and the health risks of fat are not only grossly over-exaggerated, but they may even be caused by dieting (Ernsberger and Haskew). In addition, women have a higher percentage of body fat than men, because fat is necessary for menstrual and reproductive functioning (Polivy and Herman; Bennett and Gurin).

The attack on fat can be seen as a compelling means of undermining confidence in ourselves, of subverting the potential power of our bodies, as well as of devaluing utterly our reproductive abilities. All women whether fat, average, or thin learn that fat must be the underlying and justified cause of our pain and thinness our ticket out of oppression.

The cult of thinness offers women an alternative and persuasive means of accessing power—manipulating our bodies to achieve a pre-pubescent, boyish shape, in the hope of gaining the power that being a man will bring. This is an illusory means of accessing such power. For instead of lifing us out of pain and struggle, the pursuit of thinness brings us even closer to our own despair. It causes us to divert time and energy from the search for meaning and substance in our lives to an empty preoccupation with appearance; it divides us by driving a destructive wedge between our bodies and minds, by pitting one against the other; and it traps us in a cycle of endless self-criticism and punishment.

The oppressive power of whiteness

The war waged on women's bodies is also a conflict over race and skin colour, played out in deeply held stereotypes about the value and beauty of whiteness that saturate our culture and language, and are used to colonize non-white peoples and non-western societies.

For evidence of this, just open up any popular fashion magazine. Black women, Latin American women, Southeast Asian women, South Asian women, Native women, are almost completely invisible. Overwhelmingly, the dominant image promoted in North American culture is a eurocentric one, having white skin, blond hair, blue eyes and European facial features. When images of women of colour appear in the mainstream media, they are either as close as possible to this white ideal, or they are images which reinforce racist stereotypes about the people being depicted. Think, for example, of black models such as Naomi Campbell and actresses such as Jasmine Guy and Halle Berry. Why does Naomi often appear on runways sporting long, blond locks? Why are black women with straight hair and light-skin overwhelmingly those represented in popular magazines and on television? Why do we rarely see variations in hair texture and the full range of skin colours depicted? While a wave of more empowering and diverse images of black women is emerging, this movement exists only at the fringes of popular culture.

Underlying western conceptions of beauty are deeply-held stereotypes about the meaning of whiteness and blackness. Whiteness is associated not only with physical attractiveness but with purity, goodness, wealth, intellectual superiority, and morality. Blackness, on the other hand, is seen to connote ugliness, evil, poverty, inferiority, and lack of morality (hooks; Morrison). Both the English language and the culture are infused with these values, as is our popular imagery. Think about the advertisement campaign that ran a few years ago for a multi-national, youth-oriented clothing company. The company ac-tually ran an ad that featured a blond-haired, blue-eyed white child dressed as an angel. Alongside her was the image of a brown-eyed, black child whose hair was cut to resemble horns.

Advertising also places non-western women in roles that are subservient to people from the west. One ad for an airline company states "We admit, we do train our hostesses rather young!" Depicted in the ad are young Pakistani girls who look as though they are between the ages of four and nine, and who appear delighted to serve travelers and businessmen. The advertisement contains a hidden reference to the international sex trade and its sexual exploitation of young girls. The image both alludes to and supports the parallel processes of western and male colonization: the occupation of women's bodies in the third world by western men and the colonization of the economies and cultures of the third world by the west. Another example of this trend is a recent advertisement depicting a Chinese woman who is reduced from carrying her "little red book to carrying a little red lipstick." This advertisement would not have seemed possible only ten years ago. However, with China's move towards a market-driven economy, it seems not only possible, but somehow inevitable.

Feelings of shame, self-hatred, humiliation, and unworthiness are commonly felt by women who are pressured to conform to an ideal that reinforces a myth of non-white inferiority as it enforces the superiority of white culture. (Morrison; hooks 1992, 1993). One older black woman I know said that she felt so ugly and unacceptable growing up, that she wished her hair would fall out and grow back in curly and soft. Another young woman told me about how she was harassed at school because of the size of her lips and shape of her nose. And still another described how she was taunted by other kids in her school and called degrading names because of the texture of her hair. An Hispanic friend remembered having her conceptions of beauty shaken through her socialization in school where she learned to feel ashamed of looking like her mother and aunts.

Western ideals of beauty create more than a value system; they re-create and perpetuate stereotypes that destroy the validity and integrity of non-western and non-white peoples. Ultimately, they reinforce the economic, social, and political dominance of the west.

In pursuit of perfection

The war waged on women's bodies is a war waged over our right to exist as we are, with all our imperfections and flaws, bumps, sags, wrinkles, and lines, the traits with which we were born and the evidence of life being lived out, of age and mortality. The war on women's bodies is also a war waged over our right to exist at all, with all our strengths, limitations, abilities, and vulnerabilities, in our full diversity and common humanity.

In the past decade, the number of North American women electing to go under the surgeon's knife for cosmetic reasons has more than doubled. It has been estimated that the number of women having plastic surgery in 1991 was approximately 1.5 million. Yet cosmetic surgery is not without its risks. Some women die. Many others experience debilitating complications. One woman having a "tummy tuck," for example, suffered a stroke as a result of complications from the surgery. Another had her eyesight permanently damaged and face scarred from a chemical peel that was supposed to remove wrinkles. And then there was the story of a Toronto woman who probably died from the complications of a botched liposuction operation.

In a sane world, even one death would be enough to call into serious question the ethics of performing unnecessary operations like cosmetic surgeries. Yet this has not been the case. Debates on plastic surgery see regulation—who gets to perform the operation—as *the* crucial issue, not whether it should be performed at all. Flaws in appearance have even become "diseases," needing proper medical intervention. A few years ago, the American Society of Plastic and Reconstructive Surgeons lobbied to have breast implantation classified as a *necessary* procedure. "There is a common misconception that the enlargement of the female breast is not necessary for maintenance of health or treatment of disease .... [T]hese deformities [small breasts] are really a disease which ... result[s] in feelings of inadequacy, lack of self-confidence, distortion of body image and a total lack of well-being due to a lack of self-perceived femininity."

Notions of beauty within this industry are, like the ideal itself, based on racist values. Lighter skin is better than darker skin, a straight nose is more refined than a broad one, and oval eyes are more beautiful than almond-shaped ones. In the film *Two Lies* one of the main characters decides to have cosmetic surgery in order to "enhance" the shape of ther eyes. Her two daughters experience a complex range of feelings, from rage to shame and sadness that their mother would decide to have her eyes altered. The film painfully demonstrates how western conceptions of beauty are internalized by an Asian woman. In one scene the daughters read from a cosmetic surgery book which suggests that "Oriental" women should consider opening their windows on the world by having the "hooded" sheath of skin above their eyes removed. It is my understanding that cosmetic eye operations are not only common in North America, but are the most popular form of cosmetic surgery in countries such as Japan.

Beauty is a harsh taskmaster and judge of women's worth, and the ideal is one that insists on superhuman perfection. This magnifies its effects on women with disabilities. In fact, women with disabilities are perceived and portrayed as being even more "flawed" in comparison to the beauty ideal than those without disabilities (Driedger and D'aubin). For evidence of this, think about the number of disabled women on television or in the movies. How many times do we see a woman with a disability being portrayed as powerful and sexual? As attractive and desirable? A few months ago, I learned that a flyer for a local Toronto department store had featured a model in a wheelchair. While at first glance the image seemed positive, the picture next to it featured the same woman modeling a new outfit, only this time she was shown standing! (Personal communiqué, DAWN)

In our culture, women with disabilities are almost completely invisible. This is related to the fact that they are considered "damaged goods," women who are so undesirable because of their physical flaws that they will "never get a man" (Driedger and D'aubin). When women with disabilities are represented, they are depicted as children or victims to be pitied, patronized, or taken care of. Think about the depiction of women and girls with disabilities on the posters for some charities. The images are meant to inspire benevolence and generosity, while they simultaneously evoke guilt and pity. This has had a devastating impact on women with disabilities, leaving many feeling unattractive, ashamed, and sexless.

The popularity of cosmetic surgery is an example of our western obsession with immortality, as is our preoccupation with youth and difficulty dealing with aging. The treatment of women with disabilities is an example of our preoccupation with perfection and our collective denial of our common humanity. Women's bodies, being the repository of prevailing conflicts and desires, become the landscape where the elusive pursuit of everlasting youth, perfection, and beauty is played out. Thus, it is taboo for women's bodies to age, to be less than perfect, to demonstrate that we as individuals will grow old and die, and that we have, in fact, little control over death and our own mortality.

The assault

Finally, the war on women's bodies is a desperate conflict over our humanity, and right to exist free of domination and violation; it is a literal state of siege, the invasion of our most intimate selves, where our bodies are the occupied territories, where the risks are our minds, hearts, and souls and the stakes, our very existence.

Virtually all women in our society are raised to associate self-worth with appearance. From infancy, we are encouraged to invest in appearance and are rewarded for successfully achieving the ideal of beauty. In fact, most women in North America grow up learning that having power is intimately connected to how well we can approximate prevailing ideals of beauty. We learn that beauty is both our primary commodity and spiritual mission in life, that our power is located in our bodies and in our ability to attract men. The caption of one ad reads: "Dave whistled at another woman, so I got even...." How does she get even? The young black woman purchases special cream to even out and lighten her skin tone, getting "even" with her body, her skin colour, and another woman, not her boyfriend. In this way, the man is absolved of any responsibility for harassment, and a competition based on appearance is set up between the two women for his attention and approval.

In his book *Ways of Seeing*, John Berger has stated: "Men look at women. Women watch themselves being looked at. This determines not only most relations between men and women but also the relation of women to themselves." Berger suggests that women are taught to see our bodies as reflective of our being, and at the same time, relate to our bodies as objects. For many women, the body is a mirror of the self. It is also an object that women become profoundly alienated from. This paradox leads many of us to experience our bodies as a primary site of conflict and distress. We learn to be objectified and to objectify ourselves. In being rendered objects, we are stripped of our humanity. Over and over, we see the female body dismembered, cut up and cut off; in one ad the female body is used as a prop for a bottle of skin cream; in another, we only see the woman's torso; in a third she is blind-folded by a scarf; and in a fourth, she is silenced by a man's hands which encircle and cover her mouth.

"Beautifying" the body can be seen as an eroticized act of violence against the self. Starving, trimming, tucking, and purging are all acts of self-harm. They are culturally condoned forms of self-mutilation that condition us to police our bodies, and that teach us to take pleasure in our own objectification, violation, and pain. One advertisement for a weight loss centre illustrates this point graphically. In it, a woman's torso and limbs are attached to a "passive exercise" machine (a machine designed to send small currents through the body, passively stimulating the muscles). Electric pads are affixed to different "problem areas" of the woman's body, including her breasts, and wires are running from each pad. She is standing, her legs are spread apart, and the picture is cut off just below her eyes. Looking at the advertisement, a number of questions immediately jump to mind. Why are her eyes cut out of the image? (To dehumanize?) Why are her legs spread wide apart? (To make her look more sexually vulnerable?) Why can't we see her hands and her feet? (Is she being held against her will?) The picture is obviously designed to conjure up images of bondage and sadomasochism. But it also connects the pursuit of beauty with the pain and suffering, and further eroticizes both.

I believe this theme is a common thread that is woven through the fabric of many cultures with a patriarchal tradition. In the Victorian Era, there were great public debates regarding the merits and risks of corseting. Middle- and upper-class girls started wearing stays at the age of 12 or 13. Gradually, over a period of time, the strings would be pulled tighter and tighter until the young woman achieved a tiny waist. The practice had an obviously deterimental effect on developing bones and skeletal structure as well as on the development of vital organs. Given the health risks and physical pain associated with corseting, why would so many women endure it? Delving into the underbelly of Victorian society provides some disturbing clues. Images of women stripped to their corsets, with waists spanning 14 and 15 inches are found in Victorian pornography, suggesting that Victorian men were excited by the distorted, hour-glass shape. While faded and slightly ridiculous, the once-pornographic images transcend time and place—shocking reminders of the mundane ways in which women's suffering is sexualized.

Foot binding is another example of this theme. For over a thousand years in Imperial China foot binding was practiced by upper-class women. At the ages of merely three or four, girls had their feet wrapped in cloth bindings by their mothers and female relatives. The practice was extremely painful and many young girls died as a result of infection. Yet achieving a tiny lotus foot was essential for any child who was not of peasant class or whose parents had social aspirations for her. While incapacitating, the bound foot was a powerful symbol of status and leisure. It was also a compelling symbol of captivity and immobility. It has been suggested that the practice was also sexualized. Recently, I had the chance to hold the shoes that had been worn by a Chinese woman who had had her feet bound. Spanning no more than four inches with a width of only one or two, they linger as an empty legacy of over a thousand years of pain.

Yet violence perpetrated on our bodies is not solely or even primarily self-inflicted. The objectification of our bodies and sexualization of our pain creates a culture of permissiveness towards violence against women. A few years ago a famous jeans company ran an advertisement that used an eroticized rape as a means of selling their product. Currently, a famous model is featured in an advertisement. She is crouched on all four limbs, with her breasts almost completely exposed to the viewer. Mounting her is a man whose face and torso are cut off. The look on her face is one of pain mingled with ecstacy. Seeing women splattered across magazines in this way as less than human, as inanimate objects or sexual slaves, makes it easier for men to insult, degrade, use, abuse, and even kill us (Rice and Langdon). Male violence is the inevitable culmination of these forces—the most graphic weapon used to occupy and subjugate us.

What is the connection between body image problems and sexual violence? Statistics suggest 55 per cent to 75 per cent of women with eating/weight problems have experienced some form of physical or sexual violence, including assault, rape, or sexual abuse. But what do these numbers mean? To understand the connection better, it is necessary to understand the nature of violence itself. The primary objective of any act of violence is to dehumanize. It is the attempt by one human being to invade, colonize, and enslave another. Its purpose is to turn a human being into an object, an extension or tool of another. Sexual violence involves the invasion of our most intimate selves. It transforms our bodies into a battleground, forcing us to exist in a state of siege against invasion and psychological annihilation, which is a form of death.

Through the act of violence, we struggle to maintain our integrity and human-ness, by retreating from this battleground. Through the act of violence and our retreat, our bodies become occupied territories, possessions of the perpetrators. Invasion and occupation drive a destructive wedge between our bodies, our minds, and our souls, which robs us of our humanity (Chandler).

We learn to cope with violence and the emotional repercussions of trauma by using our bodies to speak our pain. Violence drives us out of our bodies. The pain and horror of this crime is expressed through our troubled relationships with our bodies. So we develop eating and weight struggles, problems with alcohol and drugs, cut and burn ourselves, and refuse to live in our bodies and minds or leave them entirely by dissociating. In this way, the site of our violation also becomes a vehicle through which we give voice to victimization experiences in a culture where we are otherwise silenced (Rice and Langdon).

Transformation

Whenever we as women look at ourselves through the lens of our culture, we are seeing ourselves through the dominant eye. We are comparing ourselves to impossible ideals of beauty and images which only reinforce a sexist, racist, and ableist system. We are consuming images which occupy us and take our power away. When we watch ourselves through the dominant eye, we become self-critical and judgmental. We stop nurturing and loving ourselves. We end up feeling split in half—our bodies become objects to be manipulated and punished in order to be made more acceptable. We end up engaged in a war with our bodies, one that we cannot win. Society has inhabited our bodies and we have absorbed it into our skin and bones.

How do we escape this war with our bodies? I have personal experience of this struggle both as a woman who has been profoundly affected by popular images of degradation and as a woman who has personal experience of sexual violence. I have also spent many years of my life fighting to stay out of my body, relating to my body as an object, trying to protect myself by refusing to inhabit a body that I had, for a long time, ceased to call my own. How did I escape these struggles? How do any of us move beyond them? In our culture, most women have little experience of bodily integrity and affirmation, making it difficult to even conceive of liberation. Few of us have been able to survive whole in a world where there are powerful forces to undermine and divide us.

I see transformation as the dual processes of resistance and affirmation. In many ways, transformation requires us to see ourselves and the world around us through a double lens—to recognize the violence and oppression which threaten us and, at the same time, acknowledge our potential, strength, and abilities. If each one of us could build our internal resources, learn to trust our expressive and creative spirits, and develop the capacity to truly support and respect each other in spite of our differences, we could collectively find our power. Rejecting the dominant lens, struggling to come out from under occupation, finding courage to speak the stories of trauma and oppression that are buried deep within our bodies, keeping faith with our individual strengths and potential, resurrecting hope for visions of what could be, and learning again to dream our banished dreams. These are ways of reclaiming lost territory, lost history, lost memory, lost humanity—ways of taking back what has been taken away.

Originally published in CWS/cf's Summer 1994 issue, "Women and Health" (Volume 14, Number 3).

References

Andres, R. "Effect of Obesity on Total Mortality." *International Journal of Obesity* 4 (1980): 381–386.

Bennett, William and Joel Gurin. *The Dieter's Dilemma.* New York: Basic Books, 1982.

Berger, John. *Ways of Seeing.* London: BBC/Penguin Books, 1972.

Bray, G.A. "The Risks and Disadvantages of Obesity." *Major Problems in Internal Medicine* 9 (1976): 215–251.

Bruch, Hilde. *The Golden Cage.* Cambridge: Harvard University Press, 1978.

Canning, H. and J. Mayer. "Obesity: Its Possible Effect on College Acceptance." *New England Journal of Medicine* 275 (1966): 1172–1174.

Chandler, Clarissa. "The Impact of Trauma on the Body." *More Than Skin Deep Forum.* Women's College Hospital Lecture Series. Toronto. May, 1993.

Ciliska, Donna. *Beyond Dieting: Psychoeducational Interventions for Chronically Obese Women.* New York: Brunner Mazel, 1990.

Day, Dian. *Young Women in Nova Scotia A Study of Attitudes, Behaviour and Aspirations.* Halifax: Nova Scotia Advisory Council on the Status of Women, 1990.

Driedger, Diane and April D'aubin. "Women with Disabilities Challenge the Body Beautiful." *Healthsharing* (Winter/Spring 1992).

Ernsberger, P. and P. Haskew. "Health Implications of Obesity: An Alternative View." *The Journal of Obesity and Weight Regulation* 6.2 (1987): 58–137.

Gagnard, A.. "From Feast to Famine: Depiction of Ideal Body Type in Magazine Advertising, 1950–1984." *Proceedings of the 1986 Conference of the American Academy of Advertising.* Ed. E. F. Larkin. Nomman, Oklahoma, 1986.

Gortmaker, S.L., A. Must, J.M. Perrin, *et al.* "Social and Economic Consequences of Overweight in Adolescence and Young Adulthood." *New England Journal of Medicine* 329.14 (1993): 1008–1012.

Holmes, Janelle and Elaine Silverman. *We're Here, Listen to Us: A Survey of Young Women in Canada.* Ottawa: Canadian Advisory Council on the Status of Women, 1992.

hooks, bell. *Black Looks: Race and Representation.* Toronto: Between the Lines,

1992.

hooks, bell. *Sisters of the Yam: Black Women and Self Recovery*. Toronto: Between the Lines, 1993.

Hsu, G. "Are Eating Disorders More Common in Blacks?" *International Journal of Eating Disorders* 6 (1986): 113–124.

Hutchison, Marcia. *Transforming Body Image*. New York: The Crossing Press, 1985.

Morrison, Toni. *The Bluest Eye*. New York: Washington Square Press, 1970.

Morton, Patricia. *Disfigured Images: The Historical Assault on Afro-American Women*. New York: Preager Press, 1991.

Offer, D., E. Ostrov and K. Howard. *The Adolescent: A Psychological Self-portrait*. New York: Basic Books, 1981.

Polivy, Janet and Peter Herman. *Breaking the Diet Habit*. New York: Basic Books, 1983.

Polivy, Janet and Peter Herman. "The Diagnosis and Treatment of Normal Eating." *Journal of Consulting and Clinical Psychology* 55.5 (1987): 635–644.

Report on the Behaviour and Attitudes of Canadians with Respect to Weight Consciousness and Weight Control. Toronto: Canadian Gallup Poll Limited, 1984.

Rice, Carla. "The Unkindest Cut of All." *The Womanist* (Fall 1990).

Rice, Carla and L. Langdon. "Women's Struggles with Food and Weight as Survival Strategies." *Canadian Woman Studies/les cahiers de la femme* 12.1 (Fall 1991): 30–34.

Rosen, L. *et al.* "Presence of Pathogenic Weight-Control Behaviours Among Native Women and Girls." *International Journal of Eating Disorders* 7 (1988): 807–811.

Silverstein, B. *et al.* "The Role of the Mass Media in Promoting a Thin Standard of Bodily Attractiveness for Women." *Sex Roles* 14 (1986): 519–532.

Snow, J.T. and M.B. Harris. "An Analysis of Weight and Diet Content in Five Women's Magazines." *Journal of Obesity and Weight Regulation* 5 (1986): 194–214.

Walker, Alice. "Beauty: When the Other Dancer is the Self." *Black Women's Health Book: Speaking For Ourselves*. Ed. Evelyn White. Washington: The Seal Press, 1990.

"When is a Kitchen Not a Kitchen?"

Margaret Hobbs and Ruth Roach Pierson

"When is a kitchen not a kitchen?" was a question posed in January 1937 by a press release for Canada's Home Improvement Plan (HIP). Women were told that the "old-fashioned" and "inefficient" kitchens which most of them used were "not worthy of the name." Ads such as this aimed to enlist the support of women for the federal government's major job creation project during the late years of the Depression. The Home Improvement Plan, one of the few recommendations of the National Employment Commission (NEC) to be implemented by the federal government, was designed to relieve unemployment through a nation-wide scheme of residential renovation and repair. Intended to defuse radicalism among the jobless, the policy, in its media presentation to the public, operated to blur class distinctions; in actuality it may have helped to redraw and harden class lines. Paraded as a boon to the "average" homeowner, the Plan was an attempt to win over the property-owning stratum of the working class to the existing social and economic order. By the provision of low-interest loans, the securely-employed male wage earner could modernize "his" house and thus also protect "his" investment. In addition, the Home Improvement Plan presupposed and sought to entrench existing gender divisions in Canadian society. It represents one facet of the state's increasing involvement in defining what constitutes a proper home, as well as in designating the proper roles and relations between and among family members. Formulated in a climate of opinion which scapegoated women for unemployment, especially married women, the Plan is also an example of the way governments have attempted to ameliorate economic dislocation at the expense of women's autonomy in the family and the workforce.[1]

Modelled on an American plan implemented in 1934, the Canadian Home Improvement scheme offered homeowners low-interest loans to a fixed maximum of $2,000 (later $3,000) for the sole purpose of restructuring, repairing, or beautifying residential properties and farm houses as well as city homes.[2] In the minds of the National Employment Commissioners and members of the federal government more generally, the state of the nation's homes was a measure of the prosperity of the nation: rundown homes reflected a rundown economy.

Regarding the building trades as a pivotal industry, policy makers assumed that recovery in this sector would stimulate economic recovery more generally by increasing the demand for products in related industries, such as lumber, paint, insulation, linoleum, and bathroom fixtures' manufacture. Employment would also be generated for electricians, plumbers, carpenters, house painters, roofers, masons, and bricklayers, as well as certain professionals like domestic architects and engineers.[3] On the strength of the promise of job creation, the Trades and Labour Congress of Canada officially endorsed the Plan in December 1936 ("Canadian Labour Organizations Present Memoranda of Proposed Legislation to the Dominion Government"). The expected boost to employment was tied to the further expectation that the Plan would create an atmosphere of business confidence in which lending institutions would free up credit to the general public, and the general public would be encouraged to spend. The Home Improvement Plan was to straighten out a tangle of related problems: unemployment, tight credit, and the deterioration of property that was occuring in the Depression.

Having come to power in 1935 on the heels of the Bennett government, Prime Minister Mackenzie King was under considerable pressure both to appease the unemployed and to allay property owners' fears of social unrest. Urgent action was required in order to avoid the violence and disruption of previous winters, especially that of 1933–34. The government felt that mere word of the Plan could act as "a barrage against [winter] riots."[4] The Plan was especially appealing to King because it channelled "relief" to the unemployed through the respectable, responsible, propertied segment of society.

While the propertyless and the jobless were to benefit from increased employment opportunities, they were not eligible for loans.[5] Applicants had to demonstrate "moral worth" as well as ability to repay. Although good character in the first instance was defined in terms of financial security and responsibility, bank forms generally extended the concept to include conformity with prevailing norms of marriage and the family (*Hansard* 1937a; "A Job in Your Home"). The premium placed on stability in marital relations, employment, and residency was intended to weed out the unmarried and the transient.

The main target group was neither the poor nor the wealthy, but rather "ordinary credit-worthy owner[s] of residential property." A broad middle-class but so was a portion of the working-class. Advertising strategists spoke of using the image of "the humble cottage," rather than that of the baronial mansion, to attract the upper working-class and show them what a difference a few low-cost home improvements could make.[6] In these ways, the Plan worked to differentiate between strata of the working class: between the respectable and the unrespectable, the stable and the unstable, those who owned property and those who did not.

The Plan also worked to differentiate between the sexes. Very rarely did a press release acknowledge the existence of a female homeowner. For all intents and purposes, a basic characteristic of the "credit-worthy home-owner" was a male identity. Advertisers typically referred to "Mr. Home-

Owner and his wife.[7] Women were situated, by and large, in an indirect relation to the Plan; it was chiefly as dependents of men, not as home owners or labour force participants, that they were to benefit. The loans were to go to men and the employment to be generated was located in male-dominated job sectors. Nonetheless, the promotional literature cast women as central to the Plan's success in their roles as homemakers and consumers, wives and mothers.

While the first step to introducing the Plan had been to win the co-operation of banks and other lending institutions, its implementation depended on the involvement of those businesses whose interests would be served and on the employment of the most up-to-date and aggressive advertising techniques. *Chatelaine*, in co-operation with the NEC's bid for support from the housewives of Canada, declared 1937 "Home Improvement Year" on the cover of its January issue announcing a $25.00 prize every month beginning in March "for the best example of home improvements submitted" to *Chatelaine*'s "Home Improvement Contest" (35).

A powerful sales pitch was made by glorifying "the modern." Experts praised structures which were "simple, utilitarian ... efficient," and "devoid of the frills which delighted past generations." A link was made between increasing the property value of one's home, putting men to work, and keeping up-to-date. Home Improvement Plan publicity insisted that, with a little "sprucing up," an old home could become "as modern as tomorrow" (Perry; Sturrock; Fisher). To boost its Home Improvement Contest, the March 1937 *Chatelaine* featured a "dramatized presentation" of a "modernized" Winnipeg house. The "almost unbelievable changes" to the exterior were achieved by removing "a dark old verandah," a bay window and an "ugly oversized dormer," and adding a "new finish of brick veneer." In another *Chatelaine* article, architect Richard A. Fisher condemned the "clumsy front porch" for having "outlived its usefulness" since, with the increased privatization of the home, the backyard had superceded the verandah as the preferred place to sit outside. "So off with the porch!" Fisher decreed (1937a, 72; 1937b, 20; 1937c 22). In general, HIP ads advocated the elimination of all Victorian decorative detail. To our contemporary eye, the execution of many of these schemes meant the desecration of Canada's architectural heritage.

Interiors were also to be "stream-lined" and brightened. Above all, the principle of less is more was to guide renovation. Throughout the house "dark, massive and drab" were outdated; fashionable were bright or off-white walls, "cheery" furniture, and light woodwork. Exciting things could happen below stairs, too. Gone were the days when the basement was a dingy, "trash-littered" "chamber of horrors," harbouring "writhing pipes" and sooty furnaces.[8] In the era of recreation rooms, General Electric urged Canadian home owners to transform their old-fashioned cellars into clean, cheerful rooms (*Macleans* 1937c, 25). Although Home Improvement Plan promoters made every effort to assure the public that striking alterations need not be costly, most of the featured suggestions were clearly beyond the budget of ordinary Canadians.

HIP ads were aimed primarily at women in their various homemaking capacities—as mothers, wives, and housekeepers as well as consumers. In keeping with an advertising trend that developed in North America in the 1920s and 1930s, home improvement ads marshalled the opinion of "scientific experts." Ads were peppered with the advice of psychologists and home economists, as well as home decorators and architects.[9] Invocation of the experts was integral to the advertisers' strategy of playing on the fears and insecurities of the public by reinforcing consumers' "suspicions of their own inadequacies" (Marchand; Ewen). Home economists who doubled as advertising consultants helped "ad men" zero in on the special susceptibilities of the female market. HIP publicity exploited women's anxieties—especially about their appearance and homemaking talents.

Home economists also championed the extension of Frederick Taylor's "scientific management" principles from the industrial work place into the privatized home (Hayden). In the name of efficiency, household labour was to be broken down into specialized processes along the same lines as factory production, despite the fact that in the home the woman was the sole worker. Many of the renovation tips contained in HIP ads were inspired by pseudo-scientific management theory and infused with its rhetoric and imagery. The kitchen above all became the focus of "scientific" planning.

Achieving the new ideal of a "laboratory-like kitchen" involved not simply the introduction of new appliances, but their positioning in a work environment of maximum efficiency. In many older houses, kitchens were so large and badly arranged that "a woman had to be a marathon walker to prepare one meal" ("Planning for a Maidless House" 55; Alexander). Time/motion studies and diagrammatic floor plans were produced to contrast the poorly laid out kitchen of the past with the convenient modern one. Spurious quantification was cleverly utilized to lend an aura of scientific authority to the efficiency claims. In one diagram flow arrows emphasized that the orderly modern kitchen cut out much needless walking, reducing, by as much as 50 per cent, the time and energy involved in meal preparation. "How many steps make a Pie?" asked one manufacturer of plumbing and heating equipment. In the old-fashioned kitchen, over 100, this ad replied, as compared with a mere 22 in the modern kitchen (Alexander; "Why Planned Kitchens?").

Manufacturers of kitchen equipment did not hesitate to capitalize on HIP modernization schemes. Canadian General Electric, for example, sold appliances in a co-ordinated ensemble around which a total kitchen would be created. The CGE ad promised the Canadian housewife that "For a few dollars a month" she could "own a General Electric kitchen—under the new Home Improvement Plan," and thereby fulfill her dreams for a kitchen that is "trim and compact … clean and cool." Emphasizing the magically transformative power of electricity when joined with the brilliance of CGE-designed appliances, this ad tantalized women with the vision of "A kitchen where a score of tedious tasks are done quickly and economically, merely by turning electric switches" (*Macleans* 1937a: 27).

Despite efforts to draw in upper working-class women with "affordable" modernization hints, HIP ads projected an ideal world in which the perfect family was WASP, middle to upper middle class and composed of "Mr. Home-Owner," his wife "Mrs. Consumer," and their two children, a boy and a girl. In their appeal to "Mrs. Consumer," the ads conveyed conflicting messages. On the one hand, the woman was represented as a responsible "purchasing agent" with a careful "eye on her budget." She was the one who could exercise a restraining influence. On the other hand, in a universalization of the upper-middle-class women with considerable spending power, women were portrayed as spendthrifts and compulsive shoppers. The woman may have been the "purchasing agent" in the corporation of the family, but through her economic dependency, she remained accountable to her husband, the "president" (Marchand 169-170). Built into this relationship, because of the woman's need to account for every penny spent, was the wife's vulnerability to her husband's criticism of her performance as financial manager. Even the thriftiest housewife could be made to appear wasteful or frivolous from the man's perspective. Women were seen as waging a constant assault on the wallets of their husbands, an image that certain comic strips, like "Dagwood and Blondie," have helped keep alive for decades.

In the HIP appeals to women as homemakers, women were identified so closely with the home that they were encouraged to express the essence of their personalities through the rooms and furnishings of their houses, particularly the kitchen. HIP press statements typically sought to instill in women the desire to stand out from all their neighbours through unique home decoration. "Every once in a while," one ad posited, "the average homemaker wants a kitchen that is entirely individual and doesn't resemble in the slightest the yellow and blue, or the red and white or the pink and brown workshops of her friends."[10] Some ads recognized that women's confinement to the home might be a source of depression or restlessness. Paradoxically, these same ads urged women to undertake home decoration as a cure for discontent. "The redecorating of one room or an entire house can do more to soothe the troubled spirit of the true housewife than a trip to the Canary Islands," one ad maintained—as though the average home owner in Depression Canada could have contemplated such an extravagance.[11] Thus women's feelings of entrapment and yearnings for independence were subverted and channelled back into domesticity.

The ads so identified woman with home that woman and dwelling became one and the house took on a feminine persona. The homemaker was encouraged to empathize in a very personal way with the feelings of her house. "Did you ever look at your house as you approached it and think it looked dispirited and dejected?" one press release queried the Canadian housewife. "Remember how a facial or a wave will raise your own morale and let the house profit accordingly," the ad continued. Renovating the facade of a house was made analogous to giving a woman a face lift.[12]

Despite the extent to which HIP ads promoted the coalescence of woman with home, some expressed the worry that women might make the home *too* feminine an environment for the male head of household and his son. Excessive accommodation to the feminine taste for ruffles and frills threatened to overthrow the "natural" order of the patriarchal family. In a thinly disguised reference to the wife's economic dependence on her husband and consequent fear of losing him, one press release warned that "only a foolish woman plans a totally feminine house in which a man will feel out of place." Accordingly, this ad instructed the woman to go easy on the "dainty," "lady-like" touches, for such decor would "hardly ... make a man want to stay around and read the evening newspaper and spill ashes."[13] The female persona of the house notwithstanding, man's privileged place in it was to be protected and confirmed.

In general, the spatial ordering of the house and the gender identity embodied in rooms and their furnishings expressed and reinforced the sexual division of labour. The mother/wife was to give priority to the spatial needs of other family members before her own. Only after the husband got his den, the son a club room, and the daughter an attic bedroom, could the wife expect a space of her own, perhaps a sewing room (*Macleans* 1937b, 1). Ironically, like the other rooms considered women's domain, the sewing room was a site of work. The reality of the home as a place of leisure for men and work for women was thereby preserved.

As mothers responsible for the upbringing of their children, women were charged with implanting and enforcing gender divisions. Women were advised that the "home-making instincts of a little girl may be fostered or stunted by the kind of room she lives in." The responsible mother would furnish her daughter's room with "a dressing table, a desk, a comfortable chair for reading" and maybe "a coffee table from which she might dispense cocoas or orange juice to her young friends." In contrast, a boy's room might use "ships, dogs, hockey, football, or soldiers" as the decorative theme.[14] Most favoured was the nautical motif, as in a Marboleum ad in *Chatelaine* which promised that in such a room your boy would be king (1939, inside front cover).

Despite the idealization of the home as a haven of love and affection, HIP ads also recognized that the home was an arena of conflict. It was women's job, as wives and mothers, to manage tension among family members. Proper allocation of space was billed as a solution to family conflict. A Marboleum ad showed one woman boasting to her friend about how she averted a crisis in her family by creating "a smart extra room" where "Babs and Billy could practise without having to stop when I am on the phone or when their Dad wants to hear a special radio speech" (*Chatelaine* 1940, inside front cover). The subtext of these ads was that those families too poor to afford conflict resolution through "wise" allocation of space would remain caught in wrangling.

The Home Improvement Plan's intent to generate male employment by the salvaging of rundown homes was in keeping with Depression values. "Use it up, wear it out, make it do, or do without" was an oft-repeated saying of the 1930s (Ware 2). At the same time, the encouragement that the HIP gave to loosening credit and stimulating consumerism heralded an end to the period of "telling ourselves that self-denial is good" ("1937 Home Improvement Year" 41). The injunction to lift self-restraint on spending was directed, it should be noted, at the more affluent of Canadian society, the group of middle-income home owners truly targeted by the Plan. "[T]he industrial workers of Canada will wait until doomsday before they get any relief from this Bill," T. C. Church, Conservative MP, charged in the House. It was not designed to help them cope with high taxes or to fend off foreclosures. As CCF member J. S. Woodsworth pointed out, "it simply does not touch the great problem of housing that faces the country at the present time." In fact, he warned, "it may become a substitute for a more comprehensive scheme." Moreover, despite the "great hullaballoo" surrounding the promotion of the Plan, the job creation it promised was limited to a small and specialized group of workers in the building and allied trades. It did not, Woodsworth intoned, "begin to touch the great mass of the unemployed people of this country" (*Hansard* 1937b, 468, 476, 475).

While criticism of the class implications of the Plan was raised on the floor of the House and elsewhere, rarely if ever did anyone question its gender implications. This silence indicates the depth to which the priority of the male and ensuing gender divisions were unquestioningly entrenched in Canadian society. Despite evidence of widespread female joblessness, women's unemployment was simply not addressed by the Plan. Indeed, the Plan's clear assignment of women to domesticity reflected the strong opposition during the Depression to the gainful employment of the married woman and the prevailing assumption that her right to work should be sacrificed to the needs of the male breadwinner. In addition, the Plan became another arm of the state's active intervention in the home to establish norms of familial constitution and gender roles. While the wife was regarded as the financial manager, she remained answerable to her boss, the husband. The housewife's freedom to transform the environment to which she was confined was always to be limited by her prior duty to safeguard her husband's comfort and authority. Her home decorating activities were also to serve the proper gender development of her children, a task with which she, as mother, was entrusted. The Home Improvement Plan stands as an example of the Canadian state's agency in the social construction of class and gender relations. Furthermore, critical response to the Plan demonstrates the extent to which, in this period of economic distress, class inequities were visible and challenged, however feebly, while the patriarchal structuring of gender inequities was not only accepted as given but viewed as crucial to economic recovery.

Originally published in CWS/cf's Winter 1986 issue, "Women's History/L'histoire des femmes canadiennes: 2" (Volume 7, Number 4).

[1]National Archives of Canada (NAC), Record Group (RG) 27, Department of Labour Records, Vol. 3347, file 5, HIP Press Release #20; Vol. 3355, file 3, Press Release, January 15, 1937.

[2]NAC, RG 27, Vol. 3355, file 3, "Address of H. A. McLarty at Banquet of the Association of Ontario Architects," Windsor, Ontario, October 17, 1936.

[3]NAC, RG 27, Vol. 3354, file 13, "A British Building Society for Canada," 1936; Vol. 3347, file 4, Press Release #10, November 12, 1936; Vol. 3366, file 10, Press Release #156, "A Year of the Home Improvement Plan"; Vol. 3355, file 3, "Address of H. A. McLarty."

[4]NAC, RG 27, Vol. 3355, file 3, HIP Press Release, "For Release in Morning Papers of Saturday, October 17, 1936"; "Outline of Plan for Promoting and Popularizing the Home Improvement Plan" 1.

[5]NAC, RG 27, Vol. 3347, file 4, Press Release #1, "House Renovation Scheme."

[6]NAC, RG 27, Vol. 3347, file 5, "Speech of Arthur B. Purvis: Over a National Network, March 25th, 1937"; Vol. 3354, file 10, Press Release #120; Vol. 3355, file 3, "Minutes of Meeting at Cockfield, Brown & Co. Ltd., Tuesday, December 8, 1936," 4.

[7]NAC, RG 27, Vol. 3354, file 10, Press Release #83; Vol. 3347, file 5, Unnumbered Press Release; Vol. 3354, file 10, Press Release #45.

[8]NAC, RG 27, Vol. 3347, file 5, Press Release #40; "1937 Home Improvement Year"; Fisher 1937c.

[9]NAC, RG 27, Vol. 3354, file 10, Press Release #106; Vol. 3366, file 8, Press Release #70; Maclean's 1936, 1937a.

[10]NAC, RG 27, Vol. 3354, file 10, Press Release #48.

[11]NAC, RG 27, Vol. 3354, file 10, Press Release #92.

[12]NAC, RG 27, Vol. 3354, file 10, Press Release #111; "1937 Home Improvement Year."

[13]NAC, RG 27, Vol. 3354, file 10, Press Release #136.

[14]NAC, RG 27, Vol. 3354, file 10, Press Release #116 and #96.

References

"1937 Home Improvement Year." *Chatelaine* (January 1937): 41.

Alexander, John. "Replanning the Kitchen." *Maclean's* 15 April 1937: 72.

"Canadian Labour Organizations Present Memoranda of Proposed Legislation to the Dominion Government." *Labour Gazette* (January 1937): 39.

Chatelaine (January 1937).

Chatelaine (May 1939).

Chatelaine (April 1940).

Ewen, Stuart. *Captains of Consciousness: Advertising and the Social Roots of the Consumer Culture*. New York: McGraw-Hill, 1976.

Fisher, Richard A. "Modernizing an Old House." *Chatelaine* (February 1937a): 72.

Fisher, Richard A. "Before/After." *Chatelaine* (March 1937b): 20.

Fisher, Richard A. "Modernizing the Small House." *Chatelaine* (April 1937c): 22.

Hansard 29 January 1937a.

Hansard 2 February 1937b.

Hayden, Dolores. *The Grand Domestic Revolution: A History of Feminist Designs for American Homes, Neighbourhoods, and Cities.* Cambridge, MA: MIT Press, 1982.

"A Job in Your Home." *Maclean's* 15 November 1936.

Maclean's 1 December 1936.

Maclean's 1 March 1937a.

Maclean's 15 March 1937b.

Maclean's 1 October 1937c.

Marchand, Roland. *Advertising the American Dream: Making Way for Modernity, 1920–1940.* Berkeley: University of California Press, 1985.

Perry, Evan. "'Modern' Style." *Maclean's* 15 September 1937: 24.

"Planning for a Maidless House." *Chatelaine* (November 1940): 55.

Sturrock, Gordon. "Money to Loan." *Chatelaine* (November 1936): 82.

Ware, Susan. *Holding Their Own: American Women in the 1930s.* Boston: Twayne Publishers, 1982.

"Why Planned Kitchens?" Maclean Building Reports Annual. 1937: 58.

Mothering Mythology in the Late 20th Century
Science, Gender Lore and Celebratory Narrative

Pamela Courtenay Hall ━

"The myth of the natural mother" as it has developed in western cultures is not a myth in any simple sense. It is a complex and heterogeneous array of beliefs, stories, images, and perceptions connected to an equally heterogeneous array of mothering practices, social institutions, knowledge projects, and ideologies. The myth involves the representation of mothering as natural to women, essential to their being, an engagement of love and instinct that is utterly distant from the world of paid work and formal education.

It is a myth that I think most people in advanced industrial societies would not admit to believing—certainly not wholesale. And yet features of the myth are all around us. They percolate through most mothers' experiences of mothering. They often cast agonizing shadows into many women's decisions not to have children. And they serve as an implicit justification for the staggering lack of publicly-funded parenting support and education that still characterizes most western industrialized societies.

The myth of the natural mother is never told as a single story. It is communicated in shades and pieces, and it is a gradual, multi-stage, multi-media phenomenon. Threads of the myth are interwoven into literature, art, film, advertising, and of course, daily life, where it is encapsulated most tellingly in that magical incantation, "Mommy will make it better." Features of the myth are particularly prevalent in children's stories where mothers are seen taking care of children as naturally as birds fly. The recent inclusion of fathers in the scene hasn't changed the fundamental message.[1]

At its core, the myth of the natural mother involves the belief that women are *naturally* mothers—they are born with a built-in set of capacities, dispositions, and desires to nurture children; hence, mothering comes *naturally* to women. Accordingly, mothering is assumed to have the following characteristics. First, mothering is believed to be instinctive, not learned. The most important dimensions of mothering thus require *attunedness to instinct* rather than education. Mothering is also considered to be primarily an engagement of love, not work. More precisely, it is presumed that the work of mothering primarily involves love (thought of as an *unsocialized* emotion), dedication, and intuitive understanding more than it involves labour, skill, and knowledge in the economically and scientifically significant sense of these things.

Another key assumption about the work of mothering is that it primarily involves *instrumental activity* rather than *interpretive activity*. In other words, children's emotional and physiological needs are a pre-given objective reality to which the mother can respond well or badly in ways readily assessable by outside observers.[2] (This feature of the myth can come into tension with the idea that mothering is instinctive, if instinctiveness is taken to entail that mothers know their children's needs better than others can know them. But the acceptance of this idea of maternal epistemic authority is often limited to such matters as knowing when the baby is hungry and predicting diaper changes.)

Mothering is also considered to be primarily an *individual* engagement between mother and child rather than a largely *social* one. In other words, mothering is carried out primarily in private space; the mother and child are most fundamentally a single interactive dyad, only secondarily involved in interpersonal networks located in socio-cultural space.

A related feature of the myth is the belief that mothering is about bonding. A mother's "bonding" with her child from the moment of birth is seen as crucial to the child's well-being in infancy and later in life. Bonding is believed to happen most deeply with one person, which should be the mother, and to happen most effectively through breastfeeding (or at any rate, through full-time, 24-hour-a-day care). Lastly, mothering is considered essential for women. Mothering is thought to be the fulfillment of maternal drives or dispositions that are deeply (biologically) a part of all women's natures (and not, or not as fully, a part of men's).

The problematic nature of these beliefs has been well explored in feminist literature, including their historical origin in capitalist patriarchy; the gender, class, race, culture, and ability bias of the picture of mothering that they enforce; the essentialism involved in the arguments associated with these beliefs; their replication patterns; their impact on women's lives; their contribution to the persistence of sexist, heterosexist, classist, racist, ableist structures in western societies. (See e.g. Ehrenreich and English; Everingham; Johnson; Nakano Glenn *et al.*; Rich; Rothman; Thurer).

Yet despite these problems and despite the growing social support for mothers in the workplace, the myth of the natural mother persists. In this article, I explore why. I begin with the question, "Why call it myth?" and I try to uncover some of the epistemological features that have enabled this myth to persist into the late twentieth century.

My own perspective on motherhood is influenced by my experiences embracing the myth of the natural mother for my first several years as a mother, despite strong tensions between this myth I had absorbed and the facts of my maternal heritage. My mother, Mary (Rozich) Courtenay, had returned to work as a secretary in the mid-1950s against a swell of criticism from the people around her. But she had seen her family's welfare threatened by frequent lay-offs and strikes at the automobile factory where my father worked, and she was determined to do what she knew was best for her children, both materially and by her example. It was also what she *knew* was best for her. She was brimming with intelligence and organizational talents which she wanted to share on more than just the home front. Her own mother, my grandmother, Katerina (Karabogden) Rozich, was a Croatian peasant who missed only one day as a farm labourer to birth her first baby, after which she worked every day in the fields with her baby swaddled beside her.[3] Neither of these women could afford the intensive, infinitely engaged nuclear mothering that patriarchal science and back-to-nature romanticism have recommended in this century. It took me some time to discover that neither could I. And yet I still feel its tug ... to which I respond with thoughts on privilege, sharing, social parenting, and cherishing. These are still in progress.

Why "myth"?

Feminists have been deconstructing beliefs about mothering for decades using the handy epistemological category of "myth," and for good reason. "Myth" means more than "false belief," and more than "ideology," though it includes both of these within its layered array of meanings. And this is just what is needed to describe the depth, the hold, the complexity, and the problematic nature of what goes on in the myth of the natural mother. In at least some of its various forms, it is a myth in the richest sense of the term. It is "a symbolic text which presents *a story* which in turn transmits values, norms and patterns essential and fundamental for a given culture" (Mach 58; emphasis added).

The myth of the natural mother does not consist of any one particular text nor any one particular story; rather; it takes shape in a host of them. But it functions in a way that illustrates what Barthes has identified as "the very principle of myth: *it transforms history into nature*" (1972 129; emphasis added). It transmits a set of norms whose origin has become lost in the myth's pre-history. The norms thus come to be seen as "natural" rather than constructed by historical circumstances.

The phenomenon of gender lore

Such mystification of authority is typical in the proliferation of myths. But it is amplified in the case of natural mothering, as in contemporary western "gender lore" generally, by its mode of popular transmission: the vague remembering of references to scientific studies uncritically read and namelessly called in as authoritative (discussed in Robeck). Here is a mothering-focused example: "I read this study somewhere, I don't remember where, that said that babies who are breastfed are more secure in their social relationships later in life than babies who aren't."

A quintessential example of gender lore that I have encountered in my own teaching and research is this: "I read a study somewhere, I can't recall the source, that said that the part of the brain where the emotions are is more developed in women than in men." Claims of this sort are key to the production, dissemination, and resilience of essentialist thinking about mothering and about gender roles generally.

I think that what is really going on in the phenomenon of gender lore is a casual but nevertheless ritual dance. Widespread enculturation processes—in the home, in schooling, in literature, in television, in film, music, and art—antecedently make many people believe and want to believe that the gender differences which surround and constitute them are innate, and that the sexist structures they have grown up with are okay. But another strand of western enculturation—respect for the authority of western science—makes us want to have scientific evidence for the things that we believe. Hence the impetus to make reference to scientific studies to sanction our beliefs ... however fleeting, vague, and uninformed the references may be. Gender loring can thus be interpreted as a form of ritual devotion to myth, even though it is not recognized as such in the cultures where it is practised (that is, in scientistic patriarchal western cultures).[4]

But this "gender loring" is only the tip of the iceberg of the epistemological problems that lie within the myth of the natural mother: the body of scientific knowledge it so vaguely draws upon is itself formed and hardened around concealed gender biases. The creators of the various knowledge discourses that inform the myth of natural mothering have engaged in tremendously gender-biased research. For decades (and in many cases still today), child-care experts systematically ignored, devalued, and silenced the voices and knowledge of the people most centrally engaged in the phenomenon they were studying—mothers! (Ehrenreich and English; Margolis). For an even longer span of western history and also continuing today, sociobiologists and their precursors have uncritically sought justification for sex roles and gender hierarchies in human patterns unwittingly projected onto primate societies and then reflected back into the notes of ethnologists (Haraway; Hubbard; Tester). This is dominant culture become ethological discovery become ethnological discovery.

Yet another ongoing effort within science which contributes to gender entrenchment: many brain research scientists have uncritically sought interconnections between sex hormones and brain development without attending to questions of directionality of causation (i.e., are female humans *born with* brains that are significantly different from male humans, or are such statistical gender differences in brain morphology—if genuine—*the result* of years of differential training and habituation, hence differential growth? And where prenatal, are such differences genuinely related to significant differences in functional capacity later in life, beyond the sex-specific capacities of procreation and breastfeeding?). The discourse of brain-sex research seems also to be strikingly silent about related problems in phrenological escapades of the past (Hankinson Nelson; Longino; Rooney, etc.)

As a result of its problematic "knowledge" basis, the discourse of natural mothering also qualifies as "myth" in the thinnest sense of the term. It contains stories that need to be questioned, stories whose lack of questioning has harmful consequences in two areas: it hinders informed ethical evaluation of social policies affecting women, children, families, daycares, and schools; and it leads to alienation, frustration, co-optation, or unwitting diversion in many women's lives.

Finally, the discourse of natural mothering is myth-like also in the sense that it inspires many mothers to endure hardships and accomplish goals that would be difficult to achieve without such inspiration. Yet the obstacles and tasks that mothers face would be less imposing if the myth were not so strongly in place to begin with, both in their lives and in their societies. Such flickering empowerment/disempowerment may well be a distinctive feature of feminine calls to heroism in patriarchal myths.

Myth as celebratory narrative

I considered using the term "ideology" in place of "myth" to refer to the complex of beliefs, stories, and images that revolve around mothering. But I think that "myth" is a more adequate and accurate term. It is a richer concept, and I think it accomplishes something that "ideology" doesn't readily seem to. "Myth" suggests that natural mothering operates most deeply at the level of celebratory narrative—of stories passed on in celebration of traditions whose meaning and significance may be larger than life but remain nevertheless inchoate, not understood, not spoken. The term "ideology" may also suggest such subliminal or subterranean levels of influence and communication, but it does so without the full-bodied storiedness of "myth," and without the strong suggestion that what is passed on is culturally invested with the spirit of celebration (however ambiguous attitudes to mothering may be; however materially unsupported women's efforts at mothering may be).

These features of storiedness and celebration are crucial to understanding why the myth of the natural mother is still around. From storybooks to magazine ads, portrayals of mothering communicate to girls and young women that this is your purpose, this is your call to significance, this is what will make your life complete, and it will all come as naturally as falling in love. These messages aren't conveyed by direct means. They are carried by stories and images that capture a child's imagination and connect with all the other pieces she has picked up about the role of mothering in her life and society. Whether her response will be to embrace the myth, to reject it, or to reconstruct it 0 will depend upon many factors in her life, including class, culture, and family circumstances. But it is hard to live in a western industrialized society without having been touched by this myth in some way.

Getting beyond the myth

Despite decades of challenges, the myth of the natural mother continues to be reflected in Canadian and U.S. social and economic institutions, including wage standards, evaluations of economic productivity, education policy, taxation and insurance policies, divorce settlements, and reproductive technology regulation (or the lack thereof) (Griffith and Smith; Johnson; Katz Rothman). It is most blatantly present in the lack of public funding for child care, in the persistence of nuclear over social or communal conceptions of parenting, in the persistence of the property model of what it is to "have" a child, in the guilt or worry or regret that many mothers of young children feel over having to work, in the pressures felt by many "stay-at-home" mothers to refrain from seeking outside employment while their children are young. Stay-at-home mothering is an institution created by the combined forces of capitalism and patriarchy, sustained by the myth, and funded by class and race subordination. But for anyone locked in the myth's embrace, these problems are hard to see.

Yet they are important to see. The myth of the natural mother involves a dominant culture set of discourses that revolve around issues of personal *fulfillment* for women ... while for many women, mothering issues are first of all issues of bodily, family or cultural survival (Collins; Nakano Glenn *et al.*; Wong). This is particularly so for many women living in poverty; for many indigenous women, including those whose mothering traditions were violently interrupted by residential schooling (Ing); for many women of minority races and cultures living with racism; for many immigrant women coping with cultural transition (Shu); for many women living with disability; for many lesbian women dealing with homophobia; for many women living with abusive partners or lack of child support; etc. The personal fulfillment discourse needs to reckon with these social realities, as with the fact that [in 1998] a million and a half Canadian children live in poverty—that's one in every five children under the age of 18, the highest level of child poverty in Canada since the Depression of the 1930s (Callwood).

We need to work towards the redirection of material, financial, and social resources to families in need, and towards the structural and communal socializing of parenting, so that the welfare of children and the support structures for parenting are no longer restricted along nuclear family lines. The de-centring of mothering discourses is crucial to progress in these directions, because the white middle-class ideology of mothering as women's obligatory full-time biologically ordained role and source of fulfillment (performed in the context of a happy home and securely employed husband) remains a strong though now often subterranean contributor to the forces that keep child care facilities out of workplaces, public funding out of early childhood education, parenting education out of the schools, and most people in western societies out of communally and socially engaged forms of parenting.

But this doesn't mean that we have to burn every thread of the myth of the natural mother as an utterly worthless and pernicious legacy. Because on a suitably complex understanding of love, of individual, of bonding and of instinct, mothering as widely cross-culturally and historically experienced *is* about love and bonding between individual mothers and children in ways that are not simply learned, and in ways that run deeper for being life-long, for being intimate in number, and for being outside the reign of institutional structures. Plato's vision in *The Republic* of state-run, anonymous parenting is a vision that should be resisted. Nevertheless, we do need to get beyond the myth of the natural mother far enough that our hidden cultural messages about mothering neither communicate the idea that mothering is essential for women nor obscure the fact that mothering is very much about work, very much in need of social support, and centrally about contributing to there being children and young adults in the world, now and in the future—a staggeringly important thing once you stop to imagine a society without young people.

This paper was condensed from a larger manuscript entitled, "The Myth of the Natural Mother," to be submitted for publication elsewhere.

Originally published in CWS/cf's Summer/Fall 1998 issue, "Looking Back, Looking Forward: Mothers, Daughters and Feminism" (Volume 18, Numbers 2 & 3).

[1]The inclusion of fathers is certainly a good thing, but about this, two things need saying. First, it is important that the increased focus on active fathering not translate into greater energy for compulsory heterosexism and for the devaluation of single mothering and shared lesbian mothering. How to deal with this problem? By including not only fathers in the expanded stories that are told about "mothering," but partners of both genders and of all kinds of relations, including kin and social parenting. Second, as active fathering gains more press and more practitioners, it is important that we ask, What myths about fathering are coming into being? And what impact are they likely to have on children, on fathers, on mothers, *et al.*, and on social structures?
[2]Mothering as interpretative activity is the central focus of Everingham.
[3]There is a growing literature on motherhood in marginalized and oppressed groups. The conditions under which African women lived during slavery reflect some of the cruellest conditions imaginable for mothering (Shaw). These histories are important to tell and to reckon with. They also constitute important points from which to critique dominant-culture practices and institutions.
[4]Perhaps "gender loring" is not the best term for this: it would be helpful to have a term that makes (fleeting) reference to science.

References

Barthes, R. *Mythologies.* New York: Hill and Wang, 1972.
Callwood, June. "A Report on Canadian Children and Poverty." *Homemakers* (May 1997).
Collins, P. H. "Shifting the Center: Race, Class and Feminist Theorizing About Motherhood." *Mothering: Ideology, Experience, and Agency.* Eds. E. Nakano Glenn *et al.* New York: Routledge, 1994.
Ehrenreich, Barbara and Deirdre English. *For Her Own Good: 150 Years of*

Experts' Advice to Women. New York: Anchor Books, 1978.

Everingham, Christine. *Motherood and Modernity: An Investigation into the Rational Dimension of Mothering*. Philadelphia: Open University Press, 1994.

Griffith, A. I. and D. Smith. "Constructing Cultural Knowledge: Mothering as Discourse." *Women and Education*. Eds. J. Gaskell and A. McLaren. Calgary: Detsilig, 1991.

Hankinson Nelson, L. *Who Knows: From Quine to a Feminist Empiricism*. Philadelphia: Temple University Press, 1990.

Haraway, Donna. *Primate Visions: Gender, Race and Nature in the World of Modern Science*. New York: Routledge, 1989.

Haraway, Donna. *Simians, Cyborgs, and Women: The Reinvention of Nature*. London: Free Association, 1991.

Hubbard, Ruth. *The Politics of Women's Biology*. New Brunswick, NJ: Rutgers University Press, 1990.

Ing, Rosalyn N. "The Effects of Residential Schools on Native Child-Rearing Practices." *Canadian Journal of Native Education* 18 (1990) (Supplement): 67–117.

Johnson, M. M. *Strong Mothers, Weak Wives: The Search for Gender Equality*. Berkeley, CA: University of California Press, 1988.

Kaplan, A. E. *Motherhood and Representation: The Mother in Popular Culture and Melodrama*. New York: Routledge, 1992.

Katz Rothman, B. *Reproducing Motherhood: Ideology and Technology in a Patriarchal Society*. New York: Norton, 1989.

Kitzinger, S. *Women as Mothers: How They See Themselves in Different Cultures*. New York: Vintage Books, 1978.

Longino, H. *Science as Social Knowledge: Values and Objectivity in Scientific Inquiry*. Princeton: Princeton University Press, 1990.

Mach, Z. *Symbols, Conflict, and Identity: Essays in Political Anthropology*. Albany: State University of New York Press, 1993.

Margolis, Maxine L. *Mothers and Such: Views of American Women and Why They Changed*. Los Angeles: University of California Press, 1984.

Nakano Glenn, E., Grace Chang, and Linda Rennie Forcey, eds. *Mothering: Ideology, Experience, and Agency*. New York: Routledge, 1994.

Oakley, Ann. *Women's Work: The Housewife, Past and Present*. New York: Pantheon Books, 1974.

Rich, A. *Of Woman Born: Motherhood as Experience and Institution*. New York: Norton, 1976, rpt. 1986.

Robeck, E. "Teaching Heroics: Identity and Ethical Imagery in Science Education." Diss. University of British Columbia, 1996.

Rooney, Phyllis. "Feminist-Pragmatist Revisionings of Reason, Knowledge, and Philosophy." *Hypatia* 8.2 (1993).

Shaw, S. J. "Mothering Under Slavery in the Antebellum South." *Mothering: Ideology, Experience, and Agency*. Eds. E. Nakano Glenn *et al*. New York: Routledge, 1994.

Shu, Ning. "Reframing Motherhood in a Cultural Transition: The Experiences of Immigrant Chinese Mothers." Diss. University of British Columbia, 1998.

Tester, Keith. *Animals and Society: The Humanity of Animal Rights.* New York: Routledge, 1991.

Thurer, S. L. *The Myths of Motherhood: How Culture Reinvents the Good Mother.* Boston: Houghton Mifflin Co., 1994.

Trebilcot, Joyce, ed. *Mothering: Essays in Feminist Theory.* Totawa, NJ: Rowman and Allanheld, 1983.

Wong, S. C. "Diverted Mothering: Representations of Caregivers of Color in the Age of 'Multiculturalism.'" *Mothering: Ideology, Experience, and Agency.* Eds. E. Nakano Glenn *et al.* New York: Routledge, 1994.

Gender, Youth and HIV Risk

Nikki Kumar, June Larkin and Claudia Mitchell

HIV/AIDS is fast becoming a global crisis and young people, worldwide, are one of the most vulnerable groups. Within the youth population, there is strong evidence that girls are particularly at risk (UNAIDS). Our interest in gender, youth and HIV risk was inspired by the work of the Canada South African Management Program (CSAEMP), a partnership of CIDA, McGill University, and the National Department of Education in South Africa. Through CSAEMP, Mitchell and Larkin worked with South African educators and learners on the development of the educational module, *Opening Our Eyes: Addressing Gender-Based Violence in South African Schools* (Mlamleli, Napo, Mabelane, Free, Goodman, Larkin, Mitchell, Mkhize, Robinson and Smith), a document designed to educate teachers about issues related to gender-based violence. This CIDA-funded project brought to light the link between gender and HIV, a connection we are now applying to our understanding of HIV risk in Canadian youth.

The AIDS crisis in South Africa is particularly acute: the national rate of prevalence is 22.8 per cent with infection rates rising at an alarming rate, most significantly in youth (*Anthropology News*). In Canada, however, the number of reported HIV infections is also on the rise with more teens infected than ever before (Health Canada 2000). With the stark increases in incidence among women in both the industrialized and the developing world, there is growing acknowledgement that HIV/AIDS is a highly gendered disease (Simmons, Farmer and Schoepf; UNAIDS). The rise in the HIV incidence rate of both women and youth suggests that young females may be a particularly vulnerable group (Grierson; White; Wingwood and DiClemente). In South Africa, for example, the HIV incidence rate among South African girls is three to four times higher than boys (Brown).

Across the world, more than four-fifths of all HIV-infected women have contracted the virus through heterosexual transmission (Health Canada 2001; Larkin 2000; Wingwood and DiClemente). Although their political and economic situations vary, women are linked by their subordinate status in heterosexual relations. For young women, a combination of biological and social factors increases this risk (Mlamelli *et al.*). These factors are the focus of this article. This work has grown out of our involvement with the *Gendering*

Adolescent AIDS Prevention (GAAP) project, a newly formed group of Canadian and South African researchers working in the area of gender, youth, and HIV/AIDS. Our first efforts have focused on exploring gender as an HIV risk factor in the heterosexual encounters of youth. This information will provide the background for achieving our larger goal: the development of gender-sensitive HIV/AIDS prevention programs for Canadian and South African youth.

Young women and HIV risk

Biologically, young women are more vulnerable to HIV infection than young men. The risk of HIV infection during unprotected vaginal intercourse is as much as two to four times higher for women (UNAIDS). During heterosexual sex, the exposed surface area of the vagina and labia is larger in women than the vulnerable surface area in men (Simmons *et al.*). Semen infected with HIV contains a higher concentration of the virus than female sexual secretions. In general, the male-female transmission of HIV is much more efficient than female-male transmission. A single episode of unprotected intercourse is risky for women who may be receiving infected semen from a male partner. Young women are particularly vulnerable to infection through intercourse prior to menstruation when the lower reproductive tract is still developing (UNAIDS).

The presence of an untreated STD can increase the risk of HIV transmission. Women are more likely than men to have an undetected STD because the sores and symptoms may be mild or difficult to recognize (UNAIDS). Infection rates for STDs, which have increased since 1997, are highest in the 15-19 age group with girls being infected far more than boys (Picard). Thus young women, for whom general rates of chlamydia and gonorrhea are increasing the most, are at particular risk for contracting HIV during unprotected heterosexual intercourse (Sanford).

Young women's biological vulnerability to HIV infection is increased when their sexual autonomy is compromised. Gendered power relations operate to shape and constrain heterosexual practices in ways that increase young women's risk to HIV infection. Although adolescent heterosexual relationships take place within the private sphere, they are located within complicated social networks of peers where information is exchanged and sexual reputations are constructed (Holland, Ramazanoglu, Sharpe and Thomson; Holland and Thomson; Moore, Rosenthal, and Mitchell). According to the dominant femininity script, young women are not supposed to desire sex or be sexually assertive, and are further expected to resist young men's sexual advances (Gomez). Enforced through the mechanism of sexual reputation amongst peers, a young woman can be labelled a "whore" or a "slut" if she is seen as too sexually knowledgeable or assertive by her peers or male sexual partner (Holland and Thomson). Thus, an empowered, independent young woman with her own active sexual desires, who seeks sexual pleasure and sexual safety on her own terms, is not a "normal" feminine woman, but often seen as sexually and socially deviant (Holland and Thomson). It is these distinctions and accompanying judgements that serve to disempower a young woman by limiting her scope of socially appropriate behaviours within heterosexual relationships (Travers and Bennett). Therefore, the extent to which young women conform to or transgress conventional femininity in their intimate relationships depends in part on the climate of the peer culture within which they are located (Holland and Thomson).

Safer sex negotiation presents a challenge for many young women because of socio-cultural norms that have traditionally fostered female sexual passivity, innocence and/or ignorance (Suarez-Al-Adam, Raffaelli, and O'Leary). For a young woman to insist her male partner use a condom or to present a male condom to her partner is implying that she is sexually experienced and sexually assertive, and therefore, sexually promiscuous (De Oliveira). Through this deviation from the expected feminine role, she is placing herself at risk for betrayal by her male partner, either through him disclosing their sexual relationship to peers, and pegging her as sexually accessible or "easy," or insisting she is sexually experienced, and labelling her a "slut" (De Oliveira). Faced with the threat of a tarnished or "bad" reputation, many young women choose to remain submissive or ignorant with regards to male condom use and/or are coerced into sex, instances where the male determines whether or not a condom will be used during heterosexual intercourse (De Oliveira). Thus, many young women are at high risk for contracting HIV through unprotected heterosexual intercourse because they feel pressured to maintain a "good" female (sexual) reputation amongst peers.

Young women's vulnerability to HIV infection is also directly related to the structural conditions of their lives (White). Young women exist within a socially stratified system maintained by racism, economic inequality, poverty, sexism, and violence (White). Desperate economic circumstances can increase HIV risk when girls and women are forced into survival sex where condom use is difficult to negotiate. As reported by UNAIDS, for many girls and women, "sex is the currency in which they are expected to pay for life's opportunities, from a passing grade in school to a trading licence or permission to cross a border" (3). In many circumstances, clients demand unprotected heterosexual intercourse, and may often use sexual and physical violence and/ or may refuse to pay if a condom is used (Gomez; Larkin 2000). The growing demand for low-risk sexual partners has led to increased child sexual exploitation and a rise in the numbers of HIV-infected girls. Most vulnerable are girls from developing countries who are sold into the international flesh trade to service male sex tourists.

Throughout the developed world, unintended teenage pregnancies and the contraction of STDS are most common among young women from socially deprived neighbourhoods and from minority ethnic groups, which are often disproportionately economically disadvantaged. Minority ethnic groups also suffer the health-damaging effects of explicit prejudice or more subtle forms of social exclusion, and are more likely to experience difficulties assessing health and social services or to find these services culturally inappropriate or non-welcoming (Campbell and Aggleton; Larkin 2001). These factors combined with the gender inequalities faced by many young women render them at increased vulnerability for contracting HIV through unprotected, high-risk heterosexual intercourse (Campbell and Aggleton).

Hegemonic masculinity and HIV risk

Hegemonic masculinity[1] dominates the sexual cultures of youth. Dominant ideologies of masculinity portray young men as sexually active and aggressive (Gomez). Challenging hegemonic masculinity takes individual courage and may be punished by peers and partners (Holland and Thomson). Within peer groups specifically, sexual experience can provide young men with a passport to status and affirmation.

The dynamics of the adolescent male peer group can make it difficult for young men to demonstrate ignorance or innocence about sex to their male peers or even to their (female) sexual partners (Holland and Thomson). Furthermore, the pressure for young men to be sexually active and to have multiple (female) sexual partners may become so great, that those unfulfilling this expectation may be open to ridicule and homophobic bullying. This reinforces the stigmatizing of sexual minorities and supports the idea that multiple sexual partnerships with young women are the expected norm in heterosexual masculinity (Campbell and Aggleton; Holland *et. al.*; Holland and Thomson; Moore *et al.*).

For many young men, male condom use is associated with "gay" or "un-masculine" sexual activity. Therefore, in order to maintain a masculine heterosexual identity amongst peers, in particular with female sexual partners, condom use may be discouraged during heterosexual intercourse. As well, it is socially accepted and expected that men control the sexual decision-making, including the use of male condoms within heterosexual relationships (Garcia-Moreno and Watts). It is this social acceptance and encouragement of male promiscuity, sexual decision-making, and sexual aggression alongside female sexual passivity, innocence and ignorance that are some of the gendered factors that put women at greater peril for HIV infection ("U.N. officials said violence against women helps spread HIV").

Young men and young women may have a vested interest in not communicating about sex in early sexual encounters. Silence surrounding hetero-sexual activities can maintain an ambiguity between partners as to whether sex will actually happen. To mention condoms presumes that sexual intercourse will be occurring, thereby opening the possibility of sexual rejection towards the male, and an unfavourable sexual reputation for the female (De Oliveira). The risk of acquiring a tarnished sexual reputation among peers, therefore, exists for both the young man and the young woman. However, in the absence of communication, the meanings and associations of conventional masculin-ity and femininity tend to fill the silence, overshadowing the needs and desires of the individuals involved and concerns for sexual safety. Through "sponta-neous," unprotected heterosexual intercourse, then, the young man maintains his masculine sexual dignity, while the young woman maintains her proper maintains her proper sexual role through sexual passivity, innocence and/or ignorance (Suarez-Al-Adam *et al*).

In this absence of communication, the past sexual histories of the partners become silenced as well. Thus, the lack of knowledge surrounding her male partner's past sexual exploits alongside her socially expected sexual passivity prevents opportunities for condom negotiation and increases the risk for HIV infection.

(Hetero)sexuality and the privileging of male desire

Many young men have learned to approach sex from the position of sexual actor, whereas young women see themselves as the objects of sexual acts and the targets of male desire. Young women may enter heterosexual relationships aware of the sexual needs of men but without a clear sense of their own sexual self-interest (Holland and Thomson). For instance, heterosexuality and heterosexual intercourse have become based on a masculine understanding and definition of sex (Wallace and Wolf). Consequently, sexual intercourse becomes defined as solely vaginal penetration where women become per-ceived as passive recipients of the sexual act, of sexual expression, and objects of male desire (Holland *et. al*.; Wallace and Wolf). Thus, many young women find it difficult to articulate their own agency in sexual encounters, and frequently describe sex as something that happens to them (Holland and Thomson).

Michelle Fine has written extensively about the absence of a discourse of female desire in the dominant language and perspectives of sexuality. Accord-ing to Fine, when the expression of female sexuality is limited to a male-defined terrain, girls' sexual agency can be reduced to saying yes or no to sexual intercourse, a practice that may not be generated from their own sexual desire. Through being positioned as objects of male sexual desire, young women can be rendered as passive in heterosexual sexual relationships, irrespective of the existence of force or pressure on the part of male partners. The emphasis on male sexual needs, pleasures, and desires combined with a lack of discourse on heterosexual pleasure for women through which young women can both locate and further develop their own sexuality, cause many young women to collude with men in promoting and maintaining male heterosexual dominance (Holland *et. al*).

Being the object of male desire can effectively silence female desire and lead to sexual self-surveillance on the part of the young women (Puri). Self-surveillance can be manifested as "nurturance" (fulfilling the needs of their male partner) and/or pragmatism (accepting that consent to sexual experience may be easier than offering resistance) (Holland and Thomson). Furthermore, young women may have internalized beliefs about the priority of male sexual pleasure (Holland and Thomson). This, in turn, places young women in a risky situation for having unprotected heterosexual intercourse and hence, increases her chances in contracting HIV. For example, if a young woman does not derive pleasure from penetrative sex and has no discourse within which to locate her own sexuality, than the use of condoms makes little difference to her own enjoyment of sex. Thus, it becomes easy for her male partner to insist on unprotected heterosexual intercourse because *he* finds it sexually pleasurable, and *she* feels she must please him.

Accounts given by young women of their first sexual experiences illustrate the differently gendered worlds in which adolescents become sexually active. For example, some young women recall their first experience of heterosexual intercourse as something that which they "rushed" through, or wanted to get it "over and done with," all the while focusing on wanting to please their male sexual partner. Moreover, many young women believed that they were "in love" with their male partner, and therefore, engaged in unprotected heterosexual intercourse because they trusted their male partner to be safe from HIV, especially when located within steady, preferably monogamous, relationships (De Oliveira; Holland *et. al*; Holland and Thomson). However, through this "relinquishment of (sexual) control in the face of love" with male partners, young women place themselves at increased risk for contracting the fatal virus (Campbell and Aggleton, De Oliveira; Holland *et. al*; Holland and Thomson).

Gendered power relations also places pressure on young men to establish themselves as sexually masculine, and many times, this is through silencing female sexual desire and needs. Through the privileging of male sexual pleasure, it becomes clear the expression of power in sexual relationships resides with the males. One expression in this privileging is the definition of what counts as sex.

When the prevalent definition of "real sex" is the act of vaginal penetration and male ejaculation and/or orgasm, non-penetrative sexual activities are relegated to the category of foreplay (Holland *et. al*). Thus, sexual practices such as touching, mutual masturbation, and oral sex are seen either as a precursor or as an afterthought to "real" sex which is interpreted as heterosexual intercourse (Holland and Thomson). This places young women at a significant disadvantage in negotiating safer sex because male partners may insist and/or female partners may believe that heterosexual intercourse is the essence of sexuality. Thus, because the use of condoms may disrupt or lessen the pleasure for males, unprotected heterosexual intercourse can become a necessity for "real" sex to occur, placing pressure on young women to engage in unprotected, heterosexual intercourse with potentially HIV infected partners, and thus, increasing their own chance of becoming HIV infected.

Violence against young women

Dealing with sexual violence is considered to be a key factor in the fight against AIDS (Mlamelli *et al.*). In South Africa, for example, the legacy of violence that underpinned the apartheid state has led to extremely high levels of violence. A history of oppressive political practices has embedded violence as a normal part of gendered relations. The rapid spread of the HIV virus across the country and the disproportionate infection rate in females, have been linked to the high incidence of rape (Human Rights Watch; Mlamelli *et al.*). While it can be dangerous to generalize from one cultural setting to another, it is important to recognize that the connection between AIDS and gender violence is not limited to the African context. Sexual violence is a problem for women worldwide and the statistics show that Canadian women are no exception. As Holland *et al*, point out,

> On a global scale, heterosexual intercourse has emerged as a means through which HIV is now transmitted, and it appears that transmission is very widely facilitated by social factors which constrain women's control of heterosexual encounters.... (458)

A critical constraint experienced by young people wishing to practice safer heterosexual intercourse consists of the degree of control they have within sexual encounters. In general, young women have far less control over their sexual encounters than do young men. One obvious way power is manifest in heterosexual relationships is through the presence or threat of violence against young women by young men.

Sexual pressure from male sexual partners, ranging from rape to persuasion, is common in adolescent heterosexual relationships (Holland and Thompson). For many young men, sexual persuasion is a legitimate (and even requisite) component of the masculine sexual role (Holland and Thomson). However, the degree of persuasiveness determined by the male can vary, from the consistent pestering of their female partner for sexual intercourse to actual rape. For some females, sexual assault can become integrated with socially-constructed roles of proper masculine sexual behaviour and feminine sexual behaviour. The threat or actuality of sexual violence, combined with a greater biological vulnerability to infection than her male partner, renders a young woman at increased risk for HIV transmission during unprotected heterosexual intercourse. For example, the potential tearing and bleeding that occurs in the vaginal tract from forced intercourse increases the risk of HIV infection.

For young women who are particularly vulnerable to HIV infection, gender inequality in heterosexual relationships has become a serious health risk.

Conclusion

With the sharp increase in STD rates in youth, young people have become a group at high risk for HIV infection. To curb the spread of the disease, HIV/AIDS prevention programs must consider the many risk factors affecting youth. Considering that girls are particularly vulnerable to STD infection, including HIV, highlighting the role of gender in HIV transmission is crucial. In addition to acknowledging young women's biological vulnerability to HIV infection, programs must consider the ways violence and inequity in heterosexual relationships limit young women's ability to practice safer sex. This is the focus of the GAAP project. By developing ways to incorporate a gender perspective in HIV/AIDS prevention programs for youth, we are hoping to take an important step in stopping the spread of the HIV epidemic.

The authors acknowledge the support of the Social Science and Humanities Research Council (SSHRC). For more information about GAAP, check out our website at www.utgaap.info or e-mail us at gaap.project@utoronto.ca.

Originally published in CWS/cf's Summer/Fall 2001 issue, "Women and HIV/ AIDS" (Volume 21, Number 2): 35-40.

[1]Hegemonic masculinity, according to Holland and Thomson, is a "socially shared understanding of successful masculinity, constituted in opposition to femininity and other forms of masculinity including homosexuality" (64).

References

Anthropology News 40(7) (October 1999).

Brown, M. M. "United Nations Development Programme." *The New York Times.* January 11 2000.

Campbell, C., and P. Aggleton. "Young People's Sexual Health: A Framework for Policy Debate." *Canadian Journal of Human Sexuality* 8 (4) 1999: 249-262.

De Oliveira, D. L. "Adolescent Women's Ways of Seeing Sexual Risks and the Epistemological Dimension of 'Risky Sex.'" 2000. Online. http://www.ioe.ac.uk/ccs/conference2000/papers/pde/papers/deoliveira.html July 2001.

Fine, M. "Sexuality, Schooling, and Adolescent Females: The Missing Discourse of Desire." *Toward a New Psychology of Gender: A Reader.* Eds. M. Gergen and S. Davis. New York: Routledge, 1998: 375-402.

Garcia-Moreno, C. and C. Watts. "Violence Against Women: Its Importance for HIV/AIDS." *AIDS* 14 (3) 2000: 253-265.

Gomez, A. "Women and HIV/AIDS: A Gender Perspective." *Women, Vulnerability and AIDS.* Eds. A. Gomez and D. Mercring. Santiago, Chile: Latin American and Caribbean Women's Health Network, 1998: 2-10.

Grierson, J. *Peer Education Program.* Toronto: Toronto Public Health, nd.

Health Canada. "*HIV/AIDS Epi Update:* HIV and AIDS *Among Youth in Canada.*" Ottawa, 2001.

Health Canada. "HIV and AIDS Among Youth in Canada." 2000. Online http://www.hc-sc.gc.ca/hpb/lcdc/bah/epi/youth_e.html August 16 2001.

Holland, J., C. Ramazanoglu, S. Sharpe, and R. Thomson. "Feminist Methodology and Young People's Sexuality." *Culture, Society, and Sexuality.* Eds. R. Parker and P. Aggleton. London: UCL Press, 1999. 457-472.

Holland J. and R. Thomson. "Sexual Relationships, Negotiation and Decision Making." *Teenage Sexuality: Health, Risk and Education.* Eds. J. Coleman and D. Roker. Amsterdam: Harwood Academic Publishers, 1998. 59-79.

Human Rights Watch. *Violence Against Women in South Africa: The State Response to Domestic Violence and Rape.* New York: Human Rights Watch, 1995.

Larkin, J. "Gender-based Violence and HIV/AIDS Prevention Programs for Youth." Washington, D.C: Presentation at the CIES Conference, 2001.

Larkin, J. "Women Poverty and HIV Infection." *Canadian Woman Studies/les cahiers de la femme* 20 (3) 2000: 137-141.

Mlamelli, O., V. Napo, P. Mabelane, V. Free, M. Goodman, J. Larkin, C. Mitchell, H.M. Mkhize, K. Robinson, and A. Smith. "Workshop 6: Gender and HIV/AIDS." *Opening Our Eyes: Addressing Gender-based Violence in South African Schools.* Pretoria: Canada-South Africa Education Management Program, 2001. 131-138.

Moore, S., D. Rosenthal, and A. Mitchell. *Youth, AIDS and Sexually Transmitted Diseases.* London: Routledge Press, 1996.

Picard, A. "Diseases Show Ominous Rise as Safe-Sex Messages Fade." *The Globe and Mail.* 17 August 2001: A1, A8.

Puri, J. *Woman, Body and Desire in Post-Colonial India.* London: Routledge Press, 1999.

Sanford, Wendy C. *Our Bodies, Ourselves for the New Century.* New York: Simon and Schuster, 1998.

Simmons, J., P. Farmer, and B. Schoepf. A Global Perspective. *Women, Poverty and AIDS: Sex, Drugs and Structural Violence.* Eds. P. Farmer, M. Connors, and J. Simmons. Maine: Common Courage Press, 1996. 39-90.

Suarez-Al-Adam, M., M. Raffaelli, and A. O'Leary. "Influence of Abuse and Partner Hypermasculinity on the Sexual Behaviour of Latinas." *AIDS Education and Prevention* 12 (3) (2000): 263-274.

Travers, M., and L. Bennett. "AIDS, Women and Power." *AIDS as a Gender Issue.* Eds. L. Sherr, C. Hankins, and L. Bennett. London: Taylor and Francis, 1996. 64-77.

"U.N. officials said violence against women helps spread HIV." *AIDS Weekly Plus.* March 22 1999: 11.

UNAIDS. "Women, HIV and AIDS." 1999. Online. http://www.avert.org/womenaid.htm July 12, 2000.

Wallace, Ruth A. and Alison Wolf. *Contemporary Sociological Theory: Expanding the Classical Tradition.* New Jersey: Prentice Hall, 1999.

White, R. T. *Putting Risk in Perspective: Black Teenage Lives in the Era of* AIDS. Lanham: Rowman and Littlefield Publishers Inc, 1999.

Wingood, G. M. and R. J. DiClemente, R. J. "HIV Sexual Risk Reduction Interventions for Women: A Review." *American Journal of Preventative Medicine* 12 (3) (1996): 209-213.

Erasing Race

The Story of Reena Virk

Yasmin Jiwani ➤

On November 14, 1997, 14-year-old Reena Virk, a girl of South Asian origin, was brutally murdered in a suburb of Victoria, British Columbia. Reena was first beaten by a group of seven girls and one boy between the ages of 14 and 16. She was accused of stealing one of the girl's boyfriends and spreading rumours. Her beating was framed as retaliation to these alleged actions. According to journalistic accounts, the attack began when one of the girls attempted to stub out a cigarette on her forehead. As she tried to flee, the group swarmed her, kicked her in the head and body numerous times, attempted to set her hair on fire, and brutalized her to the point where she was severely injured and bruised. During the beating, Reena reportedly cried out "I'm sorry." (*The Vancouver Sun* A10). Battered, Reena staggered across a bridge trying to flee her abusers, but was followed by two of them—Warren Glowatski and Kelly Ellard. The two then continued to beat her, smashing her head against a tree, and kicking her to the point where she became unconscious. They then allegedly dragged her body into the water and forcibly drowned her. Reena's body was subsequently found eight days later on November 22, 1997, with very little clothing on it. The pathologist who conducted the autopsy noted that Virk had been kicked 18 times in the head and her internal injuries were so severe as to result in tissues being crushed between the abdomen and backbone. She also noted that the injuries were similar to those that would result from a car being driven over a body. The pathologist concluded that Reena would likely have died even if she had not drowned.[1]

This chilling murder of a 14-year-old girl was singled out by the news media and heavily reported in the local, national, and international press. The media's initial framing of the murder focused largely on "girl-on-girl" violence. The issue of racism, sexism, pressures of assimilation, and the social construction of Reena Virk as an outcast were rarely addressed. When they were addressed, it was always in the language of appearance—that she weighed 200 pounds and was five feet, eight inches tall. According to media accounts, her heaviness and height precluded her from being accepted. The assumptions regarding the validity of normative standards of beauty and appearance were significantly absent in all accounts of the story. Rather, as with dominant frameworks of meaning that are utilized to cover stories of racialized immigrant and refugees communities—Reena's difference was underscored and inferiorized.

This article focuses on the framing of the Reena Virk murder in media accounts. The aim is to draw attention to the lack of coverage and critical analysis of racism as a form of violence communicated by exclusion, scapegoating, and targetting of "others," and underpinned by the inferiorization of difference as well as its framing as deviance. Additionally, this article argues that the absence of any discussion of racism as a motivating factor in the murder is symbolic of the denial of racism as a systemic phenomenon in Canada. The absence of any mention of racism in the judicial decision concerning the murder is echoed in the news coverage of the decision, thereby privileging a particular interpretation of the case as one involving physical gang violence. Finally, the erasure of race in the discourse of the news media is made evident by the complete denial of the Virk's appearance and racialized identity and its significance in terms of her vulnerability to violence. By not referencing "race" in this context, the media were able to negate and omit any substantive discussion of racism, and at the same time, to reinforce hegemonic notions of racism—as behaviour which is simply confined to hate groups.

Racialized girls and their vulnerability to violence

A recent study conducted by the Alliance of Five Research Centres on Violence underscores the vulnerability of girls and young women to male violence. It has been found, for instance, that girls comprise 84 per cent of the reported victims of sexual abuse, 60 per cent of the physical child abuse cases, and 52 per cent of cases of reported neglect (Department of Justice). Girls are also victims in 80 per cent of the cases of sexual assaults reported to police (Fitzgerald). Many flee abusive homes and end up on the streets where they are subjected to further abuse (Alliance). The situation is compounded for marginalized girls who have to deal with the interlocking effects of racism, homophobia, classism, ableism, and sexism (Jiwani 1998b; Razack).

The Working Groups on Girls (WGG) noted in its report that immigrant and refugee girls experience higher rates of violence because of dislocation, racism, and sexism from both within their own communities and the external society (Friedman). Caught between two cultures, where their own is devalued and constructed as inferior, and where cultural scripts in both worlds encode patriarchal values, these girls face a tremendous struggle in trying to "fit." When they don't, they suffer intense backlash. In effect, what these girls experience is a double dose of patriarchy—the patriarchal values encoded in the dominant society which resonate with the patriarchal values encoded in their own cultural backgrounds.

At the core of the diversity of experiences that shape the lives and realities of girls from marginalized groups is the intensity of rejection and exclusion mediated by the mainstream of society. Faced by racism, and the compounding sexism, girls from racialized immigrant and refugee communities have few avenues of recourse available to them.[2] The obverse side of this rejection is the

overwhelming pressure to conform and assimilate into the dominant normative framework and thereby strive for at least conditional acceptance. However, the internalization of the dominant culture often leads to an inferiorization,
negation, and hatred of the self and their communities.

Cultural identity and conflict

Rather than focusing on girls' experiences of racism and sexism, many studies
have tended to concentrate on issues of cultural and intergenerational conflict
within racialized immigrant communities. To some extent, these studies have
emerged in response to prevailing occupations in the area of ethnicity and
identity retention cohering around the debate of whether such identity is
primordially rooted (Geertz; Isaacs) or situationally constructed (Keyes; Lyman
and Douglass). Further, the prevalence of these identity-oriented studies
suggests a greater degree of comfort in looking at "cultural" issues of co-
existence, conflict, and exchange, or assimilation and acculturation (Drury;
Jabbra; Kim; Rosenthal *et al.*), although more recently, this trend has shifted
(see, for example, Matthews).

Despite the use of culture as the focal point of inquiry, many of these
studies reveal that girls within racialized immigrant cultures experience a
greater degree of dissatisfaction and strain with the normative values imposed
by their own culture (Hutnik; Miller; Onder; Rosenthal *et al.*). The contextual
factors influencing and shaping this dissatisfaction tend not to be examined in
structural terms, i.e., as emanating from the subordinate position of the
cultural group in relation to the dominant society, and the construction of
racialized immigrant communities as deviant Others (Bannerji, 1993; Thobani;
Tsolidas as cited in Turnbull 163). Nor has the complex interaction of sexism
and racism shaping the lives and choices of young women been examined in
great detail in Canadian studies (for exceptions see Bourne *et al.*; Vertinsky *et
al.*). Thus, rather than focusing on how racialized girls are inferiorized and how
they internalize dominant values which embody a rejection of the self and their
cultural communities, many of the existing studies tend to frame these "Other"
communities as being problematic insofar as clinging to traditional, non-
liberatory and patriarchal cultures (see Alicea for more on this critique).

Within the context of the violence of racism, girls from marginalized
communities are often faced with systemic barriers around which they must
negotiate their survival. They may choose to try to conform and assimilate,
although this choice is often not available to them due to the exclusionary
impact of racism and/or homophobia. On the other hand, the deviant
characterization of their communities by the mainstream often forces them
into silence as they are afraid to report experiences of violence for the fear of
betraying their own communities (Burns; Razack). As Burns notes,

> Our abuse has been hidden in our communities' refusal to acknowl-
> edge the pervasiveness of violence in our lives. This refusal is not

maliciousness but a protective measure born of the legitimate fear that such information would be used as a weapon by the dominant culture. Our abuse has been hidden behind bravado and denials. The result is the creation of a climate of tolerance. (4)

Yet, it is critical to form a space whereby the specific kinds of violence that racialized girls experience can be discussed and analyzed. It is not enough to universalize their experiences within the category of "girls" or "women" (Tipper; Russell), or alternatively "youth" and "children." At the same time, focusing on culture fails to capture the structural forces of oppression that shape the lives of racialized and marginalized girls. A central issue here is the subtlety with which racism is communicated and naturalized, and how it intersects with sexism to influence the lived reality and strategies of survival of racialized girls.

As Kimberle Crenshaw notes, "Race and gender are two of the primary sites for the particular distribution of social resources that ends up with observable class differences" (97).

An analysis of how racism interlocks with other systems of domination to influence the life chances and reality of racialized girls requires acknowledging racism as a form of violence that is endemic and pervasive. Nevertheless, while it has become increasingly common to accept the structured inequality produced and reproduced by sexism, the same does not hold true for racism. Thus, rather than accepting racism as a structure of domination, similar to sexism, and as arising from a legacy of colonialism, the reality of racism has to be "proven" continually (Bannerji 1987; 1993). In part, this denial of racism is formed and informed by the dominant mediated discourses on race and racism which are powerfully communicated through the mass media.

The mass media, "race," and racism

The media play a critical role in communicating notions of "race" and racism. In effect, they help define these terms and locate them within the public imagination (Hall 1990; van Dijk, 1993). In the production and reproduction of social knowledge, the mainstream mass media are crucial vehicles in reinforcing hegemonic interpretations and interests (Cottle). Thus, how they frame race and racism is both derived from and informed by social life, and reproduced in everyday talk and thought (Smitherman-Donaldson and van Dijk; van Dijk 1987).

Previous research has documented the ways in which Canadian mainstream media communicate notions of "race" and forward particular definitions of racism (Bannerji, 1986; Indra; Jiwani, 1993; Scanlon). These definitions explain racism as arising from ignorance, increasing immigration, and economic downturns (Jiwani 1993; see also van Dijk 1993). Such explanations are privileged through various discursive means so that they appear to be meaningful and resonate with everyday social reality. "Racists" are then defined as ignorant, uneducated, and usually rural-based individuals who at times are organized into hate groups (Jiwani, 1993). At the same time, "race" is represented by allusions to cultural differences and phenotypic differences where these can be readily observed (i.e., through film footage and pictures), and through Manichean oppositions which underscore these differences within the footage itself or in the presentation of the story (see also JanMohamed; Jiwani, 1998). It has been argued that the Canadian news media communicate race and racism by "omission and commission"—at times in a deliberate manner, and at other times, through strategic absence (Jiwani 1993).

Media frames—the erasure of race/racism

As the events leading to Virk's murder unfolded in the daily papers and television newscasts, the horror of what "girls do to other girls" was highlighted and quickly overshadowed the issue of male violence. In contrast to the numerous deaths of women by their spouses and ex-spouses, Reena's death was held up as symbol of how girls are not immune to committing acts of violence. Story after story in the daily papers covered the issue of teen girl violence, quoting research to support the main contention that girls are just as dangerous as boys.[3] Even though existing research clearly links the issue of teen girl violence to the *internalization* of a dominant, patriarchal culture which values sex and power, this connection was trivialized if not side-stepped altogether (Artz; Joe and Chesney Lind). Additionally, counter evidence which demonstrates that only 3.83 per cent of violent crimes are committed by girls (Schramm) failed to hit the headlines in the same manner or intensity.

Headlines from *The Vancouver Sun* during this early period (November, 1997) framed the story in the following way: "Teenage girls and violence: The B.C. reality"; "Girls fighting marked by insults, rumours, gangs"; "Bullies: Dealing with threats in a child's life"; "Girls killing girls a sign of angry, empty lives." This last headline suggests that had girls followed a traditional (gender-based) lifestyle, their lives would not be so empty and frustrating. Throughout the coverage, the media dwelt with puzzlement on the increasing violence of teenage girls at a time when they were supposedly enjoying greater equality. Statistics indicating the growing number of girls graduating with honours, as compared to boys, were used to demonstrate this perplexing contradiction. Implicit throughout the news coverage was the sense that girls do not deserve to be violent because of the privileges they are now enjoying, and further, that girls are not used to the demands inherent in these privileges and therefore, can not cope, a disturbing echo of late nineteenth-century ideology.

At no time did the media provide any in-depth analysis of the violent nature of the dominant culture, or examine ways in which violent behaviour is internalized as a function of coping with a violent society. Nor did the media report on the kinds of violence to which girls are generally subjected to, or the differential impact of violence on girls and boys from different backgrounds. In fact, this kind of coverage only surfaced with the school murders in Littleton,

U.S.A., and the subsequent copy-cat murder in Taber, Alberta (see for instance, *The Vancouver Sun* Special Issue on Teen Violence), where suddenly, boys who were considered marginalized became the objects of public sympathy and reporting.

While the dominant filter became one of girl-on-girl violence, this subsequently shifted, albeit slightly, towards a sustained coverage of schoolyard bullies, sprinkled with some sympathetic coverage of children who are marginalized in school because they do not fit peer-group normative standards. Aside from opinion pieces written by individuals, mostly South Asian, none of the news articles discussed the issue of racialization as it impacts on girls who are physically different by virtue of their skin colour, or the pressures of assimilation that racialized girls experience in attempting to fit within their peer group culture. Interestingly, in contrast to previous patterns of coverage observed in the news accounts of the stories of young racialized women, accounts which tended to focus on issues of cultural and intergenerational conflict (Jiwani 1992), the coverage of the Reena Virk murder did neither. Instead, the coverage continued to focus on girl-on-girl violence in the immediate aftermath of the murder.

Subsequent coverage of the court appearances and sentencing of the six girls who were charged, focused on Virk's inability to find acceptance in her peer culture, and once again, emphasized her weight and height as the major contributing factors. Despite her physical difference—as a racialized girl— there was no mention, save one, of the possible motive being racism. Instead, the stories repeatedly stressed her lack of "fit" and her overweight appearance. The implication was that had Reena Virk fit the normative standards, she would have been acceptable. Normative standards in this society imply a body which is thin, white, (or exotic and beautiful), able-bodied, heterosexual, and which conforms to accepted notions of female teenage behaviour.[4] In essence, the victim is held responsible for her own fate. The issue of racism as a motive is significantly absent in early media coverage and only surfaced two years later in the coverage of the trial of one of her attackers. (Hall)

A brief interlude in the construction of the story occurred with the revelation that Virk had allegedly been sexual abused by a close family member. This underlined once again, her lack of "fit"—both within her familial culture and the external, dominant culture of her peers. The allegations were immediately denied in the detailed coverage of the eulogy delivered by an elder of the Jehovah's Witness church at her funeral. The denial was underscored by her mother's comments to reporters suggesting that Reena had been a troubled child. Journalistic accounts which stressed her inability to conform to her family's ethnic values, combined with the strict beliefs of the Jehovah Witness church, reinforced her mother's statements and helped locate the issue as one of intergenerational conflict, youth rebellion, and cultural conflict. (Beatty and Pemberton; Dirk) However, despite this obvious location and familiar terrain, these lines of inquiry were never investigated in subsequent stories. The allegations were reported again in a subsequent article which focused on a friend's disclosure of Virk's sexual abuse by a family member, but were not contextualized in reference to existing statistics on child sexual abuse and the links between violence in the home and running away from home (Kinnon and Hanvey).[5] Aside from these subdominant motifs, the framework of the story remained that of the escalating girl-on-girl violence.

Not only was Virk's racialized identity erased, but there was a significant lack of attention paid to even the *possibility* that her death was racially motivated. Almost two years later, at the trial of one of her alleged murderers, Warren Glowatski, the issue of racism was brought up by one witness—Syreeta Hartley, his girlfriend (Hall 1999a). However, aside from the brief reporting of her testimony in the daily coverage of the trial, the issue itself was neither investigated by the media nor considered to be of importance by Justice Macaulay in his decision (*R. v Warren Paul Glowatski*, 1999). This absence occurred despite the hate crimes legislation available to the courts; existing documentation of the activity of hate groups in schools and colleges campuses (Prutzman; Sidel); existing studies which highlight the vulnerability of racialized girls to violence; or the racial connotations imbuing the acts of brutality to which Virk was subjected, as for example, the stubbing of a cigarette on her forehead—the place usually used to put a *bindi* which is a common practice among various South Asian cultures.

The significant absence of any discussion or investigation of racism as a motive reflects not only a minimization of the violence of racism, but also its sheer taken-for-granted character as a non-problematic and unrecognizable element. As Hall (1990) and Essed point out, everyday racism is ingrained in the daily interactions of people of colour with the dominant society—it structures common sense reality and is thereby naturalized in an insidious way. Part of its naturalization arises from its taken-for-granted nature and embeddedness. The media's denial of racism corresponds with hegemonic definitions of racism as an activity confined to extreme hate groups, rather than as a system and structure of domination inherent in the very fabric of society and its institutions. Thus, even though Syreeta Hartley's testimony was explicit in highlighting the racial motivations of the murder, its import was minimized both by the media and the judge. As one journalist stated, "Syreeta Hartley said her former boyfriend told her that his involvement was partly motivated by racism. Virk was Indo-Canadian" (Hall 1999a: A5). The media also reported that Glowatski did not know Reena Virk and had never spoken to her.

At no time did the local or national media dwell upon or investigate the fact that Warren Glowatski had first bragged about picking a fight with a Native man (Hall 1999b). The issue of why he would first select a Native man as the target for his aggression remained unexamined and yet suggests the vulnerability of marginalized groups and the hierarchy in which they are positioned. The reporting implies that it is much easier to beat a Native man and get away with it, than it is to beat up a white male. The value of difference is thus communicated by allusion and association.

The dominant framing of "Other" cultures as deviant is naturalized and taken for granted by the dominant media, and tends to be used strategically to underline the "unassimilable character" of immigrant communities (Jiwani 1992). However, in the case of Reena Virk, there was a significant absence of any kind of cultural framing. It could be argued that the dominant media have become more sensitized to issues of cultural representations. Alternatively, the media's reluctance to use a cultural frame may be derived from the possibility that some of the girls involved in the first fight were themselves of South Asian origin. This in itself does not negate the reality that many members of a racialized community internalize the normative values and behaviours of the dominant society and reject identifiers and people of their communities. In fact, the cultural frame would have allowed the media to continue a noted tradition—that of portraying racialized communities as being sites of conflict and disturbance created by their own members (Entman; Indra). It can be argued that in this particular instance, the construction of girl-on-girl violence became a dominant filter as it better served masculinist hegemonic interests within a contextual climate of backlash against women. For the media to have focused on culture at this point would, by necessity, have involved an examination of racism as predicated on Virk's exclusion from and marginalization by her peer group, as well as the defining characteristics which resulted in her "lack of fit." Organizing and translating information within this frame would thus have resulted in a confrontation with the reality of racism and its prevalence in Canadian society, as well as the vulnerability of racialized people to racially motivated violence.

As an elite institution, the media reproduces hegemonic values, and often does so by reporting on the decisions and perspectives of other elites (van Dijk 1993). In the case of Reena Virk, the accounts which were reported on a sustained basis—each story referenced the other thereby resulting in a cumulative stock of knowledge—tended to be based on the reports or announcements of other elites. These included academics, police, and judges. Alternative interpretations based on the views of advocates were significantly absent, the exception being those cases where individuals wrote opinion pieces which were subsequently published. Thus, the complete absence of any mention of racism in Judge Macaulay's sentencing decision was echoed in the news coverage and served to secure his view of the case as the dominant and preferred interpretation—that the murder was the result of violent intent, but an intent that was unconnected to racism, sexism, or a combination thereof.

Conclusion

From the above analysis, it can be seen that the Canadian print media continue to favour and forward interpretations of race and racism which resonate with elite definitions and which reinforce hegemonic interests. In the case of Reena Virk, the critical issues facing racialized girls were never examined by the media, nor was the issue of racism dealt with in any substantive manner.

Rather, as with issues concerning child abuse, racism was relegated to the background and overshadowed by stories regarding the increasing levels of girl-on-girl violence, and the inability of Reena Virk to "fit." Thus, the issue of racism was erased from the dominant discourse, and Reena Virk's identity as a racialized young woman, has been similarly erased in terms of its significance and contribution to her vulnerability and marginality. As a young woman of colour, she was visibly different, yet her difference was only understood in terms of her weight and height and her general "inability to fit." The issue of what she needed to "fit into" was never explored, nor were the assumptions underlying normative standards of beauty and behaviour for teenage girls interrogated. Yet these issues are central to highlighting the particular ways in which racism and sexism interact in shaping the lives of racialized girls, and in contributing to their marginalization and vulnerability to violence—both as girls and as racialized others. The erasure of race and racism in this story reinforced the accepted stock of knowledge that racism is confined to the acts of organized hate groups. Thus, the structured nature of racism as a system of domination which informs everyday life and constrains the life chances of racialized peoples remains outside the dominant discourse, relegated to the margins.

Originally published in CWS/cf's Fall 1999 issue, "Immigrant and Refugee Women" (Volume 19, Number 3): 178-184.

[1]This composite is derived from the accounts presented in various newspapers and magazines over a two year period (1997-1999).
2For a discussion of racism and sexism within the school system, see Bourne *et al*.
[3]This analysis of news coverage is based on articles on the story of Reena Virk which were published in *The Vancouver Sun* during November and December in 1997. In addition, an electronic search of all articles appearing in Canadian newspapers pertaining to the decision in the Warren Glowatski trial were also examined.
[4]In their examination of girls' critique of schooling, Bourne *et al*. note that the South Asian girls in their focus groups commented on how their appearance is exoticized suggesting that this is one of the ways in which they are considered acceptable.
[5]In their review of the literature on violence against women, Kinnon and Hanvey note that, "60 to 70 per cent of runaways and 98 per cent of child prostitutes have a history of child abuse" (7).

References

Alicea, Marixsa. "'A Chambered Nautilus,' The Contradictory Nature of Puerto Rican Women's Role in the Social Construction of a Transnational Community." *Gender and Society* 11 (5) (1997): 597-626.

Alliance of Five Research Centres on Violence. *Final Report on Phase I, Violence Prevention and the Girl Child.* 1998. Research funded by the Status of Women Canada. Available online: http://www.harbour.sfu.ca/freda/

Artz, Sibylle. *Sex, Power, and the Violent School Girl.* Toronto: Trifolium Books, 1998.

Bannerji, Himani. "Now You See Us/Now You Don't." *Video Guide* 8 (40) (1986): 5.

Bannerji, Himani. "Introducing Racism: Towards an Anti-Racist Feminism." *Resources for Feminist Research* 16 (1) (May 1987): 10-12.

Bannerji, Himani, ed. *Returning the Gaze: Essays on Racism, Feminism and Politics.* Toronto: Sister Vision Press, 1993.

Beatty, Jim and Kim Pemberton. "Teen Recanted Claims Of Abuse Says Church Elder." *The Vancouver Sun.* November 29, 1997. A3.

Bourne, Paula, Liza McCoy and Dorothy Smith. "Girls and Schooling: Their Own Critique." *Resources for Feminist Research* 26 (1/2) (Spring 1998): 55-68.

Burns, Mary Violet C., ed. *The Speaking Profits Us: Violence in the Lives of Women of Colour.* Seattle, WA: Centre for the Prevention of Sexual and Domestic Violence, 1986.

Cottle, Simon. "'Race,' Racialization and the Media: a Review and Update of Research." *Sage Race Relations Abstracts* 17:2 (1992): 3-57

Crenshaw, Kimberle Williams. "Mapping the Margins: Intersectionality, Identity Politics, and Violence Against Women of Color." *The Public Nature of Private Violence, The Discovery of Domestic Abuse.* Eds. Martha Fineman and Roxanne Mykitiuk. New York: Routledge, 1994. 93-118.

Drury, Beatrice. "Sikh Girls and the Maintenance of an Ethnic Culture." *New Community* 17 (3) (1991): 387-399.

Entman, Robert. "Modern Racism and the Images of Blacks in Local Television News." *Critical Studies in Mass Communication* 7 (1990): 332-345.

Essed, Philomena. *Everyday Racism. Reports from Women of Two Cultures.* Translated by Cynthia Jaffe. Claremont, CA: Hunter House, 1990.

Fitzgerald, Robin. "Assaults against Children and Youth in the Family, 1996." *Juristat* 17 (11) Ottawa: Canadian Centre for Justice Statistics, Statistics Canada, November 1997.

Friedman, Sara Ann with Courtney Cook. *Girls, A Presence at Beijing.* New York: NGO WGG (Working Groups on Girls), 1995.

Geertz, Clifford. "The Integrative Revolution: Primordial Sentiments and Civil Politics in New States." *Old Societies and New States.* Ed. Clifford Geertz. New York: Free Press, 1963. 105-57.

Hall, Neal. "Virk's Killing Motivated by Racism, Witness Says," *The Vancouver Sun* April 15, 1999a: A5.

Hall, Neal. "Accused Changed Bloody Clothes on the Night Virk Dies, Court Told." *The Vancouver Sun.* Tuesday April 20, 1999b: A6c.

Hall, Stuart. "The Whites of Their Eyes." *The Media Reader.* Eds. Manuel Alvarado and John O. Thompson. London: British Film Institute, 1990.

Hutnik, Nimmi. "Patterns of Ethnic Minority Identification and Modes of Adaptation." *Ethnic and Racial Studies* 9 (2) (April 1986): 150-167.

Indra, Doreen. "South Asian Stereotypes in the Vancouver Press." *Ethnic and Racial Studies* 2 (2) (1979):166-189.

Isaacs, Harold. *Idols of the Tribe, Group Identity and Political Change*. New York: Harper and Row, 1975.

Jabbra, Nancy. "Assimilation and Acculturation of Lebanese Extended Families in Nova Scotia." *Canadian Ethnic Studies* 15 (1) (1983): 54-72.

Jan Mohamed, Abdul R. "The Economy of Manichean Allegory: The Function of Racial Difference in Colonialist Literature." *Critical Inquiry* 12 (1) (1985): 59-87.

Jiwani, Yasmin. "To Be or Not to Be: South Asians as Victims and Oppressors in the *Vancouver Sun*." *Sanvad* 5 (45) (1992):13-15.

Jiwani, Yasmin. "By Omission and Commission: Race and Representation in Canadian Television News." Unpublished doctoral dissertation, School of Communications, Simon Fraser University, 1993.

Jiwani, Yasmin. "On the Outskirts of Empire: Race and Gender in Canadian Television News." *Painting the Maple: Essays on Race, Gender, and the Construction of Canada*. Eds. V. Strong-Boag, S. Grave, A. Eisenberg, and J. Anderson. Vancouver: University of British Columbia Press, 1998. 53-68.

Jiwani, Yasmin. *Violence Against Marginalized Girls: A Review of the Literature*. Vancouver: FREDA, 1998b.

Joe, Karen A. and Meda Chesney-Lind. "'Just Every Mother's Angel': An Analysis of Gender and Ethnic Variations in Youth Gang Membership." *Gender and Society* 9 (4) (August 1995): 408-431.

Keyes, Charles F. "The Dialectics of Ethnic Change." *Ethnic Change*. Ed. Charles F. Keyes. Seattle: University of Washington Press, 1981. 4-30.

Kim, Jin K. "Explaining Acculturation in a Communication Framework: An Empirical Test." *Communication Monographs* 47 (August 1980): 155-179.

Kinnon, Diane and Louise Hanvey. "Health Aspects of Violence Against Women." Available online: http://hwcweb.hwc.ca/canusa/papers/english/violent.htm.

Lyman, Stanford M. and William A. Douglass. "Ethnicity: Strategies of Collective and Individual Impression Management." *Social Research* 40 (1973): 344-365.

Macaulay, J. "Reasons for Judgment in *R v. Warren Paul Glowatski*." Supreme Court of British Columbia, Docket 95773. June 2, 1999.

Matthews, Julie Mariko. "A Vietnamese Flag and a Bowl of Australian Flowers: Recomposing Racism and Sexism." *Gender, Place and Culture* 4 (1) (March 1997): 5-18.

Meissner, Dirk. "Murdered Girl Was Turning Her Life Around, Mother Says" *The Vancouver Sun*. Monday April 19, 1999. B6C

Miller, Barbara D. "Precepts and Practices: Researching Identity Formation among Indian Hindu Adolescents in the United States." *New Directions for Child Development* 67 (1995): 71-85.

Onder, Zehra. "Muslim-Turkish Children in Germany: Socio-cultural Problems." *Migration World Magazine* 24 (5) (1996):18-24.

Prutzman, Priscilla. "Bias-Related Incidents, Hate Crimes, and Conflict Resolution." *Education and Urban Society.* 27 (1) (November 1994): 71-81.

Razack, Sherene H. *Looking White People in the Eye, Gender, Race, and Culture in Courtrooms and Classrooms.* Toronto: University of Toronto Press, 1998.

Rosenthal, Doreen, Nadia Ranieri, and Steven Klimidis. "Vietnamese Adolescents in Australia: Relationships between Perceptions of Self and Parental Values, Intergenerational Conflict, and Gender Dissatisfaction." *International Journal of Psychology* 31 (2) (April 1996): 81-91.

Russell, Susan with the Canadian Federation of University Women. *Take Action for Equality, Development and Peace: A Canadian Follow-up Guide to Beijing '95.* Eds. Linda Souter and Betty Bayless. Ottawa: CRIAW, Canadian Beijing Facilitating Committee, 1996.

Scanlon, Joseph. "The Sikhs of Vancouver." *Ethnicity and the Media.* Paris: Unesco, 1977.

Schramm, Heather. *Young Women Who Use Violence: Myths and Facts.* Calgary: Elizabeth Fry Society of Calgary, 1998.

Sidel, Ruth. "Battling Bias: College Students Speak Out." *Educational Record* 76 (2,3) (Spring-Summer 1995): 45-52.

Smitherman-Donaldson, Geneva and Teun van Dijk. *Discourse and Discrimination.* Detroit: Wayne State University Press, 1988.

Thobani, Sunera. "Culture isn't the cause of violence." *Vancouver Sun* September 26, 1992: A12.

Tipper, Jennifer. *The Canadian Girl Child: Determinants of the Health and Well-Being of Girls and Young Women.* Ottawa: Canadian Institute of Child Health, September 1997.

Turnbull, Sue. "The Media: Moral Lessons and Moral Careers." *Australian Journal of Education* 37 (2) (1993): 153-168.

Van Dijk, Teun A. *Communicating Racism, Ethnic Prejudice in Thought and Talk.* United States: Sage, 1987.

Van Dijk, Teun A. *Elite Discourse and Racism.* Sage series on Race and Ethnic Relations, Volume 6. California: Sage, 1993.

The Vancouver Sun May 8, 1999: A10

The Vancouver Sun Special issue on Teen Violence May 14, 1999

Vertinsky, Patricia, Indy Batth and Mita Naidu. "Racism in Motion: Sport, Physical Activity and the Indo-Canadian Female." *Avante* 2 (3) (1996): 1-23.

Does A Lesbian Need a Vagina Like a Fish Needs a Bicycle?

Or, Would the "Real" Lesbian Please Stand Up!

Amber Dean

About five years ago I stumbled upon a comic strip from Alison Bechdel's brilliant *Dykes to Watch Out For* series that (like so many of her comics) made me laugh out loud and then shake my head in wonderment at her ability to so compellingly bring forward the very debates I'd found myself having with friends only weeks or days or maybe even hours before. This particular strip, "I.D. fixé?" (Bechdel 58-59), starts out as a debate about who "qualifies" as a dyke, and by the end of the strip leaves the reader pondering the ongoing relevance of identity categories *period* in the present "post-"(insert favourite now-under-fire-brand-of-theorizing-or-category-of-identity here) world. I was particularly struck by main character Sparrow's insistence that sleeping with a man need not entail renouncement of her "dyke" status (she self-identifies as a "bi-dyke" in the strip), while her boyfriend Stuart asserts that he considers himself to be "a butch lesbian in a straight man's body." The comic also points out how trans-identified people have the subversive potential to put identity categories into a tailspin; but (still, and perhaps stubbornly) identifying as a dyke myself, I am more intrigued by the questions the strip raises about who "qualifies" as a lesbian these days and for what reasons (and hence it is these questions, rather than the equally important and challenging questions about the subversive potential of trans-identities, that became the focus of this paper).

Around the same time, I came across a personal ad in the notoriously gender-bending lesbian sex magazine, *On Our Backs*, in which the writer insisted that only "real lesbians" need reply: according to the author of this ad, a "real" lesbian is apparently a "professional Woman who's childless, financially secure, spiritual, intelligent and likes working out and reading" and is definitely not a "Bi." Hmm, I wondered, am I missing something here? When I came out, did somebody forget to send me some important guidelines that spell out exactly what qualifies one as a "real" lesbian? Or if I *am* a real lesbian, would I just *know* the guidelines without needing to be told? Does Bechdel's Sparrow—complete with long hair, make-up, flowing dresses, and boyfriend—qualify as a "real" lesbian? Not according to the author of the *On Our Backs* personal ad, I know, but what about to others? What about Stuart, the "butch lesbian in a straight man's body"—would he qualify as a lesbian in *anyone's* eyes but his own? And who gets to decide whether one "qualifies" as a lesbian or not, anyway? In this paper, I attempt to think through some of these questions.

To be visible

When I first started to explore my lesbianism in the mid-1990s, I had long spiraling hair and liked to wear full-length skirts or flowing dress pants with V-neck blouses or sweaters and, often, long dangly earrings. I applied perfume, make-up, and hair products daily as part of my beauty regimen. As I tried to break onto the lesbian scene, I sometimes wondered if my appearance was a barrier. Did my looks somehow disqualify me as a lesbian? Similarly, a subject in Julie Melia's essay on the lesbian "continuum of resistance" describes a long-haired friend of hers who worried she "wasn't a real dyke because of her hair" (551). This connection between *looking like* a lesbian and *being* a lesbian—between appearance and identity—seems to be a common theme. A subject from Anthony Freitas, Susan Kaiser and Tania Hammidi's study on visibility issues in queer communities tells us that "if you feel you are a part of the greater lesbian community, it is important to look like you identify with that community" (99). In their short film *What Does a Lesbian Look Like?* Winnipeg performance artists Shawna Dempsey and Lorri Millan poke fun at the controversy and uneasiness surrounding what it means to "look like a lesbian": "Is she butchy, ball-busting, bad-assed with facial hair?" they ask. "Or does she strut her stuff, show some thigh, and leave a trail of kisses with her lipstick?" The question of what a lesbian looks like has been hotly contested, and has at times been used as a standard for judging who qualifies as a "real" lesbian and who does not. How much does being visibly identifiable as a lesbian relate to the question of who "qualifies" as a lesbian?

A week after my first sexual experience with a woman, I bought my first pair of cargo pants and played seriously with the idea of cutting my hair short and maybe getting a nose ring. My last lesbian lover, who was in a relationship with a man prior to me, cut her long hair drastically short within the first two weeks of our relationship. We had a running joke about who looked "dykey-er." Not long after that relationship ended, I decided it was time to (once again) go back to short hair in an effort to look more "like a lesbian." Of course, my idea of what a lesbian "looks like" is largely shaped by my own race and class backgrounds: being white, from a middle-class background, and coming to my lesbianism largely through my engagement with feminism in an academic environment, I can't help but suspect that my notion of lesbian appearance is shaped by the lingering influence of 1970s lesbian feminism. My ability to conform to this narrow notion of what a lesbian "looks like," then, is unquestionably influenced by my race and class privilege.

The subjects in Melia's study point out that there is a tendency to dramatically alter one's appearance shortly after starting to self-identify as a lesbian (550, 554). Thus I remain convinced that appearance is still intimately connected to my own and many other lesbians' sense of our identities *as* lesbians. For me, looking like what I think a lesbian is supposed to look like or occasionally adorning myself with lesbian signifiers (my current favourite is a button that reads "I got this way from kissing girls") holds several different meanings. I believe it is a way for me to be recognized by other dykes, which I secretly hope ensures my place among lesbians and communicates my sexual availability to other women (which relates to why "looking like a lesbian" seems more important at times when I'm not already in a relationship). As Freitas *et al.* indicate, "visibility is often coded for 'perceivers who matter'" (97). Visibility, then, is perhaps related as much to desire as it is to identity: being visible as a lesbian allows me to communicate my desire to others, just as being able to visibly identify other women as lesbian facilitates my desire for those women. My appearance is also a way for me to communicate to the rest of the world that I am different and proud of my difference. When I first came out I was eager to signal my resistance to hetero-normativity and my willingness to take on whatever challenges I might have to face as a result of my difference, even if this meant harassment or personal attacks.

Although some postmodernist theorizing has encouraged a shift from thinking in terms of visible/invisible bodies to terms of marked/unmarked ones, Lisa M. Walker chooses to continue to use the former, despite the "lack of clarity" she perceives in these terms (868, footnote). As she points out, the term "unmarked" is used to describe the normative body in theory, but "invisible" refers to those bodies that are *not* normative, and so the two sets of terms fail to "map directly onto each other" (868). She argues that a focus on visibility among several so-called minority groups has become a "tactic of late twentieth-century identity politics" (868). Melia points to how queer activists have privileged appearance and style as "a key part of resistance" (548), and the prevalence of the popular slogan VISIBILITY = LIFE on the t-shirts of some gay and lesbian activists has also been noted (Freitas *et al.* 84). Clearly, visibility—looking "like a lesbian"—has historically been and remains an important aspect of many lesbians' identities, and hence gets tied to debates about who qualifies as a "real" lesbian.

So what *does* a lesbian look like? Although many have suggested that at various points in history there is an identifiable (normative) lesbian appearance, or very specific standards of dress and style, what a lesbian *actually* looks like depends a great deal (of course) on the historical period, on her personal preferences, and/or on her desire to conform to these standards (Melia; Freitas *et al.*; Myers, Taub, Morris and Rothblum). It also depends a lot on her race or ethnicity, class, ability, and age. As soon as a categorical "lesbian uniform" is posited it becomes important to think about who is being excluded through this categorization of lesbian appearance. There are numerous testimonies, for example, of the unhappiness suffered by women who identified as femmes but abandoned this style (and, for a time, a femme identity) in order to continue to "qualify" as a lesbian during the heyday of the lesbian-feminist 1970s (see Millersdaughter; Faderman).

Similarly, many lesbians write about how being of colour or being from a working class background has resulted in their exclusion from gay and lesbian communities that privilege whiteness and middle or upper-class visibility (Allison; Feinberg; Khan; Law). These exclusions have caused some lesbians to struggle with their allegiance to lesbian communities, wondering whether they would have to forgo their racial or class allegiances in order to be "visible" as lesbians. Surina Khan articulates this struggle when she writes: "when I came out I identified only as a lesbian. It didn't occur to me to identify as a Pakistani lesbian" (130). Only after many years of struggling with her various identities and the intersecting impacts of racism and homophobia—often experienced *within* her queer and Pakistani communities—was Khan able to come out as and embrace a Pakistani lesbian identity. And relatedly, because predominant notions of what a lesbian "looks like" tend to privilege youthfulness, many older lesbians may struggle with perceived demands to maintain an appearance-identity connection.

The dominant construction of what a lesbian "looks like" was developed, according to Deke Law, "by white women in response to sexism in the U.S. Left and in the gay men's movement, with an apparently rigid definition for membership" (144). Law insists we must critique this construct because, whether it is expressed "through clothes, politics, or space, there is an implicit understanding that all lesbians are alike in fundamental ways" (144). This assumption has frequently resulted in the exclusion of femmes, trans-identified people, lesbians of colour, working class, disabled, and older lesbians from the category of "lesbian," which has seriously undermined the revolutionary potential of lesbian politics.

For most lesbians in the 1950s, appearance was central to both identity and community. As described so poignantly by Leslie Feinberg in hir autobiographical novel *Stone Butch Blues*, in the 1950s there were butches and femmes, and femmes partnered with butches, period. Feinberg writes about primarily working-class lesbians, and in hir novel any lesbian who strayed outside of the butch-femme formation in the 1950s and early 1960s was ostracized and failed to qualify as a "real" lesbian. At this time butch-femme was a way of life for many lesbians, but a butch or a femme was defined as much by appearance as by behavior, sexual preference, or preferred roles in sex acts (Myers *et al.*).

With the rise of second wave feminism in the late 1960s and throughout the 1970s, butch and femme came under fire. A new breed of feminist lesbians, mostly middle-class, mostly academic, and mostly white, decried the "old ways" of butch-femme (Faderman). They believed the butch-femme configurations of most lesbian relationships up to that time were merely an attempt to mirror heterosexual relationships, right down to "appearing" like a "man" or a "woman." Claiming that she wanted to break with the trappings of patriarchy entirely, the new lesbian feminist did her best to achieve an appearance that was completely androgynous, similar to the style previously known as butch (Faderman). The pressure to conform to this regulation of appearance was enormous for those who still wanted to count as "real" lesbians and wanted a place in the lesbian feminist community. The 1970s "lesbian uniform" most prevalently accepted and adhered to was created to signal this desire for androgyny: "Flannel shirts, blue jeans, work boots, no jewelry or makeup, and short hair became *de rigeur*" (Myers *et al.* 21). Indeed, as recently as 1997, some women interviewed by Anna Myers, Jennifer Taub, Jessica Morris and Esther Rothblum indicated that their extremely butch or extremely femme appearances still drew hostility from other lesbians. Clearly, such a "uniform" posed significant visibility barriers for any lesbian wanting to represent other aspects of her identity.

In the 1980s and 1990s, of course, butch-femme made a comeback. It was once again becoming acceptable among most lesbians to claim a butch or femme identity, and to construct one's appearance accordingly. Lesbians who had suppressed their femme-ness and conformed to the androgynous dress code of the 1970s now re-embraced their "femmes within" and reclaimed dresses and makeup. The term "lipstick lesbian" was no longer necessarily a pejorative (Clark 488). Similarly, challenges to the centrality of white, middle-class women's experiences in feminist and lesbian communities made by women of colour, working-class women, women with disabilities, and more recently by older women, helped to increase awareness about racism, classism, ableism, and ageism within these communities (although there is still much work to do). This made it easier for lesbians to dress in ways that also represent other aspects of our identities without (perhaps) the same level of hostility about our claims to lesbianism. The qualifications for a "real" lesbian shifted from rigid concepts of what a lesbian "looks like" to the more straighforward qualifier of one woman's attraction to or desire for another woman. Indeed, Jacquelyn Zita tells us that "lesbians are customarily defined by a preference for sexual encounters generally involving four breasts, two vaginas, and two clitorises, among other things" (112).

But while some have (re)claimed butch or femme styles and challenged rigid "lesbian uniforms," there still exists some consensus among the lesbians participating in at least one study about what constitutes "conventional dyke style—jeans, T-shirt, boots" (Melia 550) with short hair and no makeup. While I am hesitant to suggest that this "conventional dyke style" has anything to do with who qualifies as a "real" lesbian, I am also struck by the fact that I (one who knows better) still make an effort to conform to this style when I really want to "look like a lesbian," even though I know that not all—not *nearly* all—lesbians conform to these conventions.

Debates about what a lesbian "looks like" in the twenty-first century have been rekindled by the increasing appearance of lesbians in popular culture. The TV drama *The L-Word*, the first ongoing program to focus almost exclusively on lesbian life, has kicked off heated debates about whether the show's characters look enough like lesbians. I confess that until recently I refused to watch the program out of disdain for the so-called representation of lesbianism apparent in the show's advertisements: a group of thin, long-haired, extremely well-coifed, predominantly white women in expensive tailored suites and high heels is a far cry from what I would consider to be a grand achievement of lesbian visibility (which tells you something about *my* assumptions). But some dyke friends have told me that they really like the show and find it does a good job of representing lesbian life, so I decided to rent the first season to see if my assumptions would be challenged.

In the first couple of episodes of *The L-Word*, I was genuinely surprised at the derision directed towards the show's only almost-butch character, Shane, who is informed that everything about the way she dresses "screams dyke" and is therefore embarrassing to some of the other characters. Shane, despite making some gestures towards butch style, still has long hair, is painfully thin, and frequently wears make-up and low-cut, femme-like outfits, yet in one episode she is (unconvincingly) mistaken for a gay man. As Karen X. Tulchinsky notes in her primarily positive review of the show in the feminist magazine *Herizons*, *The L-Word* "has been criticized … for not representing 'real lesbians'" (17) since most of the main characters are thin, femme, wealthy women who live in fancy homes and drive sporty cars. Rather than protesting whether a femme woman "qualifies" as a lesbian, though, I believe critics of *The L-Word* (including myself) are primarily concerned with the lack of diversity among the characters: in other words, it's not the presence of femme lesbians so much as the predominance of femme style (and a very narrow representation of femme at that) at the expense of all other visible signifiers of lesbianism that is at issue.

In Canada, the feminist press has (surprisingly) been kinder to the show than the queer press: in queer bi-weekly *Xtra! West*, columnist Ivan E. Coyote points out that some of the show's advertising is specifically directed towards straight men, using the show's graphic lesbian sex to encourage a straight male audience to tune in to the show "right after the Trailer Park Boys." Coyote, a high-profile Vancouver butch lesbian, was hired to teach the program's actors about how to look and act like more "authentic" lesbians, but was disappointed to note the significant absence of crew-cuts, boots, belts, or butches among the actresses. Not to mention the entire exclusion of working-class lesbians, which Coyote argues is a gross misrepresentation of the fact that most lesbians don't have the luxury of driving fancy cars, for example, since women still bring home so much less, on average, than men. Still, the debates that the show incites about what a lesbian looks like indicate that a connection between appearance and identity is still highly relevant to many lesbians today.

Elizabeth Wilson (1990) argues that changes in style among lesbians are partly a reflection of changing styles for women as a whole. The butch-femme styles of the 1950s, she suggests, may have come about because it was becoming more and more difficult for lesbians to achieve a look that marked their difference from straight women, as mainstream fashion styles themselves became more relaxed. Pointing to how changes in mainstream fashions for women have made it more difficult to visually separate lesbians from straight women, Wilson laments "it's so hard to look deviant these days" (73). Indeed, short hair, no makeup, or clothing that would more traditionally be considered "mannish" can no longer automatically be assumed to be signs that are indicative of a lesbian, as "many of the signifiers of lesbian identity have become trendy in the avant-garde heterosexual community" (Inness 174). While some lesbians feel proud to see styles that we feel some ownership of adopted by a more mainstream audience, we are also faced with an identity challenge. After all, if there is no longer any sure way to "look like a lesbian," how will we know who the lesbians *are*?

Visibility problems

Despite the importance of appearance to an individual and communal sense of identity for many lesbians, several writers have raised some serious problems stemming from a connection between appearance and identity (Melia; Freitas *et al.*; Walker). Walker, for example, argues that privileging visibility as central to a lesbian identity causes an erasure of those lesbians whose appearance might not conform to the generally accepted standards of what a lesbian "looks like." Such an erasure or dismissal causes some lesbians to struggle precisely with this question of whether we qualify as "real" lesbians or not, putting our sense of identity in crisis and sometimes resulting in our ostracism from lesbian communities. Walker argues that these problems tend to be most profound in relationship to lesbians who—like Sparrow in the comic strip—can "pass" for straight: "Because subjects who can "pass" exceed the categories of visibility that establish identity, they tend to be regarded as peripheral to the understanding of marginalization" (868). Shuffling those who can "pass" to the sidelines of lesbian communities results in a further marginalization of such women within our already-marginalized communities and constitutes a use of oppressive tactics for the purposes of "lesbian" boundary maintenance.

Although those in queer communities who hold tightly to the *visibility = life* philosophy view passing for straight as perhaps the greatest threat to gay or lesbian identities, women who pass as straight may do so for a variety of reasons. A lesbian who shapes or adorns her body in a way that does not make her easily identifiable as such often causes others (both lesbian and straight) to react with "uneasiness, anger, or even terror" (Inness 161). Yet Melia points out the many dangers some lesbians still face if we choose to always overtly assert our lesbianism, ranging from loss of employment to harassment or assault. She argues that a "continuum of resistance" (556) should be used to expand our understanding of how passing can sometimes be a subversive strategy for lesbians. Sherrie A. Inness insists that passing at some point is inevitable for all lesbians, and argues that the roll of the onlooker is essential in determining whether a lesbian will "pass" in a given situation - in other words, whether a lesbian will "pass" in a given situation may have little to do with whether she *herself* desires to pass.

Historically, the backlash from within lesbian communities against the lesbian whose style preference is more traditionally feminine has been rooted in femme women's abilities to more easily pass as heterosexual. For some lesbians, the fact that a femme (or a bi-dyke, for that matter) can pass more readily as straight is considered a sign that femmes and bi-dykes are less committed to lesbianism or less willing to risk being identified as a lesbian, possibly out of a fear of the various ways in which lesbians are oppressed. An outright decision to pass as straight in some areas of her life may have drastic consequences for a lesbian—as a subject from Melia's research explains, "you lose friendship and community" (551). However, a closer theoretical examination indicates that femme lesbians, bi-dykes, or lesbians who, consciously or not, pass as straight in some areas of our lives, may pose a deeper threat to heteronormativity than a first glance allows. After all, there is a desire not only among some lesbians but also among many people who identify as straight to be able to visually identify a lesbian in order to ensure her exclusion from the realm of "normal," or, in the Butlerian sense, from the realm of "bodies that matter." Disruptions of what a lesbian "looks like" have the potential to confound those people who would like to continue to define the lesbian body as deviant. As Inness (1997) so astutely points out,

> the lesbian who passes as heterosexual calls into question the distinction between heterosexual and homosexual. Ultimately, she threatens to overthrow the whole heterosexual order because heterosexuality can only exist in opposition to homosexuality. (161).

So the lesbian who some would argue fails to "qualify" as a lesbian because she differs in appearance from what is *expected* of a lesbian actually has as much, if not more, potential to disrupt heteronormativity than the lesbian who looks like what she is: for some, a good argument to suggest that women like Bechdel's bi-dyke Sparrow have just as much entitlement to the signifier "lesbian" as women who have short hair, wear t-shirts, jeans and boots, swear off make-up, and have sex strictly with other women.

The lesbian "bodies that matter"

Judith Butler's theories on how certain bodies come to "matter" can be helpful in articulating how lesbians who sometimes pass as straight can present a significant challenge to heteronormativity. Although Walker has argued the limitations of Butler's earlier writings in defining the subversive potential embodied by lesbian femmes (884), in *Bodies that Matter* there are several passages that indicate Butler's belief in such a potential. For example, Butler insists that she does not wish to suggest the masculinized (or butch) lesbian and feminized fag are the "only two figures of abjection," or only two figures excluded from the category of bodies that come to matter in our society (103). Rather, she goes on to tell us that to take these two figures as the only "figures of abjection" causes us to lose sight of those figures that incorporate "precisely the kind of complex crossings of identification and desire which might exceed and contest the binary frame itself" (103). The femme "bi-dyke" would certainly be a figure for such "complex crossings."

But if there is no set definition of what a lesbian "looks like," then what sort of body "qualifies" as a lesbian body? In the 1970s, the acceptable construction of what a lesbian looked like involved, as I have discussed, appearing as androgynous as possible. Yet such restrictions on who qualifies as a lesbian are comparable to the oppressive tactics used to measure who qualifies as "human" (white heterosexual men), or as a "body that matters." The more relaxed standards for what a lesbian looks like in the late 1980s and 1990s are partly a response to a growing awareness of the fragmentation caused by the strict "lesbian policing" (Freitas *et al.* 99), or pressures from within lesbian communities to conform to normative standards for appearance. According to Butler, we have to adopt certain positions or categories (e.g. "Lesbian") while at the same time contesting or being open to contestation of the boundaries or limits of these categories, in order to develop a more "complex coalitional frame" (115). This frame would allow women to maintain different aspects of our identities (for example, our race and class backgrounds) without needing to privilege one at the expense of another. Such an understanding of how change occurs certainly encompasses the negotiations within lesbian communities over who qualifies as a "real" lesbian that have been taking place throughout the last few decades.

Still, Butler warns us to be aware of instances when "denaturalizing parodies," such as the parodies of masculinity and femininity encompassed by butch and femme, reiterate norms without questioning them (231). The subversive potential in both butch and femme, and indeed in lesbianism itself, lies in the challenge these identities pose to heteronormativity, or an understanding of heterosexuality as natural, normal, or the only sexual choice available. Butch and femme appearances can denaturalize gender, sex, and sex roles by showing how they are constructed rather than natural. But if at any point butch lesbians, femme lesbians, or lesbians in general create or "police" norms of our own, without at least being open to exceptions to or contestation of these norms, Butler warns that our radical or subversive potential will be diminished. To provide just one of many possible examples, in a particularly significant scene from Feinberg's *Stone Butch Blues*, Frankie, a butch, announces to the main character, Jess, that she's dating another butch. Frankie says "'you don't have to understand it, Jess. But you gotta accept it. If you can't, then just keep walking,'" and Jess tells us "that's exactly what I did. I couldn't deal with it, so I just walked away" (202). Jess denies that two butches in a relationship together can qualify as lesbians, and she adopts oppressive tactics for ensuring their exclusion from lesbian community, tactics that actually work to support heteronormativity rather than challenge it: as the late Audre Lorde continues to remind us, "the master's tools will never dismantle the master's house" (112).

But if there can be no boundaries to the category "lesbian," no directives for what a lesbian "looks like" (or who she necessarily sleeps with), is there *such a thing* as a lesbian? Or could *anyone* be a lesbian? Certainly some postmodernist theorizing might lead us to think so. As Cathy Griggers explains, "lesbians in the public culture of postmodernity are subjects-in-the-making whose body of signs and bodies as signs are up for reappropriation and revision" (123). In the past few years, the place of trans-identified people within lesbian communities has been a source of much debate. Zita makes note of the following signs surrounding what she calls the "precious little lesbian space there is in the world:" "Women only. Lesbians only. Women-born women only. Genetic female dykes only. No boys over the age of twelve" (122). Yet most lesbian communities have slowly started to accept that trans-identified people can and should "qualify" as lesbians if they desire to identify as such. But what about someone like Bechdel's Stuart, meaning an anatomically male human being with a penis, testes, male secondary sex characteristics and no plan to alter any of these, whose gender identity is also masculine and who would unquestion-ingly be interpreted by onlookers to be, without hesitation or doubt, a man? In Bechdel's comic strip, Stuart makes a claim to a lesbian identity. Could Stuart qualify as a "real" lesbian? Should he?

The male lesbian (?)

Can a man "qualify" as a lesbian? This is perhaps the most difficult identity question that a feminist-postmodernist-lesbian has to ponder. For some lesbians, of course, the question is also an absurd one, and may understandably seem highly irrelevant in the context of trying to survive, support a family, and deal with the day to day pressures of being an out lesbian in a homophobic culture.[1] But the male lesbian keeps popping up on our radar: five years ago there was Bechdel's Stuart, and today we're confronted with "Lisa," a "lesbian-identified-male" who becomes one of the main character's "lesbian lover" during the first season of The L-Word. Hence I remain persuaded of the importance of the figure of the male lesbian to lesbian and feminist theorizing and politics, and as such I will flesh out his theoretical and political signifi-cance in this section.

A belief in the constructed-ness of gender forms the basis of many feminist theories. A belief in the constructed-ness of sex follows close behind, and has been argued by Butler and adopted by many feminist and postmodernist theorists. If sex is a construct, then a deconstruction would certainly allow the possibility of a male lesbian, since the category "male," and, for that matter, the category "lesbian," no longer hold the same meaning. After all, Butler has insisted that it is "unclear to [her] that lesbians can be said to be 'of' the same sex" (65-66). But is the possibility of a man wanting to represent himself as a lesbian not antithetical to almost everything that lesbianism has stood for or tried to accomplish in the last few decades? Yet if the category of "lesbian" can stretch (as it mostly has and certainly must) to include those who fail to "look like" a lesbian (i.e. femme lesbians) or to always "act like" a lesbian (i.e. bi-dykes), or to those who resist narrow and essentialist meanings of the signifier "woman" (i.e. trans-identified people), what recourse (if any) do we have to argue that a man cannot "qualify" as a lesbian?

Opening the definition of "lesbian" to include women whose appearances stray from the androgynous "lesbian uniform" discussed before seems to be a far cry from opening the definition to include men. But at the same time there is certainly precedence, even within lesbian communities, for such an opening to occur. In the 1970s some lesbians tried to desexualize lesbianism, arguing that instead of being defined by her desire to have sex with other women, a lesbian was defined merely by her "woman-centered-ness" or her political commitment to other women.[2] Given such a definition of lesbianism, I certainly know a few men who could qualify. Indeed, Adrienne Rich's notion of the lesbian continuum, long hailed as the cornerstone of lesbian theorizing, contributed to a de-sexualizing of lesbianism in its attempt to marry feminist and lesbian thought. Monique Wittig has often been quoted for her infamous pronouncement that "lesbians are not women" (qtd. in Wiegman 16), leaving us to beg the question: "Can they be men?" And, in one of the only existing theoretical writings on male lesbians, Zita suggests that a male who is willing to relinquish the significance of his penis and also ask others to do so, or who is willing to engage in "sex acts, mutually interpreted as 'female' sex acts" (120), might have grounds to consider himself a lesbian and ask others to do so as well.

However, many (or most?) women who identify as lesbian might opposed the idea of men qualifying as "real" lesbians (well, for sure the woman who wrote the personal ad in *On Our Backs* would, anyhow). As Zita points out, "[t]he 'male lesbian' seems to be an oxymoron. Yet I have met more than a few. Other lesbians report similar encounters. Is there a problem here?" (107). How much weight does the opinion of other lesbians carry in the ability of a man to self-identify as lesbian? Well, Sherrie Inness argues that the roll of the onlooker is essential in determining whether a lesbian will "pass" in a given situation. Similarly, in critiquing Judith Butler's work, Susan Bordo (argues that "subversion of cultural assumptions is not something that happens in a text or to a text. It is an event that takes place (or doesn't) in the 'reading' of the text" (8). What is the likelihood that observers of the text of man-as-lesbian will read "Lesbian"? How would a man signify his lesbianism to an audience for which such a reading would basically be implausible? Even if he adorned himself in lavender labryses and double-woman symbols from head to toe, these signifiers don't tend to "signify" much for the general population anyway, and even when they do, for a reader who recognizes these signifiers but notes that they are attached to a male body, "*Oh, he's a lesbian!*" is not likely the first thought to come to mind.

Still, some men wanting to qualify as lesbians might find acceptance in a community of postmodernist-dykes willing to interpret the representation or "text" he is creating in the manner that he wants them to (think of Ginger's half-hearted acknowledgement of Stuart's lesbian potential when she grumbles that he could be "*Soft* butch. May-be" in the Bechdel comic, or of the main characters' apparently unquestioning acceptance of "Lisa" in *The L-Word*). Would such a man then qualify as a lesbian? Zita argues that even if such acceptance is found, the man who wishes to identify as lesbian is unable to control the readings of his (male) body undertaken by the outside world. "When these readings numerically outnumber the less frequent "lesbian" attributions in the charmed circle," she argues, "this external world definitively 'sexes' his body" (125). "Lisa," the lesbian-identified-male from *The L-Word*, passes as lesbian only with the support of the show's lesbian community: outside of that community he is clearly *not* read as lesbian, as his confused encounter with a straight male in episode ten makes clear. Zita points out that the outside world's reading of the subject's body as "male" also determines his access to certain types of privilege inaccessible to a subject read as "woman" or "lesbian," even if such readings occur against his will.

These readings point to the significant political consequences of the notion of the male lesbian: if he is so unlikely to be consistently identified as a lesbian, is he really making any sort of political statement through his act of claiming a lesbian identity? Is he really more politically allied with lesbians, when his male privilege remains intact? Yet we must consider that this is a slippery slope: femme lesbians, bi-dykes, lesbians of colour, working class lesbians, disabled lesbians, older lesbians, or trans-identified people may also be read most often as something other than "lesbian" or, sometimes, as other than "woman," yet to disqualify these individuals as lesbians, as outlined above, is not only highly problematic but is a practice that has been rejected by a significant proportion of lesbian communities today. Hence there seem to be potentially significant political consequences of both including and excluding men from the category "lesbian:" the consequences of excluding them risks reproducing the kind of lesbian policing that has also at times (and ongoingly) excluded large numbers of women on the basis of other forms of difference. Yet the consequences of including men in the category of "lesbian" in the present might result in an undermining of lesbian political organizing, since, as discussed, men are seldom likely to be read as "lesbian" outside of a potentially small, welcoming circle at the present moment in time.

So, can a man qualify as a lesbian—or should he? This is, at present, perhaps a question better left unanswered, although certainly an important one to ask. For a related question we would have to ponder would of course be whether the very category of "lesbian" is still relevant, important, essential, or meaningful. Consider the assertion of Sparrow, in Bechdel's comic strip, that perhaps now "identity is so much more complex and fluid than these rigid little categories of straight, gay, and bi can possibly reflect" (58-59). After providing a framework for understanding how some postmodernist theorizing has made it possible for a man to qualify as a lesbian, Zita concludes by providing us with tools for a continued exclusion of men from this category. While she agrees that readings that confer a sex to a given body, regardless of the wishes of the subject, may be "utterly constructed and arbitrary," she nevertheless reminds us that they are also "encumbering" (125).

Perhaps for the present, it might be more politically expedient for a man wishing to identify as a lesbian to instead focus his energy on deconstructing masculinity and the many restrictions that construct places on his behaviour and identity. Such a critique of masculinity might even undercut the need some men might feel to identify as lesbian, since the desire to claim a lesbian identity might stem in large part from a rejection of hegemonic constructions of masculinity ("Lisa" makes this point in the *The L-Word* when he insists that straight white men represent "everything that's wrong in the world"). However, it is equally important that we remain open to contestation of the boundaries of the category "lesbian," perhaps always with the vision of a time when it will be commonly or popularly accepted that there are more than two genders, more than two sexes, more than two sexualities—in short, what Zita describes as "a number of different ways to inhabit the body" (123). But until we have gone further in popularizing the notion that gender, sex, and sexuality are constructed, it might be more politically astute for a man who wants to qualify as a lesbian to identify himself instead as what Zita has coined a "lesbian-identified-non-lesbian-hating-male" (123).

While it may be necessary in the current political context to continue to raise questions and debate about men who wish to represent lesbianism, it is absolutely essential that we maintain a vision for a future in which such policing of the boundaries of lesbianism will become unnecessary or perhaps irrelevant. As Butler suggests, "it may be only by risking the *incoherence* of identity that connection is possible" (113, emphasis in original). Because we live in an imperfect world, it is at times politically necessary to create and maintain a working definition of "lesbian," while always remaining open to contestation of who "qualifies" as a lesbian. But perhaps in the "post-postmodern" period, the male lesbian will have his day.

Originally published in CWS/cf's Winter/Spring 2005 issue, "Lesbian, Bisexual, Queer, Transsexual/Transgender Sexualities" (Volume 24, Numbers 2/3): 93-101.

[1]Thanks to an anonymous reviewer for reminding me of this fact.
[2]Thanks to an anonymous reviewer who pointed out that there was also an effort among some lesbian feminists in the 1970s to define a "real lesbian" as a woman who had *never* had sex with a man. Clearly, these debates from the 1970s are still reverberating in our communities today.

References

Allison, Dorothy. *Two Or Three Things I Know for Sure.* New York: Dutton, 1995.

Bechdel, Alison. "I.D. Fixe?" *Post-Dykes To Watch Out For.* New York: Firebrand, 2000. 58-59.

Bordo, Susan. "Postmodern Subjects, Postmodern Bodies." *Feminist Studies,* 18 (1) (1992): 159-176.

Butler, Judith. *Bodies that Matter: On the Discursive Limits of "Sex."* New York: Routledge, 1993

Clark, Danae. "Commodity Lesbianism." *Out In Culture: Gay, Lesbian, and Queer Essays on Popular Culture*. Eds. Corey K. Creekmur and Alexander Doty. Durham: Duke University Press, 1995. 486-500.

Coyote, Ivan E. ("The B-Word: Parts 1 and 2." *Xtra! West*, Feb. 17 & Mar. 17, 2005. Online: http://www.xtra.ca. Date accessed: 05/04/05.

Faderman, Lillian. "The Return of Butch & Femme: A Phenomenon in Lesbian Sexuality of the 1980s and 1990s." *Gender in the 1990s*. 2nd Edition. Eds. E. D. Nelson and B. W. Robinson. Toronto, Nelson Canada, 1995. 40-57.

Freitas, Anthony, Susan Kaiser and Tania Hammidi. "Communities, Commodities, Cultural Space, and Style." *Journal of Homosexuality* 31 (1/2) (1996): 83-107.

Feinberg, Leslie. *Stone Butch Blues: A Novel*. New York: Firebrand Books, 1993.

Griggers, Cathy. "Lesbian Bodies in the Age of (Post)Mechanical Reproduction." *The Lesbian Postmodern*. Ed. Laura Doan. New York: Columbia University Press, 1994. 118-133.

Inness, Sherrie A. *The Lesbian Menace: Ideology, Identity, and the Representation of Lesbian Life*. Amherst: University of Massachusetts Press, 1997.

Khan, Surina. "Color Me White." *This Is What Lesbian Looks Like*. Ed. Kris Kleindienst. New York: Firebrand Books, 1999. 127-135.

The L-Word. Dir. Rose Troche. Los Angeles, CA: Showtime Networks Inc., 2004.

Law, Deke. (1999). "Evolution." *This Is What Lesbian Looks Like*. Ed. Kris Kleindienst. New York: Firebrand Books, 1999. 137-145.

Lorde, Audre. "The Master's Tools Will Never Dismantle the Master's House." *Sister Outsider: Essays and Speeches*. Freedom, CA: The Crossing Press, 1996. 110-113.

Melia, Julie. "An Honest Human Body: Sexuality and the Continuum of Resistance." *Women's Studies International Forum* 18 (5/6) (1995): 547-557.

Millersdaughter, Katherine. "A Coincidence of Lipstick and Self-Revelation." *Femme: Feminists, Lesbians and Bad Girls*. Eds. Laura Harris and Elizabeth Crocker. New York: Routledge, 1997. 119-130.

Myers, Anna, Jennifer Taub, Jessica Morris and Esther Rothblum. "Beauty Mandates and the Appearance Obsession: Are Lesbians Any Better Off?" *Looking Queer: Body Image and Identity in Lesbian, Bisexual, Gay, and Transgender Communities*. Ed. Dawn Atkins. New York: Haworth Press, 1998. 17-26.

Rich, Adrienne. "Compulsory Heterosexuality and Lesbian Existence." *Signs: Journal of Women in Culture and Society*, 5, (Summer 1980): 631-60.

Tulchinsky, Karen X. "Drama Queers." *Herizons: Women's News and Feminist Views* (Spring 2005): 16-18 & 45.

Walker, Lisa M. "How to Recognize a Lesbian: The Cultural Politics of Looking Like What You Are." *Signs* 18 (4) (1993): 866-890.

What Does A Lesbian Look Like? Dir. Shawna Dempsey and Lorri Millan. Finger in the Dyke Productions/Much Music: Winnipeg/Toronto, 1994.

Wiegman, Robyn. "Introduction: Mapping the Lesbian Postmodern." *The Lesbian Postmodern.* Ed. Laura Doan. New York: Columbia University Press, 1994. 1-22.

Wilson, Elizabeth. "Deviant Dress." *Feminist Review* 35 (Summer 1990): 66-73.

Zita, Jacquelyn N. "Male Lesbians and the Postmodernist Body." *Hypatia* 7 (4) (1992): 106-127.

Model Athletes

Advertising Images of Women in Sport in Canada, 1950-2006

Jennifer Ellison

Danica Patrick, 2005 Indy 500 Rookie of the Year, is the star of Secret Platinum anti-perspirant's 2006 ad campaign. "My Secret" reads one print ad, "deep down, I'm a girly girl." Patrick stands facing the camera, her hands on her hips, with one high-heeled and pedicured foot perched on her racing helmet. Clad in an evening gown with a tulle crinoline, Patrick's skirt is hiked slightly up to reveal one of her lean, muscular legs (*Chatelaine* 2006: 271). A television spot for the same campaign finds Patrick in a video game arcade clobbering a series of male opponents in a simulated racing game. "You ever think about being a race car driver?" she asks one young boy, who answers "no." "Good, you shouldn't" Patrick replies, calling in her next competitor. Patrick is all business in this ad, taunting and rejecting her young male opponents and laughing at their failure. In voice over she says "My secret for not breaking a sweat on and off the track? Secret Platinum" (www.secret.com). In this ad Patrick wears a plain black sleeveless shirt and her body is barely visible. What are we to make of these two seemingly different advertisements for the same product? The print advertisement celebrates Danica Patrick's unconventional femininity, her "strength with a soft touch." The television spot seems to embrace a different sort of non-conformity. Patrick's take-no-prisoners approach to her young male opponents is unexpected and funny behavior and plays against the viewers expectations of a woman in her early twenties. Is one of these ads more progressive than the other? Is Patrick less feminine in the television spot because she is not maternal? Does either of these ads take Patrick seriously as an athlete?

Images of female athletes have been used to sell a range of products to Canadian consumers throughout the twentieth century, from cigarettes to silverware, cars to hand lotion. This article will consider the Danica Patrick campaign in light of this longer history of images of women in sport. Representations of the model athlete have changed with the times, transforming as discourses of femininity, and female athleticism, have shifted. For most of the twentieth-century sport was identified with masculinity and male "self-actualization" (Felshin 182). As a consequence, "the history of women in sport" has been "a history of cultural resistance" (Hall 1996: 101). While it is important to acknowledge the contested nature of women's participation in sport, it does not necessarily follow that advertising representations of athletes are transgressive or anomalous. In advertisements sport becomes a signifier of feminine ideals of the day. Advertisements do this by simplifying more complex stories, like that of a female athlete, in such a way as to produce a new message. Through text and visual imagery these simplified messages make famous athletes more like the "every woman" to whom advertisers were making their appeal. Rather than seeing such advertising images as positive or negative, this paper will suggest that images of female athletes help us understand the historical context in which they appear. Advertising images of women, much like the athletes themselves, harness multiple social, political and cultural messages about sport for women in any given period; they show that femininity is a contested site rather than a fixed historical category.

Femininity and discourse

Femininity has tended to be seen as a factor limiting women's sporting participation by historians and sociologists of sport. In her 2004 history of women's sport in Canada M. Ann Hall argues that femininity, defined by the idea that women are biologically inferior, has restricted female sporting participation since at least the 1850s (1). Similarly, American sociologist of sport Jan Felshin coined the term "feminine apologetic" to suggest that female athletes are often compelled to dress and act in stereotypically feminine ways in order to "apologize" or compensate for their transgression of gender norms (204). Such definitions of femininity tend to imply that the real athlete is not feminine. Instead, it implies that sportswomen would be better athletes if they cast off the oppressive shackles of femininity and embraced their true selves. Rather than seeing femininity as something that scholars can separate out from the woman or the athlete, I want to consider athletes and advertisements as part of a broader discourse of femininity; one that is manifested in everyday objects and rituals such as magazines, work, clothing and food (Smith 41). Femininity is a culturally sanctioned ideal of womanhood, but it is neither determinate nor unitary. This means that femininity changes depending on the time and place, it is "intelligible only in the context of the complex of which" [it] "is part" (Smith 37-38). The contention of this paper is that such shifts in the discourse of femininity can be read through images of women. Bruno Latour's essay "Drawing Things Together," which argues that change can be understood by looking at "how a culture *sees* the *world*, and makes it visible" provides a methodological grounding for my discussion of the history of images of athletes in Canada (30).

Latour uses the term *inscriptions* to describe images, text, diagrams and the like that are used to synthesize and simplify ideas (23). Advertisements can be seen as inscriptions because they reduce information about products, a sales pitch, social messages and more to the visual. In this paper I use three qualities of Latour's inscriptions to discuss the ads. First, meaning can be created through the juxtaposition of opposing concepts, such as man and woman (Law and Whittaker 171). A second characteristic of inscriptions is optical consistency which exists when a method of visualization has a common visual vocabulary (Law and Whittaker 168). Lastly, simplification is used reduce the complexity of an inscription to a single message (Law and Whittaker 168). Such reductions can in turn be productive because they select and enhance particular qualities of an athlete for the purposes of selling. In my analysis, I will use juxtaposition, optical consistency and simplification to read the images and their text against the historical record. I have selected four ads depicting high-profile athletes at the height of their popularity. The first, a print ad from 1950, features figure skater Barbara Ann Scott selling *Timex* watches. The second from 1970 shows down-hill skier Nancy Greene modeling for *Jergens* skin lotion. Silken Laumann's 1993 television spot for *IBM* will be the third ad, and the fourth is Patrick's 2006 *Secret Platinum* campaign. These ads all appeared in Canadian magazines or on television; all but Patrick are Canadian athletes. This paper does not provide a comprehensive overview of all images of athletes in advertising, but rather provides an introduction to the history and complexity of representations of women in sport.

Model Athletes: Our most charming girls

The ideal woman of post-war Canada was thought by many to be embodied in the person of Barbara Ann Scott. Media stories about Scott, the 1948 European, World and Olympic women's figure skating champion, exhaust themselves in their descriptions of the athlete. A 1948 *Time* magazine description extends to a paragraph:

> Barbara Ann, with a peaches-and-cream complexion, saucer-size blue eyes and a rosebud mouth, is certainly pretty enough. Her light brown hair (golden now that she bleaches it) falls page-boy style on her shoulders. She weighs a trim, girlish 107 lbs., neither as full-bosomed as a Hollywood starlet nor as wide-hipped as most skaters. She looks, in fact, like a doll which is to be looked at but not touched. But Barbara Ann is no fragile mamet. She is the woman's figure skating champion of the world. ("Ice Queen" 35)

Don Morrow argues that Scott was famous as much for her good looks and charm as she was for her skating accomplishments. Morrow identifies a list of adjectives and phrases most commonly used to describe Barbara Ann in the media. Among them are "Ice Queen, Fairy Princess of Ottawa, Little Princess of the Ice, Canada's Valentine and Remarkably Beautiful Doll" (Morrow 41). Morrow goes so far as to suggest that Scott "gained far more acclaim than her achievements warranted" because her image was so well-suited to "traditional female stereotypes" (46). I am not as convinced as Morrow that such a straightforward reading of Scott's feminine appeal is possible. As the above quotation suggests, behind Scott's "saucer-size blue eyes" was a formidable competitor. Scott is "no fragile mamet" (meaning she is no weakling or baby), she is a champion.

A 1950s-era *Timex* advertisement makes a similarly positive association between Barbara Ann's achievements and her appeal as a woman. The *Timex* ad reads, "Like Men — Active Women Need a Rugged Watch says Barbara Ann Scott Olympic Skating Champion" (Milton 22). This advertisement features two photos of Barbara Ann. The larger shows Scott in her figure skates, jumping into the air and smiling at the camera. Next to it is a somewhat smaller photo of Scott washing dishes. Once again Scott's head is turned toward the camera and she smiles out at the viewer. It is unclear if the skater is wearing the *Timex Sportster* on the ice but it is clearly visible in

Barbara Ann Scott Doll © Canadian Museum of Civilization, cat. No.983.29.23, photo Harry Foster, image no. S89-1870.

the shot of Scott doing the dishes. The copy tells us "Barbara Ann Scott uses and depends upon the *Timex Sportster* … just as doctors, engineers, seamen, farmers—men in every walk of life…." She uses the watch "throughout her busy, active day—at home and on the ice…." Here Scott is represented as both an "Olympic Skating Champion" and a housewife type figure. This housewife image may explain the rather bizarre claim that the watch is "dustproof" in addition to being "waterproof and shock-resistant." Is this ad telling us that Barbara Ann Scott is "like men" or that she is just like the housewives to whom the message is directed?

The *Timex* advertisement relies on the juxtaposition of images and words in order to make its appeal to the reader. A number of possible readings of this ad are possible. How an image was read depended upon the person looking at it. The images might represent a 'before' and 'after' scenario. Scott is comfortable at home and on the ice! Or, the images might be read as prescriptive, indicating the kinds of roles appropriate to men and women of the era. Here, the active woman is a skater and a homemaker, while active men are "doctors, engineers, seamen, farmers…." Visually, the two images of Scott are consistent. In both images she is on display, looking out at the viewer, her hair is tidy, her skin is clear and her lips part in a wide smile. This optical consistency is not surprising given that figure skating lends itself to notions of femininity and would not be seen to be at odds with other feminine goals and attributes (Feder

206). However, this ad is not just drawing on Scott's femininity to sell the watch; it is also playing upon notions of equality. The text of the ad seems to be directing the reader toward a particular reading of femininity. Scott's roles, and the roles of women in general, are important. Women are "like men." Their days "at home" are "busy and active."

The *Timex* ad can further be read as a simplification of both Scott's identity and gender roles in the period. While the *Timex* ad visually represents Scott as a bride-housewife figure, such lucrative endorsements in fact allowed Scott to live independently and unmarried until later in life. She earned an estimated $100,000 a year in the early 1950s as the star of the *Hollywood Ice Revue*, as well as through sponsorship deals with Canada Dry and Eaton's, whose Barbara-Ann Scott doll was a bestseller (Hall 2006: 109). Scott was also a licensed pilot and an accomplished golfer (Scott 27). Simplifying Scott's story lends itself to advertising as a medium, but can also be understood as part of broader discourses on women's roles in the 1950s. In 1944, there were one-million Canadian women working in the public and private sectors, and an additional 40,000 working in the armed forces (Tupper 20). At the end of the war employment for returning servicemen took precedence and countless women were expected to return to their work in the home. As Mona Gleason has observed, this return to mothering and childrearing was associated with a post-war return to social order and normalcy (53). Thus, the *Timex* ad can further be understood as part of wider social concerns about the importance of child rearing and family in the post-war era.

The lady jock

Following her 1967 and 1968 World and Olympic Skiing titles, Nancy Greene's manager Doug Maxwell told *Chatelaine* that he was unsure she would be able to secure any endorsements because her "…image lacked glamour'" (MacDonald 54). Maxwell attributed Greene's eventual endorsement success to the athlete's ability to "win over" Canadians (MacDonald 54). Ads featuring Nancy Greene appeared in quite a different social and political climate for female athletes than those of Barbara Ann Scott. In Canada in the late 1960s and 1970s the women's liberation movement identified femininity as a form of socialization which limited women's potential. In turn, feminists were the subject of concern and ridicule in some parts of the Canadian media and were sometimes portrayed as radical, demanding and anti-male (Freeman 3; 135). It is within this climate that concern about the gender non-conformity of female athletes became an issue. As Helen Lenskyj has demonstrated, factors such as such as "tomboyism" and interest in "boys" games were seen as signs of "gender non-conformity and predictors of lesbianism in adult life" (97). No direct links between such anxieties about gender non-conformity and Nancy Greene's public image can be made. Nonetheless, images of Greene must be understood as part of these debates about athleticism and its impact on normalcy and femininity.

Why Mrs. Raine loves Jergens just as much as Nancy Greene does.

Mrs. Alan Raine is a housewife. She washes dishes and windows, hangs drapes. Goes shopping. Entertains friends.

Mrs. Raine loves Jergens Lotion because it keeps her hands soft and smooth. Her complexion fresh and natural-looking. And because "it's the best lotion ever for all-over skin care".

Nancy Greene, as you know, is a skier. She's used (and loved) Jergens Lotion for a long time now.

To protect her face from harsh winds, and sleet, and year-round weather extremes.

To keep her hands looking soft and nice.

To give her silky, smooth skin from head to toe.

And Nancy's not the only one. In fact, more women use Jergens than the next six lotions put together. Since Jergens makes a girl feel like a girl all over, shouldn't you be using it too?

Take it from Nancy Greene (now Mrs. Raine)—you'll love what Jergens Lotion does for you.

For beautiful skin. From Jergens.

Courtesy of Nancy Greene.
Reprinted with permission.

Lesbian athletes experienced tangible losses if they were publicly 'outed.' In 1981, professional tennis player Billie Jean King was outed in a lawsuit from a former same-sex partner (Choi 42). In the following three years alone, King lost an estimated 1.5 million dollars in sponsorship and advertising endorsements (Hargreaves 147).

A 1970 *Jergens* ad reads: "Why Mrs. Raine loves Jergens just as much as Nancy Greene does" (*Chatelaine* 1970: 8). The ad explains how both housewife Mrs. Raine and skier Nancy Greene love to use their *Jergens* brand hand lotion to keep their skin soft, revealing in the end that Nancy Greene *is* Mrs. Raine! Three images of Greene are featured in the ad. The first and smallest features Greene posing holding her skis over her shoulders. The second to largest features Greene in a sun suit, rubbing Jergens lotion into her skin. The third and largest shows Greene smiling at the camera. She is wearing a dress and arranging a bouquet of flowers. Language plays an important role in the juxtaposition of Nancy Greene the skier with Mrs. Raine the housewife. On the one side is Nancy Greene the athlete who experiences "harsh winds" and "weather-extremes" and on the other is Mrs. Raine and her "silky, smooth skin." Silky smooth skin is representative of good feminine behavior. The sensible Mrs. Raine has managed to alleviate the risk posed by Nancy Greene whose skin could have been damaged in harsh weather conditions. The text implies that Greene/Raine has triumphed for standing on the good side of this battle, the "soft, smooth" side. The "soft, smooth" side of Greene is her feminine side, a point of which the text reminds us when it says that "Jergens makes a girl feel like a girl all over...." The ordinariness of the girl/softness association is underscored by *Jergens* assumption that the reader understands what "makes a girl feel like a girl."

The language and visual imagery of the *Jergens* ad offer an optically consistent image of the skier. Unlike Scott who was portrayed actually performing her routine, Greene is shown only posing on the side of a ski hill. Downhill skiing does not lend itself to feminine display. In this way images of Greene become consistent with the image of Scott and with polished represen- tations of femininity in general. One way to read these images is to look at the placement of Greene's hands. Janice Winship argues hand placement acts as a visual cue of masculinity and femininity in advertising images. These cues can include the size of the hand, the product it is handling and painted fingernails. Another characteristic of hand placement in advertisements is the tendency for women to touch or caress a product, rather than to grip it or use the product itself (Winship 30). In the *Jergens* ad Greene jauntily props her skis on her shoulder, one hand resting on top. In the second image she rubs lotion on her neck and in the third she is holding on to a flower. In this last image Greene's engagement ring and wedding band are quite visible, which, along with the text of the ad, confirm her heterosexuality. Greene's athletic prowess here acts as a background to the more important story of the power of Jergens lotion to transform her into Mrs. Raine. Greene's manager seems to have been wrong in thinking that her image lacked glamour. Instead, her image leant itself quite well to representations of white, middle class and heterosexual women of the early 1970s.

What else can she do? Or, just do it!

The Greene and Scott ads are quite similar in that each is preoccupied with other potential roles for the athlete. More specifically, each draws on the trope of the housewife to show that athletes are just like other women. The visual language of these ads is also consistent. Both Scott and Greene are shown in forward facing poses, they smile out at the viewer and perform non-sports related tasks. They further share in common the tendency to simplify some broader anxieties about gender and sport in the era by suggesting that sport is acceptable, perhaps because neither woman otherwise departs from accepted notions of femininity. I would argue the Greene ad departs somewhat from the Scott ad in that the language and visual cues in the advertisement are less mixed. In Scott's case, sport is seen as compatible with a housewife role. In Greene's case, femininity is at risk. Diligence is required of women who spend a lot of time outdoors. They must maintain and preserve their skin through the regular use of *Jergens* lotion.

A 1993 television ad featuring Silken Laumann shares with the Green and Scott ads an investment in the question "what else can she do?" However, it departs from the earlier images in that it is less concerned with heterosexuality and women's role in the home. The television ad opens with Laumann and "Bill Meyer" standing side by side. Laumann is holding oars and Meyer is standing beside a computer. The voice over says "we've asked these experts to tell us which is easier: getting into a boat or using the IBM PS/1 personal computer…we'll also ask them to trade places." Laumann and Meyer switch, Laumann sits down at the computer hesitantly and says "…I don't know if I can

Courtesy of Silken Laumann. Reprinted with permission.

do this very well..." while Meyer smiles and gives a thumbs-up to the camera. A black screen appears with the words "five minutes later." The next image features Meyer falling in the water, struggling to sit in the boat, while Laumann is clicking away at the computer, looking up information on boating. A number of possible readings of this ad are possible. It might suggest that using the PC is easy, much easier than rowing. Another interpretation is that rowing is hard, but Laumann is adept at both. Women's duplicity in propping up masculine and feminine norms is also implied in this ad, since Laumann is obviously humoring the less competent Meyer.

Much like the Danica Patrick ad described at the beginning of this article, the humor in the *IBM* ad relies on differences in gender and competence between Laumann and her opponent. Like the Barbara Ann Scott ad from the 1950s, the juxtaposition of gender roles is part of the language of the advertisements. The ad presumes the viewers knowledge of these gender differences. A key difference is that Laumann's ad takes a "battle of the sexes" approach. It acknowledges Laumann's competence as an athlete. It thus departs from the Greene and Scott ads in asking Laumann to prove her competence at a stereotypically male activity, computers, rather than a stereotypically female activity, housework. Cheryl Cole and Amy Hribar argue that in order to understand the changing 'look' of advertisements from the 1990s and beyond it is necessary to look at the feminist critique of images of women from earlier decades. This critique "highlighted a system of represen-tation that produced damaging illusions and psychological harm and...undermined self esteem" (Cole and Hribar 350). Cole and Hribar discuss advertisers who, in apparent response to this critique, sought to affirm and empower women. The Laumann and Patrick television ads suggest that this reading of advertisements after the 1990s is appropriate. Their tongue-in-cheek approach suggests some awareness of, or irony in, shifting gender roles.

In addition to changes in the way sexes are juxtaposed, the Silken Laumann and Danica Patrick advertisements are not optically consistent with the earlier images of Greene and Scott. Part of the reason for this is that they are television campaigns and the visual language of this format is different. But beyond the change in format, the bodies of the athletes themselves have changed. Laumann is portrayed in her unitard-style rowing uniform; she has broad shoulders and muscular arms. Laumann herself has acknowledged ambiguities about the beauty of her athletic body. In 1993 she told an interviewer, "when I started becoming muscular as a rower, I really had a problem with it. In the beginning, I thought, 'oh this is ugly'" (Moore 18). Talking about her perception of herself as an adult, Laumann told another interviewer, "I love being strong ... it's a feeling of power, the feeling of being strong and looking strong is so great" (Oliver 48). Patrick's body is also notably muscular in both of her *Secret* advertisements. These images suggest that notions of acceptably feminine bodies have shifted in the last 20 years. As both Susan Bordo and Priscilla Choi have suggested, the 1980s witnessed a shift in body ideals. Active femininity, represented through a fit, toned body has become a new feminine ideal (Choi 64; Bordo 95). While not all models have been as muscled as Patrick or Laumann, shifting ideals about the appropriate size, shape and muscle tone of women's bodies make representations of these athletes acceptable. Patrick and Laumann's ads, just like those featuring Greene and Scott, are emblems of shifting discourses of femininity in the period in which they appeared.

Conclusion

The use of a female athlete as a spokes model is an endorsement of her success at sport. This endorsement of individuals such as Scott, Greene, Laumann and Patrick belies the struggles of female athletes as a group for recognition, funding and media coverage in the post-war era. Representations of individual athletes in advertisements do not necessarily work to challenge the existing sports system, to legitimize women's sport or even women's role in the public sphere. Advertisements are a part of a broader set of social, political and cultural discourses on femininity and athleticism. As such, they do not in themselves have the power to make or break feminine norms. Deconstructing the ads is nonetheless useful in thinking about the taken for granted assumptions about gender of each of the periods under investigation. What was, or is, masculine and feminine is not explicitly stated but implied in the juxtaposition of words and images; in what is said and not said about sport in the ads and more subtle cues of dress and demeanor. Images of female athletes also help us to understand sport as a social and political system. The fact that gender relations are so essential to the visual and linguistic construction of the female athlete shows us that sport has been understood as a gendered system in the decades under review.

It is also important to remember that each of the women in the advertisements chose to be there. This does not mean that each athlete had control over her representation in the ad, but it also does not mean that she was feminized against her will. Historical actors wear many sets of discursive and ideological clothes. Behaving in a way that is acceptably feminine may or may not require conscious choice or effort for the athletes featured in the advertisements. Further questions must be asked in order to develop our understanding of the relationship between women and representations of women in popular culture. It is also necessary to continue to investigate absences and gaps in popular cultural representations: what is simplified and left unsaid in advertisements? Aside from important moments in women's history of the post-war era, these advertisements are silent on questions of class, ability and ethnicity. Idealized images of women have tended to be seen as problematic because of their emphasis on femininity and passivity, but such idealizations are more distant for some women than others. For example, my longer study of images of athletes in Canadian magazines yielded only one image of a woman of colour, Charmaine Crooks (Ellison 130). In this sense, the advertisements under review both do and do not represent a change in worldview. They reveal that femininity was and is a historically shifting and contingent category. However, they also suggest that these shifts occurred within a popular culture that was represented and directed toward a limited group of people.

An earlier version of this article was published in CWS/cf's Winter 2002 issue "Women and Sport" under the title, "Women and Sport: An Examination of Advertisements Between 1950 and 2002" (Volume 21, Number 3): 77-82.

References

Bordo, S. "Reading the Slender Body." *Body/Politics: Women and the Discourses of Science*. Eds. E. F. Keller and S. Shuttleworth. New York: Routledge, 1990. 83-112.

Chatelaine. January 1970: 8.

Chatelaine. May 2006: 271.

Choi, P. Y. L. *Femininity and the Physically Active Woman*. Philadelphia: Routledge, 2000.

Cole, C. L. and A. Hribar. "Celebrity Feminism: Nike Style, Post-Fordism, Transcendence and Consumer Power." *Sociology of Sport Journal* 12 (4) (1995): 347-369.

Ellison, Jennifer. *Our Most Charming Girls: Female Athletes in Canadian Advertisements, 1975-2002*. Ottawa: M.A. Thesis, Carleton University School of Canadian Studies, 2002.

Feder, A. "A Radiant Smile from the Lovely Lady." *Women on Ice*. Ed. C. Baughman. New York: Routledge, 1995. 206-233.

Felshin, J. "The Dialectic of Women and Sport." *The American Woman in Sport*. Eds. J. Felshin, E. Gerber, P. Berlin and W. Wyrick. Reading, MA: Addison-Wesley Publishing Company, 1994. 179-210.

Freeman, B. *The Satellite Sex: The Media and Women's Issues in English Canada, 1966 to 1971*. Waterloo: Wilfred Laurier University Press, 2001.

Gleason, M. *Normalizing the Ideal: Psychology, Schooling, and the Family in Postwar Canada*. Toronto: University of Toronto Press, 1999.

Hall, M. A. "Creators of the Lost and Perfect Game." *Sport and Gender in Canada*. Ed. P. White. Don Mills: Oxford University Press, 1996. 5-23.

Hall, M. A. *The Girl and the Game: A History of Women's Sport in Canada*. Peterborough: Broadview Press, 2004.

Hargreaves, J. *Heroines of Sport*. New York: Routledge, 2000.

"Ice Queen." *Time* February 2, 1948: 35, 50-54.

Latour, B. "Drawing Things Together." *Representation in Scientific Practice*. Eds. M. Lynch and S. Woolgar. Cambridge, MA: The MIT Press, 1988. 19-88.

Law, J. and J. Whittaker. "On the Art of Representation." *Picturing Power*. Eds. G. Fife and J. Law. London: Routledge, 1988. 160-182.

Lenskyj, H. *Out of Bounds: Women, Sport and Sexuality*. Toronto: The Women's Press, 1986.

MacDonald, D. "Nancy Greene: From Olympic Star to Happy Housewife." *Chatelaine* January 1970: 22, 51-54.

Milton, S. and B. McCutcheon. *Skate: 100 Years of Figure Skating*. Toronto: Key Porter Books, 1996.

Moore, M. "Smooth as Silken." *The Toronto Sun* February 7, 1993: 18.

Morrow, D. "Sweetheart Sport: Barbara Ann Scott and the Post World War II Image of the Female Athlete in Canada." *Canadian Journal of History of Sport* 28 (1) (1987): 36-54.

Oliver, B. "Silken Steel." *The Toronto Sun* July 13, 1991: 48.

Scott, B. A. *Skate with Me*. Garden City, NY: Doubleday and Co., 1950.

Smith, D. "Femininity as Discourse." *Becoming Feminine: The Politics of Popular Culture*. Eds. L. Roman and L. Christian-Smith. London: The Falmer Press, 1988. 37-59.

Tupper, J. "Little Woman – What Now?" *Maclean's* November 1, 1944: 20, 32-33.

Winship, J. "Handling Sex." *Looking On*. Ed. R. Betterton. New York: Pandora Press, 1987. 25-39.

—— **Health**

Women's Occupational Health

Scientific Bias and Androcentric Studies

Karen Messing ——

Historically, and to a great extent today, occupational health intervention and research have concentrated on jobs typically held by men (Messing and Stellman). Men are much more likely to be compensated for occupational illness, and fewer than 15 per cent of workers in Québec's priority sectors for occupational health intervention are women (Messing and Boutin). I suggest that this is not because women have safer jobs, but because occupational health research concepts and intervention practices have been derived from examination of men's jobs. I will discuss a few examples in detail (for a more detailed treatment see Messing, Punnett, Bond *et al.* 2003).

The requirement that populations be uniform or, women keep out

In order to make valid comparisons among sub-groups, researchers have insisted that populations examined be "uniform." It is interesting to see which criteria make sub-populations non-uniform. In cancer research, uniformity might be sought by requiring study subjects to share an urban or rural environment, some nutritional habits or medical history. However, women have frequently been eliminated from samples by this criterion.

For example, in 1988, Block and her colleagues published a study of cancer among phosphate-exposed workers in a fertiliser plant. Among 3,400 workers, 173 women were eliminated with the comment "because females accounted for only about five per cent of the study population, they were not included in these analyses" (Block *et al.* 7928). However, the 38 male workers in the drying and shipping department were not considered too small a population for study: a significant rise in their death rate was noted.

Another example is a Canadian study paid for with $2 million in public funds during the 1980s, studying cancers in relation to a huge number of occupational exposures. When I asked why his study excluded women, the researcher replied, "It's a cost-benefit analysis; women don't get many occupational cancers." He did not react when it was pointed out to him that his argument was circular, nor that for women taxpayers, the cost-benefit ratio of a study excluding them was infinitely high. The resulting papers, published in peer-reviewed journals, made no attempt to justify the exclusion of women (Siemiatycki *et al.*).

There are now, in fact, some well-identified occupational cancers among women, and research in this area is increasing (Zahm and Blair 2003). Women members of the American Chemical Association have significantly high rates of ovarian and breast cancer (Walrath *et al.*). Hairdressers are especially likely to get leukemia and ovarian cancer (Spinelli *et al.*). But there is a lot of catching up to do: a 1994 survey showed that occupational cancer researchers consistently ignored or under-analysed studies on women workers: Of 1,233 cancer studies published in 1971-1990 in the eight major occupational health journals, only 14 per cent presented analyses of data on white women and only ten per cent on non-white women (Zahm *et al.* 1994).

Similar exclusions have been found in studies of occupation and heart disease. Of 36 studies relating job strain to cardiovascular disease symptoms or risk factors, reviewed by Schnall in 1994, 22 concerned only men, 12 both men and women and a meager two concerned only women. The average all-male study involved an average 2533 subjects and was therefore fairly large, expensive and definitive; the two all-female studies involved a *total* of 576 subjects (Schnall). Analogous results have been found in a more recent search of the PubMed data base for articles on the most common professions of women and men; many more articles were found on men's than on women's professions (Messing and Stellman). The exclusion of women from studies reinforces the notion that women's jobs are safe and that women's concerns about their work environment are unfounded. Inclusion of women's jobs in prevention efforts becomes hard to justify.

The requirement for objectivity or, shutting our ears to women's voices

Who is considered to be objective in documenting health problems? In order to relate working conditions to illness, researchers refer to "experts" as in the following example, taken from the occupational health literature. In a study of 13,568 workers, experts were asked to class certain jobs as exposed or not exposed to dust. Reported symptoms of dust exposure (difficulty breathing, asthma ...) were correlated with experts' ratings. The study also correlated symptoms of dust exposure with the workers' own reports of dust exposure. Not surprisingly, the workers' reports were much more highly correlated with symptoms than were the experts'. In fact, for women workers and less-educated workers, the correlation with expert estimates was quite low. Did the researchers conclude that the experts' estimates were incomplete, class-biased, wrongly applied to women's jobs or out of date? Not at all: "Factors modifying the strength of the association between two estimates of exposure [experts' vs. workers'] are potential recall determinants of exposure. This association was significantly stronger in men than in women, suggesting a better perception of exposure by men..." (Hsairi *et al.* 979).

In other words, if self-reported exposure was better related to symptoms than expert-reported exposure, the self-reports of exposures and symptoms were wrong. If educated men were closer to the experts, the men had made fewer errors than the women or the less-educated. However, it is also possible that experts' estimates of exposure according to job title are based on experience with male job-holders.

The history of menstrual problems related to work also provides examples of biased attitudes toward women. After reporting that beginning airline hostesses underwent unfavourable changes in the menstrual cycle three and one half times as often as favourable changes, early researchers commented:

> There is not enough information to explain the pathophysiology of dysmenorrhea. The frequent association of dysmenorrhea with other [*sic*] neurotic symptoms is indicative of its psychological origin" (Iglesias *et al.* 519)

This lack of respect for women's perceptions of perimenstrual pain has probably had a detrimental effect on women's health. Well over half of European and North American women of reproductive age now do paid work, and 30-90 per cent of menstruating women report lower abdominal and lower back pain associated with the menstrual periods (Woods *et al.*, Sundell *et al.*, Pullon *et al.*). But Western occupational health literature has rarely included menstrual symptoms among outcome variables. A 1983-94 search of the Medline data bank for English-language studies using as keywords "menstr-" associated with "work" or "environment" to identify articles dealing with menstruation and the occupational environment yielded only 16 articles on paid work effects on the cycle. (Fewer than 20 more have been published in the ensuing 12 years.) Overall, about a third of the papers published in 1983-94 dealt with one category of women's professional activity: sports performance. Some papers reported studies in which women were exposed to pain or cold at various stages of their cycles in order to determine pain threshold variation. Others dealt with the effects of menstruation on performance. Most of the papers on the effects of working conditions on the menstrual cycle came either from our own research group, CINBIOSE, (one by Mergler and Vézina was the first of these) or from Eastern Europe. The only paper on working conditions and premature menopause came from Poland (Stanosz *et al.*). (Two other groups have since explored this question [Cassou *et al.*; Hardy and Kuh].)

Our original requests for funding to explore the effects of working conditions on menstrual pain were refused. In fact, of nine projects presented as a research program to the Québec Institute for Research in Occupational Health and Safety, the only one refused on the grounds of insufficient priority and relevance was the one on menstrual problems. We have, in fact, never been funded for any of the work we have done on menstrual problems, although we have published four studies on the subject. With the help of unpaid students, we have found that French women who were exposed to cold and to lifting weights had more menstrual pain. When we reported our results to the collaborating physicians they called the results "cute" [*amusant*], but suggested that publicising the results would injure the scientific credibility of the research team.

Calling this sort of wilful ignorance objectivity also has repercussions for accuracy in describing occupational health in general. Back pain is an important parameter of occupational health. The prevalence of back pain has been determined in many jobs; for example, 70 per cent of hospital workers (both sexes) report back pain in cross-sectional studies. At a given time, about 12 per cent of women workers are menstruating, of whom about 50 per cent have associated pain in the lower back area, about 2.5 times as many as those who are not menstruating (Borges 2000) but almost no studies of back pain ask whether subjects are menstruating. This is an important source of inaccuracy in understanding and prevention of factors leading to back pain.

Thus, a definition of objectivity centred on the perceptions of male scientists may prevent researchers from gaining critical knowledge of use to all workers.

Choice of variables to study or, why am I so tired if I'm doing light work

A number of risky situations in work traditionally assigned to women are not subject to standards or guidelines. Those who work as sewing machine operators, still the 13th most common job for women (Institut de la statistique du Québec), suffer from increased disability which is even more prevalent if they are paid at piecework rates (Brisson *et al.*). Yet there is no standard forbidding piecework. Women with families find it particularly difficult to deal with irregular and unpredictable schedules (Prévost and Messing), yet there are no standards to prevent wide, unforeseeable variations in work schedules.

Women's physical exertions are also under-regulated and understudied. There is a large literature on the physical capacities of women and men, particularly on the ability to lift weights (Messing and Kilbom). Data have been gathered on the relative capacities of women and men to lift weights upwards of ten kg, at different angles (Fothergill *et al.*) and at different frequencies. These data have been used to establish standards for load lifting (International Organization for Standardization). Although some tests used have been shown not to be well adapted to the size and shape of the average woman (Stevenson *et al.*), and the fact that women have breasts of different sizes has usually been ignored (Tate), such data have been used both to set standards and as pre-employment screens.

Another problem is that standards have rarely been adapted to the types of exertions found more often in women's traditional work, such as very rapid manipulation of light weights (Messing). Exertion of force is now recognised in occupational health practice primarily when a large force is exerted all at once, although most women's jobs require small forces with a high degree of repetition. Sewing machine operators (Vézina *et al.*), laundry workers (Brabant *et al.*) and other factory and service workers manipulate thousands of kilograms per day, a few grams at a time. This type of job is associated with repetitive strain injury such as bursitis, epicondylitis and carpal tunnel syndrome. Concerted efforts of feminist scientists (see Punnett, Silverstein) have resulted in increasing compensation being paid to workers with repetitive strain injury, but there is as yet no suggested limit on total weight lifted in a day.

Also, the conditions of women's work have not been considered. For example, according to the international standard for manual handling (International Organization for Standardization), lifting a baby weighing 9.5kg (about a year old) is a "classical" example of vertical lifting to which they apply the standard equations to decide on the physical requirements of day care workers. One wonders whether the authors of the standard have tried to lift a screaming, wiggling child and compared the physical requirements with those involved in lifting other types of industrial loads.

Walking is rarely considered as repetitive movement and there is no suggested limit to the total distance walked in a day. Hospital workers, waitresses and cleaners, among others, may run from the beginning to the end of their shifts.

Many jobs men do involve dynamic effort, which is exerted when muscles are contracted during movement. Dynamic effort is visible: a box is lifted, a nail is hammered. Static effort is exerted when muscles are maintained in a contracted state for long periods, as in standing without moving. This type of effort creates musculoskeletal and circulatory problems due to interference with circulation. Cleaning jobs (reaching to dust high surfaces, bending over toilets) often require this type of prolonged uncomfortable posture. Static effort, exerted without movement, is invisible and has not been regulated or subjected to guidelines.

Standing without moving the feet, a type of static work, is a characteristic of women's jobs in North America in many services including cashier work, one of the top five women's jobs (Institut de la statistique du Québec). This type of exertion tends to interfere with blood circulation to and from the legs and results in strain on the musculo-skeletal system. This is a job which requires employees to handle more than ten articles per minute with weights up to 6 kg, exerting additional strain on the bones and joints, yet it is not known as a manual handling task (Vézina *et al.* 1994).

Although there has been an attempt to introduce gender-fair guidelines for manual lifting tasks (Stevenson *et al.*), few standards apply to the type of physical exertions in jobs traditionally assigned to women. As a union health and safety activist told us, "It looks like nothing, that job [sewing machine operation], it's true that it's not a manual job and it's not like a repairman who climbs telephone poles, it's less spectacular." This kind of perception makes it difficult for women to get compensation for their employment-related illnesses (Lippel *et al.*).

Adjustment for relevant confounding variables or, how to hide bad working conditions

"Adjusting" for a variable while analysing data means using a mathematical procedure to eliminate its effect. It is reasonable, for example, to adjust for smoking when examining the relationship of dust exposure to lung damage, because smoking is often an independent determinant of lung damage and might confuse the issue if those exposed to dust smoke more or less than those not exposed. We may need to add a correction factor to the lung performance of smokers before testing the relationship between dust exposure and lung damage. This procedure allows us to determine the effect of dust on the lungs while taking into account the well-established effects of smoking. Almost all epidemiological studies of occupation and health adjust for non-occupational characteristics such as smoking, previous illness, and age.

Descriptors representing the place of people in society (gender, race, class) pose a special problem for adjustment during data analysis. They may represent higher probabilities of some biological characteristics (hormonal status, blood groups, nutritional status) but they also represent probabilities of different occupational exposures. Waitresses almost always have higher levels of circulating estrogens than waiters, but they also may work in different kinds of restaurants and have different work loads. Their relaxation time after work may also be different. Adjusting for sex may be an error, if sex is a synonym for a work exposure.

Studies which examine the health of workers often find that women workers report more symptoms of poor health or psychological distress than their male counterparts. It may be thought that this is due to women's "weakness." However, since women and men have different exposures because of their different task assignments, it is appropriate to analyse exposure data for women and men separately before deciding whether differences should be ascribed to personal or work factors. However, very many researchers adjust for gender without previous examination of the data and without considering whether gender is a surrogate for some exposure parameter such as amount of repetitive work. For example, all the studies examined in a review of the relationship between jobs and carpal tunnel syndrome adjusted for gender (Hagberg *et al.*). In adjusting, the authors attribute to hormonal or other woman-specific factors the fact that women have carpal tunnel syndrome more often than men. Adjusting for sex will make it less probable that an effect of women's occupations on carpal tunnel syndrome will be found.

In a study of men and women workers in poultry processing plants, it was found that men's and women's work was so different that their work-related illnesses had little in common. Women had more illnesses than men, so it appeared that women were more susceptible to disease. Adjusting for gender would have given weight to this idea and reduced the ability to recognise illness in both sexes (Messing *et al.* 1998). Analysing the data for women and men separately allowed researchers to see that women's illnesses were associated with their specific working conditions.

Thus, the standard techniques usually used may obscure the types of suffering women experience at their jobs. Perhaps worse, they may maintain the illusion that women are physically, mentally and emotionally "the weaker sex."

Statistical significance, or why hurry to clean up the workplace

Hidden political choices made by scientists can interfere with prevention of health hazards among women. The necessity for these choices arises from the fact that there is usually a rather long interval between the first doubts about particular working conditions and the time when the final word is in on the exact level of risk. Initial studies may show a weak relationship between an exposure and an effect, so that scientists have had to set a standard for when they will believe a relationship exists. Scientists hesitate to conclude that there is a relationship if they may be wrong. Standard scientific practice is to accept that there is a risk if there is less than one chance in twenty that the observed association was due to happenstance. This means that even if the researchers would have only two chances in twenty of being wrong if they concluded that there was a risk, the study is considered to be "negative," that is, no risk has been demonstrated.

The risk of being wrong in concluding that there is a risk is called "alpha," and, as mentioned, it is almost always set at less than five per cent. Scientists would not consider themselves justified in asking an employer to change a workplace if there is more than a five per cent chance they could be wrong. Furthermore, for scientists to be really sure of their conclusions, more than one study must show the same relationship. Given the small numbers of workers in most women's workplaces, the variations in conditions between workplaces, and the large numbers of potential hazards, it is no wonder that very few dangers have been established.[1] I still remember my surprise when a colleague, at the end of a million-dollar study, rejected his only statistically-significant conclusion (of a relationship between sawdust exposure and nasal cancer), saying it needed to be confirmed. In a province where the pulp and paper industry is a major employer, it seemed to me that it was time to alert the industry to a need for prevention. But, for this scientist, rigorous methods required a confirmation before taking action.

This caution leads to delays in prevention. Tens of thousands of women worked with video display terminals (VDTs) before the first study of VDT effects on pregnancy. But pregnant women never stopped working with VDTs while the studies were done. In this and many other cases, a decision was made to place the burden of proof on the worker rather than on the employer. This is a political decision but in the scientific literature it is presented as a scientific decision as to the standard level of statistical significance, rarely questioned or explained.

How can we promote recognition of in occupational health risks of women?

We have to move away from technology and environments based on men's bodies and techniques toward technology which takes into account human diversity. We have to devise tests for strength which will allow both women's and men's capacities to be shown to best advantage. We have to re-design many jobs and consult working women to find out new ways to do them. We may even have to consider whether, in the current economic context, it is better to ask for equal salaries for women's and men's jobs rather than insisting that all traditionally higly-paid male jobs be immediately redesigned so as to make them accessible to a wider sample of body types, including more women.

However, we must avoid erring in the other direction (Messing and Stellman). Several scientific journals and medical textbooks have begun promoting so-called "gender-specific medicine" (Legato) and some scientists are trying to incorporate gender sensitivity into their practice. But it is not sufficient to "add gender and stir." Not all women have pre-menstrual syndrome, high body fat content or weak muscles, and researchers should not compensate for years of neglecting women by exaggerating or over-generaliz-ing male-female differences. For example, we have examined the treatment of sex in the occupational health literature on mercury toxicity in chloralkali plants (Messing and Stellman). In eight of the ten papers published since 2000, the old, familiar mistakes were made: in two, subjects were identified as males but the sex of referents was not stated; in one, women were explicitly excluded from study; in three, sex of subjects was not identified at all; and in two more cases, sex of the sample was stated but not taken into account and exposure categories were not broken down by sex.

In the remaining two cases, however, the authors reported on the sex of subjects and attempted to take the sex of the sample into account in examining the data. In one of these, sex was even taken into account in calculating toxic effects (Frumkin *et al.* 2001). The authors, however could not analyse the results separately by sex due to small numbers of women (6.8 per cent of those exposed, 11.4 per cent of those not exposed). Instead of using the old-fashioned method of discarding the women, they combined the data on both sexes using a sex-specific correction factor. To calculate this factor, the authors relied on the fact that women, on the average, have a higher percentage of body fat, which affects the relationship between measured body weight and mercury metabolism. However, such reliance on a generalization from population differences to individual workers could lead to misinterpretation of the data. Not all women have more body fat than all men, and nothing is known about body fat in the sample. Given that the unexposed group had 68 per cent more women than the exposed group, the use of an erroneous correction factor may have led to error, either overestimating or underestimating the effects of mercury exposure. In addition, we are not told whether women and men were exposed differentially. The companion paper that explained the calculation of exposure data by occupational group did not give any information on gender. If, as is probable, the women were found preferentially in low-exposure office jobs, the use of sex-based correction factors may have distorted the exposure-effect relationship.

Thus, treating sex and gender in occupational health is not simple, and researchers must think seriously about it. Overemphasis on difference without consideration of the mechanisms involved may do as much harm as ignoring women.

We will not be able to take generalized theoretical views on these questions, but will have to base ourselves on woman-based feminist research. This means that a context must be developed in order to encourage such research and to provide money for it. In particular, ways must be found to channel community insights into academic research. Woman-based research also requires money: this will be available if granting agencies incorporate representatives from women's labour and community groups in funding.[2] In this way women's critiques of what scientists say about them can more quickly find their way into the scientific process, and ignorance of women's working conditions will no longer lead us to believe that women's work is safe and "light."

This paper reflects conversations with many colleagues, in particular Donna Mergler, Nicole Vézina, Julie Courville, Céline Chatigny and Jeanne Stellman. I thank the Social Sciences and Humanities Research Council of Canada and the Fonds Québécois de recherche sur la société et la culture for research support.

An earlier version of this article was originally published in CWS/cf's Summer 1994 issue, "Women and Health" (Volume 14, Number 3).

[1]Not only women are affected. Any relatively powerless group (among which are blue-collar workers and women) may have the burden of proof placed on it without explicit justification.

[2]The Université du Québec à Montréal has signed agreements with the three major Québec unions, providing resources for responding to union requests (released time for professors who participate in educational activities and university seed money for research). A similar agreement was signed in 1981 with a consortium of women's groups. These agreements have led to a partnership between researchers and union women's committees, supported by the Fonds québécoise de recherche sur la société et la culture, which incorporates community representatives in its decision-making processes. They are currently funding studies of discrimination against women in workers' compensation, of the impacts and consequences of methods used to reconcile family and professional responsibility, and of ways to make women's work more visible.

References

Block, Gladys, Genevieve Matanoski, Raymond Seltser, and Thomas Mitchell. "Cancer Morbidity and Mortality in Phosphate Workers." *Cancer Research* 48 (1988): 7298-7303.

Borges, Aismara. *Les désordres menstruels chez les infirmières de la Province d'Aragua (Venezuela).* Ph. D. Thesis, Sciences de l'environnement, Université du Québec à Montréal, 2000.

Brabant, Carole, Sylvie Bédard, and Donna Mergler, "Cardiac Strain Among Women Laundry Workers Doing Repetitive Sedentary Work." *Ergonomics* 32 (1989): 615-628.

Brisson, Chantal, Alain Vinet, Michel Vézina, and Suzanne Gingras, "Effect of Duration of Employment in Piecework on Severe Disability Among Female Garment Workers." *Scandinavian Journal of Work, Environment and Health* 15 (1989): 329-344.

Cassou. B., F. Derriennic, C. Monfort, P. Dell'Accio and A. Touranchet. "Risk Factors of Early Menopause in Two Generations of Gainfully Employed French Women." *Maturitas* 26 (1997): 165-174.

Fothergill, David M., Donald W. Grieve, and Stephen T. Pheasant. "Human Strength Capabilities During One-handed Maximum Voluntary Exertions in the Fore and Aft Plane." *Ergonomics* 34 (1991): 563-573.

Frumkin H., R. Letz , P. L. Williams, F. Gerr, M. Pierce, A. Sanders, L. Elon, C. C. Manning, J. S. Woods, V. S. Hertzberg, P. Mueller, and B.B. Taylor. "Health Effects of Long-Term Mercury Exposure Among Chloralkali Plant Workers." *American Journal of Industrial Medicine* 39 (1) (2001): 1-18.

Hagberg, Mats, Hal Morgenstern, and Michael Kelsh "Impact of Occupations and Job Tasks on the Prevalence of Carpal Tunnel Syndrome."*Scandinavian Journal of Work Environment and Health* 18 (1992): 337-345.

Hardy Rebecca and Kuh Diana. "Social and Environmental Conditions Across the Life Course and Age at Menopause in a British Birth Cohort Study." *BJOG: An International Journal of Obstetrics and Gynaecology* 112 (2005): 346-354.

Hsairi, Mohammed, Francine Kauffmann, Michel Chavance, and Patrick Brochard. "Personal Factors Related to the Perception of Occupational Exposure: An Application of a Job Exposure Matrix." *International Epidemiology Association Journal* 21 (1992): 972-980.

Iglesias, R.E., A. Terrés, and A. Chavarria. "Disorders of the Menstrual Cycle in Airline Stewardesses." *Aviation, Space and Environmental Medicine* May (1980): 518-20.

Institut de la statistique du Québec. n.d. *Les 20 principales professions féminines et masculines, Québec, 1991 et 2001.* Online: http://www.stat.gouv.qc.ca/donstat/societe/march_travl_remnr/cat_profs_sectr_activ/professions/recens2001/tabwebprof_juin03-1.htm Date accessed: April 20, 2006.

International Organization for Standardization (ISO). 2003. *ISO Ergonomics*

- *Manual handling - Part 1: Lifting and Carrying.* Geneva, Switzerland: ISO 11228-1, 2003.

Legato, Marianne J., ed. *Principles of Gender-Specific Medicine.* New York: Academic Press, 2004.

Lippel, Katherine, Karen Messing, Susan R. Stock, amd Nicole Vézina. "La preuve de la causalité et l'indemnisation des lésions attribuables au travail répétitif: rencontre des sciences de la santé et du droit." *Windsor Yearbook of Access to Justice* XVII (1999): 35-86.

Mergler, Donna and Nicole Vézina. "Dysmenorrhea and cold exposure," *Journal of Reproductive Medicine* 30 (1985): 106-111.

Messing K. "ISO, ISOTTE: les normes ont-elles un genre?" *Ergonomie et normalisation.* Eds. P. Rey, E. Ollagnier, V. Gonik et D. Ramaciotti. Toulouse: Octarès, 2004. 37-47.

Messing, K. and S. Boutin. "La reconnaissance des conditions difficiles dans les emplois des femmes et les instances gouvernementales en santé et en sécurité du travail." *Relations industrielles* 52 (1997): 333-362.

Messing, K., and Å. Kilbom. "Identifying Biological Specificities of Relevance to Work-Related Health." *Women's Health at Work.* Eds. Åsa Kilbom and Karen Messing, and Carina Thorbjornsson. Solna, Sweden: National Institute for Working Life, 1998. pp. 99-120.

Messing, K. and J. M. Stellman. "Sex, Gender and Health: The Importance of Considering Mechanism." *Environmental Research* 101 (2) (2006): 149-162.

Messing, K., F. Tissot, M. J. Saurel-Cubizolles, M. Kaminski, and M.Bourgine. "Sex as a Variable Can Be a Surrogate for Some Working Conditions: Factors Associated with Sickness Absence." *Journal of Occupational and Environmental Medicine* 40 (1998): 250-260.

Messing, K., Laura Punnett, Meg Bond, Kristina Alexanderson, Jean Pyle, Shelia Zahm, David Wegman, Susan R. Stock and Sylvie de Grosbois. "Be the Fairest of Them All: Challenges and Recommendations for the Treatment of Gender in Occupational Health Research." *American Journal of Industrial Medicine* 43 (2003): 618-629.

Pullon, S., J. Reinken, and M. Sparrow. "Prevalence of Dysmenorrhea in Wellington Women." *New Zealand Medical Journal* 10 (February 1988): 52-54.

Punnett, Laura. "Soft Tissue Disorders in the Upper Limbs of Female Garment Workers." *Scandinavian Journal of Work, Environment, and Health* 11 (1985): 417-425.

Schnall, P.L., P. A. Landsbergis, and D. Baker. "Job Strain and Cardiovascular Disease." *Annual Reviews of Public Health* 15 (1994): 381-411.

Siemiatycki, Jack, Ron Dewar, Ramzan Lakhani, Louise Nadon, Lesley Richardson, and Michel Gérin. "Cancer Risks Associated with Ten Organic Dusts: Results from a Case-Control Study in Montréal." *American Journal of Industrial Medicine* 16 (1988): 547-567.

Silverstein, B. A, L. J. Fine, and T. J. Armstrong. "Occupational Factors and

Carpal Tunnel Syndrome." *American Journal of Industrial Medicine* 11 (1987): 343-358.

Snook, Steven H. and Vincent Ciriello. "The Design of Manual Handling Tasks: Revised Tables of Maximum Acceptable Weights and Forces." *Ergonomics* 34 (1991): 1197-1213.

Spinelli, J.J., R. P. Gallagher, P. R. Band, and W. J. Threlfal. "Multiple Myeloma Leukemia and Cancer of the Ovary in Cosmetologists and Hairdressers." *American Journal of Industrial Medicine* 6 (1984): 97-102.

Stanosz, S., D. Kuligowski, and D. A. Pieleszek. "Concentration of Dihydroepiandrosterone, Dihydroepiandrosterone Sulphate and Testosterone During Premature Menopause in Women Chronically Exposed to Carbon Disulphide." *Medycyna Pracy* 46 (1995): 340.

Stevenson, Joan, D. R. Greenhorn, J. T. Bryant, Janice M. Deakin, and J. T. Smith. "Selection Test Fairness and the Incremental Lifting Machine." *Applied Ergonomics* 27 (1996):45-52.

Sundell, G., I. Milsom, and P. Anderson. "Factors Influencing the Prevalence of Dysmenorrhea in Young Women." *British Journal of Obstetrics and Gynaecology* 97 (1990): 588-94.

Tate, Angela J. "Some Limitations in Occupational Biomechanics Modelling of Females." Communication March 29 2000 at the Colloque on women's environmental and occupational health, Montréal. CD-ROM, 2004.

Vézina, Nicole, Céline Chatigny, and Karen Messing. "A Manual Materials Handling Job: Symptoms and Working Conditions Among Supermarket Cashiers." *Chronic Diseases in Canada* 15 (1994): 17-22.

Vézina, Nicole, Daniel Tierney, and Karen Messing. "When is Light Work Heavy? Components of the Physical Workload of Sewing Machine Operators Which May Lead to Health Problems." *Applied Ergonomics* 23 (1992): 268-276.

Walrath, J., F. P. Li, and Shelia K. Hoar. "Causes of Death Among Female Chemists." *American Journal of Public Health* 75 (1985): 883-885.

Woods, N. F., A. Most, and G. K. Dery. "Prevalence of Premenstrual Symptoms." *American Journal of Public Health* 72 (1982): 1257-1264.

Zahm, Shelia H., Linda M. Pottern, D.R. Lewis, Mary H.Ward, and D. W. White. "Inclusion of Women and Minorities in Occupational Cancer Epidemiological Research." *Journal of Occupational Medicine* 36 (1994): 842-847.

Zahm, S. H. and A. Blair. "Occupational Cancer Among Women: Where Have We Been and Where Are We Going?" *American Journal of Industrial Medicine* 44 (2003): 565-575.

The Canadian Women's Health Movement
Looking Back and Moving Forward

Madeline Boscoe, Gwynne Basen, Ghislaine Alleyne, Barbara Bourrier-LaCroix and Susan White

You would be hard-pressed to find any one who works in, or thinks about health in Canada today who did not agree, at least publicly, on the importance of social and economic conditions such as education, housing, environment, and gender on a person's health status. This broadened approach to health reflects a profound change in thinking and can be credited, in part, to the work of the women's health movement. This social movement was the first to bring together women's own experiences with health services, and their own opinions about their health concerns, with new visions, new information, and new methods of research and outcome evaluations.

The publication of this edition of *Canadian Woman Studies* devoted to women's health and well-being provides us at the Canadian Women's Health Network (CWHN) with an opportunity to share our reflections on the past, our comments on the present, and our speculations on the future of women's health in Canada.

In the beginning

The 1960s, 1970s and 1980s saw the rebirth of the women's movement and directly associated with it, the women's health movement in Canada and around the world. Women came together to share experiences and knowledge. We looked at our cervixes, fit diaphragms, helped get each other off mood-altering drugs and "caught" babies. We shared stories about our interactions with the medical system. We started asking questions. We understood that knowledge was power and sought information. Through debate and sharing, we developed new approaches. We realized that we could understand medical information if it was presented in an accessible form. We came to recognize the impact of issues such as violence and racism on our health. We realized that those who formulated the research questions controlled the answers. We understood that women's health is a political, social and economic matter. We were, as Sue Sherwin wrote, "No Longer Patient" and would be, to quote Sharon Batt (1994), "Patient No More."

Women gathered in discussion groups, educational forums and conscious-ness-raising sessions. We created new avenues to develop our concerns and our ideas that broke down isolation and allowed for individual and group action. No one was just a "patient" or a doctor, or a nurse, or a therapist, or an academic. Health was something that mattered to all women.

The women's health movement made links and formed partnerships with other groups who shared our issues, such as:

- consumer groups and self-help movements dealing with issues such as cancer, mental health, and addictions;
- anti-racism groups and those working on equity and access issues, including First Nations and rural communities;
- those providing alternative and traditional healing;
- environmental and anti-nuclear groups;
- disability rights activists;
- medical reform groups, including those interested in health promotion and community development;
- the legal community, who helped us push companies and providers to be more responsive and responsible.

In part, the strength and endurance of the women's health movement has been a result of this network.

Shaping our issues

Over the years, the movement has focused on three main issues: the health care delivery system, the development and analysis of the social determinants of health, and a commitment to increase the participation of women in all aspects of health care.

The movement's critique of a health care system dominated by white, male health professionals began with exposing how lack of information prevented women from making informed decisions; how the power dynamics between health professionals (doctors [usually male] and nurses [female]) and between physicians and patients made it hard to question professional expertise or refuse treatment; how sexism, racism, paternalism and other power oppressions within the system led to our priorities not being addressed; how the growing pervasiveness of drugs and other technologies distorted the treatment and prevention programs women really needed (Cohen and Sinding; Beck; Status of Women Canada; Batt 2002).

Women also learned that some institutions had interests in conflict with ours. For example, the commercial push to market a drug and increase profits could supersede the obligation to make safe and effective medicines available and to do follow-up on a drug's safety.

The emphasis was on a woman-centred vision of health and wellness. We knew that improving the health status of women meant paying attention to education, economic and social policies, housing, and the environment. Gender was put up front and centre as a critical determinant of health. The analyses recognized and respected the diverse needs and realities of women's lives and the impact of these on their health status.

Women worked for the increased presence of women throughout the health care system. We looked at the research used to rationalize the existing approaches to our health concerns. We saw that women's issues and voices were absent in both asking the questions and seeking the answers and that none of it was "neutral." We saw that women were often excluded from clinical trials for new drugs and couldn't know if the medicine we were given was safe for us.

We fought for greater participation of women in all levels of the health care system, including policy making. We pressed for and finally got Women's Health Bureaus or Departments in provincial governments, women's health committees in research and professional groups such as the Medical Research Council, a Women's Health Bureau inside Health Canada, women's health research centres in Ontario, and the establishment of the Centres of Excellence for Women's Health.

Creating woman-centred programs and services

Not satisfied with just offering critiques, women's health advocates also developed programs that reflected our vision of woman-centred care (Barnett, White and Horne). When we found existing services unresponsive or unyielding to our issues, we founded new, creative ones where all women would have opportunities to learn and freely discuss their concerns. We developed more equitable, non-hierarchical ways for health service providers to work with each other—and to work with women.

These activities fuelled a new approach to women's health and health services, one that required much more than pink walls—or even "nicer" female doctors. We called for providers to listen to women's voices, putting women, not care providers, centre stage in the healthcare system. This approach, which we called a *woman-centred model*, had several themes or principles. These included: user control of health care delivery systems; establishing innovative services; creating resource centres; emphasizing self-help and peer support; obtaining appropriate and effective health promotion and education; deprofessionalizing medical knowledge and health service jobs; developing programs examining health issues in their social context; demanding equity in hiring practices; understanding that women are experts in their own needs and issues; providing continuity of care and care providers; having access to female practitioners.

From these principles came activities, programs and services. One of the earliest was *Side-effects*, a play and popular education campaign about women and pharmaceuticals that made a remarkable cross-country tour in the early 1980s (Tudiver and Hall). Other examples included the formation of home birth and midwifery coalitions, the launching of the still-published *A Friend Indeed* newsletter on women and menopause, women-centred tobacco programs, the *Montreal Health Press*, environmental action groups, women and AIDS activities, endometriosis and breast cancer action groups, the disability rights organization DAWN, feminist counselling programs, women's shelters, traditional healing study groups, *HealthSharing* magazine, sexual assault support and action groups, anti-racism work, and community-based women's services such as Le Regroupement des centres de santé des femmes du Québec, Winnipeg's Women's Health Clinic or the Immigrant Women's Health Centre in Toronto, to name a few.

These organizations, programs and services were characterized by innovation and social action. Their work recognized that women's health and well-being are deeply affected by poverty and class and by experiences of abuse and racism. Women who sought services in woman-centred programs experienced group-learning methods, peer support, or new types of care providers, such as nurse practitioners. Women experienced alternative delivery models, which increased their knowledge and sense of autonomy and competence. The programs provided examples of outreach to those women whom conventional medical service providers considered "hard to reach."

The development and evolution of these programs and services is the "happy" part of the story. Sadder, if not tragic, is that, despite women's best efforts, most of these programs and services, no matter their effectiveness, remained marginalized within the mainstream health delivery sector and/or have had their funding severely if not completely cut. Those that survive are the exception to the rule and even these have never received the funding that would make them universally accessible.

Building the Canadian Women's Health Network

In the 1970s and '80s, groups of women across the country began talking about creating a formal women's health network to create a national presence and strengthen ties among women working in women's health. They saw a need for a network of networks that would encourage dialogue and discussion about strategies and policies and empower women to make informed choices about health (Tudiver).

Networking is a challenging task in Canada with its vast geographic distances and its linguistic, cultural, and regional diversities. But women across the country rose to the task. It was a time of severe cutbacks in government spending on health and social services and far-reaching attacks on Medicare and medical care as a right in Canada. The cutbacks were targeted to the poor and the poorest of the poor—women on welfare, persons with disabilities requiring home care services, shelters and other services for abused women and children. Women's health activists knew how severely these cuts would affect women's health.

In 1993, after a decade of consultation and discussion with women across the country, the Canadian Women's Health Network was created. Eleven years later, the CWHN continues to build and strengthen the women's health movement in Canada through information sharing, education and advocacy with the goal of changing inequitable health policies and practices for women and girls.

Many of the visions expressed when the CWHN was born have become realities. The CWHN has established a national presence for women's health issues and is on the "consultation" list of the federal government and national organizations when health issues are being discussed. Our bilingual information centre now has over 2,500 organizations listed in its database and over 7,000 resources on women's health; and we are a major source for media seeking information on women's health. Our website and *Network* magazine are popular sources of knowledge. Our electronic newsletter and email discussion lists are busy and well subscribed. CWHN has links with a variety of research and policy networks.

Moving forward

Women's health concerns have become very popular and "acknowledged" in the mainstream. This has proved to be both a blessing and a curse. Women's health advocates have achieved a certain level of recognition, but are always in danger of being co-opted or used by those who control the health system. The language of the women's movement has been taken on by governments and media, but too often without a deep commitment to giving women a real voice in health care policy and planning.

We in the CWHN know that there is still much to be accomplished. Today we can identify five broad challenges ahead for women's health in Canada.

1. Health reform and health service restructuring

The erosion of our publicly-funded, not-for-profit health insurance system and the accelerating growth of a two-tiered health system is a significant women's health issue. Though women and men are both affected by government cutbacks and rising health care expenditures, they do not have the same financial resources to cope with them and the impacts are different. Women, on average, earn less than men, are less likely to have supplementary health insurance coverage through their paid employment, and are more likely to live in poverty (Donner, Busch and Fontaine). As a result, women face a greater burden when health care costs are privatized.

And it is women who bear the burden when health care services are offloaded from the institution to the home. Women provide 80 per cent of both paid and unpaid health care (Armstrong *et al.*; National Coordinating Group on Health Care Reform and Women 2002). This inequitable situation results in increased stress, poverty and social exclusion for these female caregivers.

Despite a 2002 Royal Commission on Health Care that clearly demonstrated the support for and superiority of the Canadian Medicare system (Romanow), action is missing. The Commission report itself was also lacking in almost any mention of women's health issues and concerns (National Coordinating Group on Health Care Reform and Women, 2003). The movements toward national home care and pharmacare programs seem to be fading. Primary care discussions make little if any mention of community health centres. Midwifery and feminist counselling services remain small and under-funded. Through the establishment of the Canadian Institutes of Health Research (CIHR), there has been an increase in support for academic research in gender and health. But there is little funding for innovation or demonstration projects such as support for women's second stage housing, women centred smoking cessation or addiction treatment, or mothering support.

The federal government, as well some provinces, has a commitment to undertake gender sensitive policy and program development, with, at the very least, uneven results. Provincial governments may have identified women as a priority population, produced a women's health plan or set up Women's Health departments but without much effect on care. The hopes and requests for women-centred models of care remain.

There have been and continue to be huge cuts to the groups and ad hoc organizations that have provided much of the infrastructure for the women's health movement. Women's centres, community health centres, national and regional organizations such as DES Action, *HealthSharing*, the Vancouver Women's Health Collective and innovative demonstration projects have all had their funding dramatically reduced or disappear altogether. Burnout is common, as staff members grow exhausted from unrealistic workloads to which are added the need to write seemingly endless funding proposals and reports (Scott). The loss of these groups and programs is a "double-whammy," women lose services and programs providing practical examples of women-centred approaches and also lose their work in promoting a health determinants approach in all service and policy areas.

2. The continuing medicalization of women's health

The biomedical-corporate model continues to dominate our health care system. Institutions, professional groups and corporations in the medical field have significant built-in inertia, if not conflicts of interest, with the reforms envisioned by the women's health movement and the Beijing *Platform for Action* (United Nations), and indeed, Canadian government policy statements such as *Achieving Health For All* (Epp). For most, it is business as usual.

Despite years of mobilization and analysis, women's bodies and women's health issues continue to be over-medicalized, with women seen as incompetent and *all* our health issues in need of medical intervention. Among the latest examples are the widespread prescribing of hormone replacement for all menopausal women and the increasing use of epidural anesthesia for birthing women (O'Grady; Giving Birth in Canada).

This biomedical focus on the treatment of acute medical problems continues to colour the approach of health care providers, as well as the media and politicians. In this reactive role, the health system continually allocates resources that result in questionable policy "choices," such as:

• Paying for breast cancer screening by mammography, but not for breast cancer support groups or smoking awareness and cessation programs, or for research into possible environmental causes (O'Leary Cobb).

• Directing some $100 million in federal/provincial "economic development" funds to drug companies to produce hormonal drugs for older women, with little or no support allocated to health education, menopause research, or ensuring streets are safe enough to encourage women to prevent osteoporosis through exercise (Batt 2002).

• Investing large amounts of public and private funds into "new" reproductive technologies while midwifery continues to struggle for recognition and resources to support mothering and to address environmental contaminants that may lead to infertility are basically non-existent (Hawkins and Knox).

• Over-prescribing of benzodiazepines: women are not only more likely to be prescribed benzodiazepines compared to men, but are also more likely to be prescribed benzodiazepines for longer periods of time (Currie 2003).

• Over-prescribing selective serotonin uptake inhibitors (SSRIs) to treat depression and other mental health conditions while other effective interventions such as counselling or exercise remain unfunded and under utilized—and systemic changes in workplaces and elsewhere that lead to stress and depression are ignored (Currie 2005).

It took two decades of lobbying by women's health advocates before legislation to regulate the new reproductive technologies was introduced and passed into law (*An Act Respecting Assisted Human Reproduction and Related Research*). The Act is just one step towards an overall strategy to improve the reproductive and sexual health of Canadians, a commitment made by the government several years ago in yet one more "green" paper. This strategy must include increasing access to emergency contraception and ensuring reliable, accessible information on sex education for women and girls across their life spans.

3. Quality health information for women

For women to make informed choices, we must have access to accurate, timely, women-sensitive health information. But programs that used to fund groups creating information tools no longer exist. And while the explosive growth of the Internet seems to have created access to an enormous amount of information, it is not necessarily the knowledge women need or can access. In addition, most health research continues to lack an analysis of the differences between men and women or among women (Health Canada).

Community-based health providers have responded to the demand for health information by creating material, but have been constrained by limited funding and time. By contrast, advertising by the pharmaceutical industry has continued to permeate our media, not only to promote new products to professionals with expensive sophisticated techniques, but to produce health "information" brochures and other material that really should come from impartial, trusted, non-commercial sources. These same companies push their products to women—often flouting laws that prohibit direct-to-consumer advertising (Mintzes and Baraldi).

4. Public policy—is it going to be healthy or not?

While the federal government takes pride in its progressive health policy statements, we need actions not words.

Those government policy frameworks that emphasize a broad range of health determinants and have goals to achieve population health (Federal/ Provincial/Territorial Advisory Committee on Population Health) overlap with a woman-centred holistic approach. However, many of the government's actions appear to ignore these commitments. No action has ever been taken to build in health impact assessments that would evaluate new policies or programs as possible causes of inequities in women's health.

The growing gap between the rich and the poor, both within Canada and internationally, points to a societal failure to protect citizens and increases ill health, not just for the impoverished, but for everyone (Donner, Busch and Fontaine). Poverty is increasingly becoming feminized. The dismantling of social programs such as housing and income support are felt everywhere in Canada, but this has a particular impact on the lives and health of women and children. Poverty is hazardous to women's health.

5. Changes in the Women's Health Movement

Women's health activists continue to struggle with whether or not to put our energies into modifying existing institutions or building new ones. Funding restraints makes it more difficult for *all* the services envisioned by grassroots groups to be developed. When they are (under) funded, they immediately develop long waiting lists and meeting needs becomes difficult if not impossible.

We are grappling with a sisterhood made up of women who live at different levels of power and privilege. Our sisterhood's members have many different issues, priorities, and perspectives. How to prioritize issues and resource allocation is far from clear.

Midwifery is an example of this potential stress—in effect, a competition for services between rich and poor women. Midwifery, fought for by a broad coalition of consumers, midwives, and public health staff, has finally been implemented in most provinces and territories. How can equal access for all women be ensured? Will midwifery services, in short supply at the present, be "overused" by women who have resources, while women who would most profit from midwifery services (adolescents, women with multiple problems, rural and northern women who have to leave their communities to birth) have the least chance of getting access to them? It is clear that many women would seek to improve their birth experience if they had the opportunity. What happens to the women most in need, whose voices are often absent?

Protecting our vision

The women's health movement has broadened and matured. Some of the coalitions created long ago remain, but even those that have come apart have continuing ties that have created an underlying network of individuals and groups who remain active and connected. And women need this network: the issues we have fought for remain as current and as real today as they were three decades ago. New problems have an all too familiar ring. The task is clearly not an easy one.

The changes that have been won have been the result of persistence and, at times, anger and pain. Not only has the health care system resisted us, but frequently women's wishes and concerns have been disregarded, no matter how clearly they were articulated, while at other times they have been co-opted. Gender parity in medical schools and the recognition of nurse practitioners are wonderful, but this is only a small step toward our vision. Having women in positions of power as physicians, health administrators, and politicians will continue to have some positive effect. But this is not the only mechanism that we can rely on. As we all know, women frequently experience "glass ceilings" and "sticky floors." We also know that one's values cannot be automatically assumed because of gender.

We need to move from the *personal is the political* to *the communal good is in everyone's interest*. Individual health cannot exist without social justice. As individuals, we need to work on issues that are best for the community of women, even when these are not necessarily our personal priorities. Those of us working in the health service sector will need to join other groups to advocate for the systemic changes that will remove inequities, such as poverty and racism, that so strongly affect health. We need to ensure that whatever changes are made are not merely superficial or cosmetic changes laid over a biomedical service model, with no attention paid to the broader social determinants of health.

Women's health activists need to continue to lobby to reform and adapt existing institutions and professions. But we need to be sure this work doesn't lead to losing what has been achieved with the creation of alternative and new women-centred services and service providers. We must stay on guard to protect woman-centred research. We also need to consider creating a long-term demonstration fund for community-based, consumer-controlled services, particularly for women. We are, after all, retooling an industry.

We need mechanisms throughout the system to ensure that this dynamic process continues. Grassroots groups and a diverse range of citizen voices must maintain a strong leadership role as we move forward. We know that in times of confusion and constraint, dissent and critiques can be hard to hear. We will need to continue to build new alliances and new coalitions.

The women's health movement has provided a dynamic environment for some of the most creative debates and positive visions for a better, healthier future. Given the opportunity, there is no reason why we can't take on the challenges ahead.

This paper is adapted and updated from a presentation by Madeline Boscoe, Executive Director of the Canadian Women's Health Network, to the delegates of the Canada-U.S.A. Women's Health Forum in 1996 and was edited by Ghislaine Alleyne, Gwynne Basen, Madeline Boscoe, Barbara Bourrier-LaCroix and Susan White and reviewed by the Executive Members of the CWHN's Board of Directors. <http://www.cwhn.ca>

Originally published in CWS/cf's Fall 2004 issue, "Women's Health and Well-Being" (Volume 24, Number 1): 7-13.

References

An Act Respecting Assisted Human Reproduction and Related Research. Ottawa: Ministry of Supply and Services Canada, 2004.

Armstrong, Pat, Carol Amaratunga, Jocelyne Bernier, Karen Grant, Ann Pederson and Kay Willson. *Exposing Privatization: Women and Health Care Reform in Canada.* Aurora, ON: Garamond, 2001.

Barnett, Robin, Susan White and Tammy Horne. *Voices From the Front Lines: Models of Women-Centred Care in Manitoba and Saskatchewan.* Winnipeg: Prairie Women's Health Centre of Excellence, 2002.

Batt, Sharon. *Patient No More: The Politics of Breast Cancer.* Charlottetown: Gynergy, 1994.

Batt, Sharon. *Preventing Disease: Are Pills the Answer?* Toronto: Women and Health Protection, 2002.

Beck, Christina S. *Partnership for Health: Building Relationships Between Women and Health Caregivers.* Mahwah, NJ: Lawrence Erlbaum Associates, Inc., 1997.

Cohen, May and Chris Sinding. "Changing Concepts of Women's Health: Advocating for Change." *Women's Health Forum: Canadian and American Commissioned Papers.* Ottawa: Minister of Supply and Services Canada, 1996.

Currie, Janet. *Manufacturing Addiction: The Over-Prescription of Benzodiazepines and Sleeping Pills to Women in Canada.* Vancouver: British Columbia Centre of Excellence for Women's Health, 2003.

Currie, Janet. *The Marketization of Depression: Prescribing of SSRI Antidepressants to Women.* Toronto: Women and Health Protection, 2005.

Donner, Lissa, Angela Busch, and Nahanni Fontaine. *Women, Income and Health in Manitoba: An Overview and Ideas for Action.* Winnipeg: Women's Health Clinic, 2002.

Epp, Jake. *Achieving Health for All: A Framework for Health Promotion.* Ottawa: Minister of Supply and Services Canada, 1986.

Federal/Provincial/Territorial Advisory Committee on Population Health. *Strategies for Population Health: Investing in the Health of Canadians.* Ottawa: Ministry of Supply and Services Canada, 1994.

Giving Birth in Canada: A Regional Profile. Ottawa: Canadian Institute for Health Information, 2004.

Hawkins, Miranda and Sarah Knox. *The Midwifery Option: A Canadian Guide to the Birth Experience.* Toronto: HarperCollins Canada Ltd., 2003.

Health Canada. Women's Health Bureau. *Exploring Concepts of Gender and Health.* Ottawa: Minister of Supply and Services Canada, 2003.

Mintzes, Barbara and Rosanna Baraldi. *Direct-to-consumer Prescription Drug Advertising: When Public Health is no Longer a Priority.* Toronto: Women and Health Protection, 2001.

National Coordinating Group on Health Care Reform and Women. *Women and Health Care Reform.* Winnipeg: National Coordinating Group on Health Care Reform and Women, 2002.

National Coordinating Group on Health Care Reform. *Reading Romanow: The Implications of the Final Report of The Commission on the Future of Health Care in Canada for Women.* Winnipeg: National Coordinating Group on Health Care Reform, 2003.

O'Grady, Kathleen. "Reclaiming Menopause: Another Look at HRT and the Medicalization of Women's Bodies." *Network* 5/6 (4/1) (2002): 3-4.

O'Leary Cobb, Janine. "Behind the Screens: Mammograms." *A Friend Indeed* 10(4) (2003).

Romanow, Roy J. *Building on Values: The Future of Health Care in Canada.* Final Report of the Commission on the Future of Health Care in Canada. Saskatoon: Commission on the Future of Health Care in Canada, 2002.

Scott, Katherine. *Funding Matters: The Impact of Canada's New Funding Regime on Nonprofit and Voluntary Organizations.* Ottawa: Canadian Council on Social Development, 2003.

Sherwin, Susan. *No Longer Patient: Feminist Ethics and Health Care.* Philadelphia: Temple University Press, 1992.

Status of Women Canada. *What Women Prescribe: Report and Recommendations From the National Symposium "Women in Partnership: Working Towards Inclusive, Gender-sensitive Health Policies."* Ottawa: Minister of Supply and Services Canada, 1995.

Tudiver, Sari. *The Strength of Links: Building the Canadian Women's Health Network.* Winnipeg: Women's Health Clinic, 1994.

Tudiver, Sari and Madelyn Hall. "Women and Health Services Delivery in Canada: A Canadian Perspective." *Women's Health Forum: Canadian and American Commissioned Papers.* Ottawa: Minister of Supply and Services Canada, 1996.

United Nations. Department of Public Information. *Platform for Action and the Beijing Declaration: Fourth World Conference on Women, Beijing, China, 4-15 September, 1995.* New York: United Nations, 1996.

The Shattered Dreams
of African-Canadian Nurses

Najja Nwofia Modibo ⟶

Dear Nigger:

This letter is to inform you that we don't want you to work at our hospital. We have shown you in many ways that we hate your black guts. There are too many niggers in the nursing office and you are one too many. We don't want any religious freak preaching the love of God to us. We will do everything to get rid of you. Branson [Hospital] nursing office should know better than to hire too many black niggers in the nursing office. We will run you and your principles away from here. We don't need anyone trying to be a perfect coordinator. One day your car might blow up with you in it. If you don't get the point then something will happen to you and your husband and child. Niggers are not suppose to walk around with their heads in the air.

White people should be in that position not black niggers. We got rid of one and another came. If they put another black person in that office 2 i [sic] we will continue to do the same thing. Something might happen if you walk the halls at night.

Your enemies.

Don't be foolish to tell anyong. [sic] So you have a voice box on your phone. What a laugh.

This letter is dated February 1, 1988. It was sent to one of the women I interviewed in 1993 for a research project that was spurred by media reports, during the period of 1991 through 1994, that African-Canadian female nurses from hospitals were being fired and demoted for unprofessional behaviour ("Hospital employees want inquiry into racism"; "Racism cited at Ontario hospitals"; Majtenyi; Wanagas). Institutional spokespersons identified the problem as one of ill-trained immigrant women (Henry); however, within the African-Canadian community, reports suggested that the events were an outcome of the daily experiences of racism (Hardill).

This letter expresses the contempt held by some White nurses for their African-Canadian colleagues. The letter also stands as evidence of the daily harassment and poisoned workplace environment that Black nurses endured. In this article, I present this letter to situate the everyday workplace experiences of racism that African-Canadian[1] nurses confronted in some of Toronto's hospitals in the decade that followed the letter's receipt.

The work experiences of African-Canadian Nurses

In interviews conducted with 15 African-Canadian female nurses in 1993, the women continually raised the issue of their differential treatment in the workplace. Noting that White managers did not accord them the same opportunities or professional courtesy that the managers gave White nurses, some nurses also raised the issues of verbal abuse and the reluctance of White patients and their families to be nursed by "Black hands." The latter issue of the opposition of White families to Black nurses is beyond the limits of this paper; these practices, however, disclose how micro social relations are experienced in daily encounters with "majority" culture representatives and help to perpetuate existing racial inequality. Other researchers have written that these experiences are not accidental and are linked to the political, economic, and social implications that gender and race have had on workplace hierarchy (Lawrence; Silvera; Parmar). As dictated by the common-sense notion of "masculinized sub-human creatures" (hooks 1981: 22), such views aim to brand African-Canadian nurses as inferior members of their profession.[2]

As revealed by one interviewee, the early acceptance of the Black "exotic" did not mean that she escaped being stigmatized. Speaking of her early years in the Canadian North, she noted:

> In those days ... there weren't too many people of colour in Canada; we were seen as a novelty. I must say we were treated very well; everyone was very friendly. I worked in pediatrics and of course a lot of the children had not seen Black people before then (laughter).... This was something entirely different. They would refer to me as the chocolate nurse, but it was quite amusing, really. It was a small community and whenever Black women were seen around [town] they knew we were nurses because [we] were the only people of colour in the area in 1962. So I must say I was treated very well in Thunder Bay (Ontario) and accepted by the staff and patients, generally.

Starting with the slow acceptance of Black women in the nursing profession, hospital administrators made distinctions between Black, Brown, and White nurses. Such distinctions also appeared to be linked to another distinction, that is, country of origin and ethnicity. According to Monica Boyd (1975; 1984), immigrant women's occupational attainment in Canada shows an advantage for White female immigrants from developed capitalist countries. These observations were indicated by an other interviewee in a response concerning workplace hierarchy:

The ones [nurses] from England were called graduate nurses; the ones from elsewhere were called foreign-trained nurses. The graduate nurses were allowed to wear White uniforms; the foreign-trained nurses [were told to] wear an RNA uniform. It was really degrading! I spent six months there and I told them I was leaving ... I was forced to leave because I could not take it anymore [author's emphasis]. When you see some of the [White] RNs there [at the hospital] ... so dumb, you know, it was really appalling.

As a foreign-trained nurse, you did the same work as a graduate nurse but got less pay ... just a little more than a RNA.

Hospital Administrators along with White co-workers did not consider foreign-trained nurses to have achieved the "acceptable" standards. Because their training and education were viewed to be substandard, wearing differently coloured uniforms was intended to remind the nurses themselves, their co-workers, and the general public of their perceived lower skills and social status.

Researchers such as Rina Cohen, and Makeda Silvera have also made similar observations about the hierarchical divisions based on the experiences of immigrant, African-Canadian domestic workers. For example, Cohen talked about the fact that Filipino domestics were generally assigned to care for the young in White families, whereas African-Canadians were assigned to household cleaning tasks. These experiences tended to reinforce the racialized, gendered, matriarchal, and patriarchal relations of the society. I suggest that White managers and co-workers draw on these ideological constructs to support the systemic workplace segregation of Black nurses in Toronto's health-care institutions. Society thus digests "difference" as meaning patho-logical, thereby allowing such social constructions to serve as a cover for a racist, patriarchal-capitalist exploitation that denies Black women's profes-sionalism (Carby; Collins; Young and Dickerson).

Differential treatment of Black women was experienced by the placement of women on chronic care wards. For example, when I asked one interviewee about the women's understanding of why the majority of African-Canadian nurses were located on a special floor at one of Toronto's hospitals, she answered:

They understand clearly that [it is] discrimination ... based on race... They'd tell you about shifts, how shifts were allocated, who gets to go to professional development days, training, etc. That's a pattern. They talked about one young Black woman asking to go on a particular unit because [it was] her area [of training].... She was not put where she asked [to be assigned], but others [White nurses] were given their preferences.

This individual also confirmed that such experiences were not isolated events, indicating that similar reports have been heard from nurses from other institutions. African-Canadian nurses appear to be highly represented in chronic care facilities. The interviewee noted that:

> I was not a nurse. I worked in the office and I would [visit] the floors all the time.... The unit on [the fourth floor is] where they [were] cleaning feces and bathing, lifting, and turning ... hard work.... People [patients] cannot come out of their beds. That's where the Black nurses were.... This was [my] personal observation.

Recalled in the preceding account is the manner in which institutional racism operated to marginalize women of African descent in their chosen profession. These women were continually confronted by Whites who saw nothing abhorrent in institutional and personal practices; that is, in limiting the professional development of their Black co-workers.

Similar experiences were confirmed by women who worked on the frontline of nursing care. One individual who had been recruited from Britain spoke of her early experiences.

> I was all gung-ho about it [working in the unit] because there was just so much to learn. In those days, they were starting heart surgery. Dr. Smith was pioneering heart surgery with children, and working directly with someone like [him] ... that to me ... was just wonderful. And again, I must say I never ran into prejudice at the Hospital.... I can honestly say that.

These positive experiences changed, however, when she sought employment at another large suburban hospital. A number of practices that singled out both her and other Black women indicated that a level of differential treatment was accepted in this institution.

As summer relief staff, she and other nurses were moved to other units. This particular individual was placed in the outpatient department. At the end of the summer, she was reassigned to another department because of greater workload but was subsequently demoted by the director of nursing to casual status until a part-time position became available. Over the next two years, she repeatedly asked to be made one of the part-time staff because she was in fact working part-time hours, but, as she explained,

> [The nursing director] said if there was [a part-time position, it] would have to be posted and applied for. I couldn't have it just because I was functioning in the job. I again approached Human Resources about making me a part-time worker, [pointing to] the fact that I am [sic] doing part-time hours. [Their response was to put me on] the outpatient [department's] ... payroll instead of being in a casual pool. I was put on their payroll but I was never given a part-time job; I was still a casual worker even though I did the part-time hours.

This latter development paralleled changes in Ontario provincial policy that allowed part-time workers to participate in the workplace benefits program. Those women who were part of the casual worker pool were denied benefits. Such a denial represents a pattern that undermines opportunities for job mobility, as well as the monetary rewards incurred.

The experiences described here were supported by another interviewee from a different suburban Toronto hospital. Pointing to the kinds of discussions she had with senior management regarding her job performance, the close scrutiny she received by White supervisors and co-workers, and her workload that was heavier than that of White nurses, this individual emphasized the continuing hurdles that nurses of African descent had in obtaining full-time employment at her institution. Their only option for gaining work at this institution located in their community was through a job-registry agency. In other words, access to jobs within the institutions was continually blocked. Access through the job registry meant that they were always "on call" as casual labour or were given assignments to the institution for a few weeks at a time. A casual labour status not only allowed institutions to meet their commitments when demand for medical care services increased but also allowed casuals to undertake the job requirements of full-timers who might be away on holiday, sick leave, or professional development days. These results are also supported in the research of L. Mishel, J. Berstein and J. Schmitt (257) and David Livigstone. These authors observed that workers who are designated as part-timers have poor job security and job promotion prospects. Livingstone's Canadian study also points out that in the mid-1990s, an increasing percentage of Canadians were "combining part-time jobs to become full-time workers" (70).

These findings represent some of the most common experiences of Black nurses: their inability to obtain secure employment or their being directed to areas for which they have not been trained. When they opt to take on a job for which they are not trained, they run the risk of being accused of incompetence. Such accusations ignore the ways in which micro and macro practices buttress each other. In other words, the concern here has not been in attempting to explain individual behaviours, but to make clear "that all such relations are present in and produced in the organization of activities at… [the] … everyday level as well as entering the everyday into relations that pass beyond the control of individual subjects" (Smith 134). In this context, I argue that gendered-racism should be viewed within the larger societal, economic, and political realignments being undertaken in Canadian society.

Other interviewees substantiated these observations by recounting their own experiences of job retrenchment. Retrenchment was achieved in a number of ways: in one example, the interviewee reported that as an African-Canadian nursing manager's job

> … was made redundant; she was taken out of the job and someone else was brought in from outside to replace her. Now I don't understand how a job can be redundant if somebody else is put in the same job. [The]

person who came in to take over ... naturally [it] was a White person rather than a Black.

What does this interviewee mean by "naturally [it] was a White person rather than a Black?" This individual holds up the nursing profession and Canadian society for criticism. In other words, her "interpretation and evaluation of specific experiences is a process of collecting and combining often diverse and complex information into a judgement" (Essed 70). Her evaluation of the way gendered-racism functions inside Canadian institutions is based on a set of everyday experiences on which she draws to make sense of social inequality. I inquired further about what the interviewee meant by bringing in "someone from the outside." Her answer offered a remarkable insight into the ongoing changes taking place in Ontario's medical care. The interviewee pointed out that the new nurse manager had worked in nursing but this person had never worked in a hospital; she had gained her experience in the industrial sector. According to the interviewees, this was not a unique occurrence.

As the government's privatization efforts in health care became more institutionalized, there appeared to be increasing efforts to recruit those members of the workforce who had gained their experience in the private sector in which the "new" Taylorist management strategies had been adopted.[3] The so-called redundancy of some jobs appeared to be part of the strategy of re-engineering with gendered-racist outcomes. As a result, the corporatization of health care appears to have exaggerated the already entrenched nursing hierarchy; in other words, re-engineering contributed to their deskilling and pushed African-Canadian women into the lowest levels of the profession, with White colleagues being placed in the middle to upper levels. A 1994 study (Das Gupta 1994) illustrates this gendered-racialized experience. Concerning the management of the Heritage Hospital in Toronto, the study found that it

is predominately White, while 56% of its nursing staff were people of colour, of which 30% were Black. Most of the Black nurses were working in the Chronic and Acute Care Units (which requires a great deal of lifting and tending), and they were the least represented in the specialty units. For instance, 41% of the nurses in the Chronic and Acute Care Units were Black compared to 15% White and 44% other nurses of colour. Conversely, only 13% of the nurses in the Intensive Care Unit were Black, compared to 55% White and 32% other nurses of colour. (Das Gupta 1994: 39)

The women also spoke about the lack of support from their White colleagues, few of whom took a public stand on the issue of the differential treatment of Black women. As one interviewee noted, "they [White nurses] seemed to be afraid to say the word *racism*." An interviewee who had asked some of her White co-workers to testify against the administration in a legal case that she had brought against the hospital observed that

> they recognized that the treatment [was not] fair, but they [were not] willing to say, well, this is racism.... I don't think they understand.... This particular one, she would phone me and say, "...I'm so sorry for what happened. I know it's not fair treatment, but I wouldn't go as far as saying it's racism."

The interviewee concluded, "I honestly think they don't understand what racism is all about. They would say, okay, this is unfair treatment, they are treating you different than they treat the others ... *but.*"

When asked about White co-workers' reluctance in offering public support, the interviewee responded that her co-workers said that they had "to think about [their] job[s]." Job tenure is important, but such individualistic responses, for all practical purposes, support the marginalization of Black nurses and their struggles against workplace racism. Not surprisingly, research has identified the different perceptions that Blacks and Whites have regarding racialized oppression. Liberals, conservatives, and radical Whites have displayed a general tendency to believe that Canada's employment equity programs have brought about a level playing field and that Blacks and others have nothing to complain about.

White perceptions and continuing silences about racism contribute to the "alienation of the non-recognition of the lives" (Carby 213) of African-Canadian women; further, such positions hide the fact that "White women stand in a power relation as oppressors of Black women" (Carby 214). Without this recognition and the commitment to act on alliances, sisterhood will remain only a concept. Too often, these perceptions have stood as hurdles, inhibiting White women and other women of colour from seeking alliances with women of African descent. One interviewee was very candid in this regard, pointing out that activists from the White community seemed more concerned about driving their own agenda than about acknowledging racism as a particular experience of African women:

> When we march in the streets, you don't see them (representatives from other communities). For too long, even in the god damn labour movement, when you got one Black they are thinking that is one too many. You cannot have two Blacks in any place; now when they hire one Black, they are thinking about an Asian, etc. Never mind about those Blacks who have been carrying on the struggle and doing human rights and doing anti-racist work. Suddenly, people have gotten conscious about representation. I am not able with that [i.e., I am not concerned], I am old, you all are young people, you could try with your politically [correct] moves and your intersection of oppression and all them things.... Racism is where I dey [i.e., I am].

This interviewee's narrative offers an insightful analysis of the practice of racism in modern Canadian society and points to both the difficulties of overcoming marginalization and the importance of coalition building. The interviewee also raises questions of how strategies chosen by institutions serve to perpetuate racism. This respondent is well aware that representatives from other marginalized populations are engaged in the struggle against racism; she also realizes, however, that anti-Black sentiments are deeply entrenched in Canadian society. In other words, although fighting racism is the alleged aim of many institutions, certain efforts, such as employment equity in Canada, assume a basic inequality for all groups. The interviewee's response also points to the weakness of a common approach by Canadian institutions in their hiring strategies; that is, the approach favours either the promotion of equal representation of employees from communities of colour or recruitment of a "minority" [sic] whom they believe is representative of marginalized communities in the corporate culture. These institutions are then considered diverse. This approach not only sets off a competition among marginalized groups for political and economic enfranchisement but also leaves both macro and micro racism against African-Canadians intact.

Conclusion

The brief results presented here highlight the continuing difficulties that African-Canadian nurses had with gendered-racism in Toronto's hospitals. These experiences were manifested in personal and institutional practices that effectively pushed the women into low-status jobs that were viewed as unfit for White women. I suggest that these practices are based on the socially constructed categories of gender and race (Feagan and Vera; hooks 1984).

Why did the differential experiences of White and African-Canadian nurses appear to be more pronounced in the early to mid 1990s? The restructuring of the Canadian economy and the transition in Ontario's health care were partly responsible for exacerbating underlying socio-economic arrangements that resulted in privileges for White women in the larger society. But just as important were the entrenched hierarchal relationships in the nursing profession that were challenged by the efforts of organizations such as the Congress of Black Women, Nurses and Friends Against Discrimination, and numerous individuals inside and outside the African-Canadian community. Without their undertaking, the acceptance of the nurses' human rights complaints by the Ontario Human Rights Commission (OHRC) would have been made more difficult. In 1994, the OHRC finally agreed that there was systematic racism in a hospital. Sharon Luddington, one of the nurses who had been critical to bringing the public's attention about the plight of black nurses, echoed the sentiments of many of her colleagues by stating "We have been vindicated.... We had bad management." Even Tony Canale, the Northwestern hospital chairperson, agreed that the hospital was wrong (Papp).

In addition to the sharing of $320,000 among seven nurses for "mental anguish," as well the lost of wages, the hospital was required to make a number of institutional adjustments. These were establishing a "vice-president of ethno-racial equality to oversee ridding the workplace of discrimination," developing a "human rights committee to change hospital policies in dealing with minorities," and "providing all hospital staff, doctors and volunteers with race-related training" (Papp). This settlement did not bring an end to the difficulties faced by Black nurses at other institutions. In a letter to the Ontario Minister of Health, the Ontario Nurses' Association commended the government on the resolution of the discriminatory claims that had been settled by the OHRC but warned in its correspondence, which was dated four months after the initial settlement that,

> The current Arbitration system lacks the expertise of Arbitrators who recognize discriminatory practices, despite substantial evidence to support the claim.... The union is seeing a growing number of discriminatory employer practices in the recent months that are not tied solely to racial origin, rather they cross the full spectrum of discrimination. I should also add that these occurrences are not a Toronto problem, but are spread over the entire province's health care facilities (Ontario Nurses' Association).

As a result of these concerns and the activism from a variety of interest groups, including African Canadians, the Ontario Hospitals Anti-Racism Task Force presented a document entitled "Anti-Racism Project Report" that was aimed at institutionalizing a process in the health-care sector. In part, it read that organizational change needed to include:

> Anti-Racism Policy Guidelines
> Anti-Racism Complaint Mechanism
> Anti-Racism Organizational Change Self-Assessment Tools
> Anti-Racism Education Strategy Guidelines (Ontario Hospitals Anti-Racism Task Force: iii)

These policy proposals should be praised, yet they represent small steps in addressing wider societal problems, in other words, without an understanding that racism is a fundamental problem for all Canadians, without vigorous commitment and support at the national level, each new generation of Canadians will continually be reminded of and made to relive gendered-racist experiences inside and outside of the workplace.

Because of the limited number of individuals that participated in this study, I do not claim that the experiences of African-Canadian nurses are widespread. Yet, a growing literature documenting the experiences of African-Canadians and other women of colour would not refute such a claim (Henry; James and Shadd; McKague; Ontario Nurses' Association). Additionally, in their recent article, Gina Feldberg, Molly Ladd-Taylor, Alison Li, and Kathryn McPherson discuss the continuing effects of the "restructuring" efforts implemented by hospital administrators in the 1990s as a means of holding down spiraling costs in Canadian health care delivery. In spite of the advances made by women within Canadian society, Feldberg et al. note that "feminists have had to struggle to place the needs of female employees and caregivers as well as patients on the policy agenda." More insidious are the effects of many health "reforms" such as the shift to non-hospital and outpatient care, which, as pointed out by Canadian health critics, "often led to layoffs or wage reductions for nurses and hospital workers—most of them female—while increasing the unpaid caregiving work of family and friends—again, most of them female" (Feldberg et al. 36). These effects not only mirror but also exacerbate the continuing struggles cited in this paper of the public and therefore also the private experiences of African-Canadian women within the Canadian health care delivery system. The inextricable link between the public and private effects of health care policy administration highlights the need for more research to be undertaken to address these critical issues.

Originally published in CWS/cf's Winter 2004 issue, "Women and the Black Diaspora" (Volume 23, Number 2): 111-117.

[1]Despite the contradictory nature of their citizenship, I present the women as African-Canadian, yet the reader should be aware that the majority of the women were born in the Caribbean and immigrated to Canada, or arrived through a second country, primarily the United Kingdom. Claiming Canadian citizenship does not mean that they are recognized by the society as Canadian, or that the women have broken ties to the countries of their birth. As are other immigrant populations, they are marginalized but also retain strong links with their countries of origin. They find themselves located in a kind of transnational space.

[2]See the following research for documented evidence on racism: Billingsley and Muszynski; Henry and Ginzberg; Rees and Muszynski. Other populations of colour such as Arabs, Chinese, First Nations, Japanese, and East Indians have their own horror stories to tell (see Kashmeri; Bolaria and Li; Stevenson; Sugimoto).

[3]New management practices were drawn from policies that had been implemented by manufacturing firms; although presented under different names, such schemes were based on a number of assumptions that had been identified in the work of Edward Deming. According to the Ontario Premier's Council, such practices meant "[c]ontinuous quality improvement including teamwork in everything; customer or patient satisfaction; total quality approach; employee empowerment; automation; innovation by everybody; management through vision and values; strategic choices; developing core competencies; and focusing on the interdependencies in the organization" (Armstrong et. al.: 32). In other words, there was an attempt by the supporters of these policies to undermine the market regulations that had been fixtures in most post-WWII economies, regulations that had provided some support to the most vulnerable

members of our communities: women of color, immigrants, the poor, and aged. For further discussion on how these policies have been implemented and their effects on women of colour and other workers, see Pat Armstrong et. al., Christina Gabriel, and Michele Landsberg.

References

Armstrong, Pat et al. *Medical Alert: New Work Organizations in Health Care.* Toronto: Garamond Press, 1997.

Billingsley, Brenda and Leon Muszynski. *No Discrimination Here? Toronto Employers and The Multi-Racial Work Force.* Toronto: The Social Planning Council of Metropolitan, 1985.

Bolaria, S. and P. Li Racial Oppression in Canada. Toronto: Garamond Press, 1988.

Boyd, M. "The Status of Immigrant Women in Canada." *Canadian Review of Sociology and Anthropology* 12 (1975): 406–416.

Boyd, M. "At a Disadvantage: The Occupational Attainment of Foreign-born Women in Canada." *International Migration Review* 18 (1984): 1091–1099.

Carby, Harzel. "White Woman Listen! Black Feminism and the Boundaries of Sisterhood." *The Empire Strikes Back: Race and Racism in 70s Britain.* Ed. Centre for Contemporary Cultural Studies. London: Hutchinson, 1982. 212-235.

Cohen, Rina. "Working Conditions of Immigrant Women Live-in Domestics: Racism, Sexual Abuse and Invisibility." *Resources for Feminist Research* 16 (1987): 36–38.

Collins, Patricia Hill. *Black Feminist Thought: Knowledge, Consciousness, and the Politics of Empowerment.* New York: Routledge, 1991.

Das Gupta, Tania. Analytical Report on the Human Rights Case Involving Northwestern General Hospital, Toronto: Ontario Human Rights Commission, 1994.

Essed, Philomena. *Understanding Everyday Racism: An Interdisciplinary Theory,* California: Sage Publications, 1991.

Feagin, Joe R. and Vera Hernan. *White Racism: The Basics,* New York: Routledge, 1995.

Feldberg, Georgina, Molly Ladd-Taylor, Alison Li and Kathryn McPherson. "Comparative Perspectives and American Women's Health Care Since 1945." *Women, Health, and Nation: Canada and the United States Since 1945.* Eds. Georgina Feldberg et. al. London, ON: McGill-Queen's University Press, 2003. 15-42.

Gabriel, Christina. "Restructuring at the Margins: Women of Colour and the Changing Economy." *Scratching the Surface: Canadian Anti-racist Feminist Thought.* Eds. Enaksi Dua and Angela Robertson. Toronto: Women's Press, 1999. 127-164.

Hardill, Kathy. "Discovering Fire Where The Smoke Is: Racism in the health

Care System." Towards Justice in Health, Vol. 2 No. 1, (1993) pp. 17-22.

Henry, Francis. Background Paper For The Ontario Nurses Association and The Clark Institute of Psychiatry. Toronto: York University, 1994.

Henry, Francis and Effie Ginzberg. Who Gets The Work: A Test of Racial Discrimination in Employment, Toronto: The Urban Alliance on Race Relations and The Social Planning Council of Metropolitan Toronto, 1985.

hooks, bell. Feminist Theory: From Margin to Center. Boston: South End Press, 1984.

hooks, bell. Ain't I A Woman: Black Women and Feminism. Boston: South End Press, 1981.

"Hospital employees want inquiry into racism." CBL-AM [CBC] Toronto, 18 November 1991.

Kashmeri, Zuhair. The Gulf Within: Canadian Arabs, Racism, and the Gulf War. Halifax, Nova Soctia: James Lorimer and Co., 1992.

Jones, James. Prejudice and Racism. New York: Random House, 1972.

Landsberg, Michele. "Getting rid of nurses bad medicine for hospitals." The Toronto Star, 19 May 1996.

Lawrence, Errol. "In the Abundance of the Water the Fool is Thirsty: Sociology and Black Pathology." The Empire Strikes Back: Race and Racism 70's Britain. Ed Centre for Contemporary Cultural Studies. London: Hutchinson, 1982. 95-142.

Li, Peter S. The Chinese in Canada. Toronto: Oxford University Press, 1988.

Livingstone, David. The Education-Job Gap: Underemployment or Economic Democracy, Boulder, Colorado: Westview Press, 1998.

Majtenyi, C. "Inquiry called for over race bias in Ontario's health care system." The Catholic Register 10 December, 1994.

Mishel, L., J. Bernstein and J. Schmitt. The State of Working America: 1996-1997. Armonk: M.E. Sharpe, 1997.

Ontario Hospitals Anti-Racism Task Force. Ontario Hospitals Anti-Racism Project Report. February 1996.

Ontario Nurses' Association. Internal Correspondence. 10 August 1994.

Parmar, Pratibha. "Gender, Race and Class: Asian Women in Resistance." The Empire Strikes Back: Race and Racism 70's Britain. Ed. The Centre for Contemporary Cultural Studies London: Hutchinson, 1982. 236-275.

Papp, Leslie. "Seven nurses get award in 'landmark' rights case." Toronto Star, 13 May 1994.

"Racism cited at Ontario hospitals." CFYN [M-H] Toronto, 18 November 1991.

Rees, Tim and Leon Muszynski. Eds. Racial and Ethnic Minorities in the Workplace: Resource Book, Toronto: Social Planning Council of Metropolitan Toronto, 1982.

Richardson, Boyce. "Concealed Contempt." Racism in Canada. Ed. Ormond McKague. Saskatoon: Fifth House Publishers, 1991. 65-72.

Silvera, Makeda. Silenced. Toronto: Williams-Wallace, 1984.

Smith, Dorothy E. *The Everyday World As Problematic: A Feminist* Sociology, Boston: Northwestern University Press, 1987.

Stevenson, Winona. "Colonialism and First Nations Women in Canada." *Scratching the Surface: Canadian Anti-Racist Feminist Thought.* Eds. E. Dua and A. Robertson. Toronto: Women's Press, 1999. 49-80.

Sugimoto, Howard Hiroshi. *Japanese Immigration, the Vancouver Riots, and Canadian Diplomacy.* New York: Arno Press, 1978.

Wanagas, Don. "Nurses Charge Discrimination." Toronto Sun, 14 September, 1994, P. 8.

Young, Gay and Bette J. Dickerson, Editors. *Color, Class, and Country: Experiences of Gender.* Atlantic Highlands, New Jersey: Zed Books, 1994.

"Quality Care is Like a Carton of Eggs"

Using a Gender-Based Diversity Analysis to Assess Quality of Health Care

Beth E. Jackson, Ann Pederson, Pat Armstrong, Madeline Boscoe, Barbara Clow, Karen R. Grant, Nancy Guberman and Kay Willson

In the 1990s, extensive restructuring in the Canadian health care system occurred as most provincial governments launched health care "reforms" such as: increased use of day surgery, delayed admission, and early release; de-listing of insured services and restrictions on entitlement to insured services; bed closures; and reductions in health care personnel (notably, nurses and other allied health care workers) (Armstrong *et al.*). While changes such as these have been implemented largely to control costs, governments and other payers need to demonstrate that quality is maintained and even enhanced by restructuring so that they are seen as meeting their responsibilities to taxpayers, "clients" and stockholders (Baker *et al.*; Brook, McGlynn and Cleary; Chassin; McGlynn). Governments, health care organizations and insurance companies have turned to quality assessments to provide this evidence.

In this paper, we argue that current health care quality assessments lack mechanisms to represent and respond to: 1) important structural features of the health care system (e.g. heterosexism) and 2) women's diverse experiences of care, including what the health system "costs" the women who use it. First, conventional quality assessments examine only limited dimensions of the "structure" of the health care system, conceptualizing structure in terms of the material and human resources and organizational arrangements of health care settings. This approach fails to recognize and measure important structural relations of power that constitute and shape the health care experience. Second, health quality assessments are largely concerned with "cost," defined in economic terms. Yet research into women's experiences of health care suggests that a broader conceptualization of "cost" would be useful in understanding health care quality. We discuss these missing elements in health quality assessments, illustrating them with material drawn from focus group discussions with lesbian/bisexual/queer women undertaken as part of a larger investigation of women's understanding of quality of health care in Canada. Our findings suggest that health care researchers, policy makers, workers, and recipients must critically examine what counts as evidence in quality reports and recognize the limitations arising from current conceptualizations and measurement practices. Because current quality assessments rely ultimately on individual-level, decontextualized data, their analysis of quality emerges from simple aggregation of discrete individuals and events. They miss the complex social production of health care structures, processes, and outcomes. Consequently, they do not fully capture women's experiences of health care (as patients, providers, and coordinators of care). Moreover, they envision change as emerging primarily from individual action and local institutional adjustments rather than systemic reorganization. Health-quality assessments informed by a gender-based diversity analysis would produce an explicit systemic analysis to more fully account for what creates quality health care for women.

Health-quality assessments that are informed by a gender-based diversity analysis would consider the possible implications for conceptualizing and measuring health quality from the perspectives of women and men in diverse social, economic, geographic and political locations (Health Canada). A gender-based diversity analysis recognizes not only that there are differences between women and men, but that women do not constitute a homogeneous group and that significant differences may exist *among* women. Gender-based diversity analysis rests on an understanding of intersectionality (Weber and Parra-Medina), which considers the multiple, intertwined and mutually constructed social processes underlying social experiences. For example, intersectionality recognizes that gender, race, sexuality, and social class, among other things, are not simply characteristics of individuals; rather, they are products of social systems and are continuously constructed through the actions of social actors. Accordingly, in this view, change emanates not only from individuals; it also requires systemic adjustments.

Current measurement practices

Quality assessments in health care tend to adopt either a universalist approach or a localized approach. The universalist approach, most evident in purchaser assessments of quality, standardizes health care experiences and thereby strips them of their context. In contrast, the localized approach, apparent in provider (e.g., doctors, nurses) and patient accounts of quality, focuses on particular (i.e., "local") experiences of key participants in the health care system but generally does not account for the structural conditions in which those participants are situated. Consequently, these accounts are localized but decontextualized. The discussion that follows focuses on the universalist approach, as it figures prominently in current large-scale health care reforms (the localized approach is discussed elsewhere; see Jackson 2004).

Who measures quality?

Universalist health care quality assessments, embodied in such reports as those issuing from the Standing Senate Committee on the State of the Health Care System in Canada (Kirby) and the Royal Commission on the Future of Health Care in Canada (Romanow), foreground the voices of insurers, regulators, and large-scale purchasers.[1] In such documents, quality may be *defined* broadly, including patients', providers' and population-level perspectives, but it is frequently *measured* in much narrower terms. For example, the Romanow Commission recommends that the proposed Health Council of Canada "establish a national framework for measuring and assessing the quality of Canada's health care system, comparing the outcomes with other OECD countries" (Romanow 150). However, the Organization for Economic Co-operation and Development (OECD) measurement strategies emphasize narrow outcome measures such as morbidity and mortality rates. They do so in part because international comparison is very difficult when not all participating countries collect the same kinds of information or have the resources to do so. Morbidity and mortality statistics tell us little about the social conditions of health, illness, or care and they tell us nothing about the gendered experience of well-being or caregiving. Comparison with other OECD countries, therefore, is no standard to set for quality measurement if it does not inspire us to generate more nuanced and systemic analyses of the performance of our health care system.

What is measured?

Conventional quality assessments typically measure three elements of health care: structure, process, and outcome (Donabedian; also see Campbell, Roland, and Buetow; Hogston). "Structure" frequently refers to "attributes of the settings in which care occurs"—this *could* be understood quite broadly to include, for example, social determinants of health such as racism or heterosexism, but universalist quality assessments primarily operationalize "structure" as material resources, human resources, and organizational arrangements. "Process" refers to what is actually done in giving and receiving care. This may include both practitioners' and patients' activities, and may measure both technical aspects of care (i.e., the appropriate and skilful application medical interventions) and interpersonal aspects of care (i.e., humane and compassionate treatment) (Donabedian). "Outcome" refers to the effects of care on the health status of patients and populations. Here, "health" is defined in predominantly biomedical terms, excluding other, non-medical aspects of well-being. Universalist quality assessments typically focus on narrowly defined "structure" and "outcome" measures.

What is *not* measured? When "structure" is understood simply as material and human resources and organizational arrangements in institutional settings, the social and political conditions in which health care takes place are not accounted for. But even this limited view of structure is not judged to be terribly important to health care quality: structural characteristics are viewed as "a rather blunt instrument in quality assessment" (Donabedian 1746). Minimizing the importance of structural components undermines the impact they have on more vulnerable participants in the health care system, including workers and patients, most of whom are women (Adams and Bond), and undermines the extent to which quality assessment will effect systemic change rather than sustain the status quo.

How is evidence on quality produced?

In the universalist approach to quality assessment, quality is typically defined in terms of cost containment and economic efficiency (Baker *et al.*; Brook, McGlynn and Cleary; Chassin; McGlynn). For example, while "accessibility" of health care is a key concern in the Kirby and Romanow reports, this concern is situated in a discourse of sustainability—and the sustainability of the health care system is in turn framed exclusively in financial terms. In this framework, quality is transformed into a resource to be managed, like monetary, capital or human resources, and efficiency is understood in fiscal terms and measured accordingly. Universalist quality assessments frequently rest on statistical data gleaned from administrative and billing records which reflect managerial concerns of cost efficiency; they tend to lack clinical details, information about structural conditions in which individuals provide and receive care, and information about interpersonal processes of care. Where interpersonal aspects of care *are* measured, those measurements tend to rely on standardized clinical guidelines. Such guidelines usually represent the perspectives and language of health care professionals, not patients, so while they do provide some information about clinical practice, they are poor sources of information about women's diverse experiences of receiving care. Clinical outcomes are frequently the sole outcome measures used, but these tend not to include patients' evaluations of care. And when patient satisfaction surveys are employed, they suffer from serious limitations (Hall and Dornan 1; van Teijlingen *et al.*), are rarely developed with gender issues in mind, do not contain questions specific to women's health care, are not systematically analyzed for gender differences, and are not reported separately for women and men (Weisman 19).

Universalist quality assessments standardize experience. "Standardized population health" status is often used as a crude outcome measure of quality, but tremendous diversity is smoothed over in the practice of aggregation (Grant; Jackson 2003; Kaufert). In population-level analysis aggregated data are presented as if they are applicable to "everyone" (Hayes 1994), obscuring particularity and creating the impression that the participants in the health care system, and the services they provide or receive, are interchangeable. But a standardized patient does not represent "everyone." The standard or "universal" patient (or provider) is removed from any historical and political context. For example, it is widely acknowledged that existing indicators for population health do not adequately reflect women's biological and social differences from men.[2] Despite these limitations, there remains an overwhelming urge to standardize health care experiences in quality assessments.

There are serious gaps between these universalist approaches to quality assessment and the experiences and expectations of women working in and receiving health care. To illustrate some of these gaps, we now turn to the health care experiences and expectations of lesbian/bisexual/queer women in two major Canadian cities.[3]

Structure and cost: What quality means to lesbian/bisexual/queer women

According to a focus group participant from a drop-in for lesbian/bisexual/transgendered young women:

> *Quality care is like a carton of eggs—if there is like one egg missing, it isn't a full carton, right? And then quality care is like—if you don't have—like, you have to have the trust, and respect, confidentiality, et ceteras, right? or you don't have the whole package…. You know, like you went to go buy a dozen eggs, you know, but you don't get it. It's kind of like quality care, you want the whole package but you can't have it and you just kind of feel like blah. You can't, like make your cake or something.*[4]

This account of quality in health care suggests a gap between lesbian/bisexual/queer women's experiences of care and how quality of care is frequently conceptualized and measured in current health care quality assessment frameworks. The elements of "trust, respect, [and] confidentiality" clearly point to interpersonal aspects of care, which are less frequently measured in universalist quality assessments than technical aspects or outcomes of care. These elements also point to structural conditions such as heterosexism, classism, racism, ableism, and other social relations of power that shape the interpersonal contexts in which women deliver and receive care. The accounts of lesbian/bisexual/queer participants in our study illustrate how heterosexism is a structural feature of the health care system, that is, a consistent element of the health care encounter that organizes and shapes the interactions between health care providers and those seeking their care. These participants also described how issues of sexual disclosure and psychological safety "cost" them in their encounters with health care providers. They challenged traditional notions of "cost" in economic terms with nuanced descriptions of the invisible emotional and interpersonal work generated by heterosexist assumptions in the health care system and among health care providers.

As we have noted above, "structure" is inadequately conceptualized and addressed in conventional quality assessments, neglecting the socio-political structures that shape health care. Heterosexism, which interacts with other systemic relations of power, is an important structural element that profoundly affects health care quality. Heterosexism "assumes that all people are heterosexual and incorporates mainstream attitudes that value heterosexuality more highly than other types of sexuality" (McNair). Research suggests that heterosexism limits lesbian and bisexual women's willingness to disclose their sexuality and other potentially important life issues to practitioners, possibly compromising the quality of the care they receive and their experiences of safety and trust. It can also lead to them avoiding care or being denied care (Coalition for Lesbian and Gay Rights in Ontario; McNair). One participant in our study described visiting an emergency room after she had been injured during sexual play with her partner, the result of which was significant vaginal bleeding:

> We go to the hospital, they tried to tell me I'm pregnant. I said "That's not possible." They' re convinced I've miscarriaged and maybe I've even tried an abortion. I had to, with haemorrhaging, go and find my doctor and get a note saying I was in a lesbian relationship, I am not pregnant, in order to access the facilities—and be accompanied by my gynaecologist who at that point met me at the hospital—and have to listen to everybody in the hallway going "Which one is fem? Which one is butch?" "I don't know." For hours. Now if that isn't affecting my health care....

Another participant who identifies as gender-queer and who works as a drag king spoke about how heterosexism and transphobia in mental health care made it difficult to get the help she needed:

> ... [O]nce you' re in there, uh, a lot of it are misconceptions about queer or whichever identified women can be very frustrating. It almost feels like it's not worth going in at all.... a lot of my friends are transsexuals or gender queer or just relatively open to that kind of thing. And so when [my therapist and I] were discussing incidents that had happened that upset me or I was having trouble dealing with ... she would make me, she' d be like, "okay, so when you say 'he,' that he is actually a woman?" And I' d be like, "No, no, no. That 'he' was born as a woman but is a man." ...I'm like okay, "So John and I were doing this." "So you mean John, the girl?" I'm like, "No, John the boy. So him and I did this." "But you mean she though? That's the she?" And you know, she'd force me to identify the bio, the biology of every single person that I mentioned, and it was just so incredibly frustrating and it just, it got us nowhere because from there on she knew that some of my friends couldn't fit into her perceptions.... And at one point I was just like "Okay, I'm sorry. No more. I'm going. Bye." Because it was just causing more problems than it was worth.

As this example demonstrates, for many women heterosexism combines with other systemic barriers to make access to appropriate, adequate health care particularly difficult. In the case that follows, heterosexism and combines with the complex experience of immigration and the acute lack of supportive resources for new Canadians to create substantial obstacles to appropriate health care. Consider the account of Jody and her partner Jean, who recently immigrated to Canada from China:

We haven't found a suitable family doctor. We tried two or three.... We tried to pick up some like Chinese, like ethnic, who can speak Chinese or Mandarin. Then, because doctor, we have to talk to them about a lot of private issues and a lot of, like in details. We hope, like, solve the language problem may be the primary issue. But then we tried a couple of them, not really that good. Well because, sexuality, we don't want the Chinese community to know too much about, you know, well because this is also close community sometimes. So and then we tried to find Caucasian. But then we couldn't find anybody.

Systemic heterosexism is responsible for creating substantial "invisible work" for lesbian/bisexual/queer women as they try to get health care for themselves and their families. Conventional assessments of health care system efficiency focus exclusively on expenditures related to machines, human resources and buildings and do not take into account other elements of "cost." But lesbian/bisexual/queer women must work hard to manage social interactions with health care workers and to negotiate the health care system, work that represents a significant cost to them and that must ultimately be calculated in the cost of care. For example, one participant talked about her neighbours, an elderly lesbian couple for whom she does occasional, unpaid care. The couple has been together for about 40 years; they are both housebound and require occasional hospitalization. She spoke about the work they all do to balance the need to feel safe, connected and informed in the context of a heterosexist system that does not readily acknowledge lesbian family relations:

And now when one of them goes into the hospital, the other one ... can't go to the hospital and visit or anything like that. So with respect to being a lesbian, they encounter the system I think in a very biased sense where no one would—they're listed as friends instead of being acknowledged as partners.... I've actually presented myself as the niece to one of them, um, which has worked very well because I can gain entry. And I thought to myself "Who's to say I'm not a niece?" You know, there are lots of people who are other people's aunts and there's no biological relationship. So she's my aunt. And this other woman's partner has said on the phone that she's the niece to get information about her partner. Do you know what I mean? So she's pretended to be me in order to gain access.

Invisible work to accommodate heterosexist assumptions is required in a variety of health care settings (not just hospitals and clinics). A participant who has a partner with schizophrenia talked about her experience of attending a support group for family members affected by the disease:

... [W]hen I got in I kind of assessed what was going on and I just felt like, hmm, no, this is not going to be a safe environment for me. I just don't, I'm

not going to be caring and sharing at this point.... They were very welcoming, but you know, just like anyone else. They made assumptions about who I was there for. And I just wasn't comfortable. Cause it just seemed like an extra layer of something that wasn't relevant, you know what I mean? It wasn't something that I needed to spend energy working on explaining.

Being able to build a relationship with a trusted health care provider can alleviate some of the invisible work created by uncertainty about how lesbian/bisexual/queer women's sexuality and family connections may/may not be understood or acknowledged. But finding and building a relationship with a health care provider is difficult in an environment of health care reform where efficiency (measured by money and time) is seen as the ultimate goal.

Lesbian/bisexual/queer women in our focus groups regarded "efficiency" as a synonym for "cutbacks" and argued that it leads to decreased access to health care providers, shorter visits, and a lack of continuity of care. In these conditions lesbian/bisexual/queer women do not have the opportunity to develop relations of trust with health care providers, which are crucial for them to feel safe to disclose their sexual orientation and related health care concerns (Solarz and Committee on Lesbian Health Research Priorities; Duncan *et al.*; Dobinson *et al.*; Coalition for Lesbian and Gay Rights in Ontario). For example, street-involved women talked about how it is important "to be known," and how being known is most likely when you have the same health care provider over time:

It's better if you have your doctor, your family doctor that you see every week that knows you, that knows what your problems, that knows how you are, what you like and what you don't like, and respects you. Cause you never know, you're gonna get a doctor that treats you like shit next time or who is not going to want to fucking deal with you or is not going to be too nice, you know what I mean?

And you've got to explain to a new doctor every time. I hate that.

Oh yeah, I hate that. You need to be able to trust your doctor...

Exactly.

...and you can't do that unless you know them, and you see them all the time.

Where it *is* possible to build a relationship with a trusted provider, the benefits are obvious. In one case, a participant's partner (Abby) and her partner's daughter (Kate) had a long history with a family physician:

[On a few occasions I had] to take Kate to the doctor and I keep saying there's sadly lacking a word if you' re not the biological mother but you' re a parent. There's no, like it's really easy for Abby to say "I'm Kate's mom." And I' d say "I'm her … I'm her, I made up some really crazy word. But so I always have to say "I'm one of Abby's parents." So I just said it that way…. The clinic, like I said, she had a history already with the clinic and it wasn't an issue. So we were actually quite fortunate.

The history and continuity of this relationship reduced the "cost" of negotiating the health care system for this participant, and in many ways made her encounter with the system "efficient" for all concerned.

Summary: "Quality is like a carton of eggs"

We have illustrated two ways in which the women in our focus groups challenged the discourse of conventional universalist quality assessments. What is missing in most quality assessments and the tools that are used to generate them are mechanisms to represent and systematically address women's diverse experiences, including how structural features of the health care system such as heterosexism reduce the quality of the health care experience, and what the health care system "costs" the women who use its services. Too often, the accounts of marginalized women are reduced to "preferences" or dismissed as the griping of "interest groups" rather than recognized as responses mediated by intersecting, persistent social systems such as class, race, gender, and sexuality. Given the limitations of the universalist approach to quality assessment, what might provide better evidence of quality?

We urge that quality assessments adopt a gender-based diversity approach (Jackson 2004). Quality must be understood both in the local context of women's diverse everyday experiences (as both users and providers in the health care system), and in the context of the systemic social relations of power in which those experiences are situated. Unlike a universalized approach to quality assessment, a gender-based diversity approach puts social relations of power at the centre of its analysis by measuring contextualized experiences, situated within the systemic social relations of heterosexism, racism, poverty, ableism, sexism, etc. Moreover, unlike a localized approach to health quality assessment, a gender-based diversity analysis offers such a systemic analysis and locates particular experiences of the health care system in a socio-historical and political context. These measurements give us an account of social relations in process, that is, how complex systems intersect and interact to create conditions in which quality is enhanced or compromised. Accordingly, they produce what feminist philosopher Lorraine Code calls "responsible knowledge" which is inclusive, situated, and has community/local accountability. A full, responsible account of quality in health care needs to acknowledge and address the "whole carton" of experiences, needs, and diversity, nested in complex, persistent social relations of power.

This paper is adapted from a presentation to the Third National Lesbian Health Conference, "Working Together to Create Healthy Lives," May 20-22, 2004 in Chicago.

This paper is jointly authored by members of the National Coordinating Group on Health Care Reform and Women and Dr. Nancy Guberman (Université du Québec à Montréal). Primary authors are listed first, followed by Dr. Pat Armstrong (NCGHCRW Chair) and remaining co-authors. Beth Jackson is Research Coordinator for the NCGHRCW; Ann Pederson is Policy and Research Manager for the British Columbia Centre of Excellence for Women's Health.

The National Coordinating Group on Health Care Reform and Women (hereafter, "the Coordinating Group") is a collaborative working group of the Canadian Centres of Excellence for Women's Health, the Canadian Women's Health Network, and Health Canada's Women's Health Bureau. The mandate of the Coordinating Group is to illuminate the impact of health care reforms on women and to inform health policy and practice with a gender-based analysis. The National Coordinating Group on Health Care Reform and Women, with Dr. Nancy Guberman (Université du Québec à Montréal), is currently conducting a study entitled "What Does Quality Health Care Mean to Women?" with support from the Social Sciences and Humanities Research Council and Health Canada, Women's Health Bureau.

Originally published in CWS/cf's Fall 2004 issue, "Women's Health and Well-Being" (Volume 24, Number 1): 15-22.

[1]While these reports may give a brief nod to diverse "consumer" or patient perspectives, they devote most of their attention to the concerns of the governments and organizations that finance and deliver health care. For example, Chapter Six of the Romanow Report, entitled *Improving Access, Ensuring Quality,* "ends with a recommendation that 'Governments, regional health authorities, and health care providers should continue their efforts to develop programs and services that recognize the different health care needs of men and women, visible minorities, people with disabilities, and new Canadians.' In a document that spans over 350 pages, this recommendation garners only a page and a half of commentary" (National Coordinating Group on Health Care Reform and Women 41).

[2]In a recent Health Policy Research Program initiative to develop health indicators that reflect gender and diversity, Health Canada noted, "Women and men experience health in different ways and also differ in how they perceive health and illness, set health priorities, utilize health care services and receive treatment. We lack comprehensive indicators to track these differences in a way that takes into account the context of women's and men's lives. Although many health indicators are sex-disaggregated (biological), they do not adequately capture gender (social) differences that would reflect the complexity of women's health experiences, concerns and needs and their roles

as both recipients and providers of care" (Applied Research and Analysis Directorate).

[3]The research team for the study "What does "quality health care" mean to women?" is located in British Columbia, Saskatchewan, Manitoba, Ontario, Quebec and Nova Scotia, and has conducted a total of 22 focus groups in these five provinces. Our aim has been to gather the stories of a wide range of women; accordingly, our participants have a broad range of characteristics: young women in BC and Ontario; women who are recent immigrants (six mos. to six yrs.) from Asia, Europe, the former USSR, and Haiti; ethnic Chinese women who are not recent immigrants; middle-aged, urban women; First Nations and Metis women; women in rural and "remote" areas; low-income women and their support workers; health care workers; "women of size" with chronic health problems; women with disabilities; university students; seniors; street-involved women with addictions; lesbian, bisexual, and queer women; injured workers; mothers with children in daycare.

We attempted to capture as much diversity of social location and experience as possible, however we acknowledge that some experiences are not represented here and that the absence of transsexual and transgender women's perspectives is a limitation in a study on gender and quality of health care. While each focus group may have attended to particular experiences and social locations of participants, these categories clearly intersect (e.g., there were health care workers and mothers and recent immigrant women in our lesbian/bisexual/queer focus groups; there were bisexual women in our street-involved focus group…). In this paper, we focus on how lesbian/bisexual/queer women define and experience "quality" health care.

[4]In our reporting of research participants' accounts, we have endeavoured to retain the vocabulary, syntax and cadence of their spoken words.

References

Adams, Ann, and Senga Bond. "Hospital Nurses' Job Satisfaction, Individual and Organizational Characteristics." *Journal of Advanced Nursing* 32 (3) (2000): 536-543.

Applied Research and Analysis Directorate, Health Canada. *Health Policy Research Program, Request for Letters of Intent for Secondary Research RFLOI 016 on Women's Health Indicators.* Health Canada, 2003. [cited Nov. 6 2003]. Available from http://www.hc-sc.gc.ca/iacb-dgiac/arad-draa/english/rmdd/rfp/rfp016.html.

Armstrong, Pat, Carol Amaratunga, Jocelyne Bernier, Karen Grant, Ann Pederson, and Kay Willson. Eds. *Exposing Privatization: Women and Health Care Reform in Canada, Health Care in Canada.* Aurora, Ontario: Garamond Press, 2002.

Baker, Richard, Carolyn Preston, Francine Cheater, and Hilary Hearnshaw. "Measuring Patients' Attitudes to Care Across the Primary/Secondary Interface: The Development of the Patient Career Diary." *Quality in*

Health Care 8 (1999):154-160.

Brook, Robert H., Elizabeth A. McGlynn and Paul D. Cleary. "Measuring Quality of Care–Part Two of Six." *New England Journal of Medicine* 335 (13) (1996): 966-970.

Campbell, S. M., M. O. Roland, and S. A. Buetow. "Defining Quality of Care." *Social Science and Medicine* 51 (2000): 1611-1625.

Chassin, Mark R. "Improving the Quality of Care–Part Three of Six." *New England Journal of Medicine* 335 (14) (1996): 1060-1063.

Coalition for Lesbian and Gay Rights in Ontario. *Systems Failure: A Report on the Experiences of Sexual Minorities in Ontario's Health Care and Social Services Systems.* Toronto: Coalition for Lesbian and Gay Rights in Ontario, 1997.

Code, Lorraine. *Rhetorical Spaces: Essays on Gendered Locations.* New York: Routledge, 1995.

Dobinson, Cheryl, Judy MacDonnell, Elaine Hampson, Jean Clipsham, and Kathy Chow. *Improving the Access and Quality of Public Health Services for Bisexuals.* Toronto: Ontario Public Health Association, 2003.

Donabedian, Avedis. "The Quality of Care. How Can It Be Assessed?" *Journal of the American Medical Association* 260 (12) (1988): 1743-1748.

Duncan, Kerrie, Jean Clipsham, Elaine Hampson, Carol Krieger, Judy MacDonnell, Dianne Roedding, Kathy Chow, and Donna Milne. *Improving the Access and Quality of Public Health Services for Lesbians and Gay Men.* Toronto: Ontario Public Health Association, 2000.

Grant, Karen R. "Gender-based Analysis: Beyond the Red Queen Syndrome." *Centres of Excellence for Women's Health Research Bulletin* 2 (3) (2002): 16-20.

Hall, J. A. and M. C. Dornan. "What Patients Like About Their Medical Care and How Often They Are Asked: A Meta-Analysis of the Satisfaction Literature." *Social Science and Medicine* 27 (9) (1988): 935-39.

Hayes, Michael V. "Evidence, Determinants of Health and Population Epidemiology: Humming the Tune, Learning the Lyrics." *The Determinants of Population Health: A Critical Assessment.* Eds. M. V. Hayes, L. T. Foster and H. D. Foster. Victoria, BC: University of Victoria, 1994. 121-133.

Health Canada. *Exploring Concepts of Gender and Health.* Ottawa: Women's Health Bureau, Health Canada, 2003.

Hogston, Richard. "Quality Nursing Care: A Qualitative Enquiry." *Journal of Advanced Nursing* 21 (1995): 116-124.

Jackson, Beth E. "Situating Epidemiology." *Advances in Gender Research.* Eds. M. Texler Segal, V. Demos and J. Kronenfeld. Kidlington, Oxford UK: Elsevier Ltd, 2003. 11-58.

Jackson, Beth E. *Gender (e)Quality? A Critical Review of Health Care Quality Assessment Frameworks.* Toronto, Unpublished manuscript, 2004.

Kaufert, Pat. "The Vanishing Woman: Gender and Population Health." *Sex, Gender and Health.* Eds. T. M. Pollard and S. B. Hyatt. Cambridge: Cambridge University Press, 1999. 118-136.

Kirby, Michael J. L. *The Health of Canadians: The Federal Role. Final Report on the state of the health care system in Canada. Volume Six: Recommendations for Reform.* Ottawa, ON: The Standing Senate Committee on Social Affairs, Science and Technology, 2002.

McGlynn, Elizabeth A. "Six Challenges in Measuring the Quality of Health Care." *Health Affairs* 16 (3) (May/June 1997): 7-21.

McNair, Ruth P. "Lesbian Health Inequalities: A Cultural Minority Issue for Health Professionals." *Medical Journal of Australia* 178 (12) (2003): 643-645.

National Coordinating Group on Health Care Reform and Women, with Olena Hankivsky, Beth Jackson and Marina Morrow. *Reading Romanow: The Implications of the Final Report of the Commission on the Future of Health Care in Canada for Women. Revised and updated edition.* Winnipeg, Canada: National Coordinating Group on Health Care Reform and Women, 2003.

Romanow, Roy J. *Building on Values: The Future of Health Care in Canada–Final Report.* Ottawa, ON: Commission on the Future of Health Care in Canada, 2002.

Solarz, A. L. (ed.), and Institute of Medicine. Committee on Lesbian Health Research Priorities. *Lesbian Health: Current Assessment and Directions for the Future.* Washington, D.C.: National Academy Press, 1999.

van Teijlingen, Edwin R., Vanora Hundley, Ann-Marie Rennie, Wendy Graham and Ann Fitzmaurice. "Maternity Satisfaction Studies and Their Limitations: "What Is, Must Still Be Best." *Birth* 30(2) (2003): 75-82.

Weber, Lynn and Deborah. Parra-Medina. "Intersectionality and Women's Health: Charting a Path to Eliminating Health Disparities." *Advances In Gender Research.* Eds. M. Texler Segal, V. Demos and J. Kronenfeld. Kidlington, Oxford UK: Elsevier Ltd., 2003. 181-230.

Weisman, Carol S. "Measuring Quality in Women's Health Care: Issues and Recent Developments." *Quality Management in Health Care* 8 (4) (2000): 14-20.

Racism, Sexism and Colonialism

The Impact on the Health of Aboriginal Women in Canada

Carrie Bourassa, Kim McKay-McNabb and Mary Hampton

Aboriginal women in Canada carry a disproportionate burden of poor health. Aboriginal women have lower life expectancy, elevated morbidity rates, and elevated suicide rates in comparison to non-Aboriginal women (Prairie Women's Health Centre of Excellence, 2004). Aboriginal women living on reserves have significantly higher rates of coronary heart disease, cancer, cerebrovascular disease and other chronic illnesses than non-Aboriginal Canadian women (Waldram, Herring, and Young, 2000). A significantly greater percentage of Aboriginal women living off-reserve, in all age groups, report fair or poor health compared to non-Aboriginal women; 41 per cent of Aboriginal women aged 55-64 reported fair or poor health, compared to 19 per cent of women in the same age group among the total Canadian population (Statistics Canada). In addition, chronic disease disparities are more pronounced for Aboriginal women than Aboriginal men. For example, diseases such as diabetes are more prevalent among Aboriginal women than either the general population or Aboriginal men (Statistics Canada).

Epidemiologists suggest that many of these chronic health conditions are a result of the forced acculturation imposed on Aboriginal peoples (Young 1994). Yet, for Aboriginal women, low income, low social status and exposure to violence also contribute to poor health. Aboriginal women face the highest poverty and violence rates in Canada. Joyce Green (2000) notes that in 1991 eight out of ten Aboriginal women reported victimization by physical, sexual, psychological, or ritual abuse; this rate is twice as high as that reported by non-Aboriginal women. These issues are evident in Saskatchewan where the Saskatchewan Women's Secretariat (1999) determined that at least 57 per cent of the women who used shelters in 1995 were of Aboriginal ancestry, yet they comprised only eleven per cent of the total female population. These numbers reflect the magnitude of the problem. Redressing these injustices requires awareness of the processes that create negative health consequences and mobilization of action to correct these processes. The Saskatchewan Women's Secretariat notes: "Studies have shown that health differences are reduced when economic and status differences between people, based on things such as culture, race, age, gender and disability are reduced" (44).

Gender and ethnicity have been shown to be influential determinants of health across populations. Conceptual distinctions between definitions of "gender" and "sex" have led to our understanding that the processes of sexism (such as increased exposure to violence) are more likely to contribute to women's poor health than biological or genetic differences between women and men. Similarly, conceptual distinctions between definitions of "ethnicity" and "race" in population health research suggests that "race" is used to describe natural units or populations that share distinct biological characteristics; whereas ethnic groups are seen as being culturally distinct (Polednak). In population health research, these two terms are used interchangeably, often leaving out a discussion of the processes by which racism creates conditions of poor health for certain ethnic groups (Young 1994). Racism is a biopsychosocial stressor that has severe negative health effects on racialized individuals (Clark, Anderson, Clark and Williams). Sexism is blatantly dangerous to women's health in many ways (Lips). Racism and sexism have this in common; they operate via external power structures to contribute to poor health in certain disadvantaged groups. Research suggests that culture and cultural differences also have an impact on health (Amaratunga; Wienert). However, little is written about how what we describe as culture can be the outcome of colonial processes. Cultural groups that have lived under colonization experience a legacy of oppression that adds another level of threat to their health. Indigenous Peoples as distinct cultural groups have been exposed to genocide to further the interests of colonization (Chrisjohn and Young; Tuhiwhai Smith). We will illustrate that this colonization and its contemporary manifestations in the policies and practices that affect Aboriginal women create unique threats to their health status. Our analysis will demonstrate that the process by which the definition of "Indian" is imposed by colonial legislation in Canada constitutes a form of multiple oppressions that differentially disempower Aboriginal women, conferring particular risks to their health.

Links between sexism, racism, colonialism and Aboriginal women's health

Sexism, racism, and colonialism are dynamic processes rather than static, measurable determinants of health; they began historically and continue to cumulatively and negatively impact health status of Aboriginal women. Colonialism depends on the oppression of one group by another, beginning with a process described as "othering" (Gerrard and Javed). The process of "othering" occurs when society sorts people into two categories: the reference group and the "other". Women who bear their "otherness" in more than one way suffer from multiple oppressions, leaving them more vulnerable to assaults on their well-being than if they suffered from one form of oppression. The cumulative effects have painful material, social and health consequences. We offer an example of the process of "othering" imposed on Aboriginal women through colonial legislation defining Indian identity between the years 1869-1985; these policies continue to influence women's health and well-being today. Using this example, we will deconstruct the process of colonialism and reveal its consequences for Aboriginal women and their health.

We describe ways in which the *Indian Act* differentially affects Aboriginal women and men in Canada; it is a case example of multiple oppressions. Colonial discourse has historically represented non-white populations as racially inferior. These assumptions have been used to justify social treatment of these populations that fosters inequality and social exclusion in all areas, ultimately contributing to poor health conditions in the oppressed group. Linda Tuhiwai Smith notes that racism, sexism, and colonialism (through the process of "othering") serve to describe, objectify and represent Indigenous women in ways that have left a legacy of marginalization within Indigenous societies as much as within the colonizing society. She points out that racist and sexist notions about the role of women were imposed upon Indigenous communities by white, European settlers with patriarchal consciousness. "Colonization," she notes, "is recognized as having had a destructive effect on Indigenous gender relations which reached out across all spheres of Indigenous society." Sexism, racism and colonialism have had a negative impact on Aboriginal women's identities, our sense of who we are, and where we belong. We argue that gender differences in the process of "othering" have forced Aboriginal women to challenge the racist, sexist, and colonial policies within and beyond our communities. We further suggest that accumulated disadvantage from past colonization and contemporary processes of ongoing colonization have a direct affect on Aboriginal women's access to social determinants of health and impedes their ability to develop a healthy sense of identity that can contribute to personal well-being.

Impact of Aboriginal identity on health and well-being

An insidious result of colonialism has been the externally imposed definition of Indian identity through processes that create cultural ambiguity for Aboriginal women (Mihesuah). Bonita Lawrence (1999) argues that although Euro-Canadian legislation has affected what she terms "native identity" across gender lines, it has had greater impact on Aboriginal women. Consequently, significant gaps exist between material, social and health outcomes for Aboriginal men and Aboriginal women. However, racist underpinnings of colonialism have also produced gaps *amongst and between* Aboriginal women themselves (Saskatchewan Women's Secretariat). For example, Métis women in Saskatchewan are more likely to be employed than status Indian women but less likely to be employed than non-Aboriginal women. Hence, sexism, racism and colonialism have converged to create a matrix of oppression that differentially affect specific Aboriginal groups and men and women within those groups.

Cultural identity evidently has implications for the status that women have in the external world and this has an impact on health. However, identity also has implications for feelings of self-worth and belonging, and this has an impact on health as well. A recent study conducted with Aboriginal women in Manitoba by the Prairie Women's Health Centre of Excellence found that Aboriginal women endorsed important links between health and wellness and their cultural identities. Cultural identities were inseparable from their family, history, community, place and spirituality and all of these elements were integrated into a broad and holistic understanding of health and well-being. The women acknowledged that many factors shaped their health and well-being including poverty, housing, violence and addictive behaviours, however, cultural identity served as a potential anchor to help them deal with these issues and promote health. Accordingly, they made recommendations for health practices that integrated holistic solutions that included "traditional cultural practices and understandings with respect to health and wellness" (24). This suggests that women who are Aboriginal can look to cultural identity as a foundation on which they can build healthy lives, however, for women who cannot draw on a firm sense of cultural identity, maintaining and promoting health could be more difficult. Unfortunately, there are large numbers of women who are in the latter position. It is through this removal of cultural identity and status within Aboriginal groups that Canadian legislation has produced a significant threat to the health and well-being of many Aboriginal women.

Colonization as an instrument of multiple oppressions for Aboriginal women in Canada: *Indian Act Legislation*

The *Indian Act*, passed in Canada in 1876, defined Indian identity and prescribed what "Indianness" meant. Because of the sexist specification inherent in this legislation, ramifications of the Indian Act were more severe for Aboriginal women than men, ramifications that continue to have severe impacts on our life chances today. Lawrence (2000) notes that the Act ordered how Aboriginal people were to think of all things "Indian" and created classifications that have become normalized as "cultural differences". She argues that the differences between Métis (or mixed ancestry people), non-status Indians, Inuit, and status Indians were created by the Act and those differences became accepted in Canada as being cultural in nature when, in fact, they were social constructions imposed by legislation. It should be acknowledged that cultural distinctions did and do exist within and amongst Aboriginal people; however, those cultural distinctions were never categorized nor embedded in legislation prior to 1876 and did not have the same impact until commencement of the Act. Indigenous scholars agree that the *Indian Act* has controlled Aboriginal identity by creating legal and non-legal categories that have consequences for rights and privileges both within and beyond Aboriginal communities (Lawrence 2000; Mihesuah).

One important consequence of the *Indian Act* is that status Indian women (hereafter referred to as Indian women) who married non-Indian men lost their Indian status and their band membership under this Act. Prior to 1869, the definition of Indian was fairly broad and generally referred to "all persons of Indian blood, their spouses and their descendents" (Voyageur 88) After 1869, Indian women who married non-Indians were banished from their communities since non-Indians were not allowed on reserves; this was true even if a divorce occurred (McIvor). From the government's perspective, these women had assimilated and had no use for their Indian status. The goal of assimilation was a central element of the *Indian Act 1876* because it would advance the government's policy of genocide through the process of enfranchisement: the removal of Indian status from an individual. Section 12(1)(b) of the *Act* specified that Indian women would lose their status if they married a non-Indian man. Further, Indian women could not own property, and once a woman left the reserve to marry she could not return to her reserve so she lost all property rights. This legacy of disenfranchisement was passed on to her children (Wotherspoon and Satzewich). In contrast, an Indian man who married a non-Indian woman not only retained his Indian status, but the non-Indian woman would gain status under the *Act*, as would their children. Even upon divorce or the death of her husband, a non-Indian woman who gained status under the *Act* through marriage retained her status and band membership as did her children (Voyageur). Only the identity of Indian women was defined by their husband and could be taken away. The imposition of this Euro-centric, sexist ideology on Aboriginal families was a direct disruption of traditional Aboriginal definitions of family. Under *Indian Act* legislation, enfranchised Indians were to become Canadian citizens and, as a result, they relinquished their collective ties to their Indian communities (Lawrence 1999). However, Indian women were not granted the benefit of full Canadian citizenship. Lawrence notes that until 1884, Indian women who had lost their status could not inherit any portion of their husband's land or assets after his death. After 1884, widows were allowed to inherit one-third of their husband's land(s) and assets if "a widow was living with her husband at his time of death and was determined by the Indian Agent to be 'of good moral character'" (Lawrence 1999: 56). Furthermore, if a woman married an Indian from another reserve, the *Act* stated that she must follow her husband and relinquish her band membership in order to become a member of his band. If her husband died or if she divorced him, she could not return to her reserve, as she was no longer a member. These policies governing marriage and divorce were just one of several ways that Aboriginal women were stripped of their rights and privileges. For example, from 1876 to 1951 women who married Indian men and remained on the reserve were denied the right to vote in band elections, to hold elected office or to participate in public meetings. However, Indian men were eligible to take place in all of these activities (Voyageur). Therefore, colonization was an instrument by which sexism and racism were created and reinforced on and off reserve lands, converging in diminishing power and resources available to Aboriginal women in Canada.

Passage of The *Charter of Rights and Freedoms* made gender discrimination illegal and opened the door for Aboriginal women to challenge the Indian Act.

In 1967, Aboriginal women lobbied both the federal government and Indian bands for amendment to the *Act*. Sharon McIvor notes that in *Lavell v. Her Majesty (1974)* Aboriginal women challenged the government based on the argument that the government had been discriminating against Indian women for over 100 years via the *Indian Act*. The Supreme Court of Canada, however, ruled that since Canada had jurisdiction over Indians it could decide who was an Indian and that the *Act* was not discriminatory. Continual lobbying by Aboriginal women finally resulted in action and the *Act* was amended in 1985 through passage of *Bill C-31*.

However, despite the amendment, long-standing implications of the *Indian Act* for Aboriginal women in Canada are still evident. As Lawrence notes, the government's "social engineering process" (1999: 58) via the *Act* ensured that between 1876 and 1985 over 25,000 women lost their status and were forced to leave their communities. All of their descendants lost status and were "permanently alienated from Native culture, the scale of cultural genocide caused by gender discrimination becomes massive" (Lawrence 1999: 59). She notes that when *Bill C-31* was passed in 1985, there were only 350,000 female and male status Indians left in Canada. *Bill C-31* allowed individuals who had lost status and their children to apply for reinstatement. Approximately 100,000 individuals had regained status by 1995, but many individuals were unable to regain status. Under *Bill C-31*, grandchildren and great-grandchildren were not recognized as having Indian status and, in many cases, no longer identified as Indian (Lawrence 1999; Voyageur). In addition, legislative decision still blocked Aboriginal women from full participation in their communities. For example, the *Corbiere Decision in 1999 (John Corbiere et al. v. the Batchewana Indian Band and Her Majesty the Queen)* specified that Indian women living off-reserve could not vote in band elections because the *Indian Act* stated that Indian members must "ordinarily live on reserve" in order to vote. Thus, reinstated Indian women and their children were still at a disadvantage despite having legal recognition under the *Act*.[1]

In the end, the amendments did not repair the damage of previous legislation. Kinship ties, cultural ties and participation in governance were significantly disrupted. Long term consequences for these women and their children would include the erosion of connections and rights that may have enabled them to work collectively to address social disparities.

It is ironic that the only recourse Aboriginal women have is to appeal to the federal government and judicial system—the same government and system that instituted and upheld the sexist, discriminatory and oppressive legislation for over 100 years. This government holds different principles of justice than traditional Aboriginal government, leaving women once again vulnerable to multiple oppressions. As Jan Langford writes, "If First Nations governments are built on the traditional Aboriginal way of governing where equity is built into the system, there wouldn't be a need for the 'white' ways of protecting rights" (35). However, band governing bodies are not working according to the traditional Aboriginal way, instead using legislation to exclude women and protect male privilege.

After fighting for the recognition of Aboriginal rights, Aboriginal women have found themselves at odds with some of their own community leaders. Indian women and their children have not been welcomed back to their communities. Since the 1980s, when the federal government began the process of devolution of control to Indian bands, band governments have been able to refuse band membership. It should be noted that there has been an influx of status Indians going to their bands to seek membership. However, the government has consistently refused to increase funding to those bands. Cora Voyageur notes that some bands have not given band membership to people given status by the federal government because they do not have the resources or the land base to do so. Most reserves are already overcrowded, and many feel that conditions will worsen if a rush of reinstated Indians want to return to the reserve. Some reinstated Indians are referred to as "C-31s," "paper Indians" or "new Indians" (Voyageur). In addition, many of these individuals may have previously been identifying with Métis or non-status Indian communities and were rejected not only by their Indian communities but also by the communities with which they had identified. As Lawrence (1999) reports that resistance to acknowledging the renewed status of those reinstated under Bill C-31 has been expressed throughout the Native press.

Furthermore, women have been formally excluded from constitutional negotiations as a result of patriarchal legislation that was applied in the federal government's decision to exclude them. The Native Women's Association of Canada (NWAC) has argued that the interests of individual Aboriginal women should not be overshadowed by collective social values and operational mandates that may be enshrined in customary law (Jackson 2000). However, Aboriginal women find themselves caught between bands who appeal to traditional practices to avoid action and a federal government that avoids involvement in deference to self-government (Green 2001).[2] In this way, government intrusion has succeeded in ensuring that divisions among Aboriginal people are maintained, if not more firmly entrenched.

Finally, as Lawrence (1999) argues, "Who am I?" and "Where do I belong?" are common questions among what she calls "people of mixed-race Native heritage." She examines the impact of the *Indian Act* and *Bill C-31* on Métis people in addition to Indian people and argues that the *Act* has externalised mixed-race Native people from Indianness and that this has implications for Native empowerment. What this discussion reveals is that other Aboriginal peoples have also been affected by these policies and this has likely had consequences for identity, empowerment, and quality of life of all Canada's indigenous peoples..

Implications for the health of Aboriginal women in Canada

A review of the post-contact history of indigenous peoples in Canada clearly demonstrates that direct practices of genocide have transformed into legislated control of Aboriginal identity and colonization-based economic, social and political disadvantage that disproportionately affects Aboriginal women. The government's definition of who can be called Indian, who cannot and who must exist in liminal spaces where they are outsiders both on and off reserve lands clearly has implications for citizenship, but it also has implications for access to health services and ability to maintain health and well-being. With this knowledge, we must re-examine data that suggests Aboriginal women are excessively vulnerable to cerebrovascular disease, coronary heart disease, diabetes, suicide cancer, depression, substance use, HIV/AIDS and violence/abuse in light of how colonization and post-colonial processes have conferred risks to the health of Aboriginal women, and barriers to accessing quality health care. It is these risks and barriers that contribute to rates of morbidity and mortality that are well above those of the average Canadian woman.

At a fundamental level, we understand that the colonization processes that began many years ago and continue today have material and social consequences that diminish access to social determinants of health for both Aboriginal men and Aboriginal women. Yet, as we have discussed, women have been especially marginalized through these processes and their lower social status is reflected in diminished resources and poor health. Health consequences for women have been identified, but largely within a western model of equating health with the absence of disease or illness (Newbold). The wounds that result from the cultural ambiguity imposed on Aboriginal women are harder to catalogue. They are perhaps demonstrated to us in the plight of the Aboriginal women of Vancouver's Downtown Eastside. This neighbourhood is home to thousands of Aboriginal women who have been displaced from their reserve communities and extended families (Benoit, Carroll and Chaudhry). They are socially and culturally isolated, living in poverty, and often driven to substance use, violent relationships and the street sex trade to survive and provide for their children (Benoit et al.). Their material circumstances force acts of desperation, but the damage that has been done to their cultural identities can leave them without the foundation to cultivate health and well-being in their lives. Recent initiatives that have arisen out of results from the First Nations and Inuit Regional Health Survey (National Steering Committee) may offer some hope for these women, but they are still disadvantaged in benefiting from them. First, the development of culturally-appropriate services will not be useful for women who have been excluded from the definition of that culture and excluded from the decision-making structures that will determine how Aboriginal health resources are to be designed and distributed (Benoit et al.; Grace). Second, the research that serves as the foundation of these initiatives has not included many Aboriginal women, both because women and children have been overlooked in the work (Young 2003), and because women who do not fit into research-defined categories of "Indian" (derived from Federal categories) have not been included in the data collections.

Conclusions

In conclusion, we reiterate the fact that in Canada, Aboriginal women have faced destruction in our communities, in our families as a result of multiple oppressions. Articulating the process by which the Indian Act differentially marginalizes Indian women is important for our empowerment. Devon Mihesuah notes that there has never been a "monolithic essential Indian woman ... nor has there ever been a unitary world view among tribes" (37) She argues that this never created problems for people until after colonization and resulting genocide of Indian peoples (Chrisjohn and Young). Prior to the sexist specification of the *Indian Act* Aboriginal women were matriarchal in their families. Families thrived with their Aboriginal women's strength and support. Today, Aboriginal women suffer from poorer health than non-Aboriginal women in Canada; they suffer from more chronic diseases than Aboriginal men.

Our goal in writing this paper was to clarify our understanding of the externally-imposed oppressions facing Aboriginal women: to know where to focus our fight and our healing and to show the impact on the health of Aboriginal women. This paper has not examined the impact on Métis women specifically, but they too face similar challenges as a result of colonial policies. Today we find ourselves at peace with our identities, but vigilant against the ever-present social constructions of our identities. We can see the implications this has on our well-being and the well-being of our children. As long as we buy in to the arbitrary, patriarchal, sexist, racist, socially constructed labels, we will continue to struggle not only as individuals but also as families and communities.

Originally published in CWS/cf's Fall 2004 issue, "Women's Health and Well-Being" (Volume 24, Number 1): 23-29.

[1]The *Indian Act* has had and continues to have implications for Aboriginal women in terms of identity. With the passage of *Bill C-31*, new divisions among Indian people were created. The bill limits the ability of women and their children to pass on their status beyond one generation. That is, grandchildren and great-grandchildren are generally not eligible to apply for status. In addition, while status can no longer be lost or gained through marriage, there are new restrictions on the ability to pass status on to children (Lawrence 1999). For example, the bill divides Indian people into categories by using subsections of the *Act*. A 6(1) Indian is defined as an Indian who had status in 1985. A 6(2) Indian is defined as a re-instated Indian under the *Act*. If a 6(1) Indian marries a non-status Indian (including a Métis) then any resulting child from that union will be considered a 6(2) Indian. If that 6(2) Indian child grows up and has a relationship with a non-status Indian the resulting child is a non-status Indian. Thus, once again, status can be eliminated in two generations and grandchildren and great-grandchildren are excluded. It should

be pointed out that if a 6(1) has a relationship with a 6(2), the resulting child is a 6(1) Indian. Furthermore, if a 6(2) has a relationship with a 6(2) the resulting child is a 6(1). The message is, if you don't marry back into your race, you risk losing status for your children or grandchildren. Although assimilation policy was supposedly abandoned in 1973 (announced by the Minister of Indian Affairs, Jean Chretien), long-term effects of the *Indian Act* and *Bill C-31* still promotes assimilation. The federal government effectively controls the definition of "Indianness," but communities, families and individuals live with the consequences and the confusion that arise from that control (Lawrence 1999).

[2]McIvor points out that these violations of civic and political rights of Aboriginal women are violations of their "existing Aboriginal and treaty rights" (35). She argues that the *Sparrow* decision (*Sparrow v. The Queen 1990*) was a landmark Supreme Court ruling that upheld the notion of existing Aboriginal and treaty rights and that this forms part of the inherent right to self-government protected under s. 35 of the *Constitution Act, 1982*. She maintains that self-government is central to Aboriginal nationhood, culture, and existence and, if it is central to the existence of Aboriginal nations, then the ability to determine civil and political rights of members must also be central. This right to self-government thus includes the right of women to define their roles in Aboriginal communities. She states:

> The right of women to establish and maintain their civic and political role has existed since time immemorial. These rights are part of customary laws of Aboriginal people and part of the right of self-government ... they [rights] are those which women have exercised since the formation of their indigenous societies. In some cases, these rights were suppressed or regulated by non-Aboriginal law, such as the *Indian Act*. (35)

References

Amaratunga, C. (2002). *Race, Ethnicity, and Women's Health*. Nova Scotia: Atlantic Centre of Excellence for Women's Health, 2002.

Benoit, C., D. Carroll and M. Chaudhry "In Search of a Healing Place: Aboriginal Women in Vancouver's Downtwon Eastside." *Social Science and Medicine* 56(2003): 821-833.

Chrisjohn, R. D. and S. L. Young. *The Circle Game: Shadows and Substance in the Indian Residential School Experience in Canada*. Penticton, BC: TheytusBooks Ltd., 1997.

Clark, R., N. B. Anderson, V. Clark and D. R. Williams. "Racism as a Stressor for African Americans: A Biopsychosocial Model." *American Psychologist* 54 (10) (1999): 805-816.

Gerrard, N. and N. Javed. (1998). "The Psychology of Women." *Feminist Issues: Race, Class, and Sexuality, 2nd ed.* Ed. N. Mandell. Scarborough,

ON: Prentice Hall Allyn and Bacon Canada, 1998. 103-131.

Grace, Sherryl L. "A Review of Aboriginal Women's Physical and Mental Health Status in Ontario." *Canadian Journal of Public Health* 94 (3) (2003): 173-175.

Green J. A. "Canaries in the Mines of Citizenship: Indian Women in Canada." *Canadian Journal of Political Science/Revue Canadienne de Science Politique* 34 (4) (2001): 715-738.

Green, J. A. (2000). "Constitutionalizing the Patriarchy." *Expressions in Canadian Native Studies*. Eds. R. F. Laliberte, P. Settee, J. B. Waldram, R. Innes, B. Macdougall, L. McBain and F. L. Barron. Saskatoon: University of Saskatchewan Extension Press. 328-354.

Jackson, Margaret. (2000) "Aboriginal Women and Self-Government." *Expressions in Canadian Native Studies*. Eds. R. F. Laliberte, P. Settee, J. B. Waldram, R. Innes, B. Macdougall, L. McBain and F. L. Barron. Saskatoon: University of Saskatchewan Extension Press. 355-373.

Lawrence, B. *"Real" Indians and Others*. Unpublished Ph.D. Dissertation. Toronto: UMI Dissertation Services, 1999.

Lawrence, B. "Mixed-Race Urban Native People: Surviving a Legacy of Policies of Genocide." *Expressions in Canadian Native Studies*. Eds. R. F. Laliberte, P. Settee, J. B. Waldram, R. Innes, B. Macdougall, L. McBain and F. L. Barron. Saskatoon: University of Saskatchewan Extension Press, Pgs. 69-94.

Langford, Jan. (1995) "First Nations Women: Leaders in Community Development." *Canadian Woman Studies*, Vol. 14, No. 4, pgs. 34-36.

Lips, H. M. *A New Psychology of Women: Gender, Culture and Ethnicity*, 2nd ed. Toronto: McGraw Hill, 2003.

McIvor, S. D. "Aboriginal Women's Rights as Existing Rights." *Canadian Woman Studie/les cahiers de al femme* 14 (4) (1995): 34-38.

Mihesuah, D. A. Ed. *Natives and Academics: Researching and Writing About American Indians*. Lincoln: University of Nebraska Press, 1998.

National Steering Committee. *First Nations and Inuit Regional Health Survey: Final Report*. Akwesasne Mohawk Territory, 1999.

Newbold, K. B. Problems in search of solutions: Health and Canadian Aboriginals. *Journal of Community Health* 23 (1) (1998): 59-73.

Prairie Women's Health Centre of Excellence. Living Well: Aboriginal Women, Cultural Identity and Wellness – A Manitoba Community Project. Winnipeg: Prairie Women's Health Centre of Excellence, 2004.

Polednak, A. P. *Racial and Ethnic Differences in Disease*. New York: Oxford University Press, 1989.

Razack, S. *Race, Space and the Law: Unmapping a White Settler Society*. Toronto: Between the Lines, 2002.

Saskatchewan Women's Secretariat. *Profile of Aboriginal Women in Saskatchewan*. Regina: Saskatchewan Women's Secretariat, 1999.

Statistics Canada. *Aboriginal Peoples Survey 2001: Well-Being of the Non-Reserve Aboriginal Population*. Ottawa: Cat. no. 89-589-XIE, 2001

Tuhiwai Smith, Linda. *Decolonizing Methodologies: Research and Indigenous Peoples*. New York: Zed Books Ltd., 2002.

Voyageur, C. "Contemporary Aboriginal Women in Canada." *Visions of the Heart: Canadian Aboriginal Issues*. Eds. David Long and Olive P. Dickason. Toronto: Harcourt Canada, 2000.

Wienert, D. *Preventing and Controlling Cancer in North America: A Cross-Cultural Perspective*. Westport, CN.: Praeger, 1999.

Waldram, J. B., D. A. Herring, and T. K. Young. *Aboriginal Health in Canada: Historical, Cultural, and Epidemiological Perspectives*. Toronto: University of Toronto Press, 2000.

Wotherspoon, T. and Satzewich, V. *First Nations: Race, Class and Gender Relations*. Regina: Canadian Plains Research Centre, 2000.

Young, I. M. *Inclusion and Democracy*. Oxford: Oxford University Press, 2000.

Young, T. K. "Review of Research on Aboriginal Populations in Canada: Relevance to their Health Needs." *British Medical Journal* 327 (2003): 419-422.

Young, T. K. *The Health of Native Americans: Toward a Biocultural Epidemiology*. New York: Oxford University Press, 1994.

Rural Women's Health Issues in Canada

An Overview and Implications for Policy and Research

Beverly D. Leipert ━

A review of the literature on rural health in Canada reveals that research about rural women's health is a relatively new area of scholarship. Nevertheless, the limited data reveal that within the rural Canadian context, physical, mental, and social health issues challenge women's ability to attain and maintain their health. Health policy in Canada has only recently begun to address rural health issues; health policy that specifically addresses rural women's issues is virtually nonexistent. This article summarizes key rural women's health issues and recent relevant initiatives, and suggests future directions for policy and research to advance rural women's health.

The rural Canadian context

A commonly agreed-upon definition of "rural" does not exist in Canada. The various definitions that are proposed emphasize diverse criteria, such as population size, density, labour market, or settlement context (Office of Rural Health). Although characteristics of the rural context and rural people differ for each definition, some similar themes and conclusions are evident. Approximately 95 per cent of Canada's land mass is rural, and about 30 per cent of Canada's population (about nine million people) and about 20 per cent of women live in rural settings (Kirby and LeBreton; Sutherns, McPhedran, and Haworth-Brockman). Rural settings across Canada are diverse, ranging from coastal regions on the eastern and western boundaries, prairie and agrarian regions centrally, and northern areas that are characterized by forests, lakes, and subarctic conditions. Rural Canada includes small towns, as well as rural and remote settings where few or no people live. Low population density and issues related to isolation and limited access to resources increase the further one moves from urban centers and from the forty-ninth parallel of latitude (Romanow). Rural areas also have higher unemployment levels and lower educational levels compared to the rest of the country (Kirby and LeBreton). In many small communities, young people of working age often leave to look for better opportunities, while seniors leave in search of better health care. Consequently, older individuals, children, and youth under 20 years are over-represented in rural areas (Kirby and LeBreton). In addition, more than half of Aboriginal peoples live in rural and remote Canada (Kirby and LeBreton).

The health status of people who live in rural communities, especially people in northern communities, is poorer than the rest of the Canadian population (Romanow). The life expectancy for rural people is less than the Canadian average, and disability rates, infant mortality rates, and deaths from cancer and circulatory diseases are higher in rural areas (Romanow). Indeed,

> the health of a community appears to be inversely related to the remoteness of its location ... there is ... a progressive deterioration in health as one moves from ... urban centers into the remote hinterland areas. (Romanow 162)

Rural health needs stem from a variety of sources, including occupations such as farming and mining, demographic trends such as increased seniors' populations in some rural areas, and needs associated with the large number of rural Aboriginal peoples (Kirby and LeBreton). Limitations in resources that support health, such as secure jobs and affordable food, and community attitudes and expectations can also compromise health (Leipert 2002; Report of the Northern and Rural Health Task Force). Addressing these diverse issues requires a concerted and sustained effort on the part of many sectors of society, including government and the private sector. However, rural health needs are difficult to address when limited numbers of health care personnel exist in rural Canada, and where sparse populations and challenging weather and terrain compromise health care delivery. Recruiting and retaining health care professionals is challenging in rural and remote areas, and this is further compromised by present health care personnel shortages (Rennie, Baird-Crooks, Remus, and Engel; Romanow). The financial and social costs for rural residents to travel to access care and resources elsewhere are often prohibitive and further compromise residents' ability to address health issues.

Limited research exists about rural women's health in Canada (Sutherns, McPhedran, and Haworth-Brockman). Although some knowledge is available regarding the health of Aboriginal women and farm women, research regarding the health of rural women who do not live on farms, who are from diverse cultural backgrounds, and who experience disability is more limited. In addition, more information is needed about the health of both young and elderly rural women and of women with lifestyles that do not conform to the predominant heterosexual couple-oriented rural lifestyle, such as lesbian women and women who are single, divorced, or widowed.

Nevertheless, the limited knowledge about rural women's health in Canada does reveal some common themes. For example, rural women often have difficulty accessing health care that is respectful, that includes them as equal partners, that focuses on health promotion, and that is provided by female health care providers, who are often preferred by rural women (Leipert and Reutter 2005; Sutherns, McPhedran, and Haworth-Brockman). Even if resources exist, distance and lack of transportation compromise or preclude access. In addition, rural women often carry double, triple, or quadruple workloads as they engage in commitments to family, farm, community, and employment, and this leaves little time and energy for women to attend to their own health needs (Kubik and Moore 2003a; Prairie Women's Health Centre of Excellence). As a result, rural women experience a variety of physical, mental, and social health issues that may not be as prevalent or not exist in urban counterparts.

Rural women's physical health issues

Rural women have a higher risk of dying from motor vehicle accidents, poisoning, suicide, diabetes, and cancer (Sutherns, McPhedran, and Haworth-Brockman). For rural women who live on farms, it is important to note that the agriculture industry has become Canada's most dangerous industry, with farmers being five times more likely to be killed and at risk for more disabling injuries compared to workers in other industries (Kubik and Moore 2003b). Farm machinery is designed for the male physique. When women use this type of machinery, it is usually intermittently and infrequently, such as during seeding or harvesting. These women are at risk, as they are less physically able to operate machinery and less knowledgeable about and familiar with farm equipment operation. In addition, increased use of agricultural chemicals and the tendency to focus on the safety of male farmers in the handling of these products increase women's exposure to and risks from farm chemicals (Argue, Stirling, and Diaz; McDuffie. By focusing on the health of farm men with little or no attention to the health of farm women, these women may not realize that their unprotected handling of chemically saturated clothing may pose hazards to their health. As a result, farm women may have increased risks of breast cancer, non-Hodgkin's lymphoma, and other chemically-related health effects (McDuffie).

Rural women are also at risk of physical violence and abuse (Hornosty and Doherty). Isolation, patriarchal attitudes that objectify and devalue women, and the presence of a "gun culture" where owning and using weapons are condoned and where access to weapons is enhanced, contribute to violence in the lives of rural women (Fishwick; Goeckerman, Hamberger, and Barber). Lack of access to health care providers who are sensitive to violence issues, limited or no resources such as counselors and shelters, early marriage, higher fertility rates, and lower education and employment in rural areas also contribute to rural women experiencing violence and being less able to address or get free from violent relationships (Hornosty and Doherty; Leipert 1999; Leipert and Reutter 2005).

Other physical health issues relate to risks of hunger, malnutrition, and homelessness (Ryan-Nicholls). These risks are a result of the immense stresses and strains that rural communities are undergoing and the limited understanding of and support for rural communities (Blake and Nurse; Diaz, Jaffe, and

Stirling). In many parts of rural Canada, especially on the prairies and in maritime communities, annual family incomes are some of the lowest in the country (Amaratunga 2000a; Diaz, Jaffe, and Stirling). Limited government commitment to and support for rural communities, coupled with depleted natural resources and a global economy, contribute to lower annual incomes and limited employment, housing, and other options in rural communities. Consequently, rural residents have fewer job opportunities and lower incomes which result in limited ability to access adequate food, clothing, and housing, and compromised quality of life. Fewer options for affordable housing and the high cost of food in rural and remote communities further contribute to hunger and nutrition problems and to housing that may be unstable, inadequate, or too expensive.

Women's physical health is also affected by limited access to appropriate and timely health care (Leipert and Reutter 2005; Prairie Women's Health Centre of Excellence; Sutherns, McPhedran, and Haworth-Brockman). For example, studies have shown that women in Canada do poorly if they must travel long distances to give birth. In Saskatchewan, a largely rural province, the 1993 closure of 53 rural hospitals was followed by an increase in its perinatal mortality rate (Kirby and LeBreton). Rural women experience not only limited diagnostic and treatment services, but also compromised or non-existent health promotion, illness and injury prevention, and rehabilitation resources. Some of these resources and services are delivered by care providers who parachute briefly into rural communities from elsewhere, or by telehealth technology that is used to overcome geographic distances in the provision of health care. Nevertheless, problems exist with these types of band-aid solutions. Telehealth requires adequate technology and training and effective integration into existing health delivery systems (Pong). Both telehealth and visiting providers must pay attention to communication, contexts, attitudes, and relationships with people in order to be effective. For example, if rural residents do not feel confident that visiting health care providers or telehealth advice is sensitive to their issues and contexts, they will not use these alternate service delivery systems (Leipert and Reutter 2005; Pong).

Other factors also affect women's access to the limited health care that exists in rural communities. Rural community dynamics, which are influenced by religious and conservative beliefs and values, affect rural women's access to confidential care such as birth control and abortion information (Leipert 2002). Limited and expensive transportation, physical obstacles and low incomes for women with disabilities, and language barriers for immigrant rural women and women with sensory impairment also pose challenges for care in rural communities (Prairie Women's Health Centre of Excellence; Sutherns, McPhedran, and Haworth-Brockman). Aboriginal women require care that avoids invalidating encounters such as disrespect, stereotyping, marginalization, and disregard for personal circumstances (Browne and Fiske; Leipert 2002). More appropriate are affirming encounters that encourage them as respected participants in health care, affirm personal and cultural identity, and that assist in the development of a positive, long-term relationship with the health care provider (Browne and Fiske).

Another factor that affects rural women's access is that health care in rural settings is often provided by male physicians or physicians from other countries (Kirby and LeBreton). Care that is provided by male physicians may be problematic in that the values and priorities of male physicians may influence the practice of public health nurses and female physicians in ways that are not conducive to the health of rural women (Leipert 1999). For example, male physicians in rural settings have discouraged female physicians and public health nurses from providing PAP smear services, even though some rural women will not attend a male physician for these services (Leipert 1999). In addition, male physicians have been identified as having the most negative response to women's declaration of lesbianism (Trippet and Bain) and to women's desires to be fully informed and empowered participants in health care decisions (Leipert 2002). Rural women have also noted that physicians from other countries may not be aware of or agree with Canadian women's roles and expectations regarding their care, and that this lack of cultural sensitivity on the part of physicians compromises their care (Leipert 2002; Prairie Women's Health Centre of Excellence). If only male physicians or foreign physicians are available to provide care in rural areas and women do not have the means to travel elsewhere, their access to health care may not only be compromised, it may be completely blocked. Thus, even if health care providers exist in a community, their attitudes and values can compromise women's access to health care. Rural women's access to health care can be enhanced by female public health nurses, physicians, and other care providers, as women often feel more comfortable addressing sensitive topics with another woman and they perceive that female care providers accord more respect, time, and care to women (Leipert 2002; Sutherns, McPhedran, and Haworth-Brockman).

Mental health issues

Mental health issues are as significant for rural women as physical health issues (National Rural Women's Health Conference). Despair, depression, and psychological distress are becoming increasingly common for women in rural settings in Canada (Kubik and Moore 2003b; Leipert and Reutter 2005; Sutherns, McPhedran, and Haworth-Brockman). Vast distances and sparse or declining populations compromise access to social support that helps women address isolation and loneliness (Leipert 2002). Lack of public recognition, undervaluing of women and women's work in rural settings, social exclusion, and stresses placed on resource-based economies also contribute to women's mental health issues (Amaratungam 2000b; Kubik and Moore 2003b). Women may feel invisible, underappreciated, and vulnerable in such situations. To address these feelings and economic circumstances, women may decide to take on additional responsibilities both inside and outside of the home. For example, many farm women supplement the family income through off-farm employment or increased efforts in on-farm labour (Kubik and Moore 2003a). By adding these responsibilities to their multiple family and community roles and commitments, rural women may overextend themselves and compromise their mental health in the process.

Rural expectations and community dynamics, norms, and values can also contribute to mental health issues. Rural expectations associated with hardiness and self-reliance can perpetuate the stigma that is often attached to mental illness and inhibit access to help (Leipert 2002). Rural community dynamics may include blaming and the use of minimizing language to normalize unhealthy behaviours and attitudes that contribute to mental health issues (Hornosty and Doherty). For example, women may be blamed for partners' abusive behaviours or these behaviours may be viewed as normal within a marriage relationship. In addition, rural community norms and values may signal to a woman that a "failed" relationship is her fault, and that divorce is unacceptable because it will contribute to the breakup of the family farm and jeopardize economic viability. These rural expectations, dynamics, norms, and values contribute to women's reluctance to access relationship and other mental health services, perpetuate unrealistic expectations of women, and contribute to women's acceptance of community norms and their reluctance to challenge norms that are unhealthy for women.

The nature and location of mental health services in rural communities also create health issues for women. Rural women often do not have access to a range of health-promoting resources such as alternative health care and culturally appropriate care in their communities (Browne and Fiske; Leipert 2002). Because of the stigma attached to mental health issues and the lack of anonymity that exists in small communities, mental health services that are provided in stand alone or other publicly visible ways are less or not accessible to rural women (Leipert and Reutter 2005; Sutherns, McPhedran, Haworth-Brockman). Indeed, this type of service provision may serve to further jeopardize the health of women if, for example, community members and abusive partners become aware of women's use of these services.

Social support and rural women's health

One of the main ways that women in isolated settings stay healthy is through social support (Amaratunga 2000b; Leipert and Reutter 2005). Social resources help women obtain practical, emotional, and affirmational support (House and Kahn 1985). In rural settings, informal social support from friends and family may be preferred to the formal support available from health care and other professionals. Social support helps rural women learn the how, where, when, and why of local actions and beliefs; address isolation and other challenges of rural life; and affirms women's knowledge and abilities (Leipert, 2002). By facilitating the sharing of advice, goods, and assistance, social support can also help counter the poverty that many rural women endure.

Social support is particularly important in Canada to counter the isolation that can often result from vast geography and extreme weather.

Social health issues are especially significant for particular subgroups of rural women. Elderly women may experience feelings of diminished self-worth if they do not have the social support necessary to help them maintain independence, self-competence, and mastery (Chafey, Sullivan, and Shannon). In addition, elderly women's social support needs and strengths may be misunderstood and neglected in rural areas where physical labour and the work of men are privileged (Prairie Women's Health Centre of Excellence). Rural lesbian women may experience limited social support or outright hostility and social exclusion (Isaac, Anderson, Healey, Herringer, and Perry). Disabled women may find that limitations in employment and transportation in rural communities challenge their ability to connect with others. Being a member of a minority group can create social health issues for women in rural communities that favour cultural homogeneity or that have limited cultural sensitivity (Browne and Fiske).

Social support helps rural women develop and sustain resilience in the face of hardships by assisting them in developing hardiness, confidence, and the ability to carry on; in making the best of resources and opportunities; and in advocating for change (Leipert 2002; Leipert and Reutter 2005). However, social support—and thus women's health—can be compromised by issues related to sparse populations, weather, distance, values, and resources in rural settings. Sparse populations limit the number and nature of the people and resources that are available to provide formal and informal support. For example, sparse populations may result in inadequate home care services in a rural community which, in turn, results in rural women taking up additional care responsibilities, thereby affecting women's time, energy, and other resources available for social support for themselves and others (Forbes and Janzen). The rural climate and geography affect if, when, and how often women can get together with others. Values in rural communities also affect the nature, purpose, and frequency of contact for social support. For example, women in a rural community may be encouraged to get together for quilting bees or child care purposes, but discouraged from meeting for less traditional reasons (Leipert 2002; Leipert and Reutter 2005) such as for Take Back the Night events and feminist reading groups.

Factors and consequences of the rural context for women's health

Rural women's physical, mental, and social health issues result from a number of contextual and personal factors. For all women in rural Canada, health issues arise due to limited access to health promotion, illness and injury prevention, diagnostic, treatment, and rehabilitative health care services. In addition, rural women often do not have access to alternative health care resources or to care that is respectful of their gender, culture, experiences, or perspectives (Leipert 2002; Sutherns, McPhedran, and Haworth-Brockman). Women who are more isolated, have more limited options, and who have less power to make change and address health issues tend to have greater health risks and less ability to deal with risks (Leipert 2002). In addition, personal factors such as age, health status, and financial resources affect rural women's experience of health issues. Rural older women, women with health problems, and women with inadequate financial resources have greater needs but fewer resources to address needs, which increases their vulnerability and risks. Thus, although all rural women are exposed to vulnerability and health issues, some women are in greater peril.

As a result of personal and contextual factors, rural women experience the health-related consequences of not being able to access a diverse range of appropriate services and resources to promote and sustain their health, having to postpone access to health care, or foregoing health care altogether. As a result of these consequences, rural women are likely to experience a greater number of and more severe health-related issues, live with adverse health issues longer before addressing them, and have less ability to recover from or address health-related issues.

Discussion

Rural health and rural women's health are relatively new areas of focus at the national level in Canada. In 2002, two federal government-initiated reports focused on the health of Canadians: Michael Kirby's and Marjory LeBreton's *The Health Of Canadians—The Federal Role*, and Roy Romanow's *Building On Values: The Future Of Health Care In Canada*. Each report devoted one chapter to a discussion of rural health. Both chapters explore the nature of the rural context and issues facing rural and remote communities and make recommendations to improve the health of rural residents.

Although these reports present information that is relevant to rural health in general, rural women's health is not significantly addressed. For example, recommendations from the reports focus on enhancing the numbers of health care professionals, especially physicians, in rural and remote communities, and on treatment, diagnostic and drug services. Other services and approaches that rural women require and which they are often denied or compromised in acquiring, such as respectful inclusive care, health promotion and illness, disease, and injury prevention services, and services provided by nurses, midwives, counselors, and women's health centers, receive little attention in these documents. In addition, recommendations that address the social determinants that are so important for the health of rural women are virtually nonexistent. For example, the effects of and ways to address rural sociocultural values and behaviours, rural poverty, and rural education to enhance women's health require greater emphasis in these documents. More knowledge is needed about the strengths of rural women and about how they cope and "make things work" in rural settings. This knowledge can help rural people and rural communities realize, include, and build on local capacities. In order to advance the health of women in rural Canada, it is important to remember that health is much more than the absence of illness. National reports must take a broader more inclusive perspective on the health of rural people if they are to be effective in advancing rural women's health.

In September 2003, a report prepared by the Canadian Institute for Health Information (CIHI) was released that focused on the health of Canadian women. *The Women's Health Surveillance Report* (CIHI) summarizes important information about women's health, such as gender differences and disparities in the distribution of determinants of health, health behaviours, health outcomes, and health care utilization. The report also examines health issues of vulnerable subgroups of women such as younger and older women and women with disabilities, and addresses several social and physical health issues for women across the nation. In spite of its importance, the report is limited in its explication of information about health issues of rural and remote women. Essentially, the report discusses rural women's health in terms of mortality rates, physical violence, and sexual assault in comparison with urban counterparts. Importantly, the report identifies a gap in knowledge in health information about women who live in rural and remote Canada, and notes that this gap limits policy development to address rural and remote women's health issues. General recommendations are made to enhance knowledge about rural and remote women's health.

In June 2004, the Prairie Centre of Excellence for Women's Health released a report that focused exclusively on the health of rural and remote women in Canada (Sutherns, McPhedran, and Haworth-Brockman). This report, the first to focus on rural and remote women on a national scale, summarizes much of the extant literature about rural and remote women in Canada and combines this knowledge with research conducted with rural women throughout the country to propose a policy framework and research agenda for rural and remote women's health. The report is valuable on a number of levels. For the first time, rural and remote women's health in Canada is comprehensively addressed in one document. The literature review is an important resource as it thematically summarizes the state of knowledge in many sectors, including peer-reviewed academic publications, government documents, community-based research, and conference presentations. By its highly consultative approach, employing focus groups across the country, the report also honours the knowledge, experience, and perspectives of rural and remote women throughout Canada. Research and policy recommendations in the document effectively address the realities and health issues of rural women's lives. Eleven priorities for research are proposed:

- Any aspect of rural women's health that addresses the importance of place, culture, and gender
- Creative models of rural health service
- Impacts of isolation on health
- Importance of cultural values for health

- Factors influencing the impact of rurality on health
- Moving from information to action
- Health issues across the life course
- Health issues relating to specific rural populations
- Getting beyond reports of satisfaction
- Rural definitions and depictions, and
- Rural occupational health and safety.

Three policy priorities are recommended: 1) Factor gender, place, and culture into all health policy; 2) Define health policy as more than health care services; and 3) Improve health by improving access to information, health care services, appropriate care, and decision-making.

These policy and research recommendations point to many fruitful areas of inquiry and application. They will help broaden women's health research and practice to include all of the determinants of women's health (Health Canada), not just those that focus on women's biomedical or reproductive functions. In addition, these policy and research recommendations will ensure inclusivity and diversity, which will result in relevant and meaningful information about rural women's health issues and ways to advance rural women's health. Finally, rural women's empowerment, through the promotion of voice, access, and power, will be fostered if these research and policy recommendations are enacted.

In addition to these important documentary initiatives, in 2003 the Ontario Women's Health Council, which is a branch of the Province of Ontario Ministry of Health, and the University of Western Ontario dedicated two million dollars for the creation of a Chair in Rural Women's Health Research. This Chair position, which is located at the University of Western Ontario, is the first and only academic research position in North America to focus on rural women's health. Objectives of the position include: 1) Expand the focus of rural women's health research beyond biomedical interests, 2) Develop and support leading research in rural women's health, 3) Facilitate rural women's health in curriculum development across disciplines, 4) Raise the profile of rural women's health research, and 5) Give rural women a voice in research. To advance these objectives, the Chair has engaged in a number of initiatives, including the establishment of multidisciplinary funding awards for graduate student research in rural women's health. All of the Chair initiatives are developed for the purpose of advancing knowledge about rural women's health. In addition, having a named Chair position in Rural Women's Health Research helps to insert rural women's health into the agenda of international, national, and local research, policy, practice, and community organizations, thereby assisting in the transfer of knowledge from theory to the real-life advancement of rural women. The creation of other Chair positions in rural women's health in other locations across the country would serve to further advance knowledge and policy and the health of rural women.

Conclusion

Women in rural settings in Canada experience diverse physical, mental, and social health issues. However, knowledge about these issues remains sparse. Recent reports, further research, and the creation of the first Chair in Rural Women's Health Research will help to address this knowledge deficit. However, it remains to be seen whether the political will exists to address issues and recommendations that arise from these initiatives (Nagarajan). The minimal attention accorded to rural women's health in the past indicates that substantial support for rural women's health is both timely and critical. Rural women are waiting.

I thank Dr. Angeline Bushy, Professor and Bert Fish Chair in Community Health Nursing, University of Central Florida, for her generous sharing of insights regarding the health of women in rural settings. Dr. Bushy's comments enriched the development of this paper.

Originally published in CWS/cf's Summer/Fall 2005 issue, "Women's Health and Well-Being" (Volume 24, Number 4): 109-116.

References

Amaratunga, C. Ed. *A Portrait of Women's Health in Atlantic Canada.* Halifax: Maritime Center of Excellence for Women's Health, 2000a.

Amaratunga, C. Ed. *Inclusion: Will Our Social and Economic Strategies Take Us There?* Halifax: Maritime Center of Excellence for Women's Health, 2000b.

Argue, G., B Stirling, and P. Diaz. "Agricultural Chemicals And Agri-Business." *Farm Communities at the Crossroads: Challenge and Resistance.* Eds. H. Diaz, J. Jaffe, and R. Stirling. Regina, SK: Saskatchewan Institute of Public Policy, University of Regina, 2003. 207-222.

Blake, R., and A. Nurse, Ed. *The Trajectories of Rural Life: New Perspectives on Rural Canada.* Regina, SK: Saskatchewan Institute of Public Policy, University of Regina, 2003.

Browne, A., and J Fiske. "First Nations Women's Encounters with Mainstream Health Care Services." *Western Journal of Nursing Research* 23 (2) (2001): 126-147.

Canadian Institute for Health Information (CIHI). *Women's Health Surveillance Report: a Multidimensional Look at the Health of Canadian Women.* Ottawa: Canadian Institute for Health Information, 2003.

Chafey, K., T Sullivan, and A Shannon. "Self-Reliance: Characterization of Their Own Autonomy by Elderly Rural Women." *Conceptual Basis for Rural Nursing.* Ed. H. Lee. New York: Springer, 1998. 156-177

Diaz, H., J. Jaffe, and R. Stirling, Ed. *Farm Communities at the Crossroads: Challenge and Resistance.* Regina, SK: Saskatchewan Institute of Public

Policy, University of Regina, 2003.

Fishwick, N. "Nursing Care of Rural Battered Women." *AWHONN's Clinical Issues in Perinatal and Women's Health Nursing* 4 (3) (1993): 441-448.

Forbes, D., and B. Janzen, "Comparison of Rural and Urban Users and Non-Users of Home Care in Canada." *Canadian Journal of Rural Medicine* 9 (2004): 227-235.

Goeckermann, C., L. Hamberger, and K. Barber. "Issues of Domestic Violence Unique to Rural Areas." *Wisconsin Medical Journal* 93 (1994): 473-479.

Health Canada. *Towards a Common Understanding: Clarifying the Core Concepts of Population Health.* Ottawa: Health Canada, 1996.

Hornosty, J., and D. Doherty. "Responding to Wife Abuse in Farm and Rural Communities: Searching for Solutions That Work." *The Trajectories of Rural Life: New Perspectives on Rural Canada.* Eds. R. Blake and A. Nurse. Regina, SK: Saskatchewan Institute of Public Policy, University of Regina, 2003. 37-53.

House, J., and R. Kahn. "Measures And Concepts Of Social Support." *Social Support and Health.* Eds. S. Cohen and S. Syme. Orlando, FL: Academic Press, 1985. 83-108.

Isaac, B., L. Anderson, T. Healy, B. Herringer, and T. Perry. *Out in the Cold: The Context of Lesbian Health in Northern British Columbia.* Prince George, BC: British Columbia Center of Excellence for Women's Health, 1999.

Kirby, M., and M. LeBreton, *The Health of Canadians—the Federal Role.* Ottawa: The Standing Senate Committee on Social Affairs, Science and Technology, Parliament of Canada, 2002.

Kubik, W., and R. Moore. "Changing Roles of Saskatchewan Farm Women: Qualitative and Quantitative Perspectives." *The Trajectories of Rural Life: New Perspectives on Rural Canada.* Eds. R. Blake and A. Nurse. Regina, SK: Saskatchewan Institute of Public Policy, University of Regina, 2003a. 25-36.

Kubik, W., and R. Moore. "Farming in Saskatchewan in the 1990s: Stress and Coping." *Farm Communities at the Crossroads: Challenge and Resistance.* Eds. H. Diaz, J. Jaffe, and R. Stirling. Regina, SK: Saskatchewan Institute of Public Policy, University of Regina, 2003b. 119-133.

Leipert, B. "Women's Health and the Practice of Public Health Nurses in Northern British Columbia." *Public Health Nursing* 16 (1999): 280-289.

Leipert, B. *Developing Resilience: How Women Maintain Their Health in Northern Geographically Isolated Settings.* Dissertation, University of Alberta, 2002.

Leipert, B., and L. Reutter. "Women's Health and Community Health Nursing Practice in Geographically Isolated Settings: a Canadian Perspective." *Health Care for Women International* 19 (1998): 575-588.

Leipert, B., and L. Reutter. "Developing Resilience: How Women Maintain Their Health in Northern Geographically Isolated Settings. *Qualitative Health Research* 15 (2005): 49-65.

McDuffie, H. "Women at Work: Agriculture and Pesticides." *Journal of*

Occupational Medicine 36 (1994): 1240-1246.

Nagarajan, K. "Rural and Remote Community Health Care in Canada: Beyond the Kirby Panel Report, the Romanow Report, and the Federal Budget of 2003." *Canadian Journal of Rural Medicine* 9 (2004): 245-251.

National Rural Women's Health Conference. Hershey, Pennsylvania, October 2004.

Office of Rural Health. *Definitions of Rural Summary.* Ottawa: Health Canada, 2002.

Pong, R. *Rural Health/Telehealth.* Ottawa: Health Canada, 2002.

Prairie Women's Health Centre of Excellence. *Action Plan for Women's Health in Manitoba and Saskatchewan: Key Priorities and Strategies.* Winnipeg: Prairie Women's Health Centre of Excellence, 2001.

Rennie, D., K. Baird-Crooks, G. Remus, G, and J. Engel. "Rural Nursing in Canada." *Orientation to Nursing in the Rural Community.* Ed. A. Bushy. London: Sage, 2000. 217-231.

Report of the Northern and Rural Health Task Force. Victoria, BC: Ministry of Health and Ministry Responsible for Seniors, 1995.

Romanow, R. *Building on Values: the Future of Health Care in Canada.* Ottawa: The Romanow Commission Report, 2002.

Ryan-Nicholls, K. "Health and Sustainability of Rural Communities." *Rural and Remote Health* 4 (2004). Online: http://rrh.deakin.edu.au. Accessed April 2, 2004.

Sutherns, R., M. McPhedran, and M. Haworth-Brockman,. *Rural, Remote, and Northern Women's Health: Policy and Research Directions.* Winnipeg: Prairie Centre of Excellence for Women's Health, 2004.

Trippet, S., and J. Bain. "Physical Health Problems and Concerns of Lesbians." *Women and Health* 20 (2) (1993): 59-70.

Life Interrupted

Reproductive Damage from Chemical Pollutants

Cynthia L. Cooper and Margie Kelly ──

Harm to human health, and especially to women's reproductive health, is moving up quickly on the scale of environmental concerns. This develop-ment, based on a growing understanding of the harm from small amounts of pollutants, reverberates with fundamental values of women's lives, human rights, and also may become a galvanizing issue for environmental activists.

In 1992, *Agenda 21*, the blueprint for global environmental action created for the United Nations Earth Summit in Rio, paid only passing attention to the damaging effects of chemical contamination on human health, including reproductive health. Instead, it emphasized the need to manage risks to the environment associated with chemical use. Nations were urged to "strengthen international risk assessment" of chemicals and "pro-duce guidelines for acceptable levels of exposure" for a greater number of toxic chemicals (UN 1992).

Ten years later at the Johannesburg Summit, priorities shifted. This time, the document developed by conference participants focused less on risk assessment and more on people's health, setting goals for 2020 "to use and produce chemicals in ways that do not lead to significant adverse effects on human health and the environment" (UN 2002).

What happened during that decade to raise alarm about toxic chemical pollution as a major threat to human health and sustainability of the planet? In short, environmental scientists showed that dangerous chemical contami-nation is interfering with human reproduction. Extensive chemical usage threatens the ability of women and men to bear children and to raise healthy children (Colburn, Dumanoski and Meyers).

Procreation is a fundamental human right, and is among the most momentous rights and life activities of women and men. Interference with that right through the involuntary exposure to chemicals threatens basic assump-tions about human existence and sustainability.

Recognizing that environmental contamination by toxic chemicals is compromising the ability to reproduce, women's reproductive rights advocates and environmentalists are establishing new alliances to confront the growing threat to the right to bear children and to bear healthy children.

The problem: Hormone disruption and reproduction

In January, 2003, the U.S. government released startling results from the largest survey of its citizens' body burden of environmental chemicals. The Centers for Disease Control (CDC) studied toxic chemicals in the bodies of ordinary people in the U.S. and found a wide array of toxic chemical contaminants and hormone disrupters (CDC 2003a).

Confirming the results of an earlier, smaller analysis issued by the CDC in 2001, the report explained that every single person studied bore measurable levels of pesticide products. Mercury, a toxin, was found in women of childbearing age, along with disturbing amounts of the plasticizers and phthalates, which are associated with developmental damage in animals and found in products such as cosmetics, perfume, and car interiors. Yet, the study analyzed only 116 of over 70,000 synthetic chemicals in commercial use (CDC 2003b). And no one knows the consequences to human health of combining a chemical potpourri of toxins.

The CDC study comes in the wake of new attention to the hormone-disrupting properties of chemicals. Hormone disrupters are human-made substances that interfere with the body's hormone system, upon which healthy reproduction depends (Thornton 2000). Hormones also affect human growth, development, and intelligence. The list of synthetic chemicals that cause hormone disruption is long: dioxin, PCBs (now banned but still bioaccumulated in the environment), phthalates, organochlorines, mercury, and pesticides. These chemicals can be found in food, water, building materials such as vinyl pipes and flooring, and household products, ranging from tuna to drinking water, from soft plastic bath toys to plastic food wrap, from nail polish to carpeting (Colburn et al.; Schettler, Solomon, Valenti and Huddle).

So drenched is the environment with these chemicals—air, water, and soil—that, according to Joe Thornton, author of *Pandora's Poison*, all persons (and animals) on the planet have now absorbed some chemicals into their systems, and normal bodily systems cannot break them down (Thornton 2002). They are literally inescapable. Neither social status nor geographic location nor personal precaution will fully protect a person from exposure to these contaminants (Thornton, McCalley and Houlihan).

Environmental scientists are discovering that even at very low levels of exposure, hormone disrupters can cause infertility, low sperm count, birth defects, second generation childbearing problems, early puberty, and a host of other serious medical conditions and diseases (Ford; Schettler et al.; Colborn; deFur and Raffensperger). Among the first scientists to propose the connection between environmental contamination and breast cancer were Devra Lee Davis and Mary Wolff (Davis et al.; Wolff et al.). Previously, analyses of environmental harms focused on cancer and diseases caused by major exposures; new studies look at the long-term degradation of human and animal life from minor exposures (Colborn; Steingraber; Thornton, Pandora's Poison).

The conclusion: reproduction suffers.

Minuscule amounts of chemicals may act as hormone disrupters, and the harm may be discovered only years later to children born of unsuspecting parents. It is known, for example, offspring of rodents exposed to phthalates, a very common element in consumer products, experience reduced sperm counts and altered sexual characteristics (Myers). Low levels of exposure of laboratory animals in utero to another compound, bisphenol-A, a chemical used in polycarbonate plastic, causes a lowering of the age of puberty of offspring (Myers).

Even though there is universal exposure to this potentially devastating and untested cauldron of chemicals, they are absorbed involuntarily. No one agrees to participate in a grand experiment with synthetic chemicals, or even knows that she is participating. Exposure to and bodily absorption of these chemical contaminants are not done willingly, voluntarily or by consent of those affected.

A reproductive rights approach to environmental contamination

Reproductive rights inherently encompass the right to choose to bear children, as well as the right to decline childbearing. Advocacy organizations have outlined the rights of childbearing women as including healthcare prior to pregnancy and childbirth, a healthy delivery, postnatal care, and informed consent in decisionmaking ("The Rights of Childbearing Women"). Some have called for "freedom from reproductive hazards" within the environment, workplace and home (Kolbert 306).

Existing laws and documents on reproductive rights have not yet grappled with the specific issues raised by environmental factors that cause harm to reproduction. But rights articulated both internationally and in the U.S. provide an important framework for reproductive freedoms, including the right to bear children.

International human rights

International human rights documents recognize the right to bear children and the responsibility of governments to provide enabling conditions to do so in safety, according to Laura Katzive, an international lawyer with the Center for Reproductive Rights in New York. The Universal Declaration of Human Rights, a primary international human rights document, adopted by the nations of the world in 1948, explicitly identifies the basic human right of every man and woman to "found a family" (Art. 16.1).

The Declaration further states that all people are entitled to live in a "social and international order in which their rights can be realized" (Art. 28). This affirmative right, says Katzive, can be seen as extending the obligations of governments beyond merely refraining from interfering with the right to bear children to an active duty to ensure that healthy conditions exist in which all people can exercise the right.

In addition to elaborating on the right to attain the highest standards of sexual and reproductive health, language in international documents also emphasizes "safe motherhood," a term used to underscore the importance of the right to bear children under healthy conditions (Center for Reproductive Rights). The definition of

> safe motherhood includes the reduction of pregnancy-related deaths and ill-health in infants, as well as the alleviation and elimination of environmental health hazards that affect the ability to bear children. (World Health Organization qtd. in Boland 23-24)

When applied to the problem of hormone-disrupting chemicals, the concept of "safe motherhood" serves to highlight the rights of women and men to bear children in a healthy, enabling environment.

Country laws: The United States as an example

As far back as 1942, the U.S. Supreme Court stated that the right to bear a child is a central liberty—"one of the basic civil rights of man," the Court wrote in *Skinner v. Oklahoma*. Any action by the government that would impinge on the right to bear children must meet the strictest standards of scrutiny, the Court said.

The right to bear children is part of a zone of privacy, which includes the right to use contraception and the right to make decisions about abortion. The U.S. Supreme Court acknowledged these as an integral part of the U.S. Constitution. The right to privacy protects citizens from governmental intrusion in decisions to bear children, just as it protects citizens from governmental intrusion in decisions not to bear children.

Although the U.S. Supreme Court has recognized that the right to bear children is "fundamental" (*Carey v. Population Services International*) hormone-disrupting chemicals pose a somewhat different challenge in the law. The production of the potentially-damaging chemicals is largely undertaken by corporations and, as such, does not generally involve an action by the government which can give rise to constitutional scrutiny under the scheme of law in the U.S. system. But it is legitimate to inquire whether the government has taken sufficient steps to prevent women and men from serious reproductive harm or abrogation of the right to privacy, and to insist that corporations have a legal and moral obligation to prevent harm to the fundamental right to bear children.

Taken together, international doctrines provide valuable guidance for framing a pro-choice position on the rights of women and men who desire to procreate. They appropriately place the emphasis on the adult right to reproduce and to bear healthy children. The reproductive rights and women's rights movements worldwide have been in the forefront on these topics.

DES: Consequences of hormone disruption for women's reproduction

The problems associated with DES (diethylstilbestrol), a chemical compound prescribed to pregnant women in the 1950s and 1960s to prevent miscarriage, has a terrifying connection to the litany of adverse effects on reproduction from hormone disrupters, as shown in wildlife populations. DES, while a pharmaceutical, had hormone-disrupting properties, and the experience and study of it provides much information and alarm about environmental hazards. In the case of DES, many of the daughters of the women who took that drug were unable to bear children, and are at higher risk of developing breast cancer due to in utero exposure to hormone disrupters (Palmer et al.). Scientists studying hormone disruption report similar incidences of sterility and deformed genitalia in the offspring of fish and birds exposed to synthetic chemicals (Colborn et al.; Schettler et al.). The same mechanism of hormone disruption is at work, and the results are alarming prognosticators for women facing harmful chemical exposures.

When Valerie DeFillipo, a senior director at Planned Parenthood Federation of America in Washington, DC, attended a conference on environmental contamination and hormone disruption, she saw the links. DeFillipo said she began to understand how what is put into the environment enters your body and affects reproduction, and realized its importance to the reproductive rights community in the future (see, also, Cooper). And a solid alliance between environmentalists and reproductive rights advocates could change the hearts and minds of policymakers, said Patricia Waak, former director of the National Audubon Society's Population and Habitat Program.

A precautionary approach to chemicals

Among environmental scientists, there is a growing consensus that supports a shift in the way chemicals are released into the environment. They believe that it is no longer appropriate to assume that a chemical is safe and then later to ban it or limit its usage when it is proves to cause severe damage. A "dirty dozen" of especially persistent chemicals have been targeted for complete elimination in an international treaty of 127 nations, known as the Persistent Organic Pollutants (or POPs) treaty (Reuters). But these chemicals have already caused significant harm to human health and the environment. Instead of permitting the release of chemicals, whose harm may not be known for years or decades, environmental scientists are recommending that the "precautionary principle" should be implemented. According to the precautionary principle, chemicals would be tested prior to their release, and only upon receiving completely clean results would they be released. Scientists also encourage searches for safe alternatives to existing chemicals that cause harm (Thornton 2002, 2000; Myers).

Sweden is the first nation in the world to adopt fully the precautionary principle, calling for the introduction of new goods free of hormone-disrupting chemicals and for the phase-out of harmful human-made chemicals (Swedish Government).

Conclusion: A critical opportunity to work together for environmental sustainability, better health, and greater reproductive freedom

Contamination from chemicals, without the knowledge or consent of the individuals who absorb them, unquestionably violates reproductive rights. Reproductive rights clearly include the fundamental right of women and men to have children if they so desire, and to have children whose health is not irrevocably compromised by environmental contaminants.

The effects of hormone disrupters concern people from varied backgrounds, diverse economic strata, and all geographic locations. Men as well as women are threatened by the harms caused by hormone disrupters. Reproductive rights advocates and environmentalists are natural allies, as are those in the growing environmental health movement, such as activists concerned about the environmental causes of breast, ovarian and prostate cancer.

Environmentally-conscious women's organizations and reproductive rights activists could bring new support and political clout to securing solutions to prevent future chemical contamination of the earth.

This collaboration also could be a powerful antidote to the efforts of the anti-choice movement to weaken reproductive rights by promoting "fetal rights," giving a fetus rights that are independent of, and in some cases superior to, those of the pregnant woman and virtually eliminating her rights. In the area of hormone disrupters, pro-choice thinkers can preempt any anti-choice assertions that focus on endangerment to the right-to-life of the fetus, rather than on the rights of the pregnant woman. Toxic chemicals do their harm by destroying an adult's ability to bear healthy children, and their children's ability to lead healthy lives, including healthy reproductive lives. The anti-choice arguments are neither appropriate nor necessary.

At this early stage of the debate, the opportunity exists to head off a dangerous dynamic by avoiding the model that blames and punishes mothers for their behavior during pregnancy. Individual women should not be blamed for the damage their children suffer from toxic pollutants in their food and water (Brody).

In addition, although the "common ground" with anti-choice groups is, indeed, slender in most areas, reproductive rights organizations can take the lead in challenging them to stand up against environmental toxins that affect the well-being of all persons desiring to become parents. For example, several Catholic healthcare organizations that are generally opposed to abortion and contraception have become leaders in demanding substitutes for medical products, such as mercury and plastic tubing, that damage the environment and may interfere with reproduction. Working with environmental organizations like Health Care Without Harm, many hospitals are now committed to eliminating dangerous materials, products, and processes to improve patients' health and future well-being (Leciejewski).[1]

The understanding of such rights that pro-choice advocates bring to this emerging issue can provide the framework for promoting change. And by focusing on this vital environmental concern, together environmental and reproductive rights advocates can broaden the definition and application of reproductive rights as fundamental human rights. Women's lives, and the future of the planet, may depend on it.

Originally published in CWS/cf's Fall/Winter 2003 issue, "Women and Sustainability: From Rio de Janeiro (1992) to Johannesburg (2002)" (Volume 23, Number 1): 115-119.

[1]See www.chw.edu and Healthcare Without Harm at www.noharm.org.

References

Boland, Reed. "Promoting Reproductive Rights: A Global Mandate." New York: Center for Reproductive Rights: 1997.

Brody, Charlotte. President of Health Care Without Harm, Personal Interview, July, 2002.

Carey v. Population Services International, 431 U.S. 678, 686 (1977)

Centers for Disease Control (CDC). "Second National Report on Human Exposure to Environmental Chemicals." 2003a. Online: www.cdc.gov/exposurereport.

Centers for Disease Control (CDC). "National Report on Human Exposure to Environmental Chemicals." 2003b Online: www.cdc.gov/nceh/dls/report.

Center for Reproductive Rights. "Reproductive Rights 2000 Moving Forward." Online: www.reproductiverights.org/pub_bo_rr2k.html.

Colborn, Theo, Dianne Dumanoski, and John Peterson Myers. *Our Stolen Future*. New York: Plume/Penguin 1997. [first release Dutton/Penguin 1996] Online: www.ourstolenfuture.org/basics/chemises.htm.

Cooper, Cynthia L. "Enviros and Pro-Choicers Join Forces." August 1, 2002. Online Tom Paine.com: http://www.tompaine.com/feature.cfm/ID/6097.

Davis, D. L., H. L. Bradlow, M. S. Wolff, T. Woodruff, D. G. Hoel, and H. Anton-Culver. "Medical Hypothesis: Xeno-estrogens as Preventable Causes of Breast Cancer." *Environmental Health Perspectives* 101 (1993): 372-376.

DeFillipo, Valerie. Personal Interview, July 2002.

deFur, Peter L. and Carolyn Raffensperger. "Endocrine Disrupter Backgrounder." 1996, Online: Health Care Without Harm: www.noharm.org/library/docs/Endocrine_Disrupter_Backgro.htm,pp 82-83.9.

Ford, Gillian. *Listening to Your Hormones*. Rocklin, CA: Prima Publishing, 1997.

Katzive, Laura. Personal Interview, April, 2003.

Kolbert, Kathryn. "Developing a Reproductive Rights Agenda for the 1990s." *From Abortion to Reproductive Freedom: Transforming a Movement*. Ed. Marlene Gerber Fried. Boston: South End Press, 1990. 297-306.

Leciejewski, Mary Ellen. Ecology Program Coordinator, Catholic Healthcare West, Personal Interview, April 2003.

Myers, J. P. "Transcript: Environmental Threats to Reproductive Rights." 2000. Online: National Family Planning and Reproductive Health Association (NPHJRA) www.simulconference.com/simulseminar/NFPRHA/01envthrt/transcript.html

Palmer, J. R. et al. "Risk of Breast Cancer in Women Exposed to Diethylstilbestrol in Utero: Preliminary Results (United States). 2002. Online: www.cdc.gov/des/consumers/research/recent_risk.html.

Reuters. "127 Nations Adopt Treaty to Ban Toxic Chemicals." May 22, 2001.

"The Rights of Childbearing Women." 1999. Online: Maternity Center Association http://www.maternity.org.

Steingraber, Sandra. *Living Downstream: An Ecologist Looks at Cancer and the Environment*. Addison Wesley, 1997.

Thornton, Joe. *Pandora's Poison: Chlorine, Health, and a New Environmental Strategy*. Cambridge MA: MIT Press. 2000.

Thornton, Joe. Personal Interview, April 2002.

Thornton, Joe, Michael McCally, and Jane Houlihan. "Biomonitoring of Industrial Pollutants: Health and Policy Implications of the Chemical Body Burden." *Public Health Reports* (July-August 2002): 315-323.

Schettler, Ted, Gina Solomon, Maria Valenti, and Annette Huddle, *Generations at Risk: Reproductive Health and the Environment*. Cambridge, MA: MIT Press, 1999.

Skinner v. Oklahoma ex rel. Williamson, 316 U.S. 535 (1942)

Swedish Government. The Government's New Guidelines on Chemical's Policy. Online: http://www.kemi.se/default_eng.cfm?page=/gfm_eng/default_eng.cfm.

United Nations (UN). *United Nations Environment Programme "Agenda 21."* 1992. Online: www.unep.org/Documents/Default.asp?DocumentID=52.

United Nations (UN). United Nations Johannesburg Summit. 2002. Online: www.johannesburgsummit.org/html/documents/summit_docs.html

Universal Declaration of Human Rights. Online: www.un.org/rights/50/decla.htm.

Waak, Patricia. Personal Interview, July 2002.

Wolff, M. S., P. G. Toniolo, E. W. Lee, M. Rivera, and N. Dubin. "Blood Levels of Organochlorine Residues and Risk of Breast Cancer *Journal of the National Cancer Institute* 85 (1993): 648-652.

Activism

Wench Radio

Funky, Feminist Fury

The Wench Collective ➥

This article was difficult to write. We knew that we wanted to chronicle our cultural production, which we view as activism. We also knew that the standard academic format would not accommodate the complexities of our identities. This article, much like our program, is not a monolithic voice. We do not subscribe to the notion of singular feminism.

Since Wench began as a zine years ago, the collective has gone through many changes. The shifting nature of our collective is difficult to manage at times. It is also our greatest asset. Currently, the collective consists of ten women between the ages of 21 to 30. We represent a variety of socio-economic classes, sexual identities, and ethno-cultural/religious communities and body sizes. Our collective is limited in many ways; we are all non-disabled, biological women who have had some exposure to post-secondary education. Immigrant women and Jewish women are under-represented. We work within a system of constraints (time, money, CRTC regulations) and we strive to produce programming that is feminist, anti-racist, anti-colonialist, anti-xenophobic, fat and sex positive, anti-ableist, anti-classist, religion-positive, anti-transphobic, queer-positive, anti-corporate, and free of anti-Semitism. We are not always successful. We receive criticism within and outside our collective. Each show represents hours of discussion, debate, and personal reflection. Still, we often fall short of our mandate.

This article is the product of a collective effort. A smaller committee brainstormed three possible formats and the entire collective gave input. The committee then composed a list of questions and each woman answered the questions independently. We edited only for length and spelling.

At the time of writing this article, the Wench Collective Members are: Afshan Ali (AA); Debbie Pacheco (DP); Fatima Mechtab (FM); Joanna Pawelkiewicz (JP); Mary Roufael (MR); Michelle Maloney Leonard (MML); Rebecca Saxon (RS); Renee Ferguson (RF); Ruthann Lee (RL); Rylee Crawford (RC); Tara Atluri (TA).

What's your definition of activism?

AA: My activism: learning about the various oppressions that people face on a daily basis and making a commitment to change myself as a result of that knowledge. Activism is about the struggle for justice that is at once fierce and motivated, but also flexible and open-minded. My activism is about justice, not just on the grand, lofty level of revolution, but about justice and compassion in the way I treat people immediately around me. Does that make sense?

DP: As a relatively new "activist," my definition of activism is ongoing and currently unconsolidated. My previous description of activism consisted in being socially "active" (that is attending rallies, protests, etc.) with a political consciousness. However, I now realize the narrowness of that definition; the act of being "socially active" takes many forms, just as people's primary motives for social activism may not derive from political awareness. They may be due to personal moral beliefs in social justice or to better improve their own social conditions. The one prerequisite of activism that has remained constant in my shifting definition is being active, of engaging in some way with the social.

FM: Taking my personal beliefs into a public forum and acting out my wishes for change through speech or physical action (e.g., by marching). Being seen and heard among others who share a similar ideology.

JP: An act of resistance—be it individual or collective. I especially admire people who struggle against a systemic oppression that they do not personally experience.

MML: Any resistance to the dominant culture's sexist, racist, heterosexist, homophobic, classist, fatphobic, transphobic, ableist hegemony. It could be coming out to a protest, writing a letter to an elected representative, writing a song or just getting up everyday.

MR: Basic definition: Any kind of action(s)/activities that have the potential to impact not only your life but others as well, with the goal to change a situation for the better. Can focus on different levels: e.g., interpersonal relationships, in the workplace, school, neighbourhood, community, or on an international level.

RS: I used to think that activism was letter writing, protesting/marching, sit-ins and sorts of other activities that are most often associated with activism in the media. But I think this is limiting. I think activism is about the belief in change and vision of a better society/environment. It can occur on any level, from how one lives one' life to relationships to actively working towards change in the world/society around oneself. I think the definition of activism needs to be expanded beyond mainstream images of "protestors" facing off the police to a philosophical idea about change.

RF: My definition of activism is very limited, perhaps too limited. I think that because I first "broke out" onto the "activist scene" at University of Toronto I associate it with young, urban students, male or female, middle-class, and white. I see it as something that can be worn, consumed, consuming. Activism is something that seems to define who is not rather than what people do, a way of challenging that status quo without really doing it, if that makes sense. I've become very conscious of the ways in which I have embraced these notions and I'm trying not to give myself or the work I do a name and just think of myself as doing things that need to be done. It seems strange because people who go down in history as "activists" weren't called activists at the time; they were doing what had to be done because they were hungry, tired, frustrated, dying and so on.

RL: I used to think that in order to be an activist, a person had to be an extremely outspoken, white, anarchist-type who wears face paint and carries clever placards while demonstrating at protests and rallies. My definition of activism has expanded considerably since I've come to realize that not all activists have to look or act a certain way. Even day-to-day survival can be a form of resistance to the white, patriarchal, ableist, heterosexist, capitalist society we live in. Thus for me, activism involves any form of resistance to social oppression as well as self-education about where and how oppression operates. Activism can range from challenging racist jokes, to singing songs about women loving women, to reading up on the largely untaught histories of colonialism, to organizing safe social spaces for marginalized community members (such as queer youth of colour).

RC: My definition of activism involved the will or choice to struggle against conditions one deems undesirable. It involves sacrifice and determination but both are connected to a vision of transformation.

TA: Activism: The struggle to live, not just exist. Activism is struggling everyday to carve out a safe space for yourself. A space where you can breathe the air and drink the water and not be insecure even though sometimes it feels as though the whole world has been orchestrated to produce doubt. Activism is kindness and care, humour and persistence. Activism is putting your 50 cents in the slot of the *Toronto Star* dispenser and not letting it slam shut so that the next person can read the paper for free. It is taking the time and energy to think about where other people are coming from. It is understanding that there are centuries of history behind every "Paki" or "Bitch" that someone spits in my face, but there are also centuries of history behind every word I spit back at them. Activism is my parents' immigration. It is getting a free cab ride because my driver says he'll just charge the next white guy double. Activism is making a daily effort to be a bad girl. It's fishnet stockings and graffiti. It's refusing to be a product and trying to be a producer. Oh yeah, and there is a lot of hugging involved…

Name an activist skill that you most value in yourself.

AA: Compassion.

FM: My perseverance, independence and creativity.

JP: Original thinking or what more corporate types would call "thinking outside the box." My greatest asset is definitely my family, their immigrant roots and conservative stance never fail to keep me in check and hooked into what real people, not just activists in some insular circles, are thinking.

MML: Good social skills! Also, know where to find information to find and make connections with other activists.

MR: Ability (or at least striving for) to maintain a balance between respecting process (e.g., listening, valuing consensus) and forging ahead with getting stuff done.

RS: I try to stay informed of the numerous issues and struggles that exist and not assume that the issues I'm working with are the most important. I guess I try to keep perspective. Also, I try to infuse fun into all of my activism.

RL: A general activist skill I strive for is commitment (in terms of time and responsibility) to projects and collective organizations. A more personal activist skill I value in myself is my desire and ability to listen and attempts to respectfully consider, appreciate and learn from the different perspectives and experiences of the people I meet.

RC: An activist skill that I value in myself is my willingness to risk personal comfort. (I also recognize how my identity affords me this ability because of the way I am positioned in relation to racial and class hierarchies).

TA: Humour. Sometimes I am in some triple-latte, moccachino coffee establishment and I see people talking on those head-set cell-phones or I see couples on the subway who aren't even talking or looking at each other, who are probably on their way to Ikea and are making a mental note of all the home décor merchandise they will have to purchase to fill the "committed and in love" demographic; or better yet I'm in a bookstore or restaurant and some person decides to tell me "how lucky you people are" because she just loves Mendhi or curry and I wonder how people can take the world so seriously. To combat the tyranny of seriousness that causes so much stress, I try and laugh at the world once a day; twice on weekends.

How do you think wench radio fulfills a third-wave agenda?

AA: I'm very reluctant to answer this question because I don't particularly value this notion of third wave versus second wave etc. These waves are really suspect. I mean, who is deciding when the new surfs up? Referring to today's feminism as the "third wave" parallels nasty capitalistic notions of progress. More importantly, by categorizing the various feminist movements in this way, this conceptualization of feminism as coming in waves fails to fully comprehend the critiques that are being presented today about feminism and inclusivity. Perhaps the feminism in the sixties was a second wave for white middle class women, who were seeking economic and social parity with white middle class straight men. But what about all the women who don't fall into this category? Was the feminism of the sixties a second wave for them?

DP: Wench fulfills third wave feminism in its intersectional analysis. Social and cultural critiques on Wench incorporate third wave feminism's move beyond a simplistic gender analysis of female oppression.

JP: Wench steps up to the challenge of speaking to the experiences of all young women. We realize that most women are dealing with more than just sexism.

MML: We don't need to fulfill the "third wave agenda." We *are* the third wave. We're making the agenda and it's always changing.

MR: Provides a creative outlet with a political edge for a younger generation of feminists. Strives to air an integrated analysis in show topics and content. Aims to incorporate this integrated analysis in how it works as a collective.

RS: Well, this question assumes I know what third wave means which I'm not 100 per cent sure I do. If third wave feminism means a shift away from looking at gender issues to incorporating an integrated analysis around race, class, sexuality, gender, colonization, etc., then I think wench works really hard to be third wave.

Wench goes beyond tokenism or multiculturalism to taking up all issues with an integrated analysis. We try to ensure that all parts of who we are reflect this, meaning our programming, promotional literature, language, music, the collective itself, etc.

Also, if the third wave agenda is about young women, then Wench certainly is a part of that! Not only is our programming done by and for young women, we also interview, profile, review and promote young, funky women.

RL: I'm not sure what a third wave feminist agenda is precisely but if it's about incorporating more than just gender into the analysis of social oppression then I know that Wench is trying hard to be a part of that. Wench always attempts to voice the expressions of various young women and give an analysis that is multiply focussed. I think that for each show we try to ask: how is this issue gendered, classed, raced? How does it link to the legacies of colonialism? How is it linked to heterosexism and how does it affect queer communities?

RC: Wench fulfills a third wave agenda by the mandated and continually taken-up goal of "diverse" membership bringing experience and concern in many different shapes to the collective and, ultimately, the show. I believe we struggle against becoming a middle class white woman's show. We struggle to become aware of our assumptions and to challenge our biases through anti-oppression workshop initiatives. It also "empowers" us as women to produce using technology with our own hands.

TA: Third wave agenda? It sounds like a contradiction in terms. The breaking down of the unified subject "woman," of which earlier movements were based on, has brought feminism to a place of multiple, sometimes conflicting agendas. I think what characterises the third wave is the understanding of the way in which many oppositional movements often reproduce the same hierarchies they fought against once the revolution is over. This is true for earlier western feminist movements in which male dominance was often replaced by upper class, able-bodied, heterosexual white women's dominance. Wench is very conscious of these dangers. An effort is made to let differences stand, rather than trying to subsume them under a communal voice. There is also an understanding within the collective and within what I conceive of as third wave feminism of the way in which issues of race, class, sexuality, ability are all interrelated. Hence there is an effort to challenge our own and each other's privileges.

Who are your feminist sheroes?

AA: The Wench crew. And I'm not just being silly. I am really impressed with the people I work with on the radio. There is a strong commitment to bring the best of ourselves and our progressive politics to the radio. Our segments and show ideas are provocative and mostly well-thought out. Some have been at this for three years. We take for granted that we can all just jump in front of a mike and start chatting. I also like the Bruderhoff kids in New York who put out *Blu* magazine. I'm impressed with how solid their pieces are and how they can put out such a quality magazine and only charge people pennies for it. The politics of *Blu* is reflected in the financial accessibility of the magazine. If knowledge is power, then they are truly all into sharing. Toni Morrison. Hard to explain.

DP: One of my feminist sheroes is definitely bell hooks. She successfully combines a piercing insight into social inequalities with very accessible language, even within academia and its penchant for exclusivist discourse.

FM: My friends. Women who, unlike media starlets, don't need to hype their image in order to sell themselves. I look up to women whose experiences differ from mine but with whom I can learn from, for example, my roommate who was a Riot Grrrl in high school. My friend who is a single mother who has just completed her university degree and who *also* volunteers at the Rape Crisis Centre in Hamilton. My friend Meredith in Halifax who is an artist and has reclaimed her body and sexuality through creative expression. Women who live to claim their truths and apply their experiences to everyday living.

JP: I admire Winnie Ng for her continual organizing and optimism, any musicians who place politics before profit and academics who write theory that is relevant, useful and accessible.

MML: bell hooks, T.J. Bryan, Mimi Nguyen, Rita Fatila, Jill Nagle, Deena Ladd.

MR: Angela Davis all the way; my friend Ana Sapp; Marg Delahunty/ Mary Walsh.

RS: The editors of *Bitch* magazine— that magazine rocks my world!!! It's fun, smart, political, and third wavy.

RL: Lee Maracle; Maxine Hong Kingston; Dionne Brand. Tina Turner rocks. Michelle Yeoh kicks ass. So does my mom. My pals—including the Wenches, of course.

RC: Ani Difranco, bell hooks.

TA: My mom. Yes it's a cliché, but here goes. Consider this is the "remembering your spirit" part of the article, okay? When I was 16 I discovered Gloria Steinem. I was convinced that the women in my family were victims. When I went to University I took Women's Studies and my condescension worsened. When I talk to my mother now, I realise that I got my resolve and my inability to tolerate ignorance from her. While I was busy pouring over course readers about immigrant women's labour, my mother was underemployed in the paid workforce and overworked in the domestic sphere. While

I was busy falling all over women's studies professors, my mother was instilling in my sister and I the strength to speak up even if it seems that you are speaking alone. And when I began to see cracks in the feminism that I had clung to, when I began to notice no faces or last names that looked like mine, I turned to her again. She offered me a feminism that could not be separated from racism because these things cannot be separated in our lives as brown women. I admire the patience it must have taken to immigrate from India to Canada in the late '60s, and the even greater patience to raise "Canadian" children who have internalized notions of racial and national hierarchy and who took about 21 years to realise that you were right about a lot of things—okay, most things.

What role do you think that academia can have in the feminist movement?

AA: Academia is vital to the feminist movement in that it can be a place where feminism reflects on itself, refuels itself and arms itself. As such, academia gains its value from how effectively it is, or can be, used by the feminist movement. The more esoteric academia becomes, the more useless it is to the feminist activist community.

DP: Academia can play a crucial role within the feminist movement. I guess I'm a little biased because I'm such a theory junkie. It helps me to organize and better understand the world around me and how I might function as an activist within it. However, it also works the other way around. Academic theory does not just explain or inform the social and activist goals and practices, but practical experience also informs theory. The potential danger of academia and theory is if it remains detached and divided from the practical, namely grassroots feminisms. Also, despite some changes, academia remains an inaccessible institution of privilege that is still very much raced and classed. This reflects the issues feminist academia addresses, and how they are addressed, which may not be directly pertinent or relevant to the issues feminists working at a grassroots level are dealing with. In order for academia to play a progressive role within feminist activism, the hierarchy between theory and practical must be dismantled and the line between the two must be reconceptualized and materialized as a border, where people and ideas are welcome to flow, rather than an impenetrable divide. (Idealistic, huh?)

FM: I think that before academia can reach a mass group of women the structure of it has to change. Formal education contains barriers (language, cultural, and economic) and academic feminism is biased towards middle-class white women who have the freedom to disagree and critique their surroundings. The concept and the importance of knowledge must change. What is important and valuable and to whom? Whom does it speak to and whom does it ignore?

JP: Ideally, academia should be a resource for activists. A place to do some critical thinking, a place to interrogate why certain institutions/constructs exist. Academia should complement *not* replace grassroots activism.

MML: Academics produce some kickin' theory, which influences and structures a lot of grassroots movements. It can make a space available for young women to be exposed to ideas about radical resistance and change.

MR: Important role of reflecting on different aspects of the movement itself and how it can move forward to meet present and future needs.

RS: I think that it has an important influence on a lot of young feminists. My feminist and political ideas have changed and developed because of my women's studies classes. But I think that academia needs to be taken into consideration not only when writing and studying feminist theory in the classroom but also in feminist organizations.

RL: Academia can have the role of providing a very nuanced and extended analysis of social issues and providing a space for re-thinking and challenging the dominant (read: white patriarchal, heterosexist) social order. It can't solve all of feminism's challenges—in fact, I think it's one *of* feminism's big challenges: how can academic feminist theories be transformed and translated to be more accessible? How can academic theories be applied to everyday realities and experiences and attend to social change at a material (rather than a discursive or ideological) level? Sometimes it seems like the gulf between progressive academia and the "real world" is so huge you need to sprout wings to get from one to the other.

RC: I think academia performs a function for the feminist movement by reaching into hegemony and spreading the words of feminists in "acceptable language and form." A sort of transforming from within. Feminist law, for example, can influence those whom might otherwise dismiss the feminist movement as too radical for them to pay serious attention. But this would be most effective if feminist courses were mandatory in all disciplines, and not just there for those of us who are interested enough to choose women's studies. The dangers of feminist academia are many—elitism, classism, white racism, ableism. So academia in general (and not just in women's studies or feminist courses) needs to seek a more inclusive outlook to those who can't, won't, or don't approximate the white, able, straight, wealthy western European male archetype.

TA: Women's studies classes were the first safe spaces in which I encountered women who were proud to call themselves feminists. Educational institutions can be valuable resources for activists, which is ultimately the most productive role I see them playing in the women's movement. Unfortunately, one cannot even begin to envision this until issues of access are addressed. How can we even talk about the good that academia could bring to the women's movement, when the majority of women cannot afford to attend post-secondary education? Furthermore, many of the underpaid jobs done on university campuses are done my women of colour and immigrant women.

Furthermore, one need only examine the case of Dr. Chun at the University of Toronto to see the hypocrisy of an educational institution that claims to teach from an anti-oppressive framework, while simultaneously attempting to maintain a white power structure at all costs. I can remember taking countless English classes in which I was told to examine the work from a "literary" point of view, meaning to look at it apolitically. To ask a person of colour to read nineteenth century English literature in which your people are being called less than human without referring to politics, is putting you at a disadvantage for not being able to see the world through a white lens. If tuition continues to be unaffordable and universities continue to engage in unfair, racist labour practices and canon formation the gap between the women's movement and the academy will be huge.

Conclusion

Our answers reflect our views at the moment of writing. Our views are constantly shaped by our lives, our families, communities, outside political projects, our jobs, friends, our learning process, our mood of the moment, an article we may have read in the mainstream press, a heated debate during a high holiday meal, or a fucked-up subway ad that caught our eye.

Originally published in CWS/cf's Winter/Spring 2001 issue, "Young Women: Feminists, Activists, Grrrls" (Volume 20/21, Numbers 4/1): 69-74.

Tear Gas in Utero

Quebec City

Jenny Foster ───

Neoliberal economic policies are often promoted as means of advancing democracy worldwide. However, the negotiation of these policies and their short- and long-term outcomes raise serious concerns about democratic processes and freedoms in general. The multitude of summits hosting political leaders (often joined by business representatives) are persistently confronted by demonstrators, who in turn are persistently confronted by repressive and dangerous crowd control attitudes and techniques in the name of security.

I was pissed off before the Free Trade Area of the Americas summit even began. Before the agenda was officially secret, before the fence went up around the conference site in Quebec City, and before I knew I was pregnant. I was disgusted at the arrogance of leaders who could put so much on the line— risking environmental degradation, erosion of labour standards, and increased polarization of living standards—with so little accountability for their actions. Once the conference began, the only means of communicating these concerns was on the streets outside the baracades, amid water cannons, rubber bullets, and dense clouds of tear gas. The decision to protest with six friends was a no-brainer: the stakes were so high, the process so flawed. What we didn't know was that the thousands and thousands of tear gas canisters launched randomly at demonstrators would cause unknown harm to those at particular risk in the crowds, including my unborn daughter.

We expected oppressive security measures at the Quebec Summit, includ-ing arrests and lots of tear gas. We expected a twisted form of democracy. We expected that we would have to protect each other amidst the street-level struggles. But we were going as pacifists and observers. We weren't planning to attack the six-kilometre long perimeter sheltering conference delegates from civil society. Aside from a couple of rough nights sleep and potential run-ins with security, what did we have to lose? There were only two women in our group; we agreed to keep an especially close eye on each other and make sure that we didn't get separated. Resisting neo-liberalism was worth it.

For two days we gasped, coughed and wiped away tears as we exercised our constitutional right to demonstrate. On the third day conference organizers didn't even need to spray tear gas at demonstrators. Its burning residue hung thick in the air and covered buildings, sidewalks, trees, statues, lampposts, and all other surfaces. We returned to Toronto worn out, but with strengthened resolve about the critical need to resist globalization and protect civil liberties.

When my doctor delivered the shock three weeks later that I was already five weeks pregnant, one of the first things I grappled with was the possibility that my child had been exposed to tear gas. I remembered all of the warnings circulating in Quebec City about pregnancy and tear gas. Distributed by diverse organizations, they all cautioned anyone who was pregnant, might be pregnant, or was planning to become pregnant soon to stay well clear of the noxious clouds. I had been exposed at least 12 times. To make matters worse, I soon discovered that the tear gas was mixed with methyl chloride for ease of dispersal. Methyl chloride is a known carcinogen with human toxicity to the liver, kidneys, and central nervous system. I decided not to panic. I resolved to find out as much as I could and make informed decisions about proceeding with the pregnancy.

But where to start? Astonishingly, there is no published research whatsoever related to the effects of tear gas on human pregnancy. Meanwhile, a 1989 review published in the *Journal of the American Medical Association* raised serious medical concerns about the use of tear gas as a harassing agent for dispersal of demonstrators and subdual of criminals. The authors conclude that

> The possibility of long-term health consequences such as tumour formulation, reproductive effects, and pulmonary disease is especially disturbing in view of the multiple exposures sustained by demonstrators and non-demonstrators alike in some areas of civilian unrest. (Hu, Fine, Epstein, Kelsey, Reynolds and Walker 662)

The report emphasizes the urgent need for epidemiological and laboratory research. Rarely does a refereed medical journal publish articles advancing concerns about human rights and civil liberties. However, this report makes clear links between medical uncertainty surrounding tear gas exposure and human rights. A sample of statements to this effect include the following:

> ... the evidence already assembled regarding the pattern of use of tear gas, as well as its toxicology, raises the question of whether its further use can be condoned under any conditions. (663)

> At a time when the world has recently seen the recurrence of the use of mustard gas ... it is also worthy to note that in 1969, at the United Nations General Assembly, 80 countries voted to ban the use of any chemical in war, including tear gas, under the Geneva Protocol. (663)

> It is the hallmark of repressive regimes to equate the voicing of dissent with disorder and to deny opponents the freedom of assembly and

speech, rights guaranteed universally among signatories to the Universal Declaration of Human Rights. (663)

Implementation of the *Access to information Act* reveals that the RCMP alone launched 3009 canisters of tear gas during the FTAA summit (Picard, 2001). This is a staggering figure, but represents only a portion of the tear gas dispersed. Corresponding figures for the other two security forces commissioned for the summit, the Sûreté du Québec and the Police Municipal de Quebec, are indeterminate but presumably equally high. Although data concerning the demographics of demonstrators at Quebec City have not been collected, it is fair to assume that at least half of these were women, scores of whom must also have been pregnant.

I probed my doctor for any further information whatsoever relating to tear gas and pregnancy. She came up with nothing and referred me to Motherisk, an organization run out of The Hospital for Sick Children in Toronto devoted to public education, counselling, and research pertaining to fetal risks associated with drug, chemical, infection, disease, and radiation exposure during pregnancy. Consultation with Motherisk turned up nothing either. The report I later received from Motherisk briefly concluded that "there is limited data published on effects of chlorobenzylidonemalanonitrate, a component of tear gas." (Ratnapalan, 2001)

At eight weeks, I still didn't know what I was going to do about the pregnancy. I was already feeling strong maternal instincts, protecting the young fetus with a careful diet, regular exercise, and lots of sleep. But what hazards had it been exposed to in Quebec City? Nobody could answer this question, and I had serious misgivings about basic health and prenatal development. The day before my birthday I started bleeding heavily with painful abdominal cramps. After an internal exam, my doctor diagnosed a miscarriage, one of the purported effects of tear gas exposure (stillbirth and genotoxicity are others). I was sad and angry. Strangely though, after only two days the bleeding stopped and I still felt pregnant. Blood tests confirmed that I was still pregnant, that I had probably lost a twin. A week later, I considered terminating the pregnancy. I felt that this fetus had already been exposed to undue stress, and my own anxiety level about the whole matter was very high. But after seeing an ultrasound image of the shrimp-like baby I just couldn't follow through with an abortion. I dearly wanted to hold it in my hands and tell it I loved it and would do whatever I could to protect it. Although the baby had been tear gassed and its living environment was traumatized with a miscarriage, this young sprout passed the five basic criteria defining appropriate prenatal development: it had a heartbeat, a spinal column, a yolk sac, intestines, and a brain.

Although Health Canada provides national leadership to develop health policy and enforces health regulations, it has expressed no interest in the issue of massive use of tear gas on the public. As far as I can tell, Health Canada maintains responsibility for at least three federal acts (the Food and Drugs Act, the Hazardous Materials Information Review Act, and the Hazardous Products Act) which should have caused the ministry to at least question the indiscriminant use of tear gas in Quebec City (and at other demonstrations). Yet, Health Canada raised no concerns before, during, or after the Quebec Summit.

My baby was born in early January 2002. All of the tests conducted so far tell me that she has developed in a healthy manner. But there are significant limitations to what can be tested both pre- and postnatally. Weighing a healthy 9 pounds 5 ounces at birth, my daughter has grown like a weed over the past six months. She squirms and wiggles practically non-stop, and has a twinkling two-toothed smile that captures even the most dour faces we meet. Despite vigorous growth and endearing charm, concern about the effects of tear gas linger. Specifically, the article published in the *Journal of the American Medical Association* reports that tear gas is potentially genotoxic (622).

As is the experience of most child-bearing women I know, I have encountered some negative socio-cultural response to pregnancy and pending motherhood. For example, a couple of people responded poorly to the news of my pregnancy, questioning the wisdom of bringing a baby into the world. But most were extremely supportive. I have learned to recognize the numerous ways in which pregnant women and mothers are often desexualized and infantilised. It is also true that many people feel they can comfortably overstep boundaries of decorum and baseline respect by trying to tell pregnant women and mothers exactly what they should and should not do. I encounter these irritations regularly, combined with the physical effects of hosting a gestating human being, gining birth, sleep deprivation and general exhaustion. Yet these pale in comparison to the stress and anxiety of an unstable pregnancy provoked by tear gas and the shortage of information relating to associated health risks.

There is no proof that tear gas is safe for public consumption. If anything, the scant research that has been conducted in this area indicates that there are grounds to assume it is unsafe, especially for people at particular risk. An outstanding example is risk to prenatal development. I went to Quebec City as a citizen exercising my democratic right to protest. I was Jane Public, one of over 50,000 people who felt strongly enough about globalization to stand up and be counted. There is no reasonable way that I or the vast majority could be perceived as a security threat. Yet, we were gassed repeatedly. For many people, the Quebec Summit was an intensely politicizing event. It certainly confirmed my own commitment to resisting the negative effects of globalization and fighting to protect civil liberties. But the urgent need for thorough testing of the human toxicity of tear gas prior to any further dissemination of the compounds must be underscored. This must become part of the policy agenda surrounding Canadian civil liberties, health, and safety.

Originally published in CWS/cf's Spring/Summer 2002 issue, "Women, Globaliza-

tion and International Trade" (Volume 21/22, Numbers 4/1): 165-168.

References

Hu, Howard., Jonathan Fine, Paul Epstein, Karl Kelsey, Preston Reynolds and Bailus Walker. "Tear Gas: Harassing Agent or Toxic Weapon?" *Journal of the American Medical Association* 262 (5) (1989): 660-663.

Picard, J. Christian. (Departmental Privacy and Access to Information Coordinator, RCMP). Personal communication, 4 July 2001.

Ratnapalan, Savitri. (Specialty Fellow in Clinical Pharmacology, The Hospital for Sick Children). Personal communication, 14 September 2001.

The Canadian Disabled Women's Movement

From Where Have We Come?

Pat Israel and Fran Odette

Over the past 20 years, women with disabilities have organized and strategized to ensure that our "equality" rights were highlighted and addressed within the realm of both the women's movement and the disability rights movement. The kinds of organizing that have taken place over the past two decades has resembled that of social movement, in which it's strength was in numbers and new ideas. The Disabled Women's Movement grew and flourished, demonstrating the creativity and initiative needed to have our voices heard. Even before DAWN Canada met in 1986, women with disabilities began organizing through writing about our own lives, in our own words. *Voices From the Shadows: Women with Disabilities Speak Out* by Gwyneth Matthews was one of the first Canadian publications dealing with issues for women living with disabilities. Also, in 1985 an issue of Resources for Feminist Resources dedicated an entire issue on "Women and Disability." For the first time a mainstream women's journal provided women with disabilities a forum in which to have their voices heard. This marked the beginning of an era in which women with disabilities demanded the right to take their place in the women's movement.

The momentum continued to swell, when in June 1985, women with disabilities from across Canada gathered at a national meeting to form DisAbled Women's Network Canada (DAWN Canada). This was an historic event since it was the first time that we had received funding to actually organize and come together to deal with our issues separately. Prior to this, disabled women's issues were ignored by both the disability rights movement and the women's rights movement. Many feminists did not seem to regard women with disabilities as women at all, while the disability rights movement failed to acknowledge that many of our issues were different from the issues affecting men with disabilities.

Both Canadian and US feminist researchers and writers have highlighted the work of women with disabilities internationally (i.e., Laura Hershey; D. Diane Driedger [REF MISSING]; Susan Sygall and Cindy Lewis). Today, women with disabilities around the world continue to challenge stereotypes, participate in community life and politics, and lead organizations for social change. Women with disabilities encounter multiple barriers and inspite of these barriers, continue to work to become full and equal participants in their communities. While we represent up to 20 per cent of the world's female population, many of us continue to experience the same problems and oppression faced by women everywhere. These critical concerns are also compounded by discrimination and inaccessibility related to disability. Education, training, employment, transportation and housing are oftentimes more difficult for women and girls with disabilities to access than our non-disabled sisters (Sygall and Lewis). Today despite much of our work, the contributions and concerns held by women living with disabilities is not on the agenda of the many organizations that make up the global women's movement. Women with disabilities offer a powerful untapped resource to the movement for women's human rights. Women's organizations can enrich their programs if they take proactive steps to include disabled women by creating opportunities for all women in their communities.

Laura Hershey writes, "like other women around the world, women with disabilities are emerging from isolation to organize and fight for their rights and empowerment. Disabled women are reframing their individual struggles in a larger political and social context. As they meet in grassroots groups and exchange experiences across national borders, they are forming networks of support and a new culture of shared experience and pride." Sygall and Lewis (2000) list in their work, some examples of how groups of women with disabilities are organizing for equality, some of which include:

- A national network of grassroots organizations of women with disabilities in Nicaragua, that works cooperatively to maximize support and political power throughout the country.
- The Uganda Disabled Women Association operates a revolving loan program for women with disabilities to initiate small businesses. A travelling drama group raises community awareness about women with disabilities.
- Women with disabilities in Russia are leading seminars on sexuality and reproductive health.
- In the UK, Deaf women are providing peer support, materials and training to enable Deaf women to obtain information and access to health care (Sygall and Lewis); and finally,
- Women Pushing Forward (formerly Whirlwind Women) an international women's wheelchair project, works with disabled women to build and repair their own wheelchairs, and earn additional income to support their families. Women Pushing Forward currently works with women and women's organizations in Uganda, Mexico and Nicaragua.

Prolific feminist writers living with disabilities (many of whom are part of DAWN Canada) write about the kinds of organizing and advocacy related work that we are undertaking on our own behalf. For many of us, this work is needed more than ever before. On every continent, new leaders are emerging to oppose double discrimination based on sex and disability. Whether we are working within existing male-dominated disability groups to form women's groups, or creating brand new women's organizations from the grassroots up, many determined activists are bringing a gendered perspective to the international disability-rights movement. As well, many of us are trying to meet the social and political agendas of the women attending the meetings, creating opportunities for eliminating the barriers that contribute to our isolation and offering ways by which we can nurture our own self-respect and pride. Regardless of the points that bring us together, we are developing and moving forward agendas for change, and look toward the future where inequities that are associated with disability are also inclusive of gender. There are new and emerging leaders within our communities.

While progress has been made women's NGOs must work more closely with disabled women to find creative, practical solutions to problems of access that prevent them from developing and contributing their expertise and skills. Leadership training and community projects must undertake specific outreach efforts to include women with disabilities at every level, as staff, consultants, participants, board members and evaluators.

Both here in Canada and internationally, the women's community can no longer afford to overlook the immense resources that women with disabilities offer. We invite the global women's movement to expand the gender dialogue, to reach out and include women with disabilities in all efforts to achieve justice, and women's human rights.

More than ever, issues for women with disabilities cannot "disappear" and needs to remain on the agenda. DAWN women are not afraid to uncover the realities of our lives; proud to use the word "feminist" in our literature, and strive to be inclusive of all women with disabilities. Embracing diversity and our understanding of inclusion goes beyond that of gender and disability, as we know there is so much more about who we are that needs to be recognized and acknowledged in the work we do.

However, despite our work the issue of ableism within the women's community and the movement as a whole still exists. For example, when workshops are offered that focus on issues for women with disabilities, the number of participants remains low. However, when our issues are included alongside the issues other communities of women who experience marginalization, oftentimes, the attendance increases … it's hard to know if they're really coming to hear us or not. Although while our lived experiences may be different, there are threads common to all women that bring us together. It is crucial that our concerns from the multiple locations and identities that are part of all women's experiences are not merely heard but are acted upon by those from the various movements of which we are a part, including the lesbian, gay, bisexual, trangender/transsexual, intersex and queer (LGBTTIQ) communities, the movement of women of colour and women from various ethno-specific communities as well as the disability rights movement. As we enter 2006, we can still not assume that workshops or women's conferences will be accessible or that our once non-disabled sisters who might be experiencing changes in their health and are now living with a disability will acknowledge or recognize our presence and the multitude of resources that we bring to these meetings.

The "social movement" of women with disabilities challenges the women's movement and the disability rights movement to begin acknowledging differing definitions of equality. Women who have been traditionally "marginalized" still need to be more welcomed by and included more within the women's movement and the disability rights movement. However, is this enough? More than 13 years ago, Odette interviewed 25 Canadian women with disabilities regarding their experiences with both the women's movement and the disability rights movement. Many women expressed frustration and isolation in their attempts to organize within these two movements. The notion that "difference is equated with inequality" captured many of the women's feelings of exclusion. Thus, one's "physical difference" can be and has been seen as a tool to be used against us in numerous ways.

Strides have been made, victories won, however, in writing this article, we know that there still needs to be much more work done in order for many women living with disabilities to feel that they are truly part of the movement of women—all women. Potential partnerships can exist without the appropriation of disabled women's voices. Academic women's journals are more reflective of diversity, however, more effort is needed to reflect the lived experiences of the communities of women whose voices we have not yet had a chance to learn from; including our aboriginal/First Nations sisters living with disability, Deaf and hard of hearing women, and our sisters who use augmentative and alternative communication. We need to hear more from our sisters of colour who are living with disabilities, and from our sisters who still find themselves on the fringes including trans sisters living with disabilities.

On May 19-21, 2006, DAWN Canada, with the generous support of Status of Women Canada, sponsored the Sowing the Seeds Conference. This conference came about to address issues impacting women with disabilities who "are one of the most economically, socially, legally and politically disadvantaged groups in the community. This disadvantage contributes to isolation from support networks and exclusion from decision-making processes that impacts on their lives; increasing their vulnerability to all forms of systemic discrimination and violence" (DAWN Canada). For many women living with disabilities, it has been suggested by anecdotal evidence that "the recent cutting of social programs, has resulted in the increased exclusion and isolation of women with disabilities, across Canada" (DAWN Canada).

Sowing the Seeds Conference was organized to focus on enhancing effective needed strategic development to be undertaken by DAWN Canada in order to work towards ending the isolation and exclusion of women with disabilities and to assist them toward mobilizing community; developing local strengths and leadership and effectively participate in policy and program developments aimed at improving their social conditions. This will be done in cooperation with community partners, which will facilitate the effectiveness of actions undertaken by DAWN Canada. (DAWN Canada)

Along with many women's organizations across Canada, DAWN Canada has also experienced ongoing challenges in obtaining sustainable funding. However, it continues to do much work in ensuring equality rights for women living with disabilities across Canada. Some of the activities that DAWN has carried out recently are:

• Fundraising for the Sowing the Seeds Project and preparing for the 2006 AGM and meeting;
• Participation with LEAF in the VIA Rail court case;
• Participating in the Status of Women Canada meeting—Gender equality consultation;
• Participating in Service Canada meeting;
• Participating in e-list on UN Convention on elimination of discrimination for persons with disabilities and a second e-list on women's article;
• Attended Equality national conference.

Through the participation of diverse women in the Sowing the Seeds Conference (2006), it is hoped that women's leadership skills will be developed, enhanced and strengthened thereby "enabling Canadian leaders to organize local, provincial, territorial grassroots groups of women with disabilities and support their effective participation both in the national organization as well as in Canadian society" (DAWN Canada).

We feel that change is around the corner. We are women first and belong with women's communities in the struggle to fight all women's oppressions, we have lots to offer and will not stay on the sidelines. We also need to relish in our difference. Diversity along the continuum of movement and experience is critical for our work and for our movement to survive and be true to all women. The experiences that women with disabilities bring to the women's movement are invaluable. Join with us to ensure "equality" for all women.

An earlier version of this article was published in CWS/cf's Summer 1993 issue, "Women and Disability" (Volume 13, Number 4).

References

DAWN Canada. www.dawncanada.net/conference/tindex.htm#about%20the %20confernece. Date accessed: May 2006.

Hershey, Laura. "Disabled Women Organize Worldwide to Build Unity and Power." Crip Commentary. Online: <http://www.cripcommentary.com>

Mathews, Gwyneth Ferguson. *Voices from the Shadows: Women with Disabilities Speak Out*. Canada: Women's Educational Press, 1983.

Odette, Francine. *Women with Disabilities: The Third "Sex"—The Experience of Exclusion in the Movement Toward Equality*. Independent Enquiry Project in partial requirement for Masters of Social Work Degree, Carleton University, Ottawa: Faculty of Social Work, 1993.

Stewart, Houston, Beth Percival, and Elizabeth R. Epperly, eds. *The More We Get Together*. Charlottetown: Gynergy Books, 1992.

Sygall, Susan and Cindy Lewis. "Tapping into the Power of Women with Disabilities in the International Women's Movement." *Raising Our Voices: The Newsletter of the Global Fund for Women*. July 2000.

Feminism, Peace, Human Rights and Human Security

Charlotte Bunch ⟶

Generalizations about women and peace are difficult, especially for a white U.S. American who has not experienced war first-hand, but whose government has conducted countless military operations around the globe. What I do hope to do here is to raise some questions that come from struggling from that location to be simultaneously a feminist, human rights and anti-war/anti-imperialist activist.

Acknowledging when and where we enter is a central tenet of feminist inquiry. Questions of women and peace/war are very particular, having to do with the specificity of each conflict—of time, place, race, ethnicity, class, religion, and other discrete circumstances—as well as related to various social constructions of gender, of masculinity and femininity. In that sense peace and the relation of women to war is a very local issue. And yet, women and war/peace is also a very universal subject discussed in a variety of ways for centuries. Throughout the twentieth century, and especially with the intensification of globalization and the rise of religious and ethnic fundamentalisms, feminists have found it useful to make cross-cultural comparisons, to share analysis and strategies, as well as to build international solidarities for peace.

There is a dynamic tension between the universality of this subject and the need for global action by feminists on the one hand, and the necessity of being grounded in the particulars of each situation and not overlooking real differences among women on the other.

Peace, human rights, and gender

First, what do we mean by or expect when we talk about peace? Most women's peace activism springs up around particular conflicts and does not begin with a plan for world peace. But we must ask what are the conditions necessary for a permanent peace to be achieved. We should look at the existing regional and international structures for peace making and peace keeping, like the UN, and at the assumptions of the men who created them to see if those assumptions—like the emphasis on national sovereignty—are a sound basis for peace. We must ask what it will take to en-gender these structures and transform them into more effective vehicles in the quest for peace, security and human rights for all. Otherwise, women will always be re-acting to patriarchal wars.

We face these questions today in a difficult context, made more complex by the events of September 11 in the U.S. and their aftermath. We have seen the most extensive development of nuclear, biological and other weapons of mass destruction in the last half century that would seem to serve as a sufficient argument for why global structures to ensure peace are now a necessity for human survival rather than just a desirable vision. But rather than being more peaceful, we entered the twenty-first century with many unresolved civil and ethnic conflicts and an increasingly militarized daily life where the lines between civilians and combatants seem ever murkier. We have sophisticated local and global terrorisms, a rise in the political use of religious extremism, an expanding arms trade led by the world's one remaining super-power, and the structural violence of the widening economic gap between haves and have-nots.

Indeed, one compelling argument for women playing a greater role in peace building and governance today is the perception that women could hardly make a bigger mess of the world than male leadership has done over the past centuries.

In this turbulent time, what then do women make of peace? The first aspect of peace is an end to violent/armed conflict—the absence of war—or what is called "Negative Peace." But this is not enough to ensure that armed conflict will not arise again nor does it address questions of what is needed to end all forms of violence—militarization, the structural violence of racial and economic injustice, or the ongoing violence against women in daily life.

"Positive Peace," on the other hand, is a term used to describe an "alternative vision" that leads to the reduction of all forms of violence in society and moves toward the "ideal of how society should be" (Women Building Peace Campaign of International Alert cited in Pankhurst and Anderlini). It is also concerned with justice and the larger dynamic of domination or power over "the other" as a mode of human interaction.

Indicators of the conditions of justice and equity that comprise positive peace are spelled out in the UN Universal Declaration of Human Rights, whose framers in 1948 saw the promotion and protection of human rights as critical to preventing genocide and war in the future. The UDHR spells out broad principles of both political/civil rights and socio-economic human rights that constitute a considerable commitment to justice, development and equality as the basis for positive peace. While we know these rights are not the world reality and their pursuit has been misused, nevertheless, movements seeking justice around the globe have continued to utilize the concept of human rights and the vision embodied in the UDHR as standards that their governments and the international community should uphold.

Feminist perspectives of positive peace build on the expanding world of human rights concepts and practice. Demanding the protection and promo-tion of the human rights of all as a central tenet of peace-building helps to ensure that inequities must be addressed and that peace should not be purchased at the price of simply allowing the prevailing military powers to have their way. Human rights principles also demand that the pursuit of justice not allow for the impunity of war criminals after a peace accord is reached.

Central to feminist conceptualizations of peace and human rights is the recognition of a continuum of violence against women, in which all forms of violence are seen as interrelated. The institutionalization of male dominance is maintained by violence and the threat of violence and leads us to question whether the term "peacetime" provides an accurate description of the lives of most women. As two South Asian feminists noted when responding to the question of whether feminism disrupts 'peaceful' homes, "one person's peace can be another's poison" (Bhasin and Khan).

War and armed conflict bring additional violation to women's lives, but these are linked to the gender-based violence and abuse of women in "normal" life. Thus, violence against women in war brings together the subordination of females with their membership in other targeted groups, expresses women's status as the property of the men in her community, and reflects social acceptance of violations of women more generally.

Further, when violence is tolerated in an everyday way in the family at the core of society, children come to see violence as an inevitable part of conflict and a natural way to deal with differences in all areas of the social order. Thus ending the violence of militarism, war and racism is tied to ending violence in the home. These are mutually reinforcing forms of violence that must be challenged simultaneously.

While it is primarily women activists and feminist theorists from all regions of the world who have pioneered work on the gendered nature of war and conflict (e.g. Elise Boulding, Jacklyn Cock, Cynthia Enloe, Ritu Menon, Betty Reardon, Simona Sharoni, Yayori Matsui, etc.), one "scientific" study by a male political scientist is of interest here. Joshua Goldstein has sought to show why there is so much cross-cultural consistency in gendered war roles, even when there is great diversity of cultural forms of both war and of gender roles when considered separately. He concludes what many feminists have contended that gender and war are inextricably linked: "Gender roles adapt individuals for war roles, and war roles provide the context within which individuals are socialized into gender roles. For the war system to change fundamentally, or for war to end, might require profound changes in gender relations. But the transformation of gender roles may depend on deep changes in the war system" (Goldstein 6-11).

Human security vs. national security

The term "human security" has come into greater use recently as a way to describe an integrated vision of positive peace, human rights, and development. The United Nations Development Program (UNDP) *Human Development Report*, as well as United Nations (UN) Secretary General Kofi Annan in his Millenium Report (UN 2000), speak of security less as defending territory, more in terms of protecting people. Non-govermental organizations (NGOs) have called for redefining security in terms of human and ecological needs instead of national sovereignty and borders. This requires a new social order that ensures the equal participation of marginalized groups, including women and indigenous people, restricts the use of military force, and moves toward collective global security (Hague Agenda for Peace and Justice in the 21st Century cited in Hill and Ranson).

Rita Manchanda notes:

> the human security discourse has come up from below, from peoples and groups excluded from the national security debate, defined and articulated by civil society groups, social movements and marginal groups, especially women. (1)

This term has emerged as an alternative to the state centered concept of "national security," rooted in the military security-defense domain and academically lodged with "realists" in the field of International Relations.

Feminists challenge the military paradigm by asking questions about whose security does "national security" defend? For example, in looking at East Asia, some have concluded:

> The security treaties ... that provide for U.S. bases, military operations, and port visits in South Korea, Japan, and the Philippines also compromise the security of local people. Negative social effects of the U.S. military presence on host communities include military prostitution, the abuse of local women, and the dire situation of mixed-race children fathered by U.S. military men. (Kirk and Francis 229)

Wider acceptance of the paradigm of human security holds promise for women, but we know how easily feminist perspectives can become marginalized as a concept becomes more mainstream. For example, a Joint Proposal to Create a Human Security Report from Harvard University and the UN University presented in May of 2001 outlined an ambitious plan to create a report that would map key systemic causes of armed conflict and violent crime . as well as a human insecurity index. Yet, while no group lives in greater insecurity than females around the globe, the proposal *never* once mentions women, gender, masculinity, rape, violence against women or any other concept that has emerged out of several decades of feminist work. A similar absence was reflected in a call from *Human Rights Dialogue* for essays on "Human Rights and Public Security." Much of the feminist discourse on these issues has never been read by men in the field and can still be overlooked unless women are vigilant about ensuring that the evolution of this concept fully encompasses the female half of humanity.

Efforts to advance peace and the concept of human security were set back by the events of September 11th and the ensuing resurgence of the masculine dominated discourse on defense. Media response to this crisis proved a rude reminder that when it comes to issues of terrorism, war, and national security, feminism is not on the map. There was rich discussion about these events among women on the internet, but public commentary in the Western media was dominated by male "authority" figures. Even the UN High Commissioner for Human Rights, Mary Robinson, one of the first to frame a response to 9/11 from the perspective of international law by suggesting justice for this act of terrorism be pursued internationally as crimes against humanity, rather than as a call to war, was quickly side-lined by the U.S. and the UN.

It is women who have been targeted by fundamentalist terrorism in many places from Algeria to the U.S., and it is mostly feminists from all parts of the world who have led the critique of this growing problem globally. Nevertheless, only when it became convenient for military purposes to discuss the rights of Afghan women did the issues of women and fundamentalism surface in the mainstream media. However, this discussion has not been extended to the rights of women in other conflicts, and non-Islamic fundamentalist attacks on women like those happening in Gujarat, India are not being highlighted. Thus, what could have led to an examination of threats to women's human rights posed by political fundamentalism, terrorism, and armed conflict in many guises was used instead by the U.S. and other western powers to demonize the "Islamic other" and to justify more militarization of society.

The justification of fighting against "terrorism," has been used to curtail human rights both in the U.S. and elsewhere. It has also led to an increase in defense budgets in many countries over the past year from the U.S. and Israel to Colombia and the Philippines. Meanwhile the donor countries pledges at the recent UN Financing for Development World Conference (March 2002) fell far short of what is needed to even begin to fulfill the millennium goals for advancing human security. Thus, human security as a guiding global principle is far from being embraced as a replacement for the nationalist security paradigm.

Since September 11th, governments in all parts of the world have used terrorism as an excuse to jettison commitment to some human rights in the name of fighting terrorism or providing for national or public "security." Thus, the newly gained recognition of women's rights as human rights, including rape as a war crime, which is not yet deeply entrenched, is jeopardized by the current rise in militaristic national security discourse and the accompanying eclipse in commitment to human rights. The need for articulating an approach to global security that ensures human rights and human security for all is more urgent than ever in the post September 11th world.

Women's role in peace-building

One of the areas in which there is the greatest agreement among feminists is about the gendered character of war, militarism, and armed conflict and the harm it causes women. Even where there is considerable diversity in the construction of sex roles, what is remarkable is the way in which war still operates in very specific gendered ways, and military forces use and rely on women as critical parts of the war process even as they privilege masculinity. In short, gender matters to war makers and what happens to women is not just an accidental byproduct of war or biology. Nowhere is this clearer than in the violence that women experience in war and conflict.

Since militarism is clearly gendered and women are victimized by war, does this mean that women are more peaceful or that peace is feminine? Images of women advocating for peace as those who are more nurturing and non-violent abound from the early 20th century to the Madres of Plaza de Mayo in Argentina or the Russian Mother's movement. While such images may serve a useful purpose for women in a particular time or place—particularly when these are the only roles in which society gives them legitimacy, they pose a number of problems for feminists claiming equality and agency. Since the human species has experienced so many centuries of social construction of roles based on gender, especially in relation to war, it is probably not possible to determine conclusively whether such traits are inherently biological or not. Therefore, rather than trying to prove or disprove a biological argument, it is more useful to look at the issue of what women bring to peace-building in other ways.

Women play many roles in armed conflict—not only as peacemakers or victims but also as perpetrators and supporters of war. There is a growing body of work addressing the complexity of women's relationships to war and militarism (e.g., Moser and Clark; Enloe; Turshen and Twagiramariya). Too many women commit acts of violence and support men who do so, whether in war or in the family, to say that women as a group are innately non-violent. However, it is also true that men commit the vast majority of acts of violence in the world, both against other men and against women and children—as armed forces, agents of the state and in the private sphere. Therefore it would also be absurd to claim that women and men are equally violent, or that women as a group do not have any proclivities toward resolution of conflicts non-violently—at least within the constraints of a patriarchal world where gender roles equate "manhood" with toughness under fire and female violence is generally discouraged.

While not all men are violent nor all women peaceful, a world structured by gender has produced real differences in how most men and most women experience war and violence—both as victims and as perpetrators. These gender differences are further complicated by the particularities of each culture and community, making universal generalizations about them difficult, but this does not make "women" as a political category useless. As Cynthia Enloe observes:

> To avoid seeing all women as natural allies simply because they are women, then, is crucial for building reliable causal analyses and for crafting effective strategies. However, arriving at this conclusion

does not require a person to lose all confidence in the belief that "women" is an authentic political category useful in making sense of the causes and consequences of militarization. (297)

Women peace activists have made creative use of women as a constituency to have significant impact on ending armed conflicts and have courageously intervened between groups of warring men, from Ethiopia and Somalia to South Asia. Having different life experiences than men means that women bring different issues to the table and bring awareness of different needs and different possible solutions to the process. A number of studies have begun to document the specific ways in which women generally have a more cooperative and less hierarchical approach to solving problems and are more inclusive in bringing others into the process, which can lead to giving more people a stake in the peace agreements and compromises reached (Anderlini; Boulding; Cockburn; Moser and Clark).

While women should be part of all aspects of peace processes because of the specific life experiences and perspectives they bring to the table, we must be aware that women are not all the same. Since women's lives are affected by their race, ethnicity, class, religion, history and culture and other factors, as well as gender, it is important to ensure that women are more than a token presence and that those involved represent diversity in background. From the research that has been done, having more women involved in decision-making does usually matter in the results that will be achieved especially if a critical mass of at least about 30-35 per cent is reached. However, it also matters where those women come from, what their commitment is to women's rights, and what are their overall politics.

The need for women to be part of all aspects of the peace-building process should be self-evident and does not rest on claims to their being innately more peaceful. This is a right that rests on the simple but profound principles of justice and democracy. As half or more of humanity, women have the right to be part of the decision-making on all critical activities that deeply affect their lives. Gender balance, as a democratic principle, should apply to the full range of peace-building activities.

Women's peace activism

Women's activism around peace takes many forms, often depending on a group's politics as well its values and life circumstances. In looking at examples of such activism, a variety of dilemmas and questions that feminists concerned with peace face are raised: Are feminists pacifists or do we believe in just wars and liberation struggles? Does holding military forces accountable to the rules of war and integrating women into military forces only strengthen them and reinforce social acceptance of military solutions? Do mother's movements necessarily reinforce gender stereotypes? What actions can feminists take when society is polarized around male defined or nationalistic options none of which we want to support? How do feminists who usually create non-formal and often marginal ways of working for peace get taken seriously in the formal peace-making processes?

One of the most significant forms of feminist peace organizing in the last two decades is embodied in efforts by women to cross national and ethnic lines and reach out to women of the "other" side, as well as to critique their own government or community's position. The issues of nationalism or communalism can be difficult for feminists. Some may feel that their own community oppresses women, but they may still be torn by loyalties to that community in the face of its domination by other forces or simply by virtue of being part of it. The nationalist/communitarian forces will certainly pressure or even try to force women to be loyal, often as symbols of the culture. In some cases, women feel that being a fighter for their group can be a way to prove themselves as political actors with agency. However, for women to play a significant role in ending conflict usually requires standing aside and being critical of nationalism, or at least of how the warring parties are manipulating it. There are a number of examples of women's peace initiatives that have taken this step—in Northern Ireland, Cyprus, Mali, the former Yugoslavia, the Middle East, and across the India-Pakistan border—to name a few. Central to such efforts is women's rejection of the nationalist project of dividing groups along racial/ethnic, religious, and/or cultural lines and dehumanizing "the other." In refusing this logic, activists often face violence, repression, or rejection from members of their own communities for being traitors.

Let me end with a few comments about women's global networking for peace. International solidarity has played an important role in sustaining many feminist peace activists, especially when they challenge the dominant nationalist or communalist discourse. Women have supported each other through keeping lines of communication open and accurate information flowing, with money and care packets, with counseling and hand holding, with assistance in escaping difficult situations and finding asylum, with petitions to governments, the UN, and other bodies. Global networking has also achieved a number of important gains in relation to war and armed conflict at the international level.

In the past decade, women's efforts at the UN have led to more attention to women and armed conflict, which became a full chapter of the Beijing *Platform for Action* (UN 1996) and received considerable attention at the Beijing Plus Five Review in 2000. Women raised the profile of sexual violence in war in the Ad Hoc Tribunals on the former Yugoslavia and Rwanda and made certain that issues of gender-based violence and persecution were incorporated into the Statute of the International Criminal Court. Another major breakthrough was the passage of UN Security Council Resolution 1325 on Women, Peace and Security in October of 2000, which mandates the inclusion of women in all of the peace processes as well as gender mainstreaming into all these activities. The dilemma posed by global networking at the UN is how to ensure that such gains are not simply rhetorical, and that they are implemented effectively in a gender and culture specific way at all levels.

This leads back to the importance of making sure that *women's peace activism is both local and global*, and that the dynamic tension between the universality and specificity of this work is recognized and grappled with continuously. Only through such a process can women's peace activism not only respond to the needs of each situation but also impact the larger global structures creating many of these conflicts so that we can move toward a pro-active vision of positive peace with human rights and human security at its core, rather than continue to be called upon to clean up after the endless succession of male determined armed conflicts.

This article is adapted from a paper written for the "Women and Peace Panel" at the "Women, Peace Building and Constitution-Making International Conference," 2-5 May, 2002, Colombo, Sri Lanka.

Originally published in CWS/cf's Fall 2002/Winter 2003 issue, "Women and Peace-Building" (Volume 22, Number 2): 6-11.

References

Anderlini, Sanam. *Women at the Peace Table: Making a Difference*. New York: United Nations Development Fund for Women, 2000.

Bhasin, Kamala and Nighat Khan. *Feminism and its Relevance in South Asia*. New Delhi: Kali for Women, 1986.

Boulding, Elise "Feminist Interventions in the Art of Peacemaking: A Century Overview." *Peace and Change* 20 (4) (October 1995).

Cock, Jacklyn. *Colonels and Cadres: War and Gender in South Africa*. Oxford: Oxford University Press, 1991.

Cockburn, Cynthia. *The Space Between Us: Negotiating Gender and National Identities in Conflict*. London: Zed Books, 1998.

Enloe, Cynthia. *Maneuvers: The International Politics of Militarizing Women's Lives*. Berkeley: University of California Press, 2000.

Goldstein, Joshua S. *War and Gender*. London: Cambridge University Press, 2001.

Hill, Felicity and Pam Ransson. *Building a Women's Peace Agenda*. Hague Appeal for Peace, ed. New York: New York Gender Focus Group of the Hague Appeal for Peace, 2001.

Kirk, Gwyn and Carolyn Bowen Francis. "Redefining Security: Women Challenge U.S. Military Policy and Practice in East Asia." *Berkeley Women's Law Journal* 15 (2000): 229-271.

Manchanda, Rita. "Redefining and Feminizing Security." Unpublished manuscript, 2001.

Matsui, Yayori. *Women in the New Asia*. London: Zed Books, 1999.

Menon, Ritu. "Borders and Bodies: Recovering Women in the National Interest." *Common Grounds: Violence Against Women in War and Armed*

Conflict Situations. Indai Lourdes Sajor, ed. Quezon City: Asian Centre for Women's Human Rights, 1998.

Moser, Caroline O. N. and Fiona C. Clark. Eds. *Victims, Perpetrators or Actors? Gender Armed Conflict and Political Violence*. London: Zed Books, 2001.

Pankhurst, Donna and Sanam Anderlini. *Mainstreaming Gender in Peacebuilding: A Framework for Action*. London: International Alert, 2000.

Reardon, Betty. *Women and Peace: Feminist Visions of Global Security*. Albany: State University of New York Press, 1993.

Sharoni, Simona. *Gender and the Israeli-Palestinian Conflict: The Politics of Women's Resistance*. Syracuse: Syracuse University Press, 1995.

Turshen, Meredeth and Clotilde Twagiramariya, Eds. *What Women Do in Wartime: Gender and Conflict in Africa*. London: Zed Books, 1998.

United Nations. *We the Peoples: The Role of the United Nations in the 21ˢᵗ Century*. Report of the UN Secretary General Kofi Annan to the Millennium Summit. New York: United Nations, 2000.

United Nations. *The Beijing Declaration and The Platform for Action: Fourth World Conference on Women, Beijing, China, 1995*. New York: United Nations Department of Public Information, 1996.

United Nations Development Program (UNDP). *Human Development Report 1994*. New York: Oxford University Press, 1994.

Building a Culture of Peace

An Interview with Muriel Duckworth and Betty Peterson

Evie Tastsoglou and Marie Ann Welton

We had the opportunity to interview Muriel Duckworth (94) and Betty Peterson (85) in October 2002. In this article they share and reflect on what they've learned in their long lives as war resisters and peace activists in Canada and the U.S. While examining their lifetime of struggle they remain hopeful, determined and active in opposition to the invasion of Iraq.

For peace and social justice

Evie: Both of you, Betty and Muriel, have been involved in the peace movement for a very long time. Could you tell us how you became interested in peace issues, what were the personal and larger social events at the time that made you turn your attention to the peace movement?

Betty Peterson: A thousand years ago when I was at university, particularly in 1938-39, there were rumblings of war in Europe. There used to be protests on the campus, saying things like "Hell No, We Won't Go!" I had been a very serious music student and not paying any attention to such things. But I happened to be very enamored of my future husband who was a conscientious objector and I began reading, and war seemed like such a senseless waste, as it does today. He was sent to Maine and built a little log cabin there. I came up with our child another child was born there. We were without newspapers, out in the middle of the woods, but there was a little radio with a lot of static, where we kept hearing about the terrible things that were happening. We felt very much that we were doing the right thing, working for a better world, bringing our children up in that way, believing they surely would go on and bring about a peaceful world.

At the end of the war came the news of the Holocaust. We had heard nothing, or very little in the States anyway, about the Holocaust. It came as the most horrendous shock. And then, of course, the bombing of Hiroshima, followed a few days later by Nagasaki—we could not believe that such a thing could happen. My husband and I decided to devote the rest of our lives to working for peace and social justice. We became Quakers shortly after the war and, of course, the peace testimony is a very strong part of what they believe.

Muriel Duckworth: Betty and I are just about nine years apart, so my life began nine years before hers did. I remember WWI and having nightmares about Huns and Bolsheviks coming into my bedroom to cut me up into little pieces when I was visiting my aunt in Boston, when the United States decided to go to war in 1917. I would have been nine. When I was in university from 1925-29 war was something away over there. It was nothing that I really felt involved in although we were raising money for European students who were having a hard time in Germany because of the tremendous inflation after WWI. There were people in Canada who did go to prison because they wouldn't go to war, but my husband was too old (he was 42 when the war began). He was the YMCA Secretary and he would not support it. After the war, after this terrible use of the nuclear bomb, which it wasn't easy to get news about because it was hushed up for quite a while afterwards, we thought there can't be another war, this is so terrible, nobody will ever have another war. Then, there was the testing of nuclear weapons in the Pacific and the death of a Japanese fisherman.[1] They not only used those bombs on Japan, they then tested them in the Pacific. That was really a wake-up call for everybody. There was a risk that nuclear weapons would be used. The anti-nuclear movement became strong during the 1950s in Canada and we were deeply involved. The Voice of Women (VOW) was started in Canada in 1960 because there was a feeling that women's voices should be heard and that there would be a difference in what women had to say about nuclear testing.

Betty: I think from the beginning some of us always put together peace and social justice, because without justice there is no peace. During the war, Kagawa, the great Japanese pacifist, was a model who played a big part in my life. It was just impossible to believe that so soon after WWII there was the Korean war in 1951. I was brought up in the States, and, living through the McCarthy period,[2] we had to be very careful. Communism had a great appeal to many of us at that time, and so did the Fellowship of Reconciliation (FOR), the largest international peace fellowship in the world.[3] Peace was not separated from everything else. Other organizations that I was involved in were the War Resisters League, another outstanding group that began in the United States but is also international.... As early as the 1940s, I was out at lunch counters with Bayard Rustin and Jim Farmer who were two outstanding peace and civil rights people. That was part of peace work as well, peace between people. We tested lunch counters—white people going into lunch counters or dining rooms, then black people going in, and then all of us going in together to see what would happen. Then I worked closely with the American Friends Service Committee, a very strong Quaker group in the States, similar to the Canadian Friends Service Committee here. They had many regional conferences, all over the U.S., and brought very well-known speakers, some from the Socialist Party. There was a wide range of excellent people so it was marvelous to have that exposure.

Muriel: The association that meant the most to me when I was at McGill was the Student Christian Movement. We had study groups and visiting speakers who introduced me to the Social Gospel, to pacifism, to suffering in the world, and the need for change through non-violent action. Several of the speakers were Quakers although I did not make a connection with the Quakers until 1962.... At McGill I met my husband, Jack Duckworth, eleven years older, who was a passionate and active pacifist. I began to learn about Gandhi and Kagawa. We had Norman Thomas and Harry Ward as speakers. Dr. Ward was considered such a social radical that people were booing him at McGill when he came there to speak. He taught in the Union Theological Seminary where I studied in 1929-30, just after I graduated from McGill, and where my husband was studying theology. There was a radical view of society in the seminary and pacifism was rampant. Then, coming back to Montreal the Depression was very serious until WWII provided jobs for everybody, including women (of course many of them were sent back to their kitchens when the war was over). "They" said "they" had fixed the economic system so that the Depression would never happen again...

During the '30s the major factors in my life was having children. Children ask a lot of questions, and you are not comfortable about the answers you have to give because of the state of the world. We were trying to create a world that would be different than the one creating wars. I became involved with the Home and School Movement for many years trying to get them to take a position on not having nuclear testing. At that time the mood in the Home and School was "what does that have to do with education?" so they weren't ready yet to do anything about it although they did later.

After the war we joined groups like the Fellowship for Reconstruction, the Fellowship for a Christian Social Order, and tried to do peace work in the United Church. Out of this renewal of energy in Canada and the feeling that surely, surely after Hiroshima and Nagasaki nobody ever will make war again, we began to build the new society. Out of this came the Co-operative Commonwealth Federation (CCF) (precursor of the NDP), the Canadian Association for Adult Education, and many actions for social reforms. In 1947 we moved to Halifax and I joined the Nova Scotia Association for the Advancement of Coloured People. Their members were disillusioned because the "war for freedom" (WWII) had brought them nothing.

Betty: I had to make a choice about what to do when my children were small, during the late 1950s and '60s when I lived in the suburbs outside of Chicago. It took a long time to get into the center of Chicago where all the big peace rallies were held. When the Vietnam war came along, we spoke out against it and wore buttons and did everything we could in the suburbs, but civil rights was the big thing. We lived in a very particular part of the south side of Chicago where there were wealthy enclaves of people, then there were middle-class people like us, and then there would be black communities over here, and people that worked in the steel mills over there. They were very close and you had to drive through all of them. There were opportunities all the time to work with black people for equal housing, equal schooling and all the rest. It was a very fearful time. You didn't dare use the words "human rights" and even the words "race relations" were forbidden. They would not print those words in the local paper.... We rarely felt we did enough though we would be called in the middle of the night, "there's going to be a riot, would you go down and try to calm people," or we would get called when there were crosses being burnt on black people's lawns. I was a part of a group called the South Suburban Human Relations Council that was started by a group of Jewish women, families right out of the Holocaust. We became very good friends. They were so courageous during the civil rights movement, those women who had witnessed such terrible things....

Muriel: The thing that happened after the war in Canada was the Guzenko case.[4] Guzenko was working for the Russian Embassy and defected in 1946. It was really devastating for peace activists and radicals because people they had known were arrested. Then along came the McCarthy era. During that time the Women's Peace Movement in the United States was really frightened and even felt they couldn't function. It just about this time the Canadian Voice of Women was formed in 1960 and, right after that, the Women's Strike for Peace in the United States. They were a very outspoken group. In fact, they did a lot to ridicule the Un-American Activities Committee.[5] They had testify as peace groups under scrutiny. They took children, they took flowers, and they answered their questions very lightly. Somebody asked the spokesperson, "how many members have you got?" She said she had no idea how many members they had. Also, "are there any communists?" She said, "we don't know. We don't ask questions about that." And, "do you have any fascists?" She sighed, "oh, if they would only join us." This was quite wonderful because it began to make fun of the Committee that had been terrorizing the country and all activist liberal people. This group had a part in ending the Un-American Activities Committee. Then along came the Vietnam war, which came not long after the Korean war in 1951, which was a total shock so soon after WWII. This was a critical period.

One of the best things the VOW did during the Vietnam war was to bring Vietnamese women to Canada twice. This was the Voice of Women Centennial Project, in 1967. They went across Canada and spoke in several of the cities to hundreds of people. As the national president of the VOW I accompanied them. Of course, we couldn't go to the United States, because the Vietnamese women were "the enemy." But hundreds of Americans came up to Canada to hear them speak. This action comfirmed our feeling that we had to be related to the women in other parts of the world and that we couldn't allow the government to make enemies of the women of the world. They weren't the enemy. We always tried to make connections with women who were on the other side. For instance, we were also the first women to invite Russian women to Canada, and later on to get Chinese women to come to Canada. We went to international conferences that included women who were, under the McCarthy terms, "the enemy." I still feel that one of the important roles we play as the VOW is to keep in touch with women as much as we can, women who are working for peace, wherever they are working, all over the world. During the Vietnam war, there was a committee in Toronto that had a lot of women, who were not members of VOW, knitting dark-colored garments for children who could not play outdoors in the daytime, because if they were seen in light-colored clothes they would be shot at. VOW would send these women information and try to give them a more accurate picture of what was happening in Vietnam. Too many people count on what the daily newspaper says. A function of VOW has always been to exchange ideas about what's worth reading and getting people to read it so that they can be better informed.

Evie: What are some of the other Canadian or international peace organizations that you were involved in or in contact with?

Betty: I was a very active member of the Women's International League for Peace and Freedom (WILPF) in the States and after I came to Canada as well. In 1983 I went to Europe with a group who were mostly Americans, but there were also a couple of Canadians, to protest at the NATO headquarters and participate in the big peace march in Brussels with women from all over the world. Then I got on a train and went to West Germany, East Germany, and then coming back I went to the women's camp in England, Greenham Common. It was quite exciting to meet women from all over the world who were working for the same thing. When I came back to Canada there were so many good groups that I thought I couldn't keep up with everything. There was the International Fellowship of Reconciliation and The International War Resisters League and, many others and, of course, there were Quaker groups all over the world.

Muriel: Besides VOW I belong to the United Nations Association of Canada and the National Anti-Poverty Organization, OXFAM, and the NDP. In addition, I support several other groups. When I was president of VOW, I went in 1967 to the Soviet Union and I couldn't believe I was there, me, this little farm girl from Quebec, expected to speak for VOW. There were women there from all over the world at this international conference of women for peace. In 1975, the first UN conference on women was held in Mexico City; in 1980 the second one was held in Copenhagen. I represented VOW at the first, and both VOW and Canadian Research Institute for the Advancement of Women (CRIAW) at the second. This web of women all over the world is very strong.

"Here I stand, I can do no other"

Marie: What sustains your involvement in the peace movement?

Betty: There's such need and you just have to keep going and keep involved.... The company of other people working hard, and especially women, is something that keeps me going. My involvement with the Quakers is very sustaining to me. Quakers believe that you owe something to the world for being here. So, you have faith that things are going to get better and I think in the long run they will, but you also have to put your faith into practice and get your hands and your feet moving towards that end and not give up.

Muriel: I've often quoted Martin Luther when he said "Here I stand, I can do no other." It's something inside that cannot be set aside. I couldn't live any other way. Now I haven't got the energy to do what I used to do. I have to live with that. On the other hand, I just could not look at myself in the mirror if I didn't renounce violence, devote myself to peace, love justice, and nurture. There are so many people out there who believe as I do. Many of them are my friends. I have to stand beside them. I am especially grateful to the Quakers and feminist pacifists in my life.

I had a very good experience this summer when 14 women came to my cottage in Quebec for the weekend just so we could sit in a circle and talk. These women were all are very concerned with social justice and peace issues and they came from Toronto, Ottawa, Halifax and Cambridge, Mass. Somebody asked me, "did you solve the world's problems?" We didn't solve the world problems but we were dealing with the problems you have trying to solve the world's problems. I believe, as Betty has said, that small groups are essential for working towards changing the world, groups where you would come together as equals and there is no-one at the top telling you what to think. You're there in a small group working things out among yourselves. The more people we can get doing that, the better chance we have for a decent world where people have the courage to say we will have nothing to do with war because it is the total destruction of life. This is essential to a culture of peace.

Grassroots organizing for peace: A web of women

Evie: What do you think are the major peace issues today and conflict situations where women around the world are involved and struggling to have a say in peacemaking?

Betty: I am totally absorbed in the crisis in the Middle East for the moment. I am so filled with admiration with what women are doing about peace—mothers of the disappeared in South America and the Women in Black in Israel and now all over the world. U.S. groups are picking up on this. There are many Women in Black groups, all over the world, and women's groups believing that peacemaking starts in the home. Some well-known women like Aung Sung Suu Kyi, for one, and Arundhati Roy for another, are speaking out as has Mary Robinson who has just resigned from the U.N. Human Rights Commission. Strong women like that are role models for us, speaking about issues, reaching out to other women across borders. Women are really leading the way. Also, there were two women, one from Palestine and one from Israel who came over last spring and actually spoke to the UN Security Council—all men— urging that women be included in peace negotiations.

Marie: What further roles could women play in peace-building? How could Canadian women in particular promote peace and solidarity in Canada and peace activism in other parts of the world?

Muriel: It is essential that women are represented equally with men at negotiations at the UN. I'm quite sure that very different conclusions would be reached if there were 50 percent of women. Politically, of course, it's very difficult to get in. We are not very good in Canada. We do not have a very good representation of women in politics. It takes a lot of courage for women to get involved. By the way, I should mention that Alexa (McDonough?)[6] signed that wonderful petition that has been circulating in Canada that says that war is no longer acceptable as a means of settling issues. I think we in the peace movement should keep feeding Alexa and the other women in parliament information for their role there.

Every year the VOW takes about 20 women from Canada to the United Nations. They go with questions, they go with ideas, and they stay for almost a week, visiting several of the different branches of the United Nations and having discussions with them.

Rosalie Bertell[7] did an excellent series of lectures in English in Norway about the whole nuclear thing and how dangerous it is. The Canadian Research Institute for the Advancement of Women (CRIAW) is arranging to get the lectures on videotape into Canada because it seems terribly important for everybody to have them available. People are not paying enough attention. A lot of people now have no idea what nuclear war really means.

In addition, we should urge our government to push for action on the UN Council resolution 1325 "Women and Peace and Security" passed in October 2000. This resolution calls for the increased representation of women at all decision-making levels and for "gender mainstreaming throughout peacekeeping missions" as well as "special measures to protect women and girls from gender-based violence." It is also high time to get out of NATO which has been VOW's position from the beginning, as well as the NDP's position. We should urge our government to get out from under U.S. militarism and empire-building. It will be costly but it is the only way. Children in Afghanistan, Sudan, Rwanda, Iraq, India, and Colombia are as precious as our children and our neighbours' children. Our government must never support sanctions. Economic sanctions are weapons of mass destruction. We should demand that our government take part in creating a culture of peace.

Betty: I belong to the Committee of Canadians, Arabs and Jews for A Just Peace in the Middle East and we are in close touch with people in Israel and also in Palestine. We are trying to give them as much hope as we can but it is a very difficult situation. It has been so painful for me, working in this field now, to be misunderstood by Jewish friends who have the perception that if you are appalled by what Israel is doing in the world today you are anti-Jewish. It just strikes to the heart. In the group End the Sanctions in Iraq we work closely with groups in Canada and the States exchanging ideas and speakers.... Those are the two biggest issues the world is confronting right now. People are interested in these things so we organize and pull people together whenever we can.

The politics of governments and the politics of people after 9/11

Evie: What do you think should be the immediate strategies of the peace movement in Canada and globally to address the current buildup for war? What should we be doing here in Canada to promote the cause of peace?

Betty: These are very tough times. A lot of people, myself included, are quite distressed. Since coming back from Cape Breton, however, I am encouraged by the number of things that I hear are going on both in the States and in Canada. Small groups of people are feeding into larger groups of people. One of the things I was reading said that the numbers of the anti-globalization group had dropped considerably because people are not yet certain that they want to combine their cause with peace. They are strictly anti-World Trade Organization-IMF and the World Bank. I hadn't realized that that many people were still holding back. This marvelous strong group of people who have been protesting, thousands and thousands of people, are concerned about globalization. We need to get them to spread their vision a little wider and realize that if we go to war everything else gets thrown out the window. We all have to protest going to war. It is important to see the connection between globalization and war. They are completely dependent upon each other and the way they subsidize the building of arms and the sales of arms.[8]

Muriel: War is terrorism. The American government thinks it is talking against terrorism but everything they say the other side could say about them. My daughter is very active in the peace movement in Cambridge, Massachusetts. She belongs to a group that came out of 9/11. A lot of them are relatives of people who died at that time. You probably heard the slogan, "Not in My Name," which is a very powerful response that came out of that group. They meant they were opposed to a retaliatory response by the U.S. government in their name. This last weekend there were great big anti-war rallies all over the place. There was one in Boston. I didn't see it in the paper, but I heard about it from my daughter. The Cambridge paper ignored it completely. There were about 20,000 people there and the papers didn't mention it. Maybe one of the things we should be doing is bugging the newspapers. Canadian people need to know about things like this.

Betty: We haven't talked about non-violence and it's a big subject. One writer that I admire a lot, Jonathan Steele started off by "daring to dream in Jerusalem." He envisioned thousands of Palestinians marching out of Jenin, heading toward Nablus, Jerusalem, and Ramallah. They march toward the first checkpoint and the soldiers are all shouting "stop!" but they don't stop. The soldiers shoot and some people fall dead, but they keep coming and they keep coming, and pretty soon they are joined by thousands of Israelis and international people and then the soldiers don't dare shoot at them. They keep moving, there's no stopping them. This is civil disobedience, this is non-violence. He said, of course this is only a dream, this has not happened, but it could. I thought of this in connection with the last question—the need to be totally non-violent and to support the non-violent efforts.... In this case, to know a lot of people are with you, really helps.

Originally published in CWS/cf's Fall 2002/Winter 2003 issue, "Women and Peace-Building" (Volume 22, Number 2): 115-119.

[1]On March 1, 1954, an American hydrogen bomb test at Bikini Atoll in the Pacific showered massive radioactive fallout on the Islanders and on the crew of the *Fifth Lucky Dragon*, a Japanese tuna fishing boat (War Resisters League, *With Peace on Our Wings, 1995 Peace Calendar*, New York: 1995).

[2]U.S. Senator Joe McCarthy and the House Un-American Activities Committee in the 1950s led a Communist witch hunt that persecuted and paralyzed many parts of society, thus jeopardizing peace, social justice and free-thinking initiatives for years.

[3]The Fellowship of Reconciliation (FOR) was founded in England in 1914. It is a large, interfaith, international peace organization working through action and education toward a peaceful world built upon principles of non-violence, social justice and spiritual values.

[4]Guzenko was a Soviet Army Lt. and cipher clerk in the military attache's office in Ottawa when he defected to the Canadians in September 1945. Because of his position he was able to provide Western intelligence services with extensive information on Soviet espionage in the West. As a result, many high-standing government officials were put on trial.

[5]Un-American Activities Committee (1938-1975) of the U.S. House of Representatives was created to investigate disloyalty and subversive organizations. Its main focus was anti-Communist investigations. The Committee consistently disregarded the civil liberties of its witnesses and failed to fulfill its primary purpose of recommending new legislation. From: http://www.infoplease.com/ce6/history/A0824313.html (accessed on February 12, 2003).

[6]Alexa McDonough was the leader of the NDP when this interview was taken.

[7]Rosalie Bertell, Ph.D., is a Roman Catholic nun and renowned expert on low-level radiation. Her research has earned her the "Right Livelihood Award" (the alternative Nobel prize).

[8]Since October 2002, when this interview was taken, the anti-war movement has gotten much stronger. "The great hope for right thinking people of good will is the massive protests world-wide against this war, as held on January 18 and February 15. Town and city councils, provincial and state governments in the U.S.A. and Canada join a network of local protests of hundreds and hundreds of thousands of aroused citizens demanding "Stop the War" and "Not in My Name"" (Betty Peterson, addendum, February 2003).

Violence and Poverty on the "Rock"

Can Feminists Make a Difference?

Glynis George ⟶

The 1990s were a cultural watershed in Newfoundland and Labrador. While the decline of the fishery threatened the livelihood which had sustained settlement for centuries, the public discourse regarding violence against women, children and dependent adults broadened, provoking a significant re-thinking of the way people live in this province, fondly referred to as "The Rock." As someone who has worked with activists in women's councils on the west coast, and in St. John's, I was impressed by the coordinated efforts of women who were differently positioned within govenment and community to address violence and poverty through lobbying, protest and advocacy in their paid work and in community-based initiatives.

This was particularly difficult in the 1990s when government restructur-ing and fiscal restraint generated immense changes to government services. At the same time, issues raised by women, poverty groups and labour organizations in this politically conservative climate were marginalized as the "narrow" claims of special interests which were somehow distinct from the concerns of "ordinary" citizens (Bashevkin; George). Hence, this period presented femi-nists with a formidable task. How could they address violence and poverty and its impact on women and children, given this chilly climate of change?

This paper focuses on the involvement of activists in government initia-tives that have taken place in the 1990s, specifically, the Provincial Strategy Against Violence, a government initiative undertaken in 1993. I suggest that it is the multi-dimensional character of their activism that permits the expression of a critical, grounded and substantive feminist politics. This is crucial in light of the apparent contradictory behaviour of the provincial government and its dependence on federal decision-making. On the one hand it has expanded its attention to violence and the experiences of vulnerable populations, in its plan to create "safe, caring" communities. On the other hand, the structural changes it has developed and the fiscal restraint it exercises has made these initiatives difficult to realize in a meaningful way.

While violence and poverty have been on the feminist agenda since the early 1970s, the 1990s mark a significant shift in feminist organizing. By this time, women were better positioned to participate in this process as a result of their paid work in government, as "femocrats" (Rankin and Vickers 352-60), and because they had developed a strong political and social network to make issues politically and locally meaningful (George). In this context, grass-roots organizing is central to ensuring that the complex connections between poverty and violence in the lives of Newfoundlanders are addressed in government policy and provide a basis for critical reflection on the substantive changes that underlie government rhetoric. Moreover, because these concerns are hardly peculiar to the province, this examination illustrates the centrality of grass roots organizing for sustaining feminism during times of political conservatism and structural transformation, and supports Brodie's call for an attention to the grass roots (Brodie).

Violence, poverty, activism and government in Newfoundland and Labrador

When a recent Statistics Canada report cited Newfoundland and Labrador as having the lowest rate of violence (five and four per cent), against both women and men (Government of Canada 14), Joyce Hancock, the President of the Provincial Advisory Council on the Status of Women was concerned about the effect of this statistic, or rather that its report would belie more than it revealed. It certainly resonated with the depiction of Newfoundlanders as egalitarian, friendly, and resilient folks more accustomed to being violated (at last economically) than engaging in such actions themselves. Yet, it didn't speak to the experiences of front-line workers who observe the impact of uneven or inaccessible direct services on women's experiences of violence. Moreover, it had little bearing on the interests of aboriginal women in their efforts to document the number of violent crimes which go unreported in their communities, or in their concern for the paucity of community policing in Labrador (see, for example, Pauktuutit). Indeed, the problem of violence is one that has been taken on and legitimated in the 1980s and 1990s across the province.

There was a significant increase in reports of violence and sexual abuse against women and children from the 1980s to the present. Cases of child sexual abuse for example, rose throughout the 1980s, by 5,000 per cent (Community Response Team). Moreover, while Newfoundland reported lower rates of violence for women in national surveys, a more effective documentation process was indicating that the incidence of violence against women was much higher than criminal justice statistics had reported (Government of Newfoundland and Labrador 2-3). Prominent cases, such as the sexual abuse of boys by Christian brothers at Mount Cashel orphanage galvanized public opinion. Perhaps more so than elsewhere in Canada, this latter issue brought into sharp focus the way power over dependent persons had been historically exercised in families, the church and communities.

While the concern for these forms of violence is relatively new in public discourse, economic crisis in the province is not. Periods of financial crisis have characterized Newfoundland's history, both before and after Confederation.

But the moratorium on cod fishing has intensified related social and economic problems. Although out-migration has stabilized somewhat recently, more than 20,000 persons have left the province since 1993, the year the moratorium was imposed. There has been a 75 per cent increase in those who have sought short- term government assistance between 1989 and 1996. This represent 100,000 men, women and children in a province of 500,000 people who receive only 50 per cent of the recommended annual incomes for families in official Statistics Canada assessments. Unemployment rates are twice the national average at 19 per cent, and 29 per cent amongst youth (Social Policy Advisory Committee). This has contributed to a loss in government revenue, which was already reduced by federal changes including reduced transfer payments, and funds for social assistance and unemployment insurance. Families are equally affected by the loss of local and regional government revenue.

The provincial government responded to these conditions through dramatic restructuring throughout the 1990s and a vow to create "safe, caring" communities. The dismantling of the department of social services and the denominational school system was accompanied by the creation of regional economic and regional health boards. It is in this context of restructuring, fiscal restraint and economic crisis that activists lobbied for community input in how changes would be implemented. This resulted in two government initiatives which permitted consultation from a variety of residents and community-based organizations: a Provincial Strategy Against Violence and a Social Policy Committee.

The creation of these kinds of committees is, however, no guarantee that substantive consultation will occur. Nor does the call for "safe, healthy communities," a gender- neutral discourse, necessarily attend to the interests and experiences of women and vulnerable persons.

Rather, this context of change necessitates activists to participate in many ways. As advocates, watchdogs, lobbyists and agents of government change, they seek to address the impact of changes on women with diverse problems and backgrounds.

Feminists working within and outside government had long pointed to the differential impact of the economy, labour market and training on women and men (see Provincial Advisory Council on the Status of Women; Porter; George). Moreover, violence against women and poverty had been important issues for feminists and activists in the anti- poverty and shelter movements since the early 1970s (Pope and Burnham; Hebert and Foley). Prominent cases such as Mount Cashel, as well as a few cases of women convicted of physically abusing children drew media attention which sometimes implicated men and women as equal participants in the problem of violence. By contrast, feminists acknowledge that women can be abusive, yet, they consider the cultural context in which such women are historically located as mothers, foster mothers and caregivers. This means situating the family as an institution within the larger context of Newfoundland history:

poverty, large families and powerful churches.

By the early 1990s women were positioned to develop multi-pronged, provincial wide strategies to address these problems. They lobbied to participate in the way these changes were implemented, through their participation in community-based organizations, and the Provincial Strategy Against Violence. The networks between grass roots activists and feminists working within institutions has been important in developing a feminist, inclusive process within the strategy, and for centring and communicating the experiences of women. And yet, the context of economic restructuring and restraint have impinged upon the implementation of the strategy and curtailed the input of less powerful residents.

Feminist activism and the Provincial Strategy Against Violence

The Provincial Strategy Against Violence (PSAV) began as a consultation process in 1993, and developed into the first coordinated and provincial-wide initiative in the province. The Strategy sought to create "safe caring communities" through enhanced prevention and service delivery. Its mandate was informed by the assumption that "solutions to the problem of violence against women, children and elderly and dependent adults" must be achieved through coordinated efforts of community and government (Government of Newfoundland and Labrador). The Strategy targeted specific aspects of legislation, policy, direct services, community, education, research and evaluation.

The Strategy is a plan to address violence in all areas of government in a way that incorporates community. Hence, its efficacy is directly connected to the way government departments operate and are restructured and the extent to which the diverse experiences of less powerful residents are represented. Five years later, an independent evaluation report summarized the limitations and achievements of the plan and confirmed what activists had themselves observed. Some successes had been made in the area of legislation and justice, and in the establishment of regional and community links. However, there was still a limited role for community-based players in areas of decision-making, and the strategy was unfulfilled due to a pre-occupation with government restructuring in other areas, and "government-wide restraint." Successes and limitations were significantly related to pre-existing networks and initiatives in regions as well as the larger historical context of regional disparity within the province.

For regions which had little community-based networks of persons working on these issues, the strategies appeared to be "top-down" and hence, did not always reach a wide range of residents. These problems were exacerbated by the large size of Newfoundland and Labrador which made meeting and networking difficult and expensive. Also, the cultural and racialized divisions (between whites and Aboriginals for example) contributed to feelings of distrust, and inequity. Moreover, even in those regions that were considered very well coordinated, such as Bay St. George on the west coast, government restructuring posed numerous roadblocks. Firstly, government representatives did not always give time to the "Strategy" and were often pre-occupied with implementing immense changes in their own departments. As Sharon Whalen, the coordinator of the Bay St. George Women's Council put it,

> *There were so many changes and directives coming from St. John's, that we didn't have time to absorb or interpret them never mind to consider their impact on women lives, or on our attempts to address violence.*

How then were feminists able to make an impact?

Feminists had some impact through their incorporation of a gender analysis in the creation of an inclusive process within the strategy. Also, pre-existing links at the grass roots with community-based organizations, allowed a greater range of residents to make more substantive contributions in certain regions, and to critically assess the changes that were being implemented.

The incorporation of a systemic gender analysis in all areas of the strategy would ideally inform new policies in areas of justice, policing, and education. This included the training of those who work with victims, offenders and clients. Also, the broad and systemic nature of the analysis was used to offset tensions and conflicts, such as the finger-pointing and the narrow outlook that can pre-occupy those who work in criminal justice, health and human resources on issues of child protection or the treatment of offenders. The incorporation of such an analysis however, is dependent on the ability of activists to be heard, to exchange information, and to reach those who actually implement specific projects.

Hence, feminists also attended to creating *an inclusive feminist process* through which the strategy was implemented. For example, the strategy included regional coordinating committees (along with government representatives) in its structure. Two of these, representing St John's and the Western region, were considered to have made strong substantive contributions to the "Strategy." It is noteworthy that both regions had developed community-based models *prior* to the strategy, the Interagency Committee on Violence Against Women in St. John's, and the Sexual Abuse Counseling Service in Bay St. George which had laid the groundwork for an inclusive process (see George). Moreover, activists in Bay St. George for example, had already learned to utilize government initiatives where possible and had developed strong networks to do so effectively. For example, although council members recognized the problems regarding the 1993 Royal Commission on Violence Against Women (see also Gotell) they were nonetheless, able to use the resources and information gathering process provided by the Commission, to increase awareness in the community through their media activism, and to expand their informal group for survivors of violence.

Grass roots links such as this were also important for critically monitoring the strategy and advocating for substantial community input, particularly in the context of fiscal restraint and restructuring. Activists are concerned that the mandate of the strategy will be undermined by some of the changes being implemented. For example, services previously provided by a social services department, are now accessed by two separate departments (Human Resources and Health). This change can make it more difficult for service workers to apprehend connections between financial need and the social problems women may experience with partners, in cases of separation and in terms of child welfare, or disabilities. In this case, community-based organizations and networks are increasingly important contexts for these connections to be made, in others words, for a woman's social and economic experience to be considered in her attempts to get training, or child care.

Ultimately, the Provincial Strategy has not yet produced significant increases in direct services although its mandate has been extended. To paraphrase one activist: how can you call for prevention by educating people on violence and then provide few resources for them to address the problem in their lives in a meaningful way? The Newfoundland government has invoked its "have-not" status and the effect of globalization in response to the criticism that changes within government departments or failure to develop services, are fiscally driven.

This kind of response exemplifies the dilemma that activists who work within government face. Their complex and ambiguous relationship with the state, a problem that is familiar to feminist elsewhere, (Brodie, 1998: 24) allows for some negotiation and influence. But in the context of government restraint activists need to ask broader and more critical questions. In this context, the diversity of activism at play in anti-poverty and violence networks in the province is evermore important. Aside from "femocrats" who work within the Women's Policy Office for example, there are eight women's councils which are community based and critical, yet provide services for, and are funded by government. There are also community-based organizations, such as the Provincial Association Against Family Violence, which receive ad hoc funding; and more autonomous, well-resourced groups, such as those linked to the labour movement.

Grass roots activists such as Helen Murphy, a representative of the Provincial Association Against Family Violence, who have been involved in these issues for years are well positioned to consider the impact of changes, or the absence of resources on women's lives over time.

Women (who experience transition houses) have illusions of what people can do for them; women come with enthusiasm, determination to change their living circumstances and are then faced with full extent of problem that may underlie their particular abusive situation.

This includes their place of residence (rural or urban), their lack of training and access to education, the difficulty of getting adequate legal representation or the larger changes in their sub- regional economy. Because her organization is "community-based" and has limited government funding,

Helen considers that she often acts as critic of government policies. She is also well-placed to "ask the really hard questions," including for example, whether moves toward mediation and alternate dispute resolution will reduce costs without negatively impacting on women's access to fair treatment in legal matters.

At the same time, grass roots initiatives are hardly a panacea to making change particularly when government points to its own impoverishment or powerlessness. This makes it crucial to maintain strong links between violence and anti-poverty activists and more autonomous feminist organizations, which can provide a critical public space for organized protest, and the expression of alternate ways of making change. This is exemplified by the strong networks which link a very active provincial advisory council, to annual provincial conferences, and representation on the National Action Committee (NAC). The annual Provincial Conference, to be held this October, will incorporate the "World March," an international series of meetings involving over 6000 organizations, into its program. Their March in Gander will, like its predecessor in Quebec in 1995, Bread and Roses March against Poverty, focus on the violence, poverty and structures that keep women poor, excluded and violated. Having completed more than 40 visits to communities across the province this past year, activists at the Provincial Advisory Council for the Status of Women hope to achieve widespread support for this event.

Activists recognize that their work within government and at the grassroots requires them to draw upon the gender neutral discourse of "safe" communities, or to underplay their analysis as "feminist." This poses several problems, including the "watering-down" of feminist insights, and the difficulty of actually documenting the impact of feminism itself. By focusing on activist links I do not mean to suggest that there is consensus among women who consider themselves to be feminist activists, or that all women who support these initiatives, would be comfortable with the label. At the same time, it is important to draw attention to the way women work on a daily basis to make and influences changes in the province to counter the impression that feminist activists represent the interests of a narrow few.

Originally published in CWS/cf's Fall 2000 issue, "Women 2000: Eradicating Poverty and Violence in the 21st Century" (Volume 20, Number 3): 181-185.

References

Bashevkin, Sylvia. *Women on the Defensive: Living Through Conservative Times.* Toronto: University of Toronto Press, 1998.

Brodie, Janine. "Restructuring and the Politics of *Marginalization.*" *Women and Political Representation in Canada.* Eds. Manon Tremblay and Caroline Andrew. Ottawa: University of Ottawa Press, 1998.

Community Response Team. "Proposal for Bay St. George Sex Abuse Counselling Service." Bay St. George, Newfoundland, 1993.

George, Glynis. *The Rock Where We Stand: An Ethnography of Women's Activism in Newfoundland.* Toronto: University of Toronto Press, 2000.

Gotell, Lisa. "A Critical Look at State Discourses on 'Violence against Women': Some Implications for Feminist Politics and Women's Citizenship." *Women and Political Representation in Canada.* Eds. Manon Tremblay and Caroline Andrew. Ottawa: University of Ottawa Press, 1998.

Government of Canada. 2000. *Family Violence in Canada: A Statistical Profile.* Statistics Canada, Catalogue no. 85-224-XIE, p. 14.

Government of Newfoundland and Labrador. "Towards the Year 2000: The Provincial Strategy Against Violence, An Action Plan. St. John's: Women's Policy Office, 1995.

Hancock, Joyce. Personal interview. August 2000.

Hebert, Cheryl and Jan Foley. "Building Shelter ... Taking Down Walls. *Ties That Bind: An Anthology of Social Work and Social Welfare in Newfoundland and Labrador.* Ed. Gale Burford. St. John's: Jesperson Publishing, 1997.

Murphy, Helen. Personal interview. Summer, 1999.

Pauktuutit Inuit Women's Association. "More Than They Say: Unreported Crime in Labrador." Unpublished report submitted to the Solicitor General, Canada, 1995.

Pope, Sharon and Jane Burnham. "Change Within and Without: The Modern Women's Movement in Newfoundland and Labrador." *Pursuing Equality.* Ed. Linda Kealey. St. John's: Institute of Social and Economic Research, 1993.

Porter, Marilyn. *Women and Economic Life in Newfoundland: Three Case Studies.* Report on Project 482-87-0005. St. John's: Institute of Social and Economic Research, 1990.

Provincial Advisory Council on the Status of Women. "Women of the Fishery." Educational St. John's: Planning and Design Associates Ltd., 1994.

Rankin, L. Pauline and Jill Vickers. "Locating Women's Politics." *Women and Political Representation in Canada.* Eds. Manon Tremblay and Caroline Andrew. Ottawa: University of Ottawa Press, 1998.

Social Policy Advisory Committee. *Investing in People and Communities: A Framework for Social Development.* St. John's: Report of the Social Policy Advisory Committee, 1997.

The Pictou Statement

A Feminist Statement on Guaranteed Livable Income

Lee Lakeman, Angela Miles and Linda Christiansen-Ruffman ⟶

Every issue of *Canadian Woman Studies/les cahiers de la femme* is edited by a guest editorial board of diverse women from across the country who read and discuss all the potential contents. This valued learning process for those on the editorial board contributes greatly to the quality of the journal isue, and thus also to its value for students, for the profession of women's studies, for activists, and for the women's movement as a whole. But in these times of great and increasing pressure on women and their activism, more is necessary. Women's places in the academy, centres, projects, and wings of the movement as well as women's livelihood, dignity, and autonomy are financially threatened in new ways. To write and to think creatively with political ingenuity and wisdom is difficult but essential in these circumstances.

With the issue on "Benefiting Women? Women's Labour Rights," Volume 23, Nos. 3/4 (Spring/Summer 2004) the journal had a rare opportunity to bring activism, research, and theory together in a specifically feminist process of knowledge creation. Two members of the *Canadian Woman's Studies* Executive Board and two members of the Guest Editorial Board for this issue were able to meet in Pictou, Nova Scotia with feminists from across the country for two days of intense dialogue around the themes of this issue. The mix of significant numbers of feminists from national groups with a substantial regional grassroots presence from the Atlantic region proved inspired. Participants are listed below.[1]

As a movement we are in need of much more contact with each other. We need a fuller discussion amongst ourselves that can renew our understanding of our shared feminist agendas for action. We need to restate the relevance of each of our demands to each other's campaigns. It is in that coming together of our demands and actions that our hope emerges and is sustained. We had that opportunity in Pictou and we rediscovered there that feminism is alive and fighting in Canada and demands her share of a better world.

For our initial discussions in Pictou we divided into two groups. Using the time-honoured feminist process of starting from women's experiences, the groups tackled the question of women's economic security and autonomy from different but related angles. In one group, participants shared information about the many economic security campaigns they had been involved in and reflected on how the varied issues are connected and might be advanced from a feminist point of view. Starting from sharing information about women's lives and experiences, including our increasing economic insecurity, the other group identified/imagined what changes would be needed to ensure the security and autonomy of all women.

Both groups were asked to prioritize the implications for the poorest women, Indigenous women, and immigrant women, and to include attention to international contexts. Information about the growing interest in an annual general income was provided in participants' package of materials and both groups were also invited to consider this in their discussions. Later dialogue as a whole group, informed by the themes of both earlier groups, contributed to the articulation of a feminist position on a guaranteed livable income. This is captured in the "Pictou Statement" presented here. This statement has not been endorsed by individual participants at Pictou and they have not yet had the time to take it to their respective groups for endorsement. However, it is an exciting outcome of a rare and generative feminist dialogue. We feel it represents an important advance in feminist thinking on these issues and are pleased to be able to present it here.

We expect this statement will resound in the diverse member groups of the World March of Women, in the World March of Women charter events, in labour and anti-poverty struggles, and in diverse grassroots women's groups across the country struggling on a daily and urgent basis with these issues. It will surely sugar the yeasty uprising of political activity among women refusing poverty and rewardless toil for all of us.

Originally published in CWS/cf's Spring/Summer 2004 issue, "Benefiting Women? Women's Labour Rights" (Volume 23, Numbers 3/4): 204-205.

[1]Participants at the meeting held in Pictou, NS, Sept.18-20, 2004 included: Louise Aucoin, New Brunswick Coalition for Pay Equity; Linda Christiansen-Ruffman, CRIAW-NS, Atlantic Women's FishNet, FemJEPP, FAFIA; Brenda Cranney, *Canadian Woman Studies;* Karen Dempsey, National Council of Women; Sue Genge, Canadian Labour Congress (CLC); Michelle Genge Harris, Women's Network PEI; Lucille Harper, Antigonish Wo-men's Centre, FemJEPP; Lee Lakeman, Canadian Association of Sexual Assault Centres (CASAC), World March of Women; Barbara Legault, Federation des femmes de Québec (FFQ); Bernadette MacDonald, Pictou County Women's Centre, FemJEPP; Angela Miles, *Canadian Woman Studies,* Toronto Women for a Just and Healthy Planet; Doreen Paris, Nova Scotia Advisory Council on the Status of Women; Katharine Reed, Canadian Centre for Policy Alternatives (CCPA), Antigonish Women's Centre; Angela Regnier, Canadian Federation of Students; Luciana Ricciutelli, *CWS/cf;* Michelle Ridgeway, Women's Network PEI; Jane Robinson, Canadian Research Institute for the Advancement of Women (CRIAW)-NFDL; Jenny Robinson, YWCA Canada; Gwen Wood, National Anti-Poverty Organization (NAPO).

The Pictou Statement
A Feminist Statement for a Guaranteed Livable Income

For millennia women's work, along with the free gifts of nature, has provided most of the true wealth of our communities. Women's work has been central to individual and collective survival. In all our diverse communities women can be seen to work on the principle that everybody is entitled to economic and physical security and autonomy and a fair share of the common wealth.

Women in every community, context and racial group are still denied our rightful political power over the economics governing these communities and our world. To paraphrase "A Women's Creed," for thousands of years men have had power without responsibility while women have responsibility without power. This situation must change.

Feminists insist that all activities of government and business in our nation(s) and our diverse communities should be assessed in the light of the prime value of sustaining life and social priorities of universal entitlement, human security, autonomy and common wealth. Social priorities of universal entitlement, human security, autonomy and common wealth must become central in social life and in public policy.

We refuse to accept market measures of wealth. They make invisible the important caring work in every society. They ignore the well-being of people and the planet, deny the value of women's work, and define the collective wealth of our social programs and public institutions as "costs" which cannot be borne. They undermine social connections and capacities (social currency).

We reject policies that sacrifice collective wealth and individual security in the interests of profit for transnational corporations.

Women in Canada expect full and generous provision for all people's basic needs from the common wealth. Social and collective provision for sustaining life must be generous and secure in Canada and must be delivered through national mechanisms appropriately influenced and controlled by the women of our many specific communities.

We expect all people's full and dignified participation in society including full individual and social sharing of the work and responsibility of sustaining life that has so far been gendered. Men must share equally in this work within and beyond monetary measures.

We expect our rightful share of the wealth we have created. Women's work must be recognized and valued both within and beyond monetary measures. We expect sustained and expanding collective provision for people's needs.

Women demand an indexed guaranteed living income for all individual residents set at a level to enable comfortable living.

Pictou, Nova Scotia, Sept 18-20, 2004

About the Contributors

Lauren Anderson survived her arts degree and is now gainfully employed as a technical writer, living in Kitchener-Waterloo with her husband, dog, and two very undignified cats.

Ghislaine Alleyne is the Web Site Manager and electronic communications specialist at the Canadian Women's Health Network. She is a board member and editorial committee member for *Herizons* magazine, where she specializes in issues around race, gender and identity in western popular culture. She is also a writer, editor, and community activist.

Pat Armstrong is Professor of Sociology and Women's Studies at York University. She holds a CHSR/CIHR Chair in Health Services focused on gender and also chairs the Women and Health Reform Group.

Hugh Armstrong is a Professor in the School of Social Work and in the Institute of Political Economy at Carleton University in Ottawa. He has published articles on privatization in health care, on the re-organization of work, and on state workers. With Pat Armstrong, he has written widely on women and work and on health care. Among their books are *Theorizing Women's Work* (1990), *The Double Ghetto: Canadian Women and Their Segregated Work* (Third Edition, 1994), *Wasting Away: The Undermining of Canadian Health Care* (Second Edition, 2003), and *Universal Health Care: What the United States Can Learn from the Canadian Experience* (1998). They have also co-authored several articles and reports, including a paper on health human resources for the recent Romanow Commission on the Future of Health Care in Canada, and "Thinking It Through: Women, Work and Caring in the New Millennium," a concept paper for "A Healthy Balance," a CIHR-funded research project on unpaid care work..

Angela Aujla is a sociology professor at the Humber Institute of Technology and Advanced Learning and a mom to Anushka and Indigo. Her areas of research include "race" and gender, colonialism and postcolonialism, and the South Asian diaspora.

Gwynne Basen is a member of the Canadian Women's Health Network.

Joan Borsa is an independent curator, art critic and associate professor who was recently appointed chair of the Department of Women's and Gender Studies at the University of Saskatchewan, Saskatoon. She has written extensively on Canadian contemporary art and works in the areas of curatorial, cultural and visual studies.

Madeline Boscoe, R.N., D.U. is the Executive Director and founding member of the Canadian Women's Health Network, a national voluntary organization working to raise awareness and improve the health of girls and women in Canada and advance understanding of gender based analysis—through communications, networking and action. She is also a long time staff member of the Women's Health Clinic, a feminist community health centre in Winnipeg where she coordinates the Policy advice and advocacy program. In 1994, she initiated a community based research and action project "Women and Health Reform" in Manitoba and has been a member of the National Coordinating Group on Health Care Reform and Women since 1999. In 1979, she was a founding member of the HealthSharing Collective in Toronto. She was awarded an honorary doctorate by the University of Ottawa in June 2005.

Carrie A. Bourassa is an Assistant Professor of Indigenous Health Studies at First Nations University of Canada. Carrie is in the final stages of her Ph.D. (Social Studies). Her dissertation is entitled *Destruction of the Métis Nation: Health Consequences*. Carrie's research interests include the impacts of colonization on the health of First Nations and Métis people; creating culturally competent care in health service delivery; Aboriginal community-based health research methodology; Aboriginal end of life care and Aboriginal women's health. Carrie is Métis, belonging to the Riel Métis Council of Regina Inc. She resides in Regina with her husband, Chad and her daughter, Victoria.

Barbara Bourrier-LaCroix is a member of the Canadian Women's Health Network.

Charlotte Bunch, Founder and Executive Director of the Center for Women's Global Leadership at Douglass College, Rutgers, the State University of New Jersey, has been an activist, author and organizer in the women's, civil, and human rights movements for over three decades. Previously Bunch was a Fellow at the Institute for Policy Studies and a founder of Washington D. C. Women's Liberation and of Quest: A Feminist Quarterly. She is the author of numerous essays and has edited or co-edited nine anthologies including the Center's reports on the Beijing Plus 5 process in 2000 and the World Conference on Racism in 2001. Her books also include two classics: Passionate Politics: Feminist Theory in Action and Demanding Accountability: The Global Campaign and Vienna Tribunal for Women's Human Rights. Bunch is a Distinguished Professor in the Women's and Gender Studies Department at Rutgers University.

Marlene Brant Castellano is a member of the Mohawk Nation now retired and living on Tyendinaga Mohawk Territory. She was a professor of Native Studies at Trent University, Peterborough, from 1973 to 1996 and seved as Co-Director of Research with the Royal Commission on Aboriginal Peoples.

Gulzar Raisa Charania is a former employee of the Toronto District School Board where she worked in the Equity Department. She was a long-time member of the editorial collective of *Fireweed: A Feminist Quarterly of Writing, Politics, Art & Culture* and is currently on the board of the Toronto Women's Bookstore. She is pursuing her Ph.D. in Sociology and Equity Studies in Education at Ontario Institute for Studies in Education of the University of Toronto and can be reached at grcharania@rogers.com.

Nancy Chater, B.A., M.A., M.L.A., is a Toronto-based writer and landscape architect.

Linda Christiansen-Ruffman received her Ph.D. in Sociology from Columbia University and since then has participated along with women seeking equality and justice in new forms of knowledge creation and feminist praxis. She continues to teach sociology and women's studies at Saint Mary's University and to be involved locally, nationally and internationally. She has led scholarly and women's movement organizations and is presently active in Nove Scotia's Feminist for Just and Equitable Public Policy (FemJEPP), in Canada's Feminist Alliance for International Action (FAFIA-AFAI), and in the International Feminist University Network (IFUN).

Barbara Clow is Executive Director of the Atlantic Centre of Excellence for Women's Health, Halifax, and Associate Professor Research in the Faculty of Health Professions at Dalhousie University, Halifax. She has a Ph.D. in the history of medicine from the University of Toronto and has presented and published on various dimensions of the history of medicine in Canada and the United States, in both national and international conferences and peer-reviewed journals. She is also the author of the only monograph on the history of cancer in Canada, *Negotiating Disease: Power and Cancer Care, 1900-1950* with McGill-Queen's University Press (2001).

Stephanie Baker Collins is an Assistant Professor in the School of Social Work at York University. Her recent work includes an examination of the household provisioning work of women who are members of marginalized communities. In addition, she engages in community based research on the impact of cutbacks in public services on the lives of the poorest persons in society and connects this work to advocacy for justice in public policy.

Radhika Coomaraswamy was appointed by the United Nations Secretary-General, Kofi Annan, as Under-Secretary General, Special Representative for Children and Armed Conflict in April 2006. In this capacity, she serves as a moral voice and independent advocate to build awareness and give prominence to the rights and protection of boys and girls affected by armed conflict. A lawyer by training, and formerly the Chairperson of the Sri Lankan Human Rights Commission, Coomaraswamy is an internationally known human rights advocate who has done outstanding work as Special Rapporteur on Violence Against Women (1994-2003).

Barbara J. Cooper is a retired teacher. In her Ph.D. dissertation (York University, 1989) entitled, "'That We May Attain to the End We Propose to Ourselves': the North American Institute of the Blessed Virgin Mary, 1932-1961," Cooper examined recruitment to a religious community of women in the years prior to the Second Vatican Council. She also discussed the ways in which women benefited from their choice to enter the convent and the extent to which power, and an individual's relationship to it, was a central subtext of community existence. She is currently working on a project about the first women who held fellowships in surgery in Canada.

Cynthia L. Cooper is a lawyer, journalist and author of several nonfiction books on justice topics. She has written or worked for several nonprofit organizations in the U.S., including Center for Reproductive Rights, Religious Coalition on Reproductive Choice, Amnesty International USA, The Parenting Project, and the Ford Foundation.

Brenda Cranney received her Ph.D. in Sociology from York University. She is the author of *Local Environment and Lived Experience: The Mountain Women of Himachal Pradesh* (Sage).

Lykke de la Cour teaches in the School of Women's Studies and the Social Science Division at York University. Her teaching and research interests include: women's health and disability issues in historical perspective. She is *still* trying to find the time to complete her doctoral dissertation for the History Department at the University of Toronto on "The History of the Ontario Hospital, Cobourg," a psychiatric facility for women that operated from 1902 to 1972.

Amber Dean is working on her Ph.D. in English at the University of Alberta, although she continues to be most at home in Vancouver where she still teaches women's studies courses in the summertime. Her work has been published in *Canadian Woman Studies/les cahiers de la femme*, *Fireweed*, and *Review of Education/Pedagogy/Cultural Studies*, among others, and she was guest editor of a special edition of *Kinesis* on women and Canadian prisons. Her dissertation work considers representations of murdered and missing women, and she is currently guest editing a special issue of *West Coast Line* on this topic.

Janice Du Mont, Ed.D is a Research Scientist at the Centre for Research in Women's Health, a partnership of Women's College Hospital and the University of Toronto. She is Assistant Professor in the Department of Public Health Sciences, and an Associate Member of the Graduate Department of Community Health at the University of Toronto. Her research interests include the medical and legal processing of sexual assault and woman abuse cases.

Jennifer Ellison is a Ph.D. candidate in history at York University. Her dissertation, "Large as Life: Self-Acceptance and the Fat Body in Canada, 1975-1995" is a history of fat-acceptance in Canada.

Ursula Franklin is University Professor Emerita at the University of Toronto.

Anne Forrest is Director of Women's Studies and Associate Professor in the Odette School of Business, University of Windsor. Her areas of teaching and research are women, work, unions, and collective bargaining.

Jenny Foster is an Assistant Professor in Environmental Studies at York University. Her research focus is urban political ecology.

Ruth A. Frager teaches history and women's studies at McMaster University. Her current research focuses on the campaigns against ethnic, "racial," religious, and sexist forms of discrimination in Ontario in the 1940s through the 1960s.

Lynn Gehl, Algonquin Turtle-Clan, is a second year Ph.D. student in Indigenous Studies at Trent University, Peterborough, Ontario. Drawing from her personal experience, her dissertation topic is the contemporary land claims and self-government process. Committed to producing community knowledge, Lynn also freelances for community publications such as *Anishinabek News* as well as *The Kichesippi Current*.

Sue Genge is a National Representative in the Women's and Human Rights Department at the Canadian Labour Congress in Ottawa. Sue has been involved in the union movement for more years than she will admit. An activist with CUPE and the Toronto women's movement, she was selected to represent workers on the Ontario Pay Equity Tribunal. She has been at the CLC since 1994, working on women's and gay, lesbian, bisexual and transgender issues—writing, speaking and organizing for equality.

Glynis George is an associate professor in the Department of Sociology/Anthropology, University of Windsor. She has conducted research on gender, culture and women's activism in both India and Newfoundland.

Lorraine Greaves, Ph.D. is the Executive Director of the British Columbia Centre of Excellence for Women's Health at the BC Women's Hospital and Health Centre in Vancouver, Canada. She is a sociologist, writer, educator and activist on women's health issues, particularly women's use of tobacco and violence against girls and wome.

Nancy Guberman is a full professor of Social Work at the University of Quebec in Montreal and Scientific Director of the University Affiliated Research Center on Social Gerontology at the Cavendish Health and Social Service Center. She has been involved in research on caregiving and homecare policy and practice,and research on issues and practices of the women's movement, particularly in Quebec.

Pamela Courtenay Hall has been teaching Philosophy and Environmental Studies at the University of Prince Edward Island since 2002. She is currently doing action research on sustainable agriculture/sustainable communities, and she has developed a third-year community-based education course at UPEI on Agriculture and Globalization. In this course, students do field placements on farms to develop a grounded understanding of agriculture and how it is impacted by globalization, while farmers and other agricultural experts serve as site instructors and collaborating instructors. Courtenay-Hall is also engaged in research in environmental philosophy, education, mothering and sexuality. She is the mother of Matthew Hall (19) and Stefan Hall (13).

Sylvia Hamilton is a filmmaker and writer living in Grand Pre, Nova Scotia. She was co-editor of *We're Rooted Here And They Can't Pull Us Up: Essays in African Canadian Women's History*. Her writing has been published in a variety of Canadian journals and anthologies. Her award-winning documentary films include *Black Mother Black Daughter, Speak It! From the Heart of Black Nova Scotia* and *Portia White: Think On Me*. She teaches part-time at the School of Journalism at the University of King's College in Halifax, Nova Scotia.

Mary Hampton is a registered clinical psychologist and a Professor of psychology at Luther College at the University of Regina. She has published in the areas of youth sexual health, women's reproductive health, cross-cultural psychology, and community development. Her research interests include violence against women, women's health, death and dying, and cross-cultural healing.

Olena Hankivsky is Associate Professor in the Public Policy Program and Department of Political Science and the Co-Director of the Institute for Critical Studies in Gender and Health at Simon Fraser University. She specializes in public policy and political theory and has a special interest in gender and social and health policy. She is the author of *Social Policy and the Ethic of Care* (University of British Columbia Press, 2004).

Lesley D. Harman is Professor of Sociology at King's University College at the University of Western Ontario, London, Ontario. She teaches in the areas of the sociology of deviance, social psychology, and qualitative methods. She has published two books, *The Modern Stranger: On Language and Membership*, and *When a Hostel Becomes a Home: Experiences of Women*, a community study of homeless women, as well as numerous articles and book chapters. She has conducted two subsequent community studies, forthcoming in *The River, My Soul: Women of the Thousand Islands* and *Faith Without Fear: The Emergence of the Feminine in Energy Healing*. She lives in London with her three children.

Jennifer Nicole Hines has graduated from Saint Francis Xavier University with a Bachelor of Arts, Honours in Sociology, First Class and has accepted a postition at the Antigonish Women's Resource Centre. She will continue her studies in the near future. Jennifer and her daughter, Amber, are happy and healthy as they are no longer living in poverty. An interest group called "operation groundswell," is currently working to reverse the policy that disallows women in Nova Scotia from attending university while receiving social assistance.

Margaret Hobbs is Chair of the Women's Studies Program at Trent University, where she teaches interdisciplinary courses on Canadian feminism, women and the welfare state, women's health and environment, as well as the introductory women's studies course. Her research focuses on the history of women and social welfare policy in Canada, women workers, and feminist activists and movements. She has a long-standing interest in community-based education and was one of the founders of the Trent Centre for Community-Based Education.

Franca Iacovetta, a professor at the University of Toronto, is the author of *Such Hardworking People: Italian Immigrants in Postwar Toronto* and the co-editor of several books in the areas of immigrant, women's and social history.

Ana Isla teaches in sociology and the women's studies program, at Brock University. Her current research specialties and interests are in feminism, eco-feminism, women in development, Third World women, women's micro-enterprises, political economy, political ecology, the commons, enclosure in the twenty-first century, debt crisis, globalization and global issues, social justice, racism, economic development, sustainable development, debt-for-nature swaps, poverty issues, community organizing, the subsistence perspective, the gift economy, Indigenous knowledge, bio-piracy, eco-tourism, mining, and environmental non-government organizations (NGOs).

Pat Israel is a disabled feminist who lives in Toronto with her husband, three cats, and a new addition, a small but very fast dog. She now works in the field of active living and older adults.

Beth Jackson is a Post-doctoral Fellow with the CHSRF/CIHR Chair in Health Services Research at the Institute for Health Research, York University (Toronto). Since 2001 she has been a member of the National Coordinating Group on Health Care Reform and Women, a collaborative working group of the Canadian Centres of Excellence for Women's Health, the Canadian Women's Health Network, and Health Canada's Bureau of Women's Health and Gender Analysis. Beth's research draws on feminist epistemologies and critical social studies of science to explore the conditions, contexts, tools and processes by which public health knowledge claims are made. Her current research addresses the production of women's health indicators, models of knowledge transfer/brokering/translation, quality assessments in health care, and the social determinants of LGBT health.

Yasmin Jiwani is an Associate Professor in the Department of Communication Studies at Concordia University, Montreal. Her doctorate in Communication Studies from Simon Fraser University, examined issues of "race" and representation in the Canadian television news. Prior to her move to Montreal, she was the Executive Coordinator of the BC/Yukon FREDA Centre for Research on Violence against Women and Children. Yasmin's main interests lie in mapping the intersections of intimate and systemic forms of violence, identifying viable points of intervention, and uncovering the multiple ways in which violence is understood in everyday thought and talk, and represented by the mass media. Her recent publications include: *Discourses of Denial: Mediations of Race, Gender and Violence* (University of British Columbia Press, 2006) and an edited collection with Candice Steenbergen and Claudia Mitchell titled: *Girlhood, Redefining the Limits* (Black Rose Books, 2006).

Pam Kapoor has over ten years experience as an organizer and communicator with small local organizations all the way to historic international campaigns. In 2000, she was the Canadian Organizer for the World March of Women, an unprecedented global women's campaign, and consulted in 2005 as campaigner with Make Poverty History. She has served as Executive Director of the National Anti-Poverty Organization and Coordinator of the Coalition for Women's Equality. She possesses a particular instinct for translating complex and controversial issues for mass public consumption. This ability has had an impact on political discourse at various levels. She recently steered the development of a communications strategy for Amnesty International Canada's Campaign to Stop Violence Against Women and has done the same for a range of other groups and prominent campaigns.

Margie Kelly is a communications consultant with more than ten years experience in high-profile media, marketing, and brand development for human rights and environmental organizations. Previously, Margie held the position of Communications Director for the Healthy Building Network, an environmental health organization, and for the Center for Reproductive

Rights, a legal advocacy organization based in New York City. Margie lives in Eugene, Oregon with her husband and two young children. She has been a member of the Planned Parenthood of Southwestern Oregon's Board of Directors since 2003.

Didi Khayatt is a Full Professor at York University's Faculty of Education. She is the author of a number of articles and one book. She is interested in various issues of equity including gender, race relations, and sexuality.

Mary Kinnear, FRSC, is a Professor in the History department at the University of Manitoba. Her most recent book is *Woman of the World: Mary McGeachy and International Co-operation* (University of Toronto Press, 2004).

Sandra Kirby, Ph.D., is a professor and Chair of the Department of Sociology at the University of Winnipeg. She is a former Canadian Olympic athlete who participated in rowing at the Montreal Olympic Games in 1976. Now she is an avid rower and cross country skier.

Wendee Kubik, Ph.D., is an Assistant Professor of Women's Studies at the University of Regina. She is the author of a number of articles on the changing roles of farm women and co-author (with Murray Knuttila) of *State Theories, Classical, Global and Feminist Perspectives* (third edition). She is involved in a tri-provincial longitudinal study of women who have been abused by intimate partners, as well as research in Chile with rural women and water conservation. She is currently secretary of the Canadian Women Studies Association/ACEF.

Nikki Kumar is currently a third year law student at the University of Windsor. Prior to law school, she obtained undergraduate and Master's degrees from the University of Toronto in Women's Studies and Exercise Sciences. Her research interests include health law and policy, the rights of the girl child, and research ethics.

Lee Lakeman lived for years on welfare raising her son. She has worked for 30 years as an anti-violence activist beginning in Woodstock, Ontario. Currently, she is a member of the collective operating Vancouver Rape Relief and Women's Shelter. She is the author of *Obsession With Intent: Violence Against Women* (Black Rose, 2005).

June Larkin is the undergraduate Coordinator at the Women and Gender Studies Institute and the Director of Equity Studies, University of Toronto. She is the co-coordinator of the Gendering Adolescent AIDS Prevention (GAAP) project at New College, University of Toronto. Her research areas include youth and HIV/AIDS, women and body image, gender violence and arts-based approaches to HIV research and education.

Beverly D. Leipert, Ph.D., RN, Associate Professor at the University of Western Ontario, holds the first and only academic Chair in North America in Rural Women's Health Research. Her research program focuses on rural women's health from social determinants and empowerment perspectives. Dr. Leipert has published widely and presented at many national and international conferences on the topics of rural women's health and community health nursing.

Marion M. Lynn is a founding editor of *Canadian Woman Studies/les cahiers de la femme.* She taught women's studies, psychology, and sociology courses for many years at Centennial College, Scarborough, Trent University in Peterborough, and York University in Toronto. Currently, she is a researcher and consultant on a wide variety of issues for several women's organizations and research institutes across the country. She is the editor of *Voices: Essays on Canadian Families* (Nelson, 2003) and has had numerous articles and chapters as well as a number of research reports.

Guida Man teaches at the Atkinson School of Social Sciences, York University. She has been doing research with Chinese immigrant women for over fifteen years, and has published extensively on the topic.

Notisha Massaquoi is currently a Ph.D. candidate in the Department of Sociology and Equity Studies at Ontario Institute for Studies in Education at the University of Toronto in the Department of Sociology and Ethnic Studies. She is also the Program Director for Women's Health in Women's Hands Community Health Centre for Black Women and Women of Color.

Kim McKay-McNabb, MA, is a doctoral student in Clinical psychology at the University of Regina. She is a First Nations woman and her research interests include community based research that focus on healing from the effects of colonization and residential schools. She is dedicated to assist with research within the community and has been involved for over ten years. Her interests include Aboriginal health and healing which include sexual health, HIV/AIDS and Aboriginal communities and end of life health care.

Andrea Medovarski is in the English Department at York University. Her current research focuses on second- generation Black Canadian and Black British women's writing. Her most recent articles have been published in *World Literature Written in English* and the *Arts Journal.*

Karen Messing, Ph. D., is an ergonomist, occupational health specialist and full professor in the Department of Biological Sciences of the Université du Québec in Montréal, Canada. Her current research focuses on applications of gender-sensitive analysis in occupational health, effects of prolonged standing, and constraints and demands of work in the service sector. She was co-founder and first director of CINBIOSE, a WHO-PAHO Collaborating Centre in Early Detection and Prevention of Work and Environment-Related Illness. Dr. Messing co-directs a research partnership with three Québec unions oriented towards improvement of women's occupational health. She is the author of numerous articles and of *One-eyed Science: Occupational Health and Working Women* (Temple, 1998) and editor of *Integrating Gender in Ergonomic Analysis* (1999) published in six languages by the Technical Bureau of the European Trade Union Confederation. She is on the editorial boards of *International Journal of Health Services, Women and Health, Recherches féministes, Policy and Practice in Health and Safety* and *Salud de los trabajadores*.

Angela Miles teaches in the Adult Education and Community Development Program at the Ontario Institute for Studies in Education of the University of Toronto. She is a founder member of the now dormant Feminist Party of Canada (FPC) and the still very much alive Antigonish Women's Association (AWA). She is active in the Canadian WomanStudies Association (CWSA) and the Canadian Research Institute for the Advancement of Women (CRIAW) and she is a member of Toronto Women for a Just and Healthy Planet. Her publications include a co-edited collection, *Feminism: From Pressure to Politics* (1989) and *Integrative Feminisms: Building Global Visions 1960s-1990s* (1996).

Claudia Mitchell is a James McGill Professor in the Faculty of Education, McGill University and an Honorary Professor in the School of Language, Literacies, Media and Drama Education, Faculty of Education, University of KwaZulu-Natal Her research focuses on visual and other participatory methodologies particularly in addressing gender and HIV and AIDS, teacher identity and gender, new literacies, and the culture of girlhood within broader studies of childhood and youth culture. She is the co-founder of the Centre for Visual Methodologies for Social Change, UKZN and the International Visual Methodologies Project (www.ivmproject.ca). She is the co-author/co-editor of a number of books on teacher education, girlhood, and children's popular culture An edited book *Combating Gender Violence in and Around Schools* (with Fiona Leach) will be published later this year.

Najja N. Modibo is currently an Associate Professor of Labor Studies and an adjunct faculty member at both the African American and African Diaspora Studies and the Department of Sociology at Indiana University, Indianapolis, Indiana. Najja's research focuses on women workers, globalization, immigrant labor, and gendered-racism. In his current research, he examines the impact of globalization and working-class women's responses to the global economic crisis in the Caribbean.

Patricia Monture isa Mohawk Woman from Six Nations near Brantford, Ontario. She currently resides at the Thunderchild (Cree) First Nation in

Saskatchewan with five of their six children. She is a prison activist and educator.

Sheila Neysmith is Professor in the Faculty of Social Work at the University of Toronto. Her books include *Telling Tales: Living With the Effects of Public Policy* (2005), *Restructuring Caring Labour* (2000), and *Women's Caring* (1998).

Roxana Ng is a sociologist and an activist who has been working with immigrant women since the mid-1970s. Her research and publications covers different aspects of their lives at work, in the family, and in the community. Since 1990 she has been paying particular attention to how globalization has affected the plight of immigrant garment workers, and anti-sweat organizing efforts across the Pacific. Her most recent funded research is on the labour market experiences of professional Chinese immigrant women. She teaches in the adult education and community development program at the Ontario Institute for Studies in Education of the University of Toronto, Canada

Fran Odette, a queer disabled feminist lives in Toronto and continues to actively work in the area of equality rights focusing on gender, sexual identities and disability. Fran is an educator on issues related to gender and disability with a particular focus on access to services for female survivors of violence living with disability.

Deborah Parnis, Ph.D., is an Associate Professor in the Department of Sociology at Trent University in Ontario. Her research interests include the institutional responses to sexual assault, policy analysis, cultural regulation, and the social studies of science and technology.

Ann Pederson is the Manager of Research and Policy at the British Columbia Centre of Excellence for Women's Health in Vancouver. She has a background in health promotion studies from the University of Toronto and has worked on numerous research and policy projects in the field of women's health. She has been a member of Women and Health Care Reform since its inception in 1998 and edits the Research Bulletin of the Centres of Excellence for Women's Health program.

Ruth Roach Pierson, Ruth Roach Pierson, Professor Emerita, Ontario Institute of Studies in Education of the University of Toronto, is the author of *"They're Still Women After All": The Second World War and Canadian Womanhood* (1986), co-author of *Canadian Women's Issues*, Volumes I and II (1993, 1995), editor of *Women and Peace: Theoretical, Historical and Practical Perspectives* (1987), and co-editor of, inter alia, *Writing Women's History: International Perspectives* (1991) and *Nation, Empire and Colony: Historicizing Gender and Race* (1998). She published her first book of poems, *Where No Window Was*, in 2002.

Elaine Porter is Associate Professor, Department of Sociology, Laurentian University. She is a member of the WEDGE Provisioning Research Project that examines provisioning, women and community in Ontario and British Columbia.

Marge Reitsma-Street is Professor in Studies in Policy and Social Work at the University of Victoria. She is Principle Investigator of the Wedge Provisioning Research Project.

Carla Rice is Assistant Professor in Women's Studies at Trent University where she lectures in culture, health, and psychology. A leader in the field of body image within Canada, she is founder and former director of innovative initiatives such as the National Eating Disorder Information Centre and the Body Image Project at Women's College Hospital in Toronto. Her current research explores representations and narratives of body and identity across the life-span.

Janice Ristock is Professor in Women's Studies and Associate Dean (Research) in the Faculty of Arts, University of Manitoba. She has published widely in the areas of violence against women, lesbian/gay/queer studies, and community research and organizing. She brings these interests to her teaching where she stresses the links between theory and action.

Jennifer L. Schulenberg received her Ph.D. in Sociology from the University of Waterloo, Canada in 2004. She is currently an Assistant Professor in the College of Criminal Justice at Sam Houston State University and serves as an Associate Editor for the *Canadian Journal of Criminology and Criminal Justice*. Her research has been published in government reports, journal articles, and book chapters in the areas of juvenile delinquency, sociology of the family, policing, and research methodology. She can be contacted at jls011@shsu.edu.

Rose Sheinin, Ph.D., D. Hum. Lett., D. Sci., F.R.S.C., was a Professor in the Department of Microbiology, Faculty of Medicine, and Vice-Dean of the School of Graduate Studies at the University of Toronto at the time the article in this anthology was first published. Currently, she is a Professor of Biology at Concordia University in Montreal. She continues to be interested in women and science, engineering, and technology in Canada. Since 1984, she has been researching the history of women in/and medicine in Toronto.

Dorothy E. Smith is Professosr Emerita, University of Toronto and Adjunct Professor at the University of Victoria. She has been preoccupied for the past 30 or so years with developing the implications of women's standpoint for sociology, problematizing the objectified forms of organization and social relations characteristic of contemporary society, and focusing more recently on the significance of texts for the organization of power. Her published books are: with Sara David ed. *Women Look At Psychiatry: I'm Not Mad, I'm Angry* (Press Gang, 1975); *Feminism and Marxism: A Place to Begin, A Way to Go* (New Star Books, 1977); *El Mundo Silenciado de Las Mujeres* (CIDE, 1985); *The Everyday World as Problematic: A Feminist Sociology* (University of Toronto Press, 1987); *The Conceputal Practices of Power: A Feminist Sociology of Knowledge* (University of Toronto Press, 1990); *Text, Facts and Femininity: Exploring the Relations of Ruling* (Routledge,1990); *Eine Soziologie fur Frauen* (Frigga Haug trans. and ed., Argument Verlag, 1998); *Writing the Social: Critique, Theory and Investigations* (University of Toronto Press, 1999); with Alison Griffith, *Mothering for Schooling* (Routledge, 2005); *Institutional Ethnography: A Sociology for People* (AltaMira Press, 2005) and editor of *Institutional Ethnography as Practice* (forthcoming AltaMira Press, 2006).

Candis Steenbergen is a Ph.D. candidate in the Humanities at Concordia University where she is investigating the interplay between generations, nostalgia, and feminisms in Canada. *Girlhood: Redefining the Limits* (co-edited with Yasmin Jiwani and Claudia Mitchell) was published by Black Rose in early 2006. Her work has appeared in *Dialogues: Sur La Troisième Vague Féministe* (Remue Ménage, 2005), and *Turbo Chicks: Talking Young Feminisms* (Sumach, 2001).

Lina Sunseri is of the Oneida nation of the Thames, Turtle Clan. Her Longhouse name is Yeliwi:saks, which means Gathering Stories, Knowledge. She also has Italian ancestry from her father's side. She is an Assistant Professor in the Department of Sociology, Brescia University College, University of Western Ontario. She recently defended her Ph.D. dissertation which examined the interconnection of gender, nationalism, colonialism and culture in the case of Oneida women. She can be contacted at lsunseri@uwo.ca.

Evie Tastsoglou has been teaching in the Department of Sociology and Criminology at Saint Mary's University since 1993. She is the leader of the "Gender, Migration and Diversity / Immigrant Women" research domain in the Atlantic Metropolis Centre of Excellence. She is also the mother of a ten-year-old daughter and an eight-year-old son

Sunera Thobani teaches Women's Studies at the Centre for Research in Women's Studies and Gender Relations at the University of British Columbia. She is past-president of the National Action Committee on the Status of Women, and has also been the Ruth Wynn Woodward Chair in Women's Studies at Simon Fraser University.

Leah M. Thompson is currently pursuing a graduate degree in Womin's Studies at Memorial University of Newfoundland.

Monique Trépanier is a lawyer in the law firm of Miller Thomson LLP, in

Vancouver, British Columbia. Monique was called to the British Columbia Bar in August 2004. She received her Bachelor of Laws in 2003 from the University of British Columbia and her Bachelor of Arts (Honours) in History with International Relations from the same university in 1995. She is a member of the Law Society of British Columbia and the Canadian Bar Association. Monique worked throughout and prior to law school, as a Program Coordinator and Researcher for the International Centre for Criminal Law Reform and Criminal Justice Policy (ICCLR) at the University of British Columbia. Monique has contributed to several conference papers as part of the International Society for the Reform of Criminal Law's Young Lawyers group, and is one of the contributing authors of ICCLR's *International Criminal Court Manual for the Ratification and Implementation of the Rome Statute*, 2nd ed., 2003.

Marilyn Waring is Professor of Public Policy on the Albany Campus of Massey University in Auckland New Zealand. Her groundbreaking book on women's unpaid work was the subject of the prize-winning Canadian National Film Board's documentary "Who's Counting? Marilyn Waring on Sex, Lies and Global Economics." The second edition of *Counting for Nothing* is published by University of Toronto Press. In 2003 Dr. Waring was appointed to the Board of the Reserve Bank of New Zealand

Marie Ann Welton has worked in the health care field since the mid-1960s including hospital work during the Nigeria-Biafra war. She is a community activist particularly related to women's unpaid work, complementary medicine, environmental health and the spiritual basis for activism.

Wench Collective members, at the time of writing this article, were: Afshan Ali, Debbie Pacheco, Fatima Mechtab, Joanna Pawelkiewicz, Mary Roufael, Michelle Maloney Leonard, Rebecca Saxon, Renee Ferguson, Ruthann Lee, Rylee Crawford, and Tara Atluri. The Wench Radio program ran on CIUT 89.5FM every Sunday afternoon until August 2001. After this time, the collective decided to end the show in order to pursue new projects and other commitments. Many thanks to the committee that conceptualized, complied and edited this article and the fine purveyors of coffee at Yonge and Bloor

Susan White is the Canadian Women's Health Network's Assistant Executive Director and a part-time lecturer in Religious Studies and Women's Studies at the University of Winnipeg.

Alice Olsen Williams was born in Trout Lake, 150 miles north of Kenora, in the traditional territory of her mother's people from time before memory. She received her teaching certificate from Lakehead Teacher's College, which is now the Faculty of Education at Lakehead University in Thunder Bay, Ont. Having taught in Thunder Bay and at Pic Mobert First Nation, Alice and her husband, Doug, moved to Curve Lake First Nation just north of Peterborough, Ont., where Doug was born and raised. While looking after their four children and their home, Alice completed her BA from Trent University as well as developing her skills in beadwork and sewing. In 1980 she discovered quilting, mastering the techniques which allow her to create the meticulous hand-quilting in her bed coverings and wall hangings. Gradually Alice formed the concepts which would be the basis for her distinctive style and work. Blending her cultural heritage into a unified whole, she envisions the central motif to depict the symbols and themes of Anishinaape culture, surrounded by the conventional North American quilting blocks and patterns which were developed and continue to be evolved by those women and their descendants who came to this Land from Europe, the legacy of her father's people. Through her understanding of the teachings of the Elders, Alice has created her own Life symbol. She continues to grow as an artist, searching for new ways to express the Spirit of Creation in the images of her designs.

Kay Willson lives in Saskatoon and is a research associate of the Prairie Women's Health Centre of Excellence.

Index

H

J

K

N

O

P

T

312; *see also* career, caregiving, employment, factory, garment work, family, household labour, housework, immigration, labour
Work is Work is Work Coalition, 226
World Bank, 61, 127, 217, 270, 271, 283, 612
WB, 61, 267, 269, 270, 271, 275, 283
World March of Women, 60, 127, 128, 129, 130, 401, 623
World Trade Organization, 62, 217, 225, 260, 264
WTO, 62, 64, 260, 261, 264
World Women's Congress for a Healthy Planet, 60, 64
World's Women, The, 225

Y

Yanz, Lynda, Bob Jeffcott, Deena Ladd, Joan Atlin, 266
Yates, Charlotte, 296
young women, 43, 44, 47, 48, 49, 50, 55, 97, 98, 101, 199, 202, 350, 357, 358, 388, 437, 442, 443, 444, 445, 446, 447, 448, 452, 453, 531, 537, 578, 579, 582
youth, 140, 194, 280, 329, 414, 416, 418, 442, 443, 445, 448, 449, 454, 456, 552, 577, 616
Yuval-Davis, Nira, 34

Z

Zapatista, 273
Zicklin, Gilbert, 348
Zita, Jacquelyn N., 477